天津统计年鉴

STATISTICAL YEARBOOK OF TIANJIN

1997

天津市统计局　编
Compiled by
TIANJIN Municipal Statistical Bureau
(总第十三期)

中国统计出版社
China Statistical Publishing House

让社会了解统计
让统计服务社会

高德占
一九九六年十一月

重视统计知识
提高决策水平

张立昌
九六年十一月

序

在全国人民喜迎党的“十五大”召开和热烈庆祝香港回归祖国的大喜日子里，1997 年《天津统计年鉴》又与读者见面了。

党的“十四大”以来，天津市的国民经济和社会各项事业取得了飞速的进步。国内生产总值连续五年实现“高增长低通胀”，步入了全国快速发展的先进地区行列，在天津市的历史发展中留下了辉煌的一页。

统计信息作为社会经济信息的主体，一直受到各级领导和社会各界人士的欢迎。非常荣幸的是，市委书记高德占、市长张立昌同志最近分别为统计工作书写了重要题词，充分表达了市领导对统计工作寄予的深切厚望。他们的题词将鼓舞和鞭策各级统计部门和全市统计人员不断开拓新的领域，紧紧围绕两个转变，不断深化统计改革，为天津的物质文明和精神文明建设提供更为优质的服务，为实现把天津市建设成为我国北方经济中心的宏伟目标作出更大的贡献。

编 者 说 明

一、《天津统计年鉴－1997》是一部全面反映天津市国民经济和社会发展情况的资料性年刊。本书收录了天津历史主要年份和改革开放18年来的主要统计数据，以及天津各区县和各专业部门1996年经济和社会各方面发展的统计数据。为便于读者了解天津在全国的地位、便于与兄弟省市对比，本书还编入了北京、上海和广州1996年的主要统计数据。

二、为便于读者分析和研究天津经济发展进程，本年鉴还收录了1996年《天津市国民经济和社会发展统计公报》、《天津市第三次工业普查公报》和《党的十四大以来天津经济和社会发展成就系列报告》等分析文章。

三、本年鉴的统计数据大部分取自统计年报，少部分来自抽样调查和普查资料。其他来源均在表下加注说明。

四、本年鉴对过去发表过的重要统计资料重新予以核实，有的数据做了调整。读者在使用历史资料时，凡与本年鉴有出入的，均以本年鉴为准。

五、本年鉴所使用的度量衡单位均采用国际统一标准计量单位。

六、本年鉴中部分数据的合计数和相对数由于小数位的取舍而产生的计算误差，均未做机械调整。

七、本年鉴表中的符号使用说明："空格"表示该项统计指标无数据、数据不足本表最小单位或数据不详；"#"表示其中的主要项。

八、《天津统计年鉴》自公开出版以来，受到了国内外广大读者的关心和支持，对本年鉴的内容和编辑工作提出了许多宝贵意见，对此我们深表感谢。限于我们的水平，书中难免有错误和不足，敬请广大读者继续给予批评指正，帮助我们进一步改进年鉴编辑工作，以期更好地为广大读者服务。

编　者

1997年6月于天津

(京)新登字 041 号

图书在版编目(CIP)数据
天津统计年鉴　1997/天津市统计局编.
-北京:中国统计出版社,1997.8
ISBN 7-5037-2475-7
Ⅰ.天…
Ⅱ.天…
Ⅲ.统计资料—中国—天津—1997—年鉴
Ⅳ.C832.21—54
中国版本图书馆 CIP 数据核字(97)第 12557 号

中国统计出版社出版
(北京市西城区三里河月坛南街 75 号　100826)
四二三六工厂印刷
*
787×1092 毫米　16 开本　32 印张　72 彩页　60 万字
1997 年 7 月第 1 版　1997 年 7 月天津第 1 次印刷
印数:1—5000 册
*
定价:130 元

篇目索引

篇　目	起始页码
天津概况	1
1996年天津市国民经济和社会发展统计公报	3
十四大以来天津市经济和社会发展成就	23
一、综　合	51
二、人口和劳动工资	81
三、固定资产投资	109
四、能源和原材料	141
五、财政和物价	149
六、城市建设和环境保护	157
七、人民生活和社会福利	167
八、农村经济	189
九、工　业	207
天津市第三次工业普查公报	268
十、建筑业	275
十一、交通运输和邮电通信	283
十二、批发零售贸易和餐饮业	291
十三、对外经济贸易和旅游业	311
十四、金融和保险业	329
十五、教育和科学技术	337
十六、文化体育卫生及其他	361
十七、改革开放和滨海新区	383
体制改革	384
滨海新区	389
新技术园区和区县开发小区	397
内联引资	398
各类市场	400
名牌产品与质量监督	406
大型交易会	411
十八、排名榜	413
十九、区县基本情况	431
附录	463
1　主要统计指标解释	463
2　世界主要国家(城市)统计资料	473

目　录

CONTENTS

天津概况 ………………………………………………………………………… (1)

SURVEY OF TIANJIN

1996年天津市国民经济和社会发展统计公报 ………………………………… (3)

STATISTICAL COMMUNIQUE OF TIANJIN NATIONAL ECONOMIC AND SOCIAL DEVELOPMENT, 1996

十四大以来天津市经济和社会发展成就

ACHIEVEMENT OF TIANJIN ECONOMIC AND SOCIAL DEVELOPMENT SINCE THE 14TH NATIONAL CONGRESS OF C. P. C

奋进辉煌的五年 ………………………………………………………………… (24)

STRIVED AND GLORIOUS FIVE YEARS

快速发展的天津工业 …………………………………………………………… (27)

TIANJIN INDUSTRY DEVELOPING RAPIDLY

农村经济再上新台阶 …………………………………………………………… (28)

RURAL ECONOMICS STEPPING NEW STAGE

面向国内外的天津商业 ………………………………………………………… (29)

TIANJIN COMMERCE FACING DOMESTIC AND FOREIGN GUESTS

方兴未艾的天津商品交易市场 ………………………………………………… (31)

TIANJIN COMMODITIES MARKET IN ASCENDANT

广引外资助天津腾飞 …………………………………………………………… (32)

WIDELY DRAWING FOREIGN INVESTMENT , SUPPORTING TIANJIN MARCHING FORWARD

外贸出口连创佳绩 ……………………………………………………………… (33)

EXPORTS OF FOREIGN TRADE CONTINUALLY SCORING GREAT SUCCESSES

投资为天津发展铺路奠基 ……………………………………………………… (35)

INVESTMENT FOR TIANJIN DEVELOPMENT LAYING A FOUNDATION

迈向现代化的交通邮电业 ……………………………………………………… (36)

STEPPING MODERN TRANSPORTATION AND POST AND TELECOMMUNICATION

日益兴旺的天津旅游业 ………………………………………………………… (37)

TIANJIN TOURISM FLOURISHING DAY BY DAY

正在崛起的天津滨海新区 ……………………………………………………… (39)

TIANJIN NEW COASTLINE AREA RISING ABRUPTLY

装点津城的建筑业 ……………………………………………………………… (41)

TIANJIN CONSTRUCTION DECORATING THE CITY

日趋良好的人口环境 …………………………………………………………… (42)

POPULATION ENVIRONMENTS ARE BECOMING WELL WITH EACH PASSING DAY

劳动就业多元化 ………………………………………………………………… (43)

VARIETY LABOUR EMPLOYMENT

科技兴市成果丰硕 …… (44)
SCIENCE AND TECHNOLOGY FLOURISHING THE CITY REAPED RICH FRUITS
绚丽多彩的社会事业 …… (45)
SOCIAL UTILITIES BRIGHT AND COLOURFUL
居民生活质量明显提高 …… (47)
LIVING QUALITIES OF RESIDENTS REMARKABLE RISE
走向富裕的农民家庭 …… (48)
FARMER'S FAMILY STEPPING PROSPERITY
物价调控成效显著 …… (49)
PRICE CONTROLLING REMARKABLE ACHIEVING

一、综　合
GENERAL SURVEY

1-1. 行政建制(1996 年底) …… (52)
ADMINISTRATIVE DIVISIONS(END OF 1996)
1-2. 1996 年土地面积 …… (53)
AREA OF LAND, 1996
1-3. 1996 年城市建设用地 …… (53)
CITY CONSTRUCTION LAND-USED, 1996
1-4. 1996 年气象资料 …… (54)
METEOROLOGICAL DATA, 1996
1-5. 主要年份国民经济主要指标和增长速度 …… (55)
MAIN INDICATORS AND INCREASE RATE OF NATIONAL ECONOMY IN MAIN YEARS
1-6. 国民经济主要比例关系 …… (62)
MAIN PERCENTAGE OF ECONOMIC INDICATORS
1-7. 国民经济主要指标经济类型变化 …… (64)
ECONOMIC TYPE CHANGES OF MAIN INDICATORS IN NATIONAL ECONOMY
1-8. 国民经济主要指标平均每人水平 …… (65)
PER CAPITA LEVEL OF MAIN INDICATORS IN NATIONAL ECONOMY
1-9. 平均每天社会经济活动 …… (66)
AVERAGE DAILY SOCIAL AND ECONOMIC ACTIVITIES
1-10. 改革开放以来国内生产总值和指数 …… (68)
INDICES AND GROSS DOMESTIC PRODUCTS SINCE REFORM AND OPENING TO OUTSIDE
1-11. 国内生产总值 …… (69)
GROSS DOMESTIC PRODUCTS
1-12. 国内生产总值构成 …… (69)
COMPOSITION OF GROSS DOMESTIC PRODUCTS
1-13. 改革开放以来国内支出总额 …… (70)
TOTAL DOMESTIC EXPENDITURES SINCE REFORM AND OPENING TO OUTSIDE
1-14. 总消费构成 …… (70)
COMPOSITION OF TOTAL CONSUMPTION
1-15. 1995 年九部门投入产出流量表(产品部门×产品部门) …… (71)
INPUT-OUTPUT TABLE BY 9 SECTORS, 1995(PRODUCTS DEPARTMENT MULTIPLICATION PRODUCTS DEPARTMENT)
1-16. 1995 年九部门投入产出直接消耗系数表 …… (73)
DIRECT CONSUMPTION COEFFICIENT TABLE OF INPUT-OUTPUT BY 9 SECTORS, 1995

1－17.1995 年九部门投入产出完全消耗系数表 ………………………………………………………………… (74)
OVERALL CONSUMPTION COEFFICIENT TABLE OF INPUT－OUTPUT BY 9 SECTORS, 1995
1－18.天津在全国的地位 ………………………………………………………………………………………… (75)
POSITION OF TIANJIN IN THE WHOLE NATION
1－19.1996 天津、北京、上海、广州主要经济指标 …………………………………………………………… (77)
MAIN ECONOMIC INDICATORS OF TIANJIN, BEIJING, SHANGHAI, GUANGZHOU, 1996

二、人口和劳动工资

POPULATION, LABOUR FORCE AND WAGES

2－1.改革开放以来户籍人口数、户数及人口密度 ……………………………………………………………… (82)
NUMBER OF REGISTERED POPULATION, HOUSEHOLD AND POPULATION DENSITY SINCEREFORM AND OPENING TO OUTSIDE
2－2.人口变动情况 ……………………………………………………………………………………………… (82)
CHANGES OF POPULATION
2－3.按地区分的户数、人口数和人口密度 ……………………………………………………………………… (83)
NUMBER OF HOUSEHOLDS, POPULATION AND DENSITY BY DISTRICTS
2－4.按农业非农业分的户数和人口数 ………………………………………………………………………… (84)
NUMBER OF HOUSEHOLDS AND POPULATION BY AGRICULTURE AND UNAGRICULTURE
2－5.按性别分的户籍人口数 …………………………………………………………………………………… (85)
NUMBER OF REGISTERED POPULATION BY SEX
2－6.主要年份户籍人口的城乡分布 …………………………………………………………………………… (85)
URBAN AND RURAL DISTRIBUTION OF MAIN YEAR REGISTERED POPULATION
2－7.主要年份计划生育情况 …………………………………………………………………………………… (86)
MAIN YEARS FAMILY PLANNING
2－8.人口婚姻登记情况 ………………………………………………………………………………………… (86)
MARRIAGE REGISTRATIONS OF POPULATION
2－9.1996 年户籍人口负担系数 ………………………………………………………………………………… (86)
DEPENDENTS INDICES OF REGISTERED POPULATION, 1996
2－10.1996 年各年龄组的户籍人口 …………………………………………………………………………… (87)
REGISTERED POPULATION BY AGE, 1996
1996 年全市人口变动情况抽样调查资料说明 ………………………………………………………………… (88)
SAMPLING INVESTIGATION DATAS OF POPULATION CHANGES, 1996
2－11.1996 年 6 岁及以上人口文化构成 ……………………………………………………………………… (88)
COMPOSITION OF CULTURE AGE 6 AND OVER, 1996
2－12.1996 年 15 岁及以上人口婚姻构成 ……………………………………………………………………… (88)
COMPOSITION OF MARRIAGE AGE 15 AND OVER, 1996
2－13.1996 年按地区分的家庭户规模 …………………………………………………………………………… (89)
NUMBER OF MEMBER PER HOUSEHOLD BY REGIONS, 1996
2－14.1996 年按地区分的家庭户类别 …………………………………………………………………………… (90)
TYPE OF MEMBER PER HOUSEHOLD BY REGIONS, 1996
2－15.1996 年育龄妇女分年龄和受教育程度的初婚状况 ……………………………………………………… (91)
FIRST MARRIAGE STATUS OF WOMEN AT CHILDBEARING BY AGE AND LEVEL OF EDUCATION RECEIVED, 1996
2－16.1996 年育龄妇女分年龄和受教育程度的初育状况 ……………………………………………………… (91)
FIRST FERTILITY STATUS OF WOMEN AT CHILDBEARING BY AGE AND LEVEL OF EDUCATION RECEIVED, 1996
2－17.1996 年育龄妇女分孩次生育率 ………………………………………………………………………… (91)
WOMEN AT CHILDBEARING BY BEARING RATE OF CHILD TIMES, 1996

2-18. 1996年分年龄和受教育程度的就业者身份 …… (92)
EMPLOYED PERSONS BY AGE AND LEVEL OF EDUCATION RECEIVED, 1996
2-19. 改革开放以来社会从业人员变化情况 …… (94)
CHANGES OF EMPLOYED POPULATION SINCE REFORM AND OPENING TO OUTSIDE
2-20. 社会从业人员人数 …… (95)
NUMBER OF LABOUR FORCE
2-21. 职工人数 …… (96)
STAFF AND WORKERS
2-22. 1996年国民经济各行业职工人数 …… (97)
STAFF AND WORKERS BY SECTOR OF NATIONAL ECONOMY, 1996
2-23. 市属各局(总公司)国有经济职工人数 …… (98)
STATE-OWNED STAFF AND WORKERS BY BUREAU (CORPORATION)
2-24. 1996年职工变动情况 …… (99)
CHANGES OF STAFF AND WORKERS, 1996
2-25. 城镇新就业人数 …… (99)
EMPLOYED PERSONS IN URBAN AREAS
2-26. 1996年工业、建筑业、交通运输仓储及邮电业职工人员分类 …… (100)
CLASSIFICATION OF STAFF AND WORKERS IN INDUSTRY, CONSTRUCTION, TRANSPORTATION & WAREHOUSE AND POSTAL & TELECOMMUNICATION, 1996
2-27. 合同制职工人数 …… (101)
CONTRACT STAFF AND WORKERS
2-28. 城乡私营、个体从业人员 …… (101)
LABOURERS OF PERSONAL OWNERSHIP AND INDIVIDUAL LABOURERS IN URBAN AND RURAL AREAS
2-29. 改革开放以来职工工资情况 …… (102)
STATUS OF STAFF AND WORKERS WAGES SINCE REFORM AND OPENING TO OUTSIDE
2-30. 1996年按经济类型分各行业职工工资总额 …… (103)
TOTAL WAGES OF EVERY SECTOR STAFF AND WORKERS BY TYPE OF ECONOMY, 1996
2-31. 1996年按经济类型分各行业职工人均工资 …… (104)
AVERAGE ANNUAL WAGE OF EVERY SECTOR STAFF AND WORKERS BY TYPE OF ECONOMY, 1996
2-32. 国有经济职工工资构成 …… (105)
COMPOSITION OF STAFF AND WORKERS WAGES IN STATE-OWNED UNITS
2-33. 按企、事业、机关分的职工人数和工资总额 …… (105)
NUMBER OF STAFF AND WORKERS & TOTAL WAGES BY ENTERPRISE, INSTITUTION
2-34. 市属各局(总公司)国有经济职工工资 …… (106)
TOTAL WAGES OF STATE-OWNED BY BUREAU (CORPORATION)
2-35. 其他从业人员人数及报酬(乡及乡以上) …… (107)
OTHER LABOURERS AND WAGES (AT AND ABOVE TOWNSHIP LEVEL)
2-36. 改革开放以来离退休退职人员情况 …… (107)
STATUS OF RETIRES AND RESIGNED WORKERS PAYED OUT SINCE REFORM AND OPENING TO OUTSIDE
2-37. 改革开放以来职工保险福利费发放情况(1990-1996年) …… (108)
TOTAL INSURANCE WELFARE OF STAFFS AND WORKERS SINCE REFORM AND OPENINGTO OUTSIDE (1990-1996)
2-38. 职工保险福利费构成 …… (108)
COMPOSITION OF INSURANCE WELFARES OF STAFFS AND WORKERS

三、固定资产投资
INVESTMENT IN FIXED ASSETS

3-1. 全社会固定资产投资及新增固定资产(1985—1996年) …… (111)
TOTAL INVESTMENT IN FIXED ASSETS AND NEWLY INCREASED FIXED ASSETS(1985-1996)

3－2.1996 年全社会固定资产投资和房屋建筑面积 …… (112)
TOTAL INVESTMENT IN FIXED ASSETS AND FLOOR SPACE OF BUILDING, 1996
3－3.改革开放以来国有单位基本建设和更新改造投资额 …… (113)
CAPITAL CONTRUCTION AND TRANSFORMATION INVESTMENTS OF STATE－OWNED SINCE REFORM AND OPENING TO OUTSIDE
3－4.固定资产施工项目和建成投产项目个数(不含农村集体和个人投资) …… (114)
NUMBER OF UNDER CONSTRUCTION IN FIXED ASSETS AND PUT INTO OPERATION PROJECTS(EXCLUDE RURAL COLLECTIVE－OWNED AND INDIVIDUALS)
3－5.按行业分固定资产投资额(不含农村集体和个人投资) …… (115)
INVESTMENT IN FIXED ASSETS BY SECTOR(EXCLUDE RURAL COLLECTIVE－OWNED AND INDIVIDUALS)
3－6.地方固定资产投资额(不含农村集体和个人投资) …… (116)
LOCAL INVESTMENT IN FIXED ASSETS(EXCLUDE RURAL COLLECTIVE－OWNED AND INDIVIDUALS)
3－7.地方按行业分固定资产投资额(不含农村集体和个人投资) …… (117)
LOCAL INVESTMENT IN FIXED ASSETS BY SECTOR(EXCLUDE RURAL COLLECTIVE－OWNED AND INDIVIDUALS)
3－8.1996 年工业行业固定资产投资额(不含农村集体和个人投资) …… (118)
INVESTMENT IN FIXED ASSETS OF INDUSTRY, 1996(EXCLUDE RURAL COLLECTIVE－OWNED AND INDIVIDUALS)
3－9.1996 年地方工业行业固定资产投资(不含农村集体和个人投资) …… (119)
INVESTMENT IN FIXED ASSETS OF LOCAL INDUSTRY, 1996(EXCLUDE RURAL COLLECTIVE－OWNED AND INDIVIDUALS)
3－10.基本建设和更新改造固定资产投资额(不含农村集体和个人投资) …… (120)
INVESTMENT OF FIXED ASSETS WITH CAPITAL CONSTRUCTION AND TRANSFORMATION (EXCLUDE RURAL COLLECTIVE－OWNED AND INDIVIDUALS)
3－11.1996 年工业行业基本建设施工、竣工项目 …… (121)
PROJECTS OF UNDER CONSTRUCTION AND COMPLETED IN CAPITAL CONSTRUCTION OF INDUSTRY, 1996
3－12.1996 年工业行业更新改造施工、竣工项目 …… (122)
PROJECTS OF UNDER CONSTRUCTION AND COMPLETED IN TRANSFORMATION OF INDUSTRY, 1996
3－13.能源工业固定资产投资额(不含农村集体和个人投资) …… (123)
INVESTMENT IN FIXED ASSETS OF ENERGY INDUSTRY (EXCLUDE RURAL COLLECTIVE－OWNED AND INDIVIDUALS)
3－14.城市基础设施固定资产投资额(不含农村集体和个人投资) …… (123)
INVESTMENT IN FIXED ASSETS OF BASIC INSTALLATIONS ON CITY (EXCLUDE RURAL COLLECTIVE－OWNED AND INDIVIDUALS)
3－15.地方各主管部门固定资产投资 …… (124)
INVESTMENT IN FIXED ASSETS BY LOCAL DEPARTMENTS
3－16.国民经济各行业新增固定资产(不含农村集体和个人投资) …… (125)
NEWLY INCREASED FIXED ASSETS BY SECTOR OF NATIONAL ECONOMY (EXCLUDE RURAL COLLECTIVE－OWNED UNITS AND INDIVIDUALS)
3－17.工业行业新增固定资产(不含农村集体和个人投资) …… (126)
NEWLY INCREASED FIXED ASSETS OF INDUSTRY (EXCLUDE RURAL COLLECTIVE－OWNED UNITS AND INDIVIDUALS)
3－18.1996 年固定资产投资资金来源(一)(不含农村集体和个人投资) …… (127)
SOURCES OF INVESTMENT IN FIXED ASSETS, 1996(1)(EXCLUDE RURAL COLLECTIVE－OWNED AND INDIVIDUALS)
3－19.1996 年固定资产投资资金来源(二)(不含农村集体和个人投资) …… (127)
SOURCES OF INVESTMENT IN FIXED ASSETS, 1996(2)(EXCLUDE RURAL COLLECTIVE－OWNED AND INDIVIDUALS)

3－20. 施工和竣工房屋建筑面积(不含农村集体和个人投资) …… (128)
FLOOR SPACE OF BUILDINGS UNDER CONSTRUCTION AND COMPLETED (EXCLUDE RURAL COLLECTIVE－OWNED AND INDIVIDUALS)
3－21. 1996年建设项目主要新增生产能力 …… (129)
MAIN NEWLY INCREASED CAPACITY OF CONSTRUCTED PROJECTS, 1996
3－22. 1996年重点建设项目完成情况 …… (130)
A SURVEY OF KEY CONSTRUCTION PROJECTS COMPLETED, 1996
3－23. 国有经济其他固定资产投资完成情况(1992－1996年) …… (136)
COMPLETED STATUS OF INVESTMENT IN OTHER FIXED ASSETS OF STATE－OWNED UNITS(1992－1996)
3－24. 房地产开发建设情况(1992－1996年) …… (136)
REAL ESTATE DEVELOPMENT AND CONSTRUCTION(1992－1996)
3－25. 1996年按经济类型分房地产开发建设情况 …… (137)
REAL ESTATE DEVELOPMENT AND CONSTRUCTION BY TYPE OF ECONOMY, 1996
3－26. 1996年按用途分房地产开发建设情况 …… (137)
REAL ESTATE DEVELOPMENT AND CONSTRUCTION BY USAGE, 1996
3－27. 1996年天津市区土地出让一览 …… (138)
LIST OF LAND－CONVEGANCE IN THE CITY AREA, 1996
3－28. 农村集体固定资产投资完成情况(1992－1996年) …… (140)
COMPLETED STATUS OF INVESTMENT IN FIXED ASSETS OF RURAL COLLECTIVE－OWNED UNITS (1992－1996)
3－29. 城镇和农村个人建房情况(1992－1996年) …… (140)
BUILDING CONSTRUCTION BY INDIVIDUALS IN URBAN AND RURAL AREAS(1992－1996)

四、能源和原材料
ENERGY AND RAW MATERIAL

4－1. 1996年原材料和能源消费总值(县及县以上) …… (142)
TOTAL CONSUMPTION OF ENERGY AND MATERIALS, 1996(AT AND ABOVE COUNTY LEVEL)
4－2. 1996年主要原材料消费量(县及县以上) …… (143)
CONSUMPTION OF MAJOR MATERIALS, 1996(AT AND ABOVE COUNTY LEVEL)
4－3. 1996年主要能源按国民经济行业分组消费量(县及县以上) …… (144)
CONSUMPTION OF MAIN ENERGY BY NATIONAL ECONOMLY SECTOR, 1996(AT AND ABOVE COUNTY LEVEL)
4－4. 分行业能源消费量及构成(折标准煤) …… (146)
COSUMPTION OF ENERGY AND COMPOSITION BY SECTORS(CONVERSION STANDARD COAL)
4－5. 天津市用水情况(1991－1996年) …… (147)
STATUS OF TIANJIN WATER－USED(1991－1996)
4－6. 天津市大型水库基本情况 …… (148)
STATUS OF LARGE RESERVOIR IN TIANJIN
4－7. 天津市中型水库基本情况 …… (148)
STATUS OF MIDDLE RESERVOIR IN TIANJIN

五、财政和物价
PUBLIC FINANCE AND PRICE

5－1. 改革开放以来地方财政收支额 …… (150)
TOTAL REVENUE AND EXPENDITURES OF LOCAL GOVERNMENT SINCE REFORM AND OPENING TO OUTSIDE
5－2. 地方财政收入和支出 …… (151)
REVENUE AND EXPENDITURES OF LOCAL GOVERNMENT

5－3. 1996 年区县级财政收入 …………………………………………………………………………………………… (152)
REVENUE ON DISTRICT AND COUNTY LEVEL, 1996
5－4. 1996 年区县级财政支出 …………………………………………………………………………………………… (153)
EXPENDITURES ON DISTRICT AND COUNTY LEVEL, 1996
5－5. 天津市国家税务局各项税收情况 ………………………………………………………………………………… (154)
VARIOUS TAXATIONS OF TIANJIN STATE TAX BUREAU
5－6. 改革开放以来各种物价总指数 …………………………………………………………………………………… (154)
VARIOUS PRICE INDICES SINCE REFORM AND OPENING TO OUTSIDE
5－7. 城市居民消费价格分类指数(以上年为 100) ……………………………………………………………………… (155)
URBAN OVERALL RESIDENT CONSUMER GOODS INDICES BY CATEGORY OF COMMODITIES(PRECEDING YEAR＝100)
5－8. 城市商品零售价格分类指数(以上年为 100) ……………………………………………………………………… (155)
URBAN OVERALL RETAIL PRICE INDICES BY CATEGORY OF COMMODITIES(PRECEDING YEAR＝100)
5－9. 城市农贸市场农产品成交价格分类指数(以上年为 100) ………………………………………………………… (155)
FARM PRODUCTS TRANSACTION PRICE INDICES IN URBAN FREE MARKET BY CATEGORY OF COMMODITIES(PRECEDING YEAR＝100)
5－10. 固定资产投资价格指数(以上年为 100) …………………………………………………………………………… (156)
PRICE INDICES OF INVESTMENT IN FIXED ASSETS(PRECEDING YEAR＝100)
5－11. 工业主要原材料、燃料及动力购进价格指数(以上年为 100) ……………………………………………………… (156)
MAIN RAW MATERIALS, FUELS AND POWERS PURCHASING PRICE INDICES(PRECEDINGYEAR＝100)
5－12. 主要工业产品出厂价格指数(以上年为 100) ……………………………………………………………………… (156)
FACTORY PRICES INDICES OF MAIN INDUSTRIAL PRODUCTS(PRECEDING YEAR＝100)

六、城市建设和环境保护

URBAN CONSTRUCTION AND ENVIRONMENT PROTECTION

6－1. 市政公用设施水平 ……………………………………………………………………………………………………… (159)
INDICATORS OF MUNICIPAL PUBLIC UTILITIES LEVEL
6－2. 主要年份城市房屋建筑面积 ……………………………………………………………………………………… (159)
URBAN FLOOR SPACE OF BUILDING IN MAJOR YEARS
6－3. 城市房屋建筑面积 …………………………………………………………………………………………………… (160)
URBAN FLOOR SPACE OF BUILDING
6－4. 城市燃气设备能力 …………………………………………………………………………………………………… (160)
URBAN CAPACITY OF GAS INSTRUMENT
6－5. 城市燃气销售量和用气户数 ……………………………………………………………………………………… (160)
SALES OF GAS AND HOUSEHOLDS OF USING GAS
6－6. 城市自来水 ……… (161)
URBAN TAP WATER
6－7. 城市市政设施情况 …………………………………………………………………………………………………… (161)
URBAN MUNICIPAL FACILITIES
6－8. 城市公共交通 …… (162)
URBAN PUBLIC TRAFFIC
6－9. 城市园林绿化情况 …………………………………………………………………………………………………… (162)
CITY PARKS, GARDENS AND GREEN AREAS
6－10. 1996 年公园分布 …………………………………………………………………………………………………… (163)
DISTRIBUTION OF PARKS, 1996
6－11. 城市集中供热 ……………………………………………………………………………………………………… (163)
URBAN HEAT SUPPLY
6－12. 城市环境卫生事业发展情况 ……………………………………………………………………………………… (163)

DEVELOPMENT OF CITY ENVIRONMENT SANITATION
6-13.环境保护系统基本情况 …… (164)
BASIC STATISTICS ON ENVIRONMENT PROTECTION
6-14.废气排放及处理情况 …… (164)
EMISSION AND TREATMENT OF WASTE GAS
6-15.城市环境噪声情况 …… (164)
NOISE OF CITY ENVIRONMENT
6-16.工业粉尘、工业废渣排放及处理利用情况 …… (165)
EMISSION AND TREATMENT OF INDUSTRIAL RESIDUE AND POWDER
6-17.工业废水排放及处理量 …… (165)
VOLUME OF EMISSION AND TREATMENT OF INDUSTRY WASTE WATER
6-18."三废"综合利用及污染事故处理情况 …… (166)
UTILIZATION AND TREATMENT OF POLLUTION OF WASTE GAS, WASTE WATER AND INDUS TRIAL RESIDUE
6-19.排污费征收、使用和企事业污染治理情况 …… (166)
DISCHARGE FEE USE AND TREATMENT OF POLLUTION IN ENTERPRISES AND INSTITUTION

七、人民生活和社会福利
PEOPLE'S LIVEHOOD AND SOCIAL WELFARE

7-1.城乡居民物质文化生活水平提高情况 …… (169)
IMPROVEMENT IN MATERIAL AND CULTURAL LIFE OF URBAN AND RURAL HOUSEHOLDS
7-2.城市居民家庭基本情况(1992-1996年) …… (171)
BAISC INDICATORS OF URBAN HOUSEHOLDS(1992-1996)
7-3.1996年城市不同收入水平居民家庭基本情况(按平均每人每月生活费收入分组) …… (171)
BASIC INDICATORS OF URBAN HOUSEHOLDS, 1996(BY LIVING INCOME PER CAPITA)
7-4.城市居民家庭平均每人全年消费性支出分类(1992-1996年) …… (172)
CLASSIFICATIONS OF URBAN HOUSEHOLD ANNUAL LIVING EXPENDITURES PER CAPITA(1992-1996)
7-5.1996年城市居民家庭平均每人全年消费性支出(按水平组分类) …… (173)
CLASSIFICATIONS OF URBAN HOUSEHOLD DIVIDED BY LEVEL ANNUAL LIVING EXPENDITURES PER CAPITA, 1996 (BY INCOME LEVEL)
7-6.城市居民家庭平均每人主要消费品全年购买量(1992-1996年) …… (175)
URBAN HOUSEHOLD ANNUAL PER CAPITA PURCHASES OF MAJOR COMMODITIES(1992-1996)
7-7.城市居民家庭平均每百户耐用消费品全年购买量(1992-1996年) …… (176)
URBAN HOUSEHOLD ANNUAL PER 100 PURCHASES OF DURABLE COMMODITIES(1992-1996)
7-8.城市居民家庭平均每百户耐用消费品年末拥有量(1992-1996年) …… (177)
URBAN HOUSEHOLD YEAR-END POSSESSION OF MAJOR DURABLE CONSUMER GOODS PER 100 HOUSEHOLDS(1992-1996)
7-9.城市居民家庭分水平组每百户耐用消费品年末拥有量 …… (178)
URBAN HOUSEHOLD DIVIDED BY LEVEL YEAR-END POSSESSION OF MAJOR DURABLE CONSUMER GOODS PER 100 HOUSEHOLD
7-10.农民家庭基本情况 …… (180)
BASIC INDICATORS OF RURAL HOUSEHOLDS
7-11.农民家庭劳动力文化程度 …… (180)
EDUCATION LEVEL OF LABOUR FORCE IN RURAL HOUSEHOLD
7-12.农民家庭平均每人年纯收入 …… (180)
RURAL HOUSEHOLD ANNUAL PER CAPITA NET INCOME
7-13.农民家庭平均每人年生活费支出 …… (181)

RURAL HOUSEHOLD ANNUAL PER CAPITA LIVING EXPENDITURES
7－14. 1996年农民家庭人均生活消费各项支出(按收入水平分组) ………………………… (181)
RURAL HOUSEHOLD PER CAPITA EXPENDITURES BY INCOME LEVEL, 1996
7－15. 农民家庭平均每人食品及衣着消费量 ………………………… (182)
RURAL HOUSEHOLD PER CAPITA CONSUMPTION ON FOOD AND CLOTHING
7－16. 1996年农民家庭主要食品及衣着消费量(按收入水平分组) ………………………… (183)
RURAL HOUSEHOLD CONSUMPTION ON MAJOR FOOD AND CLOTHING BY INCOME LEVEL, 1996
7－17. 年末每百户农民家庭耐用物品拥有量 ………………………… (184)
YEAR－END POSSESSION OF DURABLE CONSUMER GOODS PER 100 RURAL HOUSEHOLD
7－18. 1996年农民家庭耐用物品每百户拥有量(按收入水平分组) ………………………… (184)
POSSESSION OF DURABLE CONSUMER GOODS PER 100 HOUSEHOLD BY INCOME LEVEL, 1996
7－19. 优抚对象及优抚事业单位情况 ………………………… (185)
SPECIAL CARE TO DISABLED SERVICEMEN AND INSTITUTIONS
7－20. 社会福利事业、企业单位及工作人员数 ………………………… (185)
SOCIAL WELFARE INSTITUTIONS AND ENTERPRISES AND STAFF AND WORKERS
7－21. 1996年社会福利事业单位基本情况 ………………………… (186)
BASIC STATISTICS ON SOCIAL WELFARE AND INSTITUTIONS, 1996
7－22. 社会福利企业情况 ………………………… (186)
BASIC STATISTICS ON SOCIAL WELFARE ENTERPRISES
7－23. 抚恤、社会救济事业费及集体优待供给补助金额 ………………………… (187)
SOCIAL WELFARE RELIEF FUNDS AND COLLECTION SUPPLY SUBSIDYS
7－24. 享受补助和救济人员情况 ………………………… (187)
PERSONS RECEIVING SUBSIDIES AND RELIEF FUNDS
7－25. 城镇社区服务和残疾人分散就业情况 ………………………… (188)
BASIC STATISTICS ON URBAN WELFARE FACILIFIES AND EMPLOYMENT OF DEFORMIFY
7－26. 农村社会保障、养老保险及扶贫情况 ………………………… (188)
RURAL SOCIAL SECURITY AND OLD－AGE INSURANCE AND SUPPORTING POOR
7－27. 农村自然灾害救济情况 ………………………… (188)
BASIC STATISTICS OF RELIEF IN RURAL NATURAL DISASTER AREA

八、农村经济
RURAL ECONOMY

8－1. 天津市农工商总公司主要指标 ………………………… (190)
MAJOR ECONOMIC IDICATORS OF TIANJIN AGRICULTURE INDUSTRY AND COMMERCE CORPORATION
8－2. 1996年各区县农村基层组织和乡村建设 ………………………… (191)
BASIC RURAL UNITS AND RURAL CONSTRUCTIONS BY DISTRICTS AND COUNTIES, 1996
8－3. 改革开放以来农业发展情况 ………………………… (192)
DEVELOPMENT OF AGRICULTURE SINCE REFORM AND OPENING TO OUTSIDE
8－4. 改革开放以来农业总产值和播种面积 ………………………… (193)
GROSS OUTPUT VALUE OF AGRICULTURE AND SOWN AREAS SINCE REFORM AND OPENING TO OUTSIDE
8－5. 改革开放以来主要农产品产量 ………………………… (194)
OUTPUT OF MAJOR FARM CROPS SINCE REFORM AND OPENING TO OUTSIDE
8－6. 1996年各区县农村劳动力 ………………………… (195)
RURAL LABOR FORCE BY DISTRICTS AND COUNTIES, 1996
8－7. 1996年各区县农村固定资产构成 ………………………… (195)
COMPOSITION OF INVESTMENT IN FIXED ASSETS IN RURAL AREA BY DISTRICTS AND COUNTIES, 1996

8-8.农民家庭每户生产性固定资产原值 …………………………………………………………………… (196)
ORIGINAL VALUE OF URBAN HOUSEHOLD INVESTMENT IN FIXED ASSETS PER HOUSEHOLD
8-9.农民家庭每百户拥有生产性固定资产数量 ………………………………………………………… (196)
NUMBER OF PRODUTIVITY INVESTMENT IN FIXED ASSETS OF URBAN HOUSEHOLDS PER 100 HOUSEHOLDS
8-10.1996年各区县耕地面积 ……………………………………………………………………………… (197)
AREAS UNDER CULTIVATION BY DISTRICTS AND COUNTIES, 1996
8-11.1996年各区县农业现代化情况 ……………………………………………………………………… (197)
AGRICULTURE MODERNIZATIONS, BY DISTRICTS AND COUNTRIES, 1996
8-12.1996年各区县农业总产值和农业商品产值 ………………………………………………………… (198)
GROSS OUTPUT VALUE OF AGRICULTURE AND COMMODITIES BY DISTRICTS AND COUNTIES, 1996
8-13.1996年各区县农业增加值情况 ……………………………………………………………………… (198)
VALUE-ADDED OF AGRICULTURE BY DISTRICTS AND COUNTIES, 1996
8-14.1996年各区县主要农作物播种面积 ………………………………………………………………… (199)
SOWN AREAS OF MAJOR FARM CROPS BY DISTRICTS AND COUNTIES, 1996
8-15.1996年各区县主要农产品产量 ……………………………………………………………………… (200)
OUTPUT OF MAJOR FARM PRODUCT BY DISTRICTS AND COUNTIES, 1996
8-16.1996年各区县主要农作物单位面积产量 …………………………………………………………… (201)
MAJOR FARM CROPS OUTPUT PER HECTARE BY DISTRICTS AND COUNTIES, 1996
8-17.1996年各区县畜牧业生产情况 ……………………………………………………………………… (202)
PRODUCTS OF ANIMAL HUSBANDRY BY DISTRICTS AND COUNTIES, 1996
8-18.林业生产、果园面积及产量 …………………………………………………………………………… (203)
FORESTRY PRODUCTS ORCHARD AREA AND OUTPUT
8-19.1996年各区县渔业生产情况 ………………………………………………………………………… (203)
PRODUCTS OF FISHERY BY DISTRICTS AND COUNTIES, 1996
8-20.1996年乡镇企业基本情况 …………………………………………………………………………… (204)
BASIC OF TOWNSHIP-OWNED ENTERPRISES, 1996
8-21.1996年各区县乡镇企业主要指标 …………………………………………………………………… (206)
MAJOR INDICATORS OF TOWNSHIP-OWNED ENTERPRISES BY DISTRICTS AND COUNTIES, 1996

九、工　业

INDUSTRY

9-1.全部工业总产值和增长速度(1985-1996年) ………………………………………………………… (208)
GROSS OUTPUT VALUE OF INDUSTRY AND INCREASE RATE(1985-1996)
9-2.改革开放以来工业发展情况(街、乡及以上独立核算工业) ……………………………………… (209)
DEVELOPMENT OF INDUSTRY SINCE REFORM AND OPENING TO OUTSIDE (SUBDISTRICT-RUN, TOWNSHIP-RUN AND OVER WITH INDIPENDENT ACCOUNTING SYSTEM)
9-3.改革开放以来国有工业发展情况(街、乡及以上独立核算工业) ………………………………… (210)
DEVELOPMENT OF STATE-OWNED INDUSTRY SINCE REFORM AND OPENING TO OUTSIDE (SUBDISTRICT-RUN, TOWNSHIP-RUN AND OVER WITH INDIPENDENT ACCOUNTING SYSTEM)
9-4.工业企业单位数和工业总产值(街、乡及以上工业) ……………………………………………… (211)
NUMBER OF INDUSTRIAL ENTERPRISES AND GROSS OUTPUT VALUE OF INDUSTRY (SUBDISTRICT-RUN, TOWNSHIP-RUN AND OVER)
9-5.地方工业企业单位数和工业总产值(街、乡及以上工业) ………………………………………… (212)
LOCAL INDUSTRIAL ENTERPRISES AND GROSS OUTPUT VALUE OF INDUSTRY (SUBDISTRICT-RUN, TOWNSHIP-RUN AND OVER)
9-6.分行业工业企业单位数和工业总产值(街、乡及以上工业) ……………………………………… (213)

NUMBER OF INDUSTRIAL ENTERPRISES AND GROSS INDUSTRIAL OUTPUT VALUE BY SECTOR (SUBDISTRICT－RUN, TOWNSHIP－RUN AND OVER)
9－7.分行业国有工业企业单位数和工业总产值(街、乡及以上工业) …… (214)
NUMBER OF STATE－OWNED INDUSTRIAL ENTERPRISES AND GROSS INDUSTRIAL OUTPUT VALUE BY SECTOR (SUBDISTRICT－RUN, TOWNSHIP－RUN AND OVER)
9－8.分行业"三资"工业企业单位数和工业总产值(街、乡及以上工业) …… (215)
NUMBER OF FOREIGN INVESTMENT COOPERATION AND JOINT－VENTURE ENTERPRISESAND GROSS OUTPUT VALUE OF INDUSTRY BY SECTOR(SUBDISTRICT－RUN, TOWNSHIP－RUN AND OVER)
9－9.分行业地方工业企业单位数和工业总产值(街、乡及以上工业) …… (216)
NUMBER OF LOCAL INDUSTRIAL ENTERPRISES AND GROSS INDUSTRIAL OUTPUT VALUE BY SECTOR (SUBDISTRICT－RUN, TOWNSHIP－RUN AND OVER)
9－10.改革开放以来主要工业产品产量 …… (217)
OUTPUT OF MAJOR INDUSTRIAL PRODUCTS SINCE REFORM AND OPENING TO OUTSIDE
9－11.主要工业产品产量 …… (218)
OUTPUT OF MAJOR INDUSTRIAL PRODUCTS
9－12.工业企业主要产品销售量和产销率(街、乡及以上工业) …… (219)
SALES VALUE AND RATES OF MAJOR PRODUCTS OF INDUSTRIAL ENTERPRISES (SUBDISTRICT－RUN, TOWNSHIP－RUN AND OVER)
9－13.1996年独立核算工业企业主要财务指标(街、乡及以上工业) …… (220)
MAIN FINANCIAL INDICATORS OF INDUSTRIAL ENTERPRISES WITH INDEPENDENT ACCOUNTING SYSTEM (SUBDISTRICT－RUN, TOWNSHIP－RUN AND OVER), 1996
9－14.1996年地方独立核算工业企业主要财务指标(街、乡及以上工业) …… (223)
MAIN FINANCIAL INDICATORS OF LOCAL INDUSTRIAL ENTERPRISES WITH INDEPENDENT ACCOUNTING SYSTEM (SUBDISTRICT－RUN, TOWNSHIP－RUN AND OVER), 1996
9－15.1996年分行业独立核算工业企业主要财务指标(街、乡及以上工业) …… (226)
MAIN FINANCIAL INDICATORS OF INDUSTRIAL ENTERPRISES WITH INDEPENDENT ACCOUNTING SYSTEM BY SECTOR (SUBISTRICT－RUN, TOWNSHIP－RUN AND OVER), 1996
9－16.1996年分行业独立核算国有大中型工业企业主要财务指标(街、乡及以上工业) …… (229)
MAIN FINANCIAL INDICATOR OF STATE－OWNED LARGE－MEDIUM INDUSTRIAL ENTERPRISES WITH INDEPENDENT ACCOUNTING SYSTEM BY SECTOR (SUBISTRICT－RUN, TOWNSHIP－RUN AND OVER), 1996
9－17.独立核算工业企业主要经济效益指标(街、乡及以上工业) …… (232)
FINANCIAL RATIOS OF INDUSTRIAL ENTERPRISES WITH INDEPENDENT ACCOUNTINGSYSTEM (SUBDISTRICT－RUN, TOWNSHIP－RUN AND OVER)
9－18.地方预算内国有工业企业主要财务和经济效益指标 …… (233)
MAIN FINANCIAL INDICATORS AND FINANCIAL RATIOS OF STATE－OWNED INDUSTRIAL ENTERPRISES WITH LOCAL BUDGET
9－19.新产品试制和投产情况 …… (233)
NEW PRODUCTS TRIAL－PRODUCED AND PUT INTO PRODUCTION
9－20.1996年分地区独立核算工业企业主要财务指标(街、乡及以上工业) …… (234)
MAIN FINANCIAL INDICATORS OF INDUSTRIAL ENTERPRISES WITH INDEPENDENT ACCOUNT SYSTEMS BY REGION(SUBDISTRICT－RUN, TOWNSHIP－RUN AND OVER), 1996
9－21.大中型工业企业主要经济指标和占全市比重(街、乡及以上工业) …… (235)
MAIN ECONOMIC INDICATORS AND COMPOSITION OF LARGE－MEDIUM INDUSTRIAL ENTERPRISES AND PROPORTION (SUBDISTRICT－RUN, TOWNSHIP－RUN AND OVER)
9－22.乡镇属独立核算工业企业主要经济指标 …… (236)
MAIN ECONOMIC INDICATORS OF TOWNSHIP－OWNED INDUSTRIAL ENTERPRISES WITHINDEPENDENT ACCOUNT SYSTEM

9－23. 乡镇属分行业工业企业单位数和工业总产值 …… (237)
NUMBER OF TOWNSHIP－OWNED INDUSTRIAL ENTERPRISES AND GROSS INDUSTRIAL OUTPUT VALUE BY SECTOR
9－24. 冶金工业总公司主要经济指标 …… (238)
MAIN ECONOMIC INDICATORS OF METELLURGICAL INDUSTRY CORPORATION
9－25. 化工工业总公司主要经济指标 …… (239)
MAIN ECONOMIC INDICATORS OF CHEMICAL INDUSTRY CORPORATION
9－26. 机电工业总公司主要经济指标 …… (240)
MAIN ECONOMIC INDICATORS OF ENGINEERING INDUSTRY CORPORATOIN
9－27. 电子仪表工业总公司主要经济指标 …… (241)
MAIN ECONOMIC INDICATORS OF ELECTRICAL AND INSTRUMENT CORPORATION
9－28. 纺织工业总公司主要经济指标 …… (242)
MAIN ECONOMIC INDICATORS OF TEXTILE INDUSTRY CORPORATION
9－29. 一轻总公司主要经济指标 …… (243)
MAIN ECONOMIC INDICATORS OF FIRST LIGHT INDUSTRY CORPORATION
9－30. 二轻局主要经济指标 …… (244)
MAIN ECONOMIC INDICATORS OF SECOND LIGHT INDUSTRY CORPORATION
9－31. 医药集团有限公司主要经济指标 …… (245)
MAIN ECONOMIC INDICATORS OF MEDICAL GROUP CORPORATION
9－32. 建筑材料集团总公司主要经济指标 …… (246)
MAIN ECONOMIC INDICATORS OF BUILDING MATERIALS GROUP CORPORATION
9－33. 汽车工业(集团)有限公司主要经济指标 …… (247)
MAIN ECONOMIC INDICATORS OF AUTO INDUSTRY GROUP CO., LTD
9－34. 飞鸽自行车集团公司主要经济指标 …… (248)
MAIN ECONOMIC INDICATORS OF FLY PIGEON BICYCLE GROUP CORPORATION
9－35. 服装联合总公司主要经济指标 …… (249)
MAIN ECONOMIC INDICATORS OF CLOTHING COMPANY
9－36. 渤海化工集团工业总公司主要经济指标 …… (250)
MAIN ECONOMIC INDICATORS OF BOHAI CHEMICAL GROUP CORPORATION
9－37. 天津钢管公司主要经济指标 …… (251)
MAIN ECONOMIC INDICATORS OF TIANJIN STEEL TUBE COMPANY
9－38. 村办及村以下工业主要指标 …… (251)
MAIN INDICATORS OF INDUSTRY VILLAGE－RUN AND UNDER
9－39. 大中型工业企业主要工业技术经济指标(1995 年) …… (252)
MAIN ECONOMIC INDICATORS OF LARGE－MEDIUM INDUSTRIAL ENTERPRISES, 1995
9－40. 街、乡及以上工业主要产品生产能力(1995 年) …… (254)
PRODUCTIVE C APACITY OF MAIN INDUSTRY PRODUCTS SUBDISTRICTS－RUN, TOWNSHIP－RUN AND OVER, 1995
9－41. 大中型工业企业主要产品质量(1995 年) …… (256)
MAIN PRODUCT QUALITIES OF LARGE－MEDIUM INDUSTRIAL ENTERPRISES, 1995
9－42. 电子计算机、机械手等设备拥有量和动力机械总能力(1995 年街、乡及以上工业) …… (260)
NUNBER OF ELECTRIC COMPUTER AND MACHINERY HAND AND TOTAL CAPAITY OF KINETIC MACHINE (SUBISTRICT－RUN, TOWNSHIP－RUN AND OVER), 1995
9－43. 街乡及以上工业主要生产设备及其新旧程度(已安装设备 1995 年末价值量) …… (261)
MAIN PRODUCTIVE EQUIPMENT AND DEGREES OF INDUSTRY (FIXED EQUIPMENT VALUE BY THE END OF 1995)
9－44. 街乡及以上工业主要生产设备及新旧程度(已安装设备 1995 年末实物量) …… (265)

MAIN PRODUCTIVE EQUIPMENT AND DEGREEN OF INDUSTY (FIXED EQUIPMENT IN KIND BY THE END OF 1995)
天津市第三次工业普查公报 …… **(268)**
COMMUNIQUE ON THE THIRD INDUSTRIAL SURVEY OF TIANJIN

十、建筑业
CONSTRUCTION

10－1.建筑企业基本情况(按经济类型分) …… (277)
BASIC STATISTICS OF CONSTRUCTION ENTERPRISES BY TYPE OF OWNERSHIP
10－2.建筑企业基本情况(按专业类型分) …… (278)
BASIC STATISTICS OF CONSTRUCTION ENTERPRISES BY TYPE OF FIELDS
10－3.建筑企业基本情况(按企业资质等级分) …… (278)
BASIC STATISTICS OF CONSTRUCTION ENTERPRISES BY CLASSIFICATION OF CAPITAL AND QUALITY
10－4.改革开放以来建筑企业基本情况 …… (279)
BASIC STATISTICS OF CONSTRUCTION ENTERPRISES SINCE REFORM AND OPENNINGTO OUTSIDE
10－5.建筑企业劳动生产率 …… (279)
LABOR PRODUCTIVITY OF CONTRUCTION ENTERPRISES
10－6.建筑企业主要财务指标 …… (280)
MAIN FINANCIAL INDICATORS OF CONSTRUCTION ENTERPRISES
10－7.建筑企业工程质量、机械设备及经济效益指标 …… (282)
CONSTRUCTION QUALITY, INSTRUMENT AND FINANCIAL RATIOS

十一、交通运输和邮电通信
TRANSPORTATION, POST AND TELECOMMUNICATION

11－1.改革开放以来运输邮电业基本情况 …… (284)
TRANSPORTATION AND POSTAL SERVICES SINCE REFORM AND OPENING TO OUTSIDE
11－2.港口设施 …… (286)
PORTS FACILITIES
11－3.港口货物吞吐量 …… (286)
CARGO HANDLED AT PORTS
11－4.民用运输船舶拥有量 …… (287)
CIVIL TRANSPORT VESSELS
11－5.民用车辆拥有量 …… (287)
CIVIL MOTOR VESSELS
11－6.运输线路长度 …… (288)
LENGTH OF TRANSPORTATION ROUTES
11－7.民用航空航线里程 …… (288)
CIVIL AVIATION ROUTES
11－8.社会货物运输量和周转量 …… (289)
FREIGHT AND ROTATION VOLUME OF COMMODITIES
11－9.社会客运量和周转量 …… (289)
FREIGHT AND ROTATION VOLUME OF PASSENGERS
11－10.通信网络和设备能力情况 …… (289)
TELECOMMUNICATION NETS AND FACILITY CAPABILITIES
11－11.邮电业务量 …… (290)

POSTAL AND TELECOMMUNICATIONS SERVICES
11－12.分地区邮电局所数 …………………………………………………… (290)
NUMBER OF POST BY REGIONS

十二、批发零售贸易和餐饮业
WHOLESALE & RETAIL TRADE AND CATERING TRADE

12－1.改革开放以来社会商业发展情况 …………………………………………………… (292)
DEVELOPMENT OF SOCIAL COMMERCE SINCE REFORM AND OPENNING TO OUTSIDE
12－2.1996 年批发贸易业机构、网点及人员 …………………………………………………… (293)
INSTITUTION, OUTLETS AND PERSONS IN WHOLESALE TRADE, 1996
12－3.1996 年零售贸易餐饮业机构、网点及人员 …………………………………………………… (294)
INSTITUTION, OUTLETS AND PERSONS IN RETAIL TRADE AND CATERING TRADE, 1996
12－4.按地区分的批发零售贸易餐饮业机构、网点及人员情况(1996 年) …………………………………… (295)
INSTITUTION, OUTLETS AND AND PERSONS IN WHOLESALE, RATAIL AND CATERING TRADE BY REGIONS, 1996
12－5.按主管部门分的批发零售贸易业主要经济指标(1996 年) ……………………………………… (296)
MAIN ECONOMIC INDICATORS OF WHOLESALE AND RETAIL TRADE BY DEPARTMENT RESPONSIBLE FOR THE WORK, 1996
12－6.社会消费品零售总额 …………………………………………………… (297)
RETAIL SALES OF CONSUMER GOODS
12－7.批发零售贸易业商品购进、销售及库存总额 …………………………………………………… (298)
VALUE OF PURCHASES, SALES AND INVENTORY IN WHOLESALE AND RETAIL TRADE
12－8.批发零售贸易业商品购进总额 …………………………………………………… (299)
PURCHASES OF GOODS BY WHOLESALE AND RETAIL TRADE
12－9.批发零售贸易业商品销售和库存总额 …………………………………………………… (300)
SALES AND STOCK OF GOODS BY WHOLESALE AND RETAIL TRADE
12－10.1996 年国有批发零售贸易业主要经济指标 …………………………………………………… (301)
MAIN ECONOMIC INDICATORS OF STATE－OWNED WHOLSALE AND RETAILTRADE, 1996
12－11.1996 年批发零售贸易业主要商品销售数量 …………………………………………………… (302)
SALES QUANTITY OF MAJOR COMMODITIES IN WHOLESALE AND RETAIL TRADE, 1996
12－12.1996 年批发零售贸易业财务状况 …………………………………………………… (305)
MAJOR FINANCIAL INDICATORS OF WHOLESALE AND RETAIL TRADE, 1996
12－13.1996 年批发贸易业财务状况 …………………………………………………… (306)
MAJOR FINANCIAL INDICATORS OF WHOLESALE TRADE, 1996
12－14.1996 年零售贸易业财务状况 …………………………………………………… (307)
MAJOR FINANCIAL INDICATORS OF RETAIL TRADE, 1996
12－15.1996 年餐饮业财务状况 …………………………………………………… (308)
MAJOR FINANCIAL INDICATORS OF CATERING TRADE, 1996
12－16.批发和零售贸易餐饮业实行体制改革企业情况(1996 年) …………………………………… (309)
ENTERPRISES REFORMED IN WHOLESALE AND RETAIL TRADE, IN CATERING TRADE, 1996
12－17.城乡集市贸易主要指标 …………………………………………………… (310)
MAIN INDICATORS OF COUNTY FAIR TRADE
12－18.商品交易市场分类情况 …………………………………………………… (310)
CLASSIFICATION OF COMMODITIES MARKET

十三、对外经济贸易和旅游业
FOREIGN ECONOMY TRADE AND TOURISM

13－1.天津口岸进出口贸易总值(1981—1996 年) …………………………………………………… (312)

TOTAL VALUE OF IMPORTSARD EXPORTS TRADE IN TIANJIN PORT (1981 – 1996)
13 – 2. 天津口岸中天津经营单位进出口商品总值(按贸易性质分) …… (312)
GROSS VALUE OF EXPORTS AND IMPORTS WITH TIANJIN MANAGEMENT UNITS IN TINAJIN PORT BY (TRADE NATURE)
13 – 3. 天津口岸进出口商品总值(按系统分) …… (313)
GROSS VALUE OF IMPORTS AND EXPORTS IN TIANJIN PORT
13 – 4. 天津口岸中天津经营单位进出口商品总值(按国别、地区分) …… (313)
GROSS VALUE OF EXPORTS AND IMPORTS WITH TIANJIN MANAGEMENT UNITS IN TIANJIN PORT (BY COUNTRIES AND REGIONS)
13 – 5. 天津口岸中天津经营单位进出口商品分类 …… (314)
CLASSIFICATION OF IMPORTS AND EXPORTS WITH TIANJIN MANAGEMENT UNITS INTIANJIN
13 – 6. 改革开放以来外贸经营单位进出口商品总值 …… (314)
GROSS VALUE OF IMPORTS AND EXPORTS WITH FOREIGN TRADE UNITS SINCE REFORM AND OPENING TO OUTSIDE
13 – 7. 外贸经营单位进出口商品总值 …… (315)
GROSS VALUE OF EXPORTS AND IMPORTS IN FOREIGN TRADE UNITSTMENT
13 – 8. 外贸经营单位分国别、地区进出口总值 …… (315)
GROSS VALUE OF IMPORTS AND EXPORTS WITH FOREIGN TRADE UNITS BY COUNTRIES AND REGIONS
13 – 9. 1996 年外贸经营单位大宗商品出口总值 …… (317)
GROSS VALUE OF ALARGE AOMUNT COMMODITIES EXPORT IN FOREIGN TRADE UNITES, 1996
13 – 10. 天津口岸进出口商品检验情况 …… (317)
TESTS OF IMPROTS AND EXPROTS IN TIANJIN PORT
13 – 11. 利用外资情况 …… (318)
UTILIZATION OF FOREIGN CAPITAL
13 – 12. 实际利用外资情况 …… (318)
ACTUAL UTILIZATION OF FOREIGN CAPITAL
13 – 13. 1996 年借用国外资金情况 …… (319)
BORROWING FOREIGN CAPITAL, 1996
13 – 14. 客商投资企业协议和实际利用外资情况 …… (319)
FOREIGN CAPITAL SIGNED CONSTRANCTS AND ACTUALLY USED FOREIGN CAPITAL
13 – 15. 1996 年客商投资企业签约和投资情况(按主管系统分) …… (320)
SIGNED CONTRACTS AND INVESTMENT OF TRADERS INVESTMENT, 1996
13 – 16. 1996 年客商投资企业生产经营情况 …… (321)
PRODUCTION AND OPERATION OF TRADERS INVESTMENT, 1996
13 – 17. 1996 年新批准重点客商投资企业名单(协议外资额在 1000 万美元以上) …… (323)
LIST OF NEW APPROVED KEY TRADERS INVESTMENT ENTERPRISES APPROVED(SIGNED FOREIGN INVESTMENT OVER 10 MILLION US$), 1996
13 – 18. 接待国际旅游人数和居住天数(1990 – 1996 年) …… (325)
BASIC STATISTICS ON INTERNATIONAL TOURISTS(1990 – 1996)
13 – 19. 国际旅游外汇收入及构成情况 …… (325)
COMPOSITION AND INCOMES FORESIGN EXCHANGE FROM INTERNATIONAL TOURISTS
13 – 20. 天津接待国内旅游情况(1996 年) …… (326)
BASIC STATISTICS ON DOMESTIC TOURISTS IN TIANJIN, 1996
13 – 21. 天津市居民外出旅游情况(1996 年) …… (326)
BASIC STATISTICS ON TIANJIN TOURISTS, 1996
13 – 22. 天津接待国内游客和天津居民外出旅游消费额构成(1996 年) …… (326)
TOURISTS RECEIVED FROM DOMESTIC AND OUTSIDE AND COMPOSITION OF EXPENDITURES WITH

TOURISTS IN TIANJIN, 1996
13－23. 天津市因公出国人员(1992－1996 年) …………………… (327)
PERSONS GOING ABROAD ON BUSINESS(1992－1996)
13－24. 天津市涉外宾馆一览表 …………………… (327)
LIST OF HOTELS OPENNING TO THE FOREIGNER
13－25. 对外承包工程和劳务合作(1990－1996 年) …………………… (328)
CONTRACTED PROJECTS AND LABOR SERVICE COOPERATION WITH COUNTRIES (1990－1996)
13－26. 1996 年对外承包工程和劳务合作(分国别、地区) …………………… (328)
CONTRACTED PROJECTS AND LABOR SERVICE COOPERATION WITH COUNTRIES (BY COUNTRIES AND REGIONS), 1996

十四、金融和保险业
BANKING AND INSURANCE

14－1. 各类金融机构和人员 …………………… (330)
PERSONEL AND INSTITUTION OF VARIOUS BANKING
14－2. 1996 年外资银行在津分行一览 …………………… (330)
LIST OF FOREIGN CAPITAL BANK TIANJIN BRANCH, 1996
14－3. 改革开放以来银行系统各项存贷款余额 …………………… (331)
DEPOSITS AND LOANS IN BANK SERIES SINCE REFORM AND OPENING TO OUTSIDE
14－4. 银行现金收入和支出 …………………… (332)
CASH REVENUE AND EXPENDITURES OF BANKING SYSTEM
14－5. 金融系统信贷收支情况 …………………… (333)
CREDITS OF BANKING SYSTEM
14－6. 1996 年银行结汇售汇情况 …………………… (334)
SETTLEMENTS OF FOREIGN EXCHANGE IN CHINA BANK, 1996
14－7. 1996 年天津市保险业务情况 …………………… (334)
BUSINESS OF INSURANCE IN TIANJIN, 1996
14－8. 储蓄存款和单位存款利率表(1990－1996 年) …………………… (335)
INTEREST RATE TABLE OF SAVING AND UNITS DEPOSITS(1990－1996)
14－9. 流动资金和固定资产贷款利率表(1990－1996 年) …………………… (336)
INTEREST RATE TABLE OF CIRCULATING FUNDS AND LOANS IN FIXED ASSETS(1990－1996)

十五、教育和科学技术
EDUCATION AND SCIENCE & TECHNOLOGY

15－1. 专业技术人员 …………………… (338)
SCIENTIFIC AND TECHNICAL PERSONNEL
15－2. 1996 年专业技术人员构成 …………………… (338)
COMPOSITION OF SCIENTIFIC AND TECHNICAL PERSONNEL, 1996
15－3. 国民经济各行业专业技术人员 …………………… (339)
NUMBER OF SCIENTISTS AND TECHNICIANS OF NATIONAL ECONOMY BY SECTOR
15－4. 1996 年自然科学专业技术人员 …………………… (339)
NATURAL SCIENTISTS BY SECTOR, 1996
15－5. 1996 年社会科学专业技术人员 …………………… (340)
SOCIAL SCIENTISTS BY SECTOR, 1996
15－6. 独立科学研究和技术开发机构情况 …………………… (341)

SCIENTIFIC RESEARCH INSTITUTIONS, PERSONNEL AND FUND
15－7. 独立自然科学研究机构课题开展和投入 …………………………………………………… (341)
DEVELOPMENT AND INPUT OF STUDYING IN NATURAL SCIENTIFIC RESEARCH INSTITUTIONS
15－8. 三项专利申请受理量和批准量 …………………………………………………… (341)
THREE TYPES OF PATENT APPLICATIONS EXAMINED AND CERTIFIED
15－9. 天津市重大科技研究成果和获奖成果(1990－1996 年) …………………………………… (342)
NUMBER OF GREAT SCIENTIFIC RESEARCH AND ACHIEVEMENT, TIANJIN(1990－1996)
15－10. 1996 年天津市获国家发明奖科技成果一览 …………………………………………… (342)
LIST OF STATE INVENTMENT FRUITS, TIANJIN, 1996
15－11. 1996 年天津市获国家科技进步奖科技成果一览 ………………………………………… (342)
LIST OF STATE SICENTIFIC AND TECHNICAL ADVANCED FRUITS, TIANJIN, 1996
15－12. 高等学校科研课题开展与投入(理、工、农、医类) …………………………………… (343)
DEVELOPMENT AND INPUT OF SCIENTIFIC RESEARCH IN COLLEGES AND UNIVERSITIES
15－13. 高等学校研究发展机构科技专著和论文(理、工、农、医类)(1991－1996 年) ……………… (343)
SCIENTIFIC WORKS AND TREATISES OF RESEARCH IN DEVELOPMENT INSTITUTIONS OF COLLEGES AND UNIVERSITIES (SCIENCE ENGINEERING, AGRICULTURE AND MEDICLE)(1991－1996)
15－14. 1996 年技术监督机构人员、行政执法及科技成果情况 ………………………………… (344)
PERSONNEL AND INSTITUTION OF TECHNICAL SUPERINTENDENCE, ADMINSTRATIVE ENFORCEMENT AND SCIENTIFIC AND TECHNICAL ADVANCED FRUITS, 1996
15－15. 计量仪器检定情况(1991－1996 年) …………………………………………………… (344)
TEST OF MEASURING INSTRUMENTS(1991－1996)
15－16. 1996 年大中型工业和建筑业科技活动情况 …………………………………………… (345)
STATISTICS OF SCIENTIFIC AND TECHNICAL ACTIVITIES IN LARGE－MEDIUM INDUSTRY AND CONSTRUTION INDUSTRY, 1996
15－17. 天津市科学技术协会和所属学会科技活动 …………………………………………… (346)
STATISTICS OF SCIENTIFIC AND TECHNICAL ASSOCIATION AND INSTITUTES
15－18. 主要年份各类学校在校学生数和专任教师数 ………………………………………… (347)
NUMBER OF STUDENT ENROLLMENT AND TEACHERS BY TYPE OF SCHOOL IN MAJOR YEARS
15－19. 1996 年各类学校数、学生数及教职工数 ……………………………………………… (347)
NUMBER OF STUDENT ENROLLMENT AND TEACHER BY TYPE OF SCHOOL, 1996
15－20. 平均每万人口中有在校学生数 …………………………………………………… (348)
NUMBER OF STUDENT ENROLLMENT PER 10000 POPULATION
15－21. 各级学校女学生和女教师比重 …………………………………………………… (348)
PROPORTION OF FEMALE STUDENTS AND TEACHERS IN ALL TYPE SCHOOLS BY LEVEL
15－22. 各级学校学生升学率 …………………………………………………………… (348)
PERCENTAGE OF GRADUATES OF STUDENTS BY LEVEL, 1996
15－23. 各级学校毕业生数 …………………………………………………………… (349)
NUMBER OF GRADUATES BY LEVEL OF SCHOOL
15－24. 1996 年普通高等学校分科学生数 …………………………………………………… (349)
NUMBER OF STUDENTS ENROLLMENT IN COMMON COLLEGES AND UNIVERSTIES BY FIELD OF STUDY, 1996
15－25. 分学科研究生人数 …………………………………………………………… (350)
NUMBER OF POST GRADUATES BY FIELD OF STUDY
15－26. 研究生在学、毕业、招生及指导教师人数 ……………………………………………… (351)
NUMBER OF GRADUATES AND ENROLLMENT OF POST GRADUATES AND THEIR TEACHERS
15－27. 1996 年高等学校基本情况 …………………………………………………… (351)
BASIC STATISTICS ON COLLEGES AND UNIVERSITIES, 1996
15－28. 1996 年高等学校分科专任教师数 …………………………………………………… (351)

NUMBER OF FULL－TIME TEACHERS IN COLLEGES AND UNIVERSITIES BY FIELD OF STUDY, 1996
15－29.高等学校分科学生数 …………………………………………………………………… (352)
NUMBER OF STUDENTS ENROLLMENT IN COLLEGES AND UNIVERSITIES BY FIELD OFSTUDY
15－30.中等专业学校分科学生数 ………………………………………………………………… (352)
NUMBER OF STUDENTS ENROLLMENT IN SPECIALIZED SECONDARY SCHOOLS BY FIELD OF STUDY
15－31.技工学校分行业学生数 …………………………………………………………………… (353)
NUMBER OF STUDENTS ENROLLMENT IN TECHNICAL SCHOOLS BY SETOR
15－32.1996 年按部门分普通中学和小学生基本情况 ……………………………………………… (353)
BASIC STATISTICS ON MIDDLE SCHOOLS AND PRIMARY SCHOOLS BY DEPARTMENT, 1996
15－33.1996 年普通中小学分布情况 ……………………………………………………………… (354)
BASIC STATISTICS ON MIDDLE SCHOOLS AND STUDENTS OF PRIMARY SCHOOLS, 1996
15－34.1996 年普通中学、职业中学及小学校舍情况 ………………………………………………… (355)
TEACHING FACILITIES OF MIDDLE SCHOOLS, VOCATIONAL SCHOOLS AND PRIMARY SCHOOLS, 1996
15－35.1996 年普通中学分课程专任教师学历情况 ………………………………………………… (356)
SCHOOLING RECORDS OF FULL－TIME TEACHERS IN COMMON MIDDLE SCHOOL BY COURSES, 1996
15－36.1996 年小学分课程专任教师学历情况 ……………………………………………………… (356)
SCHOOLING RECORDS OF FULL－TIME TEACHERS IN PRIMARY SCHOOL BY COURSES, 1996
15－37.成人教育学校校数和学生情况 …………………………………………………………… (357)
NUMBER OF SCHOOLS AND STUDENTS OF ADULT EDUCATION
15－38.1996 年其他专项成人教育学生数 ………………………………………………………… (358)
STUDENTS OF OTHER SPECIFIC ADULT EDUCATION, 1996
15－39.特殊教育基本情况 ………………………………………………………………………… (358)
BASIC STATISTICS ON SPECIAL EDUCATION
15－40.1996 年技工学校培训多种人员情况 ………………………………………………………… (358)
VARIOUS PERSONNEL TRAINNING BY TECHNICAL SCHOOLS, 1996
15－41.托幼园所基本情况 ………………………………………………………………………… (358)
BASIC STATISTICS ON KINDERGARTENS AND NURSERIES
15－42.档案事业基本情况 ………………………………………………………………………… (359)
BASIC STATISTICS ON ARCHIVES
15－43.档案馆档案资料馆藏和开发利用情况 ……………………………………………………… (359)
KEEPING, DEVELOPMENT AND UTILIZATION OF DATA IN ARCHIVES
15－44.机关事业单位档案资料保存和开发利用情况 ……………………………………………… (360)
KEEPING AND DEVELOPMENT AND UTILIZATION OF ARCHIVES DATA IN GOVERNMENTORGANIZAION AND INSTITUTIONS
15－45.大型工业企业档案资料保存和开发利用情况 ……………………………………………… (360)
KEEPING AND DEVELOPMENT AND UTILIZATION OF ARCHIVES DATA IN LARGE INDUSTRIAL ENTERPRISES

十六、文化体育卫生及其他

CULTURE, SPORTS, PUBLIC HEALTH AND OTHERS

16－1.1996 年文化事业活动单位机构和人员 …………………………………………………… (363)
CULTURAL INSTITUTIONS AND PERSONNEL, 1996
16－2.电影事业基本情况 ………………………………………………………………………… (363)
BASIC STATISTICS ON FILM
16－3.电影放映情况 ……………………………………………………………………………… (363)
FILM PROJECTING
16－4.艺术事业基本情况 ………………………………………………………………………… (364)

BASIC STATISTICS ON ART
16－5. 艺术表演活动情况 …… (364)
BASIC STATISTICS ON PERFORMANCE OF ART TROUPES
16－6. 群众文化事业基本情况 …… (364)
BASIC STATISTICS ON MASS ART
16－7. 公共图书馆、博物馆和文物保护单位基本情况 …… (365)
BASIC STATISTICS ON LIBRARIES AND MUSEUMS AND CULTURAL RELIC AGENCIES
16－8. 图书出版 …… (365)
BOOKS PUBLISHED
16－9. 1996 年书籍和课本分类 …… (366)
BOOKS AND TEXTBOOKS BY CATEGORY, 1996
16－10. 杂志出版 …… (366)
MAGAZINES PUBLISHED
16－11. 报纸出版 …… (366)
NEWSPAPER PUBLISHED
16－12. 广播电台情况 …… (367)
STATISTICS OF BROADCASTING
16－13. 电视台情况 …… (367)
STATISTICS OF TV STATION
16－14. 1996 年广播和电视节目制作情况 …… (368)
PRODUCTION OF BROADCASTING AND TV, 1996
16－15. 1996 年各区县有线广播基本情况 …… (368)
BASIC STATISTICS OF WIRE BROADCASTING BY DISTRICTS AND COUNTIES, 1996
16－16. 1996 年区县电视台基本情况 …… (369)
BASIC STATISTICS OF TV STATIONS BY DISTRICTS AND COUNTIES, 1996
16－17. 1996 年有线电视基本情况 …… (369)
BASIC STATISTICS OF WIRE TV, 1996
16－18. 1996 年系统内有线电视宣传和节目制作情况 …… (369)
PROPAGANDA OF WIRE TV IN OWN SERIES AND PRODUCTION OF TV PROGRAM, 1996
16－19. 1996 年广播电视覆盖情况 …… (370)
BROADCASTING AND TV COVERING, 1996
16－20. 1996 年体育场地情况 …… (371)
STADIUMS AND GYMNASIUMS, 1996
16－21. 体委系统体育工作者 …… (371)
PERSONNEL OF PHYSICAL CULTURE AND SPORTS COMMISSIONS
16－22. 《国家体育锻炼标准》达标情况 …… (371)
UP TO NATIONAL STANDARY OF PHYSICAL TRAINING
16－23. 等级裁判员和运动员发展人数 …… (371)
CERTIFIED ATHLETES AND REFEREES BY TYPE OF SPORTS
16－24. 天津市举办运动竞赛情况(县及县以上) …… (372)
SPORTS MEETING HELD IN TIANJIN(COUNTY－RUN AND OVER)
16－25. 改革开放以来卫生机构、床位及技术人员数 …… (372)
NUMBER OF HEALTH CARE INSTITUTION, BEDS AND TECHNICIANS SINCE REFORM AND OPENNING TO OUTSIDE
16－26. 卫生事业机构 …… (373)
HEALTH CARE INSTITUTIONS
16－27. 卫生机构的床位数 …… (373)
NUMBER OF BEDS IN HEALTH CARE INSTITUTIONS
16－28. 1996 年分科医师数 …… (373)
NUMBER OF QUALIFIED DOCTOR BY MEDICAL COURSE, 1996

16－29. 卫生技术人员数 …… (374)
TECHNICIAN IN HEALTH CARE INSTITUTIONS
16－30. 1996 年按管理部门和性质分的卫生事业基本情况 …… (374)
PUBLIC HEALTH BY MANAGEMENT AND CHARACTER, 1996
16－31. 1996 年各类医院机构、床位及人员数 …… (375)
NUMBER OF HEALTH CARE INSTITUTIONS, BEDS AND PERSONNEL BY TYPE OF HOSPITAL, 1996
16－32. 县及县以上医院诊疗和病床使用情况 …… (375)
PATIENTS AND UTILIZATION OF HOSPITAL BEDS AT COUNTY LEVEL AND ABOVE
16－33. 1996 年医院和卫生院医疗情况 …… (376)
MEDICAL TREATMENT OF HOSPITAL, 1996
16－34. 农村村级卫生组织情况 …… (376)
HEALTH ORGANIZATION AT VILLAGE LEVEL
16－35. 1996 年 7 岁以下儿童保健工作情况 …… (376)
STATUS OF CHILDEN PUBLIC HEALTH AGE UNDER 7, 1996
16－36. 适龄儿童疫苗接种情况(1991－1996 年) …… (377)
STATUS OF VACCINE INOCULATION CHILDREN ON AGE(1991－1996)
16－37. 妇幼保健情况(1991－1996 年) …… (377)
PUBLIC HEALTH OF WOMAN AND CHILDREN(1991－1996)
16－38. 1996 年居民前十位死亡原因和死亡专率 …… (377)
DEATH REASON AND DEATH RATE OF 10 MAJOR DISEASE, 1996
16－39. 1996 年卫生机构技术人员技术职称状况 …… (378)
TITELS FOR TECHNICAL PERSONNEL IN HEALTH CARE INSTITUTIONS
16－40. 1996 年检察机关立案侦查经济案件情况 …… (379)
ECONOMIC CASES OF FILING AND INVERTIGATION BY PROCURATORIAL ORGANS, 1996
16－41. 1996 年法院经济纠纷案件收案和结案情况 …… (379)
FILING AND WINDING UP CASES OF ECONOMIC DISPUTE BY PEOPLE'S COURT, 1996
16－42. 1996 年法院民事案件收案和结案情况 …… (380)
FILING AND WINDING UP CASES OF CIVIL CASE BY PEOPLE'S COURT, 1996
16－43. 1996 年法院行政案件收案和结案情况 …… (380)
FILING AND WINDING UP CASES OF CRIMINAL CASE BY PEOPLE'S COURT, 1996
16－44. 调解工作 …… (380)
MEDIATION
16－45. 律师工作 …… (381)
LAWERS
16－46. 公证工作 …… (381)
NOTORIZATION
16－47. 妇联组织情况 …… (381)
WOMEN'S FEDERATION ORGANIZATION
16－48. 妇联工作情况 …… (382)
WOMEN'S FEDERATION WORKS
16－49. 1996 年基层工会组织基层情况 …… (382)
BASIC STATISTICS OF LABOUR UNION ORGANIZATION, 1996

十七、改革开放和滨海新区

REFORM, OPENING AND NEW COASTLINE AREA

体制改革

SYSTEM REFORM

1996 年经济体制改革进展情况 …… (384)

STATUS OF TIANJIN ECONOMIC SYSTEM REFORM, 1996
17－1. 1996 年新批企业集团一览 …… (385)
LIST OF NEW APPROVED ENTERPRISES AND GROUPS, 1996
17－2. 1996 年现代企业制度试点企业概况 …… (387)
SURVEY OF EXPERIMENTAL UNIT WITH MODERN SYSTEM, 1996
滨海新区
NEW COASTLINE AREA
17－3. 滨海新区主要经济指标 …… (389)
MAIN ECONOMIC INDICATORS OF COASTLINE NEW AREA
17－4. 滨海新区基础设施投资完成情况 …… (389)
COMPLETION OF INVESTMENT INFRASTRUCTURE IN CNA
17－5. 滨海新区区级财政收支情况 …… (390)
GOVERMENT REVENUE AND EXPENDITURE AT DISTRICT LEVEL IN CNA
17－6. 经济技术开发区城市建设情况(截至 1996 年底) …… (390)
URBAN CONSTRUTION IN TEDA(END OF 1996)
17－7. 经济技术开发区国民经济主要指标 …… (391)
MAIN INDICATORS OF NATIONAL ECONOMY IN TEDA
17－8. 经济技术开发区基础设施完成投资和形成能力 …… (392)
COMPLETION INVESTMENT AND FORMED ABILITIES OF INFRASTRUCTURE IN TEDA
17－9. 经济技术开发区已批准客商投资企业情况 …… (392)
BASIC STATISTICS ON APPROVED TRADER INVESTED ENTERPRISES IN TEDA
17－10. 经济技术开发区客商投资企业情况(截至 1996 年底) …… (393)
BASIC STATISTICS ON ENTERPRISES INVESTED BY TRADER IN TEDA(END OF 1996)
17－11. 经济技术开发区客商投资企业按行业分类(截至 1996 年底) …… (394)
FOREIGN INVESTMENT ENTERPRISES IN TEDA BY SECTOR(END OF 1996)
17－12. 天津港保税区主要经济指标 …… (395)
MAIN ECONOMIC INDICATORS IN PFTA
17－13. 天津港保税区招商情况 …… (395)
CANVASS BUSINESS OF PFTA
17－14. 1996 年滨海三区概况 …… (396)
SURVEY OF COASTLINE THREE AREAS, 1996
新技术园区和区县开发小区
NEW TECHNOLOGY INDUSTRIAL PARK AND DEVELOPMENT SUBDISTRICTS
17－15. 新技术产业园区基本情况(1992－1996 年) …… (397)
BASIC STATISTICS ON NEW TECHNOLOGY INDUSTRIAL PARK(1992－1996)
17－16. 12 个开发小区客商投资情况(截至 1996 年底) …… (397)
TRADER INVESTMENT IN 12 ECONOMIC DEVELOPMENT AREA(END OF 1996)
内联引资
DOMESTIC UNION AND ABSORBED CAPITAL
17－17. 1996 年天津市经济技术协作情况 …… (398)
ECONOMIC AND TECHNIQUE COOPERATION IN TIANJIN, 1996
17－18. 1996 年天津市人才协作状况 …… (398)
TALENT COOPERATION IN TIANJIN, 1996
17－19. 1996 年天津市内联引资情况 …… (399)
DOMESTIC UNION AND ABSORBED CAPITAL IN TIANJIN, 1996
各类市场
MARKETS
17－20. 人才和劳务市场情况 …… (400)
TALENT AND LABOUR MARKETS

17－21.技术市场基本情况 ……………………………………………………………………………………………… (400)
TECHNICAL MARKET
证券市场概况 …… (401)
SURVEY OF SECURITIES MARKET
期货市场 …… (401)
FUTURE MARKET
17－22.1996 年证券市场交易情况 …………………………………………………………………………………… (401)
SECURITIES EXCHANGE MARKET, 1996
17－23.上市股份公司情况(截止日期:1996 年 12 月 31 日) ………………………………………………………… (401)
STOCK HOLDER CORPORATION(END DATE:DEC. 31, 1996)
17－24.外汇调剂市场情况 …………………………………………………………………………………………… (402)
FOREIGN EXCHANGE MARKET
17－25.城市房产市场交易情况 ……………………………………………………………………………………… (402)
REAL ESTATE MARKET
17－26.1996 年主要商品交易市场基本情况 …………………………………………………………………………… (403)
MAJOR COMMODITIES BUSINESS MARKET, 1996
17－27.主要消费品交易市场各类商品交易额 ………………………………………………………………………… (404)
VOLUME OF BUSINESS IN MAJOR CONSUMPTION BUSINESS MARKET
17－28.1996 年主要消费品交易市场交易额 ………………………………………………………………………… (404)
VOLUME OF BUSINESS IN MAJOR CONSUMPTION BUSINESS MARKET, 1996
17－29.主要消费品交易市场主要商品交易量 ………………………………………………………………………… (404)
BUSINESS QUANTITY OF MAJOR COMMODITIES IN MAJOR CONSUMPTION BUSINESS MARKET
17－30.1996 年主要消费品交易市场交易量 ………………………………………………………………………… (405)
VOLUME OF BUSINESS IN MAJOR CONSUMPTION BUSINESS MARKET, 1996
17－31.主要生产资料交易市场各类商品交易额 ……………………………………………………………………… (405)
VARIOUS COMMODITIES VOLUME OF MAJOR PRODUCTION MATERIAL BUSINESS MARKET
17－32.主要生产资料交易市场主要商品交易量 ……………………………………………………………………… (405)
BUSINESS QUANTITY OF MAJOR COMMODITIES IN MAJOR PRODUCTION MEARS BUSINESS MARKET

名牌产品与质量监督

FAMOUS PRODUCTION AND QUALITY SUPERVISORY

17－33.天津市名牌产品名单 ………………………………………………………………………………………… (406)
LIST OF TIANJIN FAMOUS PRODUCTION
17－34.1996 年产品质量监督检验情况 ……………………………………………………………………………… (408)
SUPERVISORY AND TEST STATUR OF PRODUCTION QUALITIES, 1996
17－35.1996 年商品质量监督检验情况 ……………………………………………………………………………… (409)
SUPERVISORY AND TEST STATUR OF COMMOMDITIES QUALITIES, 1996
17－36.1996 年受理消费者投诉情况 ………………………………………………………………………………… (410)
BASIC STATISTICS OF COMSUMER INSTITUTION ACCEPTED CASES, 1996

大型交易会

LARGE COMMODITIES FAIR

中国天津出口商品交易会 ……………………………………………………………………………………………… (411)
THE CHINA TIANJIN EXPORT COMMODITIES FAIR
'96 年天津春季全国商品交易会 ……………………………………………………………………………………… (411)
TIANJIN SPRING NATIONAL COMMODITIES FAIR 1996

十八、排名榜

SENIORITY BY MAIN STATISTICAL INDICATORS

18－1.1996 年产品销售收入百强工业企业 …………………………………………………………………………… (414)

POWERFUL INDUSTRIAL ENTER PRISES PRODUCTION SALE INCOME, 1996
18－2. 1996 年实现利税百强工业企业 …… (415)
POWERFUL INDUSTRIAL ENTERPRISES ON REALIZATION PROFITS AND TAXES, 1996
18－3. 1996 年前 30 名地方建筑施工单位排名榜 …… (416)
THE FIRST 30 PLACES WITH LOCAL CONSTRUCTION OPERATION UNITS, 1996
18－4. 1996 年销售总额超亿元的批发贸易企业 …… (417)
WHOLESALE TRADE UNITS ON SALE VALUE OVER 100 MILLION YUAN, 1996
18－5. 1996 年销售总额超五千万元的零售贸易企业 …… (418)
RETAIL TRADE UNTIS ON SALES VALUE OVER 50 MILLION YUAN, 1996
18－6. 1996 年零售额超五百万元的餐饮企业 …… (419)
CATERING TRADE UNITS ON RETAIL VALUE OVER 5 MILLION YUAN, 1996
18－7. 1996 年农村经济总收入超过亿元的村 …… (419)
VILLAGES ON RURAL ECOMIC INCOME OVER 100 MILLION YUAN IN TIANJIN, 1996
18－8. 1996 年乡村联工业出口创汇百强企业 …… (421)
THE FIRST HUNDRED POWERFUL ENTERPRISES ON INDUSTRIAL EXPORTS WITH TOWMSHIP CORPORATION INDUSTRY, 1996
18－9. 1996 年乡村联工业销售收入百强企业 …… (422)
THE FIRST HUNDRED POWERFUL ENTERPRISES ON PRODUCTION SALE INCOMME WITHTOWNSHIP CORPORATION INDUSTRY, 1996
18－10. 1996 年乡村联工业实现利税百强企业 …… (423)
THE FIRST HUNDRED POWERFUL ENTERPRISES ON REALIZATION PROFITS AND TAXES WITH TOWNSHIP CORPORATION INDUSTRY, 1996
18－11. 1996 年客商投资企业销售收入百强企业 …… (424)
THE FIRST HUNDRED POWERFUL ENTERORISES ON PRODUCTION SALE INCOME OF TRADER INVESTED ENTERPRISES, 1996
18－12. 1996 年客商投资企业利税总额百强企业 …… (425)
THE FIRST HUNDRED POWERFUL ENTERORISES ON TOTAL VALUE OF PROFITS AND TAXES OF TRADER INVESTED ENTERPRISES, 1996
18－13. 1996 年客商投资企业出口创汇百强企业 …… (426)
THE FIRST HUNDRED POWERFUL ENTERORISES ON EXPORTS OF TRADER INVESTED ENTERPRISES, 1996
18－14. 1995 年全国同行业按销售收入排序前 20 名的天津企业 …… (427)
TIANJIN ENTERPRISES OF THE FIRST 20 PLACES WITH NATIONAL SECTORS BY SALE IN COME, 1995

十九、区县基本情况
BASIC STATISTICS OF DISTRICTS AND COUNTIES

市辖区
DISTRICTS

19－1. 和平区基本情况 …… (433)
BASIC STATISTICS ON HEPING DISTRICT
19－2. 河东区基本情况 …… (434)
BASIC STATISTICS ON HEDONG DISTRICT
19－3. 河西区基本情况 …… (435)
BASIC STATISTICS ON HEXI DISTRICT
19－4. 南开区基本情况 …… (436)
BASIC STATISTICS ON NANKAI DISTRICT
19－5. 河北区基本情况 …… (437)
BASIC STATISTICS ON HEBEI DISTRICT
19－6. 红桥区基本情况 …… (438)

BASIC STATISTICS ON HONGQIAO DISTRICT
19-7. 塘沽区基本情况 …… (439)
BASIC STATISTICS ON TANGGU DISTRICT
19-8. 汉沽区基本情况 …… (441)
BASIC STATISTICS ON HANGU DISTRICT
19-9. 大港区基本情况 …… (443)
BASIC STATISTICS ON DAGANG DISTRICT
19-10. 东丽区基本情况 …… (445)
BASIC STATISTICS ON DONGLI DISTRICT
19-11. 西青区基本情况 …… (447)
BASIC STATISTICS ON XIQING DISTRICT
19-12. 津南区基本情况 …… (449)
BASIC STATISTICS ON JINNAN DISTRICT
19-13. 北辰区基本情况 …… (451)
BASIC STATISTICS ON BEICHEN DISTRICT
市辖县
COUNTIES
19-14. 宁河县基本情况 …… (453)
BASIC STATISTICS ON NINGHE COUNTY
19-15. 武清县基本情况 …… (455)
BASIC STATISTICS ON WUQING COUNTY
19-16. 静海县基本情况 …… (457)
BASIC STATISTICS ON JINGHAI COUNTY
19-17. 宝坻县基本情况 …… (459)
BASIC STATISTICS ON BAODI COUNTY
19-18. 蓟县基本情况 …… (461)
BASIC STATISTICS ON JIXIAN COUNTY
附 1 主要统计指标解释 …… (463)
APPENDIX 1 EXPLANATORY NOTES FOR MAIN INDICATORS
附 2 世界主要国家(城市)统计资料 …… (473)
APPENDIX 2 STATISTIC INFORMATION OF MAIN STATES (CITIES) IN THE WORLD

庆祝十五大胜利召开
喜迎香港回归祖国

天津市地方铁路管理局局长：邝先福

天津市地方铁路管理局

TIANJIN ADMINISTRATIVE BUREAU FOR LOCAL RAILWAY SYSTEM

天津市地方铁路管理局成立于1983年，是天津市地方铁路归口管理部门，又是集地方铁路的客货运输、工程施工、物资器材供应、工贸商业、宾馆服务、房地产开发、仓储及广告艺术制作为一体的综合性经济实体。

建局十余年来，全局坚持“以路养路”的方针，走自建自营的道路，本着多业并举的经营策略，倡导“艰苦奋斗、从严治路、团结协作、争创一流”的企业精神，不断发展壮大，现拥有5条铁路总长160公里。地方铁路的发展为本市改革开放、工业总体布局的东移及滨海新区的开发，创造了良好的交通环境。

该局所属地方铁路建设公司、地方铁路工程公司均为天津市建筑百强企业。铁路运输连续五年位居全国地方铁路前列，1996年被评为全国地方铁路“八强企业”之首。局连续三年荣获建设部精神文明建设先进单位。

天津市地方铁路工程公司承建的绥中电厂铁路专用线是国家重点工程

地址:天津市河西区纪庄子道6号

电话:(022)23384762－66　　邮编:300060

Tianjin Administrative Bureau for Local Railway System was setup in 1983 which is a special department for local railway management, which is also a comprehensive economic entity that is engaged in passenger－cargo transportation, projects construction, goods, materials and equipment supply, industrial production and commercial business, hotel service, real estate development, warehouse service and advertisement service.

Since the establishment of the bureau, it adheres to the principle of "maintain a railway by the railway itself" and develops itself by relying on its own efforts. According to the principle of diversification and the spirit of "arduous struggle, unite and coordinate together, rigorous management and work hard to create the No.1" for the development, the bureau has been developed day by day. Now it has managed 5 railway lines of 160 kilometers. The development of local railway has been trying its best to create a comfortable transport condition to supply the reform, the eastward movement of industrial location and the development of Binhai new economic area in Tianjin.

Under the leadership of the bureau, the Local Railway Construction Company, Ltd. and the Local Railway Construction Engineering Company, Ltd. are both super－ones of "the one hundred strong enterprises" in Tianjin. Among all the local railway enterprises in China, Tianjin local railway bureau is the fifth in railway transportation. In 1996, Tianjin Local Railway Administrative Bureau was elected the first one of "the Eight Strong Enterprises" among all local railway enterprises of the whole country.

The Bureau has won the title of "Spiritual Civilized Unit" given by the State Construction Department for three years in succession.

Address: Jizhuang－zi RD, No.6, Hexi District, Tianjin

Post code: 300060

Tel: (022) 23384762－66

天津市地方铁路建设公司承建的铁路滨海大桥是天津市重点工程

天津市市内电话局
TIANJIN TELECOMMUNICATIONS BUREAU

天津市市内电话局局长：王学礼

天津市市内电话局系大型国有通信企业，现有员工5000余人。主要经营电话通信和无线寻呼等业务，为市内六区和新四区提供市话通信服务并为市内四区、新四区，滨海三区和五县提供无线寻呼和查号服务。

天津市话通信网上拥有4个独立的汇接局、2对信令转接点、71个程控交换系统、142个局号、交换机容量130万门、网上客户90万。数百万的用户线对，中断线对使客户装机、移机成为举手可得。自动无线寻呼容量达到75万门，127自动寻呼台实现全国联网卫星高速寻呼真正做到"一机在手走遍神州"。光缆敷设市内各处，为客户提供了话音、低速数据、高速数据、有线电视，视像点播等现代通信业务，形成了多种功能，高效运行的现代化综合通信网。

地址:中国天津市和平区赤峰道62号
邮编:300041
电话:(022)27110800
传真:(022)27118008

市内电话局大楼

Tianjin Local Posts and Telecommunications Administration is a large state-owned telecom enterprise with more than 5000 employees. Its major business includes telecommunication, radio calling (BP) services and so on. It supplies local telephone services for 6 downtown districts, newly setup districts, and radio calling services and telephone number looking up services for the above 2 parts and 3 coastal districts and 5 counties.

营业大厅

On Tianjin Local Posts and Telecommunications Administration' Telecom networks, there are 4 independent junction bureaus, 2 code transferring points, 71 programme-contral telephone systems, 142 post codes with a telephone installing capacity of 1,300,000 and 900,000 users already. There are millions of telephone lines and transferring lines, which enable consumers to install and move their telephone lines easily. Its auto radio calling capacity reaches 750,000 units. The 127 auto radio calling station has been using nationwide satellite networks to achieve height speed calling services, which realized—Traveling the country by one telephone. Its fiber cable installed can reach any part of the city, giving users' modern telecom services, such as sound, low speed information, high speed information transferring services, cable TV programs and video broadcasting services. Its networks have become a multi-functional high speed modern comprehensive telecom net.

Address No. 62 Chifeng Road Heping District Tianjin, China
Tel. (022)27110800
Fax (022)27118008
P.C. 300041

天津钢管公司

TIANJIN STEEL TUBE COMPANY

天津钢管公司轧管厂精整作业区

天津钢管公司是专业生产无缝钢管的国家特大型企业，也是目前我国规模最大的石油管材生产基地。年产钢60万吨，无缝钢管50万吨，其中石油套管35万吨。主要生产直径114－273mm，壁厚4.5－35mm的石油套管，高、中、低压锅炉管，管线管，结构管，液压支架管等优质合金无缝钢管。主要产品石油套管荣获国家钢铁产品质量金杯奖。公司先后通过美国石油学会(API)、中国船级社(CCS)和瑞士雅斯利(SGS)等国内外质量监督检验和测试权威机构的产品质量认证和ISO9001质量体系的认证。

总经理：张振纲

地址：天津市东丽区津塘公路

邮编:300301

电话:(022)24360165、24802625

传真:(022)24360649

天津钢管公司管加工厂套管作业线

Tianjin Steel Tube Company is a state owned large scale enterprise, specializing in producing seamless steel tube. It is also the largest producing base of crude oil tube material in scale in China. The company's annual steel producing capacity is 600,000 tons. Its seamless steel tube producing capacity is 500,000 tons with crude oil casing pipe of 350,000 tons. The company's main product items are crude oil tube with a diameter of 114－273 mm, and a wall thickness of 4.5－35 mm, high, middle and low pressure boiler tube, line tube, structural tube, hydraulic pressure supporting tube and other high quality alloy seamless steel tubes. Its main product, crude oil casing pipe, was rewarded State Steel Product Golden Cup Prize for its high quality. The company also passed various quality inspections and tests, including API, CCS, SGS and ISO9001.

General Manager Zhang Zhengang

Address: Jin－Tang Express Way, Dongli District, Tianjin Post Code: 300301

Tel: (022)24360165 24802625 Fax: (022)24360649

天津钢管公司管加工厂在线检测设备

天津汽车工业(集团)有限公司

TIANJIN AUTOMOBILE INDUSTRICAL CO., LTD (GROUP)

天津汽车工业(集团)有限公司是国有独资特大型汽车生产企业，是集供、产、销、科研、服务一体化的经济实体，是国家轿车和微型汽车定点生产基地之一。直属53家工厂(其中合资企业20家)，拥有职工近6万人。主要产品有:夏利牌系列轿车、华利牌系列微型汽车、三峰牌系列旅行客车、雁牌系列载货汽车以及各类专用汽车、铁牛牌大中型轮式系列拖拉机。资产总额96亿元，年汽车生产能力23万辆，其中夏利轿车15万辆。1996年汽车产量15.3万辆，销售收入119亿元，利税14.3亿元，在中国汽车行业中实现利润居第二位。

董事长: 纪学溦　　总经理: 张应吉

地址:天津市和平区烟台道78号

邮编:300040

电话:(022)23399926　23120045

传真:(022)23310858

Tianjin Automobile Industrial Co., LTD (Group) is a state owned large automobile producing enterprise, which is a economic entity with supplying, producing, selling, scientific researching and serving together. The company is one of China's nominated passenger cars and mini-bus producing basses, having 53 factories directly under its managements (There are 20 Joint Ventures among the total.) and 60,000 employees. Its main products includes, Xiali series passenger cars, Huali series mini-buses, Sanfeng series traveling buses, Yang Brand series trucks and special automobiles and TieNiu Brand large and middle sized wheel equipped tractors, with a total capital worth 96,000,000,000 yuan. Its annual producing capacity can reach 230,000 units of automobiles. Among it, there 150,000 Xiali passenger cars. In 1996, its automobile production volume reached 153,000 units, with a sale value of 119,000,000,000 yuan, handing in tax of 14,300,000,000 yuan, became the second by profit in China's automobile industry.

President Li Xuewen　　General manager Zhang Yingji

Address: No.78 Yantai Road, Heping District Tianjin, China

Post Code 300040

Tel. 23399926　23120045　　Fax: 23310858

厂长：吴金玉

天津市电缆总厂

TIANJIN GENERAL ELECTRICAL CABLE PLANT

天津市电缆总厂始建于1949年。自建厂以来，企业生产不断发展，企业规模不断扩大。目前，企业综合经济效益在全国电线电缆行业中居于6～7位。现有职工4700人。全部资产总值6.97亿元，为国家大型一档企业、国家二级企业。1996年被国家列为1000家重点扶持企业之一。1994年通过挪威DNV质量保证体系ISO9002认证。为国家安全特级企业，市质量管理奖单位、全国花园式工厂，重合同、守信誉企业。企业年生产能力可达3.8亿元～4亿元。销售收入3.9亿元～4.2亿元。

产品技术含量高，生产能力强。近几年来，投入1.3亿元用于企业技术改造，先后从德国、美国、芬兰等6个国家引进主要生产线和局部放电、硫化仪、硫变仪等重点检测仪器，形成较强工序配套能力。其中：橡套电缆、油泵电缆生产技术系从德国西门子公司、美国雷达公司引进的技术软件。产品采用IEC标准和部颁标准。多门类技术人员梯度结合，力量雄厚。产品先后为正负电了对撞机、大亚湾核电站、“长征”卫星等国家重点高精尖项目配套。出口东南亚、西亚、俄罗斯及部分欧洲国家。

企业形成多品种、大规模生产能力。目前企业生产有裸线类、电力电缆类、电器装备用电缆类、通信电缆类和电工专用设备等产品。并能够生产用户需求的各种非标产品。本部设有五个生产分厂和一个轮具自制配套分厂。下属2个中型企业、9年合资合作企业及一个技工学校。与本市物理研究所共同生产特种辐照电缆，同西门子公司合资利用芬兰悬链式干法生产线生产高中低压交联电缆。多年以来，在全国各省会、主要城市均设有分公司、供应站。

厂长：吴金玉　　党委书记：刘士达

厂址：天津市南开区黄河道西头　邮编：300112

电话：(022)27367851－55　电挂：2155

传真：(022)27366112　电传：23158 CBL.WK.CN

Tianjin General Electrical Cable Plant was setup in 1949. Since the foundation, the enterprise kept on developing itself, its scale became larger and larger. Now, the plant is the sixth or the seventh among the country's electrical line and cable industry in the terms of general economic benefit. There are 4700 employees in the plant, which has a total capital of 697,000,000 yuan, It is a national large scale enterprise of the second class of the first level. In 1996, the plant became one of the 1000 mainly supporting enterprises by the state. In 1994, the plant passed the DNV Quality Guaranty System by Norway and received its ISO9002 certificate, and became one security plant at special level at the same period. It also was entitled Quality Management Prize of Tianjin, a Garden Plant in the country, an enterprise respecting the contracts and reputation. The plant's producing capacity is very high with an annual producing capacity of 360,000,000 yuan to 400,000,000 yuan, with a sale revenue of 390,000,000 —420,000,000 yuan. Much more high technologies are used in its production.

Recent years, 130,000,000 yuan was invested in the plant's technological renovation by the enterprise. Many advanced equipment and assembly lines were imported respectively from Germany, the U. S, Finland and other countries, such as local electricityletting, vulcanizing instrument, sulphur changing instrument and other inspecting instruments. A comparatively stronger working procedure completing capacity was realized. Among its products, the technologies and software of rubber covered electrical cable and electrical cable for oil pump were imported from a subsidiary of Siemns in Germany and Radar Company of the united states. The IEC standard and Electrical Department standard are used by the plant. The plant has many technical staffs at different technical levels with various specialties, giving the plant a strong producing force. It has been producing accessories for positive and negative electron raming machine, Dayawan Nuclear Power Station, Long March series Satellites and the other state major highly advanced projects. Its products export to Southeast Asia, West Asia, Russia and some European Countries.

The plant can produce various products with a large scale. Now, its products can be divided mainly into 5 categories, as bare wire, electricity cable, cable for electronic appliances, Telecommunication cable and equipment used especially by electricians. There are 2 medium enterprises, 9 joint ventures and 1 technical school as its subsidiaries under its charge. It also co-produces special irradiation able with Tianjin Physics Science Institute, and high, middle and low voltage cross junction cable with Siemens jointventurely by using Finland's assembly lines. The plant has setup subsidiaries and supply stations in every major city and provincial capital.

General manager Wu Jinyu General Secretary Liu Shida

Address the west part of Huanghe Road, Nankai District Tianjin, China　P.C.: 300112

Tel. (022)27367851－55　Telegraph 2155　Fax (022)27366112　Telex (022)23158 CBL.WK.CN

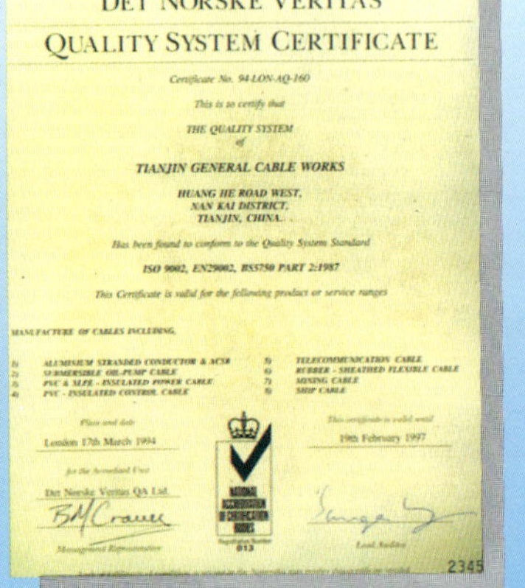
DNV
DET NORSKE VERITAS
QUALITY SYSTEM CERTIFICATE
Certificate No. 94-LON-AQ-160
This is to certify that
THE QUALITY SYSTEM
of
TIANJIN GENERAL CABLE WORKS
HUANG HE ROAD WEST,
NAN KAI DISTRICT,
TIANJIN, CHINA.
Has been found to conform to the Quality System Standard
ISO 9002, EN29002, BS5750 PART 2:1987
This Certificate is valid for the following product or service ranges
MANUFACTURE OF CABLES INCLUDING
1) ALUMINIUM STRANDED CONDUCTOR & ACSR
2) SUBMERSIBLE OIL-PUMP CABLE
3) PVC & XLPE - INSULATED POWER CABLE
4) PVC - INSULATED CONTROL CABLE
5) TELECOMMUNICATION CABLE
6) RUBBER - SHEATHED FLEXIBLE CABLE
7) MINING CABLE
8) SHIP CABLE
London 17th March 1994
19th February 1997

英国政府工贸部颁发的国际认证证书

天津环球磁卡股份有限公司

TIANJIN GLOBAL MAGNETIC CARD COMPANY, LTD

天津环球磁卡股份有限公司(即天津人民印刷厂)是国家大一型一档企业，万事达卡(Mastercard)和威士卡(VISA)国际组织在中国的首家特许制造商，国际制卡商协会(ICMA)在中国的唯一会员，银行信用卡及金融票证的国家定点生产厂家。主要从事数据卡系列产品及配套机具的研制、开发、生产、销售，承担各类金融票证及高档包装装潢产品的印制任务。

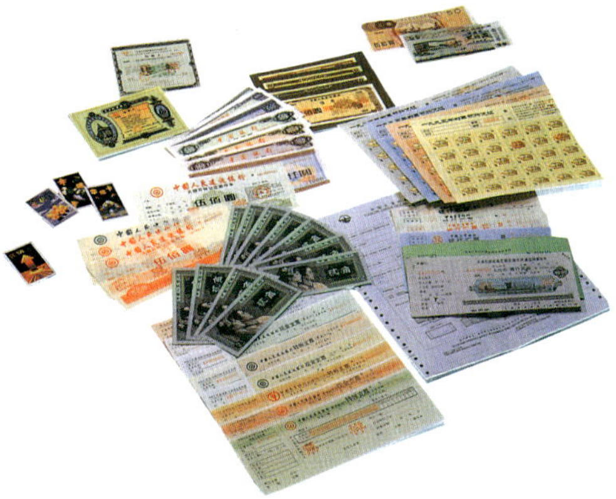

该公司是目前我国及亚太地区规模最大的磁卡制造企业，是天津市第一家上市公司，税后利润平均每年递增40%，每股税后利润由1993年0.13元提高至1996年的0.60元，在全国500多家上市公司中排名35位，天津市创利十佳企业排名第8位。公司现有注册资金1.4亿元，总资产3.86亿元，在职职工1600余人，各类专业技术人员近400人。目前，该公司正以强劲的势头向高科技的跨国企业集团迈进。

法人代表: 刘栋来

总经理: 姜肃敌

地址:天津市河西区解放南路325号

邮编:300202

电话:总机(022)28334874　28316601

传真:(022)28319333

Tianjin Global Magnetic card Company, ULtd (Tianjin People's Printing House) is a state owned first level enterprise. It is first permitted producer of Master card and VISA card, the only member company of ICMA in China. The company is also a state selected producer of bank security cards and Financial securities. The company's business fields includes data card series producing and related machinery researching developing, producing and selling. The company can receive various printing works including financial securities and high standard packaging products and so on.

The company is the largest magnetic card producing enterprise in recently China and also the Asia-Pacific area, the first listed Tianjin company in the stock market. Each year, its average profit after tax can improve 40%. Its stock prize increased from 0.13 yuan for each in 1993 to 0.60 yuan for each in 1996, which made the company became the 35th among the more than 500 listed companies in China, the 8th company among the 10 best profitable enterprises in Tianjin. Its registered capital reaches 140,000,000 yuan with a total asset of 386,000,000 yuan. There are also over 1600 employees with 400 of them having various technical titles. Now, the company is steadily working hard to become a hi-technological multi-national company (group).

Legal Representative: Liu Donglai

General Manager: Jiang Sudi

Address No.325 Jiefangnan Road, Hexi District, Tianjin

Post Code 300202

Tel: (022)28334874　28316601

Fax: (022)28319333

集团公司大楼

大港油田集团有限责任公司的前身是大港石油管理局，组织管理大港探区18744平方公里范围的石油、天然气勘探开发和油田建设。大港油田地域辽阔，油气资源丰富，勘探开发范围包括黄骅坳陷的陆地、海滩、极浅海和沧县隆起的东半部及埕宁隆起西部，地跨津—冀—鲁三省市的二十几个区县，中心地带在天津市大港区的渤海之滨，是一个油气富集的大型复合含油气区。

大港油田于1964年正式投入勘探开发，如今已经成为集油气勘探开发、油气生产、原油加工、机械修造、科研设计、施工作业、后勤服务、社会公益、多种经营为一体的大型综合性能源生产企业，截止1996年底形成了年产原油430万吨，天然气3.6亿立方米和250万吨的原油加工能力，累计为国家生产原油9349.1万吨，天然气124.2亿立方米，累计为国家上交利税47亿元。现拥有固定资产原值11.9亿元，净值60亿元，职工69000人，高、中级技术人员7300人。

大港油田是全国百家进行建立现代企业制度的试点企业，也是全国陆上石油工业系统率先进行改制的油气田，在全国21个油气田中，按原油产量排列，大港油田位居第六位。从1989年起，历年均进入全国最大500家企业之列，1995年排序列第53位。

1994年获中国人民建设银行天津市分行企业信用等级AAA级称号和天津市政府"重合同守信誉"称号，1996年大港油田集团有限责任公司建立了符合GB/T19001－1994 iat ISO9001:1994标准的质量保证体系，并整体通过了长城(天津)质量保证中心质量保证体系认证。

地址:天津市大港区　　邮编:300280
电话:(022)25922081　　25922240

炼油厂夜景

有限责任公司

NG OILFIELD GROUP CO., LTD

油田日出

中华第一人工岛

The predecessor of Dagang Oilfield Group Co., Ltd is Dagang Oilfield Adm. Bureau, which organizes and manages petroleum natural gas explorating and developing & oilfield construction of 18. 744 thousands km^2 Dagang oilfield. Dagang oilfield has large scale land, rich in oil and gas resources. The range of oilfield explorating and developing includes depressed dry land seabeach, shallows of Huang Hua city, raised eastern part of Cangxian County and raised western part of Cheng Ning County. It covers more than twenty county and district of Tianjin city. HeBei province and ShanDong province. The central section of Dagang Oilfield is located on the seashore of Bohai. It is a large scale compound petroleum natural gas district, rich in oil and gas resources.

It began to explorate and develop oilfield in 1964. Now it is a large scale unified resources production enterprise, imorporationg petroleum natural gas explorating and developing, production, crude oil processing, machinery manufacturing, scientific designing, construction, rear service, society public benefit, diversified undertakings in one. By the end of 1996, it has a certain scale with producing crude oil 4.3 million Tons, natural gas 360 million m^3 and processing crude oil 2.5 million tons in one year. It added up to produce crude oil 93.491 million tons, natural gas 12420 million m^3 and reached to 4700 million yuan of profits tax. Now it has former fixed capital value of 1190 million yuan RMB, net value of 600 million yuan RMB. It has 69 thousands staff and workers, 7.3 thousands senior engineers and engineers.

Dagang Oilfield is one of the trial unit of hundried modern enterprises system by the state, and is also the first one trial unit of the Chinese petroleum lines. Among 21 petroleum natural gas enterprises of the country, it ranked the 6th by crude oil output. From 1989 to now, it was ranked in the 500 biggest industry enterprises of the country every year and it ranked 53th in 1995

In 1994, Dagang Oilfield was awarded the Grade AAA enterprise by People's Construction Bank of China Tianjin Branch and was awarded "Put stress on prestige, faithfulness to contracts" by Tianjin Government. In 1996, Dagang Oilfield set up quality systems according to GB / T19001 – 1994 iat ISO9001:1994 and was approved by Greatwall (Tianjin) Quality Quarantee centre.

Address: Dagang District, Tianjin
Post Code: 300280 Tel: (022)25922081 25922240

公司总经理：辛鸿铎

天津市社会保险公司

TIANJIN SOCIAL INSURANCE COMPANY

天津市社会保险公司是天津市委、市政府于1992的10月批准成立的正局级事业单位，受市政府领导，是不以营利为目的的政策性社会保险经办机构。市公司在18个区县设有垂直领导的分公司，并负责对经济技术开发区、保税区、新技术产业园区3个分公司业务指导。

天津市社会保险公司办公楼外景

天津市社会保险公司总职责是承担全市各类社会保险，包括养老保险、医疗保险等方面的执行政策、业务经办、资金营运和社会服务。自成立以来，重点担负了天津市城镇国有企业固定工、劳动合同制工人、集体企业职工、外商投资企业中方职工、自收自支事业单位工作人员养老保险的具体经办工作。同时，还经办了医疗保险、农村社会养老保险的试点业务。今后随着我市经济的发展，市社会保险公司在市政府的领导下，将进一步竭诚为用人单位和广大劳动者服务，为改革、发展和稳定做出贡献。

地址：天津市河西区体院北环湖西路13门1号

电话：(022)23512904　23512910

传真：(022)23511985

邮编：300060

Tianjin Social Insurance Company was approved a bureau－level institution by Tianjin Municipal Government in October, 1992. Under the Municipal government's leadership, it became a non－profit social insurance institution of policy－oriented. It has setup subsidiaries in the 18 districts and counties of Tianjin, which are all under the company's direct leadership. The other 3 branches, locating in Tianjin Economic and Technological Development Area, the Free Trade Port Zone of Tianjin Seaport and New Technological Industrial Zone respectively, also are under its business instructorship.

The main function of Tianjin Social Insurance Company is doing various social insurances in Tianjin, including endowment insurance service, medical insurance and so on. Since its founding, the company has been doing endowment insurance for regular workers of Tianjin city and township stated owned enterprises, the workers under labor contracts, the staff of collective enterprises, the Chinese employees in foreign invested enterprises and those employees in the institutions of independent finance. In the meantime, the company still does experiment business in medical insurance and the social endowment in countryside.

Following Tianjin's economic development, the company will do more to satisfy the demand of units and their labor forces, under the leadership of the municipal government achieve its sacrifice to reformation, development and social stability.

Address No. Zeng 1, the 13th door, Huanhuxi Road Tiyuanbei, Hexi District, Tianjin, China　Post code 300060

Tel. 23512904 23512910　Fax 23511985

领导班子成员(在从左至右)：副总经理张一、总经理辛鸿铎、副总经理郭俊彦

公司和上级领导与一九九六年度公司系统先进个人合影

天津城市合作银行

TIANJIN CITY UNITED BANK

董事长冯树培，党组书记、行长、副董长彭子勤偕全体员工向各界朋友致意。

Feng Shupei, chairman to the board of directors, and Peng Ziqin, the bank party secretary & president of the bank and rice chairman to the board of directors, express their heartfelt thanks to all friends from rarious industry and commercial with all emploees of the bank.

天津城市合作银行是经中国人民银行批准，在原有66家城市信用社和城市信用社联合社的基础上改建的地方性股份制商业银行。本行在天津市工商行政管理局注册登记，是独立的企业法人。

天津城合作银行股权结构广泛，资金实力雄厚，注册资本金为人民币10亿元。截止1996年12月末，各项存款余额已达137亿元，资产总额达186亿元。现有170多个营业网点，遍布天津各个区，从业人员4200多人。是天津市首家具有独立法人地位的地方性股份制商业银行。

天津市城市合作银行的经营宗旨是以法律为依据，以效益为中心，以管理促经营，努力为社会提供一流的金融商品和优质服务，支持天津的经济发展和对外开放，为全体股东创造良好的效益。

天津城市合作银行将在继续发挥原城市信用社“灵活经营，优质服务”的基础上，勇于改革，积极开拓，稳健经营，朝着现代化的大商业银行发展。并更加注重实效，讲求信誉，发挥整体合力，快捷、简便、准确、安全地为广大客户服务。到天津城市合作银行办理业务，将是您事业成功的最佳选择。

总行地址:天津市解放北路72号　　邮编:300041　　电话:(022)23118571　　传真:(022)23118571

Being reorganized on the basis of former 66 urban credit co－operatives and united credit cooperatives, Tianjin City United Bank(there after TCUB), authorized by The People's Bank of China, is the local shareholding commercial bank, Registered with the Tianjin Adminsitration Bureau of Industry and Commerce.

TCUB has broad share structures and strong strength of capital position with registered share capital of RMB one billion yuan, At the end of 1996, all kinds of deposit balance teached RMB 13.7 billion yuan. Total assets reached RMB 18.6 billion yuan. Now the TCUB has a network of 170 operation branches located at every districts of Tianjin more than 4200 employees hired. TCUB is the first local share holding commercial bank with independent legal entity position in Tianjin.

With laws as the foundation, profits as the running center and efficient management to oprations, TCUB'S opration aims are at providing first level financial products and qualified serices for society, supporting Tianjin economic's development and opening to the outsids world and bring about a sound benefit for all the share holder.

On the basis of continuing to bring adaptable operations and excellent services by the former credit co－operatives into play, TCUB will encouragingly reform, vigorously pioneer and steadily operate, and develop itself towards the large modern commercial bank. And the bank will pay more attention to efficiency, credibility and solidarity and provide quick, handy, accurate and safe services to broad customers. Come to TCUB for business, it is the best choice to commit your business success.

Address: No.72, Jie Fang bei Rord, He Ping District, Tianjin　P.C.: 300041

Tel: (022)23118571　Fax: (022)23118571

天津市国际信托投资公司

TIANJIN INTERNATIONAL TRUST & INVESTMENT CO., LTD

总经理张长久(左二)、党委书记赵耀民(左一)向张立昌市长汇报公司发展规划

天津市国际信托投资公司成立于1980年，系非银行金融机构。经中国人民银行和国家外汇管理局批准，经营外汇和人民币业务，是国家确定的全国10个对外筹资窗口之一。公司成立17年来，充分发挥信托投资职能和对外融资窗口作用，已先后五次在日本发行债券，重点支持了天津钢管公司、天津汽车工业公司等国家和天津市重点建设项目。1995年，根据国务院和天津市领导的决定，公司成为天津钢管公司两大股东之一。公司恪守有关国际准则，按期足额支付外债本息，在国际市场享有较高信誉。

人民币业务、证券业务已具一定规模，公司全额投资的轻化实业进出口公司、津信实业公司、津信房地产建设开发公司、道克兰有限公司，也都取得较好业绩，截止1996年底，公司的总资产达95亿元。

地址: 天津市河西区友谊路6号

传真: (022)28364989

电话: (022)28364949

邮编: 300074

Tianjin International Trust and Investment Co., LTD (TITIC), established in 1980, is an non-bank financial institute. Approved by the People's Bank of China and the State Administration Bureau for Foreign Exchange, TITIC is specializing in foreign exchange business and RMB business. It is one of the ten units approved by the state in the whole country to have the right to raise foreign capital. In the past 17 years since it's established, TITIC has played full role in doing international trust and investment businesses. TITIC has issued bonds in Japan for five times, which were mainly used to support Tianjin Steel Tube Co., Tianjin Automobile Industrial Co. and other important stated owned and projects. In 1995, according to the decisions made by the State Council and leaders of Tianjin, TITIC became one of the shareholders of Tianjin Steel Tube Company. TITIC scrupulously abides international standards and pays enough capital and interests on schedule and it enjoys high prestige in the international market.

TITIC's RMB business and bonds business have well developed. The Light-Chemical Industrial Import & Export Company, Jinxin Industrial Company, Jinxin Real Estate Construction and Development Company, Daokelan Co., LTD, all are fully supported financially by TITIC, which also have achieved remarkable successes. TITIC's total capital has reached 95 hundred million RMB yuan by the end of 1996.

Address: Youyi Rd, No.6, Hexi District Tianjin

Post code: 300074 Tel: (022) 28364949 Fax: (022) 28364989

1996年12月公司成功地在日本发行第五次公募债券，张长久总经理(右二)及工作人员在发债现场

天津滨海信托投资公司

TIANJIN COASTAL TRUST AND INVESTMENT COMPANY

公司总经理: 任葆燕

天津滨海信托投资公司前身为农行天津信托投资公司,成立于1987年4月1日,注册资本1.5亿元人民币。公司是实行独立核算,自主经营,自负盈亏的经济实体,具有法人资格,实行企业化管理,在业务上受人民银行领导、管理、协调与稽核。主要经营范围包括:信托存款、委托存款、投资业务、有价证券业务、金融租赁业务、经济担保和信用见证业务等。

经过十来年的经营运作,公司实力不断发展壮大。公司坚决贯彻执行党和国家的各项方针政策,以"立足天津、面向全国、开拓进取、高效廉洁、多元筹化、稳健经营"为宗旨,以信托和证券为重点,不断扩大业务规模,增加业务种类。逐步成为一个实力雄厚、组织健全的多功能高效率的经济实体。

在公司总经理任葆燕的统一指挥和运筹下,各部门相互依存,协调运作,稳健经营极大地增强了公司的竞争力与业务经营的深度与广度。

欢迎各朋友光临惠顾!

地址:天津市和平区大沽北路138号

电话:(022)23321536

传真:(022)23321536

邮编:300040

Tianjin Coastal Trust and Investment Company was born from Tianjin Trust and Investment Company, Agriculture Bank of China, Tianjin Branch. Its company setup on April 1, 1987, with a registered capital worth 150,000,000 yuan. The company is an independent legal entity, which manages and take the responsibilities of benefits and losses by its own independently. Its business is under the leadership, administration, co-ordination and audit of the People's Bank of China. Its business fields includes, Trust Saving, Client Saving, Investment, Bonds & securities, Financial renting, Financial Guarantee and Credit Card businesses.

After more than 10 years' management, the company develops stronger and stronger. Under the Guideline of basing on Tianjin, Facing the whole country, Achieving programs, High efficiency corruption-proof, Multi-business and steady management, the company treats trust and security businesses as its main business fields. Its business scale keeps on enlarging, business fields keeps on adding. It is becoming a financially strong, multi-functional and efficient economic entity.

Under the leadership and management of the general manager, Ren Baoyan, the departments of the company assistant each other, co-ordinates with each other. The company's competitiveness and business management skill are improved.

Friends from different walks are welcomed.

Address No. 138 Dagubei Road, Heping District Tianjin. China

Tel: (022)23321536

Fax: (022)23321536 Post Code 300040

金钢桥

天津市市政工程局

TIANJIN MUNICIPAL ENGINEERING BUREAU

天津市市政工程局是天津市政府下属的唯一从事市政工程建设和养护管理的一级局，是天津市政府管理全市城市道路、桥梁、下水道、排水泵站、污水处理厂、市区防洪堤坝、地下铁路及公路等市政公路设施的主管部门。该局具有市政工程、土木工程、公路及高速公路工程、设备安装、机械制造、构件及水泥制品生产以及相应的设计、施工、科研总承包的国家一级资质企业。该局曾参加引滦入津，地下铁路，纪庄子、东郊两座污水处理厂，城市“三环十四射”，京津塘高速公路等大型市政公路工程建设。近几年他们还承担了广东、海南等十几个省及泰国、约旦、蒙古、巴基斯坦等十二个国家的市政公路工程设计、施工任务。其中天津市中山门立交桥工程获中国建筑工程质量最高奖——鲁班奖。天津中环线道路工程，天津纪庄子污水处理厂、十一经路立交桥和大连香炉礁立交桥获国家优质工程银质奖。京津塘高速公路被评为全国十大优秀公路工程之一。

该局具有世界一流的施工设备和各类专家、高级工程师、管理人员3000人。局所属有市政一、二、三、四、五、六公司，市政开发公司，建设公司，地产公司，路桥总公司，路桥工程深圳公司，成都公司等十八家企业和市政工程设计研究院，市政工程研究院等。

局长：孙增印

地址：天津市和平区重庆道118号　邮编:(022)300050

电话:(022)23394402

王顶堤立交桥

Tianjin Municipal Engineering Bureau is the only subsidiary first level bureau of Tianjin Municipality, in the field of city project construction and reservation adminstration. The bureau is the administration for Tianjin's roads, bridges, sub water pipes, water output, waste water handling, downtown anti flood dams, subways and express ways. The bureau is a first state level enterprise in capital and quality, which can receive projects as city infrastructure engineering, building construction, civil engineering, express way and free way engineering, equipment installation, machinery producing, construction parts & cement product making, and the related designing, construction and scientific research works. The bureau had participated in several projects as the input of water from Luanhe river to Tianjin, sub-way, two waste water handling factories in Lizhuangzi and Dongjia, the city's three ring roads and 14 branch roads and JIng-Jin-Tang Free Way construction. Recently the bureau also received projects and didexpress way designing and construction works in over 10 provinces as Guangdong and Hainan and about 12 countries, such as Thailand, Jordan, Mongolia, Pakistan. its Zhongshanmen Cross bridge construction work received the highest quality prize in China's Construction field, theLuban Prize. the construction works, such as Middle Ring Road construction, Jizhuangzi Waste Water Handling Factory, Tianjin, the11st Cross bridge and Xianglujiao Cross Bridge, Dalian, received silver Prize for state perfect construction. Jing-Jin-Tang Free Way construction was awarded one of the 10 perfect express way construction works in China.

There are staff of more than 3000, including various specialists, senior engineers and managerial personnel's in the bureau. Various internationally advanced construction equipment also reinforces the bureau's construction force. There are 18 subsidiary companies under its administration, such as 6 city construction and engineering companies from No.1 to No.6, City Construction Development Company, City building Company, Road & bridge General Company, Road & Bridge Construction and Engineering (Shenzhen) Company and Road & Bridge Construction and Engineering (chengdu0 Company. Tianjin City Engineering and designing Research Academy, Tianjin City Construction research Academy are alsounder its leadership.

The Executive of the Bureau Sun Zengqiu

Address: No.118 Chongqing Road, Heping District, Tianjin

Tel: (022)23394402　Post Code: 300050

中山门立交桥

公司经理: 董宏春

天津市市政工程建设公司

TIANJIN MUNICIPAL ENGINEERING CONSTRUCTION COMPANY, LTD

天津市市政工程建设公司于1992年10月18日经天津市编委、天津市建委批准正式成立。该公司同时加挂天津市市政工程局利用世界银行贷款办公室牌子，为市政工程局所属县处级事业单位。公司主要负责市政工程局世界银行贷款项目的建设管理、市政局利用外资项目的各项前期工作和项目执行管理，代表市政局推行固定资产投资项目总甲方工作，承担道路、桥梁、排水、地铁等新建工程的建设管理。

公司自组建以来，先后承担了复康路、金狮立交桥、京津公路立交桥工程，西马路、北马路、狮子林大街、芥园道、卫津路、华昌大街、长江道、大直沽五号路、金纬路道路工程，解放南路一带、宾馆一带、张兴庄一带、杨庄子一带排水工程，月牙河、南围堤河河道疏浚改造工程，光华桥、三元村、月牙河泵站工程等一大批建设项目的业主管理、建设管理，这些项目有多项被评为国家级、部级、市级优质工程。公司目前已具有丰富的建设项目管理经验，较强的建设项目管理能力、雄厚的技术实力，拥有一批高级专业人才与管理人才。

本公司坚持“立足市场、不断进取、信誉至上，精诚合作”的原则，并衷心希望和欢迎与国内外各界广泛交往、发展合作。

公司经理: 董宏春

地址:天津市和平区同安道新兴里33号　　邮编:300070　　电话:(022)23374587

Tianjin Municipal Engineering Construction Company, Ltd. was set up on 18－10,1992 approved by Tianjin Construction Committee and the Committee of Authorized Strength of Tianjin Municipal Government and at the same the company also has been named ' the Office for Using Loans Provided by the World Bank, Tianjin Municipal Engineering Bureau'. The company is an institute and is equal to a county authority that is subordinated to Tianjin Municipal Engineering Bureau (TMEB).

The main work of the company is in charge of the construction and management of projects that make use of loans provided by the World Bank, the earlier stage work and management work of projects that make use of foreign capital borrowed by TMEB. The company, on behalf of TMEB and all the first parts in contracts, is in charge of the promotion of investment for fixed assets. It also is in change of the construction and management of new roads, bridges, drainage works and subways.

Since its establishment, the company has taken part in many construction of projects, such as Fukang RD Project, Jinshi Viaduct Bridge, Jing－Jin Highway Viaduct Bridge and many roads construction, such as Xima RD, Beima RD and some drainage works such as Jiefang Bridge area drainage project, Zhangxing Zhuang Area drainage project, construction of pump stations, such as Guanghua Bridge Pump－ station, Sanyuan Cun Pump－station and Yueya River Pump－station. Many projects built by the company have been elected 'Fine Quality Projects' by the state, the department or Tianjin－City. Now the company has achieved rich experience in projects construction and management. Its ability to manage and construct projects have been enhanced by relying on its rich technical－strength and high－level personnel in special fields and management personnel.

The principle of the company is 'to face markets, to make progress continuously, to put prestige first and to cooperate with partners absolutely'. The company hopes to develop business and cooperate with friends sincerely both in China and abroad.

Manager: Dong Hongchun

Address: No. 33, Xinyili, Tongan RD, Heping District, Tianjin

Post code: 300070　　Tel: (022) 23374587

公司办公大楼

董事长、总经理：荆树明

天津市房地产发展(集团)股份有限公司

TIANJIN REAL ESTATE DEVELOPMENT CO., LTD (GROUP)

天津市房地产发展(集团)股份有限公司为天津市首家以房地产开发为主，实业投资、贸易流通为辅的多元化、多功能、跨地区、跨行业、综合型的企业集团。

(集团)公司十余年来先后开发建成体院北、王顶堤、万新村、川府新村、丁字沽二段、友谊公寓等31个功能齐全、环境优雅的居住小区，积极参与市危房改造和安居工程建设，建房面积累计达到1200多万平方米。同时，还为市重点工程中环线道路拓宽、天津站改造、煤气化等城市基础设施建设投资达5.6亿元。此外，投资兴建了吉利大厦、城建大厦(世贸广场)、华富宫大饭店、环湖大厦、滨湖大厦以及正在兴建的云翔大厦、华昌大厦、深圳(天津)皇都花园等一大批商贸服务中心。不仅取得了一定的经济效益，而且产生较大的社会效益，尤其是1993年转轨改制为股份制企业后，每年利润额均超亿元，截止目前(集团)公司拥有总资产近20亿元。(集团)公司荣获全国房地产开发综合效益百强企业之一，天津市房地产开发企业二十强之首，并多次评为市级优秀企业。

地址:和平区常德道80号　　电话:(022)23316822　23317276　邮编:300050

河北区教师村开工典礼

体北环湖大厦

Tianjin Real Estate Development Co. Ltd. (Group) is the first multi-functional, multi-business and cross regional, cross industrial enterprise group while its real estate development is its major business, industrial investment, commerce as its assistant businesses.

The group has built up 31 residential zones with sufficient equipment and beautiful environment, such as Tiyuanbei, Wangdingdi, Wanxincun, Chuanfuxincun, the second part of Dingzigu and friendship apartment buildings. It also actively participated in Tianjin housing reform and residential project, having achieved a total housing construction area of more than 12,000,000 square meters. Meanwhile, it has invested 560,000,000 yuan in Tianjin infrastructure, such as Zhonghuanxian enlargement, Tianjin Railway Station's reconstruction and Tianjin gas project. Lucky Tower, Urban Construction Tower (International Trade Square), Huafugong Restaurant, Huanhu Tower and Binhu tower, all these commercial and trade towers were invested and constructed by the group. There are also several commercial and trade centers under construction, such as Yunxiang Tower, Huachang Tower, Shenzhen (Tianjin) Huangdu Garden. In the past 10 years and more, the group not only achieved good economic benefit, but also received great social benefit. Especially in 1993,when it became Co. Ltd., it started to achieve profit, more than 100,000,000 yuan each year. By now, the group has held a total capital near 2,000,000,000 yuan. It was entitled one of the 100 strong enterprises for comprehensive real estate development benefit nationwide, and was the second to none in the 20 strong real estate development enterprises in Tianjin. The group was entitled municipal level perfect enterprise for several times.

Address No. 80 Changde Road Heping District Tianjin, China
Post Code 300050
Tel. 23316822 23317276

城建大厦

天津河川大厦

TIANJIN HE-CHUANG BUILDING

总经理：晁继

河川大厦位于天津市经济、文化、商业、金融中心南京路上，总建筑面积约5万平方米，是由香港李铭基建筑师有限公司和天津建筑设计院共同设计的，其外形为双塔式结构，高29层，是在三层裙楼商场基座上集写字楼、豪华住宅为一体的多功能综合大厦，外檐采用高级玻璃幕墙及瓷砖等进口装饰材料装修，内部设施齐全，是办公与家居的理想场所。

河川大厦聘请香港物业管理公司进行现代化物业管理。大厦内银行、超级市场、餐馆、咖啡厅、购物中心及健身俱乐部已全部开业，设在写字楼顶层的中国联通天津移动局早已开通。美国、日本、法国、新加坡、韩国、香港等国家和地区的国际大型公司和客商已相继入住。大厦出租的公寓还可提供全套家具及家用电器，并为客户提供良好的服务。

地址：天津市和平区南京路235号

电话：(022)27217001　　传真：(022)27217018

邮编：300052

天津河川大厦

Tianjin He-Chuan Building is located at Tianjin economic, cultural, Commercial and financial center-Nanjin Road. The total area of this building is about 50,000 square meters. This building was jointly designed by famous designer Li Mingji from Hong Kong and Tianjin Construction Design Academy. The Building's external form has been designed as a double-pagoda.

He-Chuan Building is a 29-storey building. The first three floors are commercial uses. Its comprehensive and multifunctional part consists of office buildings and luxurious dwellings and all facilities are available in it. The surface of this Building has been covered by high-grade glass and glazed tiles imported abroad. It is really an ideal place for living and doing business.

He-Chuan Building has been managed by Hong Kong Products Management Company by modernized style. Bank branches, super markets, restaurants, coffee bars, shopping centers and gymnasium in the building are open for enjoyment. China Liantong Mobile-phone Bureau, Tianjin Branch located on the top of this building now is also open for business. Executives and large companies from America, Japan, France, Singapore, R. Korea, Hong Kong and some other countries of the world now are entering and have been stationed here. Apartment units in it can provide furniture, all necessary facilities and good services.

Address: Nanjin RD, No. 235, Heping District, Tianjin

Post code: 300052

Tel: (022) 27217001

Fax: (022) 27217018

天津二建建筑工程有限公司

TIANJIN SECOND CONSTRUCTION ENGINEERING CO., LTD

法人代表: 李朋元

全国建筑施工企业唯一获“全国用户满意企业”奖牌

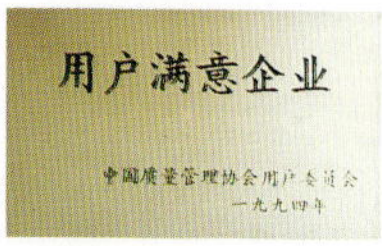

天津市第二建筑工程公司始建于1951年，1996年11月28日改制为天津二建建筑工程有限公司，是具有国家一级资质的大型建筑施工企业。

公司实力雄厚、人才济济、设备先进。具有独立承建各类大型工业建筑及高层、超高层宾馆、商厦、医院、学校、办公、住宅等民用建筑项目的施工能力。

公司依靠先进的施工技术和管理，在天津先后建成了天津新客站、水晶宫饭店、天津日报大厦、劝业场新厦等大型现代民用项目及承担了天津石油化纤、天津无缝钢管、天津十四万吨乙烯、天津十五万辆夏利轿车等国家大型重点工业项目。曾先后获得多项国家优质工程奖、建筑工程鲁班奖，1994年被评为“全国用户满意企业”，是全国建筑施工企业中唯一获得此项奖牌的单位。1995年在天津市同行业中率先通过了GB / T19002－ISO9002标准的质量认证，自1991年至今连续被天津市政府评为“重合同、守信誉”单位。

法人代表: 李朋元　　党委书记: 郑建民
地址: 天津市河北区元纬路二马路82号　邮编: 300141
电话: (022)26353214　传真: (022)26270380

Tianjin Second Construction Engineering Company was established in 1951 and its management structure was reformed and became Tianjin Second Construction Engineering Co., Ltd. This company is a large construction enterprise that has been entitled the first class national endowment by the state.

This company has been well-equipped with modern equipment, high level engineers and workers. It has the ability to build every kind of industrial buildings, high level hotels, commercial buildings, hospitals, office buildings, schools and other construction items independently.

This company, relying on advanced building technology and scientific management, has taken part in some huge buildings' construction works, such as Tianjin New Railway Station, the Crystal Palace Hotel (Tianjin), Tianjin Daily Building, the New-Building of Tianjin Quanye Bazaar and some industrial buildings, such as Tianjin Ethylene Project, Tianjin Xiali Car Project, and so on. This company has won the State-Prize for High－Quality and Luban Prize of Construction. In 1994, this company was elected the Consumer－Satisfied Enterprise in China, the only one enterprise that has won this prize among construction enterprises in China. In 1995, this company was the first one who passed GB / T 19002－ISO 9002 Standard. It has been holding the title of "respect contracts and keep promises" since 1991.

Address: Yuanwei Rd, No.82, Hebei District, Tianjin
Post Code: 300141
Tel: (022) 26353214
Fax: (022) 26270380

天津日报大厦—鲁班奖工程

天津新客站—鲁班奖工程

天津六建建筑工程有限公司

TIANJIN SIXTH CONSTRUCTION ENGINEERING CO., LTD

法定代表、总经理: 刘金友

天津六建建筑工程有限公司是有着四十多年历史的国营一级建筑施工企业。

企业具有高、中级职称的技术管理人员139名，其中高级工程师19名，正高级工程师2名。具有国家一级资质的项目经理32名。

近十年共创市优质工程21项，部样板4项，国优工程4项，为天津市唯一独获三尊鲁班奖企业。

近年来共有4项科技成果获市级以上成果奖，1996年《今晚报工程高层建筑钢管砼柱板体系的技术应用与研究》等三项技术成果，分别被评为城建系统科技进步成果奖。

本公司拥有大型机械设备353台，其中进口高塔16台，20T以上汽车吊5台，砼搅拌站4座，日产砼2000 m^3 以上。其中新引进的德国爱尔巴搅拌站生产能力150m^3/小时。砼搅拌车20辆，进口输送泵6台。

1996年6月28日，企业取得GB/T19002 ISO 9002质量体系认证。

地址: 天津市和平区多伦道274号 邮编: 300021

电话: (022)27221387 传真: (022)27315344

凯旋门大厦

The Sixth Construction (Tianjin) Company's Construction Engineering Company, LTD. is a state-owned, first-grade construction enterprise that has a long history of more than 40 years.

There are about 139 high and middle level managers and technical personnel-19 senior engineers, 2 professors and 32 project managers who have the title of state-grade intelligence.

In recent 10 years, the company has finished 21 projects which have won the title, " project of high quality" given by Tianjin Municipality, 4 projects which have won the title of "example project" given by the State Department for Construction Engineering and 4 projects which have won the title of "project with high quality "given by the state. The company is the only one enterprise that has won three Luban prizes in Tianjin.

In recent years, four items of scientific research achieved by the company, which have won prizes given by Tianjin and above provincial level. In 1996, the project of "the technology applies and research of the high story post-board system made by steel-tube for construction of Tianjin Evening Building" and other two projects have won the prizes for technical progress given by Tianjin Municipality construction unit-cycle.

The company has been equipped with 353 large size machinery equipment, of which 16 high tower cranes imported abroad, 5 crane-trucks above 20 tons, 4 cement mixer-stations which can produce cement 2000 cubic meters per day, 20 cement mixer-trucks and 6 conveyer-pumps imported from abroad.

On 28/6/1996, the company got the certification of GB/T-19002-ISO9002.

Address: Duolun RD, No.274, Heping District, Tianjin, China

Post code: 300021

Tel: (022) 27221387 Fax: (022) 27315344

日电电子有限公司程控交换机生产楼——获鲁班奖

天津市和平区房屋建筑工程公司

HOUSING CONSTRUCTION ENGINEERING COMPANY HEPING DISTRICT, TIANJIN

法定代表人：李重庆

天津市和平区房屋建筑工程公司是国家建筑施工一级资质企业。

多年来，公司把让人民住上满意的住房和向顾客提供满意的产品视为己任。工程质量连续七年在天津市施工质量大检查中排在前10名的优秀行列。1996年经审核获得GB/T19002－ISO9002国际标准认证，使企业的工程项目质量水平和经济效益水平又跃升了一个新的阶段，他们积极走向市场参与竞争，为国家和人民先后创出鲁班奖工程1项、全国十大表彰工程1项、部级样板工程3项、市级优质工程20项，做出了建筑施工企业应有的贡献。

公司施工管理经验丰富，技术力量雄厚，基建、机械施工、装饰工程先后扩展到了北京、石家庄、哈尔滨、山东、深圳、海南等地，均以良好的质量、精湛的工艺、最佳的工期，受到了甲方的赞誉，创出了企业良好的信誉和形象，赢得了较高的社会知名度。

该公司将于近期转制为天津和平房屋建筑有限责任公司。

地址:天津市和平区陕西路75号
邮编:300020
电话:(022)27307742、27307784
传真:(022)27305874

Housing Construction Engineering Company, Heping District, Tianjin is a state approved first class construction enterprise in terms of capital and quality.

The company takes " to let people live in their satisfied houses, and to give consumers satisfying products" as its task. During the continous 7 years, the company kept in the top 10 list of construction quality in each year's construction equality inspection given by Tianjin Municipal Government. In 1996, the company got its GB / T19002—ISO9002 certificate, which pushed the company's quality standard and economic benefit achieving to a new height. The company actively participated in market competition. It has achieved 1 Luban prized construction project, 1 state honored construction project,3 model construction projects at construction ministry level, and 20 municipal level perfect construction projects.

The company is equipped with rich management experiences and technological forces. In the fields of infrastructure and decoration construction, the company's business has expanded to Beijing, Shijiazhuang, Harbin, Shenzhen, Shandong and Hainan province. Its good quality, excellent technologies, best construction punctuation win its consumers' approvals, which helps setup a good reputation.

The company will be restructured into Tianjin Heping Housing Construction Co. Ltd.

Address No. 75 Shannxi Road Heping District Tianji, China
Post code 300020
Tel. 27307742 27307784
Fax 27305874

天津市华卫房地产综合开发公司

TIANJIN HUAWEI GENERAL REAL ESTATE DEVELOPMENT COMPANY

公司售房底商(门脸)

天津市华卫房地产综合开发公司成立于1992年6月，是天津市农委的直属公司。主要从事房地产开发及商品房销售，是集开发、建设、经营服务为一体，实行自主经营、独立核算、自负盈亏的全民企业。

公司成立五年来，本着“质量第一、信誉第一、用户至上”的宗旨，先后开发建设了红桥区丁字沽“桃花园东里”72000m²的住宅小区及南开区川东里5400m²的住宅楼工程，都已全部交付使用，深得广大用户的赞誉。

目前，我公司又开发了平津战役纪念馆北路的住宅楼工程，新项目房型设计新颖，布局合理，博得客户青睐。

公司经理及全体员工真诚希望与各界朋友合作，共求发展、共创辉煌。

地址：天津市南开区川府新村川东里1号楼3门101－102　邮编：300113

电话：(022)28742925

28115944　28118347

售房人员在介绍房型结构

Tianjin Huawei General Real Estate Development Company founded in June 1992, which is an attached company of Tianjin Agriculture commission. Its main business is to achieve real estate development and sell commercial houses. The company is a state owned legal entity, whose business hands reach real estate development, construction and management services.

During the past 5 years, under the guideline of Quality the First, Reputation the First, Customers are the superiority, the company has achieved many construction projects, such as the East part of Taohuayuan Garden, a 72,000 square meters' residential area in Dinzigu, Hongqiao District, Chuandongli, a residential building project of 5,400square meters in Nankai District, which two all had been put into market, and got appraisals from all walks of society.

Now, the company is constructing a residential building project located in the western road of the Museum of Ping－Jin battle. The newly design department structure is very fresh and in good order, which has won customers' desire.

The manager and staff of the company sincerely wish to co－operate with friends in various walks, and achieve mutual development and success.

Address: No.101－102 the 3rd Door of the building No.1, Chuandongli, ChuanfuXincun, Nankai District, Tianjin

Tel. (022)28742925

28115944

28118347

Post Code 300113

桃花东里七万平米住宅小区

总公司党委书记、总经理：徐金昌

红桥区房地产总公司

HONGQIAO REAL ESTATE GENERAL COMPANY

红桥区房产总公司成立于1956年，具有40多年的发展历史，是集民用公房和公用公房经营管理、房地产开发、危房改造、多元化经济为一体的全民事业单位。

总公司负责全区310万平方米的直管公房的经营管理、维修养护的繁重任务，还主动承担了全区的危房改造任务。1992年以来规划改造了全区近80万平方米的危陋平房，开发建设了19万平方米住宅小区。1996年又对丁字沽新村五段危房进行了改造，使丁字沽新村一、二、五段成为市内六区五十年代建造的工人新村第一个消号工程。

总公司为了进一步适应改革形势的发展，在原有下属八大公司的基础上又先后成立了三条石房屋修缮有限公司，成立了房屋置换中心，使房产经营以原来的粗放型向集约型转化，向专业化大房产发展。

公司总经理、党委书记徐金昌同志愿广交天下朋友，开发协作，发展经济，为振兴天津房产事业作出新贡献。

地址：天津市红桥区北门外缸店街1号
电话：(022)27352019　　邮编：300120

Hongqiao Real Estate General Company was setup in 1956, which has a history of more than 40 years. The company is a state owned career－oriented unit. Its main management fields are civil residential buildings stated owned & public buildings stated owned management, real estate development, reform of the buildings in danger and so on.

The general company is in charge of the district's state owned buildings' management of 3,100,000 square meters, which is under the direct management of the district, the repairing works and containment. The district's only old and dangerous residential building reform work is also held by the company. From 1992 until now, the company has planned and achieved 800,000 square meters' these kinds of buildings, 190,000 square meters' residential area been developed. In 1996, the reconstruction of the fifth part of Dingzigu new residential area was finished, which became the first construction project getting rid of series numbers among those workers' new residential areas built in the 1950s in the 6 downtown districts.

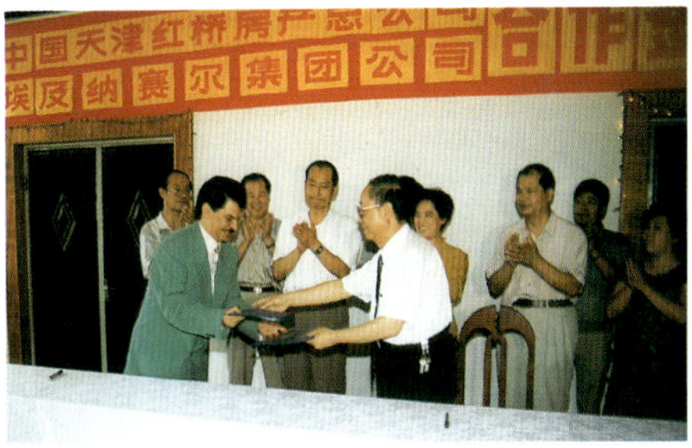

In order to be further adjusted to the national reform process, besides the 8 big subsidiary companies the general company already has the general company, one by one, setup Santiaoshi house repairing Co. Ltd. and House and Apartment Exchange Center, which change the house estate management from extensive management to intensive management, and made the company develop towards large sized Real Estate enterprise.

The general manager and general secretary, Xu Jinchang hopes to make friends all over the world, and do co－operation and development works to develop the economy, by which Tianjin's Real Estate development can be prosperous.

Address: No.1 Gangdian Street, Hongqiao District Tianjin
Post code: 300120
Tel: (022)27352019

天津市北辰区刘房子农工商联合总公司

LIUFANGZI AGRICULTURAL, INDUSTRIAL AND COMMERCIAL GENERAL COMPANY, BEICHEN, TIANJIN

发展中的——刘房子

总经理：田东平

刘房子为我市西北部一颗璀璨的明珠，被市政府评为市级明星小康村。地理位置优越，与津霸公路、中环线、外环线、子牙河形成环围。远期规划前景宏大，在九平方公里的辖区内，780余户近2700人正以饱满的热情迎接二十一世纪的挑战。

改革开放十几年的发展，村经济已初具规模。现有村办集体企业十几家，三资企业数家；农业生产逐步走上科学、规模、效益型，现已形成的津霸公路刘房子村商业一条街。为第三产业的发展起到了促进作用。工业产值在村经济的比重日渐上升，已初步形成农、工、商合理发展，相互促进，比翼齐飞良性循环之势。

几年来教育事业得到长足发展。同时加大了社会福利、社会保障的投入。村容、村貌焕然一新，治安良好，民风纯朴，已实现精神文明与物质文明的共同发展。

刘房子领导正用战略眼光审视自己，以高度的责任感率领全体人民共同努力、继往开来。我们将敞开胸怀，与各方有识之士积极合作、共创未来。

地址：天津市北辰区津霸公路　　邮编：300400
电话:(022)26654384　26650645

Liufangzi, as a shining star in Northwest Tianjin, is a Manicipal level Well-to-do Star Town with good geographic location, connected with Jin-Ba Express Way, Middle Ring Road, Extro-Ring Road and Ziya River, having a good developing potential. In its 9 square kilometers area,there are more than 780 families, nearly 2700 people, who are heartedly welcoming the challenge of the 21st century.

After more than 10 years' development since the Reform and Opening up Drive, the town's economy becomes scaled. There are over 10 township collective enterprises and several joint ventures in the town. Its agricultural production is becoming scientific efficient and on scale. A commercial street is setup in the town near Jin-Ba Express Way, which plays an important role in the development of its service industry. Its industrial production value occupies more and more in the town's economic structure. Its developments of agriculture industry and service industry become co-ordinated with each other.

Its education is also get improved rapidly. Its input in social pension and social protection system is also enlarged. The town's environment and outlook are changed freshly which is sociallysecuritied and civilized. The town is also realized co-development of spirital and material civilization.

The leaders of the town are inspecting themselves strategically, and leading its people to work hard together and success the past and looking forward the future. We are open-heartedly looking forward to actively cooperating with friends in different walks to achieve an excellent future.

Address: Jin-Ba Express Way, Beichen District, Tianjin　　Post Code 300400
Tel.(022)26654384　　26650645

环城电力

大棚蔬菜

别墅式住宅

名特优淡水品种繁育养殖基地

集贸市场的发展结出硕果

天津海洋开关厂主要生产输变电成套设备，是通过市有关部门验收合格并颁发证书的优秀单位，建厂10多年来规模逐年扩大，现已居于同行业前列。本厂还生产JYN10, TBH, GCS等高低压开关设备。

与天津商学院联建的留学生宿舍

刘房子小学

总经理：郁起

天津万盛置业发展有限公司

TIANJIN WAN SHENG REAL ESTATE DEVELOPMENT CO., LTD

万盛置业发展有限公司是专营房地产开发的合资企业，1995年成立以来，公司法人代表总经理郁起带领全体员工以企业信誉为宗旨，坚持了优质服务，优良的施工管理，开展了各项经营活动，几年来取得了优异成绩，为天津市的基本建设和改善城市优美环境做出了贡献。

特别是近年来与开发区建设集团密切合作开发了"风荷园"小区，一、二、三期总面积十七万平方米的综合性住宅小区，并以优异施工质量和先进的物业管理荣获天津市优质工程小区，被建设部评为全国城市物业管理优秀住宅小区称号。

1997年以来，我公司又自主经营开发了南开区白堤路"新技术产业园区"七万多平方米商品房住宅小区。为进一步改善城市居民的生活环境贡献我们的力量。

地址：天津市南开区红旗南路长实道福宏里1号　　邮编:300191　　电话：(022)23695612　23695614

Tianjin Wan Sheng Real Estate Development Co.Ltd. is a joint venture dealing with development.Since it was established in 1995, general manager Yu Qi has been leading staffs and workers,developing various sale works,achieving gratifying successes,making contribution to Tianjin municipality basic construct and improving the urbanist environment.'prestige first and service first ' is always the company's guidelines.

Specially in recent years,the company developed'Feng He Yuan Park'housing district with Tianjin Economic Development Area Construct Group. In the first,second,third phases of the project,the total constructionarea is 170,000 square meters,comprehensive housing district,which isawarded'Tianjin Municipality High－quality Construction Housing District'for its high quality and advanced real estate management,and is awarded'China City Advanced Real Estate Management Housing District'by the Construction Ministry of China.

Since 1997,the Company make its own managenial decision and develop'New Technique Industrial Park'in Baidi Road Nankai District.

The total area of housing district covers 70,000 square meters.Contributing our share to make further improvement on residential life environment.

Add: 1 Fugongli Changshi Road, Hongqi South Road, Nankai District, Tianjin Zip: 300191

Tel: (022)23695612, 23695614

公司外景

天津大学建筑设计研究院

ARCHITECTURAL DESIGN AND RESEARCH INSTITUTE OF TIANJIN UNIVERSITY

青岛海上皇宫

本院创建于1958年，行政上隶属天津大学，业务管理隶属国家教委计划建设司领导。是具有国家颁发的“建筑甲级”设计证书的建筑设计研究院。

本院有专门的设计力量，专业齐全、承接高级民用、公共建筑、高层建筑、高等院校教育和科研建筑的设计；承接旅游、疗养建筑、写字楼、公寓商住楼、商业等各种民用建筑和一般的工业建筑设计及装修设计、深基坑支护设计；承接城镇规划、高新技术经济开发区规划；为用户提供建设项目可行性研究、技术咨询、业务培训等服务。

威海甲午海战馆—纪念性建筑创作
荣获中国建筑学会1996年“建筑创作奖”

本院重视人才培养与职工素质的提高，坚持质量第一、一切为用户服务的原则、保证了创作质量，1987年以来28次获得国家及部委、省市级优秀设计奖，2项国家专利，1项创作奖、1项鲁班奖工程。

本院坚持科研面向工程实践，设计依靠科技进步的方针。我院从提高人员技术素质，改进设计手段入手，大力推行CAD技术，并引进了各种CAD软件，进行了软件开发工作并取得一定成果。目前，90%以上工程设计从方案、初设到施工图，均采用计算机完成。

本院招收结构工程专业的硕士学位研究生，建筑设计专业硕士研究生。

本院承担国家各部门和企业委托的科研协作。以创作与技术的优势，提高工程设计质量，赢得较高的社会信誉。

法定代表人、院长：董庆绵
院址：天津市南开区卫津路92号
电话：(022)23359044、27404752
传真：(022)23350849、23358329
邮编：300072　　电挂：1496
电传：23288　TUICO－CN

The institute was setup in 1958, which is under the charge of Tianjin University, but the institute's business management is under the leadership of the Planning Construction Department of National Education Commission. It is an Architectural Design and Research Institute with first level state rewarded Design diploma.

The institute has special designing forces, which are specialized in all the designing fields. All these make the company can hold the construction designing works, such as high level residential buildings, public constructions, skyscraper－liked buildings and higher educational colleges' teaching and researching constructions. The designing field also concerns many civil construction works, such as tourism & refreshment constructions, office buildings, commercial residential buildings and business centers, and some general industrial construction works. Decoration Designing and deep base designing works are also the institute advantages. The institute still can hold the designing works of city and town construction and high & new technological development area. Its service areas are also including construction feasibility reports, technological consulting and business technical training.

The institute pays attention to human resources' training and the improvement of its employees' technical quality. Keeping quality the superior, serving all the users are the institute's theories, which assure the institute's design quality. From 1987 to now, the institute was rewarded 28 perfect design prizes of national, department and provincial levels, 2 national patents and 1 Luban prize for construction.

Under the guideline of the institute－let scientific research works facing the real practices, designing based on the technological improvement, the institute pays attention to improving its employees' technical abilities and renovating its designing methods. CAD technology was introduced widely in the institute, many advanced CAD softwares were imported by the institute also. Its software developing work was also received good result. Now, more than 90 per cent of construction designing works from blueprint, preliminary design to construction map, are finished through computers.

The institute also can receive post－graduate students in the field of structure construction and construction designing. The institute can hold the scientific co－operations given by state departments and enterprises. The institute wins a good social reputation by improving its construction designing quality based on its designing and technological advantages.

Legal representative and director of the institute Dong Qingmin
Address: No.92 Weijin Road, Nankai District Tianjin
Post code: 300072　　Telex:23288 TUICO－CN　　Telegraph: 1496
Tel: (022) 23359044 27404752　　Fax: (022) 2335049 23358329

天津大学科学图书馆
获国家教委1991年优秀设计二等奖、邵馆项目评比一等奖

所长: 管丕恺

电子工业部第四十六研究所

THE 46TH RESEARCH INSTITUTE OF MINISTRY OF ELECTRONICS INDUSTRY

电子工业部第四十六研究所亦称天津电子材料研究所,是部属唯一的电子材料专业研究所,主要从事电子材料的研制、电子材料质量认证与检测及工业仪表开发等。硅、砷化镓等半导体材料的主要产品有:区熔硅、直拉硅、P型和N型硅外延片、硅扩散片、高压LEG-GaAs单晶、常压LEC-GaAs单晶、水平GaAs单位晶等,并具有较先进的半导体材料晶片加工设备。各种光纤及光缆的主要产品有:多模光纤、单模光纤、保偏光纤、传像光杵、大芯径、大数值孔径光纤、传感光纤、有源光纤、红外光纤等,并在特种光纤研究开发方面一直处于国内领先水平。电子部电子工业专用材料质量监督检测中心设在该所,联合国开发计划署资助项目"电子清洗ODS物质替代技术质量认证中心"设在该所。

地址:天津412信箱　电话:(022)28342662　传真:(022)28343026　邮编:300220

直径76mm半绝缘砷化镓单晶及晶片

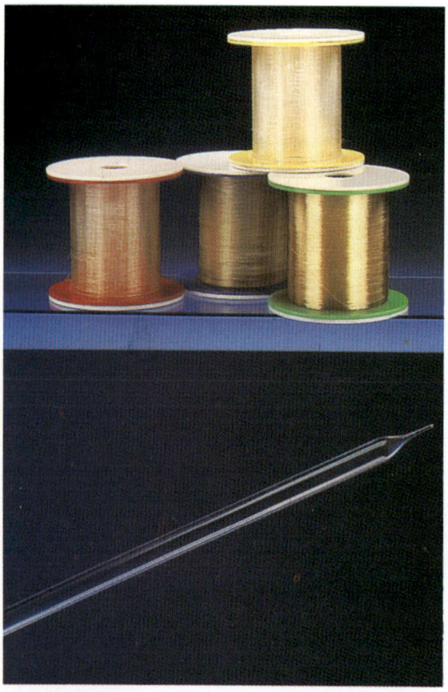

光纤预制件及光纤

The 46th Research Institute of Ministry of Electronics Industry is the exclusive electronic materials research institution subordinate to the Ministry. The Institute is mainly oriented to the development of electronic materials, material varification and characterization and the exploration and application of industry instruments. The main products of Si and GaAs crystals etc. are CZ silicon crystals, FZ silicon crystals, NTD silicon crystals and wafers, epitaxial wafers; SI-GaAs crystals, HB GaAs crystals, single and double surface polished wafers. It has advanced wafer machining equipments to ensure high precision and supper-quality. The main products of vaious optical fibers and optical cables are single mode and multi-mode optical fibers, active optical fibers, lager core optical fibers, polarzation maintaining fibers, image transimission fibers, infrared optical fibers and other development in the field of optical fiber of this country especially in the area of special optical fibers. The cente of materials characterization is built with state investment in this Institute. "Cleaning Applications Deployment Center for Replication of ODS-Free Processes Across China" is a project financed by UNDP(United Nations Development Programme).

Add: P.O.B. 412, Tianjin

Tel: (022)28342662　Fax: (022)28343026　P.C.: 300220

天津国安电气公司

TIANJIN GUO AN ELECTRICAL COMPANY

总经理: 邓幼霞

天津国安电气公司隶属于中信国安集团，拥有雄厚的资金和技术实力，立足于通讯及计算机行业，是集科研、开发、生产制造、销售于一体的高科技企业。

公司先后投资合作建立了天津津防寻呼台、天津经济信息寻呼台、徐州国安寻呼台、大同政通寻呼台，并以优质的服务和良好的信誉赢得了广大用户的赞誉。公司还可为各种寻呼台提供自动寻呼、语言信箱和汉字处理等软硬件服务。

公司承接了多项无线集群通信工程，如天津公交网跨段全双工(单工兼容)400M、150M集群系统；唐山铁路通信网跨段全双工集群系统；大连防汛台800M集群网；潍坊电厂800M集群网，以及经天津市政府批准，投资2亿多元人民币的中国联通天津GSM移动电话工程。

公司还可承接卫星通讯、有线电视、计算机网络工程、大型电子游乐设备等项目工程。

公司下属企业天津国安海运公司、天津金迈捷企划设计公司、天津国安木业工贸有限责任公司，可为广大用户提供海洋运输、广告策划、木业制造等多项服务。

公司愿凭籍雄厚的资金、技术实力以及成熟的营销网络和经验，不断开拓业务，广交国内外朋友。

地址: 天津市南开区鞍山西道445号　　邮编: 300192

电话: (022)27386688

传真: (022)27383404

Tianjin Guo An Electrical company is subordinate to Guo An group of china International Trust Investment company. It is abundant funds and strong technical force, based on communication and computer trade. It is an advanced technical enterprise with scientific researching, developing, manufacturing and sailing branchs.

Successively, Tianjin Guo An jointedly invested in Tianjin Jin Fang Paging Station, Tianjin Economic Information Paging Station, Xuzhou Guo An Paging Station and Datong Zheng Tong Paging Station that had been widely acclaimed by customers for their excellent quality and creditable reputation. Tianjin Guo An can also provide various types of paging station with hardware and software services such as automatic paging, language mail box and Hanzi word processing.

The company has signed contracts to build a number of trunking system engineering projects. They are Tianjin public communication net's cross－area duples(simplex compatible) 100M and 150M trunking system. Tangshan railroad communication net cross－area duplex trunking system, Dalian Flood Pevention Station 800M trunking system net, Weifang Power Plant 800M trunking system net, and the 200 million yuan China. Unicom Tianjin GSM Mobile Phone Project as approved by the Tianjin Municipal Government.

Tianjin Guo An Electrical Company Can undertake various engineerings of satellite communication, mobile communication, cable－TV, computer－network and large scale electric game device.

Tianjin Guo An Electrical company has subordinate enterprises as: Tianjin Guo An Ocean shipping company, Jinmaijie Advtisement Company and Guo An Wooden Company. We can provide service in ocean conve yance, advertisment scheme and wooden manufacture for customers.

Tianjin Guo An Electrical company desire with abundant funds and strong technical force, ripe sale network and expericence developing business and establish cooperate relationship with all friends at home and abroad.

Add: No.445 Anshan West Road, NanKai District Tianjin

Tel: (022)27386688

Fax: (022)27384304

Postcode:300192

美膳酒楼

MEISHAN JIULOU

美膳酒楼，一座雄踞津门的豪华美食娱乐城。座落体院北，环境幽雅。档次高、实力雄厚，是国家旅游部门涉外定点酒楼。

“松鹤”、“聚园”、多功能宴会大厅，装修豪华、设施精良。以世界名城、名贵花卉命名之高级单间，格调高雅，温馨华丽。可同时接待宾客1000余人。

正宗粤菜、鲁菜、精制各式西点。美膳酒楼曾在国内外烹饪大赛中多次获奖。美味佳肴佐以豪华歌舞厅、迷人KTV雅间，让您在品评一流佳肴的同时，尽享梦幻般的愉悦时光。

法定代表人、总经理：李全中

地址：天津市河西区体院北环湖中道10号

电话：(022)23359058　23358883

传真：(022)23359058　　邮编：300060

Meishan Restaurant is a famous luxury food and recreation centre in Tianjin, which is located in the area of TiYuanBei in good and quiet environment. It's a foreign national restaurant, designated by China National tourism department, with the advantages of high-grade and solid strength.

Mulity-function banquet halls of "SongHe" and "Juyuan" are fitted up luxuriously with excellent facilities. High-grade separate rooms, named with world-famous cities and flowers in refined style, can receive more than one thousand guests.

Customers can be served with pure Guang-Dong dishes, ShanDong cuisines and various kinds of western cakes. It has received awards many times in cooking competitions in China. Delicious food and magnificent dancing hall as well as KTV private rooms make you enjoy a dreamlike pleasant time.

Address: Huanhu Zhong Road 10 Tiyuanbei Hexi District Tianjin China

Tel: (022)23359058

23358883

P.C.: 300060

Fax: (022)23359058

全国劳动模范、公司总经理：毕玉和

天津市泰和集团公司

TIANJIN TAIHE COMPANY (GROUP)

天津市泰和集团公司位于有着“金色走廊”美称的天津市区与天津港之间，全公司面积4000余亩，职工3400人，其中具有高级技术职称的17名，中级职称的136名，并有众多的技术人员。

该公司为城郊综合外向型企业。一、二、三产业兼有，以工业、仓储业、物资贸易业、建筑业为主体。

本公司为集体所有制，是中国南方证券公司董事成员单位，流动资金8000万元，1995年度本公司总产值为4.9亿元。

天津市泰和集团公司以全国劳动模范、公司总经毕玉和同志为核心的领导班子，年富力强，素质高。我公司资金雄厚，投资环境优越，合作领域广泛，有良好的联合协作基础，愿与国内外各地区客商及朋友竭诚合作，携手共进。

地址:天津市东丽区军粮城镇东

电话:(022)24363526　24360468

电挂:天津8267

邮编:300301

Tianjin Taihe Company (Group) locates at the Golden Corridor between downtown Tianjin and Tianjin Sea Port, occupies about 4000 mu's land, having staffs of 3400. There are 17 employees with senior technological certificate, 136 with middle technological certificate and many others with technological titles.

The company is a comprehensive external – oriented enterprise located in suburbs. It does business in agriculture, industry and service sectors, industry, storage and warehouse business, material trading and construction works are its main attention.

The company is a collectively owned enterprise, which is an executive member unit of Southern China Security Company. The company's frequent capital is 80,000,000 yuan. In 1993, the total production reached 490,000,000 yuan.

The company's general manager, Be Yuhe, a state labor model, is the company's management main architecture, who is young and energetic with high business quality. The company is strong financially, has excellent investment environment, various co – operation fields, which achieve good co – operation basis. The company wished co – operated with customers and friends all over the world, and achieved co – improvement.

Address the East of JunlianchenZhen, Dongli District Tinajin, China

Tel. 24363526 24360468　Telegraph Tianjin 8267　Post Code 300301

公司领导班子

中法合营王朝葡萄酿酒有限公司

SINO-FRENCH JOINT VENTURE DYNASTY WINERY LTD.

法定代表人、总经理：高孝德

中法合营王朝葡萄酿酒有限公司始建于1980年，是我国最早成立的中外合资企业之一，主要生产王朝牌高档系列葡萄酒。合资经营17年来，企业产品的产量增加了180倍；产品的品种从单一发展成三个系列16种产品；合资各方投资额增长了70多倍。1996年年人均利税达85万元，成为亚洲规模最大的高档葡萄酒生产厂家。产品远销美国等20多个国家和地区。

王朝牌系列葡萄酒全部产品均为部优、市优，曾先后9次获国家级金奖、14次获国际金奖；1992年由于王朝酒蝉联国际金奖而被布鲁塞尔第30届评酒会授予“国际最高质量奖”称号；有关部门还将王朝酒确定为国宴用酒，通过外交部驻外使节供应处，王朝酒被供应到我国227个驻外使领馆、团、处，作为宴请和馈赠用酒。

地址：天津市北辰区兴淀公路

电话：(022)26998888　26990712

传真：(022)26990996　邮编：300402

集团公司外景

Founded in 1980, Sino-French joint venture Dynasty Winery LTD is one of the earliest foreign-invested enterprises in China. The staple products of the company are series of high-quality Dynasty wines.、The yield of the company, the volume of investment from all the parties have increased by 180 times and over 70 times respectively in more than 17 years of joint venture. Three series, 16 types of wines have been developed from just one single type of wines. Since the profit and tax per capita amount to RMB￥850,000 Dynasty Winery LTD has become the largest high-quality wine manufacturer in Asia. Dynasty wines are sold in the USA, etc., more than 20 countries and regions.

All types of Dynasty wines are awarded prizes by municipality and the ministries and have won State gold medal for 9 times and international gold medal 14 times. In 1992, Monde Selection in Brussels, Dynasty wines are awarded “ the Trophy of international High Quality ” for having won international gold medals in 5 consecutive years. Dynasty wines are served at the state banquets, moreover, in 227 Chinese embassies, consulates and offices abroad, they are selected as the wine served at the banquets or as presents by the supply office for Chines empassies abroad of the Ministry of Foreign Affair.

Address: Xingdian Rd, Beichen District Tianjin China

Tel:(022)26998888　26990712　Fax:(022)26990996　P.C.:300402

党总支书记：阎寅生

天津市东丽区河兴庄农工商总公司

（金钟宾馆）

TIANJIN DONGLI DISTRICT HEXINGZHUANG AGRICULTURE INDUSTRY & COMMERCE GENERAL COMPANY

金钟宾馆座落于河北区金种河大街外环线交口北侧，到市中心车程几分钟，宾馆面对京津塘高速公路金钟路出口；是东北三省进津必经之路，距天津国际机场十公里，交通畅通。

金种宾馆是个集餐饮、娱乐、会议、办公、旅游、休闲、健身于一体的综合型多功能娱乐城。整体建筑现代化、高雅、壮观、外观风格独特、配套设施完善，占地面积10000平米，建筑面积8794.8平米，设有客房95套，套间8个，会议厅4个，客房装修豪华，室内面积宽敞，前厅234平米内设商务服务中心，总服务台候命为宾客服务，中餐厅375.54平米，西餐厅70平米，为宾客提供中西式早餐、正餐服务。宾馆采用地下温泉热水，井深1200米，水温50度，经化验含有多种元素有良好的保健与治疗作用。设有二十条中继线程控交换机，与国际、国内、市内通讯畅通无阻；同时每个客房均设有闭路电视系统，为您通讯娱乐提供方便，备有奥的斯电梯一部，供宾客使用，宾馆采用中央空调系统，温度宜人，二楼设有豪华典雅的歌舞厅和健身房。

金钟宾馆二期工程康乐中心有温泉游泳馆、网球场、台球馆，保龄球馆等。

欢迎各界朋友光临本宾馆！

地址：中国天津河北区金钟河大街外环线交口
电话：(022)26335806
传真：(022)26337742
邮编：300240
Add: Cross of WaiHuan Road With Jin Zhong he street HeBei District Tiajin China
Tel: (022)26335806
Fax: (022)26337742
Post Code: 300240

Jin Zhong Hotel is located at the northside of cross of waihuan Road with JIN ZHONG ROAD HeBei district, only several minutes to downtown by car. The Hotel faces to the Jinzhong Road exit of high way, is the only way from three Northerneast provinces to Tianjin, and only 10 kms from Tianjin International Airport, have transport facilities.

Jinzhong Hotel is a multi entertainment palace with drinking and food, meetings, business, travel, convalesce and health. The whole building have a modern, refined, grand, unique style and perfect necessary facilities. Whole ground area 10,000m², building area 8794.8m². The hotel has 95 single room, 8 suite room and 4 conference hall. The guest room have commodious area and deluxe decorate. The lobby 234m² with the susiness center. The front desk take a warm sevice to guests all day. Chinese Restaurant 375.54m², Western-style restaurant 70m² can supply breakfast, lunch and dinner with Chinese or Western style. The hotel have a 1200 metres deep hot spring with 50℃ warm water, take health protection and treatment of disease. The hotel have twenty telephone trunk line can take a communication express domestic and international. Every room have CATV system and central air condition. Two "OTIS" elevator served for guest all day. It also has a deluxe night club and gymnasium on the second floor.

The Hotel will built hot spring swimming pool, fitness center, tennis court, billiard room and bowling alley in the second period project.

We get a warm welcome for friends of various circles and appreciate your presence.

天津静海电力发展中心

TIANJIN JINGHAI ELECTRICITY DEVELOPMENT CENTER

总经理：熊军立

静海县电力发展中心是电力局所属的第三产业，下属元亨饭店、华原科技经济开发公司、房地产开发公司、电力科技职业学校等企业。

元亨饭店位于静海火车站对面繁华的商业区，交通便利、环境优美。总面积5800平方米，饭店有标准客房，三人客房、套房、蜜月套房、豪华套房，共计52间，配有空调、暖气、闭路电视、烟感喷淋装置和现代化通讯设备。有可供300人同时就餐的中餐厅，不同风格、不同规模的宴会厅，风味餐厅和肥牛火锅以及多功能厅、商务中心、商场、卡拉ok歌舞厅，桑拿浴按摩室，会议室，购物健身娱乐设施完备。即将峻工的二期工程将使饭店的接待能力成倍增加，功能更加完善。

华原科技经济开发公司研制的引火炭，用一根火柴即可引燃峰窝煤，快速方便、清洁无烟，解决冬季煤引火难的问题。速燃烧烤炭已出口至美国、日本、港台等国家和地区。

电力发展中心与国家农业部农科院合作开发的万亩苜蓿种植区预计年产牧草可达8000吨，在满足国内市场的同时并将出口日本、韩国等家。

总裁朱希甫、总经理熊军立、客房部经理路存金携全体员工竭诚欢迎各界朋友、国内外客商的光临！

地址：天津市静海县东方红路22号

邮编：301600

电话：客房部(022)28944444

华原公司(022)28944235

传真：(022)28946873　28946874

华原公司研制的引火炭

Tianjin Jianghai Electricity Development Center is a commercial legal entity of Electricity Bureau. Under the center's charge, there are Yuanheng Hotel, Huayuan Scientific Technological Development Company, Real Estate Development Company and The Technical School of Electrical Science and Technology. Yuanheng Hotel is located in a prosperous commercial center opposite to Jinghai Railway Station with convenient transportation and beautiful environment, The Hotel's total area is 5,800 square meters with standard apartments, as 3-bed apartments, apartment units, honeymoon units, luxury units. All together, there are 52 units, which all are equipped with air-conditioners, heating, cable TV sets, fire-prevention system and modern telecommunication equipment. There are also a Chinese food dining hall with a capacity of receiving 300 guests at same time, small dining halls with different styles and scales, special dining halls and multi function halls, commercial and trade center, shopping center, dancing pools, meeting halls and a refreshment center. Its capacity will become doubled when its second period costruction works being finished.

元亨饭店高级套房

Huayuan Scientific Technological Economic Development Company produces charcoal for firing. By using a single fire-stick, the honey comb briquette can be easily burnt when the charcoal be mixed.Its products are easy, convenient and non-smoke. One of its products——quickly burning charcoal has been exported to the United States, Japan, Hong Kong and other countries and regions.

The Electricity Center setup a co-operative developing project, alfalfa farming co-operated with the Agriculture Department of China, which estimated an annual volume of 8000 tons. The products after satisfying domestic demand will be exported to Japan and P. R. Korea. President Zhu Xipu, General Manager Xong Junli, apartment manager Lu Cunjin welcome friends all over the world to enjoy themselves here, with all its employees.

Address No. 22 Dongfanghong Road Jinghai County Tianjin, China　Post Code 301600

Tel: (apartment) 022-28944444　(Company) 022-28944235

Fax 022-28946873 022-28946874

电力发展中心办公大楼

中美天津史克制药有限公司

TIANJIN SMITHKLINE & FRENCH LAB. LTD.

中美天津史克制药有限公司是天津医药公司、天津氨基酸公司与美国史克必成公司按照中华人民共和国法律和美国食品药品管理局规定的GMP要求，在中国合资兴建的，以生产、加工、分装和销售供人用的制剂和原料药为经营范围的现代化制药企业。总投资额为1794万美元。

该公司第一期工程－制剂厂是按照美国FDA的规定和现行优质生产规范的标准设计、兴建，于1987年10月19日建成投产，主要生产片剂、胶囊、油膏三种剂型，年生产能力12亿片(粒、支)，代表产品是肠虫清、泰胃美、康泰克、芬必得、康得、百多邦等。

第二期工程—原料厂于1992年10月14日竣工投产，主要生产化学原料药及中间体，其代表产品为6－氨基青霉烷酸(6－APA)，年生产能力150吨，全部出口。

史克公司占地面积67,600平方米，建筑面积27,000平方米，白色的楼群，美观整洁。该公司拥有具有八十年代国际先进水平的制药设备和监测设备，同时拥有缓释胶囊及青霉素裂解等项先进工艺技术。先进的电脑管理、工艺管理、GMP管理、质量管理、市场开发和销售网络，标志着该公司生产和管理的现代化水平。

中美史克现有员工626名，其中外籍员工9名，双方共同经营、管理企业。

中美史克制药有限公司是目前我国合资制药企业中规模较大、发展较快、产品品种新、生产技术好、人员素质较高的企业之一。自1988年起连续被评为天津市外商投资先进技术型企业；1989年取得中国GMP认证书；1991－1992年成为中国500家最佳经济效益工业企业之一；1993－1994年被评为中国最大的500家外商投资工业企业；1993－1994年被评为全国双优外商投资企业；1994年被评为天津市最大(百强)工业企业；1994年被评为首届全国十佳医药三资企业。

The Sino－American Tianjin Smith Kline & French Laboratories, Ltd(TSKF) is a joint venture formed by the Tianjin Medicinal Corporation and the Tianjin Amino Acid Corporation with SmithKline－Beecham Pharmaceuticals of the United States in accordance with the laws of the Chinese People's Repulic and the good manufacturing practice(GMP) stipulations of the Food & Drug Administration(FDA) of the United States. TSKF is a modern pharmaceutical joint venture for the production, processing and sub－packaging of human Pharmaceuticals and chemicals. Its total investment is USD 17.94 million.

Phase I of the joint venture, the Pharmaceutical Plant, was designed as per GMP requirements of the FDA, and was launched on October 19, 1987. It manufactures primarily 3 dosage forms, i.e. tablets, capsules and ointments. Its annual ouput is 1.2 billion capsules / tablets, and its principal products are Zentel 200 & 400, Tagamet 400 & 800, Contac, Contac SCF (severe cold formula), Fenbid and Bactroban. etc.

Phase II of the joint venture, the Chemical Plant, was launched on October 14, 1992, for the manufacture of 6－Aminopenicillanic Acid (6APA), an intermediate in the manufacture of synthetic penicillins. Its annual production capacity is 150 tons all of which are for export.

TSKF occupies a land area of 67,600 square meters, of which the built－up area is 27,000 square meters. The factory is a beautiful white building complex, and is equipped with manufacturing equipment and instrumentation of the 1980s. It is also endowed with the Spansule technology (sustained release technology) as well as the modern enzymation technology. Modern production and management in TSKF are reflected in its computer, process, GMP and Quality management as well as its market development and sales network.

Currently, TSKF has 626 employees of which 9 are expatriates. The enterprise is jointly run by the tow partners.

The fixed assets as at the end of 1994 totaled RMB 197 million, and its annual sales was RMB 696 million.

Currently, TSKF is one of the biggest pharmaceutical joint ventures in China through its rapid development, innovative products, modern production technology and best people. Since 1988, it has continually been given the following awards;

1."Advanced Technology Enterprise" among enterprises with foreign investment;

2.1989,"The GMP Confirmation Certificate;

3.1991－1992, it is ranked amongst the 500 industrial enterprises with the best economic benefit in China.

4.1993－1994, it is ranked amongst the 500 biggest industrial enterprises with foreign investment in China.

5.1993－1994, it is awarded the title of "Shuang You" (double excellence i. e. assessed against forex generated through exports & pre－tax profit) enterprise with foreign investment in China.

6.1994, it is ranked amongst the biggest "Bai Qiang" (100 best) industrial enterprises in Tianjin.

7.1994, it is ranked amongst the 10 best pharmaceutical enterprises with foreign investment in China.

天津市腫瘤醫院

TIANJIN TUMOR HOSPITAL

院长：郝希山

天津市肿瘤医院

天津市肿瘤医院是一所集医疗、教学、科研和预防为一体的三级甲等肿瘤专科医院，我国著名的肿瘤防治基地之一。设病床743张，年门诊量12万人次，收治病人7000多人次，每年完成手术6000余例。对乳腺癌和头颈肿瘤外科治疗达到国际先进水平，对肿瘤的综合治疗研究居国内前列。现有职工1200余人，其中专业技术人员1014人。著名肿瘤专家有张天泽、李树玲、郝希山等。中国抗癌协会总部设在该院。

地址:天津市河西区体院北环湖西路

邮编:300060

电话:23359929－38

Tianjin Tumor Hospital is a Class 3－grade A tumor－special hospital that consists of medical treatment, teaching, projects research and prevention work. It is one of the famous bases for tumor medical treatment and prevention in our country. There are about 743 hospital－beds in it. Every year the hospital makes diagnosis and gives treatment to patients for about 120,000 person－times and takes in and gives treatment to patients for more than 7000 person－times. It gives operations to patients for more than 6000 cases. It has reached the international level in the treatment of breast cancer and head－neck tumor and it also ranks first in tumor comprehensive treatment and research in our country.

Now there are about 1200 staff members in the hospital, of which, 1014 are personnel in specific fields. Professor Zhang Tianze, Professor Li Shuling and Professor Hao Xishan are experts in tumor research and treatment. The General Office of China's Anticancer Association has been setup and working in it.

Address: The West Huanhu Way, Hexi District, Tianjin

Post code: 300060

Tel: (022) 23359929 － 38

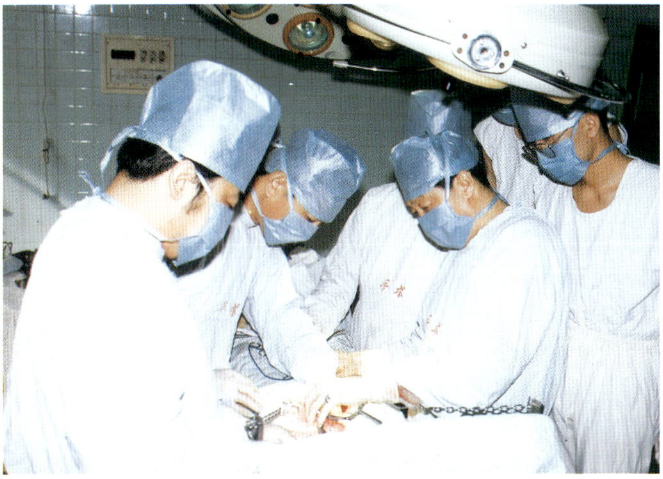

郝希山院长亲自主持手术

天津市中药制药厂

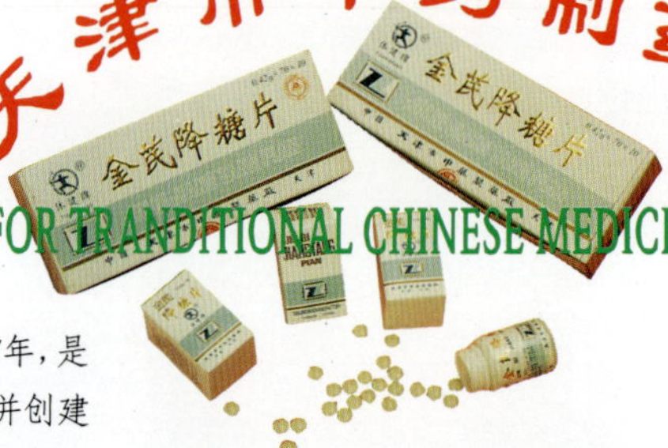

TIANJIN FACTORY FOR TRANDITIONAL CHINESE MEDICINE PRODUCTION (TFTCMP)

天津市中药制药厂始建于1957年，是由老字号隆顺榕与乐仁堂提炼部合并创建成中药药材提炼、工艺专业化中成药制造的中型企业。本厂致力于中成药研究数十年，于五十年代在国内率先推出中成药片剂，八十年代推出颗粒剂，成为我国中成药剂型改革的先驱之一。

中药制药厂拥有片剂、液剂、颗粒剂三条生产线，产品以长城、体健为商标计100余种。厂生产设备先进，技术力量雄厚，设有国家级技术中心，拥有高精尖检测仪器，对中成药进行研究。对产品主要成份进行定性、定量分析，于1992年开发出主治泌尿系统感染的癃清片、治疗糖尿病的金芪降糖片。

本厂以处方严谨、工艺精细、质量上乘、成品优良著称，其中藿香正气水、冲剂；小儿金丹片先后多次获得国家优质产品银质奖，藿香正气水在全国同行评比中连续三次夺得第一名，精制银翘解毒片、牛黄解毒片、黄连上清片、羚羊感冒片获市优，精制银翘解毒片获部优，本厂生产的“长城牌”精制银翘解毒片等近40个品种远销港、澳、新加坡、马来西亚、日本、美国等地区，出口产值超千万元，产品在国内外享有很高的声誉，成为天津市中药行业中的创汇大户。

厂长：张连城

地址:天津市河北区雁门路3号　邮编:300232

电话:(022)26340130

传真:(022)26340128

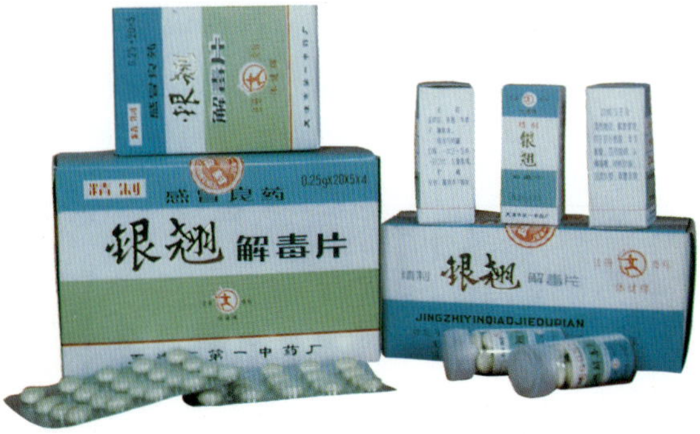

By combining the two old Brand name shops – Longshunrong and one part of old Le Rentang, Tianjin Factory for Traditional Chinese Medicine Production (TFTCMP) was setup in 1957.The factory is a middle – size factory that abstracts traditional Chinese medicine and designs traditional Chinese medicine especially. The factory has done traditional Chinese medicine research for decades. In 1950s, the factory took the lead in making tables of traditional Chinese medicine in China. In 1980s, the factory created pellets of traditional Chinese medicine and became one of the advanced preparation reformers for traditional Chinese medicine.

The factory now has three production assembly lines – powder preparation production line, tablets' preparation production line and pellets' preparation production line. The trade – marks of its products produced by the factory are "the Great Wall" and "Tijian", which consist of more than 100 items of products. The factory has been well equipped with advanced equipment and high level technical personnel. A state – level technical center also setup in here. The technical center has more advanced precision instrument that can do research work for traditional Chinese medicine, and also can do quantity analysis and quality analysis for its products. In 1992, the factory had developed new tablets' preparation (Longqing) for the treatment of urinary system disease and tablets' preparation (Jinqi)for the treatment of diabetes.

The factory has been celebrated for its prescription regorous, high quality and excellent products. Some products produced by the factory, such as "Huoxiang Zhengqi Water" (powder preparation and medicine to be taken after being mixed with boiling water), "XiaoerJindan"(-tablets' preparation for children) has won "Silver Medals for Excellent Product" given by the state for many times. "HuoxiangZhengqi Water" has been won No.1 three times when competing with factories of the same product in three continuous years. "Refined Yinqiao Antidote Tablets", "Niohuang Antidote Tablets," "Huanglian Shiangqing Tablets" and "Lingyang Ganmao Tablets" have won the titles of "Excellent Products" given by Tianjin, "Refined Yinqiao Antidote Tablets" has won the title of "Excellent Product" given by the State Department of Health. "The Great Wall" trade – mark products, such as "Refined Yinqiao Antidote Tablets" and 40 kinds of products produced by the factory have been exported to Hong Kong, Macao, Singapore, Malaysia, Japan and America and other countries in the world. The output value of products for export has exceeded ten million RMB yuan. The factory now is one of the important enterprises that can earn more foreign currency for the state and enjoys high prestige for its good products both in China and abroad.

Address: Yianmen RD, No.3, Hebei District, Tianjin

Post code: 300232

Tel: (022) 26340130　　Fax: (022) 26340128

天津市第五中药厂

TIANJIN THE FIFTH TRADITIONAL CHINESE MEDICINE FACTORY

天津市第五中药厂前身是宏仁堂，它是一个具有七十余年历史的老厂。它以生产面散剂型为传统，生产胶囊剂型为特色，产品涉及内、外、妇、儿、皮肤各科，共六十余个品种。该厂具有历史悠久、产品独特、工艺精良、疗效确切的特点，在国内外享有很高的声誉，于一九九三年被国家国内贸易部授于“中华老字号”荣誉称号。

为了与国际市场接轨，使我们的中药迈出国门走向世界。该厂近几年来，改扩建了厂房，生产设备也随着发展不断更新，全部实现了机械化或半机械化，使中成药生产开始纳入了现代化工业的轨道，产品的产量和质量都有了很大提高。该厂以产品质量过硬取信于社会，同时也注重新产品的开发研制工作。不久，该厂将会推出更好的新药投放市场，创造更好的社会效益和经济效益。

红花牌®

血府逐瘀胶囊具有活血化瘀、行气止痛之功效，是治疗血瘀症的必备良药。临床病症涉及内、外、妇、儿、皮肤及五官各科共六十余种。血府逐瘀胶囊是由桃仁、红花等名贵中药材组成，采用科学方法提炼精制而成的胶囊剂型，具有疗效显著、服用方便、易于吸收、无毒副作用的优点。它源于古典医籍，成方久远，为历代医家所推崇的活血化瘀代表方，又结合现代科技提炼精制而成。自问世以来，先后被列为国家基本药物、国家中药保护品种以及天津市公费医疗报销药品。

地址：天津市和平区河北南路334号
邮编:300050
电话:(022)23391035
传真:(022)23328158

Tianjin The FIfth Traditional Chinese Medicine Factory, its former name was 'Longren Tang', is an old factory with a history of more than 70 years. Its traditional products are power and its special product is 'capsule'. More than 60 kinds of products produced by the factory can be used by internal department, surgical department, gynecology department, pediatric department and dermatological department. The factory with its distinguishing features – a long history, special quality products, advanced technology and good curative effect, is famous both in China and abroad. In 1993, the factory won the honorary title 'China's Time – Honored Brand' given by the Internal Trade Department of China.

In order to combine the factory's production with the international market and to sale traditional Chinese medicine in the world, it has extended its workshop and updated its equipment in recent years. Production of the factory has been realized modernization or semi – modernization. The quality and quantity of products made in the factory have been improved and trusted by customers. At the same time more and more new products have been developed which will be appeared on the market. More and more social and economic benefit will be created.

Xuefu Zhuyu Capsule

The function of Xuefu Zhuyu Capsule is a good traditional Chinese medicine which can make blood move actively, cure extravasated blood and relieve pain. It can be produced in more than 60 different units which can be used in internal department, surgical department, gynecolog department, pediatric department, dermatological department and 'wuguan' department. Xuefu Zhuyu Capsule has been refined by scientific method which consists of some famous materials of traditional Chinese medicine, such as peach-nuts and safflower.It is a good curative effect Chinese medicine which can be easy taken and absorbed. It is nonpoisonous and free from side effects. The formula of Xuefu Zhuyu Capsule has been learned from ancient medical books with a long history. It has been appreciated doctors in the past years. Now it has been refined by scientific methods and rated as the basic medicine of the state. It also has been rated as one of protective Chinese medicine. In Tianjin it has be used as medicine which can be payable by public health service.

Address: No.334, Hebeinan RD, Heping District, Tianjin　P.C.: 300050
Tel: (022)23391035
Fax: (022)23328518

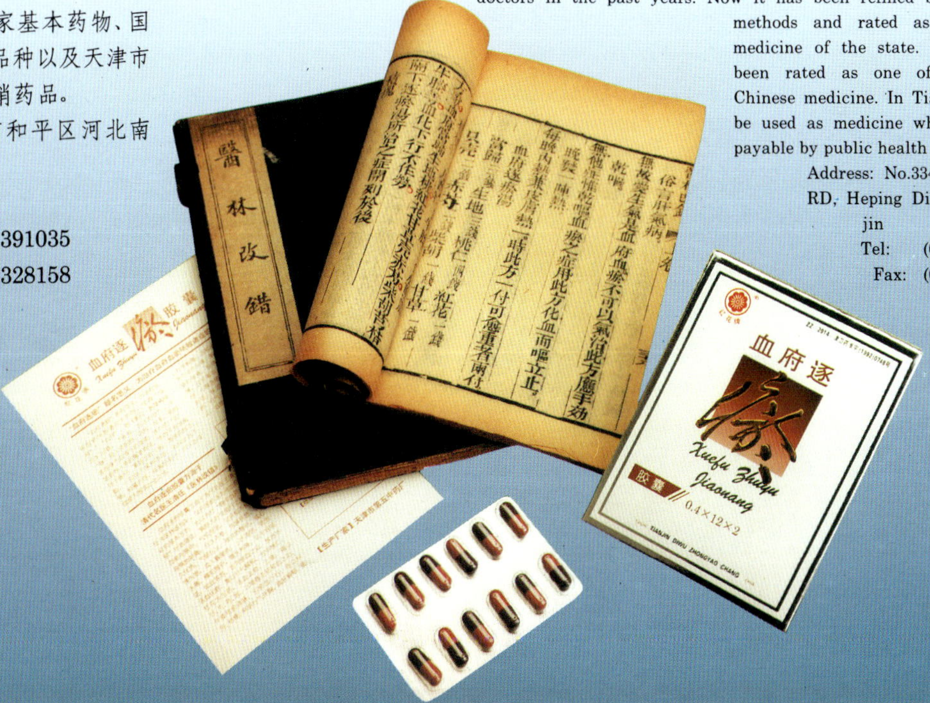

天津轮胎橡胶工业有限公司

TIANJIN RUBBER TIRE INDUSTRICAL CO., LTD

董事长、总经理:李玉梁

海豚 DOLPHIN　　解放 JIEFANG

天津轮胎橡胶工业有限公司为国家大型企业,化工部轮胎制造重点单位,天津市工业百强企业。

公司拥有员工4300人,占地面积19万平方米。已形成大规模综合配套能力产品体系,生产载重车、乘座车、工业车、马车和农机等5个系列百余种规格的轮胎。海豚牌、解放牌轮胎销往29个省、市、自治区,远销东南亚、东欧、美国及非洲、阿拉伯国家和地区。1996年工业总产值完成4.55亿、销售收入4.58亿,利税5300万元。

天津轮胎橡胶工业有限公司

目前,公司拥有与韩国、日本等合资企业4个及10全资子公司和15个控股公司、3个联营企业。通过产品结构调整、技术改造及现代企业公司机制的运作,到2000年,将跨入全国轮胎工业十强行列,公司将建立具有多元投资主体、多元产业结构、多元经营模式的企业集团。

地址:天津市河西区怒江道1号
电话:(022)28340895　　28340896
传真:(022)28340924
邮编:300220

Tianjin Rubber Tire Industrial Co. Ltd. is a state owned large size enterprise, which is also a major tire producing unit of chemical industrial department, one of the 100 strong industrial enterprises.

The company has 4,300 employees, occupies 190,000 square meters land. Its has setup a producing mechanism for comprehensive accessories producing in large scale. It can produce 5 series, more than 100 kinds of tires for lorries, passenger－cars, industrial automobiles and horse-power carriages and farming machinery. Its products with brand names as Dolphin and Liberation, have been selling to 29 provinces, municipalities and autonomous regions. In Southeast Asia, East Europe, The United States, Africa and Arabian countries can its products be found in their markets. In 1996, the company's total industrial output value realized 455,000,000 yuan with tax handing in of 53000000 yuan.

Recently the company has setup 4 joint ventures with P. R. Korea, Japan and so on, 10 wholly invested subsidiaries, 15 stock holding companies and 3 joint operatives. After the adjustment of its product structure, the renovation of technologies and the operation of modern enterprise corporation machinism, the company will become one of the first 10 tire industrial companies in China in 2000, At that time, the company will be changed into a multi－invested, multi－industrial structured and multi-management structured corporate (group).

Address No.1 Nujiang Road, Hexi District, Tianjin, China
Tel. (022)28340895, 28340896 Fax (022)28340924 P.C.:300220

轮胎硫化机组

天津國際聯合輪胎橡膠有限公司

TIANJIN UNITED TIRE & RUBBER INTERNATIONAL CORPORATION, LTD

天津国际联合轮胎橡胶有限公司系中外合资企业(大型二档)。

该公司是我市目前规模较大的中外合资企业和全国最大500家中外合资企业之一，也是全国系列化生产工程轮胎的唯一专业厂家。

该公司产品规格、品种齐全，生产的产品已经实现系列化。可根据用户的要求，设计制造具有良好的耐切割、耐穿刺、耐高温、耐磨耗等性能的工程轮胎，以适应多种作业条件。产品规格由12.00－24至36.00－51共87个规格、41种花纹类型、746个花纹品种，可为国内外多种型号的工程机械、矿用汽车、农业、林业机械、沙漠车辆及其它建工机械、采矿设备等配套。年生产能力为15000吨。

自一九八九年以来，连续被天津市外经贸委确认为“天津市外商投资先进技术型企业”，并获得“天津市最大百强工业企业”、“天津市最大三资企业”、“全国外商投资先进技术型企业”。

法人代表：杨士杰

地址：天津市河西区东江道50号　邮编：300220

电话：(022)28340824

传真：(022)27350402

Tianjin United Tire & Rubber Corporation, Ltd. is a Sino－foreign joint－venture.

It is one of Tianjin's large－scale joint－ventures and is also among China's 500 largest joint－ventures. It is the only factory in the country that manufactures serial heavy equipment tires.

The products of the corporation are full in size and variety and are serialized. The corporation is able to design and manufacture, according to the demands of the users, heavy equipment tires that are cut－resistant, pierce－resistant, heat－resistant and wear－resistant to meet various operational requirements. There are 87 sizes from 12.00－24 to 36.00－51, and in 746 patterns of 41 categories. These tires can serve the various needs of domestic and foreign made heavy equipment, automobiles for mine, agricultural machinery, forestry machinery, desert vehicles as well as other construction machinery and mining equipment. The capacity of production is 15,000 metric tons per year.

Since 1989, the corporation has been reconfirmed consecutively by the Tianjin Municipal Commission of Foreign Economy as a Tianjin Advanced Technical Enterprise of Foreign Investment. It has also won the titles of one of Tianjin Largest TOP 100 Industrial Enterprise, Tianjin Largest Foreign Investment Enterprise and National Advanced Technical Enterprise of Foreign Investment.

Legal Person Representative: Yang Shijie

Address: 50 Dongjiang Road, Hexi district, Tianjin

Tel: (022)28340824

Fax: (022)27350402

PostCode: 300220

天津阳光集团公司

TIANJIN YANG GUANG GROUP CO.

董事长、经济师：边宝臣

总经理、经济师：姬辉庭

天津阳光集团公司，是集生产、科研、商贸、运输和餐饮服务为一体的综合性大型企业。公司总占地面积23万M^2，总建筑面积4万M^2，地理环境优越、交通便利(位于河东区卫国道，东距外环线6公里，西距中环线1公里)。

公司现已形成以化工为支柱、金属制品及加工、运输、商业服务为辅助的产业群体。1995年公司总收入达1.1亿元。

地址：中国天津河东区卫国道128号

电话：(022)24342636 24513735 传真：(022)24513732

下属12家企业

天津东光特种涂料总厂	电话：(022)24341762
天津阳光大酒店	电话：(022)24513726
天津阳光福利五金制品厂	电话：(022)24342619
天津阳光剪板厂	电话：(022)24340297
天津阳光汽车运输队	电话：(022)24342274
天津阳光金属结构厂	电话：(022)24341646
天津星火化工研究所	电话：(022)24342307
天津阳光建筑涂料厂	电话：(022)24340384
天津合天钢铁有限公司	电话：(022)24349547
天津阳光汽车配件机电五金经营部	电话：(022)24342093
天津市辉伯塑料管件有限公司	电话：(022)24342919
天津市有机化肥厂	电话：(022)24341646

Tianjin Yang Guang Group Co. is a big comprehensive enterprise consisting of manufacturing, scientific research, domestic commerce and international trade, dining and drinking services. This Co. occupies a land area or 230,000 sq.m and building area of 40,000 sq.m. Geographic location is excellent and traffic is convenient(located at Wei Guo Road, Hedong District, 6 km east to Wai Huan Line, 1 km west to Zhong Huan Line).

Now the Co. has constituted chemical industry as its pillar and associated with metal product processing, transport and commercial services as subsidiaries. The total turnover in 1995 reached 110 million yuan.

12 ENTERPRISES UNDER

TIANJIN DONG GUANG SPECIAL PAINT GENERAL FACTORY	Tel:(022)24341762
TIANJIN YANG GUANG RESTAURANT	Tel:(022)24513726
TIANJIN YANG GUANG FU LI METAL WARE FACTORY	Tel:(022)24342619
TIANJIN YANG GUANG PLATE SHEARING FACTORY	Tel:(022)24340297
TIANJIN YANG GUANG TRUCK TRANSPORY SERVICE TEAM	Tel:(022)24342274
TIANJIN YANG GUANG METAL STRUCTURAL PRODUCTS FACTORY	Tel:(022)24341646
TIANJIN SPARK CHEMICAL INDUSTRY INSTITUTE	Tel:(022)24342307
TIANJIN YANG GUANG BUILDING PAINTS FACTORY	Tel:(022)24340384
TIANJIN HE TIAN IRON & STEEL CO., LTD.	Tel:(022)24349547
TIANJIN YANG GUANG AUTO PARTS ELECTRONIC AND METAL PRODUCTS DEPARTMENT	Tel:(022)24342093
TIANJIN HUIBO PLASTIC PIPE－SPARES CO., LTD.	Tel:(022)24342919
TIANJIN ORGANIC MANURE FACTORY	Tel:(022)24341646

天津阳光集团

天津市华明集团公司

TIANJIN HUAMING COMPANY (GROUP)

董事长、总经理：刘乃兰

华明集团是天津市东丽区华明镇办企业，占地66000平方米，总建筑面积28000平方米，拥有固定资产5000万元，流动资金2400万元，产值超两亿元，集科技、工业、贸易、运输为一体，二、三产业兼有的城郊型、外向型、福利性的综合企业集团。十几年来，华明集团坚持自我积累、自我完善、滚动发展，逐步完善的精神，走过了一条艰苦创业之路，取得了产值效益逐年增长的好势头；1996年完成产值2亿元，利税2200万元。为实现“九五”规划和乡镇企业第二次创业的宏伟目标，即到2000年，集团实现产值5亿元，利税5000万元，达到翻两番，提高(产值效益翻两番、职工生活水平普遍提高)的目标而奋斗。

董事长兼总经理刘乃兰荣获1996年天津市劳动模范称号并荣获国家民政部最高荣誉奖“孺子牛”奖。被评为全国企业家和全国优秀女企业家，市优秀企业家称号。集团公司连续被评为天津市文明单位、东丽区模范集体。

地址:天津市东丽区外环线三号桥东　　邮编:300300

电话:(022)24370805

传真:(022)24710576

Tianjin Huaming Company (Group) is a township enterprise located at Huamingzhen, Dongli District, Tianjin, which occupies 66000 square meters' land with a total construction area of 28000 square meters,fixed asset of 50,000,000 yuan, frequent capital of 24,000,000 yuan and production value worth more than 200,000,000 yuan.The company's business concentrates in industrial and service sectors, such as includes technological development, industry, trade and transportation, which is an urban-countryside connected, external oriented and social beneficial comprehensive enterprise group. During the past more than 10 years, keeping on accomondating by itself, improving upon itself and development and amending step by step, developing by hardworkship, Huaming Group's productive value and benefit increased year by year with good prospects. In 1996, the group achieved a productive value of 200,000,000 yuan and handed in tax of 22,000,000 yuan. In order to achieve the nineth five-year-plan and countyship enterprise's second period development —— To the year 2000, the group can achieve a productive value of 5000,000,000 yuan, hand in tax of 50,000, 000 yuan, with its productive value and benefit increase 100% for twice, employees' living standard increases commonly, the group is working harder and harder.

The group's president and general manager, Li Nailan, was entitled municipal level labor model in 1996, received Ruziniu prize awarded by China Civil ministry, who was awarded state entrepreneur, state perfect female entrepreneur, city level perfect entrepreneur in the years. The company (group) was entitled Tianjin Civilized Unit, Model Unit of Dongli District.

Address: The East of No.3 Bridge, Waihuanxing, Dongli District Tianjin, China

Tel: (022)24370805

Fax: (022)24710575　　Post Code 300300

天津德塔科技集團有限公司

TIANJIN DELTA SCIENTIFIC TECHNOLOGY GROUP

总经理：陈金城

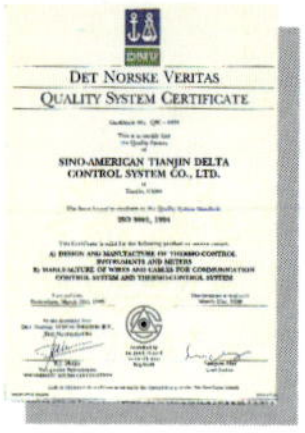

天津德塔科技集团，是在1984年建立的天津市节能仪表厂的基础上，坚持走依靠科技、依靠人才、创新产品之路发展壮大起来，业经天津市经济体制改革委员会批准的，天津市首家民营科技集团。

天津德塔科技集团的宗旨是：以一流的技术，一流的管理，一流的产品，一流的服务，创世界名牌。1995年率先在同行业通过ISO－9001国际认证；1996年被命名为天津名牌产品。先后被天津市评为新产品开发先进企业，被天津市北辰区命名为科技先导型企业。许多产品获得全国新技术新产品银奖、优秀奖，国家科技成果证书，天津市科技进步二、三等奖。

天津德塔科技集团现有产品：交联和铜塑电力电缆，自控温伴热电缆，农用10千伏埋地电缆，高温防火电缆，计算机多对屏蔽电缆，补偿线缆，医用电缆，本安防爆电缆，低烟无卤电缆，热偶热阻，智能仪表，测温合金材料，双金属温度计，多孔钛过滤材料，多孔钛净化设备。全营养叶面肥“地中宝”，轻型旋压皮带轮及提供工程成套产品和设备，同时该公司还涉及到国际贸易、房地产、餐饮等领域。

天津德塔科技集团的产品，不仅是我国电力、化工、石油等系统的定点生产厂家，为国内多项重点工程配套，而且已远销美国、意大利、巴基斯坦、孟加拉、马来西亚、印度尼西亚等国。

地址：天津市京津公路引河桥北西侧
电话：(022)26971551　26970552　26970774
传真：(022)26972454
邮编：300400

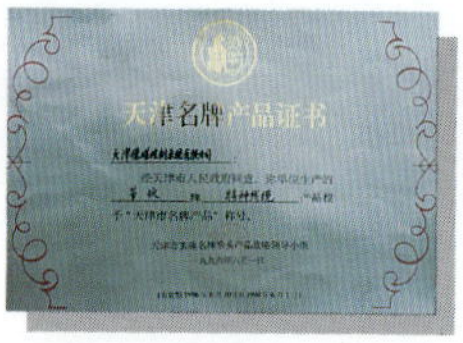

Tianjn Delta Scientific Technology Group was setup on the basis of Tianjin powersaving instrument and meter plant, which was setup in 1984. Supported by scientific technologies, human resources and the continuous product renovation works, the company developed healthily, and became the first private owned scientific technology group approved by Tianjin Economic System Reform Commission.

Tianjin Delta's Theory is to use first class technology, management, products and services to create world famous brand name. In 1995, it was the first in the industry, to get ISO9001 certificate. Its products were entitled famous brand name products in 1996. It also was entitled advanced enterprise for new product development by Tianjin, scientific technological pioneering enterprise by Beichen District. Many of its products received state silver prizes for new technology and qualified products, state scientific achievement certificate and Tianjin scientific improvement prize the second and third level.

Tianjin Delta's products are, cross connected and copper plastic electric cable for power transferring, temperature－auto controlled electric cable, underground 10 KW electric cable for farming,auto－temperature fire－proof electric cable, multi－end shield electric cable for computer, compensation circuit cable, medical electric cable, explosionproof electric cable, low－smoke & non－halogen electric cable, intelligent instruments, temperature－sensor alloy materials, double metal thermograph, multi hole titanium filter materials, multi hole titanium cleansing equipment, fertilizer for leaf—'Dizhongbao', light size revolving－pressing belt pulley. The company can supply all products and equipment for projects totally. At the same time, the company's business touch also reaches international trade, real estate development and restaurants.

Tianjin Delta is an appointed enterprise, which supply accessories for major projects in power generating, chemical industrial and petrol industries. Its products can be found in international markets, such as the United States, Italy, Pakistan, Bangladesh, Indonesia and so on.

Address: The west side of Northern Yinheqiao bridge Jing－Jin expressway, Tianjin, China　Post code:300400
Tel: (022)26971551 26970552 26970774　Fax: (022)26972454

本公司多次获奖的控制、补偿、高温防火及计算机五大系列电缆

天津裕华经济贸易总公司

TIANJIN YU HUA ECONOMY & TRADE CO.

法定代表人、总经理:刘泰来

天津裕华经济贸易总公司(其前身为天津化工采购供应站)始建于1953年,是集批发零售、生产加工、内贸外贸为一体的多功能、综合性国有大型商业企业。经国家批准具有自营进出口权,并设有海关监管库、保税库。经营面积达35万平方米。

总公司辖设26家经营、生产企业;6家联营合资企业。开展自营、代理进出口及国内批发、零售、加工、代购、代销、代接、代储、代运业务。

经营国产及进口化工、染料、油漆、颜料、中间体、食品添加剂、粮油、食品、畜产品、纺织纤维、纺织品、丝织品、服装、轻工业品、陶瓷品、工艺品、橡胶制品、运输工具、机械及设备、工农具、仪器仪表。

天津裕华经济贸易总公司全体员工恪守"敬业克勤、创业克俭、求实高效、协力拓展"的企业精神,愿与海内外客商广交朋友,竭诚欢迎海内外客商前来洽谈进出口贸易,洽谈代理进出口、合资、合作、来料加工、来件装配、补偿贸易、易货贸易、转口贸易及国内贸易。

地址:天津市和平区新华路183号
电话:总机(022)27124719、27124720
传真:(022)27125947、27121580
电挂:3651　　邮编:300041

Tianjin Yu Hua Economy & Trade Corporation(Tianjin Chemical Purchasing & Supplying Station) was established in 1953, a large commercial enterprise with multiple function of wholesale, retail, producting, processing domestic & foreign trade. It has obtained the import and export right after being approved by the Ministry of Foreign Trade and Economic Cooperation. TYETC has customs warehouse and bonded warehouse, which are about 350 thousnads square for business area.

TYETC, with its 26 subsidiaries, 6 comestic enterprises, has developed general trading, agent for import and export trade and domestic wholesale, retail, processing business as well as agent for godds buying and selling, receiving, warehouseing and transporation.

Running domestic and import chemical raw materials, dyestuff, pigment, paint, intermediate, food additives, grain oil, foods, animal products, textile fibre, textile, silk fabrics, garment, light industrial products, pottery and porcelain, handicraft articles, rubber products, means of transport, machinery and equipment, tools and farmtools, instruments.

公司主体营业大楼

The whole staffs of TYETC have scrupulously abided by the spirit of "Work industriously, Start the undertaking frugally, Work realistically in high-efficiency, Develop jointly", and wish to make friends with commercial circles all over the world, and warmly welcome all the customers at home and abroad to hold talks for import and export trade, agency, joint-venture, cooperative operation, processing with supplied material, assembing parts supplied by clients, compensation trade, barter trade, entrepot trade and interior trade.

Add: 183 Xinhua Road Heping District Tianjin China
Tel:(022)27124719、27124720
Fax:(022)27125947、27121580
Cable:3651　　P.C.:300041

1991年1月11日，李鹏总理在市委书记谭绍文陪同下视察津英

津英纺纱有限公司

JINYING SPINNING CO., LTD

津英纺纱有限公司、李七庄纺纱有限公司和津高捻线有限公司，均系天津市纺织品联合进出口公司与英国绵丰集团合资经营企业。投资总额已达4100万美元，中外双方各占50%。合资期限分别为20年和50年。三个公司原料全部进口，产品全部出口，且在国际市场上具有较强竞争能力，已经形成“三位一体”，拥有6万多纱锭，13,456倍捻纱锭和2370绣花捻线纱锭，1000余名员工，年出口创汇2500美元，具有较大规模和世界一流技术装备的合资经营企业。

津英公司自1990年6月14日开业六年来，累计出口创汇7120万美元，实现利税1121万美元。李七庄公司从合作经营到合资经营六年来，累计出口创汇3533万美元，实现利税443万美元。津高项目1996年二季度开业投产后，预计年出口创汇470万美元。从上述数字不难看出，公司是在盈利中运营，在国际市场竞争中不断发展壮大。

李鹏总理，有关国家首脑要员，以及我市主要领导和国家有关部门领导人，先后莅临公司参观视察。津英公司还作为天津市外经贸委优选的唯一的一家外商投资企业代表，于1994年12月赴北京参加“全国引进工作十五年成果展览会”。公司开业运营以来，连年荣获国家及市政府授予的“双优”、“最佳”外商投资企业，天津市“工业百强企业”、“人均出口创汇前十名企业”等荣誉称号并于一九九一年跨入“中国规模最大的500家外商投资工业企业”行列。

地址：中国天津市西青区李七庄津涞公路
电话：(022)23382847 23380940
传真：(022)23383935 邮编：300381

津英、李七庄纺纱有限公司董事长温聚和亲切会见英国绵丰纱线部主席花漫田先生

Jinying Spinning Co., Ltd, Liqizhuang Spinning Co., Ltd and Jinco Filament Twisting Co., Ltd are three joint-venture enterprises. The shareholders are Tianjin Textile Import and Export Union and Coats Viyella Plc(from the United Kingdom). The total investment of these three companies are USD 41 million, They are export-oriented enterprises, the raw material totally imported, employing more than 1,000 workers and staff members. There are 60,000 spindles, 13,456 twisting spindles and 2,370 filament twisting spindles, with strong competitive ability in the international marker. The export value is up to USD 25 million per year. The investment duration Period of these three companies is 20 and 50 years respectively.

For Jinying Spinning, since starting operation on 14th June, 1990, the accumulated export value is USD71.2 million, the total profit before tax is USD11.21 million. Liqizhuang Spinning, the operatin from co-operation to joint-venture for 6 years, the accumulated export value is USD35.33 million and the total profit is USD4.43 million. Jinco Filament Twisting Co., Ltd was put into production in the 2nd quarter 1997, The estimated export value will be USD4.7 million.

For the past few years, the companies were visited by many central & municipal goverment officials, even by primier Li Peng and many guests from other countries. Jinying Spinning was selected, as unique representative from foreign enterprises, by Tianjin Commission of Foreign Economical Relations & Trade to attend the "Achievement Exhibition for Opening and Reform 15 years" which was held in December 1994 in Beijing. They have acquired "Double Excellent", "Double Fine" enterprises with foreign investment and "The First 10 Enterprises with Export Value / Employee" rewards many times by Tianjin Municipal Government and state. It was also listed in "The Largest 500 Industrial Enterprises with Foreign Investment" in 1991.

Add: Jinlai Road Liqizhuang Xi Qig District Tianjin China Zip:300381
Tel:(022)23382847 23380940 Fax:(022)23383935

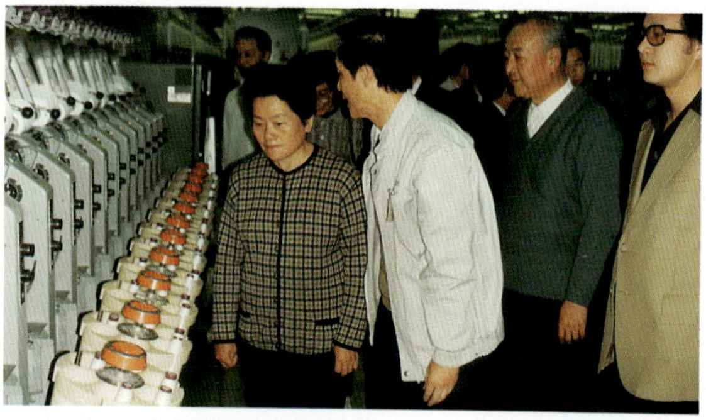

1992年1月19日，中国纺织工业部部长吴文英在温聚和董事长陪同下视察津英

天津市永安百货购物中心

TIANJIN YONGAN SHOPPING CENTER

天津龙门大厦永安百货公司是由香港永安国际有限公司投资的，天津市唯一的一家香港独资大型百货商场。

香港永安已经创建九十周年，在国内、香港及东南亚一带享有很高的信誉和知名度。今天永安已经发展成为一个业务多元化的上市公司，经营范围涵盖了香港及海外地产投资、百货业、按揭服务、电脑、餐饮等，是一个实力雄厚的集团公司。

随着香港的回归，我们投资于第二大工业城市天津，建立了天津永安百货公司，这个具有现代化、先进的电脑管理系统、一流的购物环境、一流的商品、一流的服务的商场。十几万个品种、加上特式的进口商品，丰富了天津的市场，满足了人民的需求。我公司开展的“货物齐备服务殷、永安家庭幸福多”的活动，也得到了天津人民的厚爱和支持。

地址：天津市河北区龙门大厦　邮编：300010

电话：(022)24211298　传真：(022)24211101

Tianjin Yongan Department Store Company, Dragon Gate Tower, invested by Yongan International Co., Ltd (Hong Kong), is the only large department store invested uniquely by Hong Kong.

Yongan International Co., Ltd has been founded for 90 years, achieving a high reputation in China, Hong Kong and the Southeast Asia. Now, the company has become a listed multi－business company, whose business field covers real estate development, sale, mortgage service, computer, restaurant & Hotel and so on in Hong Kong and overseas. It is a financially strong company (group).

Following the return of Hong Kong to the motherland, the company made investment in Tianjin, the 2nd largest industrial city and setup Tianjin Yongan Department Store Company. The company is shopping Center with first class commodities, services and shopping environment, which is equipped with modern advanced computer management system. The company put all together more than 0.1 million kinds of commodities, addition to many imported commodities, into market, which enriches Tianjin's market, satisfies people's demand. The activity－With all kinds of commodities and good service, families become fortunate in Yongan, organized by the company, received Tianjin people's love and support.

Address Dragon Gate Tower, Hebei District Tianjin, China

Post Code 300010

Tel. 24211298　Fax 24211101

法人代表、厂长: 王景义

天津市鼎牌燃气具总厂

TIANJIN DING BRAND GAS APPLIANCES FACTORY

Tripod

天津鼎牌燃气具总厂是具有20多年历史的燃气具生产厂家，拥有固定资产2200万元，各种生产及检测设备400余台(套)；该厂下设四个专业生产厂(灶具、热水器、电器、模具分厂)，生产“鼎牌”系列家用燃气灶，燃气热水器、餐厅大灶及厨房用具；家用电器；立管燃烧器；民用、工业用调压器(柜)等六大类60个品种，并承揽各种模具及冲压件的加工业务，是中国建筑机械行业重点企业。

自1985年起该厂用5年时间进行全面技术改造，从日本引进了先进的燃气具生产技术及设备，使产品上了一个台阶，在国内燃气具行业中居领先地位，产品远销欧、亚、非等21个国家和地区，1993年又打入美国市场。鼎牌燃气具以其优良的质量，美观的外型，完善的售后服务，受到广大消费者的普遍欢迎。

地址:天津市南开区南开四马路
电话:(022)27372876，27372397
传真:(022)27372372
邮编:300100　　电挂:4355

阀体装配车间

阀芯研磨车间

Tianjin Ding Brand Gas Appliances Factory is a gas appliances enterprise of more than 20 years of history, with fixed capital worth 22,000,000 yuan and various production and inspection equipment of more than 400 units. It has 4 subsidiaries specializing in cooking ranges, water heaters, electric appliances and industrial models. They produce 60 kinds of products including Ding brand series, such as household gas cookers, gas water heaters, big cookers for restaurants and other kitchen staff, household appliances, burning equipment, voltage regulators for civil and industrial uses. The processing of models and reinforced parts also in its business field. It is a pillar enterprise in construction machinery in China.

Since its setting up in 1985, it took 5 years to finish its comprehensive technological reform, imported advanced gas appliances producing technologies and equipment from Japan, which push its products on a new height, and taking a leading role in gas appliances producing industry in China. Its products can be see in more than 21 countries and regions. In 1993, its products entered The U. S. market. The ding series with their high quality, beautiful out designing, satisfying after-sale services win consumers' approval from different walks.

Address Simalu Road Nakai District Tianjin, China
Post code 300100
Tel. (022)27372876, 27372397
Fax (022)27372372　　Telegraph 4355

中国农业机械华北公司

THE NORTH CHINA CORPORATION OF NATIONAL AGRICULTURAL MACHINERY CORPORATION

总经理：杨书德

中国农业机械华北公司是隶属于国内贸易部的国有大型流通企业，始建于1960年，公司内设10个分公司，共有15个业务部门，销售市场网络覆盖全国二十九省市，较为固定的销售单位达300多家；日益发展的外向型经济、进出口业务，又广泛地吸引了境外客商前来合资合作，至九三年，公司年销售额已突破七亿元，名列全国农机行业的前列。中国农业机械华北公司始终弘扬“效益、竞争、团结、廉俭”的企业精神，坚持以市场为导向，以高质量服务为依托的发展方针，倡导全体员工确立“为了方便用户，宁可麻烦自己”的经营作风，在努力开拓多层面经营工作的同时，以可靠的信誉结交了各界朋友，也多次赢得了部级“优质服务”先进单位、市级先进企业等光荣称号。谨此，公司愿意与海内外各界人士继续精诚合作，共同分享走向成功的喜悦。

The North China Corporation of National Agricultural Machinery corporation is a state-owned large enterprise under the Ministry of Domestic Trade initially established in 1960. The corporation consists of 10branch companies with 15 business departments. Its sale channels cover 29 provinces and cities of the country, with more than 300 fined supply units. The rapidly developing external economics with an imported and exported business have attracted foreign travelling traders the end of 1993, the corporation's annual sales reached RMB 700 millions.

The corporation always carries on the enterprise spirit of "efficiency, competition, unity, honesty and thrifiness". It persists in the policy of "being guided by the market, depending on good services", advocation the staff and workers to carry on the business style making the custormers very convenient. In the process of the great efforts to develop a many-sided business, the corporation has come to know friends from all circles, and gained the honor title of Advanced Unit of "Good Services" awarded by the Ministry Advance Enterprise which is awarded by the city. We welcome friends from all circles both inside and outside the sea to cooperate sincerely with us to share the pleasure of being successful.

地址：天津市和平区赤峰道10号

邮编：300041

电话：(022)23394240

Add: No.10 Chifeng Road Heping District Tianjin, China

Tel: (022)23394240　　Post Code:300041

董事长、总经理：韩贵义

天津天钢集团有限公司

TIANJIN STEEL (GROUP) COMPANY, LTD

天津天钢集团有限公司是国家大型一档企业，冶金部重点钢铁企业，天津冶金工业的龙头厂。现有职工15560人。主要生产设备有100吨平炉两座；20吨转炉三座；3～5吨电炉四座；φ750/550初轧机一台套；20吨R5250－70～150(mm)方坯连铸机及25万吨180×700～1200(mm)板坯连铸机各两台套；平立交替全无扭高速线材轧机一台套。具有年产钢160万吨，初轧坯40万吨、连铸方坯55万吨、连铸板坯65万吨，高速线材35万吨的生产能力。主要产品有：碳素结构钢、优质碳素钢、低合金钢、合金结构钢、锅炉用钢、造船用钢、压力容器用钢、高速线材及钢铸件等。九五年末公司总资产37.68亿元，其中固定资产原值11.48亿元，净值5.72亿元(不含高线厂)。公司注册资本9.99亿元。

地址：天津市河东区张达庄大街1号
电话：(022)24311263　传真：(022)24310758
邮编：300180
Address: No.1 Zhang Da Zhuang Street
HeDong District　P.C.: 300180
Tel: (022)24311263 Fax:(022)24310758

Tianjin Steel(Group) Co., Ltd(TSC) is the national large, first class and key iron and steel enterprise of the State Metallurgical Ministry, and the leading one of Tianjin metallurgical industry.

It has 15,560 employees. As for the equipment, there are two 100t open hearth furnaces, three 20t converters, four 3～5t electric furnaces, one set of 750 / 550 blooming mill, two 20t R5250－70～150(mm) continuous foundry machine for square blanks, and two 250,000 t 180×700～1200(mm) continuous foundry machine for plate blanks. One set of vertical and horizontal high speed warpageless wire rod mill. The annual production capability is 1,600,000t steel, 400,000t blooming blanks, 550,000t continuous square blanks, 650,000t continuous plate blanks, and 350,000t high speed wire rods.

从美国摩根公司引进具有九十年代国际水平的高速线材轧机

The main products of TSC are carbon constructional steel, high class carbon steel, low alloy steel, alloy constructional steel; steel for boilers, ship building, and pressure cotainers; high speed wire rods and steel castings.

The total assets of the company by the end of 1995 was 3,768,000,000 yuan RMB, among whom, there is 1,148,000,000 yuan RMB for fixed assets, the net value was 572,000,000 yuan RMB (not include high speed wire rod factory). The registered capital of the company is 999,000,000 yuan RMB.

从德国德马克·曼内斯曼公司引进的超低头板坯连铸机

天津市广播电视局

TIANJIN RADIO AND TELEVISION BROADCASTING ADMINISTRATIVE BUREAU

天津广播电视塔

天津市广播电视局既是市政府主管广播电视宣传和广播电视事业发展的职能部门，又是新闻宣传单位。局机关13个职能处(室)，下属天津人民广播电台、天津电视台(均为副局级)及天津有线电视台等11个局直属单位，全局共有正式职工2200人。

天津人民广播电台于1949年1月15日开始播音，全台每天播出7套节目，总发射功率161千瓦，覆盖面积的人口达1亿左右。

天津电视台于1960年3月20日正式播出节目，全台每天播出6套节目。自办3套节目，每天播出32小时，自制节目能力达7小时。总发射功率为120千瓦，混合覆盖率达95%。

天津市有线电视台1994年7月18日开播，全台每天播出共26套节目，自办2套节目，每天总播出时间为35小时30分。市区县台已与市有线电视台实现联网，有线电视入网已达75万户。

地址:天津市和平区卫津路143号　邮编:300070
电话:(022)23359788　23359514

Tianjin Radio and Television Broadcasting Administrative Bureau is a government organ that in charge of radio and television broadcasting and radio and television development. It also places its role as a unit for news and propaganda. There are 13 functional divisions(offices) within the bureau. More than 11 direct subsidiary units, such as Tianjin People's Radio Broadcasting Station, Tianjin TV Station and Tianjin Cable TV Station, which are the bureau's subsidiaries. There are 2200 employees in the bureau who make the bureau running.

Tianjin Radio Broadcasting Station started on the air on January, 15, 1949. 7 units of programs can be listened to each day, with a total launching power rate of 161 kW. Its total radio broadcasting coverage can reach about 100 million people.

Tianjin TV station started its broadcasting on March 20, 1960. There are totally 6 units of programs can be enjoyed by TV watchers each day. Among the 6 units of programs, 3 of them are organized by the station its own, which can be watched for 32 hours each day. Its own produced programs occupy 7 hours a day. Its total lunching power rate is 120Kw, with a total mixed coverage of 95 per cent.

Tianjin Cable TV Station signed on July 18, 1994. There are all together 26 units of programs can be watched each day with 2 units organized by its own among the total. Its total broadcasting can reach 35 and a half hours a day. The station has been netted with stations of districts and counties in Tianjin. There have been 750,000 familyhood users in the cable net.

天津广播电视国际新闻中心

Address: No. 143 Weijin Road, Heping District Tianjin, China
Tel. 23359788　23359514　　Post Code 300070

天津港田发动机有限公司

TIANJIN GANGTIAN ENGINE CO., LTD

天津港田发动机有限公司是天津港田集团公司与加拿大某公司的合资企业。于1993年成立。注册资金160万美元，职工500余人。固定资产4000多万元。公司生产摩托车及发动机为主，摩托车产品有6个系列13个品种，其中有3种已获国家专利。公司在董事长兼总裁龚世权及总经理的领导下，经济效益快速增长，1996年创产值4个亿。是天津市中外合资企业利税大户，获1996年度天津市外商投资企业最佳效益奖。龚世权先生荣获“五一”奖章和全国劳动模范称号。公司总经理决心向国际标准(ISO9000)接轨，提高产品质量及管理水平，满足国内国际市场需求。

董事长兼总裁:龚世权　　总经理:龚兆杉

地址:天津市津南区双港镇海河湾村

电话:(022)28582053　　传真:(022)28589640

邮编:300350　　电挂:4428

董事长兼总裁: 龚世权

Tianjin Gangtian engine Co., Ltd is a joint-venture which was build by Tianjin Gangtian group company and a Canada company. It was set up in 1993. It's fonds is $1,600,00, and has over 500 members. It's real estate is RMB40,000,000. Motor and engine are the main product of this company, the motor products has 6 lines, 13 kinds, among these there are 3 kinds have been honoured the nation exclusive right. The company was led by Gong Shiquan the board of director and the general manager, the economic grew up rapidly. In 1996, the company made the product value of RMB 4 billon. The company is the important joint-venture which can hand in much tax to the country. Mr Gong Shiquan was honoured the "May First" medal and was chosen to be the Label Modal of the country. The General manager is determined to do their efforts to get up with the world standard(ISO9000) raise the product quality and managment level, meet the need and require of the domastic and world market.

Board of director and Chief director: Gong Shiquan

General manager: Gong Zhao Shan

Add: Haihewan Shuangguang Village Jinnan District Tianjin

Tel: (022)28582053

Fax: (022)28589640

P.C.: 300350　　Telex: 4428

天津市恒兴顺集团

TIANJINHENGXINGSHUN GROUP

恒兴顺集团董事长兼总经理：张印朋

天津恒兴顺集团是国家农业部首批命名批准的国家级企业集团。是天津市颇具影响的骨干企业，是天津汽车工业最大的配套产品制造商。它的主体产业是为天津轻型微型汽车配套生产冲压件和橡胶件。1995年，集团拥有固定资产2.3亿元，年产值5.5亿，实现利税6000万元。集团董事长兼总经理张印朋是全国乡镇企业家、天津市劳动模范和五一劳动奖章获得者。

恒兴顺集团始建于1984年。经过十几年的发展形成了汽车冲压、橡胶制品、边境贸易、建筑、装饰为一体的综合性集团。企业拥有大冲线三条，小冲线两条组焊线二条，固定点线二条，橡胶制品生产线一条，各种设备500多台套。形成了年产夏利15万台、大发10万台，各种专用汽车5万台的综合配套能力。

恒兴顺集团一贯重视企业管理，不断提高企业技术含量。1994年从国外引进5台具有九十年代水平的大型冲压设备。使产品上了新档次。集团十分重视技术人才的作用，不断提高职工的综合素质，形成了占职工总数50％的技术人才队伍，实现了由粗放经营向集约化经营的转变。

风扬长宜放眼量，恒兴顺集团要在本世纪末建成面向全国走向世界、跨地区、跨国界的企业集团。集团的奋斗目标是：一、开拓国外市场建成高科技含量、高附加值的合资企业；二、向未来投资建成培养企业专用人才的恒兴学院；三、九五期间增长率不低于22％，1997年建成恒兴别墅新村，全体员工将全部搬入新居。

集团位于天津汽车城内，环境优美、交通便利，水电资源充足、信息通讯发达、投资环境良好。

董事长张印朋挚全体员工欢迎各届朋友合作，共同发展、共同繁荣。

地址：天津市西青区京福公路微型汽车厂对过
电话：(022)27392406　传真：(022)27398831　邮编：300380

Tianjin Hengxingshun Group is one of the nation1sd－class enterprise groups first named by the Ministry of Agriculture Ministry. It is a backbone company in Tianjin and is the largest auto－mobile accessory manufacturer of Tianjin automobile industry. It mainly makes punching and rubber products. in 1995, the group had fixed assets worthing RMB 230 million, annual output value of RMB 550 million, profits tax of RMB 60 million. The group director Zhang Yinpeng is a national town and township entrepreneur, Tianjin labor model and the winner of May. I medal.

Hengxingshun Group is first established in 1984. After more than ten years of developing, it has come to be a comprehensive group concerning automobile punching, rubber products, frontier trade, archetecture and decoration. It has 3 large punching, 2 small punching lines, 2 group welding lines, 2 fixed point lines, 2 rubber product lines and 500 sets of equipments. It froms and accessor capability for 150,000 Charade, 100,000 Daihatsu and 50,000 special cars per year.

Hengxingshun Group always pays attention to enterprise management and the technical ratio has been raising all the time. Five large size punching equipment was imported from overseas which has raised the quality of the products. The group attaches much importance to technical personnel and the performance of the staff has been improving. The technical personnel enjoy 50% of the total staff. It is transferred rom extensive operation to intensive operation.

Hengxingshun Group is planning to be built to a trans－regional and transnational enterprise group. The struggle aims of the group are: 1. Opening overseas markets to set up high technical content and high added value joint ventures. 2. Establishing the Hengxing Insitute to educate personnel for exclusive use of the group. 3. During the ninth five year period the growth rate should not be lower than 22%. In 1997, the Hengxing villa will be built for all the staff to live in.

Hengxingshun group is placed in the Tianjin automobile city. The enviornment is beautiful. The transportation is convinient. It has sufficient water and electricity resources and the information and telecommunication system is developed. So the investing enviornment is fine.

The director Zhang Yinpeng with the total staff welcome friends from all circles to cooperate with us for mutual developmetn and prospery.

Add: Jing Fu Road Xi Qing District Tianjin
Tel: (022)27392406
Fax: (022)27398831
Postcode: 300380

天津针织集团公司

TIANJIN TEXTILE COMPANY (GROUP)

公司领导班子

天津针织集团公司是具有自营进出口权的专业生产针织产品的大型企业集团公司，公司下属二十家生产企业，一个研究所，一所专业技术学校，四家合资企业。

公司拥有固定资产原值5亿元，净值3.6亿元，各种主要生产设备3000多台套，其中有从国外引进的八十年代末期先进水平的生产设备500多台套，年生产能力可达生产各类针织品约一亿件。

公司主要生产经营的品种有：各种绒衣裤、棉毛衫裤、汗衫背心，各种袜子以及T恤衫，运动服装，各种时装、套装、儿童服装，经编装饰布渔网具、网布等，产品不仅畅销全国各地，而且出口远销欧、美、澳、日、中东等50多个国家和地区，公司拥有享誉国内外的梅花、菲米丽、白玫瑰名优品牌的针织服装和三花、丹顶鹤名优品牌的各类袜子，深受广大消费者欢迎。

天津针织集团公司所属骨干企业

单位	法人代表	电话
天津针织集团公司	刘世军	27617651
天津针织厂	黄克俊	24310768
天津针织运动衣厂	王群力	27365957
天津市针织一厂	李本良	27366987
天津市经纬针织厂	范志新	27365453
“三花”袜业有限公司	刘振龙	26312900
“丹顶鹤”针织有限公司	马志强	27271525

Tianjin Textile Company (Group), with an independent import & exporting right, is an enterprise group of a large scale, which is specializing in textile producing. It has 20 subsidiaries, a research institute, a textile technical school and 4 joint ventures. The company's fixed capital is worth 500,000,000 yuan with a net value of 360,000,000 yuan. It has 3,000 producing units. Among them, there are more than 500 equipment imported from abroad with technological level agreed with the late1980s'. Its total producing capacity can reach about 100,000,000 units.

Its main products are various sweats and cotton pants°shirts, sweaters, stockings, T shirts, sporting suits, fashions, suits, children's suits, fishnet clothing and so on. Its products are not only selling domestically, but also export overseas, in Europe, the United States, Australia, Japan and the Middle East, all together, more than 50 countries and regions. The company's products with famous clothes brand names including MeiHuaFeimili, White Rose and stocking brand names as Three Flowers and Red-Crowned Crane, are deeply welcomed by customers.

The company (group) foundation includes,

Tianjin Textile Company (Group)
Legal Representative Liu Shijun Tel: 27617651
Tianjin textile Plant
Legal Representative Huang Kejun Tel: 24310768
Tianjin Textile Sporting Suit Plant
Legal Representative Wang Qunli Tel: 27365957
Tianjin No. 1 textile Factory
Legal Representative LI Benliang Tel: 27366987
Tianjin Jingwei Textile Factory
Legal Representative Fan Zhixi Tel: 27365453
Three Flowers Stocking Co. Ltd.
Legal Representative Liu Zhenlong Tel: 26312900
Red-Crowned Crane Textile Co. Ltd.
Legal Representative Ma Zhiqiang Tel: 27271525

天津市塑料集团有限公司

TIANJIN PLASTICS CO., LTD (GROUP)

集团公司法定代表人: 孙学敏

天津市塑料集团有限公司是按现代企业制度，经过资产重组建成的具有法人资格的国有独资公司，为大型一档企业，有进出口经营权，是中国百家最大塑料制品企业和天津市百强工业企业之一。下设五家分公司，拥有九家全资及控股子公司，四家参股企业，资产总额4.3亿元。以生产农地膜、BOPP薄膜、人造革、聚氨酯制品为主，加工能力3.5万吨。近几年，经营范围又拓展到进出口贸易、房地产开发、工程安装、建筑装饰、商业服务业等领域。

天津塑料集团是以天津市塑料集团有限公司为核心，联合所属子公司、控参股企业和其它国有、集体、合资等50余家企、事业法人单位共同组成。现有资产14.6亿元，塑料制品加工能力10万吨，管理经验丰富，技术力量雄厚，工艺装备先进，主要产品已形成塑料包装材料、建筑及装饰材料、农渔用塑料制品、日用塑料制品、工业材料及配件、塑料机械及模具等六大系列，800多个品种，近4000个规格，拥有一批国家、部、市级优秀产品和具有先进技术水平的产品。

集团公司法定代表人: 孙学敏
地址:天津市南开区鞍山西道西湖村大街108号　邮编:300073
电话:(022)27376301－4
传真:(022)27376272

Under the modern enterprise machinism, after capital reconstruction,Tianjin Plastics Co.,ltd (group) becomes a large state owned enterprise of first level with legal entity and independent import & export right, which is one of the 100 most large plastics producing enterprises in China, the one of the 100 most strong enterprises in Tianjin. The company has 5 branch companies, 9 uniquely invested and controlled subsidiaries and join management by stockholding, with a total capital worth 430,000,000 yuan. The company's main products are land plastic film for farming, BOPP plastic film, manmade leather, polyester plastics, and so on, having a total processing capacity of 35,000 tons. Recent years, the company's business field was enlarged to import & export trading, real estate development, construction & installing, constructive decoration, commercial services and so on. Tianjin Plastics Co., Ltd (Group) is the main force of Tianjin Plastics Group. The group is made up by 50 enterprise legal entities and institutional legal entities with a total capital worth 1,460,000,000 yuan, a processing capacity of 100,000 tons. The group has rich management experience technologies and advanced equipments. Its products can divided into 6 large series, including plastic packaging material, construction & decoration material, farming and fishery use plastics, household plastics, industrial plastic material and parts, plastic machinery and models, all together, more than 800 kinds of products, nearly 4000 units. Many of its products are state, ministrial and municipal level perfect products with advanced technologies.

由国外引进的离型纸法人造革生产线，无论设备及产品的质量在国内均处于领先水平。

The legal representative of the company (group) Sun Xuemin
Address No.108 Xihucun Avenue, Anshanxi Road, Nankai District Tianjin, China
Tel:(022)27376301－4
Fax:(022)27376272
Post Code 300073

天津釀

TIANJIN

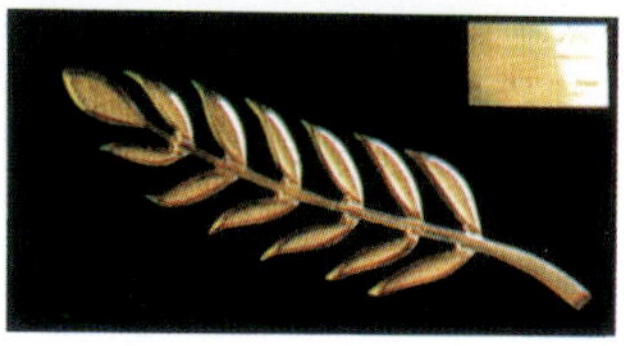

国际金桂奖

中国食品博览会金奖

国家银奖

天津酿酒厂是由津门九家百余年历史的直沽名酒厂合并组成发展起来的，在全国50家名优酒大厂中名列第24位。

自1985年以来，该厂荣获天津市先进企业、百强企业、重合同守信誉单位，1989年晋升为国家二级企业，1995年又被评为全国质量管理先进单位。

“津牌”津酒1984年以来连续获国家优质银奖荣誉，并与本市传统名酒“直沽牌”直沽高梁酒双双获得“国际金桂奖”，进入国际名酒之林。“新港牌”佳酿，1995年被评为“中国大众名白酒”。近年来该厂实施名牌战略，适应国内外市场，推出高品味的“帝王珍品”津酒、津酒液、新包装津酒及佳酿醇、直沽醇等适销对路的新产品。此外，该厂生产的“玉羊牌”玉羊露酒1995年在香港获“世界名牌消费品”殊荣，并大量出口。

多年来，该厂坚持“以质量取胜、以信誉赢人，以酒为媒广结天下友”的经营方针，进一步开拓国内外市场，振兴天津白酒工业，让天津名优酒，名扬全世界。

地址:中国天津市经桥区丁字沽三号路
电话:(022)26372833
传真:(022)26372837
电挂:6840　邮编:300131

ERY

Tianjin Winery has been established and developed based on 9 famous wines that had more than hundred years' history. It is the No.24 among the 50 famous winery enterprises in the country.

Since 1985, Tianjin Winery has won the titles of "Advanced Enterprise", one of "the One Hundred Strong - Enterprises" and "the Unit which Respects Contracts and Keeps One's Promise". It had been promoted the Second Enterprise of the State in 1989 and elected "the Advanced Unit for Quality Management" in the country.

"Jinjiu" with the trademark - "Jinpai", has been won "the Silver Prize for Fine Quality" given by the state and at the same time won "the Prize of 'Jingui'" together with famous wine named "Zhigu Pai" and "Zhigu Gaoliang" made in Tianjin. It has been one of the famous wine in the international mark.

"Jianiang" with the trademark - "Xingang Pai", had been named "Famous White Wine for Ordinary People".

Recently, the factory has carried its development strategy to create famous products and developed markets both in China and abroad, it has produced high quality new products, such as "Jinjiu, "'Jinjiu Ie", "Jianiang Chun" and "Zhigu Chun". Another product named "YuyangPai" win had won the title of "the Famous Consumer Goods of the orld" in Hong Kong in 1995 and exported abroad more and more since hen.

For many years, the factory has carried out the principle of "win upon high quality, win upon keeping promise and make friends with people all over the world upon high quality wine". The factory is now working hard to develop markets both in China and abroad and making Tianjin wine be well known in the world.

Address: Dingzi Gu, No.4 Way, Hongqiao District, Tianjin
Post code:300131
Tel: (022) 26372833
Fax: (022) 26372837

天津五金矿产进出口集团有限公司

TIANJIN METALS & MINERALS IMPORT & EXPORT GROUP CO., LTD

天津五金矿产进出口集团有限公司是国内成立最早的国有专业进出口公司之一。

天津五金矿产进出口集团有限公司主要经营黑色金属、有色金属、非金属矿产品、化工原料、机电产品、轻工产品、橡胶制品、纺织品、服装、粮油、食品、土畜产品的进出口以及补偿贸易、加工贸易、易货贸易、转口贸易、边境贸易;办理运输、广告等项业务;提供咨询、仓储服务并兼营国内贸易和房地产业务。

The Tianjin Metals & Minerals Import & Export Group Co., Ltd. is one of the earliest state-owned corporations specialized in import and export.

The Tianjin Metals & Minerals Import & Exoport Group Co., Ltd. deals mainly with the import and export of ferrous metals, nonferrous metals, nonmetallic minerals, chemical raw materials, mechanical and electrical products, light industrial products, rubber products, textiles, garments, cereals and oils, foodstuffs, native produc and animal by products; it also conducts c tion trade, processing trade, barte border trade; it can provide ding transport, advertising warehousing service, as well as e al trade and real estate.

总经理:陈玉昆

地址:天津市河西区湘江道47号 邮编:30

电话:(022)28248890或28240166转

传真:(022)28248636

电子信箱:MINMETAL@PUBLIC. TPT. TJ. CN

General Manager: Chen Yu-Kun

Address: 47. Xiangjiang Road, Tianjin, China.

P.C.: 300200

Tel: (022)28248890 or

28240166(exchange)

Fax:(022)28248636

E-main: MINMETAL@PUBLIC. TPT. TJ. CN

天津光电通信(集团)有限公司

TIANJIN OPTICAL & ELECTRICAL COMMUNICATION (GROUP) CORPORATION

天津光电通信(集团)有限公司(电子工业部国营第七五四厂)系技术密集型老军工企业,是国家暨天津市大型骨干企业。"七五"、"八五"期间经国家批准立项,先后投资两亿多进行重大技术改造,现已发展成光通信、传真通信及移动通信为主产业、资产联接或经营承包关系为纽带的光电通信产业集团。

主要生产经营:有线传输类有PDH,SDH及CATV光传输系列产品、UF系列为主的传真机、无线及保密传真、TDS-1局用数字程控交换机;移动通信类有无线寻呼系统、承接短波及超短波通信"指挥中心"工程;专用电子类有视频辐射及音频干扰系列产品、铁路电脑售票机及软票系统、电力负荷无线遥控系统、电梯开门机系列;器件类有各种变压器、滤波器、点火线圈、声表滤波器及磁芯系列。

地址:天津市河西区泰山路6号 邮编:300211 电挂:4040
电话:(022)28308980 28306901 传真:(022)28331568

移动通信设备组装线

传真机生产线

Tianjin Optical & Electronic Communication (Group) Corporation, or the No.754 State-run Factory of Ministry of Electronics, is an experienced technology-intensive military enterprises. It is one of the large-sized key enterprises both nation-wise and city-wise. As approved by the state, more than 200 million yuan were invested in this enterprise during the 7th and the 8th Five-Year Plan periods for major technological renovation. It has been developed into an industrial group of optical-electrical communication that majors in optical communication, facsimile communication and mobile communication, and links up by asset association and contractual relationship.

It manufactures and does business in wire transmission such as PDH,SDH and CATV optical transmission serial products, facsimile machines chiefly in the UF series, wireless and scrambled facsimile, TDS-1 digital programme-controlled telephone switch house. In mobile communication there are wireless beeper system and construction of "commanding center" for shortwave and ultra shortwave communications. For special electronic items there are serial products of video frequency radiation and audio frequency interference, railroad computerized ticket machine and soft ticket system, electrical power payload wireless remote control system and serial products of elevator door opener. For devices there are various transformers, filters, ignition coils, SAW filters and serial magnetic cores.

Address: 6 Taishan Road Hexi District Tianjin
Post Code: 300211
Cable: 4040
Tel: (022)28308980 28306901
Fax: (022)28331568

光电端机生产线

城建学院院长：姚怀德

天津城市建设学院

TIANJIN URBAN CONSTRUCTION INSTITUTE

天津城市建设学院是一所城建类高等学校，主要为城乡建设培养和输送德、智、体全面发展的高级工程技术人才。学院占地面积321亩，总建筑面积12万平方米。巍峨壮观的13层教学主楼，能藏书120万册的图书馆，现代化设施装备的实验中心及公寓化管理的学生宿舍，为学生提供了良好的学习条件和生活环境。

学院确立以本科教育为主的办学思路，兼办专科和成人高等教育，并积极创造条件发展研究生教育，初步形成了多层次的办学格局。现设建筑系、土木工程系、热能工程系、建筑材料系、管理工程系、市政与环境工程系等6个系和9个本科专业。有本、专科在校生2908人，专任教师241人，兼职教师46人。其中有高级职称教师154人。几年来，学院充分发挥自己的特色，贴紧行业办学，受到社会欢迎，招生分数高于全市普通院校水准，毕业生连年抢手。特别是1996年顺利通过国家教委本科教学工作合格评价后，教学管理日趋规范化，教学基本建设不断加强，科研工作突飞猛进。现承担了许多国家级、部委级及横向科研课题，使近3年来科研经费达到900多万元，注重把科研成果迅速转化为生产力，在产、学、研结合方面闯出了一条新路。

地址：天津市西青区津静公路
电话：(022)23792015
传真：(022)23792528
邮编：300381

市领导到学院指导工作

Tianjin Urban Construction Institute is an urban construction higher education school with a task of raising and sending wholly developed senior construction engineers for urban construction. It occupies area of 321 Chinese mu with a total construction area of 120,000 squaremeters. It has a main education building of 13 floors, a library That can hold 1,200,000 books, an advanced technologies equipped experimental lab center and student dormitories with apartment management style, which supplies students with convenient studying condition and living environment.

4-year college education is the institute's main focus. 2 and 3-yearcollege education and adult high education are also setup here. It is trying hard to develop post-graduate education. A multi-level education structure has been primarily found. There are 6 departments here, such as the Department of Construction, the Department of Civil Engineering, the Department of Heating resource engineering, the Department of construction Materials, the Department of Management Engineering and Municipal and Environmental engineering, and 9 under-graduate majors. Its total student number has reached 2,908, with a teaching staff of 241 and adjunct teaching staff of 46. Among the total teaching staff, there are 154 teachers with senior intellectual certificate. Recent years, the institute develops its education according to the industrial needs by developing its own characteristics, which are welcomed by all social walks. Its entrance exam mark is higher than other institutes and universities in Tianjin. Its graduates are in short supply every year. Specially in 1996, after passing National Education Commission's Qualification Estimate, the educational management becomes standardized step by step, its education environments are reinforced more and more, the researching works develop much more efficiently. Many state-level, ministry-level and co-sponsored scientific research projects were achieved, which makes its researching capital reached 9,000,000 yuan in recent 3 years. It also pays attention to the transfer of scientific research fruits to production, which paved a new way of connecting producing, educating and researching.

Address Jinggong Road, Xiqing District Tianjin, China
Post code 300381
Tel. (022)23792015 Fax (022)23792528

城建学院主教学楼

天津市建工设计院

TIANJIN INSTITUTE OF ARCHITETUREL ENGINEERING DESIGN

院长：刘太平

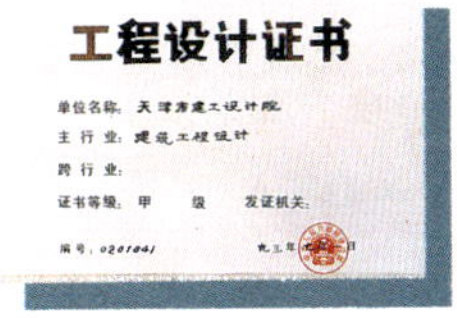
工程设计证书
单位名称：天津市建工设计院
主行业：建筑工程设计
跨行业：
证书等级：甲 级 发证机关：
编号：0201041

天津市建工设计院为国家级设计单位，技术力量雄厚，设备先进，专业齐全。天津市建工设计院下设五个综合设计所和地基开发所、电子计算中心、技术情报所等16个生产和管理部门。可为建设单位提供各类建设工程项目的策划、评估、可行性研究等设计前期的技术咨询服务；城乡规划设计；工程地质勘察；建筑工程设计；工程项目总承包以及工程建设监理等全方位服务。

我院建立了一整套严格的质量保证体系，多年推行全面质量管理并在同行业中率先贯彻GB／T19000－ISO9000系列标准，执行GB/T19001－92/ISO9001－87《质量体系－设计/开发、生产、安装和服务的质量保证模式》，依据ISO/DIS10013《质量手册编制指南》建立了符合国际惯例的质量体系，并于1994年12月通过了长城(天津)质量保证中心的认证。

我院对沿海地区的工程地质状况有较深入的研究，具有杂土椿加固软弱地基等技术，并擅长对高层建筑、超高层建筑、大型商业建筑特别是轻型框架结构的工程设计。

建院几十年来，为不同用户设计了一大批不同类型的大、中型民用建筑、工业建筑、高层、超高层建筑、大型商场、写字楼、商贸楼、医院、高层公寓、工业城等设计项目，并有多项工程获国家、市级优秀设计奖。

我院的方针是：以管理促质量，靠质量保信誉，以质量争市场，靠质量创效益。

我院愿以最好的设计质量，最快捷的设计速度，最优质的服务，竭诚为各国内外用户服务。

天津市永基花园

地址：天津市南开区灵隐道兴泰里30号
邮编：300193
电话：(022)27380781
传真：(022)27388421
电挂：天津9042

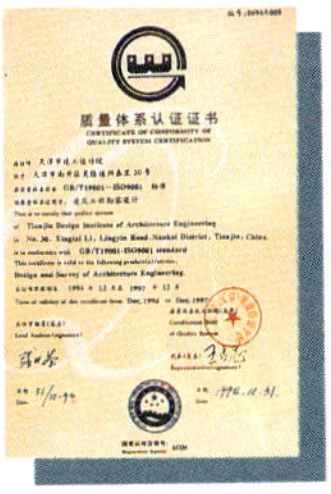
质量体系认证证书

Tianjin Institute of Arechitecturel Engineering Design is the first－class designing enterprise of the country with strong technical strength, up－to－date equipment and complete specialities. The subsidiaries are: 5 Comprehensive Design Institute, Ground Development Institure, Computer Centre, Technical Information Institute, etc. 16 production and management departments in all.

Our Institute is capable of providing construction units with preliminary－stage technical consultation and service of programme, evaluation and feasibility study for various construction engineering projects and services in every field such as rural and urban planning design, engineering geologic survey, rachitecturel engineering design, engineering projects general contracting, and engineering construction supervision, etc.

Our institute has set up a complete set of strict quality guarantee system and pursued entire quality managment over the years. It was first in the same trade to carry out GB／T1900－ISO9000 series standard and GB／T19001－92／ISO9001－87,《Quality System Quality Guarantee Model of Design《Development, Manufacture, Installation and Service》, it established quality system up to international practice in accordance with ISO／dis10013《Quality Manual & Guild》- and got the authorization of Great Wall (Tianjin) Quality Guarantee Centre in December 1994.

Our Institute has a thorough knowledge and deep study about engineerign gelogic situation of coastal areas and possessses the technology of strengthening soft foundation by mixed ois pile, and it is expert in the design of high buildings, super－high buildings, largescale commercial buildings, especially the engineering design of light frameswork structure.

In the past tens of year after establishment, our institute has designed a great deal of large and intermediate scale residential buildings, industrial buildings, high buildings, superhigh buildings, large department stores, office builings, commercial and trade buildings, hospital, high apartment buildings, industrial city, etc. of different types for different customers, Many projects have heen awarded municipal and national "Excellent Design Prize".

The principle of our institute is: to improve the quality by management, guarantee the credit by quality, win the market by quality and make profits by quality.

Our institute would like to provide the customers from home and abroad with thebest designing quality, quick designing speed and top quality service.

Add: 30, Xingtaili, Lingyindao, Nankai District, Tianjin
P.C.: 300193 Tel:(022)27380781
Telex:(022)27388421 Cable: Tianjin 9042

天津立达房地产公司

TIANJIN LIDA ESTATE COMPANY

立达公寓E、F、H座为庭院式高层公寓楼小区，总建筑面积6.5万平方米，该小区布局新颖别致，由架空庭院联接9层板式楼和2栋24层的塔楼，庭院地下为2层车库，塔楼周围是2层服务用裙房，公寓楼内1梯3户，各种设施一应俱全。

天津立达房地产公司成立于1987年，是隶属于天津立达(集团)公司的二级城市综合开发专营公司。

公司自成立以来，本着信誉至上、服务精良、平等互利的原则，依托天津立达集团的整体优势，积极参与天津市及国内外房地产开发建设，先后投资兴建了立达国际商场，乐园宾馆，合资兴建了涉外住宅小区——宾侨新村。近年来，在宾桥新村内建成了立达公寓A、B、C、D座。在友谊路合作开发了天达住宅小区一期工程。今年，在宾桥新村和天达小区分别兴建总建筑面积近10万平方米的高层公寓和写字楼。

公司总经理钱伟荣女士真诚期望与各界朋友合作，携手共同发展房地产事业。

公司地址：天津市南开区卫津南路46号

电话：(022)23910208　23912359　传真：(022)23918860　邮编：300381

Tianjin Lida Real Estate Company(TLREC) was set up in 1987 under Tianjin Lida(Group) Company(TLC), who is a Grade II professional comprehensive urban area development unit.

Since the opening of the company, TLREC has taken part in Tianjin and other domestic and foreign real estate development and construction projects, based on the advantage of TLC and the principle of credit first, quality service, equality and mutual benefit. TLREC invested to build Lida International Business Centre, Leyuan Hotel, and built Binqiao village, a place for foreigners, in the form of joint venture. In Binqiao Village, TLREC has built Lida apartment A,B,C, and D. In Youyi Road, TLREC cooperated with other unit to develop the Phase I engineering of Tianda residential subdistrict. This year, TLREC will build highrise apartment and office building in Binqiao Village and Tianda subdistrict for around 100,000-square meter construction area.

Madam Qian Weirong, General Manager of TLREC, sincerely wishes to cooperate with friends of all walks of life to develop the real estate career.

Address: 46 Weijinnan Road Nankai District Tianjin 300381

Tel: (022)23910208 23912359　Fax: (022)23918860

立达公寓C、D座

立达公寓A、B座

天津市远东房地产开发公司

TIANJIN YUANDONG REAL ESTATE DEVELOPMENT COMPANY

公司总经理：汪润丰

天津市远东房地产开发公司成立于1992年，是隶属于民政系统的城市综合开发专营公司。

公司成立以来，本着勤奋拼搏、服务好客户的宗旨，以平等互利的原则，紧紧围绕天津市的危改任务，积极参与房地产开发建设。先后投资开发建设了河北区、南开区两个区的危改工程二处。另有商品住宅小区几处以及和平区的高级写字楼等，总建筑面积近8万平方米。

目前我公司正开发建设的项目有：河西区内综合写字楼、公寓、别墅、和平区黄金宝地的金融大厦、物资贸易科技中心大厦等项目，总建筑面积约8万平方米。

公司总经理汪润丰先生真诚期望与各界朋友合作，携手共同发展房地产事业。

地址：中国天津和平区气象台路新河里七号
电话：(022)23375071　23355100　　传真：(022)23374266　邮编：300070

Tianjin Yuandong Real Estate Development Company setup in 1992, which is a comprehensive urban real estate development company under the leadership of Tianjin Civil Administrative bureau.

Since the setup, the company follows its theory, Working hard, Serving customers well and fairness & co–benefiting, obeys Tianjin's Old and endangered houses' reform task, actively participates in Tianjin's real estate development construction. In Hebei and Nankai Districts, there 2 this kind of construction works invested and developed by the company. There are also some commercial residential housing zones in Tianjin and high advanced office buildings in Heping District, which have been constructed by the company. Its total construction area is near 80,000 square meters.

Nowadays, there are also several projects under development and construction, such as office, residential and cottage buildings in Hexi District, Financial Tower, Material, Trade & technological Tower in Heping District's commercial golden area, with a total construction area of about 80,000 square meters.

General manager, Wang Runfeng sincerely hopes to do co-operation with friends all over the world to develop real estate industry.

Address No. 7 Xinheli, Qixiangtai Road, Heping District Tianjin, China
Tel. (022)23375071　23355100
Fax:(022)23374266　　Post Code 300070

河西区房管局局长：李汕源

天津市河西区房地产管理局

TIANJIN HEXI DEVELOPMENT MANAGEMENT DISTRICT

天津市河西区房地产管理局座落在河西区黄埔南路2号。现有职工3000人，掌管各类房屋近500万平方米，所属基层单位27个，各类企业61个。近年来，区局致力于房地产事业的发展，经营逐步由粗放型向集约型转变，形成了以经营、开发、物业、供热四大支柱为主体，不断向市场经济转化的经营格局，具有较强的专业化管理和经营实力，在社会和同行业中具有一定的影响。

地址:天津市河西区黄埔南路2号
电话:(022)28355483
传真:(022)28352300
邮编:300201

龙都房地产经营大厅

河西区房管局办公楼

Tianjin Hexi District Real Estate Administration is located at No.2 Huangpu South Road Hexi District. There are 3000 Workers and staff members. It handles 5 million square meters houses of Varions Kinds. The administration subordinates 27 basic units and 61 enterprises of Various Kinds. IN recent years, this District Administration devotes itself to the development of real estate. The management has been transformed progressively from extensive type to intensive type and has formed a management structure which takes development, management, real estate and heating as main line and radiates overall to social field. It has reatively strong stength of specialized management and business. It has a fixed influence in the society and the same industry.

Add: No.2 HuangPu Nan Road He Xi District Tianjin
Tel: (022)28355483
Fax: (022)28352300
P.C.: 300201

天津市河西区建设开发总公司

CONSTRUCTION AND DEVELOPMENT GENERAL COMPANY HEXI DISTRICT TIANJIN

法人代表、公司总经理：王文凯

天津市河西区建设开发总公司成立于1984年，是改革开放后天津市首批组建的房地产开发企业，直属于河西区人民政府，是具有独立法人地位的全民所有制企业。

总公司经济实力雄厚，人才济济，其中高、中、初级各类工程专业技术人员占职工总数60％以上。公司注册资金2321万元，流动资金2.2亿元，为国家一级资质综合开发企业和天津市金融信用等级三A企业。

公司成立十几年来，先后在河西区大沽路、文明里、紫金新村、平山道、三水道、重华南里、谦德庄、纯真里、三义庄等十几片住宅小区进行了开发建设、共兴建各类房屋近140万平方米，工程合格率100％，优良率占40％以上。其综合配套能力和居住环境规划都达到较高水平。

公司主要从事房地产综合开发、商品房经营、建筑设计、房屋拆迁和房屋物业管理等。公司一贯坚持"质量第一、信誉至上"的经营宗旨，竭诚欢迎海内外各界朋友惠顾和投资合作。

地址：天津市河西区绍兴道新28号

电话：(022)23110473　　23312660

邮编：300203

公司即将竣工的财院东居民小区

Construction And Development General Company, Hexi District, Tianjin was founded in 1984, which was among the first group of comapny who were setup to do real estate development since the reform and opening up drive in Tianjin. The company is directly under the leadership of Hexi District People's Government of Tianjin, which is a state owned enterprise with legal entity.

The general company is strong in finance with various human resources under its leadership. There are more than 60 per cent of its employees who have senior, middle and junior technical titles. The company's registered capital is 23,210,000 yuan with a frequent capital of 220,000,000. It is a state first level comprehensive real estate development company in quality and capital. It is also a 3A company for its financial trust in Tianjin.

During its over 10 year's operation, the company had achieved over 10 residential area's construction works in Dagu Road, Hexi district, Wenmingli, Zijinxincun, pingshan Road, Sanshui Road, Chonghuananli, Qiandezhuang, Chunzhenli and Sanlizhuang with a total construction area of near 140,000,000 square meters. All its construction works passed construction quality inspection with a perfection rate of over 40 per cent. Its construction works' comprehensive conveyance capacity and residential environment designing reached a high standard already.

The company mainly specializes in real estate comprehensive development, commercial residential building management operation, residential houses' removement and housing management. The company keeps on regarding quality and reputation the first priority, who is sincerely welcoming friends all over the world to come and make investment and co-operation here.

Address No.28 (new) Shaoxing Road, Hexi District, Tianjin

Tel: (022)23110473　　23312660

Post Code: 300203

正在施工的三义庄二期高层建筑

申银万国证券股份有限公司 天津营业部

THE TIANJIN BUSINESS OFFICE OF SHENYIN INTERNATIONAL SECURITY CO., LTD

申银万国证券股份有限公司天津营业部位于天津市和平区西康路宜昌道76号，是全国最大的证券公司—申银万国证券股份有限公司在天津开设的营业部，也是外埠在天津开设最早的营业部，于1992年11月筹建后开业，营业大厅面积800平方米，中户室400平方米，还有部分大户室。

经过改造后的电脑设备，采用586微机，这在目前是全市最先进的，新增的跑道提高了报单速度，新安装的发电机及2台UPS，避免了因停电造成的行情中断现象，保证了股民交易的正常进行。申银万国证券公司天津营业部，欢迎各界朋友到我部投资。

申银万国证券股份有限公司天津营业部总经理：华丽英

地址：天津市和平区西康路宜昌道76号　　邮编:300070

电话:(022)23374082

传真:(022)23376582

The Tianjin Business office of Shenyin International security Co. Ltd. is located at No.76, Yichang Road, Xikang Street, Heping District of Tianjin, the security company is the largest security company in China. The business office the company setup in Tianjin is also the earliest business office the companies of other provinces setup in Tianjin. In November 1992, the office was opened for business after finishing its preliminary preparing work . The total business area of the business hall is 800 square meters. Its customers' room of middle size is 400 square meters. There are also some large customers' rooms.

After the reconstruction, the company's computer equipment is upgraded, 586 series were equipped, which is the more advanced in Tianjin, now. The newly added 'electrical road' improves the speed of report units.The newly installed electricity generator and 2 UPS help the office avoid electricity caused stock information transferring breaking, which can assure the stock brokers' daily exchange processes. The Tianjin business office of ShenYin security Company welcomes friends all over the world to make investment in its office in Tianjin.

The general manager of the Tianjin Business Office of ShenYin International Security Co. Ltd. Hua Liying

Address: No.76 Yichang Road, Heping District, Tianjin

Tel: (022) 23374082　　Fax: (022)23376582　　Post code: 300070

董事长: 王作安

天津百货商务贸易总公司

TIANJIN GENERAL MERCHANDISE BUSINESS COMPANY

天津百货商务贸易总公司是中国北方最大的日用百货商品批发商。是中国百货商业协会常务理事单位和全国鞋帽、日用百货、钟表缝纫机专业委员会主任单位。

总公司拥有5000多万元固定资产、12万平米营业设施和周转仓库及相适应的运输能力。年度购销额最高达14亿元人民币，被授予“天津批发商业支柱企业”。以总经销、总代理等方式经销国内外的名、特、优的日用百货、劳保用品、家用电器、针纺织品、鞋帽、室内装饰品及相关的原材料，品种规格达2.3万个。多年来以“敬业、求实、拼搏”的企业精神赢得了国内外客商的信赖，建立了稳固的购销网络。企业内部在财务管理系统、商业微机应用、商品质量检测居同行业领先地位。竭诚欢迎各界人士前来洽谈、发展贸易、共办实业。

地址: 天津市和平区滨江道30号
电话: (022)27303053
27300984
27302186
传真: (022)27303053
邮编: 300041
电挂: 2068

Tianjin General Merchandise Business Company is the biggest department merchandise wholesaler in the north of China. It is the standing member of the general merchandise committee of China and the head unit of the special committee for shoes and hats, daily merchandise, watch and sewing machine.

The general company has 50 million yuan fixed assets, 120 thousand square meter business store, storehouse and relevant transporting capacity. The annual total sales reaches 1400 million yuan, it was conferred the title "Pillar Company of Tianjin Wholesale Business". By the manner of general agency and general commission sell, it sells the famous, special and high quality merchandise of daily use , protecting clothes, family electric and electricity facilities, knit, spinning and weaving goods, shoes and hats, indoor decorated materials and relative raw and processed materials. The variety has reached to 23000. For many years, the company obeys on the spirit "honest, reality, work hard"and wins the reputation of users in China and abroad.It has built a stable business network. The financial manage system, computer application and product quality control inside the company are at the advanced level compared with the same trades. We whole heartedly welcome the people belonged to various circles to develop together with us.

Address: 30 Binjiang Avenue, Heping District, Tianjin City
Tel: (022)27303053
27300984,27302186
Fax:(022)27303053
Postcode: 300041
Cable: 2068

天津星光橡塑有限公司

TIANJIN STARLIGHT RUBBER & PLASTIC CO., LTD

天津星光橡塑有限公司是由天津汽车进出口公司、台湾中光橡胶工业股份有限公司及香港星愿橡塑有限公司三方合资经营，是生产汽车用密封条之专业厂，于1995年4月正式投产开业。

该公司自成立以来，秉持“品质第一、顾客优先”之品质政策，“和谐、务实、卓越”之经营理念，并在1996年9月通过英国亚士力(SGS)公司ISO9002的认证，更体了该公司对产品品质的执着与决心。

该公司有先进的技术后盾，结合中国优秀敬业的职工与不断完善的管理制度，得到各方客户的支持与好评，现已向天津微型、郑州日产、沈阳金杯、南京依维柯、武汉万通、安徽江淮、长春三友等汽车厂正式供货。

该公司全体职工衷心希望有机会为各方需求客户服务，盼望能为中国汽车及相关产业尽一分心力!

地址:天津市西青区中北斜乡曹庄村西

星光路1号

邮编:300112

电话:(022)27395051－5

传真:(022)27395050

Tianjin Starlight Rubber & Plastic Co., Ltd is a joint venture invested by Tianjin Automobile import & export Company, Taiwan Zhongguang Rubber & Plastic Industrial Co., Ltd and Hong Kong Xingyuan Rubber & Plastic Co., Ltd, which is specializing in producing automobile used strip sealant. The company was setup and opened for business in April, 1995.

Since the setup, Quality is the first, Customers are second to none become its police, Harmony, Dealing with concrete matters relating to works, Outstandingness become its management theory. In September, 1996, the company passed SGS's ISO9002 Certificate, which shows more the company's strict attitude and determination towards its products.

Supported by advanced technologies, supplied by Chinese excellent employees and improving management system, the company receives its customer's supports and appraisal. It has started to provide products to Tianjin Mini, ZhengZhou RICHAN, SHENYAN GOLDEN CUP, NANJING YIWACO, WUHAN WANTONG, ANHUI JIANGWEI, CHANGCHUN SANYOU, and other automobile factories.

The employees sincerely wish had chance to provide services to customers from various walks, made sacrifice to China's automobile industry and industries concerned.

Address: No.1 Xingguang Road, the west of Caocunzuang, ZhongbeixieXiang, Xiqing District, Tianjin, China

Post Code: 300112

Tel: 27395051－5

Fax: 27395050

天津市橡胶机带厂 异型胶带技术经营服务部

THE TECHNOLOGICAL AND MANAGEMENT SERVICE DEPARTMENT FOR SPECIAL-SHAPED ADHESIVE TAPE OF TIANJIN RUBBER MACHINE-TAPE FACTORY

法人代表: 崔志宏

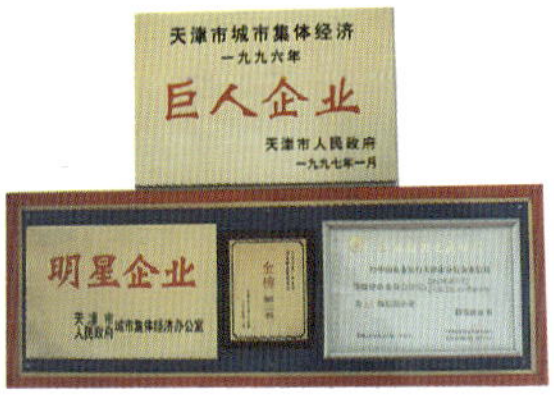

天津市橡胶机带厂异型胶带技术经营服务部是以经营各种异型胶带为主，融技、工、贸为一体的生产经营企业。

其生产与经营主要产品有国家标准、国际标准与非标的各种胶带，其中注册金钟牌商标的农机带、食品输送带、花纹输送带、窄V带、联组V带以及同步齿型带等产品畅销全国，深受农场、矿山、油田、冶金、化工等行业欢迎，享有盛誉。

该企业重视产品质量，品种齐全，服务周到，1994年曾被评为天津市化工行业综合指标金榜第二名，1994年、1995年连续被命名天津市集体经济明星企业，1996年又被天津市经委系统评为先进企业，同时天津市人民政府又授于“巨人企业”称号。由于该企业重视企业信用，1995年被天津市农行评审AA级信用单位，1996年又被农行评为AAA级信用单位。

法人代表崔志宏愿与各界朋友真诚合作、共图宏业。

地址:天津市南门外大街356号

电话:(022)27223533　　27221545　　23697930

传真:(022)27212268

电挂:9201

邮编:300100

运输带车间全景

The Technological and Management Service Department for Special Shape Adhesive Tape of Tianjin Rubber Machine-Tape Factory is a production and management enterprise. It mainly deals in all kinds of special-shaped adhesive tapes and at the same time deals in technological and industrial production and trade.

The enterprise can produce and deal in products of International Standard and the State Standard such as different kinds of adhesive tape. Its poducts with the registered trademark 'Golden Bell', such as adhesive tapes for agricultural machine, food conveyer belt, figured conveyer belt, narrow V belt, combined V belt and synchromesh gear belt have been saled all over the country and appreciated by farms, mining industry, oil fields, metallurgical industry and chenical industry.

The enterprise has been paying more attention to products quality, variety of products and good service. In 1994 the enterprise was chosen the No. 2 on Tianjin Trade Golden-list for Comprehensive Index. In 1994 and 1995, it was named as 'Bright Star Collective Enterprise' continuously. In 1996, it was chosen as the Advanced Enterprise by Tianjin Economic Committee and was given the title of 'Giant Enterprise' by Tianjin Municipal Government. It was chosen the Enterprise of AA Class in 1995 and was chosen the Enterprise of AAA Class by Tianjin Agricultural Bank for its high reputation.

Legal representative: Cui Zhihong

Adress: No.356, Nanmenwai Street, Nankai District, Tianjin

Post code: 300100

Tel: (022) 27223533 27221545 23697930

Fax: (022) 272122688

鸿起顺饭馆(老字号)

鸿起顺餐饮有限责任公司

HONGQISHUN RESTAURANT COMPANY, LTD

鸿起顺餐饮有限责任公司(前身鸿起顺饭馆)始建于1936年，已有60多年的历史，是津门老字号，座落在天津市河西区大沽路427号，所属三个直营店鸿起顺饭庄、风味食廊鸿起顺饭庄、鸿起顺饭馆(老字号)，建筑面积3800平方米。经营品种：各种回民风味炒菜、冷拼、西点、清真烤鸭、水饺、烧麦、自制酱制品、批发、零售烟酒等等。多年来在各级领导的关怀帮助下和广大顾客的厚爱光顾，使企业两个效益逐年提高，连续两年成为天津市餐饮业经营首户(1996年营业收入3681万元，利润303.5万元，税金185万元)。本店始终坚持经济实惠、薄利多销、面向工薪的经营方针，靠艰苦创业起家、靠改革开拓发展，使企业已具有一定的规模，现在鸿起顺直营店高、中、低档具备，技术力量雄厚，就餐环境优雅，为广大顾客、穆斯林兄弟提供良好的就餐环境。

曾荣获市特模集体六届，全国五 • 一劳动奖状，全国民族团结进步先进集体，全国职业道德建设先进集体，天津市商业系统十面红旗，天津市精神文明建设标兵单位，天津市优秀企业等。

风味食廊鸿起顺饭庄

Hongqishun Restaurant Company. Ltd (Hongqishun Restaurant originally) founded in 1936, having a history of over 60 years, is one of the eldest in Tianjin, which is located in No.427 Dagu Road, Hexi District, Tianjin, having 3 directly managed restaurants (Hongqishun Restaurant [original], Hongqishun eating house, Hongqishun special food restaurant)with a total construction area of 3800 square meters. Its business items includes various Muslin dishes, cool dishes, grain food, Muslin Fred Duck, JIaozi and so on, whole sale, selling of hard drinks and cigarettes are also in its business. For many years, under kindly help from Tianjin Government leaders of various levels and customers of different walks' support, the enterprise's social and economic benefits improved annually and became the best company in the field of eatables and drinkable for 2 years continuously(in 1996, its business income reached 36,810,000 yuan with a profit of 3,035,000 yuan and handing in tax of 1,850,000 yuan). The company always holds economical, sale with low benefit and large business scale, satisfying salary earners mainly as its theory, keeps on hard work and develops by reform and creating new business fields and style. The company's business has on large scale. the company's 3 directly managed restaurants at high, middle and low consumption level respectively can provide good eating environment of Muslin brothers of different walks with efficient technical skills. The company has been rewarded state May 1st Prize and entitled state nationality unifying and improving colective, Advanced State Professional Normal construction Collective, One of the 10 Red Flags in Tianjin's business system, Tianjin Spiritual Civilization construction Model Unit and Tianjin Perfect Enterprise.

鸿起顺饭庄

鸿起顺饭馆地址:天津市河西区大沽路南路444号 电话:(022)28301448
鸿起顺饭庄地址:天津市河西区大沽南路668号 电话:(022)28328038
风味食廊鸿起顺饭庄地址:天津市河西区西南楼风味食廊A区2号 电话:(022)28306040

Address of Hongqishun restaurant (original)
No.444 Dagunan Road, Hexi District, Tianjin Tel. 28301448
Address of Hongqishun eating House
No.668 Dagunan Road, hexi District, Tianjin Tel. 28328038
Address of Hongqishun Special Food Restaurant
No.2, Part A, Xinanlo Special Food Mall, Hexi District,Tianjin
Tel. 28306040

天津市统计信息咨询服务中心

TIANJIN STATISTICAL INFORMATION & CONSULTANCY SERVICE CENTRE

主任: 刘金江

天津市统计信息咨询服务中心，是以统计局为依托的，为社会进行顾问咨询、市场调查、信息服务的窗口部门。十年来，我们用优质的服务为社会各界提供了大量的统计信息，成功的进行了全国电梯市场预测、分类药品市场份额观测、主要家用电器全国销售观测、房地产市场研究等专项的市场研究和投资可行性研究，积累了大量的资料和专业技术。

本中心作为中国重点城市信息研究会和天津科技咨询业行业协会的理事单位，与全国大中城市的统计信息部门及天津市的科技咨询机构有着密切的联系，形成了比较稳定的信息交换网络，有能力承担全国性或地区性的信息资料提供及市场研究项目。

中心的特点是：以全国和地方的统计信息网络为依托，以统计信息网络的信息和统计调查结果为资源，利用自己的专业优势和人才优势，采用统计学、经济学、市场学以及各种跨学科的研究手段和抽样调查、典型调查、普查的方法，将大量的统计信息和市场信息开发出来，服务于社会，服务于企业的生产经营实践。

我们的服务方针是：重信誉、讲及时、求准确、见效果。

地址:天津市和平区泰安道32号
电话:(022)23127746　23191114
传真:(022)23127814
邮编:300040

Tianjin Statistical Information & Consultancy Service Center,under the jurisdiction of Tianjin Statistical Bureau,is engaged in consultancy,market research and information service for the public.In recent ten years,the Center has offered plenty of statistical information of Tianjin and of nation as well to all walks of life of society.The Center has successfully conducted national elevator market prediction,classified medicine market share survey,and many other market research and investmant feasibility study projects,accumulating a vast amount of data and acquiring various special techniques.

As a member of Council of China Major City Statistical Information & Consultancy Service Association,the Center has close relation with various statistical information & consultancy departments of large and medium-sized cities nation-wide,forming a steady information exchange network,is capable of offering national and regional information and data,and of undertaking market research projects.

The Center features are: Relying on national and regional statistical information network,making use of resources of statistical information network and results of statistical survey,utilizing our profession and personnel advantages,apply statistics,economics,market economics and varions interdiscipline research means and sampling survey,typical survey,census,develop alarge quantity of statistical information and market information , serving society,serving productive and marketing practice of enterprises.

Our service policy is:prestige,promptness,accuracy and good results.

Director:Liu Jinjiang
Add:32 Taian Road,Heping District Tianjin
Tel:(022)23127746　231911141
Fax:(022)23127814
Zip:300040

天 津 概 况

天津—中央直辖市，中国北方最大的沿海开放城市。地处华北平原东北部，渤海之滨，素有渤海明珠之称。总面积 11 919.7 平方公里，常住户籍人口 898.45 万人，其中市中心地区 369.32 万人。全市辖 13 个区、5 个县。天津历史悠久，得河漕、海运和渔盐之利，由普通渔村发展成为中国北方商品集散中心。元朝即为京畿要地。明初设卫筑城。公元 1860 年被辟为通商口岸。后逐步发展成为中国第二大工商业城市。

(一)区位优势明显。天津地处中国北方黄金海岸的中部，不仅毗邻首都，还是华北、西北广大地区的出海口，是中国北方对内对外开放两个扇面的轴心，是亚欧大陆桥中国境内距离最短的东部起点。天津港是中国北方最大的综合性贸易港口，拥有全国最大的集装箱码头，与世界上 170 多个国家和地区的 300 多个港口保持着贸易往来。天津滨海国际机场有多条国际国内航线，是华北地区最大货运中心。天津铁路枢纽是京山、京沪两大铁路干线的交汇处。天津公路四通八达，交通基础设施建设有了长足发展。目前，天津已形成以港口为中心的海陆空相结合、立体式的综合性的现代化的运输网络。

(二)经济进入较快发展时期。经过多年的努力，天津的经济结构得到优化，已形成汽车及机械装备、电子、化工、冶金四大支柱产业。在全国越来越占有重要地位。商贸金融中心作用进一步增强。这些都为天津国民经济持续、快速、健康发展创造了有利条件。从 1992 年起，天津经济连续 5 年保持两位数增长，后 3 年超过全国平均增长水平。这预示着今后一个时期，天津的经济仍保持着较快发展速度，为实现跨世纪的宏伟目标奠定了坚实基础。

(三)全方位对外开放的格局已经形成。天津从 1984 年实施外向型经济发展战略以来，对外开放不断向高层次、多领域发展，形成了以开发区、保税区、新技术产业园区和 12 个区县开发区为骨架的多领域、多层次、全方位的对外开放格局。吸引了大批客商特别是国际知名大公司、大财团前来投资，目前，已有欧、亚、美、澳各大洲的 90 多个国家和地区在津投资。世界排名前 500 家跨国公司，在津投资办厂的已有 189 家，合作项目 207 个。天津连续几年利用外资增长幅度居全国前列。

(四)滨海新区建设全面启动。这是天津经济发展布局调整的一个大动作。初步规划在滨海地区 350 平方公里范围内，借鉴特区和浦东的经验，充分利用滨海地区的有利条件，建立一个以港口、开发区、保税区为基础，新型产业和外向型经济为主导，基础设施完备、服务功能齐全、辐射和带动能力很强，面向 21 世纪的高度开放的现代化经济新区。是中国北方开放度最大、政策最优惠，完全按照国际惯例运作的改革开放综合实验区，是经济发展最理想的区域，是天津的希望所在。建区三年，滨海新区取得了令人瞩目的业绩。三年间，国内生产总值年均递增速度达到 27.8%，高出全市的速度近 1 倍，占全市的比重由 1993 年的 21%上升到 1996 年的 29.1%。滨海新区作为天津最大的经济增长点对全市经济的带动作用越来越明显，对全市的经济贡献率由 1994 年的 29.8%提高到 1996 年的 43.2%。1996 年滨海新区实现国内生产总值 320.3 亿元，比上年增长 28.3%；固定资产投资完成 157.1 亿元，增长 3.1%；工业总产值 701.4 亿元，增长 40.2%。

(五)人才和科技力量雄厚。天津是中国科技人才最密集的地区之一，拥有 20 所高等院校，150 多个自然科学研究机构，各类专业技术人员 59 万人，研究开发能力强，各科研机构已初步形成自己的研究特色，每年都有一批科研成果达到国内和国际的先进水平。天津有 280 多万职工，技艺素质较高，能很好地适应现代化生产的需要。

(六)社会秩序稳定。天津始终坚持“两手抓、两手都要硬”的方针，取得了良好的成效。

社会治安状况一直保持全国最好地区之一，形成了良好的社会环境。天津人朴实憨厚、聪明勤劳、热情好客、有强烈的敬业精神。

1996 年，是天津实施“九五”计划的第一年，是改革开放和现代化建设取得显著成绩的一年。全年实现国内生产总值 1 102.4 亿元，比上年增长 14.3%，增幅居全国第二位。第一产业增长 8.2%，粮食生产在大灾之年又获丰收，总产量达 20.7 亿公斤；第二产业增长 14.3%，工业总产值完成 2 522.4 亿元，增长 24.66%；第三产业增长 15.4%，占国内生产总值的比重达 40.6%。社会消费品零售总额实现 470 亿元，增长 25.1%。外贸出口实现 40.5 亿美元，增长 35.1%。全社会固定资产投资完成 435.8 亿元，增长 10.8%。财政收入完成 137.45亿元，按可比口径增长 15.8%。商品零售物价涨幅 5.1%，比去年回落 5.5 个百分点。国有企业改革步伐加快；对内对外开放水平明显提高；商贸金融中心功能不断增强；城市基础设施建设步伐加快，城市管理继续加强，环境综合整治定量考核再次评为全国第一；科技兴市战略加快实施，精神文明建设成效显著，“五个一工程”连续三年满堂红；人民生活进一步改善，解困工作力度加大，改善城乡人民生活的 20 件实事全部兑现。在肯定 1996 年天津各条战线的工作成就的同时，也要清醒地看到还存在着许多问题。如企业调整改组的步伐较慢，相当一部分国有企业生产经营困难，虽有所好转，但亏损面和亏损额仍较大。对此，需要高度重视，认真对待，下大力量解决。要依靠全市人民，同心同德，奋发图强，为实现天津经济和社会事业更快更好的发展而奋斗。

（陈　芳）

1996年天津市国民经济和社会发展统计公报

天津市统计局

1997年2月26日

1996年,是实施“九五”计划的第一年,全市各地区、各部门按照市政府提出的“工作创一流、‘九五’高起步、实现翻两番”的总体要求,艰苦奋斗,扎实工作,开拓进取,积极推进两个根本性转变,全市国民经济继续保持了快速健康发展的势头。三次产业全面发展,对外开放进一步扩大,市场繁荣,物价涨幅明显回落,城乡居民实际生活水平进一步提高,各项社会事业取得新的进展,实现了“九五”良好开局。据统计1996年全市国内生产总值为1 102.10亿元,比上年增长14.3%,提前4年实现了比1980年翻两番的目标。其中第三产业增加值446.20亿元,增长15.5%,占国内生产总值的比重由上年的38.7%上升为40.5%,人均国内生产总值由上年的10 380元增加到12 293元。全市财政收入完成137.45亿元,按可比口径计算比上年增长15.8%。经济生活中存在的主要问题是:经济结构调整的步伐还比较慢,经济增长质量和效益还不高,企业亏损面和亏损额还比较大,部分企业职工生活还比较困难。

一、农　业

农业生产在大灾之年仍取得较好收成。1996年全市农业增加值71.08亿元,比上年增长3.7%。全年粮食总产量207万吨,比历史最好水平的上年下降0.2%,粮食亩产达305公斤,“菜篮子工程”取得新的成效,主要副食品生产稳定增长。主要农副产品产量如下:

	单　位	1996年	比上年增长(%)
粮食总产量	万吨	207	-0.2
棉　　花	万吨	0.51	-54.5
油　　料	万吨	3.13	-21.9
水　　果	万吨	21.21	6.5
蔬　　菜	万吨	452.71	4.3
肉类总产量	万吨	22.59	6.4
其中:猪肉	万吨	13.09	7.6
禽　　蛋	万吨	24.44	1.5
奶　　类	万吨	11.36	2.1
水 产 品	万吨	16.80	9.4
年末生猪存栏	万头	87.78	-0.2
当年出栏肉猪	万头	173.07	6.2

农业生产条件继续得到改善。1996年末全市拥有农业机械总动力558.02万千瓦,比上年增长4.8%;载重汽车2.71万辆,增长1.5%;全年农村用电量38.82亿千瓦小时,增长19.3%。

二、工业和建筑业

工业生产持续快速发展。1996年全市工业增加值527.58亿元,比上年增长15.1%;全市工业总产值 2 109.80 亿元,增长 22.7% 。各种经济类型工业全面加快发展,全部国有工业总产值(包括"三资"企业、股份制和联营企业中国有部分在内的全部国有经济)比上年增长 13.9%,"三资"工业增长 34.5%,乡办工业增长 32.7%。轻重工业同步增长。

1996 年全市乡及乡以上工业总产值 1 314.81 亿元,比上年增长 19.3%,其中重工业总产值 699.17 亿元,增长 18.8% ,轻工业总产值 615.64 亿元,增长 20.0%。轻重工业比例为46.8:53.2,与上年比例相同。

大中型企业生产稳步提高。全年大中型工业企业完成工业总产值 646.34 亿元,比上年增长 9.7%,占全市乡及乡以上工业总产值的 49.2%,其中国有大中型工业企业生产增长 6.7%,快于上年的增长速度。

工业产品结构随着市场变化继续得到调整,一批适销对路产品大幅度增产。主要工业产品产量如下:

	单位	1996 年	比上年增长(%)
天然气	亿立方米	7.57	持平
原　油	万吨	646.60	17.4
原　盐	万吨	218.66	16.6
发电量	亿千瓦小时	112.65	-7.4
生　铁	万吨	159.43	-2.2
钢	万吨	199.12	34.7
成品钢材	万吨	129.65	-11.5
水　泥	万吨	171.54	0.5
平板玻璃	万立方米	184.03	-17.3
纯　碱	万吨	63.64	0.8
烧　碱	万吨	32.65	1.7
机制纸及纸板	万吨	24.37	-0.4
农用化肥	万吨	10.23	1.4
塑　料	万吨	17.16	6.7
塑料制品	万吨	7.58	-0.2
染　料	万吨	3.00	6.3
化学纤维	万吨	6.90	-24.6
合成洗涤剂	万吨	11.73	10.6
金属切削机床	台	337	-29.7
程控交换机	万门	112.58	10.6
电子计算机	部	76	-19.2
汽　车	万辆	15.27	16.7

其中:夏利轿车	万辆	8.80	35.4
摩托车	万辆	14.80	-25.5
内燃机	万千瓦	627.14	18.7
纱(混合数)	万吨	10.30	-5.0
毛　线	吨	7 156	-16.3
布(混合数)	亿米	3.01	-11.1
服　装	亿件	1.03	8.3
卷　烟	万箱	16.02	-15.7
照相机	万架	79.28	1.2 倍
缝纫机	万架	9.34	-25.5
家用洗衣机	万台	60.01	0.1
家用电冰箱(柜)	万台	0.60	-82.4
电视机	万部	149.49	-7.3
其中:彩电	万部	115.79	5.7
自行车	万辆	101.51	-50.9
录像机	万部	63.72	56.8

工业经济效益不理想。1996 年全市乡及乡以上独立核算工业企业产品销售收入完成 1 542.23亿元,比上年增长 13.8%,产销率为 97.4%,比上年下降 0.5 个百分点。实现利税 137.81 亿元,比上年增长 0.1%,其中实现利润 65.31 亿元,下降 1.7%。

建筑业生产稳步发展。1996 年全市建筑业完成增加值 57.24 亿元,比上年增长 10.6% 。全年建筑安装施工企业完成产值 158.29 亿元, 比上年增长 6.1%;房屋建筑施工面积 1 531.37 万平方米,增长 1.3% ;房屋建筑竣工面积 350.85 万平方米,减少 14.5% 。

三、国内商业和市场物价

1996 年全市批发零售贸易餐饮业增加值完成 98.46 亿元, 比上年增长 15.4%。国内商业总购进 675.53 亿元,总销售 721.16 亿元,分别比上年增长 8.0%和 5.1%。

零售市场繁荣活跃。全市社会消费品零售总额 470.04 亿元,比上年增长 25.8% ,其中吃的商品增长 25.7%,穿的商品增长 27.1% ,用的商品增长 25.6% 。

商品批发交易市场取得新的进展。1996 年全市主要商品批发市场成交额(不含集贸市场) 4 071.57亿元,比上年增长 2.9 倍。其中, 期货交易额 3 873.53 亿元,增长 6 倍。

物价涨幅明显回落。1996 年全市城市商品零售价格和城市居民消费价格涨幅分别比上年回落 5.5 个和 6.3 个百分点,在全国和 35 个大中城市中继续保持较低水平。1996 年各类价格指数如下(以上年为 100):

1. 城市商品零售价格指数	105.1
2. 城市居民消费价格指数	109.0

其中：	食品类	106.7
	衣着类	104.8
	家庭设备及用品	103.4
	医疗保健	106.6
	交通和通讯工具	100.8
	娱乐教育文化用品	107.8
	居　住	137.1
	服务项目价格指数	117.4

四、对外经济与国内区域合作

对外开放取得新的进展。利用外资保持增长势头，1996年全市新签“三 资”企业项目1 087个，协议外资金额39.24亿美元，比上年增长1.9%。大项目明显增多，全年签约500万美元以上的项目115个，比上年增长29.2%。截止1996年底，全市累计签约“三资”企业项目已达10 497个，协议外资金额达到156.3亿美元。1996年全市实际利用外资29.84亿美元，比上年增长41.4%，其中外商直接投资20.06亿美元，增长31.9%。截止1996年底，全市已累计实际利用外资108.87亿美元，其中外商直接投资57.6亿美元。

作为全市对外开放前沿的滨海新区对全市经济的带动作用越来越明显。1996年滨海新区实现国内生产总值320.29亿元，比上年增长28.3%，占全市国内生产总值的比重由上年的26.3%上升到29.1%；固定资产投资完成157.05亿元，增长3.5%；工业总产值512.67亿元，增长40.2%。开发区、保税区发展势头强劲。1996年开发区国内生产总值比上年增长60.6%，工业总产值增长56.2%；外贸出口增长55.7%；保税区国内生产总值增长1.3倍。

进出口贸易进一步发展。1996年天津口岸进出口总值216.85亿美元，与上年持平，其中进口93.96亿美元，增长5.0%，出口122.89亿美元，下降4.0%。天津外贸出口创历史最高水平。全年外贸进出口总值82.97亿美元，比上年增长31.2%，其中进口总值42.48亿美元，增长24.1%；出口总值40.49亿美元，增长39.6%。在全市外贸出口中“三资”企业出口21.52亿美元，增长1.1倍，占全市外贸出口的比重由上年的34.5%上升到53.2%。全市出口结构进一步改善，机电产品出口量14.84亿美元，增长79.9%。

对外经济技术合作继续发展。1996年对外承包工程和劳务合作新签合同1 320个，合同金额1.58亿美元，完成营业额8 809万美元。

国际和国内旅游业发展加快。1996年共接待国际旅游人数23.33万人次，比上年增长16.3%，其中外国人20.02万人次，增长23%。国际旅游外汇收入1.52亿美元，增长14.4%。1996年天津市接待国内旅游人数2 452.73万人次，旅游收入199.65亿元。

国内区域经济合作迈出较大步伐。1996年末全国各地区、各部门来津开设的办事机构已达1 404家，当年签订经济技术联合协作项目11 815项，吸引外地在津投资协议额51.39亿元，比上年增长25.8%，实际利用内资32.15亿元，增长42.3%。

五、交通运输和邮电通信业

1996年全市交通运输、邮电业增加值107.32亿元，比上年增长14.7%。各种交通工具运输量完成情况：

	单位	1996年	比上年增长(%)
货运量(发送量)	万吨	28 246.5	-0.6
其中:天津地区	万吨	23 381.4	-0.5
铁路	万吨	7 539.6	-1.3
其中:天津地区	万吨	2 674.5	-1.8
公路	万吨	19 491.0	0.9
水运	万吨	1 205.2	-16.9
民航	万吨	10.7	1.2倍
货物周转量	亿吨公里	1 472.8	-22.8
其中:天津地区	亿吨公里	984.4	-29.6
铁路	亿吨公里	712.1	-3.6
其中:天津地区	亿吨公里	223.7	-2.7
公路	亿吨公里	41.2	-0.2
水运	亿吨公里	219.5	-36.2
旅客发送量	万人次	4 469.5	-7.8
其中:天津地区	万人次	3 114.0	-5.7
铁路	万人次	2 929.1	-12.5
其中:天津地区	万人次	1 573.6	-12.6
公路(长途)	万人次	1 496.0	2.2
民航	万人次	44.4	18.7
港口货物吞吐量	万吨	6 188.3	6.9
其中:出口	万吨	4 839.1	6.3
进口	万吨	1 349.2	9.2
机场货物吞吐量	万吨	11.7	1倍
机场旅客吞吐量	万人次	88.8	17.3

邮电通信业快速发展。全年邮电业务总量完成25.68亿元,比上年增长37.2%。1996年末全市程控交换机总容量169万门,当年净增19万门,电话机拥有量174.65万部,比上年增长28.8%,全市平均每百人拥有电话机19.4部,比上年增加4.2部。其中,市话普及率达到每百人32.8部。

六、金融和保险业

金融保险业发展明显加快。1996年全市新增各类金融机构224家,累计2 557家,其中外资银行保险机构25家。1996年天津市金融保险业增加值107亿元,比上年增长25.1%。金融市场发展较快。全年证券市场成交额79.8亿元,比上年增长4.19倍。调剂外汇总额22.27亿美元。

金融形势保持稳定。1996年末全市金融机构各项存款余额1 391.62亿元,比年初增加313.86亿元;各项贷款余额1 325.49亿元,比年初增加211.52亿元,存款增加大于贷款增加

102.34亿元。1996 年全市银行现金收入 1 696.42 亿元,比上年增长 32.0%;银行现金支出 1 704.67亿元,增长33.7%;收支相抵,货币净投放 8.25 亿元。

保险业发展加快。1996 年全市保险业承保总额 2 555.01 亿元。保费收入 17.41 亿元,比上年增长 40.7%,其中:财险保费收入 10.81 亿元,增长 17.8%;人身保费收入 6.6 亿元,增长 1.1 倍。

七、城市公用和房地产业

1996 年城市公用事业取得新的发展,城市载体功能继续提高。1996 年末城市铺装道路长度 3 165公里,面积 3 483 万平方米。公共电汽车营运线路 257 条,比上年增加 30 条,营运长度5 848 公里,增长 13.1%。年末城市居民家庭燃气气化率 92.8%。全市城市居民住宅集中供热面积 1 806万平方米,热化率 29.7%。1996 年末全市城市居民人均公共绿地面积 3.41 平方米,建成区绿化覆盖率 19.3%,分别比上年提高 0.21 平方米和 1.6 个百分点。

房地产业平稳发展。1996 年天津市房地产业增加值为 22.44 亿元,比上年增长 4.0%。全市房地产开发投资 71.48 亿元,比上年增长 2.9%,其中住宅 建设投资 43.01 亿元,下降 3.1%,住宅竣工面积 362 万平方米,增长 13.1%,其中平房改造竣工面积 289 万平方米。

八、科学技术、环境保护

科学研究取得丰硕成果。1996 年全市科技成果登记 936 项,其中达到国际领先水平 40 项, 国际先进水平 170 项。科技成果利用率有所提高。全年获国家发明奖 5 项,国家科技进步奖 11 项。建成重点实验室 6 个。为加速国民经济的信息化,天津“信息港”建设开始启动。

1996 年全市申请专利 1 743 项,授权 899 项。自 1985 年到 1996 年底,全市累计申请专利 14 487项,已批准授权 8 194 项。

技术市场成交活跃。1996 年全市共签订技术合同 8 348 份,合同成交额 13.35 亿元,比上年增长 10.13% 。

新技术产业园区迅速发展。当年新建企业 516 家,年末累计已达 2 752 家,从业人员 4.49 万人, 全年技工贸总收入 91.32 亿元,比上年增长 36.1%;总产值 89.57 亿元,增长 45.9%;实现利税 10.11 亿元,增长 37.0%。

全市环保事业取得新的进展。1996 年已建立环境监测站 20 个,自然保护区 5 个,烟尘控制区 55 个,烟尘控制区面积达 487 平方公里,其中市内 209.43 平方公里。

九、教育、文化、卫生、体育

各级各类教育事业全面发展。1996 年末全市共有普通高等院校 20 所, 在校本专科学生 7.14 万人,毕业生 1.84 万人,在学博士研究生、硕士研究生分别为 1 119 人和 5 159 人,毕业博士研究生、硕士研究生分别为 239 人和 1 517 人;成人高校 44 所, 在校学生 6.2 万人,毕业生 1.66 万人;普通中专 78 所,在校学生 6.7 万人,毕业生 1.33 万人。南开大学、天津大学和天津医科大学进入国家“211 工程”工作进展顺利。

普及九年义务教育进一步发展。普通中学 734 所,比上年增加 18 所,在校学生 49.36 万人,毕业生 12.07 万人;小学 3 027 所,比上年减少 189 所,在校学生 87.98 万人,毕业生 14.57 万人,小学毕业生升学率97.0%。中小学办学条件继续得到改善。

文化事业健康繁荣。1996年末全市共有艺术表演团体18个,文化馆19个,博物馆14个,公共图书馆31个,电影院、影剧院、开放礼堂及俱乐部127个。全年共出版各类杂志4 686.5万册,出版各类报纸5.39亿份,出版各类图书8 917.1万册。“五个一工程”连续三年获得“满堂红”。

医疗卫生条件进一步改善。1996年末全市共有医疗卫生机构4 171个,其中医院245个。年末全市医院拥有病床3.6万张;全市拥有专业卫生技术人员7.10万人,其中医生3.3万人。

体育事业形势喜人。第35届世界体操锦标赛申办成功。在全国重大比赛中天津市运动员获8枚金牌,18枚银牌,14枚铜牌。全民健身运动蓬勃开展。

十、固定资产投资

1996年全市全社会固定资产投资完成435.31亿元,比上年增长10.7%,其中地方全社会投资325.20亿元,增长5.0%。全市国有单位投资358.51亿元,增长7.6%;集体所有制单位投资59.3亿元,增长19.3%;城乡个人投资17.5亿元,增长69.9%。

投资结构进一步调整。第三产业完成投资163亿元,增长14.4%。工业投资得到加强。1996年全市国有工业完成投资193.46亿元,比上年增长4.1%,其中石油、电力等基础原材料和能源工业投资107.93亿元,占工业投资比重55.8%。工业技术改造加快。1996年地方工业技术改造投资完成49.57亿元,增长17.0%。

重点项目建设进展顺利。全市55个重点建设项目完成投资89.9亿元,已有蓟县电厂、天津钢管公司海绵铁工程、金钢桥改造工程、夏利轿车零部件工程、大沽化工厂聚氯乙烯重点技改工程、天津造纸四、五厂扩建工程等16项重点工程竣工投产和交付使用。

十一、人口、就业和人民生活

1996年末全市常住人口948.19万人,比上年末增加6.36万人,增长0.7%;全年人口出生率为10.09‰;死亡率为6.53‰;人口自然增长率为3.56‰。年末户籍人口为898.45万人,比上年末增加3.78万人。计划生育工作取得积极成效。

1996年末全市职工人数为282.05万人,其中国有单位职工194.22万人;集体单位职工59万人,其他单位职工28.84万人。1996年全市人才市场和劳务市场179.02万人进场择业洽谈,44.42万人达成初步意向。

城乡居民收入继续增加,生活水平进一步提高。1996年全市职工工资总额210.23亿元,比上年增长13.8%,全市职工平均工资7 629元,增长17.4%,扣除价格因素实际增长7.7%;城市居民人均生活费收入5 525.48元,比上年增长19.4%,扣除价格因素实际增长9.5%;人均生活费支出4 679.61元,增长15.2%,扣除价格因素实际增长5.7%。农民人均年纯收入3 142元,比上年增加611元,增长24.1%;人均年生活费支出2 100元,增长22.3%。

城乡居民储蓄存款大幅度增加。1996年末城乡居民储蓄存款余额724亿元,比年初增加173.81亿元,其中城镇居民储蓄存款余额615.34亿元,比年初增加155.02亿元;农村居民储蓄存款余额108.66亿元,增加18.79亿元。

城乡居民居住条件进一步改善。1996年末城市人均居住面积达到7.74平方米,比上年增加0.22平方米,农村居民人均居住面积21.83平方米,比上年增加2.37平方米。

社会福利事业进一步发展。1996年全市民政事业各种福利院床位7 742张，收养5 323人，救济18.44万人次，全市社区服务设施1 737个，全市农村社会保障网络覆盖率27%。市政府为全市城乡居民办的20件实事全部兑现。

注：1.增加值是指一定时期内国民经济各个部门的企业、事业、行政单位及个体经营者生产和提供最终使用的产品和劳务的价值。

2.国内生产总值指一个国家(或地区)在一定时期内所生产和提供最终使用的产品和劳务的价值，即国民经济各部门增加值之和。

3.国内生产总值、增加值按当年价格计算，增长速度按可比价格计算。

4.1996年各项统计数据均为快报数。

(1997年4月5日在《天津日报》发表)

STATISTICAL COMMUNIQUE ON THE 1996 NATIONAL ECONOMIC AND SOCIAL DEVELOPMENT OF THE CITY OF TIANJIN

Feb.26, 1997

1996 is the first year of carrying out the 9th Five – Year Plan (The 9th – Five). All regions and departments of the city followed the overall requirements of "Creating first – rate work, high starting point for the 9th – Five, and realizing the target of redoubling the GDP" put forward by the city party committee and the municipal government, fought indefatigably, worked in solid steps, explored for new advances and positively pushed forward the two fundamental changes. The national economy of the city continued to keep a trend of healthy development. The three enterprises had all round development. The city opened even wider to the outside world than before. Market prospered. The scale of price rise fell conspicuously. The actual living condition of the urban and rural population further upgraded. All social causes and projects achieved new progress. The opening game of the 9th – Five did well. tatistics show that the 1996 Gross Domestic Production(GDP) of the city to be 110.21 billion yuan, a growth of 14.3 percent over the previous year and realized the target of redoubling the value of 1980 four years ahead of schedule. Of which, the value – added of the tertiary industry was 44.62 billion yuan and that increased 15.5 percent over the previous year. Its share in the GDP rose from 38.7 percent in 1995 to 40.5 percent. The per capita GDP increased from 10,380 yuan in 1995 to 12,293 yuan. The city's fiscal income was 137.45 billion yuan, increased 15.8 percent than 1995 as calculated by the comparables. The major problems existed in economic life were the following: the pace of the adjustment of economic structure was still relatively slow, the quality and result of economic growth were not high, the number of loss – suffering enterprises and the amount of losses were still quite large, and the life of the employees of a part of enterprises was still rather difficult.

Ⅰ. Agriculture

The agricultural production reaped pretty good harvest in a year having major disaster. The value added of the city's agriculture was 7.108 billion yuan in 1996, up by 3.7 percent over the previous year. The total grain production was 2,070,000 tons, which was 0.2 percent less than the previous year, the best year of all times. Grain production per mou reached 305kg. The "Food Basket Engineering Project" made new accomplishments and the production of major foodstuffs grew steadily.

The yield of major agricultural products and non - staple food:

	UNIT	1996	INCREASE FROM PREVIOUS YEAR(%)
Total grain production	10,000 tons	207	-0.2
Cotton	ditto	0.51	-54.5
Oil - bearing crops	ditto	3.13	-21.9
Fruits	ditto	21.21	6.5
Vegetables	ditto	452.71	4.3
Meat	ditto	22.59	6.4
of which: Pork	ditto	13.09	7.6
Poultry eggs	ditto	24.44	1.5
Milk	ditto	11.36	2.1
Aquatic products	ditto	16.80	9.4
Pigs in stock by year's end	10,000 heads	87.78	-0.2
Pigs slaughtered during the year	ditto	173.07	6.2

The conditions for agricultural production continued to improve. By end of 1996, the total power of the city's agricultural machinery reached 5.5802 million kilowatts, up by 4.8 percent over the previous year; trucks 27,100, up by 1.5 percent, and rural consumption of electricity was 3.882 billion kilowatt - hours, 19.3 percent higher than the previous year.

Ⅱ. Industry and Construction

Industrial production was in continued rapid development. In 1996, the total value added of industry reached 52.758 billion yuan, up by 15.1 percent over the previous year. The Gross Industrial Output Value (GIOV) of the city was 210.98 billion yuan, up by 22.7 percent. There were all round accelerated development in industries of various types of economy. The GIOV of entire state - owned industry (all of the state - owned part of the foreign investment involved enterprises, share - holding ownership enterprises and jointly - run enterprises inclusive) increased 13.9 percent, foreign investment involved industry increased 34.5 percent, and township industry increased 32.7 percent.

The light and heavy industries grew in the same pace. The total Industrial Output Value from rural township and above in 1996 was 131.481 billion yuan, up by 19.3 percent over the previous year. Of which, the production of heavy industry was 69.917 billion yuan and up by 18.8 percent, and light industry was 61.564 billion yuan or 20 percent up over the previous year. The ratio of light industry to heavy industry was 46.8:53.2, the same as the last year.

The production of large and medium sized enterprises grew steadily. The large and medium sized industrial enterprises accomplished 64.634 billion yuan of GIOV and increased 9.7 percent over the previous year. Their share in the GIOV of all of the city industry from township and above reached 49.2 percent. Among growth of the large and medium industrial enterprises, production of the state - owned ones grew 6.7 percent and the growth was faster than the previous year.

The structure of industrial products continued to achieve adjustment along with the changes in the market. The production of a number of products that are suitable and popular grew in large scale. The production of major industrial products is listed as the following:

	UNIT	1996	INCREASE FROM PREVIOUS YEAR(%)
Natural gas	100 million cubic meters	7.57	no change
Crude oil	10,000 tons	646.60	17.4
Salt	ditto	218.66	16.6
Electricity	100 million - kW/h	112.65	-7.4
Pig iron	10,000 tons	159.43	-2.2
Steel	ditto	199.12	34.7
Rolled steel	ditto	129.65	-11.5
Cement	ditto	171.54	0.5
Plate glass	10,000 square meters	184.03	-17.3
Soda ash	10,000 tons	63.64	0.8
Caustic soda	ditto	32.65	1.7
Machine - made paper and paper board	ditto	24.37	-0.4
Chemical fertilizer for agriculture	ditto	10.23	1.4
Plastics	ditto	17.16	6.7
Plastic products	ditto	7.58	-0.2
Dyes	ditto	3.00	6.3
Chemical fibre	ditto	6.90	-24.6
Synthetic detergents	ditto	11.73	10.6
Metal cutting machine tools	1 set	337	-29.7
Programme controlled telephone exchanges	10,000 sets	112.58	10.6

Electronic computers	1 set	76	-19.2
Motor vehicles	10,000	15.27	16.7
of which: Xiali cars	10,000	8.8	35.4
Motorcycles	10,000	14.0	-25.5
Internal combustion engines	10,000kw	627.14	18.7
Yarn(all varieties)	10,000 tons	10.3	-5.0
Woolen yarn	ton	7 156	-16.3
Fabric(all varieties)	100 million meters	3.01	-11.1
Garments	100 million pieces	1.03	8.3
Cigarettes	10,000 boxes	16.02	-15.7
Cameras	10,000	79.28	1.2 times more
Sewing machines	10,000	9.34	-25.5
Home use washing machines	10,000	60.61	0.1
Home use refrigerators and freezers	10,000	0.60	-82.4
TV sets	10,000	149.49	-7.3
of which: Color TV	10,000	115.79	5.7
Bicycles	10,000	101.51	-50.9
VCRs	10,000	63.72	56.8

The economic results of the industry was not ideal. In 1996, the sales income of the products of all the city's independently accounted industrial enterprises from township and above was 154.223 billion yuan, or 13.8 percent increase over the previous year. The production/sales rate was 97.4 percent, 0.5 percentage point lower than the previous year. Profit and tax were 13.781 billion yuan or 0.1% growth, in which profit was 6.531 billion yuan or 1.7% decrease.

The production of construction industry progressed steadily. In 1996, the city's construction industry accomplished value added 5.724 billion yuan, up by 10.6 percent over the previous year. The construction and installation enterprises accomplished 15.829 billion yuan production value as an increase of 6.1 percent over the previous year. On-going housing construction space for the year was 15.3137 million square meters, an increase of 1.3 percent. Housing space that completed construction in the year was 3.5085 million square meters, and a cut of 14.5 percent as compared to the previous year.

Ⅲ. Domestic Commerce and Market Prices

In 1996, the value added of the city's wholesale, retail, trade and restaurants reached to 9.846 billion yuan, grew 15.4 percent over the previous year. The total purchase of domestic commerce was 67.553 billion yuan, and the total sales 72.116 billion yuan. The increase was 8.0 percent and 5.1 percent respectively.

The retail market was active and booming. The city's total retail amount of social consumer goods was 47.004 billion yuan, up by 25.8 percent over the previous year. Of which, foodstuffs increased 25.7 percent, clothing 27.1 percent and daily use articles 25.6 percent.

The market for wholesale trading of goods made new progress. In 1996, the total sum of transactions of the major wholesale markets(not including rural trade fairs) reached 407.157 billion yuan as increased for 2.9 times. Of which, the transaction of the futures reached 387.353 billion yuan, a six times increase from the previous year.

The decrease of the scale of price rise was obvious. In 1996, the scales of retail price of urban commodities and the consumer price of urban residents fell 5.5 and 6.3 percentage points respectively. They are on a rather low level among 35 large and medium sized cities across the country. The following are Tianjin's various price indexes of 1996(taking the previous year as 100):

1. City commodity retail price index	105.1
2. City resident consumer price index	109.0
of which: Foodstuffs	106.7
Clothing	104.8
Household facilities and articles	103.4
Medical and health care	106.6
Transportation - communication	100.8
Recreational, educational and cultural articles	107.8
Housing	137.1
Service items price index	117.4

Ⅳ. Foreign Economic Relations and Domestic Regional Cooperation

New progress was achieved in the opening to the outside world. The foreign capital used kept a trend of growth. In 1996, the number of newly signed contracts(agreements) of projects with foreign capital was 1,087, and the amount of utilization of foreign capital through signed contracts (agreements) by investment was 3.924 billion US dollars, up by 1.9 percent over the previous year. The number of large projects increased conspicuously. The were 115 project contracts each worth over 5 million US dollars signed in 1996, up by 29.2 percent over the last year. By end of

1996, the city hosted in aggregate 10,497 projects of foreign investment involved enterprises, and the total amount of agreed foreign capital reached 15.63 billion US dollars. The total value of foreign capital used in 1996 was 2.984 billion US dollars, up by 41.4 percent over the previous year. Of which, direct foreign investment reached 2.006 billion US dollars, up by 31.9 percent. By end of 1996, the foreign capital actually used in aggregate was 10.887 billion US dollars, and of which 5.76 billion US dollars were direct foreign investment.

As the fore front of the city's opening to the outside world, the role of a locomotive as played by the New Coastal Region became growingly apparent. In 1996, the GDP of the New Coastal Region was 32.029 billion yuan, or up by 28.3 percent over the previous year. Its share in the city's GDP rose from 26.3 percent to 29.1 percent. The region's investment in fixed assets accomplished 15.705 billion yuan, increased by 3.5 percent. The GIP of the region was 51.267 billion yuan, up by 40.2 percent. TEDA and the Tianjin Port Free Trade Zone enjoyed a strong trend of development. As compared to the previous year, the 1996 GDP of TEDA increased 60.6 percent, its GIOV increased 56.2 percent and foreign trade export increased 55.7 percent. The GDP of the Tianjin Port Free Trade Zone increased 1.3 times over the previous year.

Import and export trade further developed. In 1996, the total import - export went through Tianjin was 21.685 billion US dollars, similar to that of the previous year. Of which, import was 9.396 billion US dollars and up by 5 percent; export was 12.289 billion US dollars and decreased 4 percent. During the year, Tianjin's own foreign trade export reached its historical high. The city's annual import - export reached 8.297 billion US dollars and increased 31.2 percent over the previous year. Of which, import was 4.248 billion US dollars and increased 24.1 percent; export was 4.049 billion US dollars and increased 39.6 percent over the previous year. Among the city's export value the export of foreign investment involved enterprises was 2.152. billion US dollars, an increased of 1.1 times. Its share in the city's export rose from 34.5 percent to 53.2 percent. The structure of the city's export gained further improvement. The export of electro - machinery reached 1.484 billion US dollars and that was a growth of 79.9 percent.

Foreign economic and technical cooperation and international tourism continued to develop. In 1996, 1,320 new contracts of contracted construction project and labor service collaboration were signed, and the amount involved in these contracts reached 158 million US dollars. The actual turnover was 88.09 million US dollars.

International and domestic tourism developed in a faster pace. In 1996, international tourists received were 233,300, up by 16.3 percent over 1995. Of which, 200,200 were foreigners, up by 23 percent. The foreign exchange income of international tourism was 152 million US dollars, up by 14.4 percent. During the year the city received 24.5273 million domestic tourists and the income from domestic tourism was19.965 billion yuan.

Domestic regional economic cooperation made big strides in 1996. By end of the year there were already 1,404 offices set up in Tianjin by various regions and branches across the country. Agreement of 11,815 economic and technical association and cooperation projects were signed during the year. They brought to Tianjin agreed investment from other parts of the country amounted to 5.139 billion yuan and was a 25.8 percent increase from the previous year. The actual use of domestic capital was 3.215 billion yuan and increased 42.3 percent over 1995.

Ⅴ. Transportation and Post – Telecommunications

In 1996 the valued added of the city's transportation and post – telecommunications was 10.732 billion yuan, up by 14.7 percent over the previous year. The following shows the performance of various means of transportation:

	UNIT	1996	INCREASE FROM 1995 (%)
Volume of cargo shipped	10,000 tons	28,246.5	-0.6
# Tianjin area railway	ditto	23,381.4	-0.5
Of which: Railway	ditto	7,539.6	-1.3
# Tianjin area railway	ditto	2,674.5	-1.8
Highway	ditto	19,491.0	0.9
Waterway	ditto	1,205.2	-16.9
Airway	ditto	10.7	1.2time more
Volume of freight transport	100 million ton/km	1,472.8	-22.8
# Tianjin area railway	ditto	984.2	-29.6
Of which: Railway	ditto	712.1	-3.6
# Tianjin area railway	ditto	223.7	-2.7
Highway	ditto	41.2	0.2
Waterway	ditto	719.5	-36.2
Volume of passengers transported	10,000 man/time	4,469.5	-7.8
# Tianjin area railway	ditto	3,114.0	-5.7
Of which: Railway	ditto	2,929.1	-12.5
# Tianjin area railway	ditto	1,573.6	-12.6
Highway (Long Distance)	ditto	1,496.0	2.2
Airway	ditto	44.4	18.7

Cargo handled at sea port	10,000 tons	6,188.3	6.9
of which: Export	ditto	4,839.1	6.3
Import	ditto	1,349.2	1 time more
Cargo handled at airport	ditto	11.7	105.3
Passengers handled at airport	10,000 man/time	88.8	17.3

Post and telecommunications progressed rapidly. Total turnover of post and telecommunications in 1996 was 2.568 billion yuan, increased by 37.2 percent as compared to the previous year. By end of 1996 the capacity of programme controlled telephone exchanges reached 1.69 million gates, of which 190,000 gates were added during the year. The number of telephone subscribers reached 1.7465 million, up by 28.8 percent over the previous year. Every one hundred residents owned 19.4 telephone sets and that is 4.2 telephones more than 1995. Of which, popularization of telephones in the urban area has reached 32.8 per hundred.

Ⅵ. Finance and Insurance

Finance and insurance business saw rapid development notably. 224 new financial institutions were set up in 1996 and that made the total of Tianjin's financial institutions 2,557. Of which, 25 were foreign banking and insurance institutions. In 1996, the city's value added in the fields of finance and insurance was 10.7 billion yuan, up by 25.1 percent over the previous year. The financial market developed rather fast. The sum of securities market transactions reached 7.98 billion yuan and the growth was 4.19 times over 1995. The total of swapped foreign currency was 2.227 billion US dollars.

The financial situation kept stable. By end of 1996, savings in various forms in the financial institutions totaled 139.162 billion yuan, increased 31.386 billion yuan over the beginning of the year. Net loans were 132.549 billion yuan, increased 21.152 billion yuan over the beginning of the year. The increase of the savings was 10.234 billion yuan more than the increase of loans. Cash revenue of all banks in the city for 1996 was 169.642 billion yuan, up by 32 percent over the previous year. Cash payment was 170.467 billion yuan, up by 33.7 percent. The net placement of currency was 0.825 billion yuan.

The development of insurance business accelerated. The total insured amount was 255.501 billion yuan in 1996 and the premium received was 1.741 billion yuan, up by 40.7 percent over 1995. Of which, the income of property insurance premium was 1.081 billion yuan and the increase was 17.8 percent; income of personal insurance premium was 660 million yuan and the increase was 1.1 time more.

Ⅶ. Urban Utilities and Realty Business

In 1996 the industry of urban utilities achieved new progress and the city's function of a carrier continued to upgrade. By end of 1996, the city has 3,165 kms of paved ways that covered 34.83 million square meters of space. The operating bus and trolley lines reached 257 and that was 30 lines more than the previous year. The total length of the operating lines was 5,848 kilometers, up by 13.1 percent. By the year's end the rate of gasification of fuel gas for urban households reached 92.8 percent. The space of urban residential housing warmed up by central heating reached 18.06 million square meters and the rate was 29.7 percent. By the year's end the per capita public green-land of the urban districts was 3.41 square meters. The rate of green coverage of the newly constructed area was 19.3 percent. They were up 0.21 square meters and 1.6 percentage points over the previous year respectively.

The realty business developed in a steady pace. In 1996, the value added of Tianjin's real estate was 2.244 billion yuan, up by 4 percent over 1995. The investment of real estate development was 7.148 billion yuan, up by 2.9 percent over 1995. Of which, investment of residential housing was 4.301 billion yuan, decreased by 3.1 percent. The residential space that completed construction was 3.62 million square meters, up by 13.1 percent, and in which the completed space of reconstruction of one – storied houses was 2.89 million square meters.

Ⅷ. Science – Technology and Environment Protection

Scientific research was fruitful. In 1996, 936 items of research results of science and technology were registered in Tianjin. Of which, 40 items were in the lead internationally and 107 items reached advanced international level. The application of scientific results was enhanced. During the year, 5 projects received State Invention Award, 11 projects State Scientific Progress Award. 6 key laboratories completed construction. To facilitate the informationization of the national economy, the construction of Tianjin "information harbor" was launched.

In 1996, 1,743 items applied for patent in Tianjin and 899 patents were approved. By end of 1996, 14,487 items in aggregate had applied for patent in Tianjin, and 8,194 items had been patented.

The transactions of the technological market were vigorous. In 1996, 8,348 technological contracts were signed, involving 1.335 billion yuan and that was up 10.1 percent over the previous year.

The Hi – tech Industry Park developed rapidly. 516 new enterprises were established in 1996. By end of the year there were already 2,752 enterprises in aggregate employing 44,928 employees. The total income of technology industry and trade for 1996 was 9.13 billion yuan, up by 36.1 percent over 1995. The total value of production was 8.96 billion yuan, up by 45.9 percent. Tax – profit was 1 billion yuan, up by 37 percent.

The cause of environment protection made new progress. In 1996, there set up 20 environment monitoring stations, 5 natural protection areas, and 55 smoke and dust control areas. The space of smoke and dust control areas reached 487 square kilometers and in which 209.43 square kilometers were in the urban districts.

Ⅸ. Education, Culture, Public Health and Sports

Education developed all roundly in all levels and all categories. By end of 1996, there were 20 regular higher education institutions which enrolled 71,400 and graduated 18,400 students. Students working for doctoral and master degrees were 1,119 and 5,159 respectively. 239doctoral degrees and 1,517 master degrees were conferred. There were 44institutions for adult higher education that enrolled 62,000 students and graduated 16,600. There were 78 regular specialized secondary schools that enrolled 67,000 students and graduated 13,300. The work of getting Nankai University, Tianjin University and Tianjin Medical University into the State's "211 Engineering Project" progressed successfully.

The popularization of Nine-Year Obligatory Education witnessed further development. There were 734 ordinary secondary schools and that was 18 more than the previous year. These schools enrolled 493,600 students and graduated 120,700. There were 3,027 primary schools and 189 less than the previous year. They enrolled 879,800 pupils while graduated 145,700. 97 percent of the primary school graduates entered secondary schools. The condition for running primary and secondary schools continued to improve.

Cultural and art undertakings prospered healthily. By end of 1996, there were 18 art-performing groups, 19 cultural centers, 14 museums, 31public libraries, and 127 cinemas, theatres, public auditoriums and clubs. The total publication of periodicals for 1996 was 46.865 million copies, and the total newspaper publication was 539.32 million copies. 89.171 million copies of books were published. Tianjin won all five of the "5-1 Engineering Projects" three years in a row.

Conditions for medical care and public health further improved By end of 1996, the city had 4,171 medical care and public health facilities, and of which 245 were hospitals. By end of the year the hospitals had 35,975 sick beds, There were 71,014 technical personnel for health care and of which 32,975 were doctors.

The situation of the cause of sports was good. Tianjin was successfully appointed as the site of the 35th World Championship of Gymnastics. In important national contests Tianjin won 8 gold medals. 18 silver medals and 14 bronze medals. The project of National Physical Exercises continued to develop vigorously.

Ⅹ. Investment in Fixed Assets

The city completed investment in fixed assets 43.53 billion yuan, up by 10.7 percent over the previous year. Of which, total local investment was 32.52 billion yuan, up by 5 percent. The total investment by state-owned outfits was 35.851 billion yuan, up by 7.6 percent, investment by collective-owned outfits was 5.93 billion yuan, up by 19.3 percent. The personal investment in urban and rural areas was 1.75billion yuan, up by 69.9 percent over 1995.

The structure of investment underwent further readjustment. Investment in tertiary industry was 16.3 billion yuan, up by 14.4percent. Investment in industry was intensified. In 1996, state-owned industry invested 19.346 billion yuan, up by 4.1 percent over the previous year. Of which, investment in basic materials and energy industries like petroleum and electric power was 10.793 billion yuan and that covered 55.8 percent of the total industrial investment. The pace of industrial technical renovation quickened. The 1996 investment for the technical renovation of local industry was 4.96 billion yuan, up by 17 percent.

The construction of key projects progressed successfully. 8.99 billion yuan were invested in the city's 55 key construction projects. There were 16 key projects that completed construction and turned over the key. Among them, Jixian Power Plant, Sponge Iron Project of Tianjin Steel Tube Corporation, the rebuilding of Jingang Bridge, PVC Key Renovation Engineering Project of Dagu Chemical Factory, and the expansion project of Nos. 4 and 5 Paper Mills.

Ⅺ. Population, Employment and People's Life

By end of 1996, there were 9.4819 million residents in Tianjin. It was 63,360 more than the previous year, grew by 0.7 percent. Tianjin's birth rate was 10.09 per thousand, mortality was 6.53 per thousand, and the natural growth rate of the population was 3.56 per thousand. By year's end, the registered population was 8.9845 million, which was 37,800 more than the previous year. The family planning work gained positive results.

By end of 1996 the total employed was 2.8205 million. Of which, 1.9422 million were in the state-owned units, 590,000 in collective-owned units, and 288,400 in other units. By year's end, 1.7902 million people had gone to the human resources market and labor market to engage in job selection and negotiation, and 444,200 reached the stage of initial intent.

The income of urban and rural residents continued to increase, and the level of living was further upgraded. The total per capita wage of the employees reached 21.023 billion yuan in 1996, up by 13.8 percent. The city's annual per capita wage was 7,629 yuan, up by 17.4 percent. Eliminating the price factor, the actual increase was 7.7 percent. The annual per capita income for living expenses of urban residents was 5,525.48 yuan, up by 19.4 percent. Eliminating the price factor, the actual growth was 9.5 percent. The annual per capita for expenditure of urban residents was 4,679.61 yuan, up by 15.2 percent. Eliminating the price factor, the actual increase was 5.7 percent. The net annual per capita income of rural residents was 3,142 yuan, up by 611 yuan or 24.1 percent. The per capita annual expenditure was 2,100 yuan, up by 22.3percent.

The savings of the urban and rural residents grew in large scale. By end of 1996, their savings reached 72.4 billion yuan, or 17.381 billion yuan more than the beginning of the year. Of which, 61.534billion yuan were savings of urban and township residents which increased 15.502 billion yuan from the beginning of the year. 10.866 billion yuan belonged to the rural residents which increased 1.879 billion as compared to the beginning of the year.

The housing conditions of urban and rural residents made further improvements. By end of 1996, per capita housing space in the urban area reached 7.74 square meters, up by 0.22 square meter. In the rural area it was 21.83 square meters, and up by 2.37 square meters.

The cause of social welfare made further developments. In 1996, there were 7,742 beds in welfare institutions of civil affairs and they accommodated 5,323 people. 184,400 men/times were benefited from relief work. There 1,737 community service facilities across the city. The rate of coverage of rural social protection network was 27 percent. The 20 realistic items the municipal government promised to do for the city's urban and rural residents were all fulfilled.

Notes:

1. Value added is the value of end - use product or labor produced and provided by enterprises, facilities, administrative units and individual entrepreneurs of all sectors of national economy during a certain period of time.
2. Gross Domestic Production (GDP) means the value of end - use products and labor produced and provided by a country (or region) during a certain period of time, in other words, the sum of the value added of all sectors of national economy.
3. Gross Domestic Production and value added are calculated according to the price of the year, and the speeds of growth are calculated by comparable prices.
4. All statistical data for 1996 are not final.

(Published on Tianjin's Daily April 5, 1997)

十四大以来天津市经济和社会发展成就

ACHIEVEMENT OF TIANJIN ECONOMIC AND SOCIAL DEVELOPMENT SINCE THE 14TH NATIONAL CONGRESS OF C.P.C

1992－1996 年累计完成国内生产总值 3 694.99 亿元

1992－1996 年累计完成全社会固定资产投资 1 541.41 亿元　年均增长 30.6%

1996 年城市居民人均生活费收入达到 5 525 元

国内生产总值（亿元）

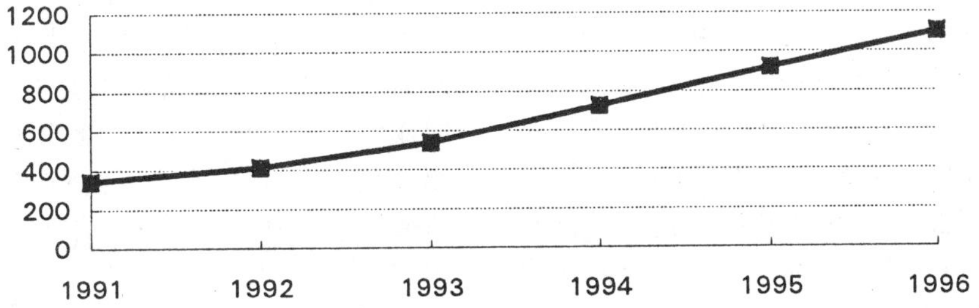

全社会固定资产投资（亿元）

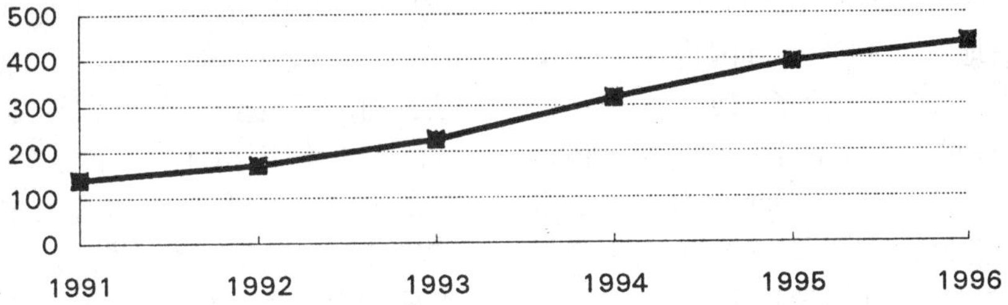

城市居民人均生活费收入（元）

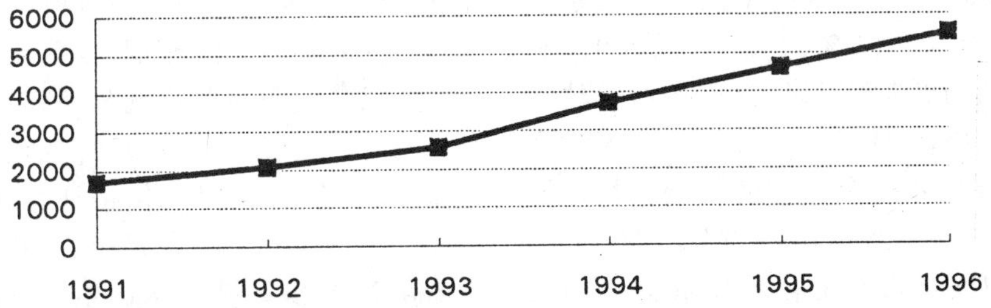

奋进辉煌的五年

——十四大以来天津市经济和社会发展成就

党的十四大以来，1992至1996年的5年间，天津人民在市委、市政府正确领导下，认真贯彻党的十四大和邓小平同志南巡讲话精神，抓住难得的历史机遇，动员和依靠全市人民，深化改革，扩大开放，艰苦拼搏，开拓进取，国民经济和社会各项事业跃上新的台阶，使天津步入全国经济发展较快地区行列，为实现“九五”计划和跨世纪的宏伟目标奠定了坚实的基础。

一、“三、五、八、十”四项奋斗目标取得突破性进展

1994年市第十二届人代会第二次会议提出天津市“三、五、八、十”奋斗目标，即：到1997年提前3年实现国内生产总值比1980年翻两番；用5至7年时间基本完成市区成片危陋平房改造任务；用8年的时间将国有大中型企业嫁接、调整、改造一遍；用10年左右的时间基本建成滨海新区。全市各部门为实现这一目标，齐心协力，取得了突破性进展。

国内生产总值提前4年翻两番，步入全国经济发展较快地区行列。全市国内生产总值由1991年的342.75亿元增加到1996年的1 102.4亿元，按可比价格计算，平均每年递增13.4%，提前4年实现了比1980年翻两番的目标。综合经济实力显著增强，人均国内生产总值由1991年的3 943元迅速提高到1996年的12 270元。5年来，天津经济发展的一个显著特点是，经济总量连续5年保持两位数增长速度。1992－1996年全市国内生产总值分别比上年增长11.7%、12.1%、14.3%、14.9%和14.3%；特别是1994年以来，国内生产总值连续3年超过全国平均增长水平，增长幅度都在14%以上，天津已步入全国经济发展较快地区行列，1996年增幅曾居全国各省(市、区)的第二位。根据中国城市经济社会发展评价中心评定，天津社会经济发展综合水平在全国30个省、市、自治区中多年来保持名列第三位。

重点建设步伐加快，危陋房屋改造取得突破性进展。1992至1996年5年间，是天津历史上固定资产投资最多的时期。5年间全市全社会固定资产投资累计完成1 541.41亿元，平均每年308.28亿元，年均递增30.6%。5年来多渠道筹集建设资金，先后建成和投产了15万辆微型汽车、55万吨无缝钢管、14万吨乙烯等一大批在全国有影响的重点大项目，为天津经济发展增添了后劲。与此同时，用5至7年时间基本完成市区成片危陋平房改造工程，带动了全市房地产、住宅和城市建设的全面发展。5年间全市住宅建设累计投资214.62亿元，住宅竣工面积累计达1 898万平米，年均递增70%。危陋平房改造取得突破性进展，已经完成或大部分完成了土城、谦德庄、中山门、王串场、万德庄、丁字沽等一批难点大片危陋平房改造地段。1992至1996年间，全市累计新增固定资产达到1 106.8亿元，年均递增39%，强有力地支撑了天津经济的持续、快速发展。

国有企业改革逐步深入，嫁接改造调整步伐加快。5年来，现代企业制度试点累计达到214户，组建了168个股份有限公司和有限责任公司。通过多元投资等形式，使国有工业企业资产负债率由1994年的79%下降到1996年的70%。工业系统国有大中型企业嫁接改造累计达195户，使一批老企业焕发了生机。发展壮大了夏利轿车、无缝钢管、冰箱压缩机、电梯、摩托车、摩托罗拉通讯电子设备、皮质激素等一大批新的名牌拳头产品，畅销国内外市场，增强了天津产品的辐射功能。

滨海新区迅速崛起，成为全市经济最大的增长点。滨海新区自规划建设以来，一直保持了强劲的发展势头，1996年实现国内生产总值320.29亿元，按可比价格计算比1993年增长1.1倍，平均每年递增27.8%，比全市平均增幅提高1倍，滨海新区国内生产总值占全市的比重由1993年的21%上升到1996年的29.1%，对全市经济增长的贡献率由1994年的29.8%提高到43.2%。外向型经济发展迅速，1996年滨海新区外贸出口17.46亿美元，占全市外贸出口的比重达到43.1%，比1994年增长2倍，平均每年递增72%；1996年滨海新区协议利用外资18.67亿美元，占全市协议外资的47.6%。5年来的新区建设不仅为10年建成滨海新区打下良好的基础，而且已成为带动全市经济发展的龙头地带。

二、经济结构进一步得到调整，新的经济发展格局正在形成

5年来，全市在加快经济发展的同时，加大了经济结构调整的力度，并取得积极进展。

三次产业结构发生明显变化。5年来，在第一产业稳步增长、第二产业不断调整优化的同时，第三产业发展明显加快，第三产业占全市国内生产总值的比重由1991年的34.8%上升到1996年的40.6%。三次产业比例由1991年的8.5:56.7:34.8，变化为1996年的6.4:53.0:40.6。

农村经济结构形成了农、林、牧、副、渔全面发展，农、工、建、交、商共同繁荣的局面。乡镇企业二次创业再创佳绩，成为农村经济的主体。非农业产值占农村全社会总产值的比重由1991年的81.9%提高到1996年的89.9%。

工业经济结构进一步得到调整。一是工业结构向重工业倾斜，轻重工业比重由1991年的49.9:50.1，1996年变化为43.1:56.9。二是“三资”工业超过国有工业成为天津市工业（乡以上）最大的主力，1996年全市国有工业和“三资”工业总产值所占比重分别由1991年的72.8%和5.7%变化为30.8%和45.8%。三是经过对大中型工业企业嫁接、改造与调整，天津工业逐步形成了具备一定规模优势的四大支柱产业和一大批名牌拳头产品。1996年，四大支柱产业产值占全市乡以上工业总产值的比重由1991年的42.3%提高到52.7%。

三、对外开放水平明显提高，为天津经济发展焕发了勃勃生机

5年来，天津市把进一步扩大对外开放、提高对外开放的层次和水平，作为加快全市经济发展的重要举措，利用外资步伐明显加快。这5年是天津市历史上利用外资最多，来津落户的国际知名大公司、大财团最多，利用外资的大项目和现有企业增资最多的时期。1992至1996五年累计有176家国际跨国公司、知名大企业来津落户，连续几年利用外资增长幅度居全国前列。

1992－1996年累计签订“三资”企业项目达9 606个，协议直接利用外资147.52亿美元，实际利用外资达到53.14亿美元，分别占历年累计的91.5%、94.4%和92.3%。以开发区、保税区、新技术产业园区和12个区县开发小区为骨架的多领域、多层次、全方位对外开放格局已经形成。

开发区主要经济指标继续在全国保持领先地位。截至1996年，共签约“三资”企业项目2 744家，协议利用外资60.25亿美元。1996年实现外贸出口14.5亿美元，占全市外贸出口的比重由1991年的7.1%提高到35.8%。

保税区发展势头强劲。截至1996年，保税区已批准“三资”企业2 773家，协议外资达到17.4亿美元。1996年保税区进出区货物总值27.01亿美元，比去年同期增长1.1倍。

对外贸易发展迅速。1996年口岸进出口总值达216.85亿美元，比1991年增长1.37倍，年均递增18.9%。1992至1996年5年间天津外贸出口总值累计达到131.42亿美元，相当于“七五”时期实现外贸出口总值的1.7倍，平均每年递增20.3%。“三资”企业外贸出口已占全市外贸出口的半壁江山，1996年“三资”企业外贸出口21.52亿美元，占全市外贸出口总值的比重由1991年的7.5%提高到53.1%。

四、市场体系建设取得重大突破，商贸中心功能不断增强

党的十四大以来，随着社会主义市场经济的发展，天津市市场体系建设取得了重大进展，各类要素市场建设全面发展，形成了一批在北方地区和全国都有一定名气和影响的生产资料和商品批发交易市场。到1996年已初步形成了以14个国家级市场为龙头，22个区域级市场为骨干，602多个初级市场为基础的比较完善的市场体系，大型商贸活动成交活跃。1996年全市主要商品批发市场商品成交总额4 071.16亿元。

零售市场繁荣活跃。5年来，天津市零售

市场商品货源充裕，消费者购买踊跃，新建和改扩建了永基商城、吉利大厦、滨江商厦、劝业新厦、世界商厦等一批大型商场，营业面积超过1万平米的零售商场达到6家，购物环境明显改善。社会消费品零售总额由1991年的159.44亿元，增加到1996年的470.04亿元，5年平均每年递增42.9%，是历史上增长最快的时期。

五、国民经济运行实现"高增长、低通胀"，改革和发展取得丰硕成果

1992－1996年天津经济是在国家加强宏观调控、实现国民经济"软着陆"的大背景下运行的，全市各部门在市委、市政府领导下，坚持加大改革开放力度与促进经济结构调整并举，加强宏观调控与保持经济快速、健康发展并举，努力扩大经济总量与注意提高经济运行质量并举，保证了国民经济的持续、快速、健康发展，成为全国经济发展中实现"高增长、低通胀"的典范，实现了在经济发展的基础上"企业多留、财政多收、职工多得"的目标。

宏观调控取得积极成效，物价水平在全国保持较低水平。5年来，市委、市政府一贯坚持把稳定物价作为全市经济发展和宏观调控的首要目标，运用市场与计划相结合的多种经济手段，整顿流通领域秩序，丰富市场供应，使天津市的物价水平一直处于全国较低水平，提高了经济运行的质量。1996年城市商品零售价格总指数由历史最高的1994年115.6%回落到105.1%，回落了10.5个百分点；城市居民消费价格指数由1994年的124.0%回落到109.0%，回落了15个百分点。

企业经济效益改善。1996年全市乡以上独立核算工业实现销售收入1 498.67亿元，比1991年增长1.8倍，年均递增22.7%；实现利税总额139.73亿元，增长1.7倍，年均递增21.6%，其中实现税金72.14亿元、增长1.2倍、年均增长17.4%，实现利润67.6亿元、增长2.3倍、年均增长27.2%。

财政体制改革进展顺利，财政收入在国民经济持续、快速、健康发展的基础上大幅度增长。1992－1996年5年累计完成地方预算内财政收入329.11亿元，是"七五"时期的1.34倍。

金融保险业迅速发展。到1996年末，全市共有各类金融机构达2 578家，其中外资银行在津分行12家；全市金融机构各项存款余额1 391.62亿元，比1991年增加1 055.06亿元，5年增长3.1倍；各项贷款余额1 325.49亿元，比1991年增加838.06亿元，增长1.7倍。保险业发展加快，1996年全市保险业承保总额2 488.21亿元，保费收入17.18亿元。

城乡居民收入大幅度提高，生活水平进一步得到改善。随着经济发展加快，城乡居民收入大幅度增加，全市职工年平均工资由1991年的2 724元增加到1996年的7 643元，扣除价格因素年均增长7.6%；城市居民人均生活费收入由1991年的1 698.67元增加到5 525元，扣除价格因素实际平均每年增长11.3%，明显高于"七五"时期3.6%的速度；农民人均纯收入由1991年的1 169元，增加到1996年的3 142元，增长1.7倍，年均增长22%。城镇居民人均居住面积由1991年的6.80平方米增加到1996年的7.7平方米。

六、"科教兴市"战略成效显著，社会各项事业全面进步

科学研究取得丰硕成果。1992－1996年5年累计完成重大科学技术研究成果3 124项，其中获国家发明奖32项，国家科技进步奖77项。全市5年累计申请专利8 549项，批准授权5 592项。"信息港"工程开始启动。

教育事业蓬勃发展。1996年末全市有高等教育院校20所，在校本专科学生7.14万人，比1991年增长43%；在学硕士、博士研究生分别为5 159人和1 119人，分别是1991年的1.77倍和2.67倍；成人高校44所，在校学生6.3万人；普通中专78所，在校学生6.7万人；南开大学、天津大学和天津医科大学进入国家"211工程"进展顺利。

卫生、广播、体育事业全面发展。医疗卫生条件进一步改善，1996年末全市共有医疗卫生机构4 171个，其中各级医院476个；医院拥有病床3.6万张；全市拥有专业卫生技术人员7.1万人，其中医生3.8万人。广播电视塔的建成使发射机功率提高一倍，电视节目套数由

4 套增加到 11 套，电视覆盖率由 1991 年的 89％提高到 1996 年的 95％。1996 年末全市共有体育场地 4 721 个，天津体育馆的建成和第 43 届世乒赛在天津成功举办，中国首届京剧艺术节取得圆满成功，大大提高了天津的知名度，取得了良好的社会效益。

精神文明建设成果喜人。“五个一工程”连续三年满堂红，和平区社区精神文明建设成为全国典型，公安消防、武警、工商等战线涌现出一批全国先进集体和个人，6 个区县获得全国双拥模范称号，社会治安继续保持全国最好地区之一。

综上所述，党的十四大以来，全市经济和社会发展取得了辉煌成就。目前，天津面临着良好的环境和机遇，只要我们充分利用和发挥已有的基础和优势，抓住机遇，同心同德，艰苦奋斗，深化国有企业改革，努力提高经济运行质量，进一步调整和优化经济结构，“九五”时期后四年天津经济和社会各项事业将会继续保持快速、健康的发展势头。一个北方商贸金融中心，技术先进的综合性工业基地和全方位开放的现代化国际港口大城市——21 世纪的新天津，将以崭新的姿态屹立在人们面前。

（杜　威）

快速发展的天津工业

党的十四大以来，天津市工业各系统在市委、市政府的领导下，认真贯彻邓小平同志南巡讲话精神，解放思想，大胆实践，以市场为导向，深化国有企业改革，优化资源配置，加大结构调整力度，使天津工业经济的发展迈上了新台阶。

工业经济快速发展，工业实力进一步增强。1992 年以来，天津工业经济总体规模显著扩大，发展水平明显提高。到 1996 年末，全市街乡及以上工业企业有11 073个，比 1991 年增加 4 254 个；工业总产值为1 354.50亿元，比 1991 年增长 1.6 倍，年均递增20.6％，比“七五”时期加快 14.3 个百分点。

主要经济效益指标大幅度增长。1996 年，全市乡及乡以上独立核算工业增加值为 347.56亿元，按可比价格计算，比 1991 年增长 92.9％，年均递增 14.0％；工业企业销售收入 1 498.67亿元，比 1991 年增长 1.8 倍，年均递增22.7％；实现利税总额139.73亿元，增长1.7 倍，年均递增 21.6％，其中实现税金72.14亿元，增长1.2倍，年均递增 17.4％；实现利润 67.60亿元，增长 2.3 倍，年均递增 27.2％。

大中型工业企业发展加快。1996 年，天津市拥有大中型工业企业 737 个，比 1991 年增加 243 个。大中型工业企业拥有资产总额 1 770.08亿元，比 1991 年增加 4.5 倍，年均递增40.5％；销售收入 1 053.05 亿元，增长1.7 倍，年均递增 22.3％，利税总额 106.07 亿元，增长 1.7 倍，年均递增 22.1％。大中型企业在全市工业经济中占主导地位。1996 年大中型企业占全部工业企业的比重：资产总额为 73.7％，增加值为 73.1％，销售收入为 70.3％，利税总额为75.9％。

主要工业产品产量明显增加，名牌拳头产品迅速崛起。近年来，面对日益激烈的市场竞争，市委、市政府下大力量培育、扶持名牌、骨干拳头产品，并制定了一系列的发展战略、方针和政策，如实施了“八年内把国有大中型企业嫁接、改造、调整一遍”，“二二二工程”，“扶强扶优”以及对国际名牌企业优惠招商、合资等重要举措，收到了显著的效果。近几年，一大批名牌拳头产品如夏利、华利汽车、康师傅方便面、奥的斯电梯、石油套管、NEC 程控交换机、王朝葡萄酒、摩托罗拉通讯设备、雅马哈电子琴、梅兰日兰断路器、环球磁卡、虹志电脑、轮式拖拉机等迅速崛起，并在国内、国际市场占有了一席之地。

经过 5 年的发展，天津市主要工业产品生产能力明显提高，产量大幅度增加。1996 年天津市基础原材料产品钢、钢材、生铁、发电量、原油、天然气等产量分别比 1991 年增长11.1％至 1.2 倍；彩电、家用洗衣机、服装、机制纸及纸板等轻纺产品产量分别增长 57.6％至99.3％；汽车产量完成 15.32 万辆，比 1991 年增长2.4 倍，其中夏利轿车完成 8.78 万辆，比 1991 年增长 6.8 倍；一些高科技产品从无到有，迅速成长壮大，填补了天津市工业的空白，如程控交换机1996年产量达113.14万门,录像机产量达60.02万台。

工业经济结构继续得到调整,经济格局趋于多元化。近年来,天津市加大"招商引资"的力度,多渠道、全方位的吸引外资,随着"三资"工业和乡镇工业的迅猛发展,工业所有制结构呈现出多种经济成份并存,竞相发展的格局。非国有工业特别是"三资"工业在全市工业经济中所占份额显著上升,国有工业比重相对下降。1996年在全市工业总产值中,国有经济占30.8%,集体经济占18.7%,分别比1992年降低41.1和0.3个百分点;1996年"三资"工业占45.8%,在全市工业经济中所占份额上升了40.4个百分点,经过近几年的发展,"三资"工业已经成为天津市工业经济增长与效益增长的主要支撑点。

优化资源配置,产业结构调整效果显著。1992年至1996年,全市工业坚持以市场为导向,发挥天津工业的整体优势,优化资源配置,重点发展了以乙烯、聚脂、蛋氨酸"三大化"为重点的化工工业;以无缝钢管、高速线材、冷轧薄板、钢丝绳为重点的冶金工业;以汽车、摩托车、数控机床为重点的机械装备产业和以程控交换机、录像机、通讯设备为重点的电子新技术工业,以带动天津市工业结构的优化。1996年,天津市四大支柱产业总产值完成714.15亿元,比1991年增长1.8倍,年均递增22.6%,占全市乡以上工业总产值的比重由1991年的42.3%提高到1996年的52.7%,提高了10.4个百分点。

为适应市场及国家产业政策要求,全市工业结构继续向重工业倾斜。1996年,轻工业资产总额占全市工业的35.5%,比1991年降低7.3个百分点;重工业资产总额占64.5%,比1991年提高了7.3个百分点。总产值占全市工业中的比重,1996年轻工业为43.1%,重工业为56.9%。

1992-1996年5年间,天津工业克服资金紧张、历史包袱沉重等困难,在激烈的市场竞争中,开拓进取,工业生产持续增长,经济效益有所提高,产业和产品结构得到进一步调整,四大支柱工业初步形成,为把天津建设成为技术先进的综合性工业基地迈出了坚实的步伐。

(王　勇)

农村经济再上新台阶

党的十四大以来,随着国民经济发展的进一步加快,天津市农村经济的发展,进入了改革开放以来的第二个较快发展时期。

粮食产量迈上了新台阶;新一轮"菜篮子工程"的实施,为繁荣市场和社会的稳定做出了贡献;乡镇企业开始了"二次创业"的历程,继续成为农村经济乃至全市经济的新增长点。在生产发展的基础上,农民收入增加,生活水平和质量进一步提高,截止1996年底,全市已有90%以上的村成为小康村,其中小康明星村72个,小康乡镇19个,充分显示了全市农村经济实力显著增强。农村经济持续稳步发展。1996年第一产业增加值达到70.53亿元,按可比价格计算,比1991年增加了43.1%,五年间平均每年增加7.4%。

1996年农村社会总产值达到1 410亿元,较1991年的322亿元,增加1 088亿元。按可比口径计算,增长1.5倍。平均每年递增20.1%。农村经济结构得到调整,高效型农业发展迅速。随着天津市农村经济全面发展和结构调整,非农产值占全部产值的比重,由1991年的81.9%,1996年上升到89.9%。非农产业成为天津市农村经济的支柱产业。

农业经济继续向"两高一优"效益型转变。尤其是效益较高、市场需求较大的畜牧业生产得到了较快发展,其产值占农业总产值的比重由1991年的28.1%提高到33.5%,种植业产值比重下降了6.0个百分点。

农业基础地位进一步加强,有效供给水平逐年提高。按照市委、市政府提出的"服务城市,富裕农民"的农村工作思路,全市农产品产量,尤其是肉、蛋、奶、菜、鱼等副食品产量大幅度增加,绝大部分农副产品实现了自给有余。

粮食生产在耕地减少,自然灾害频繁的情况下,一靠科技,二靠投入,合理调整种植结构,从1991年至1996年的五年中,有两年跨上了20亿公斤的新台阶。1995年获得了历史最高水平,达到 20.75 亿公斤。1996 年,大灾之年仍获得较好的收成,比 1991 年 19.8 亿公斤增产 4.5%。5 年累计生产粮食达 100.7 亿公斤,平均每年 20.1 亿公斤。为 2000 年全市粮食产量达到 22.5 亿公斤的目标奠定了基础。

全市菜蓝子工程进一步发展。1996 年肉类总产量达到 22.68 万吨,比 1991 年的 13.05 万吨增长了73.1%;禽蛋产量达到 24.44 万吨,增加 3.1 万吨,增长 14.2%;奶类产量达到 11.33万吨,增长了28.9%;蔬菜总产量达到 452.7万吨,比 1991 年的282.6万吨增长了 60.2%;水产品产量达到16万吨,较 1991 年增长了48.1%。

农业产品商品率稳步提高。商品率由 1991 年的 71.6%提高到 79.2%。尤其是畜牧业产品商品率 1996 年达到 93.3%,与 1991 年相比又提高了 8.0 个百分点。市场供给水平进一步提高。

乡镇企业成为全市经济的新的增长点。近年来乡镇企业克服了市场销售不畅,效益有所下降等不利条件,在"二次创业"活动中,针对市场需求积极调整生产结构和产品结构,挖潜增效,继续为农村经济的发展起保驾作用。截止 1996 年底,全市共有乡镇企业 9.6 万家,从业人员达到 113.7 万人。占全市农村劳动力总数的 68.9%。与 1991 年相比,分别增加 5.6 万家和 19.0 万人。

1996 年全市乡镇企业实现销售收入 1 150 亿元,创利税 137.5 亿元,出口交货值 142 亿元,实现增加值 243.1 亿元。与 1991 年相比,销售收入增加了 5 倍,利税总额增长了 4.6 倍,出口交货值增长了 4.3 倍。全市乡镇企业固定资产原值 1991 年为 58.4 亿元,1996 年超过 200 亿元。

继 1993 年静海县乡镇企业产值超过 100 亿元之后,西青区、武清县、津南区、宝坻县先后登上了超百亿元台阶。乡镇工业是天津市乡镇企业的主导产业,其产值占全市工业总产值的比重,1996 年已经接近 50%,出口交货值比重已经超过 50%。乡镇工业生产已经撑起全市工业生产的半边天,并成为全市经济发展的新的增长点。

农村经济发展速度与效益同步增长。1992- 1996 年农村经济逐步向效益型转变,"两高一优"农业迈出了新的步伐。1996 年全市农村经济总收入达到 985.3 亿元,比 1991 年的 219.9 亿元增长了 3.5 倍,年递增 35.1%。

农村经济纯收入达到 171.6 亿元,增加 109.1 亿元,增加 1.70 倍。农业劳动生产率逐年提高。1996 年每一劳动者创造的农业总产值达到 4 680 元,较 1991 年的 3 395 元,增长 37.8%,年平均递增 7%。1996 年每亩耕地创造农业产值 0.22 万元,比 1991 年的 0.1 万元增长 1.1 倍。

随着农村经济的增长,农民收入大幅度增加。全市农民纯收入在 1991 年人均 1 169 元的基础上,1996 年达到 3 142 元。五年间增长 1.7 倍。年均增加 395 元。其中,1996 年比 1995 年增加额达到 611 元,增加额与增幅为近几年之首。1996 年全市 175 个贫困村,人均纯收入已达 1 550 元,提前一年超额完成人均 1 300元的扶贫攻坚目标。随着农民收入的逐年增加,生活水平明显提高。富裕起来的农民正朝着小康目标迈进。

(殷保军)

面向国内外的天津商业

1992 年党的十四大以来,在市委、市政府正确领导下,全市认真贯彻落实十四大和邓小平南巡讲话精神,根据天津的发展特点,制定了要把天津建成北方商贸金融中心和国际港口大都市的战略目标,进一步加大改革力度,扩大对外开放,加快市场体系建设积极推进两个根本性转变,全市大流通、大贸易、开放型商贸中心的构架已初步形成。

流通领域改革力度加大,各类商业全面发展。近年来,全市流通体制改革进一步深化,企业结构调整步伐加快,转变了营销观念,全市市场机制和企业经营机制改革取得重大突破。一是市场经济类型主体出现了重大变革,打破过去以国有企业为主体的商业经济格局,形成了国有、集体、私营、个体、联营、股份制、外商投资、港澳台投资等多种经济类型并存竞相发展的新格局。非国有商业经济份额呈逐年上升趋势，其发展速度明显快于国有商业经济，1996年与1991年相比，社会消费品零售额增长4.97倍，平均每年递增42.9%，明显快于同时期国有商业年均增长10%的速度。1996年非国有商业经济完成社会消费品零售额占全市社会消费品零售总额的比重已达到62%，在全市商业市场中起着举足轻重的作用。二是转换企业经营机制取得重大突破。新的经营方式极大地焕发了企业活力。租赁经营、承包经营、国有民营、连锁经营、租壳卖瓤、职工自营、资产经营、集团经营、有限责任公司、股份合作等新的经营方式如雨后春笋竞比高低。这类企业截止1996年底已达6 000多家，占全市私营以上贸易企业总数的三分之一以上。全市已初步形成多种经济类型，多种经营方式的贸易企业全面、稳定、竞相发展的可喜局面。

流通环境进一步改善。经过统筹规划，改造调整，一个布局合理，市级商业中心区和准市级商业中心区与居民新区商业网点相互配套的营销网落基本形成，市场载体进一步拓宽。截止1996年末全市批发零售贸易业和餐饮业网点已达18.66万家，比1991年扩充1.1倍，净增9.8万家。经营场地在万米以上的大型购物中心由1991年的7家发展到22家，其中销售额超亿元的大型零售商场18家，比1991年增加11家。天津劝业场经过扩建改造，营销规模进入全国大型零售商场十强之列。

随着流通体制改革和市场体系的不断完善，天津市流通规模不断扩大，商品市场货丰价稳，在津举办的各类大型商品交易会的数量不断增加。据统计，仅1996年，在天津举办的各类展销会、交易会等大型经贸活动达20多次。周边地区人员来津购物、餐饮已成为时尚，对全市国民经济发展起了较大的推动作用。1992年至1996年的五年间是天津市贸易流通历史上整体规模发展最快的时期。1996年全市批发零售贸易业商品购进总额完成980.73亿元，比1991年增长1.4倍，平均年递增19%；商品销售总额完成1 035.88亿元，比1991年增长1.61倍，平均年递增21.1%。贸易流通业增加值由1991年的27.64亿元发展到1996年的98.46亿元，占全市国内生产总值的比重由1991年的8%上升到1996年的8.93%。

基础设施投入不断增加，经济实力不断壮大。近年来全市加大对商业基础设施建设的投入，使商业经济实力不断壮大。1992年至1996年5年间，批发零售贸易业、餐饮业企业累计完成固定资产投资31亿元。一批新建的大型商业设施拔地而起，一些名牌老店经过改造，重新焕发了青春。截止1996年末全市贸易业固定资产原值已达113.30亿元，比1991年增加2.87倍，固定资产净值92亿元，增长3.16倍，固定资产新旧程度为81.2%，比1991年提高5.7个百分点。商业经济实力的壮大，使其在全市社会经济发展中的作用不断增强。吸纳就业人数由1991年42万人增至1996年的59万人，增长40.5%。5年间累计为国家创利税39亿元，相当于同时期固定资产投资的1.26倍，取得了较好的投资效果。

零售市场货丰价稳，购销两旺，保持持续发展的好势头。近几年，天津市消费品市场总供给货源充足，品种丰富。特别是天津市物价调控成效显著，居民消费心理稳定，消费水平明显提高。社会消费品零售总额连续几年保持高速增长的势头。1992至1996年社会消费品零售总额累计实现1 602.4亿元，比“七五”时期增长2.8倍，其中1996年实现的社会消费品零售总额就相当于“七五”时期总和的82.1%。

随着经济的发展和生活水平的提高，居民消费观念不断更新，呈现出新的消费特点。一是消费从量的需求转向质的需求；二是由重物质消费转向物质与精神结合的消费；三是大众同向消费转向多元化消费；四是对新型商品的接受能力和购买能力增强。这些消费观念和行为的变化，使许多新型消费品悄然兴起，骤然热销。

农村市场近几年发展加快，显示出农村市场的巨大潜力。1996年县及县以下消费品零售额实现78.7亿元，比1991年增长5.7倍，平均年递增46.4%，占全市消费品零售总额的比重达 17%，比 1991 年提高 10 个百分点。

1996 年是“九五”计划的第一年，全市贸易业主要指标均实现了“九五”开局高起步，市场全面繁荣稳定。这预示着天津市正以稳健的步伐，大踏步地向建成北方商贸中心的战略目标迈进。

（张俊堂）

方兴未艾的天津商品交易市场

党的十四大以来，在邓小平南巡讲话精神鼓舞下，天津市委、市政府把加快市场建设，培育市场体系作为发展天津经济、实现建成北方商贸金融中心战略目标的重要举措。通过统筹规划，合理布局，积极扶持，规范管理，市场的建设和发展取得了显著成效。

市场规模不断扩大，大型市场发展迅猛。截止 1996 年底，全市城乡各类市场已经发展到 638 个，比 1992 年增加了 219 个。市场结构层次逐步趋于合理，一个以 14 个国家级市场为龙头，22 个区域性市场为骨干，602 个初级市场为基础的多层次、多门类的市场体系初步形成。天津的国家级及区域性批发市场大都是 1992 年以后新建和扩建的。其后，迅速发展壮大，并带动了市场的整体发展，活跃了城乡商贸，促进了全市经济增长。

市场机制不断完善，综合服务功能提高。迅速崛起的大型商品批发市场不同于一般的初级简单交易，国家级生产资料批发市场从建立开始就参照国际惯例，以现代化通讯设备、规范化的交易方式，多功能的综合服务，实现了市场建设的高起步。为物资供销及生产企业开辟了一个公开、公正、公平的交易场所。不同专业的批发市场还建立了大容量、高质量的信息网，指导供销企业的交易行为。例如北洋(天津)钢材批发市场把“全国钢材市场信息”作为产业来发展。“天津纺织原材料市场信息”则是集结了纺织市场等全国各地纺织行情为客户提供服务。吸引了全国各地的企业来津交易。会员单位数也已由 1993 年的 218 家增加到 410 家。

区域性市场更加注重了市场的自身管理和市场服务功能的完善。汽车交易市场是天津市建立较早、发展较快、经营规模较大的专业性市场，通过几年来的发展，已具备了一套严格完整的市场管理体系。消费品批发市场不断扩大经营面积，改善经营环境，为客户提供方便的交易条件。红旗路农贸批发市场、何庄子蔬菜批发市场、大胡同小商品批发市场规模不断扩大，知名度逐年提高。

市场交易方式趋于多样化，期货交易方式向国际化接轨。商品批发市场更新观念，不断改革，在交易方式上进行了大胆的探索和尝试。北洋(天津)批发交易市场、钢铁炉料交易市场、北方食糖批发交易市场相继推出过多种交易方式，如多品种的中远期现货合约，代理合作、销售协议，远程通讯交易以及北洋市场连续 4 年通过市场网络和实物交割网举办的全国钢材交易会等。交易形式的逐步规范和尝试，为天津市期货业的迅速发展打下了基础。天津市唯一的天津联合期货交易所就是由北洋钢材、钢铁炉料、北方食糖三家交易所合并建立，经历了分散、集中统一的过程。各类市场不断总结经验和教训，把规范化运作看成是期货交易存在和发展的基础。现已有比较稳固的期货交易品种，红小豆、铜铝等品种已初具规模。会员结构也已有了很大改变，在 150 家会员单位中，期货经纪公司占 60 多家。期货交易活跃，交易额剧增，1996 年期货交易额达到3 873.53亿元，比 1994 年同期增长 1.6 倍。在全国15家期货交易所中列居第四位。

交易规模大幅度增长，集散辐射作用进一步增强。1996 年全市重点商品批发市场交易额达到 4 071.16 亿元，比 1993 年增长 18 倍。其中化工产品和成品油交易活跃，新旧汽车交易一直保持旺销。由于汽车交易的客户来自全国各地，保证了车源丰富，不仅有各类地产、国产及进口轿车，又有国产、进口各类大中型柴油、汽油等车辆，稳定的供货渠道，使商品经营无淡季。天津的“大发”、“夏利”占总交易量的 70%左右。红旗路、何庄子、赵沽里、金钟路四大蔬菜批发市场日上市蔬菜占全市消费量 50%。红旗路、何庄子两个蔬菜批发市场，业务联系遍及全国 26 个省市、1 500 多个进货基地、上千个专业批发商,批发范围深入东北、西北地区。蔬菜类包括了南北方的大部分莱品,各类果品四季丰盈,水产品更是鲜活诱人。大胡同批发市场的日用品和服装在全国的知名度与日俱增,交易额增幅较大,1996年全年成交17.2亿元,成为全国小商品批发中心。

短短的几年,天津商品批发市场建设从初级走向规范,从单一数量增加向注重提高层次方向发展,在联接生产-流通-消费的中间环节中地位日益显现,其规模的不断发展壮大,必将对天津市建成北方商贸中心起到极大的推动作用。

(林 燕)

广引外资助天津腾飞

党的十四大以来,中国经济发展进入了一个新的历史时期。天津作为环渤海地区港口大都市,改革开放整体格局进一步完善,技术先进的综合性工业基地和商贸金融中心的龙头作用初步形成,利用外资规模扩大,为天津经济腾飞注入了新的生机活力,促进了天津经济持续、快速、健康的发展。

利用外资进入最好的历史发展时期,1992年以来,天津利用外资取得突破性进展,1992年签定直接利用外资项目1 702个,协议外资额12.19亿美元,实际利用外资2.31亿美元,吸引外资规模超过了改革开放前13年的总和,协议外资项目和协议外资额分别比前13年增长89.5%和52.6%,实际利用外资已占前13年实际利用外资额的34.2%,从此天津直接利用外资步入快速增长时期。1992-1996五年间,全市共批准直接利用外资项目9 606个,协议外资额147.5亿美元,实际利用外资53.14亿美元,分别占历年累计的91.5%、94.4%和92.3%,以平均每年25.2%、81.9%和84.4%高速增长。远远高于“七五”时期平均增长水平。同时,三项指标均超过全国平均递增速度11.9个、40个和26.9个百分点,增幅居京、津、沪、穗四市之首。随着天津招商引资力度的加大,在全国的地位也明显上升,利用外资项目、协议外资额和实际利用外资占全国的比重逐年扩大,分别由1991年的2.7%、1.6%和2.2%,上升到1996年的4.5%、5.7%和4.7%。截止1996年底天津已累计批准直接利用外资项目10 497个,协议外资额156.3亿美元,实际利用外资108.87亿美元,其中客商直接投资57.59亿美元。

五年间天津直接利用外资实现了从数量型向质量型的转变,投资总额超过500万美元以上的大项目逐年增多,使全市外商单项投资水平明显提高,由1991年的55.5万美元,上升到1996年的361万美元。

天津已成为国际跨国公司、知名大企业的投资热点地区。1992-1996五年间,共有176家国际跨国公司、知名大企业来津投资,签定项目265个,协议外资额56.38亿美元,如:美国的摩托罗拉公司、瑞士的雀巢公司、英国的英荷壳牌公司、法国的通用电气阿尔斯通股份有限公司、德国的西门子控股公司、日本的丰田、三菱、住友、松下公司、韩国的三星、大宇、金星集团等。一大批技术含量高、资金密集、生产规模大、产品竞争力强的项目带动了天津产业和产品结构的调整,截至1996年底,在津投资的国际跨国公司和知名大企业累计达190多家,签定项目288个,协议外资额57.89亿美元,在目前世界最大的500家企业中,在津投资的有33家,签约项目74个。

由于天津投资环境日益完善,投资回报丰厚,增强了外商投资信心,增资企业逐年增多,1994至1996三年间,共有609家企业追加外资额26.37亿美元,占新批协议外资额的23.4%。

嫁接改造国有老企业成果丰硕。1992-1996五年间,天津工业系统共批准嫁接改造项目450个,协议外资额24.36亿美元。国有老企业通过引进外资,实现资产重组,使老企业焕发出新的生机与活力。如:迅达摩托车厂与日本合资的本田摩托车有限公司,七一二厂与韩国合资的通广三星电子有限公司,合成洗涤剂厂与德国合资的汉高洗涤剂有限公司,海河冰箱压缩机公司与意大利合资的扎努西电气机械压缩机有限公司等嫁改项目都取得了显著的经济和社会效益。这些项目涉及电子、机械、化工、食品等众多行业，对天津产品的升级换代起到了极大的促进作用。截止1996年底，全市工业系统累计批准嫁改项目527个，协议外资额27.18亿美元。

三资企业为天津经济腾飞注入新的活力。随着天津利用外资迅猛发展，开业投产企业迅速扩大。1996年已达到3 377家，比1992年的772家扩大了3.4倍，三资企业主要经济指标占全市的比重逐年扩大。1996年全市三资企业实现增加值146.21亿元，占全市国内生产总值的比重由1992年的0.4%上升到1996年的13.3%，19 96年三资企业实现总产值704.59亿元(现价)，其中，工业总产值699.94亿元，占全市乡以上工业总产值的43.2%，比1992年提高36个百分点。1996年，三资工业企业实现利税总额71.0 9亿元，占全市独立核算工业企业利税总额的51.6%，比1992年提高了50.4个百分点。三资企业固定资产投资完成62.97亿元，占全市固定资产投资的17.4%，比1992年提高16.5个百分点。三资企业出口21.52亿美元，占全市外贸出口总额的53.1%，比1992年提高40个百分点。三资企业已成为天津经济发展中的生力军和新的经济增长点。

外商投资结构进一步优化、第三产业吸引外资迅速扩大。随着国家鼓励外商投资交通、能源、基础设施等行业优惠政策的出台，天津外商投资产业结构日趋优化，特别是天津港保税区的创建，为天津第三产业的发展提供了良好的外部条件。使天津外商投资以工业型项目为主体的格局有所变化，第三产业投资明显加快，1992－1996五年间，共批准第三产业项目4 106个，协议外资额52.19亿美元，分别占五年累计全部项目的比重达42.7%和38.9%，而“七五”时期仅占7.5%和21.6%；分别提高了35.4个和17.3个百分点。房地产业、国际贸易成为外商投资的热点，房地产业的发展，加快了天津危陋平房改造的进程，香港新世界、恒基兆业集团等一批国外的公司财团与天津签定房地产业项目，加速了城区改造和安居工程的实施。

经济技术开发区、保税区和新技术产业园区在全国保持领先地位。天津经济技术开发区已成为中国北方最具吸引力的投资热点地区，截至1996年底，开发区累计批准来自62个国家和地区的外商投资企业2 744家，协议外资额60.25亿美元，外商实际到位资金21.27亿美元。居31个国家级开发区之首。

天津港保税区自1991年建区以来，以优质的服务、良好的区位和特殊的优惠政策吸引了73个国家和地区外商来区投资，协议外资额达20亿美元，以每年成倍的速度增长，6年间累计实现国内生产总值18.3亿元，进出区货物总值达65.4亿美元，进出口19亿美元，税收4.07亿元，1996年与1992年相比，四项指标分别增长237倍、16.5倍、17.3倍和50.4倍。保税区已初步形成面向世界、辐射京、津、华北和西北的国际贸易窗口和国际物流进出基地。

新技术产业园区充分发挥高科技优势，批建了一批技术含量高、市场前景广阔的科技产业项目，累计批准外商投资企业332家，协议外资额16亿美元。全区1996年实现技工贸总收入达96.96亿元，比上年增长44.2%。高科技产品在天津占有重要地位，有4项达到国际领先水平，39项达到国内领先水平。目前已形成了计算机及外部设备、通讯设备、软件技术等十多种系列产品，园区作为天津发展高技术产业基地，位居全国新技术产业园区前列。

(佟承建)

外贸出口连创佳绩

党的十四大明确提出了中国经济体制改革的目标是建立社会主义市场经济体制。在探索建立社会主义市场经济体制的过程中，外贸体制改革逐步深化，天津的外向型经济年年跨上新台阶，对外贸易创历史最高水平，外贸出口加快，规模逐年扩大，出口商品结构、市场结构和经营结构进一步改善。外贸企业集团化、实业化、国际化进程加快。天津对外贸易的快速增长，有力地促进了全市经济的快速健康发展。

外贸体制改革的逐步深化、为对外贸易的发展提供了良好的外部环境。党的十四大以来，中国外贸体制发生了深刻的变化。国家陆续取消了外贸出口的指令性计划,各类外贸企业对取消出口补贴,实行出口退税制已经逐步适应,外贸自负盈亏机制深入人心。取消外汇上缴,实行汇率并轨,不仅促进和保持了人民币汇率的稳定,也极大地调动了外贸企业出口创汇的积极性。1995年《对外贸易法》的颁布和实施,既使对外贸易企业的管理有法可依,又进一步规范了外贸经营秩序,也更加符合国际通行的规则。1996年国家对外经贸政策进行了一系列的调整,再次调低了出口退税率,取消了外商投资企业的进口设备关税减免的待遇。推行了加工贸易银行保证金台帐管理。天津外贸企业经受了这一系列政策调整的考验,保持了贸易总量的增长。1996年全市外贸进出口总值82.97亿美元,比1991年增长3.1倍。平均每年递增32.7%。外贸出口加快,规模逐年扩大,增幅在全国处于领先水平。天津外贸出口由1991年的16.06亿美元,发展到1996年的40.49亿美元,增加24.43亿美元。5年间,每年跨上一个新台阶,平均每年递增20.3%,比全国同期平均增幅高出4.3个百分点,扭转了改革开放以来出口增幅低于经济增长的被动局面。1996年,天津外贸出口额在全国居第8位,增幅居各省市之首。1992至1996年,累计出口达到131.42亿美元,相当于“七五”时期的1.7倍,1992年外贸出口从谷底走出,当年创汇17.52亿美元,比上年增长9.1%。1993至1996年,随着各类企业对自负盈亏机制逐步适应和汇率并轨后的良性效应,促进了出口的快速增长。1993年出口19.42亿美元,1994和1995年出口分别达到24亿美元和29.98亿美元。1996年出口跃升到40.49亿美元,实现了外贸出口新的突破。

外贸出口经营格局改变,三资企业成为全市出口创汇主体和新的增长点。近几年,天津对外贸易连年取得突破性进展,主要是得益于市委市政府把扩大开放和利用外资作为推动全市经济发展的重要举措。在已经开业经营的三资企业中,多数企业步入收获成熟期,出口创汇实力明显增强。1996年三资企业出口21.52亿美元,占全市出口比重由1991年的7.5%提高到1996年的53.1%,成为全市出口创汇的主体,超过专业公司所占份额。其中:摩托罗拉(中国)电子有限公司全年出口6.48亿美元,成为在全市创汇规模最大的企业。三美电机有限公司出口2.81亿美元,三星电机有限公司和雅马哈电子乐器有限公司分别出口1.31亿美元和1.03亿美元,天美汽车配件、北洋集装箱、北海粮油、三星电子、通广三星、中美史克、牧津纤维、爱普生有限公司等数十家三资企业年创汇都超过千万美元。三资企业出口已成为拉动全市出口增长的决定因素。三资企业创汇实力的增强,不仅使其成为全市出口创汇新的增长点,也打破了原有专业公司包揽天下的格局,形成了三资企业、专业公司、和工贸公司“三分天下”竞相发展的新局面。专业外贸公司按照自负盈亏的要求,克服历史上沉重挂帐包袱、高换汇成本、资金紧缺和税率波动等困难的制约,在调整中发展,1996年出口13亿美元,比1992年增长4.2%。服装公司、亿利达集团、纺织品、五矿、机械进出口公司出口超过1亿美元。工贸公司经受国际市场的考验,在发挥生产技术优势的同时,努力开拓国际市场,出口创汇由1991年的1.53亿美元,发展到1996年的5.97亿美元,平均每年递增31.3%。

外贸出口结构调整显现活力,促进了出口的增长,带动了全市产业产品结构的优化。1992年以来,天津出口商品结构的改善,也极大地促进了全市出口的增长。主要表现在:一是贸易结构发生变化,来料加工、补偿贸易等灵活贸易方式的贸易规模扩大。五年间,通过灵活贸易方式出口平均每年递增31.8%,1996年,来料加工占全市出口额的比重达11.1%,比1991年提高了4.3个百分点。二是大宗骨干商品出口扩大。1996年出口额在1 000万美元以上的大宗商品有58个,比1991年多30个,出口额34.93亿美元,比1991年增长6.8倍,平均每年递增50.7%,占全市出口总额的比重由1991年的27.9%上升为1996年的86.3%。三是机电产品出口大幅度增长。1996年,科技含量高、附加值大的机电产品出口14.84亿美元,比上年增长80%,占全市出口额的比重由1991年的23.5%,上升到1996年的36.7%,外贸出口结构的调整,表明天津的出口增长方式,正在由速度型向效益型转变。

拓展国际市场,多元化市场战略取得显著成效。党的十四大以来,天津实施市场多元化战略取得显著成效。各经营单位为老的出口商品探寻新的出口市场,为小的商品拓展大的海外市场。目前天津已与170多个国家和地区之间发生贸易往来。其中:香港、日本、美国、韩国已成为位居前列的重要贸易伙伴。1996年对香港地区出口11.21亿美元,对日本出口8.84亿美元,对美国出口5.91亿美元,对韩国出口2.61亿美元,分别比1991年增长2.3倍、2.9倍和2倍。韩国已成为天津近两年开拓的海外新兴主体市场。天津外贸对亚洲出口达到27.22亿美元,对非洲出口0.84亿美元,分别比1991年增长2.2倍和2.1倍。多元化市场战略的实施,不仅有利于促进对外贸易的发展,而且有利于分散贸易风险和增强抵御贸易保护主义的能力。

(程新娣)

投资为天津发展铺路奠基

党的十四大以来,在向社会主义市场经济转轨过程中,天津固定资产投资建设取得显著成就:投资结构继续得到调整和改善,能源交通邮电等设施的建设取得突破性进展,投资向第三产业倾斜,房地产市场异军突起,为天津经济持续快速发展以及对外开放做出了新贡献。

1992-1996年的5年间,天津市全社会固定资产投资累计完成1 540.84亿元,年均递增30.6%,其中国有经济完成投资1 273.64亿元,占全市投资的82.7%,年均递增29.6%。5年全市累计新增固定资产1 106.8亿元,平均每年递增39%,固定资产交付使用率为71.8%,1996年每一元固定资产投资新增国内生产总值为0.504元,高于1992年的0.440元和“七五”时期的0.336元的水平。

工业投资仍为各行业之首,投资重点向能源原材料基础产业倾斜。5年累计全市国有集体工业投资711.03亿元,占全部投资的54.8%,居国民经济各行业之首,其中能源投资266.3亿元,占工业投资的37.5%,新增发电机组容量152万千瓦,石油开采能力年增长288万吨。在工业投资中以机械电子化工为代表的高新技术产业投资显著增加。其中15万辆夏利轿车、摩托罗拉(中国)电子有限公司、14万吨乙烯工程等大项目的建成,成为天津工业的支柱行业,给天津国民经济注入勃勃生机。

技术改造步伐加快。五年来全市用于更新改造投资为451.26亿元,年均递增36%,高于全市平均增长速度5.4个百分点。其中工业技术改造投资额完成232.2亿元,年均递增25.4%。通过技术改造,各企业更新了设备,提高了产品质量、增加了花色品种,增添了企业自我发展和市场的竞争力。

住宅建设力度加大。1994年市政府提出用5-7年的时间基本完成市区成片危陋平房改造任务。随着全市危陋平房改造工程的全面推进,带动了城市住宅建设的发展。1992-1996年全市用于住宅建设的投资214.62亿元,占全市国有及集体经济投资比重的16.6%,住宅竣工面积1 898万平方米,占全市各类房屋竣工面积的63.6%,住宅房屋竣工面积以年均70%的速度递增,1996年人均住宅居住面积达7.7平方米,比1991年提高了0.9平方米。住宅供热发展迅速。近年来,全市供热面不断加大,到1996年末全市居民住宅集中供热面积达1 806万平方米,比1991年增加1.8倍,热化率达30%,形成热电联产、地热区域集中供热和锅炉房供热三种供热方式。

投资向第三产业倾斜。5年间第三产业累计投资561.8亿元,年均递增57.9%,投资比重由1991年的21%提高到1996年的46.1%,为全市第三产业的快速发展增添了后劲。在第三产业投资中,加大了对交通邮电市政公用等城市基础设施的投资力度,城市载体功能不断提高。五年来邮电通讯业快速发展,投资83.9亿元,相当“七五”时期的11倍。新增市内电话自动交换机148.5万门,为电话的普及和通讯的现代化创造了条件。市政公用事业完成投资50.5亿元,平均每年递增54%。1993

年建成第二座污水处理厂，日处理污水40万吨，使天津的污水处理率由35%提高到58.1%，减少了对渤海湾的污染。结合城市改造拓宽了长江道、金纬路、卫津南路等城市道路，人均道路面积由1991年的6.8平方米提高到1996年的7.5平方米。金钢桥改造采光技术工艺先进，为津城又添一景。为响应市政府"让天津绿起来"的号召，在43届世乒赛期间开展了空前的绿化和美化城市区街的活动，栽植树木，开辟绿地，垂直绿化，初步建成了591片庭院式绿化小区，改善了市民生活和工作环境。教育文化事业的投入逐年加大，五年累计投资25.4亿元，平均年递增18.4%，新增大专院校席位2 500个，中等院校席位4.85万个，小学生席位1.86万个。1992－1996年，科学研究投资6.32亿元，金融保险投资3亿元，分别以61.7%和39.2%的年均速度递增。

房地产业迅速崛起。在天津市批准注册的各类房地产开发企业由90年代初的20家发展到1996年的852家。随着房地产企业数量的增多，投资额和施工面积也不断扩大，5年累计完成投资额189.25亿元，平均每年翻一番，施工面积由1991年的117.7万平方米增加到1996年的988.7万平方米，年均递增53%，房地产销售市场稳中有升，五年累计竣工商品房面积达1 091.8万平方米，销售面积达409.5万平方米，销售额由1991年的3.63亿元增加到1996年的30.51亿元，年均增长53%。

重点项目建设取得突破性进展。5年来天津市加大重点建设的力度，突出安排全市举足轻重的重点工程和特大型项目。5年来全市共兴建重点建设项目199个，累计投资404.43亿元，占全市国有投资的31.7%，其中建成投产的重点项目117个。如55万吨无缝钢管工程、14万吨乙烯工程、摩托罗拉电子工程、天津港东突堤12个深水泊位、15万辆微型汽车、造纸四、五厂、科技馆、天津日报、广播新闻中心等。这些重点工程的建成投产，为保持全市国民经济持续快速发展，为城市载体功能的提高和人民生活的改善奠定了物质基础。

（马　兰）

迈向现代化的交通邮电业

党的十四大以来，天津的交通运输和邮电通信业走上了快速发展的道路。全市运输邮电业增加值从1991年的27.13亿元，上升到1996年的98.91亿元，按可比价格计算，增长153.0%，年均递增20.4%，比全市国内生产总值增长速度高7个百分点。1992－1996的5年间，全市运输邮电业累计完成固定资产投资151.79亿元，平均每年投入30.36亿元；5年累计新增固定资产103.50亿元。港口、铁路、邮电等一大批基础设施和重点工程项目相继建成并投入使用，使天津市的交通运输和邮电通信整体水平实现了重大突破，进一步提高了城市载体功能，改善了投资环境，增强了经济发展后劲，为加快天津向现代化、国际化港口城市迈进奠定了坚实的基础。

现代化的交通运输体系保证了国民经济动脉的畅通。5年来，全市各类交通工具累计完成货物运输量111 118万吨，年均递增8.3%；累计发运旅客15 693万人次，年均递增4.1%。天津机场面向全国，面向世界，全方位、多渠道地吸引中外航空公司参与天津航空市场的竞争，目前已开辟国内航线29条，国际航线4条，地区航线1条，每周航班达到260班次。1995年，经国家验收通过，天津机场正式升格为滨海国际机场，彻底打开了天津通往世界的空中大门。1996年，天津机场完成旅客吞吐量88.8万人次，货邮吞吐量11.7万吨，分别比1991年增加80.53万人次和11.4万吨。铁路天津站改建后，接发客车能力达126列，货车62列，候车能力达1万人。地方铁路经过几年艰苦建设，成效显著。周芦铁路线、津南铁路线和李港铁路延伸线相继建成通车，使地方铁路运营里程增加了一倍，并实现了地方铁路与国家铁路接轨。地方铁路运量平均每年以10.5%的速度递增，1992－1996年累计完成货运量3 540万吨，有力地支持了地方经济建设，为加快天津滨海新区发展、开发天津港南疆港区打下良好的基础。

港口是天津最大的自然优势。早在1996年邓小平同志视察天津时就指出，港口和市区之间有很大优势，发展潜力很大。党的十四大以来，天津港深化体制改革，拓宽筹资渠道，加大投入力度，使港口保持了持续、快速的发展。1992－1996年，用于港口的基本建设投资累计达27.7亿元，改扩建万吨级泊位12个，新增生产能力551万吨，港口规模不断壮大。目前天津港拥有各类泊位72个，其中万吨级泊位48个。1996年，天津港货物吞吐量突破6 000万吨，集装箱吞吐量突破80万TEU，创历史最高水平。5年来，天津港累计完成货物吞吐量23 275万吨，年均递增21.0％，国际标准集装箱301万TEU，年均递增19.0％，远远超过全国港口平均增长速度；五年累计实现利润15.5亿元，在沿海港口中处于领先地位。继1994年我国第一艘第四代集装箱船在天津港成功首航之后，1996年我国第一艘第五代集装箱船又在天津港鸣响了首航的汽笛。现在天津港与世界160个国家和地区的300多个港口保持着货运业务往来，有40多条定期班轮航线。天津港正朝着多功能、综合型、国际性、现代化方向发展。

党的十四大以来，天津邮电业的发展进入了黄金时期。邮电通信行业抓住机遇，高起点，高速度，超常规发展，实现了邮电通信适度超前于国民经济发展的战略目标。5年来，邮电业务总量平均每年以42.0％的速度递增，1996年达到25.7亿元，相当于1991年的5.78倍；业务收入从1991年的3.82亿元，增加到1996年的22.25亿元，年均增长42.3％。

1992－1996年，也是天津通信建设史上最为辉煌的时期。天津市通信业立足于长远发展，采取“以规模投入，形成规模建设，实现规模装机”的重大举措，5年内累计完成固定资产投资84.89亿元，使天津市的通信能力和技术水平在短时期内实现了历史性巨变。1993年，天津本地网电话顺利完成六位升七位，并在全国率先实现程控化。1994年组织了以市话为重点的通信发展大决战，当年完成固定资产投资25.6亿元，使天津本地网交换机总容量突破100万门，成为继北京、上海之后，全国第三个容量超百万门的城市，1年净增57.2万门，相当于天津电话94年发展的总和。至1996年末，局用交换机总容量已达到169.4万门，5年累计净增139万门；长途交换机容量达到7.67万路端，5年累计净增7.19万路端。同时，通信业的发展在高新技术领域取得重大突破。卫星通信地球站的建成，填补了天津市长途通信技术的空白；分组交换网、数字数据网、计算机互联网相继开通，智能网、可视电话会议网等网络建设已初见成效，标志着天津通信技术的发展已达到世界先进水平。

随着通信建设的快速推进，电信业务迅猛发展，服务水平大幅度提高，服务质量明显改善。至1996年末，全市电话客户达到122.9万户，其中移动电话客户达到15万户，分别比1991年增加90万户和14.9万户；电话普及率达到每百人19.4部，其中市区达到每百人31.7部，分别比1991年增加了15部和25部。无线寻呼业务从无到有，发展之快，更如雨后春笋，至1996年末，仅邮电系统经营的无线寻呼用户即达到33.4万户，比1991年增加32.4万户。

天津邮政业务一直保持稳步增长趋势，在全国邮政专业中名列前矛。“绿卡工程”开始启动，新建并开通电子化邮局(所)54处；邮政枢纽二期改造工程顺利完成，信函自动分拣机正式投产，结束了百年来人工分拣信函的历史。邮电通信业的快速发展，有力促进了全市国民经济持续快速增长，为把天津建成现代化的国际港口大都市提供了物质技术基础。

(陶玉华)

日益兴旺的天津旅游业

党的十四大以来，天津旅游业持续、快速发展。国际旅游已成为全国发展最快的地区之一，国内旅游起步高、发展快，旅游业的综合接待能力进一步增强，产业规模继续扩大，水平不断提高，旅游业为繁荣天津经济、促进对外开放发挥着重要作用。

国际旅游实现两次重大突破，旅游外汇收入持续增长。1992至1996年间是天津国际旅游发展最快的时期，1996年接待海外游客达23.3万人次，比1991年增长1.4倍。5年间，累计接待海外游客84.41万人次，平均每年递增18.8%，高于同期全国旅游业的平均增长速度，是天津"七五"时期的1.3倍。成为全国旅游业发展最快的地区之一。5年间，天津旅游外汇收入5.06亿美元，平均每年递增34.8%。

天津旅游业是伴随着改革开放而不断发展壮大的。1992年开始进入快速发展时期。党的十四大以来，市委、市政府高度重视旅游业的发展，将其列为天津第三产业中优先发展的一个重要产业，提出了发展"大城市、大旅游、大产业"的战略构想，制定了天津发展旅游业的长远规划，确定了扶植旅游业发展的若干政策，使天津旅游业发展步入了快车道。1992年，天津抓住'92友好观光的有利时机，开展了一系列大型的宣传促销活动，在全社会形成了'92友好观光的热烈气氛，当年接待海外游客首次突破10万人大关，创汇首次突破5千万美元大关。1995年天津举办世乒赛，海外宾客聚集津门，当年共接待20.06万人次，在1992年的基础上翻了一番，创汇达1.33亿美元，比1992年增长1.6倍。

党的十四大以来，天津重视国际旅游客源市场的开发，本着"海外抓促销、国内抓建设"的方针，加大对外宣传促销力度，使天津国际旅游客源市场形成了"全方位、多元化、多源头、多渠道"的格局，5年间，先后开辟了韩国、独联体市场，拓宽了东南亚和香港市场，巩固了日本市场，恢复和发展了欧美市场。几年来，天津市有组织、有计划地参加了各主要客源国和地区的旅游交易会和巡回促销活动。在有影响的海外旅游宣传媒介进行了有针对性的宣传和广告发布，邀请了有实力的海外旅行商和旅游记者来津实地考察、交流，并通过外事、经贸、科技、文化、教育多种对外交流渠道扩大客源招揽。此外，还推出了修学旅游、经贸旅游、养生保健旅游，包机旅游和海外游船等多项旅游项目。5年间，天津各涉外宾馆共接待外国人41.34万人次，平均每年递增19.1%，华侨0.38万人次，平均每年递增35.9%；港澳台同胞15.97万人次，平均每年递增3.1%。外国人来津居前列的国家和地区有日本15.43万人次、韩国9.52万人次、美国4.48万人次、新加坡1.95万人次、德国1.66万人次、英国1.21万人次、独联体1万人次，平均每年递增速度均在10%以上。

国内旅游业迅速崛起，显示出强劲的发展势头。据抽样调查资料显示：1996年天津共接待国内游客2452.73万人次，旅游收入199.65亿元，显示出旺盛的生命力和巨大的发展潜力，成为天津第三产业前景广阔的新兴行业之一。

天津国内旅游始于80年代初期，90年代不断发展，尤其是近几年发展迅猛。由于全市经济持续快速增长，居民收入明显增加，人民生活水平不断提高，加之双休日和带薪假期的实行，使人们可自由支配的闲暇时间成倍增长，新闻媒体加大旅游宣传力度，使居民的旅游意识增强，旅游愿望迫切，这些因素为国内旅游的发展奠定了广泛的客源基础和必要条件。

天津在抓国际旅游促销的同时，注重抓国内旅游的促销。近年来，在坚持"立足本市、依托北京、主攻周边，全面推进"的市场策略指导下，通过各种渠道开展促销活动。1992年以来，天津发挥经贸繁荣、海滨环境优美和物价水平较低的优势，围绕每年的主题活动，开发了丰富多彩的旅游项目，形成了"月月有活动、季季有高潮"的旅游氛围。同时还根据国内游客的不同需求，开发和推广四大产品系列，即：都市观光、津郊风情、专项旅游和商贸会议系列，吸引了大批国内游客。特别是京、津一日游更为火爆，据抽样调查资料显示：1996年，天津接待北京市民到天津一日游的游客达266.87万人次，占国内旅游人数的10.9%；旅游花费8.88亿元，占国内旅游收入的4.4%。目前，天津已成为北京及周边地区的旅游热点。

天津旅游业综合接待能力增强，旅游基础设施和交通状况明显改善，景区、景点的开发取得新的进展。天津不断加强旅游业软、硬件的建设，综合接待能力不断增强。5年间，新增涉外宾馆22座，新批国际、国内旅行社30家，截止1996年底，已拥有涉外宾馆57座、客房8千多间，床位1.7万张。国际、国内游行社达104家，其中：国际旅行社20家。涉外定点餐馆60家,旅游定点商店54家。全国旅游商品定点生产企业8家,旅游文化娱乐场所和文物景点12处。

旅游基础设施和旅游交通有了明显改善。开辟了天津至国内一些主要旅游城市的航线,开通了天津至汉城的国际航班,开展了天津与莫斯科、基辅的包机业务。截止1996年底已开通的国际、国内航线达23条。天津至北京、天津市区至蓟县的旅游列车4对。京津塘高速公路全线通车,市内交通"三环十四射"道路已经完成,天津至日本神户、韩国仁川的客货班轮的开航,使天津市初步形成了陆海空立体交通网络。此外,通往各主要景区景点的公路交通也得到了进一步改善,大大增强了城市的载体功能,为天津旅游业的快速发展提供了条件。

旅游景区、景点的开发建设取得了新的进展。"一个中心,两个侧翼"的景观格局已经形成,市中心区以海河为风景轴线的游览区,本着"活跃水面,繁荣两岸"的精神,各类游船、游艇不断增多,海河公园设施建设进一步完善。此外还陆续修建了天塔、天津科技馆、近代名人蜡像馆、海河皇宫、平津战役纪念馆、周恩来、邓颖超纪念馆、扩建了大悲院等重要景观、景点。在蓟县盘山修复了云罩寺、万松寺,建成了盘山缆车索道、"八十七神仙卷"石刻画。在黄崖关长城修复了水关和毛主席墨迹碑林及名联堂等。并对蓟县千年古刹独乐寺等文物古迹进行了全面维修,使蓟县一翼的旅游资源得到了较好的开发利用。以天津海滨浴场为龙头,塘沽为腹地的滨海地区旅游资源,得到了迅速发展,天津海滨浴场四年来开发建设海滩2.2平方公里,围海修建了海水浴场和温泉泳池,建设了一批星级酒店、高档别墅、各类餐馆及运动娱乐等设施。此外,黄港水库和大港区的官港森林公园的建设开发也已起动,使滨海一翼的资源开发初具规模。"杨村小世界",石家大院、东丽湖度假村、团泊湖旅游风景区等别具特色的旅游产品相继推出。近年来,天津在景区、景点开发和建设中注重引入市场机制,发挥国家、集体、个体、外资的各自优势共同开发建设,取得了明显的经济效益和社会效益。

(张　辉)

正在崛起的天津滨海新区

1994年市第十二届人代会第二次会议确定"利用十年左右时间基本建成滨海新区"。3年来,在市委、市政府的领导下,滨海新区各单位和市各有关部门紧紧抓住这一难得的历史机遇,发挥优势,开拓进取,奋力拼搏,使新区的经济建设呈现"一年一变样,三年大变样"的可喜局面。

新区建设以她辉煌的业绩,向世人展示出生机勃勃、充满希望的发展前景。滨海新区已经成为天津最大的经济增长点,成为我国吸引外资热点地区之一。

经济发展持续、快速,对全市经济带动作用明显增强。1996年滨海新区实现国内生产总值320.29亿元,按可比价格计算比1993年增长1.1倍。平均每年递增27.8%,比同时期全市平均递增14.5%的水平高出近1倍。为全市国内生产总值提前四年翻两番作出了突出的贡献。随着新区经济的快速发展,滨海新区对全市的带动作用逐年提高,1994年滨海新区对全市的经济增长贡献率为29.8%,1996年提高到43.2%。新区国内生产总值占全市国内生产总值的比重由1993年的21%,提高到1996年的29.1%,平均每年上升2.6个百分点,超额实现了滨海新区国内生产总值占全市比重每年递增两个百分点的目标。

滨海新区综合经济实力显著加强。1996年滨海新区人均国内生产总值高达31 865元,比全市平均水平高1.6倍,1993至1996年平均增速高达26.8%,比全市平均递增13.8%速度高出13.0个百分点。较好地实现了市委、市政府提出的"新区带动老城区,新老并举,共同发展"的战略构想。

滨海新区建设全面推进,载体功能明显增强。滨海新区开发建设的3年间,是其历史上固定资产投资最多,建设规模最大的时期。自1994年至1996年,新区累计完成固定资产投资417.48亿元,占全市同期投资总量的36.4%,3年平均增长幅度27.9%。投资力度的不断加大,不仅为新区基础设施的完善、重点工程项目的建设创造了条件,而且也为新区投资结构和投资环境的进一步优化起到了"催化"作用。

为了改善投资环境,滨海新区坚持城市基础设施要先行的方针,经过科学布局,统一协调,基础设施面貌大为改观。自 1994 至 1996 年末,滨海新区共完成基础设施投资 62.54 亿元,建成交通、能源、通讯、给排水、环境治理等工程 120 项。其中 1996 年投资 26.3 亿元,比 1994 年的 15.64 亿元增长了 68.2%,建设项目由 20 个增加到 60 个。天津港南疆港区、北疆港区泊位改造,有力地促进了港口建设,使港口的整体功能不断完善。截止 1996 年底,天津港港口泊位增加到 73 个,其中万吨级以上的泊位 48 个,拥有可停靠和装卸第四代、第五代集装箱泊位 8 个。1996 年天津港口吞吐量达 6 188万吨,是 1993 年港口吞吐量 3 719 万吨的 1.66 倍。塘沽至汉沽的公路建成通车,为新区构筑现代化大交通网络创造了良好的条件。

滨海新区建区三年来,安排了一批在全市举足轻重的重点工程和特大型项目,尤其是为配合天津工业东移的战略目标,相继建设了本市历史上最大、投资上百亿元项目的无缝钢管工程、14 万吨乙稀工程等。自 1994 至 1996 年,滨海新区被列入国家和市级的重点项目有 34 个,完成投资 95.24 亿元,占全市重点项目投资总额的 35.1%。从而为滨海新区经济的持续发展增添了后劲。

外贸出口迅速扩大,利用外资取得突破性进展。几年来,作为本市对外开发开放前沿的滨海新区,积极扩大对外经济往来,外向度水平不断提高。据市外经贸委统计,1996 年滨海新区外贸出口 17.46 亿美元,比 1994 年增长 1.96 倍,两年平均递增 72.0%。占全市外贸出口比重由 1994 年的 19.7%上升到 43%。

在利用外资方面,特别是滨海新区首次对外打出自己的"旗帜",倍受中外客商的青睐,已成为国际资本竞相投资的热点,招商引资取得了突破性进展。自建区至 1996 年,滨海新区新签约三资企业项目 2 354 个,协议外资金额 53.12 亿美元,1996 年滨海新区新批三资企业 606 家,协议利用外资 18.67 亿元,分别占全市的 55.7%和 47.6%。

新的工业经济发展格局正在形成。随着滨海新区跨世纪经济发展奋斗目标的确定,滨海新区紧密围绕工业发展布局、产业结构和工业经济运行质量,积极开拓、善谋实干,不断加大发展的力度。新区建设三年来,工业生产迅速发展,1996 年滨海新区完成工业总产值 701.44亿元,比 1993 年增长 2.8 倍,平均每年递增 40.0%,占全市工业总产值的比重由 1993 年的 17.7%提高到 27.8%,成为推动全市工业发展的重要力量。

从工业发展的格局看,滨海新区已由传统的"长芦盐"制造区、近代造船业,以及"三角牌"制碱为代表的化学工业,石油开采和石油加工工业,逐渐发展为集冶金加工,电子信息、生物工程等七大产业为代表的高新技术工业为先导,以化工、冶金为基础,出口加工工业发达的新型工业体系。

滨海新区社会各项事业全面发展。滨海新区的开发不仅仅是项目和土地的开发,而是全社会的整体开发,由于滨海新区正确处理了经济和社会协调发展的关系问题,使得各项社会事业取得了新的成绩。

科技、教育事业进一步发展。1995 年塘沽海洋高新技术开发区被升格为国家级,将原规划面积 4.54 平方公里扩大为 24 平方公里;大港区以中塘星火密集区为龙头的高新技术产业迅速崛起,获国家星火奖,居全国同类地区之首;滨海新区创办的第一所正规大学"天津大学滨海工商管理学院"在塘沽正式成立,将成为滨海新区培养高层次工商管理人才的基地。截止 1996 年,滨海新区共有中小学 265 所。

文化卫生事业进一步完善。1996 年末,滨海新区有区级文化馆 3 个,公共图书馆 6 个,电影院、影剧院 16 个。市、区级医疗防治体系进一步健全,滨海新区共有医院 53 所,拥有病床 4 411 张,比上年增加 96 张。

三年来,滨海新区取得的令人瞩目的业绩证明,只要我们坚持市委、市政府提出的"十年基本建成滨海新区"的跨世纪目标不动摇,不断加大新区的对外开发开放力度、不断在改善投资的“软、硬”环境上继续下大力量，滨海新区必将成为天津再现辉煌的强大动力。

（陈孔政　寇　枫）

装点津城的建筑业

党的十四大以来，随着改革开放的不断深入，天津建筑业迅速发展、经济实力不断增强，呈现出以国有大中型企业为骨干，城镇集体企业、乡镇企业、外商及港、澳、台合资企业竞相发展的新格局。建筑业生产持续快速增长，施工技术和装备水平明显提高，施工质量进一步改善。1996 年建筑业总产值、劳动生产率与利税总额均创历史最高水平；与此同时，天津市建筑业的快速发展带来了城市建设日新月异，高楼大厦林立，居民生活居住水平逐步提高，国际化大都市的轮廓初见端倪。

建筑业生产持续快速增长。1996 年全市建筑业完成增加值 57.36 亿元，按可比价格计算比 1991 年增长了 2.6 倍，5 年间平均递增 28.9 %；1996 年全市建筑业完成总产值 173.57亿元，比 1991 年增长了 3.8 倍，平均每年递增 36.8%；全市房屋建筑施工面积为 1 579.53万平方米，比 1991 年增长了 1.7 倍，平均每年递增 22.1%。国有建筑企业主导地位进一步巩固，综合实力显著增强。1996 年全市国有建筑企业完成施工产值 146.63 亿元，占全行业的 84.5%，在全国 30 个省市中居第 11 位，比 1991 年前移了二位；施工面积达 1 276.39万平方米，占全行业的 80.8%，在全国居第 12 位，比 1991 年前移了 6 位。

建筑行业配套发展，施工领域不断拓宽。随着全市国民经济的发展和人民生活水平的不断提高，建筑企业在稳定发展传统行业的同时，积极开拓新的施工领域，管线安装业，装饰装修业等有了长足的发展，特别是装饰业发展迅猛，目前装饰企业已占全部施工企业总数的 24%，形成了土建、安装、装饰等门类齐全、行业配套的建筑产业大军，施工技术正向高、精、尖、深的方向发展，近年来，天津还出现了一些集勘察设计、建筑安装、设备制造、装饰装修及房地产开发为一体的综合型总承包建筑集团公司，成为天津市建筑行业中举足轻重的骨干力量。

施工技术水平显著提高。1991 年以来，天津市建筑施工企业凭借实力和技术优势，相继承接和建成了一大批形体高大、造型复杂、技术先进的能源、原材料、交通邮电、城市基础设施、商贸和文化科技体育建设项目等，主要有：无缝钢管工程、乙烯工程、蓟县、陈塘庄及杨柳青电厂、天津港东突堤及南疆开发工程、日贷通信工程、国际新闻中心、卫星通信地面站、吉利大厦、劝业场新厦、百货大楼扩建工程、夏利汽车扩建工程、天津日报、今晚报社新址工程、众多的高层写字楼和举世闻名的天津体育中心工程等。这些工程广泛采取深基础施工，泵送混凝土、滑模现浇、支模、大跨度施工、金属网架结构和玻璃幕外装饰，标志着天津市勘察设计和施工、安装工艺技术水平又登上了一个新台阶。建筑企业现代化水平进一步提高。5 年以来，天津市建筑业的自身建设进一步加强，整体素质明显提高。1996 年施工企业固定资产投资额为 8.71 亿元，比 1991 年增长 9 倍多，截止 1996 年底，全市施工企业固定资产原值达 72.59 亿元，相当于 1991 年的 2.6 倍。全市国有施工企业的技术装备率达 7 677元/人，比 1991 年增长 80.3%。5 年间先后引进众多的国外先进施工设备，机械化施工正在替代传统的手工作业，不仅大大减轻了劳动强度，改善了施工质量，而且提高了劳动生产率，1996 年全市建筑业全员劳动率高达 59 724元/人，比 1991 年增长了 2.3 倍，创历史最好水平。

建筑业市场日益完善。为适应社会主义市场经济的发展，建筑业市场不断完善，投、招标工程覆盖面逐年扩大。1996 年全市 140 家国有施工企业实行投招标承包工程达 1 789 个，占全部施工项目总数的 31.9%，比 1991 年增加 16.9 个百分点，实行投招标承包工程的房屋建筑施工面积为 438.97 万平方米，占全部施工面积的 34.4%，比 1991 年增加了 15 个百分点；与此同时，建筑业产品质量进一步提高。天津电视塔、国际大厦、天津空港、滨江商厦和大程控等工程先后荣获国家建筑业最高质量奖——鲁班奖。施工企业特别是国有建筑企业不论是按竣工工程项目个数,还是按竣工面积计算的优良品率均比1991年有较大的提高。

企业经济效益稳步提高。1996年全市建筑施工企业实现利税6.28亿元,比1991年增加了4倍,平均每年递增38.1%,实现了建筑业生产与效益的同步增长。近几年来,随着建筑业改革的不断深化,以项目法施工作为企业转换机制的突破口,在天津市全面推广,调动了广大管理人员、工程技术人员和工人群众的积极性,企业亏损面逐年缩小,1996年全市施工企业亏损面为22.1%,成为1991年以来的最低点。

目前,天津市建筑业正在按照全市"九五"规划和2010年远景规划,积极推进两个根本性转变,进一步发展壮大经济实力,加快建设现代企业制度,在市场竞争中重组生产要素,推动施工企业从劳务型向管理型转换,积极开拓外埠及海外市场,努力提高建筑行业经济效益,将建筑业发展成为天津市国民经济的重要支柱产业之一。

(王大维)

日趋良好的人口环境

党的十四大以来,天津市国民经济持续、快速、健康发展。人口作为社会经济发展的重要驱动因素出现了显著的变化:人口规模得到有效控制,人口素质显著提高,人口结构不断优化,为天津的社会经济持续发展营造了良好的人口环境。

人口数量得到有效控制。进入90年代,天津市出现了一些人口高增长的内在趋势。一是由于农村经济体制改革后,户营经济对劳动力的强烈需求,持续地刺激着农民家庭多生子女的欲望;二是经济体制改革向纵深推进,城乡间的"壁垒"开始打破,城乡之间人口往来日趋频繁,且规模迅速扩大;三是育龄妇女年均递增速度比总人口年均增速高20%以上,全市20-29岁生育高峰期育龄妇女每年保持在70万人,为人口控制工作增加了难度。但是,由于近年来中国政府对人口问题提高到实现可持续发展的战略高度来认识,逐步改变了过去以外部行政约束为主的人口控制模式,开始走上依靠社会经济发展的拉动,灵活运用"利益导向"杠杆,促使育龄人口更新生育观念以实现人口控制目标的轨道。全市人口数量控制取得明显成效。育龄妇女总和生育率由1991年的1.60降至1996年的1.29;人口出生率由1991年的11.94‰降至1996年的10.09‰,人口自然增长率由6.16‰降至3.56‰;总人口的增长速度急剧收缩,由1991年的2.81%降至1996年的0.68%,党的十四大以来全市年均常住人口为934.24万人,比计划少3.89万人,全市常住人口由1991年的908.89万人增加到1996年的948.19万人。

人口文化素质明显提高。社会主义市场经济的建立和发展,对人们应具备的文化素质提出了更高的要求,人们的求知欲变得非常强烈。党的十四大以来,天津市人口的文化素质朝着现代化不断迈进,为社会经济的持续快速发展提供了潜能。一是,总人口的平均受教育程度目前已达到初中三年级在学的水平,比1990年整整提高了一个学期;15岁及以上文盲人口减少11.34万人,粗文盲率由8.96%,降至7.17%;18-22岁人口中大学生的比重由8.29%,上升到12.42%;每千人拥有大学文化程度的人口增长34.04%。二是,城乡人口的文化素质同步提高,市中心区平均受教育程度达到高中一年级水平,五县地区平均受教育程度达到初中一年级末期的水平;另外,五县7-14岁少年儿童中有文化人口的比重目前已高达99.01%,说明党的"十四大"以来九年义务教育的普及和"希望工程"的效果显著。三是,妇女文化水平提高较快。全市18-35岁女性人口中有大学生12.84万人,比1990年时增长39.77%,比同龄男性人口的增长幅度高21.9个百分点,目前该年龄组女性与男性人口平均受教育程度之差,比1990年下降30%。四是,目前从业人员中受过各层次教育者的比重高达97.06%;具有大专及以上学历的有45.39万人,比1990年增长40.35%。

人口的自然结构和社会经济结构进一步

优化。党的十四大以来社会经济的快速发展和人口控制的巨大成效，使人口的自然结构、社会经济结构进一步优化，如人口的年龄结构、人口的城乡结构较以往更科学、合理。一是，目前全市15－64岁人口占总人口比重高达70.22%，是90年代以来的最高值；0－14岁低龄人口占21.63%，15－64岁人口的负担系数为42.41%，均为90年代以来的最低值。说明天津市目前正处于劳动力人口比重高，被抚养人口比重低的“黄金季节”。二是，乡镇企业的崛起推动了农村地区工业化的发展，从而加速了农村人口城镇化的进程。据户籍人口统计，天津市县镇的个数由1990年的24个，增加到1996年的43个，人口规模随之由68.37万人，增加至114.32万人。同时，劳动非农化的扩展也将继续加速未来农村人口的城镇化进程。

（王金才　沈　重）

劳动就业多元化

党的十四大以来，改革开放的步伐不断加快，天津市国民经济和社会发展整体水平迅速提高，劳动力就业结构和工资水平发生显著变化。劳动就业方式已由过去的“千军万马过独木桥”发展为多种就业渠道并存的新格局。就业渠道的拓宽，一方面促进了就业人数的增加，另一方面也推动了就业结构的日趋合理。天津市人才市场，劳务市场在劳动力资源配置方面发挥着越来越重要的作用，人才市场化、劳务市场化观念和市场择业行为正在形成；同时，与人民生活水平密切相关的职工工资以平稳的发展速度逐年增加。

据统计，1996年末天津市劳动力资源总数已达708.8万人，占全部人口比重的78.9%。在劳动力资源中，劳动力（即从业人员与失业人员之和）达520.2万人，比1991年增加32.2万人，其中从业人员为512万人，增加32.3万人，劳动力资源利用率达72.2%。

近年来，市委、市政府十分重视再就业工程，据劳动部门统计，1996年全市安置城镇就业人员8.9万人，比1991年多安置1.2万人。除此之外，1996年各级劳动服务公司还安置1.5万人，其中安置初次就业人员4 611人，富余人员7 291人。

1992－1996年天津市劳动就业情况，有以下几个特点：

第一，劳动力就业结构日趋合理。在深化企业改革，转换经营机制的过程中，企业自主权不断扩大，产业结构逐步得到调整。伴之而来的劳动力就业结构也发生了很大的变化：

一是职工人数大幅度减少，私营和个体经济从业人员增加。职工人数减少的主要原因是作为经济主体的国有、集体经济吸纳劳动力的能力减弱，1991年以来职工人数逐年减少，1996年末国有、集体经济职工分别为194.3万人和59.6万人，比上年末减少2.7万人和4.6万人。国有、集体职工占全市职工总数的比例由1991年的97.9%下降到1996年的89.4%。但是，非公有制经济的三资及其他所有制职工人数随着对外开放的扩大而持续增加，截止1996年底，三资及其他所有制职工达30.1万人，比上年增加1.7万人，比1991年增长3.9倍。增减因素相抵后，1996年全市职工人数比上年减少5.6万人，比1991年减少近7.6万人。在职工人数减少的同时，随着市场经济的发展，城镇个体和私营经济异军突起，迅速发展壮大，已逐渐成为劳动力就业的重要途径之一。1996年底，天津市个体私营从业人员已达51.2万人，比上年增加5.5万人，比1991年增加42.2万人。

二是城乡劳动力双向流动方兴未艾。乡镇企业从业人员1996年已达113.7万人，比1991年增加19万人，截止到1996年底，从城镇到乡镇企业就职人员达5.3万人。城镇职工正在转变一次择业保终身的就业观念，就业空间随着人们观念的更新而变的更为广阔，1996年城镇职工的流动率达2.0%；在农村表现为大量的农村剩余劳动力转向非农业生产经营活动，仅1996年农业劳动力比上年减少15万人，而乡镇企业从业人员增加13.1万人，这说明农村劳动力的流向分为两部分，一部分涌向城市进入城镇的“合资”企业、餐饮服务业、建筑施工等行业 另一部分相当数量的农村劳动力充实到了乡镇企业，天津农村有着大量的潜在富余劳动力,这些人全部进城务工显然是不可能的,其根本的出路还是发展农村经济,那么乡镇企业既是发展农村经济的手段之一,又是吸纳农村富余劳动力的主渠道,乡镇企业还为城镇一部分选择待遇好、适合发挥个人才干、特长的人员提供了就业空间。可见,乡镇企业逐渐成为城乡劳动力双向流动的纽带。

三是三次产业就业结构发生变化。1992至1996年5年间,天津市第一产业就业人数平均每年下降2.7%。第二产业平均每年增长0.3%,第三产业平均每年增长4.9%。三次产业结构发生了较大变化,第一产业由1991年的19.7%,下降到1996年的16.0%;第二产业由49.5%,下降为47.2%;第三产业由30.9%上升为36.8%。劳动力由第一,第二产业向第三产业转移的趋势加快。1993年以来,一些新兴的第三产业如房地产业、信息咨询业、广告业等迅速发展,拓宽了就业空间,为天津市跨入现代化城市奠定了基础。

第二,市场机制在劳动力资源的配置上发挥着举足轻重的作用。解决就业问题的一项主要措施是加强就业服务,培育和发展劳动力市场。近年来,天津市的劳动就业服务体系不断完善,初步形成了以市区劳动力市场为主体、行业民间职业介绍所为补充,联通城乡覆盖全市的就业服务网络,1996年进入人才市场和劳务市场招工的单位2.03万户,179万人次进场择业,44.42万人次通过市场达成初步就业意向,进场择业人次数和达成初步就业意向分别比上年增长11.8%和17.2%。

随着天津经济发展的加快,职工收入大幅度增加。职工工资总额由1991年的79.7亿元增加到1996年的212.1亿元,5年间增长1.7倍。由于分配关系的变化,职工收入渠道不断增多,分配呈多元化特征,在职工收入中除工资性收入以外还包括非工资性收入,而且随着时间的推移,非工资性收入所占比重逐年上升。1996年含非工资性收入的职工年人均收入比1991年增长近2.2倍。1996年职工年人均工资为7 643元,增长1.8倍,扣除物价因素,平均每年递增20.8%,三资及其他经济职工工资水平增长较快,1996年三资、股份及其他所有制职工年人均工资达10 522元,比上年增加1 874元。国有和集体职工年人均工资为8 072元和4 745元,分别增加了1 109元和607元,其他所有制职工年工资水平与国有、集体三者之间的比例1991年为1:0.84:0.60,1996年变化为1:0.77:0.45。

(时少林　吕金福)

科技兴市成果丰硕

党的十四大以来,天津市认真贯彻实施“科技兴市”的战略方针,以科技为先导,为经济建设提供强有力的技术支撑,积极为科技成果的涌出铺路搭桥,努力为科技成果尽快转化为生产力提供条件,使科技工作迈上新台阶。

科技研究结硕果。1992－1996年天津市取得重大科技成果3 124项,其中:国家发明奖32项,国家科技进步奖77项。在1996年936项重大科技成果中,国际领先水平40项,国际先进水平170项。科技在为经济主战场服务方面取得了新的进展,科技成果利用率达到76.19%,仅1996年由科技成果转换为生产力的项目创产值151.8亿元,科技出口创汇158.5亿元。

科技投入明显增强。近几年来,以科技为先导,促进了经济发展,提高了各级领导的科技意识,增强了科技人力与经费的投入。有利于科技进步的环境进一步得到改善。截止1996年底,天津市拥有各类专业技术人员59万人,平均每万名职工拥有科技人员2 079人,比1991年增加106人。独立科研机构科技人员1.7万人,高等院校科技人员2.9万人,比1991年增长16.0%。1996年,工业企业科技人力投入明显增加。大中型工业企业科技人员由1991年的2.4万人发展到1996年的3.5万人,增长了45.8%。其中:科学家和工程师达到2.2万人;研究与发展人员达到1.2万人。同时科技经费投入也明显加大。1996年大中型工业企业科技活动经费支出总额达10.9亿元,比1991年增加7.8亿元,增长了2.5倍。其中:开发新产品用款3.6亿元,比1991年增长1.6倍;研究与发展经费达到5.4亿元。

技术市场日趋活跃。1991年以来，天津市技术市场登记点逐年增加，技术市场交易活动更加活跃。截止1996年底，天津市拥有技术贸易机构1 046个，技术市场职工人数1.66万人，其中：专职人员1.44万人，占职工总数的87.0%。近几年来，技术市场已成为促进技术成果迅速转化为现实生产力的主渠道。1996年天津市通过技术市场缔结了技术合同8 348项，技术合同金额13.35亿元，平均每项技术合同含金量为15.99万元，比1991年含金量增长3.3倍。

技术监督部门执法力度加大。天津市技术监督工作坚持质量、计量、标准化等日常监督与综合执法相结合，全面加大了监督和执法力度，不断提高执法水平。有力地促进了产品质量和行业管理水平的进一步提高。截止1996年底，天津市拥有技术监督机构51个，专业技术监督人员1 645人。全年对近3 000种产品质量进行了监督抽查；对4 700个商店及企业、156个市场、2 636批次的定量包装商品等进行了监督检查；并出动执法人员3.6万人次，查处违反技术监督有关法律法规案件4 378件，其中较大案件141件，比上年同期增长40%。

专利意识不断增强。近几年来，天津市加强了专利的宣传工作，使单位和个人都增强了申请专利的意识。1992－1996年天津市累计申请专利8 549项，已批准授权5 592项。在1996年申请专利1 743项中，个人发明申请专利1 208项，占总数的69.3%，比1991年所占比重提高3.7个百分点。专利工作的实施带来了可观的经济效益，1996年天津市实施专利项目191项，其中：列入计划项目85项，国家项目22项。新增产值5.5亿元，新增利税1.3亿元。

科技园区快速发展。天津市科技园区自建区以来经济发展保持了快速发展的好势头。截止1996年底，园区企业累计达到2 752家，当年新增企业516家，从业人员6.3万人，比1991年增加5.3万人，增长了5.3倍。技工贸总收入达97.0亿元，比1991年增加了92.3亿元，增长了19.6倍。利润总额达到6.3亿元，比1991年增长了11.6倍。创历史最高水平，显示出良好的发展前景。

（郭秀兰）

绚丽多彩的社会事业

1992年以来，天津市社会各项事业在邓小平同志视察南方重要讲话和党的十四大精神鼓舞下，伴随着改革开放和现代化建设的步伐阔步前进。教育、文化、卫生、体育等各项事业都取得了可喜的成绩。

教育事业硕果累累。全市各级各类教育事业全面发展，截止1996年末，全市共有普通高等院校20所；在校本、专科学生7.14万人，当年毕业生1.84万人，分别比1991年增长了43%和21.9%。硕士以上学历教育步伐加快，博士和硕士研究生数量不断增加，1996年在校博士、硕士研究生分别为1 119人和5 159人，分别是1991年的2.67倍和1.77倍；毕业博士和硕士生分别为239人和1 517人，是1991年的2.23倍和1.34倍。1992至1996年高校向社会输送各级各类专业人才累计达7.8万人。

为适应深化改革对在职人员素质不断提高的要求，成人教育规模有所扩大，截至1996年，全市共有成人高校44所，在校学生6.3万人，毕业生1.66万人。5年间有近8.36万人取得了成人高等学历。

普通中专教育进一步发展，并在办学方向、学科设置和招生与毕业方式上做了调整和改革，增设了适应市场经济和社会急需的国际金融、计算机、营销、物业管理、旅游等多种学科。增加了委培生和自费生的比例，推出了双向选择的改革举措。截至1996年底全市普通中专已达78所；在校学生6.7万人，毕业生1.33万人，比1991年分别增加80.1%和19.8%。

普及九年义务制教育成绩显著。1994年天津市通过了“普九”验收，18个区县的“普九”主要指标都达到或超过国家和市颁标准，提前6年在全国率先实现了普及九年义务教育。天津市在“普九”达标的基础上，积极努力，巩固已有的成果。1996年全市共有普通中学734所，比1991年增加了37所；在校学生和毕业生分别为49.36万人和12.07万人。小学3 027所,在校学生和毕业生分别为87.98万人和14.57万人。教学质量逐年提高,小学完成率和初中完成率分别达93.7%和85.7%,小学辍学率和初中辍学率分别为0.2%和1.2%,比1992年下降5.49和6.54个百分点。师资水平不断提高,近年来天津市在联合国儿童基金会无偿援助60万美元基础上,又先后投资400多万人民币,建成了功能齐备、设施先进的四大中师培训中心,目前天津市有95.7%的小学教师达到了中专以上学历,82.68%的初中教师达到了大专以上学历,其中20%以上的初中教师取得了大学本科学历,使天津市跨入了全国初高等教育师资培训先进省市之列。

文化事业百花争艳。1991年以来,全市的文化艺术与各项事业一样进入了繁荣发展时期。截止1996年,天津市共有文化馆19个,博物馆14个、公共图书馆31个、街道乡镇文化馆近200个。全市共有艺术演出团体18个;本着推出精品,繁荣文艺的方针,创造出一系列观赏性、艺术性强的剧目,1996年共演出3 542场,累计观众404万人次。社会文化娱乐市场有序、健康发展,目前,全市共有歌厅、舞厅、卡拉ok厅569家,文化娱乐的繁荣兴旺,既充实了天津市人民的文化生活,陶冶了人民的情操,也改善了天津的投资环境。

改革开放为天津电影业注入了新的活力,5年间,天津电影制片厂摄制了一批优秀影片,其中1996年摄制的《童年的风筝》荣获了中国电影“华表奖”、“五个一工程奖”。全市已拥有642个电影放映单位,其中影剧院、电影院、开放礼堂及俱乐部127个,国产影片与进口影片异彩纷呈,教育性、观赏性、艺术性、互为交融,使观众开拓了眼界,陶冶了情操。

出版事业蓬勃发展。近年来,天津的各种书报杂志象雨后春笋迅速发展,1996年出版各类杂志4 686.5万册,各类报纸5.39万份,各类图书8 917万册,全市群众读书看报,重信息,学知识已蔚然成风。

天津电视台和广播电台经过几年的改革和发展,进入了繁荣时期。1996年天津市无线广播电台有1座,县有线广播电台为12个,乡有线广播电台220个。平均每日播出时间也由1991年的69小时增加到1996年的96小时。广播覆盖率达100%。电视节目套数从4套增加到11套;平均每周播出时间由133小时增加到428小时。电视覆盖率为95%,比1991年提高了6个百分点,丰富多彩、生动有趣的广播电视节目已成为居民生活中的重要组成部分,各区县有线电视的推广和普及更使群众业余生活锦上添花。

卫生事业稳步发展,医疗卫生条件进一步改善。近年来,天津新扩建了一批医疗卫生结构,天和医院,中医药研究院及其附属医院先后开诊,医疗急救中心和120急救电话投入运行,社会办医不断发展,从根本上改变了就医难的问题。1996年全市有医疗卫生机构4 171个,比1991年增加874个,年末全市医院拥有病床3.6万张;全市拥有医护卫生专业技术人员7.10万人,其中医生3.8万人。

防病能力不断增强。近年来,全市积极推行计划免疫保偿制,使“四苗”接种率大大提高,疫苗所控制疾病明显下降,全市已连续4年末发现脊灰病例,连续5年无白喉发生,连续5年无新生儿破伤风出现,其它疾病的发病率和死亡率也都有不同程度的下降。

卫生保健工作取得新的进展。近年来,天津市积极做好日常保健工作,同时对儿童和孕妇保健当作重点来抓,1996年天津市7岁以下儿童保健覆盖率和孕妇保健覆盖率分别为90.6%和95.83 %,保健工作的强化,提高了生命质量。与人们卫生条件关系较大的食盐加碘、改水、改厕工作力度加大,目前,天津市有85%的居民食用碘盐,90.6%的居民饮用安全卫生的自来水。

体育事业成绩喜人。天津市城市建设快速发展和体育设施的不断完善,已具备举办大型赛事的功能,一大批高素质的裁判队伍已形成,申办第35届世界体操锦标赛成功。专业运动员再创新成绩,在1996年全国重大比赛中全市运动员荣获8枚金牌、18枚银牌和14枚铜牌。

群众性体育活动方兴未艾。1996年共有各类体育场馆4 721个,除供专业人员训练外,绝大部分已对群众开放，假日和空闲时间群众在体育馆游泳、打球、健身已成锻炼和休闲的重要方式。中、小学体育锻炼达标工作取得新的成绩，全市已有94.7%的中学生和92.9%的小学生达到了体育锻炼标准，德、智、体全面发展成为学校培养学生的目标。

党的十四大以来，天津市国民经济的快速发展给社会各项事业带来了蓬勃的生机，在创造发达的物质文明的同时，开创了精神文明建设的新局面。社会事业全面进步，成绩斐然，为改革开放营造了良好环境，进一步促进了天津经济持续、健康、协调的发展。

（梁朝晖）

居民生活质量明显提高

党的十四大以来，随着全市物质文明建设和精神文明建设步伐的加快，城镇居民的物质和文化生活发生了巨大变化，生活质量显著提高，总体水平已达小康标准。

居民收入快速增长，收入渠道不断拓宽。据对天津市城镇居民家庭生活调查资料显示：1996年城镇居民人均生活费收入5 525元，比1991年增长2.3倍，扣除价格因素影响，实际增长59.3%，平均每年递增9.8%，是历史上增长较快的时期。平均每户家庭总收入达17 200元。从收入构成上看：工资性收入仍是居民家庭收入的主体；非工资性收入增幅快于工资性收入增长，而且渠道不断拓宽，呈多元化特征。

随着国民经济总体水平的提高，国家工资制度改革步伐的不断加快，公务员制度的推行和企业经济效益的提高，使职工工资有了较大的增加。1996年城镇居民家庭人均工资性收入3 679元，与1991年相比，五年间增长2.2倍。平均每年递增26.1%。工资性收入占居民家庭全部收入的61.6%，仍是居民家庭收入的主体。

非工资性收入增幅快于工资性收入增长，渠道不断拓宽，来源呈多元化。1996年居民家庭人均非工资性收入2 297元，比1991年增长2.3倍。从增长原因看：一是个体劳动者收入增长显著，1996年居民家庭人均个体劳动收入113元，5年间增长7.9倍。二是随着职工就业渠道的拓宽和职工从事第二职业等原因使其他劳动收入大幅度增加，1996年居民家庭人均其他劳动收入303元，比1991年增长7.2倍。三是财产性收入增势强劲，随着企业股份制的推行，股票、债券等有价证券发行量的增加，居民的金融交易日趋活跃，投资意识不断增强。1996年居民人均从储蓄、股票、债券等有价证券所取得的红利、利息收入96.68元，比1991年增长4.9倍。

1991年以来，城镇居民的消费水平再上新台阶，生活质量不断提高，消费结构日趋合理，消费热点不断涌现。1996年城镇居民人均消费性支出4 680元，比1991年增长2.0倍，扣除价格因素，5年间实际增长44.5%，平均年递增7.6%。吃、穿、用等各项消费呈全面增长态势。食品支出占消费性支出的比重(恩格尔系数)逐年下降，由1991年的58.6%下降到1996年的51.3%，城镇居民总体消费水平已基本达到小康。

食品消费质量进一步提高，消费比重逐年下降。据调查，1996年城镇居民人均购买食品支出2 403元，比1991年增长1.6倍。营养结构日益改善，高蛋白、低脂肪食品和方便、快捷的主副食品消费量增加。植物油、牛羊肉、鲜蛋、鲜瓜果消费量逐年上升，到1996年人均消费植物油8.9公斤，牛羊肉6.7公斤，鲜蛋17.9公斤，鲜瓜果64.8公斤，分别比1991年增长2.3%、13.6%、26.1%和6.9%。随着收入的增加，城镇居民在外就餐支出大幅度增加，1996年城镇居民人均在外用餐支出347元，比1991年增长2.6倍。

衣着消费增势平稳，成衣化趋势明显。1996年城镇居民人均衣着消费支出584元，比1991年增长1.8倍，购买成衣比重到1996年达59.8%。平均每百人购买服装644件，其中：百人购买男装232件，购买女装291件，男装消费增幅明显快于女装，男装消费主要是对高档名牌西装和皮衣需求增加。

耐用消费品拥有量明显增加，新型家电不断涌现，消费热点层出不穷。居民对大件耐用消费品需求向多功能、高档次方向发展。1996

年人均用于购置大件耐用消费品支出235元，比1991年增长1.1倍。彩电趋向于大屏幕多功能的名牌产品，电冰箱(柜)日趋高档名牌化，空调器、微波炉、摄相机、高档组合音响、影碟机、电脑等新产品迅速进入家庭，到1996年末，平均每百户拥有彩电107.4台、电冰箱(柜)108.2台、录像机35.4台、高级组合音响13.4台、空调器15.2台、摄相机0.6台、电脑2.8台、影碟机2.6台、微波炉1.6台。

交通通讯消费方兴未艾、日趋现代化。家庭安装电话、身带BP机、手持移动电话、外出乘出租车成为近几年居民消费新时尚。到1996年人均用于交通通讯支出251.27元，比1991年增长9.8倍。人均支出交通费75.05元、电讯费63.77元，分别比1991年增长5.2倍和29.3倍，其中人均支出出租汽车费35.41元。到1996年末百户拥有电话机55.4部、移动电话0.8部。

居民家庭医疗保健支出增势迅猛。随着居民自身保健意识的增强，保健用品及服务需求显著增加。1996年人均用于医疗保健及服务支出141元，比1991年增长5.6倍。其中：人均药费、保健用品及滋补药品支出增长6.3倍、医疗保健服务支出增长3.4倍。

教育投入不断增加，成人教育持续升温，精神文化生活日益丰富。1996年人均用于教育支出258元，比1991年增长4.8倍。其中成人教育人均支出12.07元，比1992年增长6倍，体现出居民更加注重对子女的教育投入和自身文化素质的提高。居民在物质生活不断改善的同时，用于精神文化消费迅速增加，各种文化娱乐消费支出1996年达到81.39元，比1991年增长1.9倍；人均旅游消费支出比1992年增长3倍。

居民居住条件明显改善。随着住房制度改革的不断深化，居民住宅建设及危陋房改造工程的加快，使居民的住房条件明显改善，消费支出增加。据城镇居民住户抽样调查：1996年城镇居民人均住房使用面积11.9平方米、居住面积7.7平方米，住房成套率达72.8%，独用厨房户占83.2%，使用管道煤气和液化气户占98.8%，有30.6%的居民户安装了暖气。居住条件的改善带动了住房装饰和卫生、厨房设备的现代化，到1996年人均住房装饰支出比1992年增长2倍，百户拥有各种电炊具28.2件、淋浴热水器39.4台、抽油烟机43.6台。

(张庚新)

走向富裕的农民家庭

党的十四大以来，中国改革和现代化建设进入了一个新的发展阶段。随着社会主义市场经济的建立，农村经济呈现出新的生机和活力，农民的生产积极性空前高涨，农民收入快速增长，1996年天津市农民人均纯收入达3 142元，比1991年的1 169元增长1.7倍，平均每年递增22%，年均增加395元。生活水平明显提高，消费结构向营养型、享受型过渡，富裕起来的农民正朝着小康目标迈进。

乡镇企业为农民增收创造了条件。十四大以来，天津市乡镇企业保持高速发展势头，规模的扩大、新建企业的兴起，容纳了更多的农业剩余劳动力，既壮大了集体经济，又增加了农民收入。1996年，农民从乡镇企业得到的收入人均达815元，比1991年增长2.1倍，人均增加533元，年均增长达25%。乡镇企业收入已成为农民收入的主要来源，1996年农民从集体和乡镇企业得到的收入已占纯收入的39%。

农民从国家政策中得到丰厚的实惠。十四大以来，国家加大了价格改革力度，多次大幅度提高了棉花和粮食收购价格，加之市场机制作用的增强，粮食及主要农副产品的市场价格均有不同程度的提高，使农民受益颇丰。1996年农民人均农业收入1 189元比1991年增长1倍，人均增加706元。

农村二、三产业发展为农民收入快速增长提供了广阔前景。在家庭经营中，部分农户专营或兼营工业、建筑、运输、商业等二三产业，扩大了收入来源。1991年以来，农户经营二、三产业收入递增23%。1996年人均二、三产业收入281元，比1991年增长1.8倍。

各区县的农民收入普遍增长，高收入户明显增多，脱贫致富成效显著。近年，各级领导把增加农民收入作为重要工作目标，增加对农业的投入，引导农民走向市场，开拓收入来源，各区县农民收入普遍大幅度提高。十四大前的4年间天津市大部分区县年均增幅不超过10%，而十四大以来大部分区县收入增幅都在20%以上，这表明天津市农民收入整体提高。十四大以来，天津市农民各收入层次也均有提高，高收入户明显增加，低收入户大幅度下降。1996年人均纯收入在2 000元以上的户所占比重已达80.6%，比1992年高出65.9个百分点，其中人均收入在4 000元以上的户也已占23.5%；人均收入万元户已不鲜见。1 000元收入以下的户比重仅为1.5%，比1992年下降32.7个百分点。1996年，天津市提前一年完成扶贫攻坚计划，175个贫困村全部脱贫，走上了富裕之路，生活质量有很大提高。

农民生活质量大为改善，消费结构明显改观。十四大以来，随着收入大幅度增长，农民的消费支出随之增大，生活质量明显提高。1996年农民用于生活的支出年人均2 101元，年递增速度21%，比1991年增长1.6倍。农民消费观念逐步转变，吃、穿、住、用及文化生活得到全面改善。食品消费质量提高，膳食结构趋向合理。1996年，人均食品支出763元，比1991年人均增长85%，其中副食消费人均417元，比1991年增长1.5倍，增加247元。1996年比1991年人均消费植物油增长28%，蛋类消费增长32%，鱼虾类增长36%，猪肉消费量略减。酒类消费量特别是啤酒消费量增加较多。农民的食品消费正由吃饱向吃好转变，副食消费由过去的高热量、高谷物食品转向高营养、高蛋白食品，饮食结构趋向合理科学。

衣着消费额大幅增长，农民穿衣着装已趋于城市化、时装化和高档化。十四大以来，农民在改善饮食的同时，注重穿衣打扮，衣着支出大幅度增长。1996年人均衣着支出253元，比1991增长2倍。1996年与1991年相比农户购买的各类服装、毛线织品及鞋类均有较大幅度增长，而且质量提高，注重款式与时尚，特别是农村青年，追求时装新潮流，代表了农民服装变化的趋势。

农民居住条件明显改善，住房质量进一步提高。十四大期间，农户的建房从增加面积向注重房屋和居住环境转变，从实用型向享受型转变，从单一型向多功能型转变。1996年人均居住21.83平方米，比1991年增加4.67平方米。每间房屋建房价值达7 559元，比1991年的2 449元，增长2倍多。砖木结构和钢筋混凝土结构的住房面积占96%，大部分农村居民已住上了庭院式楼房。卫生设施、暖气设备已进入农家，购买商品房和装修热正在农村兴起。

家庭大件耐用品增加。十四大以来，随着购买力的增强和住房条件的改善，大件家电和耐用品快速进入农家，拥有量猛增。1996年，电风扇、洗衣机、电冰箱的拥有量每百户分别为139台、76台和52台，分别比1991年增长81%、81%和4.7倍，用于文化生活的电视机，1996年每百户拥有110台，其中彩电74台，比1991年的31台增长2倍。照相机每百户拥有9台；屋内陈设的大件家具每户6件多。抽油烟机、吸尘器、空调器也进入农家。当今农户居室明亮，陈设焕然一新，体现了时代的风貌。

（张永庆）

物价调控成效显著

党的十四大以来，天津市委、市政府在抓住机遇加快经济发展的同时，不断加快价格改革和调控的力度。经过几年的努力，取得了显著效果，不仅较好地实现了价格机制的转换，而且物价涨幅也连续几年在全国保持了较低的水平。

从1993年放开粮食价格以后，全市95%以上的消费品价格已经基本放开，市场调节的作用明显增强，放开价格后的两年曾一度引发了物价的过快上涨。1994年下半年以来，随着国家宏观调控政策的贯彻实施，市委、市政府加大了对市场物价的调控力度，加强了对市场的管理，使过高的物价涨幅得到了有效地遏制。从1995年开始，价格涨势明显减弱，至1996年居民消费价格涨幅回落为9%，商品零售价格涨幅回落为5.1%，涨幅比最高的1994

年回落了15和10.5个百分点，比1991年涨幅回落1.2和2.9个百分点。

近几年，为稳定食品价格，天津市始终把"菜篮子工程"建设作为一项重要工作。一是建立了扶持菜篮子生产基金，加大了对"菜篮子工程"建设的投入，如1993年针对猪肉价格放开后的市场情况，天津市拨专款用于扶持生猪的生产；1995年在全国肉蛋生产受饲料涨价影响滑坡时，又一次拨专款无偿用于种禽的生产，同时发放低息贷款用于扶持5个万头猪场的改造。二是大力发展蔬菜的生产，扩大蔬菜的种植面积，到1996年全市蔬菜种植面积达到130.99万亩，比1991年增长了54.3%。三是新建扩建以何庄子、红旗路、金钟路为代表的大型农贸批发市场12个，为本地和外地菜进入天津市场提供了交易场所。四是建立居民生活必需品的储备制度，合理利用风险基金。市委、市政府在加大对"菜篮子工程"投入的同时，对粮、油、肉、蛋、糖等居民生活必需品增加了储备，设立了市场风险基金，在货源紧张时保证了主要商品的市场供应，稳定了物价。如1995年面对小麦市场价格不断上升和各项生产费用不断增加，适时启动粮食储备和市场风险基金，增加了对面粉生产的补贴。不仅使国营粮店的面粉价格始终保持稳定，而且基本上满足了市民的需求。五是在加大资金投入的同时，注意了发挥各职能部门的作用，将调控任务分解到各有关职能部门，具体负责菜篮子产、供、销各个环节的工作，加强了各个部门的协作，形成了对市场物价齐抓共管的良好环境，提高了政府对市场物价的调控能力。由于措施得力，天津市的菜篮子工程有了较大的发展，加之粮食连续几年的丰收，使天津市食品市场货源充足，价格涨势明显减弱，1996年食品类价格比上年仅上涨了6.7%，比涨幅最高的1994年回落21.8个百分点，比1991年的涨幅回落4.4个百分点。

严格控制地方出台项目，适时适度推进价格改革，几年来市委、市政府为了控制物价过快上涨，严格贯彻执行国家的调控措施，严格控制天津市调价项目的出台，适时适度地推进价格改革，合理解决积累多年的价格矛盾。1994年当放开商品的价格涨势较猛，影响物价总水平上涨较大时，国家和市管商品及服务项目的价格，除富强粉价格上调外，没有任何调价项目的出台，1996年市场调节价格涨势减弱，天津市适度上调了房租、民用电、液化气、管道煤气、煤和部分邮电费、学杂费等价格。虽然这一年居住类和服务项目类价格涨幅较高，但是全年物价总水平上涨幅度仍然较低，保持了天津市物价连续几年在全国处于较低水平。

强化市场物价管理，规范市场经营行为。从1994年初开始，市委、市政府做出决定，对富强粉、高烹油、大米、标准粉实行限价销售，同时还建立了对食糖、牛奶、酱油、醋、火柴、洗衣粉、卫生纸、托儿费、医疗费等28种居民基本生活必需品和服务项目的提价审批、申报、备案制度，对肉、蛋、菜价格分别实行批零差率、零售指导价和最高限价的管理。强化各项行政事业性收费，几年来，先后取消了不合理收费项目300多项，有效地抑制了乱收费、乱涨价之风，为规范市场价格行为先后制定、实施了一系列法规和管理办法，紧紧围绕整顿市场价格秩序，加大物价的监督检查力度，提倡平等竞争，保护合法经营，严厉打击价格欺诈、价格垄断和非法牟取暴利等不法行为，对稳定市场物价起到了一定的作用。

随着经济体制改革的不断深化，近几年天津市工业品市场商品丰富，货源充足，价格相对平稳。特别是由于购买力分流，受供求关系影响，大件耐用消费品价格下降，如音响、录放像机、摄像机等；由于控制了社会集团消费，使一些机电产品价格下滑，如轿车、客车、计算机等。

1991年以来，天津市在控制市场物价方面取得明显成效，实现了低通货膨胀条件下的较快经济发展，为保证居民生活水平的稳步提高和社会的稳定做出了贡献。

（于海芳）

一、综　合

GENERAL SURVEY

1996 年国内生产总值	1 102.40 亿元
其中:第三产业	447.44 亿元
第三产业占全部国内生产总值比重	40.6%
1996 年人均国内生产总值	12 270 元

国内生产总值(亿元)

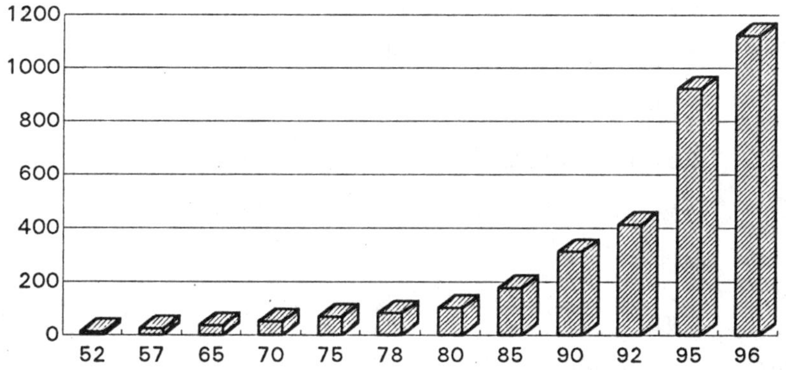

国内生产总值增长速度(以上年为100)

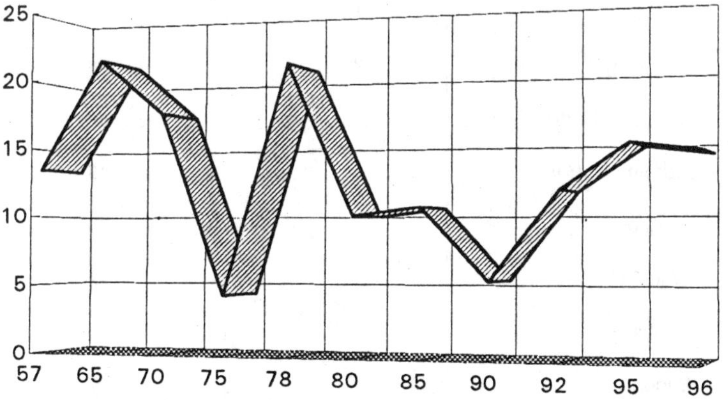

1-1 行政建制
ADMINISTRATIVE DIVISIONS
（1996年底）
END OF 1996

单位：个
Unit：Number

项目	Item	街道办事处 Subdistrict Offices	居民委员会 Resident's Committee	镇政府 Town Governments	乡政府 Township Governments	村民委员会 Village Committees
全市	**Total**	**132**	**2 741**	**75**	**145**	**3 833**
一、市辖区	**Districts Under City Administration**	**132**	**2 667**	**30**	**30**	**708**
1.市内六个区	Six Central Districts	101	2 114			
和平区	Heping	12	258			
河东区	Hedong	20	345			
河西区	Hexi	20	370			
南开区	Nankai	18	438			
河北区	Hebei	16	355			
红桥区	Hongqiao	15	348			
2.滨海三个区	Three Coastal Districts	24	339	5	17	151
塘沽区	Tanggu	13	204	1	7	36
汉沽区	Hangu	6	84	1	6	58
大港区	Dagang	5	51	3	4	57
3.其他四个区	Other Four Districts	7	214	25	13	557
东丽区	Dongli	4	66	6	1	109
西青区	Xiqing		46	4	5	149
津南区	Jinnan	1	32	7	3	173
北辰区	Beicheng	2	70	8	4	126
二、市辖县	**Counties Under City Administration**		**74**	**45**	**115**	**3 125**
宁河县	Ninghe		20	5	17	285
武清县	Wuqing		14	12	22	741
静海县	Jinghai		15	10	18	384
宝坻县	Baodi		17	7	28	766
蓟县	Jixian		8	11	30	949

资料来源：天津市民政局。
Information Source：Tianjin Civil Administration Bureau.

1－2 1996年土地面积

AREA OF LAND, 1996

指 标	Item	面 积 Area (平方公里) (sq. km)	占全市土地总面积比重 Percentage To Total Area (%)
全市土地总面积	**Total Land Area**	**11 919.70**	**100**
耕地面积	Cultivated Land	4 856.09	40.74
园地面积	Garden And Green	373.24	3.13
林地面积	Forest Land	342.27	2.87
牧草面积	Prairie Grasland	5.94	0.05
居民点及工矿用地	Land For Residents And Industry	2 183.45	18.32
交通用地面积	Transportation Land Use	329.37	2.76
水域面积	Water Land	3 150.89	26.43
未利用土地面积	Unused Area	678.45	5.70

资料来源:天津市规划局。
Information Source: Tianjin Municipal Planning Burean.

1－3 1996年城市建设用地

CITY CONSTRUCTION LAND－USED, 1996

指 标	Item	面 积 Area (平方公里) (sq. km)	占城市建设用地比重 Percentage To City Land－used (%)
建成区面积	**City－Scaled Area**	**374.30**	
城市建设用地	**City Construction Land－Used**	**370.35**	**100**
居住用地	Dwelling	97.13	26.2
公共设施用地	Public Instruments	35.13	9.5
工业用地	Industry	97.62	26.4
仓储用地	Warehouse	29.69	8.0
对外交通用地	Traffic	18.34	5.0
道路广场用地	Road and Square	29.44	7.9
市政公用设施用地	Public Instruments Of Municipal Administration	7.61	2.1
绿 地	Green land	17.49	4.7
特殊用地	Special	37.90	10.2

资料来源:天津市建委。
Information Source: Tianjin Municipal Urban And Rural Construction Commission.

1-4 1996年气象资料

METEOROLOGICAL DATA, 1996

地 区 District		最高气温 Highest Temperature (℃)	最低气温 Lowest Temperature (℃)	全年平均气温 Annual Average Temperature (℃)	平均湿度 Average Moisture (%)	日照时数 Hours Of Sunshine (小时/年) hours/year	降雨量 Precipitation (毫米) (mm)
全市平均	**City Average**	**35.2**	**-11.8**	**12.1**	**62**	**2 429.2**	**554.3**
塘沽区	Tanggu	34.1	-10.3	12.7	59	2 410.8	431.8
汉沽区	Hangu	34.2	-14.2	11.7	65	2 695.0	396.6
大港区	Dagang	35.3	-10.6	12.3	62	2 645.3	406.2
东丽区	Dongli	36.2	-11.4	12.3	61	2 534.3	397.2
西青区	Xiqing	35.5	-10.6	12.2	62	2 333.5	472.1
津南区	Jinnan	35.9	-10.7	12.1	63	2 582.5	366.1
北辰区	Beichen	35.5	-12.8	12.1	62	2 251.0	512.7
宁河县	Ninghe	33.8	-12.0	11.8	68	2 333.7	539.3
武清县	Wuqing	35.0	-11.2	12.3	62	2 315.7	773.9
静海县	Jinghai	36.3	-11.0	12.4	58	2 473.6	550.8
宝坻县	Baodi	34.9	-13.0	11.5	61	2 492.4	803.4
蓟 县	Jixian	35.1	-12.0	12.2	56	2 083.1	1 001.0

地 区 District		无霜期 Non-Frosting Period (天)Day	雾天数 Foggy Days (天)Day	最长连续降雨天数 Longest Precipitation Days (天)(Day)	最大日降雨量 longest Per Day Precipitation (毫米)(mm)	最长无降雨日数 longest Non-Precipitation Days (天)(Day)	最大积雪深度 Maximum Depth Of Snow (厘米)
全市平均	**City Average**	**219**	**21**	**6**	**89.1**	**73**	**2**
塘沽区	Tanggu	213	11	4	54.9	82	2
汉沽区	Hangu	243	27	4	52.9	82	3
大港区	Dagang	243	22	6	73.4	73	1
东丽区	Dongli	214	26	7	56.1	68	2
西青区	Xiqing	243	22	6	85.5	82	1
津南区	Jinnan	214	20	5	59.2	59	2
北辰区	Beichen	243	28	5	65.2	68	1
宁河县	Ninghe	214	13	6	125.2	82	2
武清县	Wuqing	243	12	6	204.8	68	2
静海县	Jinghai	204	35	6	58.6	67	3
宝坻县	Baodi	188	23	6	109.4	82	1
蓟 县	Jixian	171	7	7	123.8	61	2

1－5 主要年份国民经济主要指标和增长速度

MAIN INDICATORS AND INCREASE RATE OF NATIONAL ECONOMY IN MAIN YEARS

年 份 Year	户籍人口数 Registered Populations (万人) (10 000 Person)	社会从业人员数 Total Employments (万人) (10 000 Person)	#职工人数 Staffs and Workers	国内生产总值 Gross Domestic Products (亿元) (100 000 000 Yuan)	人均国内生产总值 Per Capita GDP (元/人) (Yuan/person)	社会劳动生产率 Society Labour Productivity (元/人) (Yuan/person)	农业总产值 Gross output Value Of Agriculture (亿元) (100 000 000 Yuan)
1952	439.22	159.50	45.18	12.80	299	825	2.73
1957	529.65	186.50	86.24	24.11	468	1 311	3.23
1962	595.63	203.80	106.48	24.25	414	1 166	2.77
1965	637.80	227.50	120.30	35.96	571	1 602	4.82
1970	652.70	270.20	135.81	50.99	791	1 960	5.20
1975	702.86	328.60	181.46	69.73	1 011	2 232	5.39
1978	724.27	366.70	217.40	82.65	1 160	2 335	6.72
1980	748.91	394.78	242.69	103.52	1 392	2 714	9.25
1985	804.80	455.98	276.48	175.71	2 198	3 890	20.44
1986	814.97	466.90	280.20	194.67	2 406	4 219	26.93
1987	828.73	470.93	281.53	220.00	2 682	4 692	32.93
1988	839.21	465.15	281.36	259.64	3 117	5 548	44.49
1989	852.35	469.79	284.38	283.34	3 353	6 061	51.82
1990	866.25	470.07	284.31	310.95	3 621	6 617	54.86
1991	872.63	479.67	291.56	342.75	3 943	7 218	58.05
1992	878.97	485.73	293.97	411.24	4 696	8 520	62.15
1993	885.89	503.10	293.45	536.10	6 075	10 843	70.62
1994	890.55	513.00	291.94	725.14	8 164	14 273	94.97
1995	894.67	515.30	289.59	920.11	10 308	17 896	133.25
1996	898.45	512.00	283.98	1 102.40	12 270	21 462	142.29
平均每年递增% Average Annual Increase Rate%							
1953－1957	3.8	3.2	13.8	12.8	8.8	9.0	3.8
1958－1962	2.4	1.8	4.3	－1.8	－4.3	－4.2	－2.6
1963－1965	2.3	3.7	4.2	15.3	12.6	12.4	18.8
1966－1970	0.5	3.5	2.5	7.7	7.1	4.6	1.1
1971－1975	1.5	4.0	6.0	7.2	5.7	3.3	1.1
1976－1980	1.3	3.7	6.0	7.3	6.0	3.1	3.5
1981－1985	1.4	2.9	2.6	9.3	7.7	5.7	9.7
1986－1990	1.5	0.6	0.6	5.2	3.7	4.4	10.7
1991－1995	0.6	1.9	0.4	11.7	10.9	9.8	7.1
1953－1996	1.6	2.7	4.3	8.0	6.3	5.1	5.2
1979－1996	1.2	1.9	1.5	9.2	7.8	7.0	8.8
1981－1990	1.5	1.8	1.6	7.3	5.7	5.0	10.2
1992－1996	0.6	1.3	－0.5	13.4	12.8	11.8	7.1
1996 比 1995	0.4	－0.6	－1.9	14.3	13.6	14.4	7.2

注:1.本表国内生产总值、人均国内生产总值及农业总产值按现行价计算,速度按可比价计算。2.社会劳动生产率按现价国内生产总值计算,速度按可比价计算。

Note:1. Gross Domestic products, per capita GDP and gross output value Of agriculture are at current prices, increase rate are based on comparable prices. 2. Society Labour productivity are at current prices Of GDP, speed are based on comparable prices.

1－5 续表 1
Continued

年 份 Year	工业总产值 Gross Output Value Of Industry （亿元）（100 000 000 Yuan）	轻工业 Light Industry	重工业 Heavy Industry	金融系统存款余额 Deposits Of Financial System （亿元）（100 000 000 Yuan）	#城乡居民储蓄存款余额 Savings Deposit Balance Of Rural and Urban Residents	金融系统贷款余额 Loans Of Financial System （亿元）（100 000 000 Yuan）
1952	19.70	16.36	3.34	2.66	0.50	0.46
1957	40.43	29.00	11.43	3.06	1.05	10.91
1962	45.39	29.12	16.27	10.29	0.93	24.96
1965	66.35	39.08	27.27	12.14	1.57	25.25
1970	102.77	54.83	47.94	14.48	1.59	39.04
1975	145.56	74.46	71.10	25.48	2.88	68.59
1978	157.90	81.48	76.42	32.85	4.02	80.14
1980	195.94	106.00	89.94	44.05	7.96	102.66
1985	319.47	164.22	155.25	114.25	29.38	191.04
1986	344.73	174.84	169.89	129.14	40.52	224.49
1987	405.49	205.51	199.98	156.48	54.95	260.12
1988	521.10	267.48	253.62	176.44	62.72	296.18
1989	634.24	317.43	316.81	203.44	89.71	341.60
1990	679.94	354.50	325.44	263.21	126.92	415.91
1991	786.60	392.29	394.31	336.56	163.18	487.43
1992	997.91	465.48	532.43	467.81	202.66	624.82
1993	1 401.84	530.05	871.79	586.12	269.70	768.57
1994	1 754.30	760.80	993.50	800.56	394.57	927.05
1995	1 879.65	752.03	1 127.62	1 079.97	549.97	1 113.95
1996	2 522.42	1 175.17	1 347.25	1 391.62	724.00	1 325.49
平均每年递增％ Average Annual Increase Rate％						
1953－1957	16.6	13.5	29.5	2.8	16.0	88.4
1958－1962	0.4	－1.3	4.5	27.5	－2.4	18.0
1963－1965	15.5	12.8	20.6	5.7	19.1	0.4
1966－1970	10.3	7.5	14.5	3.6	0.3	9.1
1971－1975	8.5	6.7	10.6	12.0	12.6	11.9
1976－1980	6.0	7.7	4.1	11.6	22.5	8.4
1981－1985	9.7	10.1	9.1	21.0	29.9	13.2
1986－1990	10.5	10.2	11.2	18.2	34.0	16.9
1991－1995	20.7	16.3	25.0	32.6	34.1	21.7
1953－1996	10.9	9.5	13.9	15.3	18.0	19.8
1979－1996	13.8	13.4	14.1	23.1	33.4	16.9
1981－1990	10.2	10.1	10.1	19.6	31.9	15.1
1992－1996	23.3	21.2	25.3	32.8	34.7	22.1
1996 比 1995	24.7	31.8	19.5	29.1	31.6	19.0

注：1. 本表工业总产值按现行价计算，1995、1996 年为新规定，其他为原规定，速度按可比价计算，以下各表同。2. 金融系统存、贷款余额为当年年末数。

Note：1. Gross output value Of industry are current prices, Increase rate are based on comparable prices. They are new stipulation, Others are former stipulation, 1995－1996, Same to next Tables. 2. Deposits and Loans Of Financial System are All by the End Of 1996.

1－5 续表 2
Continued

单位:亿元
Unit:100 000 000 Yuan

年 份 Year	市场货币流通量 Market Money Currency	地方财政预算内收入 Local Goverment Budgetary Revenue	地方财政预算内支出 Local Government Budgetary Expenditures	全社会固定资产投资额 Total Investments in Fixed Assets	#地 方 Local Government	社会新增固定资产 Newly increased Fixed Assets
1952	0.54	3.88	1.08	1.03	0.32	
1957	0.97	7.99	1.63	2.40	1.13	
1962	1.52	9.77	2.49	1.86	1.33	
1965	1.38	13.33	3.50	2.91	1.84	
1970	1.81	28.02	6.40	6.17	4.34	
1975	2.30	39.17	10.61	16.25	8.88	
1978	2.50	39.25	14.51	20.30	10.03	
1980	3.79	40.94	14.67	23.92	14.77	17.84
1985	9.50	48.21	26.97	65.90	53.27	42.62
1986	12.25	54.50	34.85	71.91	53.02	56.39
1987	14.60	55.87	31.16	76.44	55.35	61.04
1988	21.50	44.81	34.99	82.61	54.96	63.28
1989	24.67	46.49	39.26	83.88	53.77	69.55
1990	26.91	44.88	40.20	87.69	57.47	65.16
1991	32.00	58.09	47.47	128.95	93.14	74.11
1992	42.00	63.05	46.52	169.88	123.85	102.27
1993	52.00	74.96	51.27	226.56	176.14	140.01
1994	65.00	50.15	72.32	315.97	256.88	261.12
1995	70.00	61.90	93.33	393.18	309.75	300.86
1996	85.00	79.04	113.21	435.82	325.71	313.12
平均每年递增% Average Annual Increase Rate%						
1953－1957	12.4	15.5	8.6	20.9	36.8	
1958－1962	9.4	4.1	8.8	24.4	45.6	
1963－1965	－3.2	10.9	12.0	26.4	20.7	
1966－1970	5.6	16.0	12.8	6.7	4.2	
1971－1975	4.9	6.9	10.6	22.0	14.0	
1976－1980	10.5	0.9	6.7	6.4	7.7	
1981－1985	20.2	3.3	12.9	20.8	27.0	23.6
1986－1990	23.1	－1.4	8.3	6.8	1.0	13.4
1991－1995	21.1	21.2	18.3	36.8	43.3	35.1
1953－1996	12.2	8.4	11.2	13.8	16.5	
1979－1996	21.6	7.2	12.1	17.5	21.1	
1981－1990	21.7	0.9	10.6	16.8	19.0	17.9
1992－1996	21.6	18.8	19.0	30.6	33.1	39.4
1996 比 1995	21.4	15.8	21.3	10.8	5.2	4.1

注:1.财政收支为当年决算数,按可比口径计算 1996 年全市财政收入完成 137.45 亿元,增长速度按可比口径计算。2.固定资产投资的平均递增速度按累计法计算。

Note:1. Budgetary revenue and expenditures are fina account, in1995 budgetary reventue overfulfiled 13 745 000 000 Yuan based on Comparable prices. Increase Rate on Comparable Prices. 2. Average annual increase rate Of investment In fixed assets is used accumulate method.

1-5续表3
Continued

年份 Year	房屋竣工面积 Floor Space Of Buildings Completed (万平方米)(10 000 sq.m)	#住宅 Residential Housing	社会货运量 Freight Traffic (万吨)(10 000 tn)	港口货物吞吐量 Cargo Handled At ports (万吨)(10 000 tn)	邮电业务总量 Tele-communication Services (万元)(10 000 Yuan)	社会消费品零售总额 Retail Sales Of Consumer Goods (亿元)(100 000 000 Yuan)
1952			1 748	74	894	7.19
1957			2 984	284	935	10.55
1962			3 498	391	1 436	12.31
1965			3 450	549	1 621	12.32
1970			4 837	817	1 660	14.57
1975			6 766	826	2 385	21.18
1978			9 241	1 131	2 710	25.21
1980	395.3	239.0	13 949	1 192	3 163	34.64
1985	598.1	342.1	18 249	1 856	5 290	64.11
1986	620.3	328.6	18 525	1 818	6 158	81.39
1987	451.3	215.4	18 400	1 725	7 244	95.56
1988	414.5	195.1	16 693	2 190	10 061	121.28
1989	383.4	194.9	15 543	2 437	12 538	134.30
1990	363.3	189.5	15 929	2 063	32 735	139.89
1991	361.2	193.8	18 308	2 378	44 527	159.44
1992	406.9	199.4	17 522	2 929	61 063	181.20
1993	467.3	286.5	21 640	3 719	97 062	227.42
1994	636.4	438.6	23 783	4 652	132 465	303.37
1995	736.5	486.9	24 040	5 787	187 195	375.64
1996	725.1	494.7	24 133	6 188	256 978	470.04
平均每年递增% Average Annual Increase Rate%						
1953-1957			11.3	30.9	0.9	5.5
1958-1962			3.2	6.6	9.0	0.8
1963-1965			-0.5	12.0	4.1	4.0
1966-1970			7.0	8.3	0.5	3.9
1971-1975			6.9	0.2	7.5	7.7
1976-1980			15.6	7.6	5.8	8.9
1981-1985	12.4	12.2	5.5	9.3	10.8	9.3
1986-1990	-9.6	-13.7	-2.7	2.1	24.9	6.5
1991-1995	12.3	18.1	8.6	22.9	41.7	9.3
1953-1996			6.1	10.6	11.9	6.6
1979-1996			5.5	9.9	23.8	9.4
1981-1990	4.5	3.1	1.3	5.6	17.7	7.8
1992-1996	17.1	23.5	5.7	21.1	42.0	11.9
1996比1995	-1.5	1.6	0.4	6.9	37.3	19.1

注:1.房屋竣工面积不含农村集体和个人建房数。2.社会货物运输量为辖区内数字。3.邮电业务总量1989年以前为1980年不变价,1989年以后为1990年不变价,增长速度按可比价计算。4.计算社会消费品零售总额增长速度时已扣除物价因素。

Note:1. Floor space Of buildings completed exclude rural collecture-owned and individual houses. 2. Figures Of freight traffic are center districts. 3. Before 1989 telecommunication services are at 1980 constant prices, After 1989, They are at 1990 constant prices, Normal increase speed are based on caparable prices. 4. Calculating increase speed Of retail sales Of consumer goods without price sectors.

1－5 续表 4
Continued

年 份 Year	实际利用外资额 Foreign Capital Actually untilized (万美元) (us$ 10 000)	#客商直投 Direct Foreign Investments	海关进出口总额 Total Value Of Imports & Exports (亿美元) (us$ 100 000 000)	#出口 Exports	外贸进出口总额 Total Value Of Exports in Foreign Trade (亿美元) (us$ 100 000 000)	#出口 Exports
1952						
1957					2.50	2.48
1962					2.40	2.34
1965					3.54	3.42
1970					3.58	3.18
1975					8.86	7.72
1978					9.88	8.64
1980	271	271			18.27	15.42
1985	7 558	4 409	96.18	20.07	14.86	11.53
1986	15 771	4 287	96.82	26.37	16.64	12.55
1987	24 610	5 491	89.98	32.85	20.13	15.17
1988	48 352	2 395	102.77	38.78	22.78	16.82
1989	43 699	8 134	106.30	39.70	22.14	16.86
1990	33 467	8 315	85.95	42.53	22.10	17.86
1991	48 144	9 388	91.37	46.48	20.20	16.06
1992	83 122	23 138	104.61	54.60	23.76	17.52
1993	93 502	54 120	125.04	66.03	27.76	19.42
1994	177 642	101 499	161.67	86.81	33.12	24.00
1995	211 010	152 064	217.46	127.81	65.46	29.98
1996	298 358	200 587	216.85	122.89	82.97	40.49
平均每年递增% Average Annual Increase Rate%						
1953－1957					－0.8	－1.2
1958－1962					13.8	13.5
1963－1965					0.2	－1.4
1966－1970					19.9	19.4
1971－1975					15.6	14.8
1976－1980					－4.1	－5.7
1981－1985	94.6	74.7			8.3	9.1
1986－1990	34.7	13.5	－2.2	16.2	7.1	5.5
1991－1995	44.5	78.8	20.4	24.6	24.3	10.9
1953－1996						
1979－1996					12.5	9.0
1981－1990	61.9	40.8			1.9	1.5
1992－1996	44.0	84.5	18.9	21.5	32.7	20.3
1996 比 1995	41.4	31.9	－0.3	－3.8	26.7	35.1

1-5续表5
Continued

年份 Year	职工工资总额 Total Wages Of Staff and Workers (亿元) (100 000 000 Yuan)	#国有经济 State-owned Units	职工年平均工资 Average Annual Wages (元) (Yuan)	#国有经济 State-owned Units	城市居民人均生活费收入 Annual Per Capita Income Available for living Of Urban Households (元) (Yuan)	城市居民人均消费性支出 Annual Per Capita Expenditure Available for Living Of Urban Household (元) (Yuan)
1952	2.56	2.56		573	182	176
1957	5.05	5.05		749	225	216
1962	7.11	7.11		685	235	238
1965	8.48	7.29	714	745	240	234
1970	8.58	7.17	652	673	261	255
1975	10.66	8.61	618	663	302	295
1978	14.00	11.51	640	690	361	345
1980	19.32	15.77	820	865	492	475
1985	34.14	24.69	1 250	1 223	812	771
1986	41.50	30.08	1 498	1 455	988	949
1987	46.09	34.03	1 651	1 622	1 095	1 071
1988	55.16	41.66	1 975	1 972	1 232	1 279
1989	64.02	48.37	2 262	2 274	1 375	1 291
1990	69.38	55.50	2 438	2 611	1 522	1 440
1991	79.73	62.34	2 724	2 912	1 699	1 586
1992	91.56	71.97	3 118	3 383	2 080	1 907
1993	116.78	90.32	4 080	4 410	2 579	2 322
1994	154.04	116.07	5 364	5 806	3 725	3 301
1995	184.80	135.22	6 501	6 963	4 626	4 064
1996	212.05	154.34	7 643	8 072	5 525	4 680
平均每年递增% Average Annual Increase Rate%						
1953-1957	12.1	12.1		3.3	2.1	2.0
1958-1962	4.7	4.7		-3.9	-1.4	-0.3
1963-1965	10.0	4.6		6.7	4.5	3.2
1966-1970	0.6		-1.4	-1.5	2.3	2.1
1971-1975	4.4	3.7	-1.1	-0.3	2.9	3.0
1976-1980	11.2	11.5	4.5	4.9	8.9	8.6
1981-1985	8.4	5.8	5.3	3.7	7.0	6.6
1986-1990	5.2	7.4	4.4	5.2	3.6	3.5
1991-1995	5.2	3.4	5.3	5.3	8.0	6.4
1953-1996	6.6	5.8		2.4	4.2	3.9
1979-1996	7.1	6.4	5.7	5.6	7.1	6.4
1981-1990	6.8	6.6	4.8	4.4	5.2	5.0
1992-1996	5.5	4.0	6.6	6.3	9.8	7.7
1996比1995	5.3	4.7	7.9	6.4	9.6	5.6

注：1985年以后职工工资总额，职工平均工资中包括肉价补贴，计算工资总额、平均工资、城市居民生活费收入及支出平均增长速度时已扣除物价因素。

Note: After 1985, Total Wages Of staff and workers are include meat allowances; caculating average increase speed Of total wages average wages, Annual income and expenditure available for living Of urban households without price sectors.

1-5 续表 6
Continued

年 份 Year	农民人均纯收入 Annual Per capita Net Income Of Farmers (元) (Yuan)	农民人均生活消费支出 Annual Per Capita Expenditure Available for Farmers (元) (Yuan)	各类学校在校学生数 Student Enrollment by Level Of School (万人) (10 000 Persons)	国有单位自然科技人员数 Natural Science and Technology Personnal In State-owned Units (人) (Person)	医院床位数 Hospital Beds (张) (sheet)	卫生技术人员数 Medical Technical Personnal (人) (Persons)	#医生 Doctors
1952			57.14		3 457	8 481	3 326
1957			83.92		6 156	15 124	5 522
1962			106.37		10 521	23 858	8 627
1965			148.10		11 266	26 393	10 585
1970			148.17		11 361	23 591	9 046
1975			169.71		15 961	33 734	12 326
1978	153	132	162.30	102 022	17 288	40 653	15 776
1980	278	208	139.06	127 803	18 753	50 662	20 474
1985	564	426	121.09	194 837	25 191	60 412	25 555
1986	635	480	123.10	203 276	27 247	62 897	26 750
1987	749	539	124.25	214 700	28 371	63 067	27 222
1988	891	714	125.33	235 120	30 640	63 924	29 968
1989	1 020	781	129.42	261 393	32 224	65 766	31 619
1990	1 069	733	134.97	271 761	33 382	67 485	32 034
1991	1 169	796	138.01	280 986	35 124	68 887	32 385
1992	1 410	923	140.78	287 709	36 035	69 815	32 320
1993	1 593	1 011	145.27	290 789	36 724	70 920	33 026
1994	1 956	1 274	149.67	241 958	37 157	71 217	33 373
1995	2 531	1 717	155.28	248 739	37 280	71 806	33 693
1996	3 142	2 101	161.40	265 924	38 284	71 014	32 975
平均每年递增% Average Annual Increase Rate%							
1953-1957			8.0		12.2	12.3	10.7
1958-1962			4.9		11.3	9.5	9.3
1963-1965			11.7		2.3	3.4	7.1
1966-1970					0.2	-2.2	-3.1
1971-1975			2.8		7.0	7.4	6.4
1976-1980			-3.9		3.3	8.5	10.7
1981-1985	15.2	15.4	-2.7	8.8	6.1	3.6	4.5
1986-1990	13.6	11.5	2.2	6.9	5.8	2.2	4.6
1991-1995	18.8	18.6	2.8	-1.8	2.2	1.2	1.2
1953-1996			2.4		5.6	4.9	5.4
1979-1996	18.3	16.6		5.5	4.5	3.1	4.2
1981-1990	14.4	13.4	-0.3	7.8	5.9	2.9	4.6
1992-1996	21.9	21.4	3.2	-1.1	1.7	0.6	0.4
1996 比 1995	24.1	22.4	3.9	6.9	2.7	-1.1	-2.1

注:1994 年以后自然科技人员按普查新标准划分。
Note: Natural science and technology personal are on new standard Of census, After 1994.

1－6　国民经济主要比例关系

MAIN PERCENTAGES OF ECONOMIC INDICATORS

单位：%
Unit：%

指　标	Item	1980 年	1985 年	1990 年	1995 年	1996 年
1. 社会从业人员比例	Type Of Industry As Percentage Of Employment					
第一产业	Primary Industry		21.7	19.9	16.1	16.0
第二产业	Secondary Industry		50.0	49.4	48.0	47.1
第三产业	Tertiary Industry		28.2	30.7	35.9	36.8
2. 国内生产总值比例	Type Of Industry As Percentage Of GDP					
第一产业	Primary Industry	6.3	7.4	8.8	6.9	6.4
第二产业	Secondary Industry	70.0	65.0	57.7	54.5	53.0
第三产业	Tertiary Industry	23.7	27.6	33.5	38.6	40.6
3. 工业总产值比例	Ratios Of Gross Output Value Of Industry					
轻工业	Light Industry	54.1	51.4	52.1	40.0	46.6
重工业	Heavy Industry	45.9	48.6	47.9	60.0	53.4
4. 农林牧渔业总产值比例	Ratios Of Gross Output Value Of Farming, Forestry, Animal Husbandry And Fishery					
农　业(种植业)	Farming	78.4	67.6	63.3	64.0	63.4
林　业	Foresting	0.5	1.3	0.8	0.6	0.7
牧　业	Animal Husbandry	17.6	25.0	26.8	27.5	27.4
渔　业	Fishery	3.5	6.1	9.1	7.9	8.5
5. 固定资产投资比例	Percentage Of Investment In Fixed Assets					
第一产业	Primary Industry	2.0	1.8	2.6	0.3	0.2
第二产业	Secondary Industry	67.8	55.8	68.0	53.4	61.5
第三产业	Tertiary Industry	30.2	42.4	29.4	46.3	38.3
6. 固定资产投资资金来源比例	Percentage Of Source Of Investment in Fixed Assets					
国家预算内投资	Government Budgetary Appropriations	51.5	20.2	9.1	2.7	1.4
国内贷款	Domestic Loans	10.1	24.8	23.0	23.6	20.7
利用外资	Foreign Investments	7.1	4.6	16.9	23.1	21.1
自筹投资	Private Construct Funds	31.3	37.0	36.6	36.0	44.4
其他投资	Others		13.4	14.3	14.6	12.5

1－6 续表
Continued

单位：%
Unit：%

指 标 Item		1980 年	1985 年	1990 年	1995 年	1996 年
7. 基建投资中能源运输邮电投资比例	Energy Industry Transportation, Post And Telecommunication Services As Percentage Of Investment In Fixed Assets Of State－Owned units					
能源工业	Energy Industry	13.2	17.0	45.7	25.7	33.6
运输邮电业	Transportation, Post And Telecommunication Services	6.8	9.8	15.0	10.2	11.6
8. 货运量比例	Ratios Of Volume Of Freight Traffic					
铁 路	Railways	15.0	14.2	14.0	11.3	11.1
公 路	Highways	79.3	79.5	77.4	80.4	80.8
水 运	Waterways	5.7	4.5	6.6	6.3	6.2
民 航	Civil Aviation					
管道运输	Pipelines		1.8	2.0	2.0	2.0
9. 能源使用比例	Ratios Of Energy Consumption					
第一产业	Primary Industry				2.7	2.4
第二产业	Secondary Industry				69.8	71.0
第三产业	Tertiary Industry				18.8	15.4
10. 财政收入占国内生产总值比例	Revenue As percentage Of GDP	49.2	39.6	25.1	15.7	15.0
11. 固定资产投资占国内生产总值比例	Investments In Fixed Assets As Percentage Of GDP	23.1	37.5	28.2	42.7	39.5
12. 基建拨款占财政支出比例	Capital Construction Appropriate As Percentage Of Government Expenditure	31.2	41.8	10.6	19.2	20.5
13. 文教科卫事业费占财政支出比例	Culture, Education, Science And Health Funds As Percentage Of Government Expenditure	16.3	17.9	24.2	23.5	17.8

1－7　国民经济主要指标经济类型变化

ECONOMIC TYPE CHANGES OF MAIN INDICATORS IN NATIONAL ECONOMY

单位：%
Unit：%

指　标	Item	1980年	1985年	1990年	1995年	1996年
1.社会从业人员数	Employments					
国有经济	State－owned	47.6	45.0	46.2	39.2	38.9
城镇集体经济	Urban Collective－owned	13.8	15.3	13.3	13.3	12.3
城镇个体经济	Urban Individual	0.2	1.0	1.1	2.4	2.7
乡村劳动力	Rural Social Labor Force	38.3	38.4	37.9	37.9	38.1
2.社会固定资产投资额	Investments In Fixed Assets					
国有经济	State－Owend	92.5	82.2	82.3	62.3	59.4
集体经济	Collective－Owned	6.2	11.2	12.0	14.9	15.3
其他经济	Others	1.3	6.6	5.6	22.8	25.3
#"三资"经济	"Foreign－Funded Economy"				16.2	16.6
3.乡及乡以上工业总产值	Gross Output Value Of Industry Enterprises					
国有经济	State－Owned	83.1	79.8	74.4	42.1	35.3
集体经济	Collective－owned	16.7	18.4	18.9	15.1	17.3
其他经济	Others	0.2	1.8	6.7	42.8	47.4
#"三资"经济	"Foreign－Funded Economy"		0.4	3.6	37.7	43.1
4.乡及乡以上工业增加值	Net Output　Value Of Industry Enterprises					
国有经济	State－Owned	83.6	79.7	74.2	53.4	43.9
集体经济	Collective－Owned	16.4	18.9	18.5	13.2	16.2
其他经济	Others		1.4	7.4	33.4	39.9
#"三资"经济	"Foreign－Funded Economy"				28.1	34.5
5.乡及乡以上利税总额	Total Pre－tax Profits Of Enterprises					
国有经济	State－Owned	86.8	83.3	77.2	33.6	26.5
集体经济	Collective－Owned	12.8	15.3	16.2	13.4	16.6
其他经济	Others	0.4	1.4	6.6	52.9	56.9
#"三资"经济	"Foreign－Funded Economy"			3.8	47.0	51.5
6.社会消费品零售总额	Retail Sales Of Consumer Goods					
国有经济	State－Owned	69.7	58.4	43.9	27.8	24.6
集体经济	Collective－Owned	28.9	31.5	28.9	17.6	21.2
其他经济	Others	1.4	10.1	27.2	54.6	54.2
#个体经济	Individual	0.1	7.1	20.8	13.3	15.2
农民对非农业居民零售	Farmers Selling At Retail To Nonagricultural Residents	1.3	3.0	5.8	24.9	27.2

注：1.1980年工业总产值构成按1980年不变价计算。2.社会消费品零售总额的比例关系1992年以前按社会商品零售总额计算。3.第四项数据1990年以前按净产值计算。4.1994、1995年国有经济中不含"三资"和股份制经济。

Note：1. Composition Of gross output value Of industry are at 1980 constant prices. 2. Percentage Of retail sales Of consumer goods were caculated with retail sales Of commodities before 1992. 3. Data for Fourth Item caculated on Net Output Value before 1990. 4. State－owened in1994、1995 exclude "Foreign Capital"and "Stock Owership".

1-8 国民经济主要指标平均每人水平

PER CAPITA LEVEL OF MAIN INDICATORS IN NATIONAL ECONOMY

指 标	Item	1985年	1990年	1995年	1996年
1.国内生产总值 (元)	Gross Domestic Products (Yuan)	2 198	3 621	10 308	12 270
2.地方财政收入 (元)	Local Government Revenue (Yuan)	603	522	1 315	1 533
3.地方财政支出 (元)	Local Government Expenditures (Yuan)	337	468	1 046	1 263
4.社会固定资产投资(元)	Investments In Fixed Assets (Yuan)	824	1 020	4 404	4 861
5.工业总产值 (元)	Gross Output Value Of Industry (Yuan)	3 993	7 913	21 058	28 134
6.主要工业产品产量	Output Of Major Industrial Products				
原 油 (吨)	Crude Oil (tn)	0.47	0.55	0.70	0.72
天然气 (立方米)	Naturl Gas (cu.m)	71	43	85	85
发电量 (千瓦时)	Electricity (kwh)	1 008	1 104	1 497	1 517
钢 (吨)	Steel (tn)	0.14	0.19	0.19	0.22
钢 材 (吨)	Rolled Steel (tn)	0.18	0.21	0.48	0.49
水 泥 (吨)	Cement (tn)	0.23	0.16	0.22	0.23
布 (米)	Cloth (m)	55	57	56	44
纱 (公斤)	Yarn (kg)	14.9	13.6	13.8	11.7
7.农业总产值 (元)	Gross Output Value Of Agriculture (Yuan)	255	638	1 493	1 587
8.主要农产品产量	Output Of Major Farm Products				
粮 食 (公斤)	Grain (kg)	176	220	232	231
棉 花 (公斤)	Cotton (kg)	3.0	1.8	1.3	0.6
油 料 (公斤)	Oil-Bearing (kg)	8.5	5.4	4.5	3.5
蔬 菜 (公斤)	Vegetable (kg)	189	312	486	505
肉 类 (公斤)	Meat (kg)	8	14	24	25
蛋 类 (公斤)	Eggs (kg)	13	22	27	27
奶 类 (公斤)	Milks (kg)	5.4	8.9	12.5	12.7
水产品 (公斤)	Aquatic Products (kg)	6.1	12.7	17.2	19.0
水 果 (公斤)	Fruits (kg)	8.2	11.8	22.3	23.7
9.居民消费品零售额(元)	Total Retail Sales Of Personal Cosumption (Yuan)	801	1 628	4 208	5 243
10.城市居民主要商品购买量	Perchase Volume Of Major Products Of Urban Overall Residents				
粮 食 (公斤)	Grain (kg)	144.0	136.2	109.3	113.5
食用植物油(公斤)	Edible Vegetable-oil (kg)	6.3	8.1	8.4	9.0
猪牛羊肉 (公斤)	Pork Beef and Mutton (kg)	19.0	27.7	20.4	23.2
蛋 类 (公斤)	Eggs (kg)	14.7	14.4	18.5	18.2
蔬 菜 (公斤)	Vegetable (kg)	171.5	150.1	119.0	136.1
鱼 (公斤)	Fish (kg)	8.7	9.4	9.7	9.8
鲜乳品 (公斤)	Milk (kg)	6.84	8.34	7.05	7.39
干鲜瓜果 (公斤)	Fresh and Dried Fruit (kg)	40.1	56.6	55.3	65.7
服 装 (件)	Garment (piece)	2.2	2.3	5.8	6.4
皮 鞋 (双)	Leather Shoes (pair)	0.7	0.8	2.5	2.5
11.外贸出口商品总值(美元)	Total Value Of Export Commodites ($)	144	208	336	452
12.社会货物运输量(吨)	Freight Traffic (tn)	22.8	18.5	26.9	26.9

1-9 平均每天社会经济活动

AVERAGE DAILY SOCIAL AND ECONOMIC ACTIVITIES

指 标	Item	1985年	1990年	1995年	1996年
一、全市每天创造的财富	Daily Productions				
国内生产总值 (万元)	Gross Domestic Products (10 000 Yuan)	4 814	8 519	25 208	30 202
工业总产值 (万元)	Gross Output Value Of Industry (10 000 Yuan)	8 753	18 628	51 497	69 107
农业总产值 (万元)	Gross Output Value Of Agriculture (10 000 Yuan)	560	1 503	3 651	3 898
地方财政收入 (万元)	Local Government Revence (10 000 Yuan)	1 321	1 230	3 215	3 766
外贸出口总额 (万美元)	Total value Of Export In Foreign Trade (US$ 10 000)	316	489	821	1 109
实际利用外资 (万美元)	Foreign Capital Actually Untilized (US$ 10 000)	20.7	91.7	578	817
竣工房屋建筑面积(万平方米)	Floor Space Of Buildings Completed (US$ 10 000)	1.64	1.00	2.02	1.99
主要工业产品产量	Output Of Major Industrail Products				
钢 (吨)	Steel (tn)	3 067	4 568	4 701	5 507
钢材 (吨)	Rolled Steel (tn)	4 022	4 897	11 791	12 079
水泥 (吨)	Cement (tn)	2 880	3 346	5 496	5 695
原油 (吨)	Crude Oil (tn)	10 264	12 863	17 009	17 715
原盐 (吨)	Sait (tn)	4 862	4 720	6 038	6 048
发电量 (万千瓦时)	Electricity (10 000 kwh)	2 210	2 599	3 662	3 727
汽车 (辆)	Motor Vhicles	57	74	359	420
电视机 (台)	Television (set)	2 472	3 943	4 406	4 311
自行车 (辆)	Bicycle	15 429	14 704	15 791	10 453
手表 (只)	Wrist Watches	11 835	14 368	5 638	13 528
布 (万米)	Cloth (10 000 m)	121	135	136	109
主要农产品产量	Output Of Major Farm Pruducts				
粮食 (吨)	Grain (tn)	3 850	5 171	5 684	5 671
肉类 (吨)	Meats (tn)	195	326	582	621
蛋类 (吨)	Eggs (tn)	291	511	659	670
蔬菜 (吨)	Vegetables (tn)	4 151	7 346	11 895	12 403
奶类 (吨)	Milks (tn)	118	208	305	311
水产品 (吨)	Aquatic Products (tn)	134	297	421	465
二、全市每天消费量	Daily Consumptions				
社会消费品零售总额 (万元)	Total Retail Sales Of Social Consumption (10 000 Yuan)	1 757	3 832	10 291	12 878

1-9 续表
Continued

指 标		Item		1985 年	1990 年	1995 年	1996 年
主要消费品零售量		Volume Of Retail Sales Of Main Consumption					
布(含化纤布)	(万米)	Cloth	(10 000 m)	18.01	13.55	2.13	2.00
呢 绒	(万米)	Woolen Piece Goods	(10 000 m)	2.67	1.86	0.34	0.36
绸 缎	(万米)	Silk And Satin	(10 000 m)	6.25	4.44	0.46	0.38
皮 鞋	(万双)	Leather Shoes	(10 000 pair)	1.21	1.43	1.19	0.95
电视机	(台)	Television Sets	(set)	767	603	374	455
电冰箱	(台)	Refrigerators	(set)	129	328	223	295
洗衣机	(台)	Washing Machines	(set)	411	169	207	257
自行车	(辆)	Bicycle		2 118	897	643	638
生活用煤、气、水、电		Coal, Gas, Water And Electricity For Living					
煤	(万吨)	Coal	(10 000tn)	1.07	0.85	0.86	0.89
液化石油气	(吨)	Liquefied Petrolem Gas	(tn)	85	72	110	158
天然气和煤气	(万立方米)	Natural Gas And Coal Gas	(10 000 cum)	2.7		76.4	66.6
水	(万吨)	Water	(10 000 tn)		67.3	65.0	65.2
电	(万千瓦时)	Electricity	(10 000 kwh)	108	220	393	464
三、每天其他经济活动		**Other Daily Economic Activities**					
社会货物运输量(天津辖区内)	(万吨)	Freight Traffic	(10 000 tn)	50.0	43.6	65.9	66.1
客运量	(万人次)	Passenger Traffic	(10 000 person times)	8.2	6.0	9.1	8.6
港口吞吐量	(万吨)	Cargo Handled At ports	(10 000 tn)	5.1	5.7	15.9	17.0
铁路客运人数	(万人次)	Passenger Traffic By Railway	(10 000 person times)	6.0	4.6	4.9	4.3
公共电汽车客运人数	(万人次)	Passgenger Traffic By Buses	(10 000 person times)	230.1	192.8	152.9	140.0
出版图书	(万册)	Books Published	(10 000 copies)	71.4	35.8	19.0	22.8
出版报纸	(万份)	Newspapers Published	(10 000 copies)	131.5	105.2	147.1	153.3
出版杂志	(万册)	Magazines Published	(10 000 copies)	29.0	12.0	13.1	13.5
邮寄函件	(万件)	Letters		18.4	20.3	33.4	30.1
电 报	(万份)	Telegrams	(10 000 copies)	0.6	0.7	0.3	0.2
接待来津旅游人数	(人次)	Accommmodated Tourists		135	153	358	332
四、每天的人口和婚姻动态		**Daily Population Changes And Marriages**					
出生人口	(人)	Borths	(person)	306	415	231	217
死亡人口	(人)	Deaths	(person)	127	148	142	157
结婚对数	(对)	Marriages	(couple)	269	212	174	177
离婚对数	(对)	Divcorces	(couple)	9	19	30	34

注:1.1995、1996 年主要消费品零售量中不含农贸市场、个体及工业自销数。2.生活用煤为零售量,生活用水为城市数。
Note:1.1995、1996 Volume Of retail sale Of major products exclude agriculture market individual and industry self-selled. 2. Coal for Living are Volume Of Retail Sales, Water for Living are Number Of Urban.

1－10　改革开放以来国内生产总值和指数

INDICES AND GROSS DOMESTIC PRODUCTS SINCE REFORM AND OPENING TO OUTSIDE

年　份 Year	国内生产总值 Gross Domestic Products	第一产业 Primary Industry	第二产业 Second－ary Industry	工　业 Industry	建筑业 Cons－truc－tion	第三产业 Tertiary Industry	#运输邮电业 Transpor－tation Postal and Telecmmuni－cations Services	商　业 Com－merce	人均国内生产总值(元/人) Per Capita GDP (Yuan)
绝对数(亿元) Value(10 000 000 Yuan)									
1978	82.65	5.03	57.53	54.39	3.14	20.09	4.79	6.95	1 160
1979	93.00	6.54	64.76	60.95	3.81	21.70	5.51	7.41	1 272
1980	103.52	6.53	72.43	67.35	5.08	24.56	6.36	7.12	1 392
1981－1985	668.64	43.86	450.67	410.80	39.87	174.11	44.16	54.90	
1981	107.96	5.18	76.77	70.86	5.91	26.01	6.70	8.52	1 433
1982	114.10	7.00	79.59	72.03	7.56	27.51	6.59	7.24	1 488
1983	123.40	7.60	84.11	76.33	7.78	31.69	7.58	8.89	1 583
1984	147.47	11.13	95.97	87.47	8.50	40.37	11.60	14.61	1 868
1985	175.71	12.95	114.23	104.11	10.12	48.53	11.69	15.64	2 198
1986－1990	1 268.60	116.52	774.42	703.19	71.23	377.66	96.51	89.42	
1986	194.67	16.51	122.49	111.06	11.43	55.67	13.89	17.40	2 406
1987	220.00	19.63	136.96	123.99	12.97	63.41	14.46	20.36	2 682
1988	259.64	26.21	159.58	145.35	14.23	73.85	16.61	21.55	3 117
1989	283.34	26.85	175.88	159.07	16.81	80.61	21.30	14.26	3 353
1990	310.95	27.32	179.51	163.72	15.79	104.10	30.25	15.85	3 621
1991－1995	2 935.34	204.65	1 632.80	1 475.71	157.09	1 097.89	263.08	263.59	
1991	342.75	29.26	194.41	177.56	16.85	119.08	27.13	27.65	3 943
1992	411.24	30.26	230.61	210.00	20.61	150.37	35.66	41.05	4 696
1993	536.10	35.39	302.48	275.04	27.44	198.23	47.60	51.21	6 075
1994	725.14	46.53	404.08	361.27	42.81	274.53	66.55	65.41	8 164
1995	920.11	63.21	501.22	451.84	49.38	355.68	86.14	78.27	10 308
1996	1 102.40	70.53	584.43	527.07	57.36	447.44	98.91	97.97	12 270
比上年增长% Increase Rate Than Last Year(%)									
1978	20.9	15.6	23.3	21.1	67.9	16.0	50.3	2.2	19.6
1979	10.0	17.4	10.4	10.4	10.7	7.0	14.1	5.8	7.2
1980	10.0	－0.2	11.4	10.6	22.0	8.7	12.0	－6.8	8.1
1981	4.8	－20.9	7.0	6.6	12.2	4.8	4.5	18.7	3.4
1982	4.3	12.9	3.5	2.4	17.5	5.3	－1.9	－15.3	2.5
1983	8.3	9.2	6.0	6.0	6.3	14.8	14.7	22.4	6.6
1984	19.3	22.8	16.6	17.5	6.2	25.9			17.7
1985	10.6	21.1	10.5	10.0	16.5	8.8	－5.7	0.2	9.2
1986	5.8	8.0	5.5	5.0	11.8	6.0	8.1	1.3	4.5
1987	7.6	6.0	8.3	8.2	8.9	6.3	9.9	2.3	6.1
1988	5.8	7.7	7.7	8.3	1.2	0.4	－5.9	－5.7	4.1
1989	1.6	11.4	－1.9	－2.2	1.2	9.3	19.3	－24.8	0.2
1990	5.4	4.6	1.1	2.0	－8.4	16.4	39.6	2.7	3.8
1991	6.0	3.4	5.5	5.8	2.1	7.5	－0.9	30.0	4.7
1992	11.7	0.7	11.5	12.4	1.2	14.6	20.0	34.9	10.8
1993	12.1	7.4	12.9	13.6	3.6	11.7	24.0	9.2	11.2
1994	14.3	5.3	14.7	14.1	22.7	15.6	24.5	11.9	13.6
1995	14.9	6.3	14.1	14.5	9.9	17.9	20.6	11.1	14.4
1996	14.3	8.2	14.3	14.6	10.1	15.4	13.2	12.9	13.6

1－11 国内生产总值

GROSS DOMESTIC PRODUCTS

单位：亿元；%
Unit：100 000 000 Yuan；%

指 标	Item	1995 年	1996 年	1996 比 1995 年增长% 1996 Incr－ease Rate than 1995	构 成 Composition 1995 年	构 成 Composition 1996 年
国内生产总值	**Gross Domestic Products**	**920.11**	**1 102.40**	**14.3**	**100**	**100**
第一产业	Primary Industry	63.21	70.53	8.2	6.9	6.4
第二产业	Secondary Industry	501.22	584.43	14.3	54.4	53.0
工 业	Industry	451.84	527.07	14.6	49.1	47.8
建筑业	Construction	49.38	57.36	10.1	5.3	5.2
第三产业	Tertiary Industry	355.68	447.44	15.4	38.7	40.6
农林牧渔服务业	Services Of Farming, Forestry, Animal Husbandry And Fishery	0.68	0.16	－74.3	0.1	
地质勘探水利管理业	Geological Prospecting And Water Conservancy	3.24	2.64	－24.9	0.4	0.2
交通运输和仓储业	Transportation And Warehouse	74.50	83.05	10.4	8.1	7.5
邮电通讯业	Postal And Telecommunication	11.64	15.86	32.0	1.3	1.5
批发零售贸易餐饮	Wholesale Trades and Foodservices	78.27	97.97	12.9	8.5	8.9
金融保险业	Banking and Insurance	81.40	107.00	25.9	8.8	9.7
房地产业	Real Estate Management	16.85	26.29	34.0	1.8	2.4
社会服务业	Social Services	45.43	56.46	9.5	4.9	5.1
卫生体育社会福利业	Health Care Sports and Welfare	7.21	8.57	8.9	0.8	0.8
教育文艺广播电影电视	Education Culture Radio and Television	15.97	17.75	2.1	1.7	1.6
科研综合服务业	Scientific Research and Polyechnical Services	6.27	10.24	9.7	0.7	0.9
国家政党社会团体	Government Agencies and Organization	11.96	19.41	11.7	1.3	1.8
其他行业	Other Industry	2.26	2.04	－24.6	0.3	0.2

1－12 国内生产总值构成

COMPOSITION OF GROSS DOMESTIC PRODUCTS

单位：亿元
Unit：100 000 000 Yuan

指 标	Item	1990 年	1991 年	1992 年	1993 年	1994 年	1995 年	1996 年
国内生产总值	**Gross Domestic Products**	**310.95**	**342.75**	**411.24**	**536.10**	**725.14**	**920.11**	**1 102.40**
劳动者报酬	Compensation Of Laborers	139.52	150.68	169.33	225.62	328.69	422.48	545.24
固定资产折旧	Depreciation Of Fixed Assets	47.65	54.43	67.63	71.73	97.52	137.40	174.01
生产税净额	Net Value Of Production Tax	25.07	37.55	41.14	67.09	95.48	122.33	134.54
营业盈余	Business Surplus	98.71	100.09	133.14	171.66	203.45	237.90	248.61

1－13　改革开放以来国内支出总额

TOTAL DOMESTIC EXPENDITURES SINCE REFORM AND OPENING TO OUTSIDE

单位:亿元　　Unit:100 000 000 Yuan

年份 Year	国内支出总额 Total Domestic Expenditures	总消费 Total Consumption	居民消费 Resident Consumption	农业居民 Agricultural Residents	非农业居民 Nonagricultural Residents	社会消费 Public Consumption	总投资 Total Investment	固定资产形成 Fixed Assets Formation	库存增加 Inventory Increase	货物和服务净出口 Net Export Of Foods and Services
1978	82.65	30.18	26.52	6.89	19.63	3.66	26.40	18.55	7.85	26.07
1979	93.00	34.01	29.90	8.00	21.90	4.11	33.27	23.91	9.36	25.72
1980	103.52	39.62	35.48	9.58	25.90	4.14	35.66	25.56	10.10	28.24
1981－1985	668.64	276.09	234.46	73.79	160.67	41.63	238.76	211.90	26.86	153.79
1981	107.96	43.72	37.31	10.46	26.85	6.41	25.06	25.00	0.06	39.18
1982	114.10	47.22	40.72	12.86	27.86	6.50	34.81	32.36	2.45	32.07
1983	123.40	52.92	45.20	13.96	31.24	7.72	41.94	38.27	3.67	28.54
1984	147.47	60.37	50.63	16.98	33.65	9.74	48.30	48.67	－0.37	38.80
1985	175.71	71.86	60.60	19.53	41.07	11.26	88.65	67.60	21.05	15.20
1986－1990	1 268.60	592.54	466.56	135.95	330.61	125.98	607.64	447.83	159.81	68.42
1986	194.67	82.11	68.66	20.67	47.99	13.45	101.10	75.89	25.21	11.46
1987	220.00	97.23	76.31	22.99	53.32	20.92	92.70	81.63	11.07	30.07
1988	259.64	126.42	97.16	28.73	68.43	29.26	142.27	96.85	45.42	－9.05
1989	283.34	143.10	109.05	32.00	77.05	34.05	137.20	95.43	41.77	3.04
1990	310.95	143.68	115.38	31.56	83.82	28.30	134.37	98.03	36.34	32.90
1991－1995	2 935.34	1 310.94	1 007.59	247.74	759.85	303.35	1 662.11	1 349.41	312.70	－37.71
1991	342.75	165.26	130.16	34.66	95.50	35.10	163.65	144.19	19.46	13.84
1992	411.24	190.08	147.90	38.58	109.32	42.18	227.18	185.12	42.06	－6.02
1993	536.10	244.85	186.31	47.11	139.20	58.54	315.61	246.16	69.45	－24.36
1994	725.14	323.76	241.56	55.78	185.78	82.20	430.90	361.45	69.45	－29.52
1995	920.11	386.99	301.66	71.61	230.05	85.33	524.77	428.48	96.29	8.35
1996	1 102.40	494.91	370.94	91.75	279.19	123.97	611.51	504.25	107.26	－4.02

注:本表按当年价格计算。

Note:This tatble is at current prices.

1－14　总消费构成

COMPOSITION OF TOTAL CONSUMPTION

项目	Item	绝对值(亿元) Value(100 000 000Yuan) 1995年	1996年	构成(%) Composition(%) 1995年	1996年
总消费	**Total Consumption**	**386.99**	**494.91**	**100**	**100**
一、居民消费	**Residents Consumption**	**301.66**	**370.94**	**78.0**	**75.0**
1.农业居民	Agriculture Residents	71.61	91.75	100	100
自给性消费	Self－sufficieny Consumption	15.35	13.41	21.4	14.6
商品性消费	Commodity Consumption	42.38	52.68	59.2	57.4
文化生活服务性消费	Consumption Of Culture And Life Services	6.21	10.80	8.7	11.8
住房及水电消费	Housing Water And power Consumption	7.67	14.86	10.7	16.2
#住房消费	Housing Consumption	5.89	13.25		
2.非农业居民	Nonagriculture Residents	230.05	279.19	100	100
商品性消费	Commodity Consumption	173.37	202.57	75.4	72.6
文化生活服务性消费	Consumption Of Culture And Life Services	45.79	57.89	19.9	20.7
住房及水电消费	Housing Water And power Consumption	10.89	18.73	4.7	6.7
#住房消费	Housing Consumption	6.78	12.79		
二、社会消费	**Public Consumption**	**85.33**	**123.97**	**22.0**	**25.0**

1－15 1995年九部门投入产出流量表(产品部门×产品部门)

INPUT－OUTPUT TABLE BY 9 SECTORS, 1995 (PRODUCTS DEPARTMENT MULTIPLICATION PRODUCTS DEPARTMENT)

单位:万元

Units:10 000 Yuan

产出 Output / 投入 Input		中间使用 Intermediate Use				
		农业 Agricul－ture	工业 Industry	建筑业 Constru－tion	交通邮电业 Transpor and Postal Telecom－munication Services	商业 Commerce
总投入	**Total Input**	**1332500.00**	**22306900.00**	**1864500.00**	**1776713.53**	**2358886.43**
中间投入合计	**Intermediate Inputs**	**7000400.00**	**17788500.00**	**1370700.00**	**978687.53**	**1512812.43**
农业	Agriculture	182728.63	677853.96	1042.13		105915.76
工业	Industry	370155.27	15038715.32	1108318.78	653815.26	640472.08
建筑业	Constrction		1423.39	61.96	4360.90	10388.64
交通邮电业	Transportation and Postal Telecommunication Services	6139.43	502494.31	145565.68	155921.55	152430.26
商业	Commerce	51515.49	682927.24	58582.60	40034.49	183295.16
公用事业及居民服务业	Public Utilities & Residents Services	9244.33	149762.24	26405.05	24367.18	89571.87
文教卫生科研事业	Culture, Education, Health Care and Scientific Research	914.37	194207.41	13648.22	62654.11	13593.29
金融保险业	Banking and Insurance	79702.48	541116.13	17075.58	37534.04	317145.37
行政机关	Administrative Organization					
最初投入合计	**Priamry Inputs**	**632100.00**	**4518400.00**	**493800.00**	**798026.00**	**846074.00**
固定资产折旧	Depreciation Of Fixed Assets	24500.00	909000.00	35300.00	203458.00	41342.00
劳动者报酬	Compensation Of Laborers	493300.00	1726500.00	321100.00	358623.00	514277.00
生产税净额	Net Value Of Production Tax	8400.00	891900.00	55600.00	117392.00	－6092.00
营业盈余	Business Surplus	105900.00	991000.00	81800.00	118553.00	296547.00

产出 Output / 投入 Input		中间使用 Intermediate Use				
		公用事业及居民服务业 Public Ut－ilities & Residents Services	文教卫生科研事业 Culture, Education, Health Care and Scientific Research	金融保险业 Banking and Insurance	行政机关 Administr－ative Org－anization	中间使用合计 Total Intermediat Use
总投入	**Total Input**	**1364900.04**	**715800.00**	**1163000.00**	**398300.00**	**33281500.00**
中间投入合计	**Intermediate Inputs**	**702900.04**	**421300.00**	**349000.00**	**256100.00**	**24080400.00**
农业	Agriculture	12014.78	14139.00	0.00	0.00	993694.26
工业	Industry	452845.84	328847.39	230340.63	182367.05	19005877.62
建筑业	Constrction	59023.20	4040.74	3218.00	2077.77	84594.60
交通邮电业	Transportation and Postal Telecommunication Services	35873.24	23486.86	69590.41	47683.33	1139185.07
商业	Commerce	39786.59	16759.06	17875.79	8765.40	1099541.82
公用事业及居民服务业	Public Utilities & Residents Services	72048.67	12797.21	24656.35	13671.44	422524.34
文教卫生科研事业	Culture, Education, Health Care and Scientific Research	5163.11	15802.48	2486.08	969.50	309438.57
金融保险业	Banking and Insurance	26144.61	5427.26	832.74	565.51	1025543.72
行政机关	Administrative Organization					
最初投入合计	**Priamry Inputs**	**662000.00**	**294500.00**	**814000.00**	**142200.00**	**9201100.00**
固定资产折旧	Depreciation Of Fixed Assets	122400.00	7800.00	28100.00	2100.00	1374000.00
劳动者报酬	Compensation Of Laborers	392300.00	240800.00	57500.00	120400.00	4224800.00
生产税净额	Net Value Of Production Tax	69600.00	6800.00	78800.00	900.00	1223300.00
营业盈余	Business Surplus	77700.00	39100.00	649600.00	18800.00	2379000.00

1 - 15 续表
Continued

单位:万元
Units:10 000 Yuan

投入 Input \ 产出 Output		最终使用 Final Use 总消费 Total Consumption 居民总消费 Total Consumption Of Households 农业居民 Agricul-tural Residents	非农业居民 Non-agric-ultural Residents	小计 Subtotal	社会总消费 Public Consum-ption	合计 Total	资本形成总额固定资本形成 Fixed Asset Formation
中间投入合计	**Intermediate Inputs**	**716100.00**	**2300500.00**	**3016600.00**	**853300.00**	**3869900.00**	**4284800.00**
农业	Agriculture	139950.89	181707.34	321658.23	0.00	321658.23	
工业	Industry	345755.47	1613237.42	1958992.89	76626.76	2035619.65	2166942.71
建筑业	Constrction						2077410.51
交通邮电业	Transportation and Postal Telecommuni-cation Services	13217.69	75999.51	89217.20	1596.14	90813.34	23071.07
商业	Commerce	124082.96	183237.99	307320.95	80652.29	387973.24	17375.71
公用事业及居民服务业	Public Utilities & Residents Services	52917.98	135087.94	188005.92	34243.26	222249.18	
文教卫生科研事业	Culture, Education, Health Care and Scientific Research	40175.01	111229.80	151404.81	261800.00	413204.81	
金融保险业	Banking and Insurance				81.55	81.55	
行政机关	Administrative Organization				398300.00	398300.00	

投入 Input \ 产出 Output		最终使用 Final Use 资本形成总额 Gross Capital Formation 库存增加 Inventory Increase	资本形成合计 total Capital Formation	净流出 Net Exports	最终使用合计 Total Final Use	总产出 Gross Output
中间投入合计	**Intermediate Inputs**	**962900.00**	**5247700.00**	**83500.00**	**9201100.00**	**33281500.00**
农业	Agriculture	177457.48	177457.48	-160309.97	338805.74	1332500.00
工业	Industry	521126.47	2688069.18	-1422666.43	3301022.40	22306900.00
建筑业	Constrction		2077410.51	-297505.11	1779905.40	1864500.00
交通邮电业	Transportation and Postal Telecommuni-cation Services	100623.05	123694.12	423021.01	637528.47	1776713.53
商业	Commerce	163693.00	181068.71	690302.66	1259344.61	2358886.43
公用事业及居民服务业	Public Utilities & Residents Services			720126.51	942375.69	1364900.04
文教卫生科研事业	Culture, Education, Health Care and Scientific Research			-6843.39	406361.42	715800.00
金融保险业	Banking and Insurance			137374.72	137456.27	1163000.00
行政机关	Administrative Organization				398300.00	398300.00

1－16 1995年九部门投入产出直接消耗系数表

DIRECT CONSUMPTION COEFFICIENT TABLE OF INPUT－OUTPUT BY 9 SECTORS，1995

产出 Output / 投入 Input		中间使用 Intermediate Use			
		农业 Agriculture	工业 Industry	建筑业 Constrution	交通邮电业 Transpor and Postal Telecommu－nication Services
总投入	**Total Input**	**1.000000**	**1.000000**	**1.000000**	**1.000000**
中间投入合计	**Intermediate Inputs**	**0.525629**	**0.797444**	**0.735157**	**0.550841**
农业	Agriculture	0.137132	0.030388	0.000559	
工业	Industry	0.277790	0.674173	0.594432	0.367991
建筑业	Constrction		0.000064	0.000033	0.002454
交通邮电业	Transportation and Postal Telecommunication Service	0.004607	0.022526	0.078072	0.087758
商业	Commerce	0.038661	0.030615	0.031420	0.022533
公用事业及居民服务业	Public Utilities & Residents Services	0.006938	0.006714	0.014162	0.013715
文教卫生科研事业	Culture, Education, Health Care and Scientific Research	0.000686	0.008706	0.007320	0.035264
金融保险业	Banking and Insurance	0.059814	0.024258	0.009158	0.021126
行政机关	Administrative Organization				
最初投入合计	**Priamry Inputs**	**0.474371**	**0.202556**	**0.264843**	**0.449159**
固定资产折旧	Depreciation Of Fixed Assets	0.018386	0.040750	0.018933	0.114514
劳动者报酬	Compensation Of Laborers	0.370206	0.077398	0.172218	0.201846
生产税净额	Net Value Of Production Tax	0.006304	0.039983	0.029820	0.066073
营业盈余	Business Surplus	0.079475	0.044426	0.043872	0.066726

产出 Output / 投入 Input		中间使用 Intermediate Use				
		商业 Commerce	公用事业及居民服务业 Public Ut－ilities & Residents Services	文教卫生科研事业 Culture, Education, Health Care and Scientific Research	金融保险业 Banking and In－surance	行政机关 Administr－ative Org－anization
总投入	**Total Input**	**1.000000**	**1.000000**	**1.000000**	**1.000000**	**1.000000**
中间投入合计	**Intermediate Inputs**	**0.641325**	**0.514983**	**0.588572**	**0.300086**	**0.642983**
农业	Agriculture	0.044901	0.008803	0.019753		
工业	Industry	0.271515	0.331779	0.459412	0.198057	0.457864
建筑业	Constrction	0.004404	0.043244	0.005645	0.002767	0.005217
交通邮电业	Transportation and Postal Telecommunication Services	0.064620	0.026283	0.032812	0.059837	0.119717
商业	Commerce	0.077704	0.029150	0.023413	0.015370	0.022007
公用事业及居民服务业	Public Utilities & Residents Services	0.037972	0.052787	0.017878	0.021201	0.034324
文教卫生科研事业	Culture, Education, Health Care and Scientific Research	0.005763	0.003783	0.022077	0.002138	0.002434
金融保险业	Banking and Insurance	0.134447	0.019155	0.007582	0.000716	0.001420
行政机关	Administrative Organization					
最初投入合计	**Priamry Inputs**	**0.358675**	**0.485017**	**0.411428**	**0.699914**	**0.357017**
固定资产折旧	Depreciation Of Fixed Assets	0.017526	0.089677	0.010897	0.024162	0.005272
劳动者报酬	Compensation Of Laborers	0.218017	0.287420	0.336407	0.049441	0.302285
生产税净额	Net Value Of Production Tax	－0.002583	0.050993	0.009500	0.067756	0.002260
营业盈余	Business Surplus	0.125715	0.056927	0.054624	0.558555	0.047201

1-17 1995 年九部门投入产出完全消耗系数表

OVERALL CONSUMPTION COEFFICIENT TABLE OF INPUT AND OUTPUT BY 9 SECTORS, 1995

投入 Input \ 产出 Output		中间使用 Intermediate Use 农业 Agriculture	工业 Industry	建筑业 Constrution	交通邮电业 Transpor and Posta Telecommu-nication Services
中间投入合计	Intermediate Inputs				
农业	Agriculture	1.210442	0.134186	0.090811	0.062595
工业	Industry	1.299824	3.581484	2.342493	1.600428
建筑业	Constrction	0.002182	0.003184	1.003408	0.005366
交通邮电业	Transportation and Postal Telecommunication Services	0.054477	0.108683	0.161488	1.151011
商业	Commerce	0.098480	0.131303	0.123470	0.087927
公用事业及居民服务业	Public Utilities & Services Residents	0.025802	0.036548	0.042298	0.034931
文教卫生科研事业	Culture, Education, Health and Scientific Research Care	0.015342	0.037091	0.035346	0.056666
金融保险业	Banking and Insurance	0.119040	0.115948	0.092601	0.079909
行政机关	Administrative Organization				

投入 Input \ 产出 Output		中间使用 Intermediate Use 商业 Commerce	公用事业及居民服务业 Public Ut-ilities & Residents Services	文教卫生科研事业 Culture, Education, Health Care and Scientific Research	金融保险业 Banking and In-surance	行政机关 Administr-ative Org-anization
中间投入合计	Intermediate Inputs					
农业	Agriculture	0.111618	0.068631	0.094302	0.033970	0.074496
工业	Industry	1.440503	1.487200	1.844419	0.869822	1.932123
建筑业	Constrction	0.008934	0.047502	0.008633	0.004895	0.009190
交通邮电业	Transportation and Postal Telecommunication Services	0.133985	0.084317	0.097195	0.094968	0.194614
商业	Commerce	1.146325	0.091687	0.096856	0.051416	0.099972
公用事业及居民服务业	Public Utilities & Residents Services	0.064013	1.074476	0.040541	0.033320	0.059572
文教卫生科研事业	Culture, Education, Health Care and Scientific Research	0.025241	0.021546	1.043521	0.013920	0.027805
金融保险业	Banking and Insurance	0.200213	0.075524	0.074278	1.033579	0.071785
行政机关	Administrative Organization					1.000000

1-18 天津在全国的地位

POSITION OF TIANJIN IN THE WHOLE NATION

指 标		Item		1992年 天 津 Tianjin	1992年 占全国比重 As Percentage to National (%)	1996年 天 津 Tianjin	1996年 占全国比重 As Percentage to National (%)
一、年末户籍人口	(万人)	Registered Population(Year-End)	(10 000 person)	878.97	0.8	898.45	0.7
二、社会从业人员	(万人)	Total Employment	(10 000 person)	485.70	0.8	512.00	0.7
三、国内生产总值	(亿元)	Gross Domestic Products	(100 000 000 Yuan)	411.24	1.7	1 102.40	1.6
第一产业		Primary Industry		30.26	0.5	70.53	0.5
第二产业		Secondary Industry		230.61	2.0	584.43	1.8
第三产业		Tertiary Industry		150.37	1.5	447.44	2.1
四、财政、金融		Public Finance And Banking					
地方财政收入	(亿元)	Local Government Revence	(100 000 000 Yuan)	63.05	1.5	79.04	1.1
地方财政支出	(亿元)	Local Government Expenditures	(100 000 000 Yuan)	46.52	1.1	113.21	1.4
银行存款余额	(亿元)	Banking Deposit	(100 000 000 Yuan)	376.19	2.0	1 057.47	1.5
银行贷款余额	(亿元)	Banking Loans	(100 000 000 Yuan)	539.53	2.5	1 108.78	1.8
五、工业总产值	(亿元)	Gross Output Value Of Industry	(100 000 000 Yuan)	997.91	2.7	2 522.42	2.5
轻工业		Light Industry		465.48	2.7	1 175.17	2.6
重工业		Heavy Industry		532.43	2.7	1 347.25	2.5
六、主要工业产品产量		Output Of Major Industrial Products					
钢	(万吨)	Steel	(10 000 tn)	183.45	2.3	200.99	2.0
生 铁	(万吨)	Pig Iron	(10 000 tn)	162.21	2.1	169.04	1.6
水 泥	(万吨)	Cement	(10 000 tn)	144.58	0.5	207.88	0.4
平板玻璃	(万重量箱)	Plate Glass	(10 000 weight cases)	226.18	2.4	211.14	1.4
发电量	(亿千瓦时)	Electricity	(100 000 000 kwh)	98.62	1.3	146.04	1.3
原 油	(万吨)	Crude Oil	(10 000 tn)	491.76	3.5	646.60	4.1
天然气	(万立方米)	Naturl Gas	(10 000 cum)	41 200.00	2.6	75 800	3.8
农用化肥	(万吨)	Chemical Fertitizers	(10 000 tn)	7.84	0.4	11.31	0.4
化学农药	(万吨)	Chemical Pesticides	(10 000 tn)	2.01	7.2	2.95	6.9
汽 车	(万辆)	Motor Vehicles	(10 000)	7.57	7.1	15.27	9.9
金属切削机床	(万台)	Metalcutting Machines	(10 000)	0.13	0.6	0.12	0.8
电视机	(万台)	Television Sets	(10 000)	140.99	4.9	157.34	5.1
化学纤维	(万吨)	Chemical Fibers	(10 000 tn)	8.35	3.9	8.82	2.6
纱	(万吨)	Yarn	(10 000 tn)	10.86	2.2	10.51	2.1
布	(亿米)	Cloth	(100 000 000 m)	4.30	2.2	3.97	2.3
机制纸及纸版	(万吨)	Marchine-Made Papers And Paperboards	(10 000 tn)	33.32	1.9	45.89	2.2

1-18 续表
Continued

指　标	Item	1992年 天　津 Tianjin	1992年 占全国比重 As Percentage to National (%)	1996年 天　津 Tianjin	1996年 占全国比重 As Percentage to National (%)
家用电冰箱　（万台）	Household Refrigerators (10 000 set)	9.27	1.9	0.29	
家用洗衣机　（万台）	Washing Machines (10 000 set)	32.5	6.7	60.02	5.6
自行车　（万辆）	Bicycles (10 000)	457.4	11.2	381.52	13.6
手　表　（万只）	Watches (10 000)	438.57	5.1	493.77	1.3
空调器　（万台）	Air Conditioners (10 000 set)			5.6	0.9
七、农林牧渔业总产值（亿元）	Gross Output Value Of Farming, Forestry, Animal Husbandry And Fishery (100 000 000 Yuan)	62.15	0.7	142.29	0.6
八、主要农产品产量	Output Of Major Farm Products				
粮　食　（万吨）	Grain (10 000 tn)	198.74	0.5	207.0	0.4
肉　类　（万吨）	Meats (10 000 tn)	11.20	0.4	22.68	0.4
蛋　类　（万吨）	Eggs (10 000 tn)	21.34	2.1	24.44	1.3
水产品　（万吨）	Aquatic Products (10 000 tn)	11.10	0.7	16.99	0.5
九、社会固定资产投资（亿元）	Investments In Fixed Assets (100 000 000 Yuan)	169.88	2.2	435.82	1.8
#国有经济	State-owned	137.81	2.6	258.78	2.1
十、运输、邮电	Transportation, Postal And Telecommunication Service				
港口货物吞吐量　（万吨）	Cargo Handled At Ports (10 000 tn)	2 929	5.5	6 188	7.3
社会货物运输量　（万吨）	Freight Traffic (10 000 tn)	17 522	1.7	24 133	1.9
#公路货运量	Highway Freight Traffic	13 562	1.7	19 491	2.0
邮电业务总量　（万元）	Postal And Telecommunication (10 000 Yuan)	61 063	2.1	256 978	1.9
十一、商业、外贸、外经	Commercial, Foreign Trade And Foreign Economy				
商品购进总额　（亿元）	Final Purchases (100 000 000 Yuan)	450.76	4.2	980.73	2.5
商品销售总额　（亿元）	Final Sales (100 000 000 Yuan)	479.73	4.5	1 035.88	2.4
社会消费品零售总额（亿元）	Total Value Of Retail Sales (100 000 000 Yuan)	181.20	1.9	470.04	1.9
外贸出口商品总值（亿美元）	Total Value Of export Commodities (US$ 100 000 000)	17.52	2.1	40.49	2.7
实际利用外资额　（亿美元）	Foreign Capital Actually Utilized (US$ 100 000 000)	8.31	4.3	29.84	5.4
十二、教育、科技、卫生	Education Science And Culture				
高等学校数　（所）	Higher Education Institutions (Number)	26	2.5	20	1.9
高等学校在校学生数（万人）	Students Enrollment Of High Schools (10 000 person)	5.21	2.4	7.14	2.4
中等专业学校在校生数（万人）	Students Enrollment Of Specialized Secondary Schools (10 000 person)	3.88	1.6	6.7	1.6
普通中小学在校生数（万人）	Students Enrollment Of Regular Secondary Schools And primary Schools (10 000 person)	125.39	0.7	137.33	0.7
国有单位专业技术人员数（万人）	Scientific And Technical Personal In State-Owned Units (10 000 person)	55.30	3.1	56.67	2.8

1－19 1996年天津、北京、上海、广州主要经济指标

MAIN ECONOMIC INDICATORS OF TIANJIN, BEIJING, SHANGHAI, GUANGZHOU, 1996

项 目	Item	天津市 Tianjin	北京市 Beijing	上海市 Shanghai	广州市 Guangzhou
土地面积(平方公里)	Land Area (sq. km)	11 919.7	16 807.8	6 340.5	7 434
＃城市建成区面积	City－Scaled Area	374.3	487.7	412.0	262
年末户籍人口(万人)	Registered Population (10 000 person)	898.45	1 077.7	1 304.43	656.05
＃非农业	Unagriculture Population	513.15	709.7	932.14	403.27
人口出生率 (‰)	Birth Rate (‰)	10.09	8.02	5.2	12.03
人口自然增长率(‰)	Natural Growth Rate (‰)	3.56	2.68	－2.3	6.32
年末全部从业人员数(万人)	Total Employments (Year－end) (10 000 person)	512.0	660.2	792.93	392.89
＃城镇个体劳动者	Urban Individuals	13.75	22.9	7.74	32.98
1.职工人数	Staff And Workers	283.98	460.6	456.75	202.80
＃国有单位	State－Owned Units	194.32	349.0	312.53	130.06
2.第一产业	Primary Industry	82.1	72.5	79.4	92.16
第二产业	Secondary Industry	241.4	260.1	411.98	136.41
第三产业	Tertiary Industry	188.5	327.6	301.55	164.32
职工工资总额(亿元)	Total Wages For Staff And Workers (100 000 000 Yuan)	212.05	442.4	492.75	239.56
＃国有单位	State－Owened Units	154.34	339.4	348.96	167.25
职工年平均工资(元)	Average Annual Wage (Yuan)	7 643	9 579	10 663	11 813
＃国有单位	State－Owened Units	8 072	9 645	11 015	12 868
平均工资指数(实际工资,上年＝100)	Average Annual Wage Indices (Actual Wage)(Preceding Year＝100)	107.9	105.7	108.7	106.3
国内生产总值(亿元)	Gross Domestic Products (100 000 000 Yuan)	1 102.40	1 615.7	2 902.27	1 444.94
第一产业	Primary Industry	70.53	83.5	71.58	81.16
第二产业	Secondary Industry	584.43	683.1	1 582.5	675.39
＃工 业	Industry	527.07	541.4	1 439.14	581.46
第三产业	Tertiary Industry	447.44	849.1	1 248.12	688.39
人均国内生产总值(元)	Per Capita Gross Domestic Products (Yuan)	12 270	15 044	22 275	22 183
国内生产总值指数(上年＝100)	Indices Of Gross Domestic Products (Preceding year＝100)	114.3	109.2	113.0	112.6
第一产业	Primary Industry	108.2	97.0	105.0	105.3
第二产业	Secondary Industry	114.3	107.4	111.1	113.4
第三产业	Tertiary Industry	115.4	112.3	117.8	112.4
人均国内生产总值指数 (上年＝100)	Per Capita Indices Of Gross Domestic Products (Preceding year＝100)	113.6	108.5	112.8	111.0
全社会固定资产投资总额(亿元)	Total Investment In Fixed Assets (100 000 000 Yuan)	435.82	876.9	1 952.06	638.94
＃国有单位固定资产投资	State－Owned Investment In Fixed Assets	258.78	545.7	1 079.44	317.21
社会新增固定资产投资(亿元)	New Increased Investment In Fixed Assets(100 000 000 Yuan)	313.12	427.5	1 199.10	444.16
地方财政收入(预算内)(亿元)	Local Government Revenue(In Budget) (100 000 000 Yuan)	79.04	150.9	288.49	85.24
地方财政支出(预算内)(亿元)	Local Government Expenditures (In Budget) (100 000 000 Yuan)	113.21	187.4	342.66	121.91
金融系统年末存款余额(亿元)	Deposits Of Financial System (Year－end) (100 000 000 Yuan)	1 391.62	4 378.9	3 870.98	2 712.98
＃城乡居民储蓄存款余额	Saving Deposits Of Urban And Rural Residents	724.00	1 707.0	1 868.34	1 293.23
金融系统年末贷款余额(亿元)	Loans Of Financial System (Year－end) (100 000 000 Yuan)	1 325.49	2 082.8	2 852.66	1 605.22
银行现金收入(亿元)	Cashing Revenue Of Banking (100 000 000 Yuan)	1 696.42	3 178.3	3 469.05	5 409.04
银行现金支出(亿元)	Cashing Expenditure Of Banking (100 000 000 Yuan)	1 704.67	3 141.9	3 650.54	5 422.76

注：上海的金融系统年末存贷款余额为银行存贷款余额数。

Note: Deposits and loans of Shanghai financial system (year－end) is the data of banking.

1-19 续表1
Continued

项　目	Item	天津市 Tianjin	北京市 Beijing	上海市 Shang-hai	广州市 Guang-zhou
保险业务承保额　(亿元)	Insurance Value　(100 000 000 Yuan)	2 488.21			5 962.88
保险业务保费收入　(亿元)	Permiums　(100 000 000 Yuan)	17.18	38.7	52.40	102.33
保险业务赔款支出　(亿元)	Settlements　(100 000 000 Yuan)	6.26		15.0	13.28
城市商品零售价格指数 (上年=100)	Price Indices Of Urban Overall Retail (Preceding year=100)	105.1	107.3	105.0	104.3
城市居民消费价格指数 (上年=100)	Price Indices Of Urban Overall Resident Consummer (Preceding year=100)	109.0	111.6	109.2	108.2
工业品出厂价格指数 (上年=100)	Industrial Products Producer Price Indices　(Perceding Year=100)	100.9	100.7	97.59	101.4
原材料及动力购进价格指数 (上年=100)	Purchasing Price Indices Of Raw Material And Power (Perceding Year=100)	99.0	100.3	97.58	104.5
每一农村劳动力负担人口(人)	Dependents Per Rural Labour (person)	0.45	0.45	0.42	0.59
每一城市就业人口负担人口(人)	Dependents Per Urban Employee (person)	0.36	0.41	0.95	0.70
城镇居民人均生活费收入(元)	Annual Per Capita Income Available For Living Of Urban Households (Yuan)	5 525	6 885	7 721	9 379
城镇居民人均生活费支出(元)	Annual Per Capita Expenditure Available For Living Of Urban Households (Yuan)	4 680	5 729	6 763	8 093
农民人均纯收入(元)	Annual Per Capita net Income Of Farmers　(Yuan)	3 142	3 580	4 846	5 165
农民人均生活费支出(元)	Annual Per Capita living Expenditure Of Expenditure Of Farmers　(Yuan)	2 101	2 656	3 868	3 531
城市住宅竣工面积(万平方米)	Completed Floor Space Of Urban Residences　(10 000 sq.m)	494.73	870.4	1 872.65	1 155.26
城市人均居住面积(平方米)	Per Capita Living Floor Space Of Urban (sq.m)	7.74	9.33	8.5	10.08
农村人均居住面积(平方米)	Per Capita Living Floor Space Of Rural (sq.m)	21.83	25.74	45.47	31.63
乡村劳动力(万人)	Rural Labor Force (10 000 person)	167.92	164.2	226.82	158.97
年末实有耕地面积(万公顷)	Caltivated Areas(year-end)(10 000 ha)	42.58	34.4	28.72	12.82
农业总产值(当年价)(亿元)	Gross Output Value Of Agriculture (Current Price)　(100 000 000 Yuan)	142.29	168.9	200.95	142.91
农业总产值指数(上年=100)	Indices Of Gross Output Value Of Agriculture(Perceding Year=100)	107.2	99.1	108.3	106.6
乡及乡以上工业企业单位数(个)	Numbers Of Industry Enterprises At and Above Township Level (Number)	11 073	16 905	15 595	8 433
#国有经济	State-owned Enterprises	2 069	4 827	3 612	1 035
全部工业总产值(当年价)(亿元)	Total Gross Output Value Of Industry (Current Price)　(100 000 000 Yuan)	2 522.42	1 853.3	5 126.22	2 068.58
#乡及乡以上	Township Level And Above	1 666.26	1 632.2	4 329.52	1 630.38
#国有经济	State-owned Enterprises	587.86	887.0	1 678.62	424.67
集体经济	Collective-owned Enterprices	287.61	277.4	533.87	193.95
股份制经济	Stock Owership Enterprises	41.74	21.2	349.88	81.87
“三资”经济	“Foreign-funded Industry”	718.77	421.1	1 505.15	900.14
轻工业	Light Industry Enterprises	678.68	522.4	1 875.79	942.39
重工业	Heavy Industry Enterprises	987.58	1 109.8	2 453.73	687.99
工业总产值指数(上年=100)	Indices Of Gross Output Value Of Industry(Perceding Year=100)	124.66	109.2	115.5	116.9

1-19 续表 2
Continued

项 目	Item	天津市 Tianjin	北京市 Beijing	上海市 Shang-hai	广州市 Guang-zhou
独立核算工业企业主要指标	Main Indicators Of Industrial Enterprises with Independent Accouting System				
企业单位数 (个)	Number Of Enterprises	10 490	15 002	15 007	4 903
工业总产值(现价)(亿元)	Gross Output Value Of Industry (CurrentPrice)(100 000 000 Yuan)	1 635.96	1 522.3	4 247.12	1 545.68
工业销售产值(现价)(亿元)	Sales Output Value Of Industry (CurrentPrice)(100 000 000 Yuan)	1 573.50	1 498.6	4 174.62	1 495.94
工业增加值 (亿元)	Added Value Of Industry (100 000 000 Yuan)	347.56	478.3		426.67
年底固定资产原价(亿元)	Original Value Of Fixed Assets (Year-end)(100 000 000 Yuan)	1 338.28	1 632.0	2 987.71	1 056.90
固定资产净值 (亿元)	Net Value Of Fixed Assets (100 000 000 Yuan)	979.96	1 045.0	1 956.46	803.13
流动资产年末合计(亿元)	Total Circulating Funds (year-end) (100 000 000 Yuan)	1 118.55	1 293.9	3 155.29	1 051.06
产品销售收入(亿元)	Product Sales Revenue (100 000 000 Yuan)	1 498.67	1 580.1	4 250.51	1 436.04
利税总额(亿元)	Total Pre-Tax Profits (100 000 000 Yuan)	139.73	122.5	441.61	174.25
利润总额(亿元)	Total After-Tax Profits (100 000 000 Yuan)	67.60	33.1	210.68	75.77
资金利税率(%)	Pre-Tax Profits Rate (%)	7.21	5.41	8.66	10.44
增加值率 (%)	Rate Of Added value Of Industry (%)	21.25	27.07	25.41	24.85
工业全员劳动生产率(按增加值)(元/人)	Overall Labor Productivity (According to Added Value) (Yuan/person)	20 993	23 445	29 745	45 415
全部流动资金周转次数(次)	Turnover Times Of Circulating Funds (times)	1.43	1.3	1.4	1.49
能源消费总量 (万吨标准煤)	Total Energy Consumption (10 000 tn Of sce)	1 611.27		3 602.34	1 715.90
亿元工业产值能源消费量(万吨标准煤)	Per 100 000 000 Yuan Value Of Energy Consumption(10 000 tn Of sce)	0.95		1.66	
港口泊位 (个)	Berths at Port	75		138	169
#万吨级以上	10 000 tonnage Level and Above	48		69	37
港口货物吞吐量(万吨)	Cargo Handled at Port (10 000 tn)	6 188		16 402	8 510
社会货运量(万吨)	Freight Transport(10 000 tn)	24 133	32 906	45 106	23 315
社会货物周转量(亿吨公里)	Freight Traffic Turnover (100 000 000 tn.km)	1 051.54	317.5	3 756	3 076.96
社会客运量(万人次)	Passenger (10 000 person.times)	3 125	9 798.9	5 197	15 638
邮电业务总量(1990 年不变价)(亿元)	Posts and Telecommumications Service (at 1990 Constant Prices) (100 000 000 Yuan)	25.7	72.9	76.20	57.85
电话交换机装机总容量(万门)	Switchboards Capacity (10 000)	169.41	442	455.5	204.46
批发零售贸易业、餐饮业网点数(万个)	Whole Sale Trade and Services Outlets(10 000)	18.69	29.4	19.64	26.02
#个体	Individual	16.46	17.2		14.02
餐饮业网点数(万个)	Outlets In Catering Trade (10 000)	2.58	3.7	2.53	1.81
#个体	Individual	2.41	2.9		1.46

1－19 续表 3
Continued

项　目	Item	天津市 Tianjin	北京市 Beijing	上海市 Shang－hai	广州市 Guang－zhou
社会消费品零售总额(亿元)	Retail Sales Of Consumer goods (100 000 000 Yuan)	470.04	969.7	1 161.3	686.44
海关进出口总额(亿美元)	Total Value Of Imports and Exports (US＄ 100 000 000)	216.85	53.9	528.70	432.84
＃出口（亿美元）	Exports(US＄ 100 000 000)	122.89	20.9	272.13	230.93
外贸进出口总额(亿美元)	Total Value Of Imports and Exports In Foreign Trade(US＄ 100 000 000)	82.97	39.6	222.63	104.84
＃出口（亿美元）	Exports(US＄ 100 000 000)	40.49	23.6	132.38	65.14
当年实际利用外资额(亿美元)	Foreign Capital Actual Used Current Year(US＄ 100 000 000)	29.84	15.5	75.10	26.00
＃客商直接投资	Direct Foreign Investments	20.06	12.5	47.16	23.32
年末累计实际利用外资额(亿美元)	Foreign Capital Actual Used (Upto Year－end)(US＄ 100 000 000)	108.87	89.7	271.76	110.52
＃客商直接投资	Direct Foreign Investments	57.59	66.3	189.57	90.10
接待(过夜)旅游人数(万人次)	Accommodated Tourists (10 000 person times)	12.11	218.9	143.19	1 552.96
涉外旅馆数(个)	Numbers Of Tourist Hotel	56	254	315	315
旅游外汇收入(万美元)	Total Foreign Exchange Incomes from Tourism (US＄ 10 000)	15 191	225 200		99 200
"三资"企业情况	Foreign Capital Enterprises				
企业单位数(个)	Numbers Of Enterprises	3 377	4 586		8 423
从业人员数(万人)	Employments (10 000 persons)	32.32	36.3		46.88
利润总额（亿元）	Total After－tax Profits (100 000 000 Yuan)	43.93	2.9		
年末实有出租汽车数(辆)	Numbers Of Taxies (Year－end)	27 565	59 493	38 554	15 143
年末实有铺装道路面积(万平方米)	Area Of Paved Roads(Year－end) (10 000 sq. m)	3 539	3 806.9	3 755	2 030
园林绿地面积（公顷）	Area Of Green public And Gardens (ha)	3 151	5 147.4	7 231.1	27 248
环境噪声达标面积(平方公里)	Area Of Noise Reaching Standards (sq. km)	129	240	233	166
各级各类学校数（个）	Schools by Level and Type	4 303	4 049	2 634	2 238
＃高等学校	Institutions Of Higher Education	20	65	41	25
各级各类在校学生数(万人)	Student Enrollment by Level and type Of School(10 000 persons)	161.40	202.8	221.84	133.29
＃高等学校	Institutions Of Higher Education	7.14	18.2	14.79	9.92
独立自然科研与技术开发机构数(个)	Institutions Of Research and Development Of Personal (In Natural)	139	305	233	644
科技机构中从事科技活动人员数(人)	Personal Enrollment In Sciences and Technology Institution(person)	77 248	81 572	75 912	15 816
卫生机构数(个)	Health Care Institutions	4 171	6 470	5 200	1 987
卫生技术人员数(万人)	Medical Technical Personal (10 000 persons)	7.10	11.7	10.95	5.25
＃医生	Doctors	3.30	5.4	5.24	2.24
卫生机构床位数(万张)	Beds Of Health Care Institution (10 000 sheet)	3.96	6.70	7.00	3.43
社会福利院数（个）	Numbers Of Social Welfare Homes	12	305	23	150

二、人口和劳动工资

POPULATION, LABOUR FORCE AND WAGES

1996 年年末户籍人口	898.45 万人
1996 年人口自然增长率	3.56‰
1996 年年末社会从业人员	512 万人
1996 年职工年平均工资	7 643 元

户籍人口数(万人)

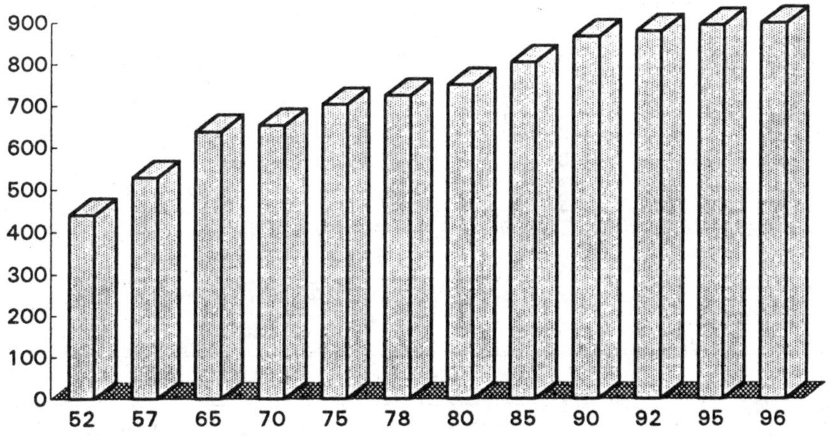

职工年平均工资(元)

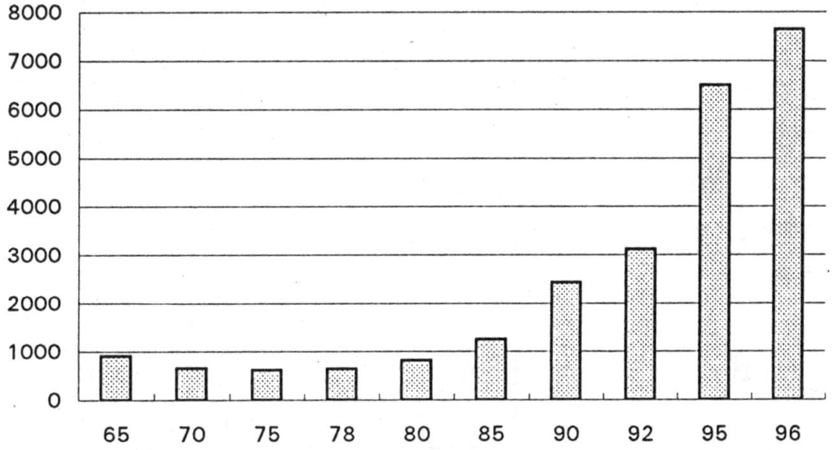

2-1 改革开放以来户籍人口数、户数及人口密度

年份	户数(万户)	人口数(万人)	农业	非农业	人口年增长率(%)	人口密度(人/平方公里)
1978	171.82	724.27	365.82	358.45	1.60	607
1979	174.77	739.42	358.85	380.57	2.09	619
1980	179.67	748.91	356.29	392.62	1.28	627
1981	188.61	760.32	359.57	400.75	1.52	637
1982	196.63	774.92	364.22	410.70	1.92	649
1983	203.47	785.28	365.72	419.56	1.34	658
1984	209.96	795.52	358.43	437.09	1.30	666
1985	216.86	804.80	359.11	445.69	1.17	674
1986	221.81	814.97	367.92	447.05	1.26	682
1987	230.71	828.73	374.05	454.68	1.69	694
1988	241.46	839.21	371.83	467.38	1.26	703
1989	249.44	852.35	375.73	476.62	1.57	714
1990	258.42	866.25	380.81	485.44	1.63	725
1991	262.78	872.63	382.31	490.32	0.74	730
1992	266.77	878.97	384.17	494.80	0.73	736
1993	270.77	885.89	385.91	499.98	0.79	741
1994	273.86	890.55	386.52	504.03	0.53	745
1995	276.89	894.67	386.73	507.94	0.46	749
1996	279.62	898.45	385.29	513.15	0.42	752

注:1.历年人口密度均按现调整后土地面积进行计算。2.人口年增长率是指年末人口本年比上年增长百分率。

2-2 人口变动情况

指标	单位	全市		市辖区		市辖县	
		1995年	1996年	1995年	1996年	1995年	1996年
人口自然增长数	人	32 669	21 793	7 407	865	25 262	20 928
人口自然增长率	‰	4.00	3.56	1.25	0.15	8.36	6.88
出生人数	人	84 451	79 070	39 881	36 840	44 570	42 230
人口出生率	‰	10.23	10.09	6.75	6.22	14.75	13.88
死亡人数	人	51 782	57 277	32 474	35 975	19 308	21 302
人口死亡率	‰	6.23	6.53	5.50	6.07	6.39	7.00
人口机械增长数	人	11 613	14 341	9 974	13 066	1 639	1 275
人口机械增长率	‰	1.30	1.60	1.69	2.21	0.54	0.42
人口迁入数	人	43 306	41 680	35 628	33 778	7 678	7 902
人口迁入率	‰	4.85	4.65	6.03	5.70	2.54	2.60
人口迁出数	人	31 693	27 339	25 654	20 712	6 039	6 627
人口迁出率	‰	3.55	3.05	4.34	3.50	2.00	2.18

注:全市的人口出生率、死亡率、自然增长率为人口抽样调查数据,其他均为公安年报数据。

2－3 按地区分的户数、人口数和人口密度

地　区	户　数（万户）		1996年平均户规模（人/户）	人口数（万人）		1996年平均人口数（万人）	1996年人口密度（人/平方公里）
	1995年	1996年		1995年	1996年		
全市常住人口	**281.14**	**285.60**	**3.3**	**941.83**	**948.19**	**945.01**	**795**
全市户籍人口	**276.89**	**279.62**	**3.2**	**894.67**	**898.45**	**896.56**	**752**
一、市辖区	**192.97**	**194.77**	**3.0**	**591.36**	**593.12**	**592.24**	**1 368**
市内六区	123.07	124.34	3.0	368.71	369.32	369.02	22 015
和平区	15.00	14.99	3.1	47.58	47.18	47.38	47 183
河东区	20.75	21.06	3.0	61.83	62.04	61.94	15 906
河西区	22.94	23.22	3.0	68.16	68.52	68.34	18 520
南开区	24.11	24.46	3.0	71.95	72.54	72.25	18 601
河北区	20.60	20.80	3.0	61.61	61.55	61.58	22 798
红桥区	19.67	19.80	2.9	57.58	57.48	57.53	27 370
滨海区	29.84	30.15	3.1	92.77	93.35	93.06	414
塘沽区	14.61	14.73	3.1	44.82	45.05	44.94	594
#开发区	0.01	0.02	4.4	0.07	0.10	0.08	
汉沽区	5.71	5.74	2.9	16.72	16.72	16.72	378
大港区	9.52	9.67	3.3	31.23	31.58	31.41	299
其他四区	39.31	39.55	3.2	127.64	128.26	127.95	671
东丽区	9.37	9.49	3.1	29.71	29.85	29.78	623
西青区	9.10	9.14	3.3	30.23	30.57	30.40	542
津南区	11.00	11.01	3.3	36.23	36.29	36.26	932
北辰区	9.85	9.91	3.2	31.47	31.55	31.51	659
天津铁厂	0.75	0.74	3.0	2.24	2.19	2.22	
二、市辖县	**83.91**	**84.85**	**3.6**	**303.31**	**305.33**	**304.32**	**403**
宁河县	9.81	9.90	3.5	34.72	34.90	34.81	244
武清县	22.54	22.70	3.5	79.05	79.35	79.20	504
静海县	14.24	14.23	3.5	49.01	49.41	49.21	334
宝坻县	16.55	17.13	3.7	63.37	63.86	63.62	423
蓟　县	20.77	20.88	3.7	77.17	77.81	77.49	489

注:1.常住人口是天津市人口抽样调查结果推算数据,户籍人口是公安年报数据。2.计算人口密度时已将天津铁厂人口剔除。土地面积(除市中心六区)为调整后数据。

2-4 按农业非农业分的户数和人口数

地　区	户籍户数(万户)				户籍人口数(万人)			
	非农业户数		农业户数		非农业人口		农业人口	
	1995年	1996年	1995年	1996年	1995年	1996年	1995年	1996年
全市总计	**167.40**	**170.31**	**109.48**	**109.31**	**507.94**	**513.15**	**386.73**	**385.29**
一、市辖区	**156.29**	**158.62**	**36.68**	**36.15**	**472.04**	**475.36**	**119.32**	**117.76**
市内六区	122.34	123.63	0.73	0.71	366.59	367.34	2.12	1.98
和平区	15.00	14.99			47.58	47.18		
河东区	20.72	21.03	0.03	0.04	61.74	61.95	0.09	0.09
河西区	22.76	23.05	0.18	0.17	67.68	68.08	0.47	0.45
南开区	23.77	24.11	0.34	0.35	70.90	71.49	1.05	1.06
河北区	20.57	20.78	0.03	0.03	61.56	61.50	0.05	0.05
红桥区	19.51	19.68	0.15	0.12	57.13	57.14	0.45	0.34
滨海区	22.24	23.07	7.60	7.08	68.58	70.66	24.19	22.70
塘沽区	11.84	12.41	2.77	2.32	36.30	37.83	8.52	7.22
#开发区	0.01	0.02			0.07	0.10		
汉沽区	4.25	4.36	1.46	1.39	11.94	12.11	4.78	4.61
大港区	6.14	6.31	3.37	3.37	20.34	20.71	10.88	10.87
其他四区	10.96	11.19	28.35	28.36	34.62	35.17	93.02	93.08
东丽区	2.80	2.89	6.57	6.61	9.20	9.33	20.51	20.52
西青区	2.33	2.35	6.77	6.79	7.34	7.60	22.89	22.97
津南区	2.66	2.67	8.34	8.33	7.69	7.72	28.54	28.56
北辰区	3.17	3.28	6.67	6.63	10.39	10.52	21.08	21.03
天津铁厂	0.75	0.74			2.24	2.19		
二、市辖县	**11.12**	**11.69**	**72.80**	**73.16**	**35.90**	**37.80**	**267.41**	**267.53**
宁河县	2.45	2.51	7.36	7.40	6.13	6.30	28.59	28.60
武清县	2.52	2.66	20.03	20.04	8.13	8.47	70.92	70.88
静海县	2.18	2.22	12.06	12.01	6.55	6.79	42.46	42.62
宝坻县	2.01	2.25	14.53	14.88	7.15	8.00	56.22	55.86
蓟　县	1.95	2.06	18.81	18.82	7.95	8.23	69.23	69.58

2-5 按性别分的户籍人口数

单位:万人

地　　区	男性人口		女性人口		性别比(女=100)	
	1995年	1996年	1995年	1996年	1995年	1996年
全 市 总 计	**453.24**	**454.78**	**441.44**	**443.67**	**102.67**	**102.50**
一、市辖区	**299.07**	**299.69**	**292.29**	**293.42**	**102.31**	**102.14**
市内六区	185.24	185.35	183.46	183.97	100.97	100.75
和平区	23.03	22.80	24.54	24.38	93.84	93.50
河东区	31.27	31.33	30.56	30.70	102.30	102.06
河西区	34.10	34.24	34.05	34.29	100.14	99.85
南开区	36.57	36.81	35.39	35.73	103.33	103.04
河北区	31.17	31.14	30.44	30.42	102.40	102.38
红桥区	29.10	29.03	28.48	28.45	102.18	102.02
滨海区	48.54	48.78	44.23	44.57	109.72	109.43
塘沽区	23.35	23.43	21.48	21.62	108.71	108.33
#开发区	0.04	0.06	0.03	0.04	155.38	141.69
汉沽区	8.52	8.52	8.19	8.20	104.03	104.01
大港区	16.66	16.83	14.56	14.75	114.42	114.05
其他四区	64.14	64.44	63.50	63.82	101.01	100.97
东丽区	14.99	15.06	14.72	14.79	101.81	101.79
西青区	15.15	15.32	15.08	15.25	100.43	100.49
津南区	18.15	18.18	18.08	18.11	100.35	100.40
北辰区	15.85	15.88	15.61	15.67	101.53	101.32
天津铁厂	1.15	1.13	1.09	1.06	105.33	106.86
二、市辖县	**154.17**	**155.08**	**149.15**	**150.25**	**103.36**	**103.22**
宁河县	17.63	17.70	17.09	17.20	103.11	102.96
武清县	39.85	39.98	39.20	39.36	101.67	101.58
静海县	24.94	25.13	24.07	24.28	103.60	103.48
宝坻县	32.14	32.38	31.23	31.49	102.88	102.82
蓟　县	39.62	39.89	37.55	37.92	105.49	105.19

2-6 主要年份户籍人口的城乡分布

指　　标	1978年	1980年	1985年	1990年	1992年	1995年	1996年
人口数(万人)	724.27	748.91	804.80	866.25	878.97	894.67	898.45
城　镇	355.18	385.75	432.55	476.07	485.19	498.50	504.55
乡　村	369.09	363.16	372.25	390.18	393.78	396.17	393.90
构　成(%)							
城　镇	49.0	51.5	53.7	55.0	55.2	55.7	56.2
乡　村	51.0	48.5	46.3	45.0	44.8	44.3	43.8

注:城镇人口指市辖区和县辖镇的非农业人口。

2-7 主要年份计划生育情况

单位:%

指　　标	1978年	1980年	1985年	1990年	1992年	1995年	1996年
计划生育率	71.97	84.12	96.31	95.73	93.23	97.54	97.85
一　孩　率	52.16	74.33	89.78	73.19	80.00	80.11	82.32
二　孩　率	31.29	21.27	9.93	22.76	17.42	17.76	16.90
多　孩　率	16.55	4.40	0.29	4.05	2.58	2.13	0.79
晚　婚　率	95.18	96.52	63.34	57.97	58.29	62.76	63.85

资料来源:1985年以前数据取自《天津市人口统计与调查》;1990年以后计划生育率、晚婚率为计划生育委员会年报数;孩次率为历年人口抽样调查数据。

2-8 人口婚姻登记情况

单位:对

指　　标	1978年	1980年	1985年	1990年	1992年	1995年	1996年
结婚对数合计	**63 342**	**115 324**	**98 005**	**77 210**	**74 364**	**63 620**	**64 735**
市辖区	**44 288**	**80 727**	**70 887**	**50 374**	**47 247**	**40 764**	**41 155**
#市内六区			42 384	29 500	24 623	20 632	20 927
滨海区			12 066	7 931	9 333	8 598	9 179
市辖县	**19 054**	**34 597**	**27 118**	**26 836**	**27 088**	**22 808**	**23 535**
合计中:恢复结婚对数	257	294	208	357	383	580	584
离婚对数	**1 481**	**2 349**	**3 390**	**6 967**	**8 069**	**10 912**	**12 264**

资料来源:结婚对数是民政事业统计年报数,离婚对数是民政事业统计年报和法院统计年报数。

2-9 1996年户籍人口负担系数

单位:%

地　　区	总负担系数	负担少儿系数	负担老年系数	老化指数
全　　市	**38.88**	**27.12**	**11.76**	**43.37**
市辖区	**35.17**	**23.24**	**11.93**	**51.34**
市内六区	36.60	22.50	14.10	62.63
滨 海 区	30.14	22.09	8.05	36.45
其他四区	34.88	26.13	8.75	33.50
市辖县	**46.71**	**35.31**	**11.40**	**32.30**

2-10　1996年各年龄组的户籍人口

单位:万人

年龄组	总计	按性别分组		按地区分组		
		男	女	市辖区	#市内六区	市辖县
一、按学龄人口分组						
0-3岁	27.09	14.44	12.65	14.59	6.84	12.50
4-6岁	31.43	16.47	14.96	16.40	8.60	15.03
7-12岁	85.56	44.09	41.47	49.92	31.38	35.64
13-15岁	45.53	23.42	22.11	30.14	19.66	15.39
16-18岁	37.09	18.94	18.15	23.39	14.19	13.70
二、按婚育人口分组						
进入法定婚龄人口	11.45	5.97	5.48	7.35	4.04	4.10
育龄妇女人口(15-49岁)	259.62		259.62	173.08	105.87	86.54
三、按劳龄人口分组						
进入劳龄人口(国内标准)	11.49	5.93	5.56	7.36	4.82	4.13
(国际标准)	14.17	7.32	6.85	9.08	5.62	5.09
劳动年龄内人口(国内标准)	574.98	300.12	274.86	387.52	236.14	187.47
(国际标准)	646.92	326.57	320.35	438.81	270.36	208.11
退出劳龄人口(国内标准)	7.89	3.85	4.04	5.60	3.48	2.29
(国际标准)	6.15	3.16	2.99	4.31	3.11	1.84
四、按老年人口分组						
60岁及以上人口	114.66	56.23	58.43	80.31	57.68	34.35
65岁及以上人口	76.08	37.10	38.98	52.35	38.11	23.73
80岁及以上人口	10.29	4.57	5.72	6.61	4.79	3.68

注:进入法定婚龄人口标准为男22岁、女20岁;进入劳龄人口、劳动年龄内人口、退出劳龄人口的国内标准分别是男16岁、16—59岁、60岁和女16岁、16—54岁、55岁;国际标准男女均为15岁、15—64岁、65岁。

1992与1996年劳动适龄人口状况图

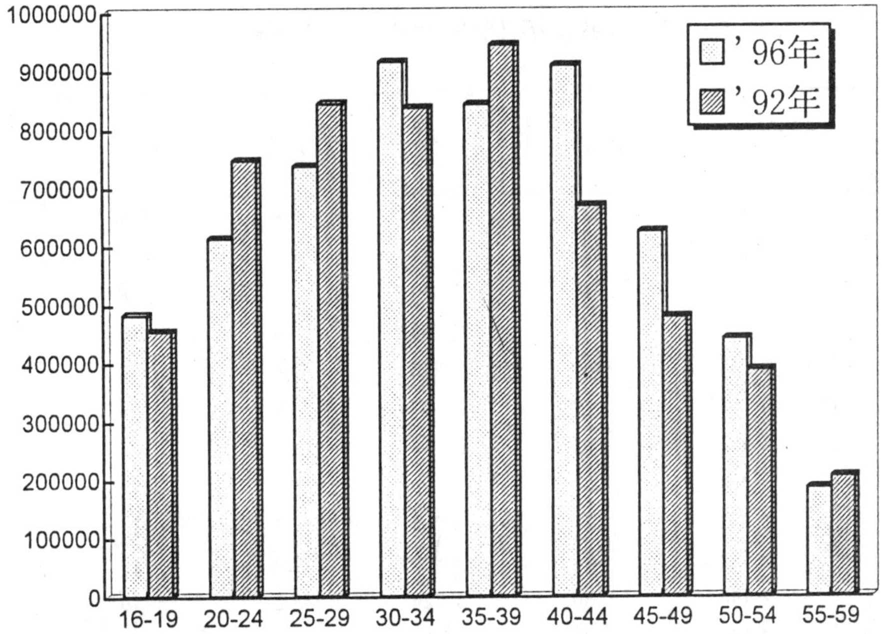

1996年全市人口变动情况抽样调查资料说明：

按照国家统计局统一部署，天津市进行了1996年度人口变动情况抽样调查，此次调查范围涉及全市18个区县中的63个街、乡、镇的95个居、村委会，并从中抽取了126个调查小区。人口抽样调查时点为1996年10月1日零时，调查登记1995年10月1日零时至1996年9月30日24时一年间的人口变动情况。经过调查员逐人逐户现场登记与核对，实际调查样本量为15395户，51046人，其中市辖区人口占66.2%，市辖县人口占33.8%。这次人口变动抽样调查在95%的把握程度下，人口出生率的抽样误差为±0.46‰，人口死亡率的抽样误差为±0.33‰，调查结果均在样本设计的误差允许范围之内。以下表2-11至2-18为这次人口变动抽样调查机器汇总数据。

2-11 1996年6岁及以上人口文化构成

单位：人

年 龄	6岁及以上人 口	#大专及以上	高 中	初 中	小 学
总 计	**47 759**	**2 342**	**8 222**	**17 121**	**15 432**
6-9 岁	3 623				3 302
10-14岁	4 241		6	1 725	2 499
15-19岁	3 152	68	1 139	1 599	330
20-24岁	3 280	253	838	1 758	401
25-29岁	4 322	365	898	2 316	694
30-34岁	5 265	374	1 532	2 589	670
35-39岁	4 732	235	1 723	1 804	831
40-44岁	4 985	266	701	2 303	1 464
45-49岁	3 390	228	453	1 148	1 345
50-54岁	2 424	174	356	749	907
55-59岁	2 052	147	268	422	840
60-64岁	2 158	113	138	309	838
65岁以上	4 135	119	170	399	1 311

2-12 1996年15岁及以上人口婚姻构成

单位：人

年 龄	合 计	未 婚	初 婚有配偶	再 婚有配偶	离 婚	丧 偶
总 计	**39 895**	**6 037**	**30 622**	**658**	**299**	**2 279**
15-19岁	3 152	3 128	24			
20-24岁	3 280	1 910	1 354	5	8	3
25-29岁	4 322	495	3 733	46	43	5
30-34岁	5 265	182	4 918	85	67	13
35-39岁	4 732	77	4 507	73	56	19
40-44岁	4 985	91	4 746	75	41	32
45-49岁	3 390	55	3 190	66	21	58
50-54岁	2 424	17	2 236	64	15	92
55-59岁	2 052	27	1 800	49	12	164
60-64岁	2 158	30	1 724	62	9	333
65岁以上	4 135	25	2 390	133	27	1 560

2－13　1996年按地区分的家庭户规模

单位:户

地　区	家庭户户数	一人户	二人户	三人户	四人户	五人户	六人及六人以上户
全　市	**15 355**	**771**	**2 396**	**6 622**	**3 417**	**1 420**	**729**
一、市辖区	**10 700**	**622**	**1 815**	**5 261**	**1 903**	**775**	**324**
市内六区	6 592	531	1 213	3 369	939	381	159
和平区	1 099	133	236	520	134	53	23
河东区	1 069	87	176	571	150	65	20
河西区	1 057	55	208	593	133	48	20
南开区	1 296	109	214	676	188	75	34
河北区	978	73	158	442	188	68	49
红桥区	1 093	74	221	567	146	72	13
滨海区	1 925	41	303	856	463	186	76
塘沽区	713	10	115	320	170	63	35
汉沽区	456	20	56	164	119	72	25
大港区	756	11	132	372	174	51	16
其他四区	2 183	50	299	1 036	501	208	89
东丽区	530	14	73	315	96	21	11
西青区	500	14	85	233	120	36	12
津南区	697	14	76	317	174	76	40
北辰区	456	8	65	171	111	75	26
二、市辖县	**4 655**	**149**	**581**	**1 361**	**1 514**	**645**	**405**
宁河县	755	39	95	150	258	135	78
武清县	923	32	111	336	264	135	45
静海县	1 000	25	130	428	275	91	51
宝坻县	885	12	114	204	318	130	107
蓟　县	1 092	41	131	243	399	154	124

2-14 1996年按地区分的家庭户类型

单位:户

地 区	单身户	一 对夫妇户	二代户	三代及以上户	一代与其他户	二代与其他户	三代及以上与其他户
全 市	**783**	**1 823**	**9 756**	**2 561**	**83**	**227**	**122**
一、市辖区	**634**	**1 354**	**6 782**	**1 625**	**61**	**165**	**79**
市内六区	541	859	4 058	998	37	76	23
和平区	136	147	638	146	15	14	3
河东区	87	130	658	173	5	15	1
河西区	55	166	695	121	4	12	4
南开区	111	148	819	201	3	12	2
河北区	77	95	579	192	5	18	12
红桥区	75	173	669	165	5	5	1
滨海区	43	238	1 254	283	11	69	27
塘沽区	10	94	471	121	4	9	4
汉沽区	20	52	228	86	5	53	12
大港区	13	92	555	76	2	7	11
其他四区	50	257	1 470	344	13	20	29
东丽区	14	66	406	40	1	2	1
西青区	14	67	336	56	7	5	15
津南区	14	69	476	129	1	2	6
北辰区	8	55	252	119	4	11	7
二、市辖县	**149**	**469**	**2 974**	**936**	**22**	**62**	**43**
宁河县	38	71	471	146	2	11	16
武清县	33	85	563	221	5	14	2
静海县	25	113	687	145	7	15	8
宝坻县	12	96	556	201	2	12	6
蓟 县	41	104	697	223	6	10	11

2－15　1996年育龄妇女分年龄和受教育程度的初婚状况

单位：人

年　龄（岁）	初婚人数合　计	大专及以　上	高　中	初　中	小　学	不识字或识字很少
总　计	**12 018**	**618**	**2 716**	**5 103**	**3 038**	**543**
15－19	17		1	8	6	2
20－24	801	25	129	493	144	10
25－29	2 028	140	410	1 092	360	26
30－34	2 655	181	796	1 208	405	65
35－39	2 337	91	832	803	520	91
40－44	2 483	103	333	989	866	192
45－49	1 697	78	215	510	737	157

2－16　1996年育龄妇女分年龄和受教育程度的初育状况

单位：人

年　龄（岁）	初育人数合　计	大专及以　上	高　中	初　中	小　学	不识字或识字很少
总　计	**11 365**	**543**	**2 530**	**4 809**	**2 954**	**529**
15－19	8		1	2	4	1
20－24	532	11	58	344	112	7
25－29	1 823	97	351	1 011	342	22
30－34	2 590	171	775	1 182	400	62
35－39	2 307	89	814	795	518	91
40－44	2 452	100	322	976	863	191
45－49	1 653	75	209	499	715	155

2－17　1996年育龄妇女分孩次生育率

单位：‰

年　龄（岁）	生育率	一孩生育率	二孩生育率	多孩生育率
总　计	**34.86**	**28.70**	**5.89**	**0.27**
15－19	3.39	3.39		
20－24	117.61	115.36	2.25	
25－29	93.13	81.49	10.71	0.93
30－34	22.90	10.69	11.45	0.76
35－39	12.20	1.63	10.57	
40－44	1.63	0.82	0.82	
45－49	0.60		0.60	

2-18 1996 年分年龄和受教育程度的就业者身份

单位:人

受教育程度与年龄	在业人口	城镇单位从业人员	乡镇企业从业人员	私营个体雇员	私营个体雇主	自营劳动者	乡村从业人员	其他
总计	**29 461**	**12 864**	**2 781**	**987**	**426**	**2 463**	**9 719**	**221**
15-19 岁	1 282	258	384	121	7	68	428	16
20-24 岁	2 885	1 075	476	183	18	246	863	24
25-29 岁	3 968	1 503	423	171	72	383	1 384	32
30-34 岁	4 906	2 122	455	186	81	488	1 547	27
35-39 岁	4 466	2 518	289	126	62	352	1 093	26
40-44 岁	4 679	2 416	341	91	77	366	1 368	20
45-49 岁	2 960	1 456	167	48	60	218	994	17
50-54 岁	1 719	771	90	19	18	137	675	9
55-59 岁	1 104	428	53	19	12	86	487	19
60-64 岁	749	190	57	14	10	63	398	17
65 岁以上	743	127	46	9	9	56	482	14
大专及以上	**1 980**	**1 934**	**10**	**5**	**8**	**11**	**6**	**6**
15-19 岁	3	3						
20-24 岁	180	176	2			1	1	
25-29 岁	361	348	1	1	3	1	3	4
30-34 岁	372	365	2		1	2	1	1
35-39 岁	235	231		1	1	2		
40-44 岁	266	264		1		1		
45-49 岁	223	216	2		2	3		
50-54 岁	160	157	1	2				
55-59 岁	111	109	1		1			
60-64 岁	45	43	1				1	
65 岁以上	24	22				1		1
高中	**6 472**	**5 131**	**262**	**119**	**71**	**271**	**584**	**34**
15-19 岁	137	107	11	3		4	8	4
20-24 岁	752	594	43	28	5	21	54	7
25-29 岁	860	662	38	10	10	39	95	6
30-34 岁	1 480	1 104	76	31	20	80	163	6
35-39 岁	1 676	1 325	50	27	24	74	170	6
40-44 岁	679	556	24	9	5	29	56	
45-49 岁	420	378	9	4	4	8	16	1
50-54 岁	273	243	7	5	1	2	15	
55-59 岁	140	122	1	2		10	4	1
60-64 岁	37	27	2			4	2	2
65 岁以上	18	13	1		2		1	1

2-18 续表

单位:人

受教育程度与年龄	在业人口	城镇单位从业人员	乡镇企业从业人员	私营个体雇员	私营个体雇主	自营劳动者	乡村从业人员	其他
初　中	**12 717**	**5 009**	**1 599**	**595**	**249**	**1 210**	**3 948**	**107**
15-19岁	860	139	279	87	6	47	294	8
20-24岁	1 575	286	356	123	11	173	611	15
25-29岁	2 085	465	297	115	54	250	886	18
30-34岁	2 378	619	301	122	53	298	966	19
35-39岁	1 712	901	131	73	28	138	426	15
40-44岁	2 221	1 462	127	42	46	161	368	15
45-49岁	1 027	682	52	19	30	72	166	6
50-54岁	499	265	34	6	11	39	141	3
55-59岁	213	114	12	3	7	15	60	2
60-64岁	78	40	6	5	1	10	11	5
65岁以上	69	36	4		2	7	19	1
小　学	**6 814**	**693**	**820**	**245**	**88**	**760**	**4 150**	**58**
15-19岁	277	9	92	30	1	17	124	4
20-24岁	357	17	74	29	2	48	185	2
25-29岁	628	27	77	42	5	87	386	4
30-34岁	604	26	71	31	7	86	382	1
35-39岁	730	58	95	23	9	94	447	4
40-44岁	1 310	101	172	37	26	155	814	5
45-49岁	1 130	165	95	22	21	110	709	8
50-54岁	641	96	46	5	5	72	411	6
55-59岁	479	79	31	12	3	36	309	9
60-64岁	364	67	39	8	8	28	208	6
65岁以上	294	48	28	6	1	27	175	9
不识字或识字很少	**1 478**	**97**	**90**	**23**	**10**	**211**	**1 031**	**16**
15-19岁	5		2	1			2	
20-24岁	21	2	1	3		3	12	
25-29岁	34	1	10	3		6	14	
30-34岁	72	8	5	2		22	35	
35-39岁	113	3	13	2		44	50	1
40-44岁	203	33	18	2		20	130	
45-49岁	160	15	9	3	3	25	103	2
50-54岁	146	10	2	1	1	24	108	
55-59岁	161	4	8	2	1	25	114	7
60-64岁	225	13	9	1	1	21	176	4
65岁以上	338	8	13	3	4	21	287	2

2-19 改革开放以来社会从业人员变化情况

单位:万人

年份	从业人员合计	按城乡分组				
		城镇	国有经济	集体经济	其他经济	个体与私营经济
1978	366.70	217.50	168.30	49.10		0.10
1979	380.54	230.24	178.20	52.04		0.10
1980	394.79	243.59	188.08	54.61		0.90
1981	413.20	255.00	194.02	59.88		1.10
1982	420.52	262.02	198.91	61.61		1.50
1983	435.53	270.33	201.27	66.96		2.10
1984	447.29	276.39	201.29	71.42	0.98	2.70
1985	455.98	281.08	205.26	69.71	1.51	4.60
1986	466.90	284.50	209.97	68.47	1.76	4.30
1987	470.93	286.63	212.10	66.89	2.54	5.10
1988	465.15	286.64	213.99	64.33	3.04	5.28
1989	469.79	289.91	217.32	63.45	3.61	5.53
1990	470.07	290.01	217.26	62.55	4.50	5.70
1991	479.67	300.58	219.34	66.17	6.05	9.02
1992	485.70	303.70	212.73	72.39	8.85	9.73
1993	503.10	312.70	210.90	75.50	16.30	10.00
1994	513.00	318.60	206.50	71.40	24.40	16.30
1995	515.30	319.80	202.10	68.40	29.20	20.10
1996	512.00	317.10	199.10	62.80	31.00	24.20

年份	乡村	按三次产业分组			职工人数	#国有经济	城镇集体经济
		第一产业	第二产业	第三产业			
1978	149.20				217.40	168.30	49.10
1979	150.20				230.24	178.20	52.04
1980	151.20				242.69	188.08	54.61
1981	158.20				253.90	194.02	59.88
1982	158.50				260.53	198.91	61.62
1983	165.20				268.23	201.27	66.96
1984	170.90				273.69	201.29	71.42
1985	174.90	99.13	228.04	128.73	276.48	205.26	69.71
1986	182.40	96.06	231.02	139.86	280.20	209.97	68.47
1987	184.30	94.12	232.03	144.78	281.53	212.10	66.89
1988	178.51	91.19	229.85	144.11	281.36	213.99	64.33
1989	179.88	93.46	231.57	144.76	284.38	217.32	63.45
1990	180.06	93.63	232.17	144.27	284.31	217.26	62.55
1991	179.09	94.27	237.24	148.16	291.56	219.34	66.17
1992	182.00	92.50	238.40	154.80	293.97	212.73	72.39
1993	190.40	89.00	245.20	168.90	293.45	206.52	70.89
1994	194.40	85.60	246.50	180.90	291.94	201.75	66.21
1995	195.50	82.90	247.10	185.30	289.59	197.01	64.19
1996	194.90	82.10	241.40	188.50	283.98	194.32	59.62

2-20 社会从业人员人数

项目	绝对数（万人）			构成（%）	
	1995年	1996年	1996比1995年增长数	1995年	1996年
从业人员合计	**515.3**	**512.0**	**-3.3**	**100.0**	**100.0**
按经济类型分					
国有经济	202.1	199.1	-3.0	39.2	38.9
集体经济	238.2	230.7	-7.5	46.2	45.1
私营经济	15.7	18.7	3.0	3.1	3.7
个体经济	30.1	32.5	2.4	5.8	6.4
联营经济	2.1	2.1		0.4	0.4
股份制经济	6.2	7.2	1.0	1.2	1.4
"三资"经济	20.8	21.4	0.6	4.0	4.2
外商投资经济	12.9	15.0	2.1	2.5	2.9
港、澳、台投资经济	7.9	6.4	-1.5	1.5	1.3
其他经济	0.1	0.3	0.2		0.1
按三次产业分					
第一产业	82.9	82.1	-0.8	16.1	16.0
第二产业	247.1	241.4	-5.7	48.0	47.2
工　业	217.5	211.0	-6.5	42.2	41.2
采掘业	9.9	10.0	0.1	1.9	2.0
制造业	203.8	198.2	-5.6	39.6	38.7
电力、煤气业及水的生产和供应业	3.8	2.8	-1.0	0.7	0.6
建筑业	29.6	30.4	0.8	5.7	5.9
第三产业	185.3	188.5	3.2	36.0	36.8
地质勘察业、水利管理业	2.4	2.0	-0.4	0.5	0.4
交通运输、仓储及邮电通信业	30.7	31.6	0.9	6.0	6.2
批发和零售贸易、餐饮业	67.6	69.7	2.1	13.1	13.6
金融、保险业	3.7	3.9	0.2	0.7	0.8
房地产业	2.8	2.2	-0.6	0.5	0.4
社会服务业	19.4	18.6	-0.8	3.8	3.6
卫生、体育和社会福利业	8.6	7.5	-1.1	1.7	1.5
教育、文化艺术及广播电影电视业	20.2	19.7	-0.5	3.9	3.9
科学研究和综合技术服务业	5.5	6.2	0.7	1.1	1.2
国家机关、政党机关和社会团体	14.3	13.7	-0.6	2.8	2.7
其　他	10.1	13.4	3.3	2.0	2.6

2－21 职工人数

单位:百人

项目	职工人数 1995年	职工人数 1996年	职工人数 1996比1995年增长%	#女职工人数 1995年	#女职工人数 1996年	#女职工人数 1996比1995年增长%
总计	**28 959**	**28 398**	**－1.9**	**12 360**	**12 023**	**－2.7**
按经济类型分						
国有经济	19 701	19 432	－1.4	7 927	7 739	－2.4
集体经济	6 419	5 962	－7.1	3 081	2 859	－7.2
联营经济	211	205	－2.8	103	95	－7.8
股份制经济	611	687	12.4	234	269	15.0
"三资"经济	2 011	2 085	3.7	1 012	1 053	4.1
外商投资经济	1 246	1 464	17.5	634	766	20.8
港澳台投资经济	765	621	－18.8	378	287	－24.1
其他经济	6	27	350.0	3	8	166.7
按隶属关系分						
中央	4 621	4 525	－2.1	1 576	1 536	－2.5
地方	24 338	23 873	－1.9	10 784	10 487	－2.8
按国民经济行业分						
农、林、牧、渔业	190	173	－9.0	68	57	－16.2
#农业	95	76	－20.0	40	31	－22.5
工业	14 903	14 395	－3.4	6 746	6 489	－3.8
采掘业	921	927	0.7	306	298	－2.6
制造业	13 604	13 199	－3.0	6 319	6 104	－3.4
电力、煤气及水的生产和供应业	378	269	－28.8	121	87	－28.1
建筑业	1 830	1 912	4.4	457	495	8.3
地质勘察业、水利管理业	232	194	－16.4	60	44	－26.7
交通运输、仓储及邮电通信业	1 760	1 838	4.4	463	500	8.0
交通运输和仓储业	1 606	1 669	3.9	404	436	7.9
邮电通信业	154	169	9.7	59	64	8.5
批发和零售贸易、餐饮业	3 447	3 241	－6.0	1 676	1 540	－8.1
#批发和零售贸易业	3 197	2 983	－6.7	1 535	1 402	－8.7
餐饮业	240	234	－2.5	137	130	－5.1
金融、保险业	339	366	8.0	149	168	12.8
房地产业	257	212	－17.5	101	77	－23.8
社会服务业	1 340	1 262	－5.8	567	548	－3.4
卫生、体育和社会福利业	769	735	－4.4	481	469	－2.5
#卫生	713	689	－3.4	461	451	－2.2
体育	25	21	－16.0	7	6	－14.3
教育、文化艺术及广播电影电视业	1 925	1 925		1 036	1 044	0.8
教育	1 779	1 709	－3.9	977	964	－1.3
文化艺术业	105	169	61.0	43	63	46.5
广播电影电视业	42	47	11.9	16	17	6.3
科学研究和综合技术服务业	516	600	16.3	175	208	18.9
国家机关、政党机关和社会团体	1 258	1 287	2.3	319	291	－8.8
其他行业	193	258	34.2	62	93	50.0

2-22 1996年国民经济各行业职工人数

单位:百人

项目	国有经济	#地方	集体经济	其他经济	#"三资"经济	股份制经济
总计	**19 432**	**15 441**	**5 962**	**3 004**	**2 085**	**687**
按国民经济行业分						
农、林、牧、渔业	163	163	9	1		
#农业	75	75	1			
工业	8 655	7 110	3 243	2 496	1 893	433
采掘业	925	157	3			
制造业	7 486	6 790	3 223	2 488	1 892	426
电力、煤气及水的生产和供应业	244	163	17	8	1	7
建筑业	1 511	902	386	15	8	6
地质勘察业、水利管理业	193	76	1			
交通运输、仓储及邮电通信业	1 442	725	346	49	27	20
交通运输和仓储业	1 276	723	344	48		19
邮电通信业	166	2	2	1		1
批发和零售贸易、餐饮业	1 555	1 450	1 450	236	76	138
#批发和零售贸易业	1 427	1 325	1 341	215	56	137
餐饮业	115	112	102	17	17	
金融、保险业	263	4	51	51		51
房地产业	180	179	12	19	9	10
社会服务业	904	823	270	88	61	4
卫生、体育和社会福利业	711	709	22	2		
#卫生	669	667	21			
体育	21	21				
教育、文化艺术及广播电影电视业	1 898	1 685	26	1		
教育	1 685	1 537	24	1		
文化艺术业	167	102	1			
广播电影电视业	46	46	1			
科学研究和综合技术服务业	487	242	77	36	9	25
国家机关、政党机关和社会团体	1 281	1 199	2	5		
其他行业	187	174	65	5	2	

2－23　市属各局(总公司)国有经济职工人数

单位:人

局(总公司)	年末人数 1995年	年末人数 1996年	年末人数 1996比1995年增长数	年平均人数 1995年	年平均人数 1996年	年平均人数 1996比1995年增长数
一、经委系统						
机电工业总公司	87 254	83 840	－3 414	87 332	82 812	－4 520
电子仪表工业总公司	62 353	59 419	－2 934	57 630	57 811	181
冶金工业总公司	86 129	83 485	－2 644	86 785	84 234	－2 551
化学工业总公司	48 666	46 231	－2 435	46 881	41 548	－5 333
纺织工业总公司	130 461	126 398	－4 063	123 875	117 105	－6 770
一轻总公司	80 041	76 464	－3 577	76 459	70 036	－6 423
二轻局	31 736	32 859	1 123	31 692	33 048	1 356
医药局	17 829	16 075	－1 754	17 802	15 806	－1 996
汽车工业(集团)有限公司	33 624	29 946	－3 678	33 438	30 589	－2 849
服装联合总公司	3 332	3 140	－192	3 316	3 280	－36
渤海化工集团公司	6 736	21 728	14 992	6 818	21 921	15 103
长芦盐务管理局	16 753	365	－16 388	17 055	388	－16 667
飞鸽自行车集团公司	21 461	20 591	－870	21 571	19 782	－1 789
二、农委系统						
农林局	1 260	1 234	－26	1 243	1 231	－12
农工商总公司	17 340	15 221	－2 119	15 765	14 228	－1 537
水产局	5 566	3 295	－2 271	5 615	3 369	－2 246
三、建委系统						
建工集团总公司	48 014	45 336	－2 678	48 727	44 565	－4 162
建筑材料集团总公司	25 661	24 119	－1 542	26 591	24 519	－2 072
市政工程局	32 308	31 782	－526	32 279	31 892	－387
房地产管理局	39 244	37 575	－1 669	39 169	37 628	－1 541
公用局	41 820	38 766	－3 054	41 225	38 724	－2 501
四、交委系统						
港务局	20 760	20 874	114	20 733	20 752	19
交通局	20 180	19 883	－297	19 190	18 526	－664
五、商委系统						
粮食局	36 447	37 419	972	36 540	37 270	730
益商集团总公司	27 489	22 494	－4 995	27 014	22 885	－4 129
食品工贸集团总公司	24 591	23 702	－889	23 322	21 600	－1 722

注:1996年长芦盐务局部分单位转入渤海化工集团公司。

2－24 1996年职工变动情况

单位:百人

项 目	合 计	按经济类型分			按企事业机关分		
		国有经济	集体经济	其他经济	企 业	事 业	机 关
一、职工增加合计	**1 825**	**957**	**405**	**463**	**1 538**	**226**	**61**
1.从农村招收人员	228	113	25	90	215	11	2
2.从城镇招收人员	222	52	46	124	211	9	2
3.复员转业军人	23	19	2	2	14	3	6
4.大中专毕业生	347	258	14	75	241	90	16
#技校毕业生	106	67	4	35	101	5	
5.调入职工	495	315	86	94	367	96	32
#市外调入	20	13	2	5	15	5	
6.其 他	510	200	232	78	490	17	3
二、职工减少合计	**2 347**	**1 447**	**620**	**280**	**2 065**	**233**	**49**
1.离退休退职人员	670	492	134	44	542	113	15
2.开除、除名、辞退	194	108	31	55	186	7	1
3.终止、解除合同	252	132	51	69	242	7	3
4.调出职工	563	382	122	59	459	80	24
#调至市外	11	9	1	1	8	3	
5.其 他	668	333	282	53	636	26	6

2－25 城镇新就业人数

单位:万人

年 份	合 计	国有经济	集体经济	“三资”经济	私营、个体经济	临时劳务
1990	8.1	1.5	0.8	0.3	0.1	5.4
1993	7.1	0.1	0.5	1.4	0.3	4.8
1994	7.3	0.4	0.5	1.1	0.5	4.8
1995	8.7	0.5	0.5	1.1	0.8	5.8
1996	8.9	0.5	0.5	1.1	0.7	6.1

注:1995年“临时劳务”中含1.2万下岗人员,1996年“临时劳务”中含1.3万下岗人员。

2-26　1996年工业、建筑业、交通运输仓储及邮电业职工人员分类

单位:百人

项　目	职工人数	按劳动岗位分组				
		工人和学徒	工程技术人员	管　理人　员	服　务人　员	其　他人　员
一、工　业	**14 395**	**8 229**	**842**	**1 518**	**868**	**2 938**
1.按经济类型分						
国有经济	8 655	4 704	519	886	633	1 913
集体经济	3 243	1 849	114	302	136	842
联营经济	170	104	5	15	7	39
股份制经济	433	283	38	60	17	35
"三资"经济	1 893	1 289	166	255	75	108
其他经济	1					1
2.按隶属关系分						
中央单位	1 767	1 048	157	224	253	85
地方单位	12 628	7 181	685	1 294	615	2 853
二、建筑业	**1 912**	**946**	**178**	**300**	**139**	**349**
按经济类型分						
国有经济	1 511	684	142	247	123	315
集体经济	386	256	34	49	15	32
联营经济	1					1
股份制经济	6	4	1		1	
"三资"经济	8	2	1	4		1
其他经济						
三、交通运输、仓储及邮电通信业	**1 838**	**1 006**	**146**	**254**	**135**	**297**
按经济类型分						
国有经济	1 442	833	138	206	106	159
集体经济	346	149	4	32	25	136
联营经济	3		1	1		1
股份制经济	20	12	2	5	1	
"三资"经济	27	12	1	10	3	1
其他经济						

2－27 合同制职工人数

单位:百人

项 目	1995年			1996年		
	全 市	#国有经济	集体经济	全 市	#国有经济	集体经济
总 计	**10 630**	**7 334**	**1 245**	**16 297**	**11 035**	**3 085**
农、林、牧、渔业	59	58	1	105	100	4
工 业	7 668	5 016	793	10 406	6 768	1 730
采掘业	250	250	1	249	247	2
制造业	7 248	4 600	790	10 012	6 385	1 726
电力、煤气及水的生产和供应业	170	166	2	145	136	2
建筑业	757	713	42	1 243	1 138	101
地质勘察业、水利管理业	26	25		20	19	1
交通运输、仓储及邮电通信业	616	555	28	1 476	1 249	193
批发和零售贸易、餐饮业	1 028	674	242	2 213	1 192	858
金融、保险业	20	2	17	26	5	16
房地产业	50	28	19	40	32	6
社会服务业	244	125	85	495	324	120
卫生、体育和社会福利业	34	33	1	35	32	3
教育、文化艺术及广播电影电视业	36	34	2	43	42	1
科学研究和综合技术服务业	32	20	7	77	38	31
国家机关、政党机关和社会团体	46	45	1	51	51	
其他行业	14	6	7	67	45	21

2－28 城乡私营、个体从业人员

单位:万人

项 目	1995年			1996年		
	合 计	私 营	个 体	合 计	私 营	个 体
总 计	**45.76**	**15.71**	**30.05**	**51.19**	**18.72**	**32.47**
#城 镇	20.15	7.70	12.45	24.18	10.43	13.75
按国民经济行业分						
农、林、牧、渔业	0.05	0.03	0.02	0.12	0.05	0.07
工 业	12.45	8.14	4.31	13.00	8.88	4.12
#制造业	12.43	8.14	4.29	12.96	8.88	4.08
建筑业	0.42	0.30	0.12	0.58	0.49	0.09
交通运输、仓储及邮电通信业	3.39	0.32	3.07	3.57	0.44	3.13
#公路运输业						
批发和零售贸易、餐饮业	24.02	4.72	19.30	28.17	6.81	21.36
#餐饮业	4.55	0.11	4.44	4.73	0.16	4.57
社会服务业	4.95	1.86	3.09	5.45	1.90	3.55
卫生、体育和社会福利业						
科学研究和综合技术服务业						
其他行业	0.48	0.34	0.14	0.30	0.15	0.15

资料来源:天津市工商局。

2-29 改革开放以来职工工资情况

年份	职工工资总额(亿元)	国有经济	集体经济	其他经济	#"三资"经济
1978	14.00	11.50	2.50		
1979	16.34	13.48	2.86		
1980	19.32	15.77	3.55		
1981-1985	126.99	98.38	26.02		
1981	19.93	16.04	3.89		
1982	21.03	16.97	4.05		
1983	22.90	18.20	4.70		
1984	28.99	22.48	6.44	0.07	
1985	34.14	24.69	6.94	0.18	
1986-1990	276.15	209.64	49.85	3.41	
1986	41.50	30.08	7.87	0.26	
1987	46.09	34.03	8.42	0.41	
1988	55.16	41.66	9.62	0.63	
1989	64.02	48.37	11.31	0.86	
1990	69.38	55.50	12.63	1.25	
1991-1995	626.91	475.92	98.83	52.16	
1991	79.73	62.34	15.42	1.97	
1992	91.56	71.97	16.51	3.08	
1993	116.78	90.32	19.21	7.25	4.03
1994	154.04	116.07	21.69	16.28	9.50
1995	184.80	135.22	26.00	23.58	16.49
1996	212.05	154.34	27.14	30.57	21.77

年份	职工平均工资(元)	国有经济	集体经济	其他经济	#"三资"经济
1978	640	690	478		
1979	732	781	565		
1980	820	865	667		
1981	805	845	674		
1982	820	865	672		
1983	868	916	721		
1984	1 071	1 132	900		
1985	1 250	1 223	995	1 272	
1986	1 498	1 455	1 149	1 479	
1987	1 651	1 622	1 256	1 630	
1988	1 975	1 972	1 475	2 212	
1989	2 262	2 274	1 691	2 479	
1990	2 438	2 611	1 866	2 946	
1991	2 724	2 912	2 114	3 455	
1992	3 118	3 383	2 285	3 553	
1993	4 080	4 410	2 780	5 869	5 167
1994	5 364	5 806	3 370	7 100	6 699
1995	6 501	6 963	4 138	8 648	8 629
1996	7 643	8 072	4 745	10 522	10 879

注:1.1993年以前各项指标中均不含洗理、交通费。2.1985-1989年"工资总额"、"人均工资"中含肉类价格补贴,其分组不含。

2－30 1996年按经济类型分各行业职工工资总额

单位:万元

行 业	国有经济	#地方	集体经济	其他经济	#"三资"经济	股份制经济
总 计	**1 543 422.3**	**1 115 217.0**	**271 357.8**	**305 711.5**	**217 702.7**	**74 415.0**
按国民经济行业分						
农、林、牧、渔业	8 964.7	8 959.2	530.6	115.7	36.8	
#农 业	3 626.0	3 620.5	91.0			
工 业	630 131.9	461 958.4	129 791.9	252 669.0	196 001.8	48 062.7
采掘业	108 862.2	15 386.8	189.2			
制造业	490 077.8	429 375.7	128 479.2	251 458.2	195 913.6	46 940.1
电力、煤气及水的生产和供应业	31 191.9	17 195.9	1 123.5	1 210.8	88.2	1 122.6
建筑业	124 452.4	61 000.5	24 971.7	1 165.6	773.9	343.3
地质勘察业、水利管理业	21 389.7	6 785.7	80.0			
交通运输、仓储及邮电通信业	153 593.1	68 775.9	12 989.2	7 723.0	4 254.2	3 172.4
交通运输和仓储业	132 141.5	68 659.2	12 899.2	7 648.2	4 238.6	3 119.6
邮电通信业	21 451.6	116.7	90.0	74.8	15.6	52.8
批发和零售贸易、餐饮业	116 400.0	105 303.1	69 035.8	22 678.9	6 791.9	13 151.6
#批发和零售贸易业	107 563.1	96 651.4	64 167.2	21 158.9	5 335.2	13 129.0
餐饮业	7 344.3	7 192.3	4 554.1	1 142.4	1 101.7	
金融、保险业	29 420.9	556.5	5 689.6	6 737.2	12.6	6 724.6
房地产业	16 148.0	15 992.4	714.7	2 009.1	976.1	1 023.5
社会服务业	64 994.2	60 286.6	14 918.3	8 955.7	7 642.0	289.0
卫生、体育和社会福利业	63 443.4	63 252.7	1 281.8	41.9		
#卫 生	59 552.3	59 361.6	1 203.8	8.1		
体 育	2 140.2	2 140.2		10.2		
教育、文化艺术及广播电影电视业	145 550.1	124 690.4	1 171.0	36.2		
教 育	124 913.3	111 132.4	1 067.5	36.2		
文化艺术业	16 168.9	9 090.1	62.3			
广播电影电视业	4 467.9	4 467.9	41.2			
科学研究和综合技术服务业	41 343.1	18 936.2	5 918.9	2 821.6	1 063.0	1 647.9
国家机关、政党机关和社会团体	110 913.9	103 706.5	99.9	353.5		
其他行业	16 676.9	15 012.9	4 164.4	404.1	150.4	

2-31 1996年按经济类型分各行业职工人均工资

单位:元

行业	国有经济	#地方	集体经济	其他经济	#“三资”经济	股份制经济
总计	**8 072**	**7 407**	**4 745**	**10 522**	**10 879**	**10 991**
按国民经济行业分						
农、林、牧、渔业	5 690	5 691	5 749	9 331	8 000	
#农业	5 245	5 246	5 385			
工业	7 463	6 724	4 174	10 490	10 821	11 220
采掘业	11 658	9 776	7 478			
制造业	6 757	6 556	4 161	10 475	10 823	11 137
电力、煤气及水的生产和供应业	12 120	10 514	6 024	15 004	7 475	16 293
建筑业	8 210	6 964	6 721	8 151	9 369	6 577
地质勘察业、水利管理业	11 117	9 006	7 692			
交通运输、仓储及邮电通信业	10 822	9 765	4 408	15 726	16 090	15 760
交通运输和仓储业	10 528	9 773	4 403	15 897	16 153	16 056
邮电通信业	13 069	6 593	5 233	7 480	7 800	7 543
批发和零售贸易、餐饮业	7 726	7 516	4 877	9 677	9 120	9 537
#批发和零售贸易业	7 760	7 531	4 897	9 911	9 677	9 562
餐饮业	6 828	6 850	4 623	6 945	6 973	
金融、保险业	11 255	14 492	11 091	13 493	21 000	13 484
房地产业	9 045	9 015	5 764	10 585	11 079	10 144
社会服务业	7 116	7 385	5 546	10 411	12 581	7 118
卫生、体育和社会福利业	9 059	9 052	5 912	4 708		
#卫生	9 040	9 033	6 028	9 000		
体育	10 532	10 532		7 286		
教育、文化艺术及广播电影电视业	7 712	7 451	4 608	4 209		
教育	7 465	7 289	4 535	4 209		
文化艺术业	9 583	8 795	4 387			
广播电影电视业	9 850	9 850	9 156			
科学研究和综合技术服务业	8 443	7 807	8 030	8 969	11 957	7 697
国家机关、政党机关和社会团体	8 757	8 743	6 529	7 442		
其他行业	8 894	8 650	6 594	8 050	8 744	

2－32 国有经济职工工资构成

项 目	1990 年	1992 年	1995 年	1996 年	1996 比 1995 年增长％
一、绝对数（万元）					
工资总额	555 045.8	719 664.3	1 352 214.5	1 543 422.3	14.1
计时和计件标准工资	299 740.5	369 739.8	631 033.4	730 110.9	15.7
奖金和计件超额工资	118 925.3	160 774.9	308 395.9	324 363.8	5.2
各种津贴	117 900.8	169 237.0	377 178.5	437 641.3	16.0
加班加点工资		19 431.6	27 949.6	35 071.6	25.5
其他工资	18 479.2	481.0	7 657.1	16 234.7	112.0
二、构成（％）					
工资总额	100.0	100.0	100.0	100.0	
计时和计件标准工资	54.0	51.4	46.7	47.3	
奖金和计件超额工资	21.4	22.3	22.8	21.0	
各种津贴	21.3	23.5	27.9	28.4	
加班加点工资		2.7	2.0	2.3	
其他工资	3.3	0.1	0.6	1.0	

注：1. 1990、1992 年工资总额及构成中不含洗理费、上下班交通补贴费。2. 1990 年“其他工资”中含加班加点工资。

2－33 按企、事业、机关分的职工人数和工资总额

项 目	合计		企业		事业		机关	
	1995 年	1996 年	1995 年	1996 年	1995 年	1996 年	1995 年	1996 年
一、职工人数（百人）	**28 959**	**28 398**	**23 517**	**22 893**	**4 278**	**4 319**	**1 164**	**1 186**
中 央	4 621	4 525	3 908	3 825	603	618	110	82
地 方	24 338	23 873	19 609	19 068	3 675	3 701	1 054	1 104
#国有经济	15 645	19 432	11 114	14 059	3 498	4 203	1 033	1 170
二、职工工资总额（万元）	**1 848 028**	**2 120 491**	**1 495 645**	**1 669 860**	**271 681**	**344 948**	**80 701**	**105 683**
中 央	406 502	473 325	352 302	409 247	45 538	56 874	8 662	7 204
地 方	1 441 526	1 647 166	1 143 343	1 260 613	226 143	288 074	72 039	98 479
#国有经济	982 873	1 543 422	693 202	1 100 515	219 009	338 533	70 661	104 373
三、职工年平均工资（元）	**6 501**	**7 643**	**6 494**	**7 500**	**6 398**	**8 007**	**7 002**	**9 008**
中 央	8 805	10 278	9 012	10 517	7 598	8 971	8 009	8 983
地 方	6 054	7 118	5 980	6 861	6 201	7 840	6 897	9 010
#国有经济	6 392	8 072	6 373	7 992	6 304	8 073	6 903	9 020

2－34　市属各局(总公司)国有经济职工工资

局　(总公司)	工资总额（万元）			年平均工资（元）		
	1995年	1996年	1996比1995年增长%	1995年	1996年	1996比1995年增长%
一、经委系统						
机电工业总公司	52 924.7	52 994.5	0.1	6 060	6 399	5.6
电子仪表工业总公司	30 742.9	31 091.6	1.1	5 335	5 378	0.8
冶金工业总公司	72 136.9	69 386.7	－3.8	8 312	8 237	－0.9
化学工业总公司	27 421.8	29 179.2	6.4	5 849	7 023	20.1
纺织工业总公司	61 902.4	62 321.0	0.7	4 997	5 322	6.5
一轻总公司	41 611.2	43 372.2	4.2	5 442	6 193	13.8
二轻局	12 477.1	12 609.4	1.1	3 937	3 815	－3.1
医药局	13 744.8	13 250.5	－3.6	7 721	8 383	8.6
汽车工业(集团)有限公司	40 093.4	42 886.0	7.0	11 990	14 020	16.9
服装联合总公司	2 005.8	2 628.7	31.1	6 049	8 014	32.5
渤海化工集团公司	6 668.0	21 862.1	227.9	9 780	9 973	2.0
长芦盐务管理局	14 420.8	537.8	－96.3	8 455	6 405	－24.2
飞鸽自行车集团公司	10 798.0	9 249.4	－14.3	5 006	4 676	－6.6
二、农委系统						
农林局	632.4	840.1	32.8	5 088	6 532	28.4
农工商总公司	6 891.1	7 584.9	10.1	4 371	5 331	22.0
水产局	2 800.5	2 292.4	－18.1	4 988	6 804	36.4
三、建委系统						
建工集团总公司	30 861.0	30 598.4	－0.9	6 333	6 866	8.4
建筑材料集团总公司	13 919.6	14 143.9	1.6	5 235	5 769	10.2
市政工程局	20 859.7	25 628.4	22.9	6 462	8 036	24.4
房地产管理局	22 819.5	25 902.5	13.5	5 826	6 884	18.2
公用局	30 177.7	33 953.4	12.5	7 320	8 768	19.8
四、交委系统						
港务局	30 001.6	36 132.0	20.4	14 470	17 411	20.3
交通局	7 298.6	7 882.2	8.0	3 803	4 255	11.9
五、商委系统						
粮食局	20 784.5	23 758.3	14.3	5 688	6 375	12.1
益商集团总公司	18 948.1	15 672.4	－17.3	7 014	6 848	－2.4
食品工贸集团总公司	12 595.4	13 166.8	4.5	5 401	6 096	12.9

2－35　其他从业人员人数及报酬

（乡及乡以上）

行　　业	人　数（百人）			劳动报酬(万元)		
	1995 年	1996 年	1996 比 1995 年增长％	1995 年	1996 年	1996 比 1995 年增长％
总　　计	**1 010**	**888**	**－12.1**	**45 036.2**	**63 574.0**	**41.2**
农、林、牧、渔业	1			8.2	10.7	30.5
工　业	352	319	－9.4	24 107.5	30 071.9	24.7
采掘业	69	71	2.9	2 956.6	9 069.5	206.8
制造业	279	240	－14.0	21 016.1	20 818.7	－0.9
电力、煤气及水的生产和供应业	4	8	100.0	134.8	183.7	36.3
建筑业	142	108	－23.9	4 883.7	6 049.5	23.9
地质勘察业、水利管理业	4	4		162.0	165.6	2.2
交通运输、仓储及邮电通信业	37	38	2.7	1 658.0	3 544.5	113.8
批发和零售贸易、餐饮业	185	152	－17.8	6 139.1	6 305.9	2.7
金融、保险业	15	21	40.0	661.8	2 277.2	244.1
房地产业	9	7	－22.2	316.5	316.8	0.1
社会服务业	60	57	－5.0	3 541.4	3 880.8	9.6
卫生、体育和社会福利业	19	17	－10.5	390.4	634.6	62.6
教育、文化艺术及广播电影电视业	46	52	13.0	1 134.0	1 689.2	49.0
科学研究和综合技术服务业	21	20	－4.8	829.3	7 528.8	807.9
国家机关、政党机关和社会团体	111	83	－25.2	1 025.4	805.8	－21.4
其他行业	8	10	25.0	178.9	292.7	63.6

注：其他从业人员指国有经济、城镇集体经济和其他所有制经济（不含乡镇企业、私营经济和个体经济）职工以外的从业人员。

2－36　改革开放以来离退休退职人员情况

年　份	离退休退职人数（万人）					离退休退职人员与在职职工之比（以在职职工为100）
		国有经济	集体经济	其他经济	民政部门	
1978	9.90					4.6
1979	22.70					9.9
1980	28.10					11.6
1981	30.70					12.1
1982	32.40					12.4
1983	33.30					12.4
1984	37.20					13.6
1985	40.83	29.17	10.69	0.10	0.87	14.8
1986	44.38	29.83	13.64	0.08	0.83	15.8
1987	48.22	33.61	13.64	0.10	0.87	17.1
1988	53.75	39.11	13.68	0.08	0.88	19.1
1989	55.04	40.65	13.43	0.16	0.80	19.4
1990	57.27	42.83	13.41	0.24	0.79	20.1
1991	59.66	44.50	14.12	0.27	0.77	20.5
1992	65.28	49.17	14.67	0.89	0.55	22.2
1993	70.50	53.00	14.70	2.10	0.70	24.0
1994	73.10	54.50	14.60	3.30	0.70	25.0
1995	75.54	56.78	14.81	3.30	0.65	26.1
1996	82.98	62.92	15.79	3.64	0.63	29.0

资料来源：天津市劳动局。

2－37 改革开放以来职工保险福利费发放情况

(1990－1996年)

年份	在职职工保险福利费用总额(万元)	国有经济	集体经济	其他经济	非在职职工保险福利费用总额(万元)	#国有经济
1990	139 845.4	119 652.8	18 481.4	1 711.2	129 376.1	104 841.0
1991	140 657.4	119 221.4	19 673.9	1 762.1	144 560.2	117 737.4
1992	159 177.4	135 834.4	20 354.2	2 988.8	185 463.7	153 317.7
1993	144 493.5	122 511.0	14 253.6	7 728.9	251 992.2	206 578.8
1994	158 059.0	129 005.1	15 737.5	13 316.4	327 492.6	269 674.8
1995	189 544.7	156 124.7	16 000.8	17 419.2	410 644.5	338 645.3
1996	223 400.0	180 295.8	20 887.0	22 217.2	524 404.2	434 679.1

年份	在职职工人均保险福利费(元)	国有经济	集体经济	其他经济	非在职职工人均保险福利费(元)	#国有经济
1990	491	563	273	404	2 265	2 412
1991	481	557	270	309	2 340	2 611
1992	542	638	283	346	2 841	3 082
1993	505	598	206	626	3 574	3 898
1994	578	653	272	581	4 480	4 948
1995	667	804	255	639	5 436	5 964
1996	850	953	405	1 013	6 320	6 908

注:1.非在职职工劳保福利费含民政部门支付。2.1993年以来在职职工劳保福利费已剔除上、下班交通补贴,洗理卫生费。3.本资料来源于市劳动局、民政局。

2－38 职工保险福利费构成

单位:万元

在职职工保险福利费	1995年	1996年	非在职职工保险福利费	1995年	1996年
合　　计	**189 544.7**	**223 400.0**	**合　　计**	**410 644.5**	**524 404.2**
集体福利设施、事业补贴费	25 296.3	24 396.8	离休费	20 466.1	25 606.8
文体宣传费	4 907.5	9 155.5	退休费	212 696.8	285 601.1
医疗卫生费	118 390.4	136 303.5	退职生活费	2 380.1	3 202.0
丧葬抚恤救济费	2 649.8	3 250.0	医疗卫生费	70 787.8	78 434.5
生活困难补助	3 129.9	4 103.1	丧葬抚恤救济费	3 618.7	4 850.3
计划生育补贴	4 055.8	4 343.3	交通费补贴	1 977.1	2 521.3
冬季取暖补贴	19 588.4	28 387.7	冬季取暖费	6 682.7	10 351.4
其　他	11 526.6	13 460.1	其　他	89 633.8	108 931.2

注:非在职职工保险福利费构成中不含民政部门支付。

三、固定资产投资

INVESTMENT IN FIXED ASSETS

1996年全社会固定资产投资	435.82亿元
1996年社会新增固定资产投资	313.12亿元
1996年社会房屋竣工面积	725.13万平方米
其中:住宅	494.73万平方米

全社会固定资产投资额(亿元)

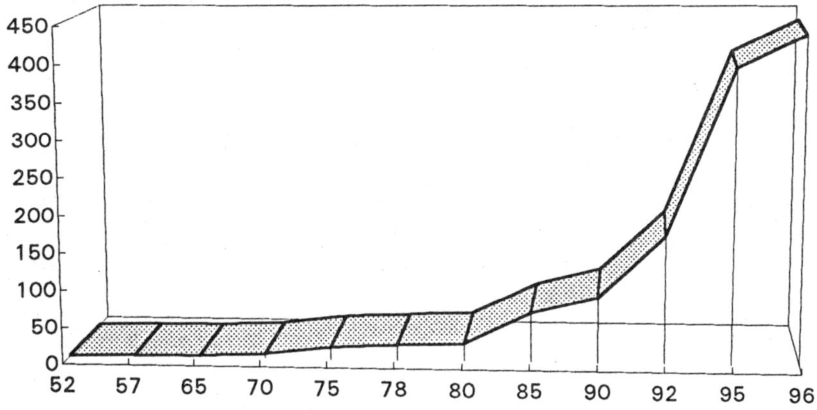

1996年固定资产投资三次产业构成

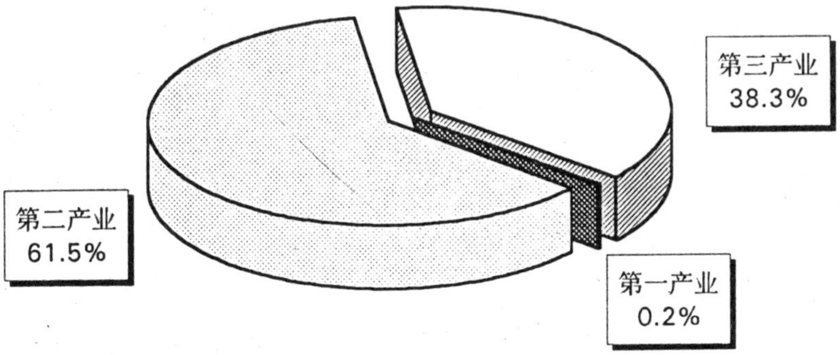

3－1　全社会固定资产投资及新增固定资产

（1985－1996年）

年　份	全社会	国有经济	集体经济	#农　村	个体经济	#农　村
投资额（亿元）						
1985	65.90	54.16	7.39	3.04	4.35	3.93
1986－1990	**402.53**	**329.03**	**42.71**	**31.08**	**30.79**	**26.64**
1986	71.91	61.03	5.93	2.73	4.95	4.24
1987	76.44	61.32	9.53	6.59	5.59	4.31
1988	82.61	66.11	9.01	6.53	7.49	7.12
1989	83.88	68.39	7.68	5.75	7.81	6.61
1990	87.69	72.18	10.56	9.48	4.95	4.36
1991－1995	**1 234.54**	**1 024.85**	**166.69**	**145.27**	**42.98**	**36.99**
1991	128.95	109.69	12.18	10.84	7.08	6.68
1992	169.88	137.81	25.21	23.59	6.86	6.08
1993	226.56	187.83	30.51	27.34	8.22	6.36
1994	315.97	265.32	40.14	36.98	10.51	8.51
1995	393.18	324.20	58.65	46.52	10.33	9.36
1996	435.82	351.60	66.67	57.35	17.55	15.28
平均每年递增（%）						
1981－1990	16.8	14.7	18.3	33.2		45.2
1986－1990	6.8	6.6	－20.0	24.9	20.0	10.3
1991－1995	36.8	37.1	41.2	40.0	19.0	18.2
1992－1996	30.6	29.3	46.6	45.6	14.1	10.6
1996比1995	10.8	8.5	13.67	23.3	69.9	63.3
新增固定资产（亿元）						
1985	42.62	32.26	6.01	3.04	4.35	3.93
1986－1990	**315.42**	**239.26**	**45.37**	**34.47**	**30.79**	**26.64**
1986	56.39	46.12	5.32	2.73	4.95	4.24
1987	61.04	46.02	9.43	6.59	5.59	4.31
1988	63.28	47.06	8.73	6.82	7.49	7.12
1989	69.55	50.40	11.34	8.78	7.81	6.61
1990	65.16	49.66	10.55	9.55	4.95	4.36
1991－1995	**878.36**	**698.11**	**137.24**	**128.77**	**43.01**	**36.99**
1991	74.11	54.99	12.03	10.85	7.09	6.68
1992	102.27	73.24	22.17	21.26	6.86	6.08
1993	140.00	105.82	25.96	24.11	8.22	6.36
1994	261.12	216.98	33.63	32.36	10.51	8.51
1995	300.86	247.08	43.45	40.19	10.33	9.36
1996	313.12	246.63	48.94	41.61	17.55	15.28
平均每年递增（%）						
1981－1990	17.9	14.9	29.8	34.5	47.5	45.2
1986－1990	13.4	13.4	14.1	28.7	11.8	10.3
1991－1995	35.1	36.7	33.8	35.1	19.0	18.2
1992－1996	39.4	42.1	37.8	38.4	14.1	10.6
1996比1995	4.1	－0.2	12.6	3.5	69.9	63.2

注：本表国有经济中包括“三资”、股份制、联营、私营经济，与历年口径可比。

3-2 1996年全社会固定资产投资和房屋建筑面积

项　目	合　计	#国有经济	集体经济	股份制经济	"三资"经济	个体经济
一、投资总额(亿元)	**435.82**	**258.78**	**66.67**	**19.16**	**72.42**	**17.55**
1.按构成分						
建筑工程	226.68	135.14	32.62	8.87	31.53	17.55
安装工程	31.24	23.11	3.04	2.33	2.73	
设备工器具	121.20	59.42	29.36	3.29	29.07	
其他费用	56.70	41.11	1.65	4.67	9.09	
2.按建设性质分						
新　建	142.95	67.47	27.83	0.99	37.66	
扩　建	141.99	110.31	13.31	1.91	7.67	
改　建	69.32	43.10	15.12	7.85	3.22	
其　他	10.06	4.50	3.15	0.03	2.38	17.55
3.按生产性与非生产性分						
生产性	272.86	161.35	55.74	9.92	49.23	
非生产性	162.96	97.43	10.93	9.24	23.19	17.55
#住　宅	78.67	44.44	6.12	4.79	9.23	13.51
4.按三次产业分						
第一产业	18.90	0.25	3.07			15.28
第二产业	272.37	138.26	52.23	8.91	48.83	
第三产业	144.55	120.27	11.37	10.25	23.59	2.27
二、房屋建筑面积(万平方米)						
房屋施工面积	2 536.8	1 167.2	482.3	135.6	279.8	456.6
#施工住宅	1 487.4	741.7	127.2	83.1	100.8	425.7
竣工房屋面积	1 470.0	567.3	343.1	38.5	61.0	456.6
#竣工住宅	965.5	378.3	93.0	31.4	33.7	425.7

注:按建设性质分组不包括房地产开发投资。

3－3 改革开放以来国有单位基本建设和更新改造投资额

年份	基本建设投资额（亿元）	按隶属关系分		按建设性质分		新增固定资产（亿元）	固定资产交付使用率（%）
		中央	地方	新建	改、扩建及其他		
1978	15.28	9.26	6.02	8.70	6.58	12.08	79.06
1979	18.83	10.23	8.60	12.62	6.21	13.81	73.34
1980	17.20	8.77	8.43	9.66	7.54	13.17	70.87
1981－1985	**110.37**	**33.70**	**76.57**	**48.50**	**61.86**	**93.89**	**85.07**
1981	16.27	6.64	9.63	6.03	10.23	18.81	115.61
1982	19.41	4.92	14.49	10.82	8.58	16.37	84.34
1983	21.85	6.07	15.78	10.90	10.94	22.88	104.71
1984	21.99	5.87	16.12	9.85	12.14	17.65	80.26
1985	30.85	10.30	20.55	10.89	19.96	18.18	58.93
1986－1990	**165.98**	**90.16**	**75.83**	**62.28**	**103.70**	**95.84**	**57.74**
1986	25.56	11.65	13.91	8.89	16.67	17.90	70.03
1987	29.39	17.61	11.78	10.06	19.33	17.56	59.75
1988	33.32	20.50	12.82	12.58	20.75	18.04	54.14
1989	37.65	19.84	17.81	12.92	24.72	22.91	60.85
1990	40.06	20.55	19.51	17.84	22.22	19.42	48.48
1991－1995	**495.69**	**169.32**	**326.41**	**267.77**	**227.96**	**349.66**	**70.54**
1991	64.18	21.18	42.99	37.78	26.40	21.47	33.45
1992	80.14	30.50	49.64	44.24	35.90	36.06	44.00
1993	75.70	30.50	45.20	36.17	39.53	36.25	47.89
1994	115.88	34.92	80.96	58.61	57.27	123.04	106.18
1995	159.74	52.22	107.52	90.97	68.77	132.84	83.16
1996	169.48	68.55	100.93	95.32	74.16	124.95	73.73

年份	更新改造投资额（亿元）	按隶属关系分		按建设性质分		新增固定资产（亿元）	固定资产交付使用率（%）
		中央	地方	新建	改、扩建及其他		
1978							
1979	4.72	1.18	3.54		4.72		
1980	4.93	0.62	4.31		4.93	3.15	63.89
1981－1985	**60.41**	**7.91**	**52.50**	**5.45**	**54.95**	**39.90**	**66.05**
1981	4.74	0.79	6.66	0.18	7.27	4.36	58.52
1982	10.64	1.80	8.84	0.28	10.37	6.76	62.69
1983	9.56	0.83	8.73	0.22	9.34	7.55	78.97
1984	12.14	2.04	10.10	1.25	10.89	8.53	70.26
1985	20.61	2.44	18.17	3.53	17.09	12.70	61.62
1986－1990	**136.69**	**19.32**	**117.37**	**19.95**	**116.74**	**121.90**	**89.18**
1986	31.51	3.19	28.32	7.33	24.18	24.83	78.80
1987	27.76	3.43	24.32	5.55	22.21	25.35	91.32
1988	29.54	4.12	25.43	3.07	26.47	25.83	87.44
1989	24.72	5.10	19.62	2.18	22.54	23.75	96.08
1990	23.15	3.47	19.68	1.81	21.34	22.14	95.64
1991－1995	**356.76**	**59.10**	**297.67**	**44.57**	**312.19**	**268.44**	**75.24**
1991	32.71	5.54	27.17	3.80	28.91	22.54	68.91
1992	45.72	8.23	37.49	5.33	40.39	29.74	65.05
1993	66.75	11.99	54.77	6.27	60.48	44.73	67.01
1994	115.36	14.52	100.84	12.66	102.70	89.72	77.34
1995	95.57	18.82	76.75	16.51	79.06	81.71	85.50
1996	107.93	28.70	79.23	11.02	96.91	63.97	59.27

注：本表国有经济中包括“三资”、股份制、联营、私营经济，与历年口径可比。

3-4 固定资产施工项目和建成投产项目个数

(不含农村集体和个人投资)

单位:个

项目	施工项目		全部建成投产项目		项目投产率(%)	
	1995年	1996年	1995年	1996年	1995年	1996年
总计	**1 852**	**1 918**	**1 101**	**1 293**	**59.4**	**67.4**
基本建设	574	663	279	393	48.6	59.3
#国有经济	512	626	247	386	48.2	61.7
更新改造	1 205	1 197	786	868	65.2	72.5
#国有经济	1 112	1 106	755	813	67.9	73.5
其他投资	73	58	36	32	49.3	55.2
按行业分						
农、林、牧、渔业	30	22	16	11	53.3	50.0
工业	699	837	406	594	58.1	71.0
采掘业	4	16		9		56.3
制造业	483	433	242	267	50.1	61.7
电力、煤气及水的生产和供应业	212	388	164	318	77.4	82.0
建筑业	43	45	22	18	51.2	40.0
地质勘察业、水利管理业	41	31	26	20	63.4	64.5
交通运输、仓储及邮电通信业	214	254	139	184	65.0	72.4
批发和零售贸易、餐饮业	70	73	37	38	52.9	52.1
金融、保险业	43	29	21	16	48.8	55.2
房地产业和社会服务业	195	160	91	92	46.7	57.5
房地产业	128	83	51	38	39.8	45.8
社会服务业	67	77	40	54	59.7	70.1
卫生、体育和社会福利业	39	35	21	29	53.8	82.9
教育、文化艺术及广播电影电视业	146	155	71	96	48.6	61.9
科学研究和综合技术服务业	127	28	99	16	78.0	57.1
国家机关、政党机关和社会团体	182	223	134	159	73.6	71.3
其他行业	23	26	18	20	78.3	76.9

注:本表项目个数不含房地产开发企业个数。

3-5　按行业分固定资产投资额

（不含农村集体和个人投资）　　单位:万元

项　　目	合　　计		＃国有经济	
	1995 年	1996 年	1995 年	1996 年
固定资产投资总额	**3 363 355**	**3 609 168**	**2 450 914**	**2 587 824**
一、按三次产业分				
第一产业	8 182	5 468	8 086	2 475
第二产业	1 796 965	2 219 658	1 294 222	1 382 619
第三产业	1 558 208	1 384 042	1 148 606	1 202 730
二、按行业分				
农、林、牧、渔业	2 857	2 475	2 857	2 475
工　业	1 882 428	1 945 006	1 362 371	1 356 117
采掘业	315 243	436 121	315 243	416 579
制造业	1 303 778	1 124 441	783 853	555 094
电力、煤气及水的生产和供应	263 407	384 444	263 275	384 444
建筑业	53 557	31 370	53 254	26 502
地质勘察业、水利管理业	26 731	30 468	26 731	30 468
交通运输、仓储及邮电通信业	385 918	381 504	384 780	363 393
批发和零售贸易、餐饮业	44 629	66 112	27 929	44 989
金融、保险业	12 834	11 145	9 813	10 050
房地产业和社会服务业	806 428	923 013	444 483	537 028
房地产业	768 074	766 423	412 709	385 258
社会服务业	38 354	156 590	31 774	151 770
卫生、体育和社会福利业	6 146	8 952	5 814	8 880
教育、文化艺术及广播电影电视业	76 770	60 422	75 992	60 187
科学研究和综合技术服务业	13 722	14 526	13 579	14 526
国家机关、政党机关和社会团体	43 065	95 406	36 150	94 692
其他行业	8 270	38 769	7 161	38 517

项　　目	集体经济		股份制经济		“三资”经济	
	1995 年	1996 年	1995 年	1996 年	1995 年	1996 年
固定资产投资总额	**121 309**	**93 243**	**129 082**	**191 573**	**636 539**	**724 222**
一、按三次产业分						
第一产业						
第二产业	24 306	18 267	52 475	89 053	432 720	488 309
第三产业	97 003	74 976	76 607	102 520	203 819	235 913
二、按行业分						
农、林、牧、渔业						
工　业	24 003	10 245	52 475	89 053	432 720	488 309
采掘业						19 542
制造业	23 911	10 245	52 435	89 053	432 720	468 767
电力、煤气及水的生产和供应	92		40			
建筑业	303	4 868				
地质勘察业、水利管理业						
交通运输、仓储及邮电通信业	1 022	746		1 301	116	14 914
批发和零售贸易、餐饮业	2 261	2 408	8 173	17 472	5 422	1 243
金融、保险业	3 021	1 095				
房地产业和社会服务业	89 607	72 637	67 956	83 747	198 281	219 756
房地产业	89 607	72 637	67 956	83 747	192 541	214 936
社会服务业					5 740	4 820
卫生、体育和社会福利业	202	72				
教育、文化艺术及广播电影电视业		235	180			
科学研究和综合技术服务业			143			
国家机关、政党机关和社会团体	50	685				
其他行业	840	252	155			

3－6　地方固定资产投资额

（不含农村集体和个人投资）

单位：万元

项　　目	1995年	#基本建设	更新改造	1996年	#基本建设	更新改造
固定资产投资总额	**2 529 007**	**1 075 189**	**767 461**	**2 508 063**	**1 009 297**	**792 269**
1.按构成分						
建筑工程	1 075 918	333 319	260 003	1 255 391	448 203	277 580
安装工程	166 378	99 168	46 479	140 186	71 417	58 524
设备工器具	834 953	388 984	405 296	667 799	284 568	347 380
其他费用	451 758	253 718	55 683	444 687	205 109	108 785
2.按建设性质分						
新　建	874 349	710 898	157 616	860 184	756 932	93 320
扩　建	686 273	330 967	333 134	494 172	148 886	337 306
改　建	266 333	29 453	235 753	411 774	73 571	337 817
其　他	46 801	3 871	40 958	55 974	29 908	23 826
3.按生产性与非生产性分						
生产性	1 553 897	901 189	622 401	1 345 750	730 470	597 554
非生产性	975 110	174 000	145 060	1 162 313	278 827	194 715
#住　宅	552 478	17 335	88 844	536 836	37 993	83 689
4.按行业分						
农、林、牧、渔业	2 822	1 496	1 326	2 020	1 504	516
工　业	1 293 950	846 595	423 645	1 129 072	646 417	472 410
采掘业	7 164		7 164	24 481	19 542	4 939
制造业	1 215 452	803 436	388 306	1 013 042	568 840	433 957
电力、煤气及水生产和供应业	71 334	43 159	28 175	91 549	58 035	33 514
建筑业	39 516	5	39 511	15 631	6 625	4 206
地质勘察业、水利管理业	18 150	14 516	3 634	23 036	19 122	3 914
交通运输、仓储及邮电通信业	238 236	68 456	168 758	206 398	92 602	113 050
批发和零售贸易、餐饮业	33 241	17 287	13 693	43 164	16 990	23 766
金融、保险业	8 225	3 411	1 793	6 320	4 460	765
房地产业和社会服务业	767 315	33 962	77 262	889 792	81 890	121 943
房地产业	728 961	4 988	68 722	737 034		51 075
社会服务业	38 354	28 974	8 540	152 758	81 890	70 868
卫生、体育和社会福利业	6 130	5 803	125	8 952	8 388	492
教育、文化艺术及广播电影电视	65 245	54 781	10 464	44 521	43 201	1 085
科学研究和综合技术服务业	8 207	4 400	3 807	8 011	4 112	3 899
国家机关、政党机关和社会团体	40 520	21 292	19 178	93 096	47 239	45 172
其他行业	7 450	3 185	4 265	38 050	36 747	1 051

注：按建设性质分组不包括房地产开发投资。

3－7　地方按行业分固定资产投资额

（不含农村集体和个人投资）　　单位:万元

项　　目	1995 年	1996 年	
			#国有经济
固定资产投资总额	**2 529 007**	**2 508 063**	**1 496 576**
一、按三次产业分			
第一产业	2 822	2 020	2 020
第二产业	1 333 466	1 144 703	551 014
第三产业	1 192 719	1 361 340	943 542
二、按行业分			
农、林、牧、渔业	2 822	2 020	2 020
工　业	1 293 950	1 129 072	540 183
采掘业	7 164	24 481	4 939
制造业	1 215 452	1 013 042	443 695
电力、煤气及水的生产和供应业	71 334	91 549	91 549
建筑业	39 516	15 631	10 831
地质勘察业、水利管理业	18 150	23 036	23 036
交通运输、仓储及邮电通信业	238 236	206 398	197 861
批发和零售贸易、餐饮业	33 241	43 164	22 256
金融、保险业	8 225	6 320	5 225
房地产业和社会服务业	767 315	889 792	503 807
房地产业	728 961	737 034	355 869
社会服务业	38 354	152 758	147 938
卫生、体育和社会福利业	6 130	8 952	8 880
教育、文化艺术及广播电影电视业	65 245	44 521	44 286
科学研究和综合技术服务业	8 207	8 011	8 011
国家机关、政党机关和社会团体	40 520	93 096	92 382
其他行业	7 450	38 050	37 798

项　　目			
	集体经济	股份制经济	“三资”经济
固定资产投资总额	**93 175**	**190 081**	**715 925**
一、按三次产业分			
第一产业			
第二产业	15 045	89 053	488 309
第三产业	78 130	101 028	227 616
二、按行业分			
农、林、牧、渔业			
工　业	10 245	89 053	488 309
采掘业			19 542
制造业	10 245	89 053	468 767
电力、煤气及水的生产和供应业			
建筑业	4 800		
地质勘察业、水利管理业			
交通运输、仓储及邮电通信业	746	24	6 617
批发和零售贸易、餐饮业	2 408	17 257	1 243
金融、保险业	1 095		
房地产业和社会服务业	72 637	83 747	219 756
房地产业	72 637	83 747	214 936
社会服务业			4 820
卫生、体育和社会福利业	72		
教育、文化艺术及广播电影电视业	235		
科学研究和综合技术服务业			
国家机关、政党机关和社会团体	685		
其他行业	252		

3－8　1996年工业行业固定资产投资额

（不含农村集体和个人投资）

单位:万元

项　　目	合　计	#国有经济	集体经济	股份制经济	“三资”经济
总　　计	**1 945 006**	**1 356 117**	**10 245**	**89 053**	**488 309**
采掘业	**436 121**	**416 579**			**19 542**
煤炭采选业	19 542				19 542
石油和天然气开采业	411 640	411 640			
非金属矿采选业	4 939	4 939			
制造业	**1 124 441**	**555 094**	**10 245**	**89 053**	**468 767**
食品加工业	29 770	3 904			25 866
食品制造业	5 138		40		5 018
饮料制造业	4 580	3 156			474
烟草加工业	4 023	4 023			
纺织业	33 976	16 614	120		17 242
服装及其他纤维制品制造业	190	190			
皮革、毛皮、羽绒及其制品业	51		51		
家具制造业	650	650			
造纸及纸制品业	91 651	91 464			187
印刷业、记录媒介的复制	5 358	1 553		3 805	
文教体育用品制造业	359	359			
石油加工及炼焦业	69 251	67 443	300		1 508
化学原料及化学制品制造业	274 035	149 827	174	80 701	43 281
医药制造业	18 465	2 454		1 648	14 363
化学纤维制造业	20 357	19 357			1 000
橡胶制品业	61 220	945	1 662		58 613
塑料制品业	3 880	3 812			68
非金属矿物制品业	33 662	27 473			6 189
黑色金属冶炼及压延加工业	66 840	66 840			
有色金属冶炼及压延加工业	233	33			
金属制品业	21 293	9 602			11 691
普通机械制造业	38 763	28 813	552	432	8 966
专用设备制造业	5 808	5 793		15	
交通运输设备制造业	71 286	34 652	6 929		29 705
电气机械及器材制造业	8 541	5 002		508	3 031
电子及通信设备制造业	252 483	8 728	246	1 944	241 565
仪器仪表及文化办公用机械制造业	2 557	2 407	150		
其他制造业	21		21		
电力、煤气及水的生产和供应业	**384 444**	**384 444**			
电力、蒸汽、热水的生产和供应业	326 209	326 209			
煤气生产和供应业	33 053	33 053			
自来水的生产和供应业	25 182	25 182			

3－9　1996年地方工业行业固定资产投资

(不含农村集体和个人投资)

单位:万元

项　　目	合　　计	#国有经济	集体经济	股份制经济	“三资”经济
总　　计	**1 129 072**	**540 183**	**10 245**	**89 053**	**488 309**
采掘业	**24 481**	**4 939**			**19 542**
煤炭采选业	19 542				19 542
非金属矿采选业	4 939	4 939			
制造业	**1 013 042**	**443 695**	**10 245**	**89 053**	**468 767**
食品加工业	29 770	3 904			25 866
食品制造业	5 138		40		5 018
饮料制造业	4 580	3 156			474
纺织业	33 976	16 614	120		17 242
服装及其他纤维制品制造业	190	190			
皮革、毛皮、羽绒及其制品业	51		51		
家具制造业	650	650			
造纸及纸制品业	91 651	91 464			187
印刷业、记录媒介的复制	5 358	1 553		3 805	
文教体育用品制造业	359	359			
石油加工及炼焦业	1 808		300		1 508
化学原料及化学制品制造业	250 273	126 065	174	80 701	43 281
医药制造业	18 465	2 454		1 648	14 363
化学纤维制造业	14 526	13 526			1 000
橡胶制品业	61 220	945	1 662		58 613
塑料制品业	2 956	2 888			68
非金属矿物制品业	33 662	27 473			6 189
黑色金属冶炼及压延加工业	66 840	66 840			
有色金属冶炼及压延加工业	233	33			
金属制品业	21 293	9 602			11 691
普通机械制造业	38 763	28 813	552	432	8 966
专用设备制造业	4 190	4 175		15	
交通运输设备制造业	64 573	27 939	6 929		29 705
电气机械及器材制造业	8 110	4 571		508	3 031
电子及通信设备制造业	251 829	8 074	246	1 944	241 565
仪器仪表及文化办公用机械制造业	2 557	2 407	150		
其他制造业	21		21		
电力、煤气及水的生产和供应业	**91 549**	**91 549**			
电力、蒸汽、热水的生产和供应业	33 539	33 539			
煤气生产和供应业	33 053	33 053			
自来水的生产和供应业	24 957	24 957			

3－10 基本建设和更新改造固定资产投资额

（不含农村集体和个人投资）

单位：万元

项 目	1995年	基本建设	更新改造	1996年	基本建设	更新改造
固定资产投资总额	**2 553 143**	**1 597 435**	**955 708**	**2 774 054**	**1 694 756**	**1 079 298**
一、按隶属关系分						
中 央	710 493	522 246	188 247	972 488	685 459	287 029
地 方	1 842 650	1 075 189	767 461	1 801 566	1 009 297	792 269
二、按构成分						
建筑工程	983 349	655 974	327 375	1 203 482	814 698	388 784
安装工程	239 607	168 653	70 954	263 148	140 246	122 902
设备工器具	952 475	465 287	487 188	879 425	428 949	450 476
其他费用	377 712	307 521	70 191	427 999	310 863	117 136
三、按建设性质分						
新 建	1 074 770	909 687	165 083	1 063 425	953 247	110 178
扩 建	1 044 305	616 404	427 901	1 099 644	599 162	500 482
改 建	369 789	57 877	311 912	541 881	103 342	438 539
其 他	64 279	13 467	50 812	69 104	39 005	30 099
四、按生产性与非生产性分						
生产性	2 061 905	1 272 272	789 633	2 107 995	1 245 984	862 011
非生产性	491 238	325 163	166 075	666 059	448 772	217 287
#住 宅	160 957	64 971	95 986	208 109	114 355	93 754
五、按行业分						
农、林、牧、渔业	2 857	1 531	1 326	2 475	1 959	516
工 业	1 774 279	1 227 225	547 054	1 835 356	1 177 462	657 894
采掘业	231 097	169 493	61 604	336 716	218 881	117 835
制造业	1 279 867	844 432	435 435	1 114 196	629 390	484 806
电力、煤气及水的生产和供应业	263 315	213 300	50 015	384 444	329 191	55 253
建筑业	53 254	6 424	46 830	26 502	15 782	10 720
地质勘察业、水利管理业	26 731	23 037	3 694	30 468	26 554	3 914
交通运输、仓储及邮电通信业	384 896	162 285	222 611	380 758	196 036	184 722
批发和零售贸易、餐饮业	42 368	27 795	14 573	63 704	22 825	40 879
金融、保险业	9 813	7 812	2 001	10 050	8 970	1 080
房地产业和社会服务业	111 224	33 962	77 262	207 910	85 722	122 188
房地产业	73 710	4 988	68 722	51 320		51 320
社会服务业	37 514	28 974	8 540	156 590	85 722	70 868
卫生、体育和社会福利业	5 944	5 819	125	8 880	8 388	492
教育、文化艺术及广播电影电视业	76 770	66 130	10 640	60 187	56 992	3 195
科学研究和综合技术服务业	13 722	9 393	4 329	14 526	9 870	4 656
国家机关、政党机关和社会团体	43 015	22 237	20 778	94 721	47 449	47 272
其他行业	8 270	3 785	4 485	38 517	36 747	1 770

3-11 1996年工业行业基本建设施工、竣工项目

项　　目	施工项目（个）	全部建成投产项目（个）	建成项目投产率（%）	投资额（万元）	新增固定资产（万元）	固定资产交付使用率（%）
总　　计	**110**	**56**	**50.9**	**1 177 462**	**911 352**	**77.3**
采掘业	**3**	**1**	**33.3**	**218 881**	**100 638**	**46.0**
煤炭采选业				19 542	19 542	100.0
石油和天然气开采业	3	1	33.3	199 339	81 096	40.7
非金属矿采选业						
制造业	**64**	**29**	**45.3**	**629 390**	**507 902**	**80.7**
食品加工业	5	2	40.0	29 722	12 635	42.5
食品制造业	2	1	50.0	3 383	2 803	82.9
饮料制造业	1			950	950	100.0
烟草加工业						
纺织业	10	9	90.0	721	870	120.7
家具制造业	1	1	100.0	650	650	100.0
造纸及纸制品业	1			683	683	100.0
印刷业、记录媒介的复制						
文教体育用品制造业						
石油加工及炼焦业	3	1	33.3	57 908	9 240	16.0
化学原料及化学制品制造业	5	3	60.0	116 394	161 110	138.4
医药制造业	4			14 379	109	0.8
化学纤维制造业	1			1 000	100	10.0
橡胶制品业	1			58 500		
塑料制品业	3	2	66.7	924	324	35.1
非金属矿物制品业	5	2	40.0	12 384	390	3.1
黑色金属冶炼及压延加工业	1			45 861	99 000	215.9
有色金属冶炼及压延加工业						
金属制品业	3	2	66.7	4 271	390	9.1
普通机械制造业	3	1	33.3	3 178	5 080	159.8
专用设备制造业	2	2	100.0	250	250	100.0
交通运输设备制造业	3	1	33.3	26 269	183 501	698.5
电气机械及器材制造业	4	1	25.0	1 231	150	12.2
电子及通信设备制造业	5			248 637	26 809	10.8
仪器仪表及文化办公用机械制造业	1	1	100.0	2 058	2 858	138.9
电力、煤气及水的生产和供应业	**43**	**26**	**60.5**	**329 191**	**302 812**	**92.0**
电力、蒸汽、热水的生产和供应业	33	20	60.6	286 701	286 207	99.8
煤气生产和供应业	6	4	66.7	24 929	8 747	35.1
自来水的生产和供应业	4	2	50.0	17 561	7 858	44.7

3－12　1996年工业行业更新改造施工、竣工项目

项　目	施工项目(个)	全部建成投产项目(个)	建成项目投产率(%)	投资额(万元)	新增固定资产(万元)	固定资产交付使用率(%)
总　计	**707**	**522**	**73.83**	**657 894**	**416 187**	**63.26**
采掘业	**12**	**8**	**66.67**	**117 835**	**115 871**	**98.33**
煤炭采选业						
石油和天然气开采业	2			112 896	106 500	94.33
非金属矿采选业	10	8	80.00	4 939	9 371	189.73
制造业	**350**	**222**	**63.43**	**484 806**	**269 009**	**55.49**
食品加工业	1	1	100.00	48	44	91.67
食品制造业	3	3	80.00	1 715	6 931	404.14
饮料制造业	5	4		3 630	3 598	99.12
烟草加工业	1			4 023		
纺织业	13	11	84.62	33 135	15 915	48.03
服装及其他纤维制品制造业	1	1	100.00	190	190	100.00
造纸及纸制品业	4	1	25.00	90 968	14 926	16.41
印刷业、记录媒介的复制	3	3	100.00	5 358	3 665	68.40
文教体育用品制造业	1	1	100.00	359	857	238.72
石油加工及炼焦业	18	17	94.44	11 043	9 433	85.42
化学原料及化学制品制造业	71	43	60.56	157 467	66 946	42.51
医药制造业	50	47	94.00	4 086	4 010	98.14
化学纤维制造业	17	13	76.47	19 357	25 832	133.45
橡胶制品业	17	12	70.59	1 058	1 089	102.93
塑料制品业	2			2 956	1 227	41.51
非金属矿物制品业	11	4	36.36	21 278	4 640	21.81
黑色金属冶炼及压延加工业	30	15	50.00	20 979	12 402	59.12
有色金属冶炼及压延加工业	2	1	50.00	233	33	14.16
金属制品业	18	8	44.44	17 022	19 090	112.15
普通机械制造业	24	11	45.83	35 033	23 243	66.35
专用设备制造业	10	1	10.00	5 558	3 824	68.80
交通运输设备制造业	19	7	36.84	38 088	37 644	98.83
电气机械及器材制造业	12	4	33.33	7 273	3 937	54.13
电子及通信设备制造业	13	11	84.62	3 600	9 099	252.75
仪器仪表及文化办公用机械制造	4	3	75.00	349	434	124.36
电力、煤气及水的生产和供应业	**345**	**292**	**84.64**	**55 253**	**31 307**	**56.66**
电力、蒸汽、热水的生产和供应	229	197	86.03	39 508	25 688	65.02
煤气生产和供应业	91	71	78.02	8 124	4 115	50.65
自来水的生产和供应业	25	24	96.00	7 621	1 504	19.73

3－13　能源工业固定资产投资额

（不含农村集体和个人投资）　　单位：万元

部　门	固定资产投资		#基本建设		更新改造	
	1995年	1996年	1995年	1996年	1995年	1996年
总　计	**603 253**	**840 153**	**410 926**	**568 877**	**108 009**	**171 571**
石油和天然气开采业	307 679	411 640	169 493	199 339	54 040	112 896
电力、蒸汽、热水的生产和供应业	232 791	326 209	195 867	286 701	36 924	39 508
石油加工及炼焦业	51 740	69 251	37 650	57 908	14 010	11 043
煤气生产和供应业	11 043	33 053	7 916	24 929	3 035	8 124
能源投资占全市固定资产投资比重(%)	**22.6**	**29.0**	**25.7**	**33.6**	**11.3**	**15.9**

3－14　城市基础设施固定资产投资额

（不含农村集体和个人投资）　　单位：万元

部　门	固定资产投资		#基本建设		更新改造	
	1995年	1996年	1995年	1996年	1995年	1996年
总　计	**678 624**	**910 844**	**397 014**	**599 981**	**280 496**	**310 117**
交通运输、仓储及邮电通信业	385 918	381 504	162 285	196 036	222 611	184 722
#铁　路	6 087	7 607	430	1 268	5 657	6 339
公　路	5 493	5 523	1 453	3 184	3 081	1 752
水　运	1 157	2 635	1 157	2 635		
航　空	1 892	5 173	1 652	2 890	240	2 283
仓储业	4 586	18 969	1 575	16 697	3 011	2 272
邮电通信	230 162	204 245	35 469	62 897	194 693	141 348
电力蒸气、热水生产和供应业	232 791	326 209	195 867	286 701	36 924	39 508
煤气生产和供应业	11 043	33 053	7 916	24 929	3 035	8 124
自来水的生产和供应业	19 573	25 182	9 517	17 561	10 056	7 621
公共服务业	29 299	144 896	21 429	74 754	7 870	70 142
城市基础设施占全市固定资产投资比重(%)	**20.2**	**25.2**	**24.9**	**35.4**	**29.3**	**28.7**

3－15　地方各主管部门固定资产投资

单位:万元

项　目	固定资产投资		#基本建设		更新改造	
	1995 年	1996 年	1995 年	1996 年	1995 年	1996 年
市农林局	1 369	1 394	1 274	1 354	95	40
市水利局	17 685	22 886	14 051	18 972	3 634	3 914
市水产局	717	85	55	85	662	
冶金工业总公司	31 106	50 035	3 988	23 179	27 118	26 856
化工工业公司	16 569	98 063	3 714	1 865	12 776	94 362
机电工业总公司	29 722	28 861	129	2 629	29 593	26 232
电子仪表工业总公司	50 243	74 305	6 725	67 744	42 930	6 165
一轻工业总公司	76 503	126 973	2 814	1 437	73 160	125 536
二轻工业总公司	18 068	5 426	130	1 225	15 681	4 201
纺织工业总公司	33 017	47 725		1 162	32 787	46 443
医药总公司	21 609	5 604	2 530	899	18 971	4 705
建材集团	12 899	27 906	5 013	10 624	7 887	17 282
长芦盐务局	7 564	100			7 654	100
渤海化学工业集团	31 513	81 655	300		31 213	81 655
市汽车工业(集团)有限公司	221 858	79 440	152 762	23 897	51 392	49 271
市公用局	22 178	24 838	18 425	7 707	3 753	17 131
建工集团	6 352	3 218			6 352	3 218
市市政工程局	88 989	104 710	85 124	98 930	3 865	5 780
市房地产管理局	19 045	3 057			19 045	3 057
市园林管理局	2 800	4 221	480	2 448	2 320	1 773
市环境卫生管理局		2 698				2 698
市环境保护局	2 172	768		251	2 172	517
天津港务局	60 741	72 453	46 535	46 751	14 206	25 702
市交通局	4 688	2 619	1 244	1 194	2 485	1 058
邮电管理局(地方部分)	158 363	118 917	6 600	34 304	151 763	84 613
市粮食局	13 358	5 122	10 655	2 460	2 353	2 662
益商集团	6 739	9 000			6 739	9 000
市第二商业局	873		570		303	
市对外贸易局(地方部分)	2 413	2 252	100	90	2 313	2 162
天津市经济技术开发区管委会	288 744	325 625	227 316	7 233	61 428	54 721
市科学技术委员会	665	1 738	665	1 738		
市高等教育局(地方部分)	7 233	3 841	7 233	3 841		
市教育局	14 235	19 730	4 573	7 202	9 662	12 528
市卫生局	2 762	4 248	2 762	4 248		
市体育运动委员会	370	644	370	644		
市文化局	1 198	8 240	948	8 060	250	180
市新闻出版管理局	749	1 553			749	1 553
市广播电视局	15 144	822	15 144	822		
市公安局	3 120	9 094	3 120	8 794		300
市劳改工作管理局	2 409	380	844	280	1 565	100
市民政局		324		324		

3－16　国民经济各行业新增固定资产

（不含农村集体和个人投资）　　单位:万元

项　目	全　市		#基本建设		更新改造	
	1995年	1996年	1995年	1996年	1995年	1996年
总　计	**2 503 344**	**2 539 533**	**1 328 421**	**1 249 521**	**817 070**	**639 708**
一、按隶属关系分						
中　央	827 922	714 625	599 075	386 987	150 562	224 231
地　方	1 675 422	1 825 008	729 346	862 534	666 508	41 477
二、按行业分						
农、林、牧、渔业	2 798	1 959	1 612	1 438	1 186	521
工　业	1 695 520	1 437 490	1 080 805	911 352	532 080	416 187
采掘业	208 295	313 329	82 751	100 638	53 178	115 871
制造业	1 085 234	790 042	624 638	507 902	450 327	269 009
电力、煤气及水的生产和供应业	401 991	334 119	373 416	302 812	28 575	31 307
建筑业	18 185	223 300	4 625	12 299	13 257	10 001
地质勘察业、水利管理业	25 868	31 606	21 955	29 061	3 913	2 545
交通运输、仓储及邮电通信业	287 660	216 397	119 479	113 652	167 159	102 269
批发和零售贸易、餐饮业	37 047	15 629	23 479	4 129	11 425	9 132
金融、保险业	11 601	8 313	7 141	6 880	1 117	803
房地产业和社会服务业	348 205	682 675	17 482	75 466	62 618	71 339
房地产业	330 122	577 841	2 588		59 479	41 971
社会服务业	18 083	104 834	14 924	75 466	3 139	29 368
卫生、体育和社会福利业	9 089	8 418	8 762	7 974	125	372
教育、文化艺术及广播电影电视业	29 665	38 558	19 294	35 989	10 371	2 569
科学研究和综合技术服务业	11 872	9 067	8 835	5 367	3 037	3 700
国家机关、政党机关和社会团体	21 568	60 088	11 761	40 649	9 707	18 754
其他行业	4 266	7 003	3 191	5 265	1 075	1 516

3－17 工业行业新增固定资产

(不含农村集体和个人投资)　　单位:万元

项目	基本建设			更新改造		
	1995年	1996年	1996比1995年增长%	1995年	1996年	1996比1995年增长%
总计	**1 080 805**	**911 352**	**－15.7**	**532 080**	**416 187**	**－21.8**
采掘业	**82 751**	**100 638**	**21.6**	**53 178**	**115 871**	**117.9**
煤炭采选业		19 542				
石油和天然气开采业	82 751	81 096	－2.0	51 053	106 500	108.6
非金属矿采选业				2 125	9 371	341.0
制造业	**624 638**	**507 902**	**－18.7**	**45 032**	**269 009**	**497.4**
食品加工业	639	12 635	1 877.3	99	44	－55.6
食品制造业	415	2 803	575.4	71	6 931	9 662.0
饮料制造业	16 635	950	－94.3	119	3 598	2 923.5
纺织业		870		2 495	15 915	537.9
服装及其他纤维制品制造业					190	
家具制造业		650		31		
造纸及纸制品业	6 367	683	－89.3	287	14 926	5 100.7
印刷业、记录媒介的复制				15	3 665	24 333.3
文教体育用品制造业				221	857	287.7
石油加工及炼焦业	40 292	9 240	－77.1	15 242	9 433	－38.1
化学原料及化学制品制造业	347 966	161 110	－53.7	41 849	66 946	60.6
医药制造业	5 865	109	－98.1	22 880	4 010	－82.5
化学纤维制造业		100		8 453	25 832	205.6
橡胶制品业				1 601	1 089	－32.0
塑料制品业	3 013	324	－89.2	22 546	1 227	－94.6
非金属矿物制品业	300	390	30.0	3 257	4 640	42.5
黑色金属冶炼及压延加工业	61 664	99 000	60.5	66 523	12 402	－81.3
有色金属冶炼及压延加工业				8 856	33	－99.6
金属制品业		390		39 530	19 090	－51.7
普通机械制造业		5 080		108 565	23 234	－78.6
专用设备制造业	2 950	250	－91.5	5 910	3 824	－35.3
交通运输设备制造业	18 039	183 501	917.2	18 471	37 644	103.8
电气机械及器材制造业	1 605	150	－90.7	4 022	3 937	－2.1
电子及通信设备制造业	118 888	26 809	－77.5	51 803	9 099	－82.4
仪器仪表及文化办公用机械制造业		2 858		2 400	434	－81.9
电力、煤气及水的生产和供应业	**373 416**	**302 812**	**－18.9**	**28 575**	**31 307**	**9.6**
电力、蒸汽、热水的生产和供应业	357 378	286 207	－19.9	25 494	25 688	0.8
煤气生产和供应业	3 927	8 747	122.7	1 376	4 115	199.1
自来水的生产和供应业	12 111	7 858	－935.0	1 705	1 504	－11.8

3－18　1996年固定资产投资资金来源（一）

（不含农村集体和个人投资）　单位:万元

项　目	合　计	基本建设	更新改造	房地产开发	其　他
本年资金来源合计	**3 798 559**	**1 705 589**	**1 052 594**	**918 953**	**121 423**
1.上年末结余资金	**277 838**	**46 192**	**114 488**	**111 772**	**5 386**
2.本年资金来源合计	**3 520 721**	**1 659 397**	**938 106**	**807 181**	**116 037**
(1)国家预算内资金	47 840	32 247	8 515	6 998	80
(2)国内贷款	727 135	304 278	168 769	251 175	2 913
(3)债　券	22 200	21 000	300	900	
(4)利用外资	742 516	549 260	105 565	87 691	
＃对外商直接投资	447 493	319 200	77 551	50 742	
对外借款	272 263	216 570	26 495	29 198	
＃统借统还	26 438	1 610	15 383	9 445	
(5)自筹资金	1 562 029	621 979	587 080	240 988	111 982
中央各部门自筹	84 996	36 025	48 971		
市自筹	146 410	124 695	21 679		36
区自筹	217 578	106 442	111 116		20
县自筹	30 315	19 563	10 260		492
企、事业单位自有资金	1 082 730	335 254	395 054	240 988	111 434
＃发行股票	12 946		12 946		
(6)其他资金来源	419 001	130 633	67 877	219 429	1 062
＃集　资	72 510	7 397	48 428	16 192	493

注:本表数据是指固定资产资金实际投入数。

3－19　1996年固定资产投资资金来源（二）

（不含农村集体和个人投资）　单位:万元

项　目	合　计	＃国有经济	集体经济	股份制经济	"三资"经济
本年资金来源合计	**3 798 559**	**2 639 627**	**132 221**	**200 627**	**813 439**
1.上年末结余资金	**277 838**	**148 237**	**20 595**	**14 250**	**92 812**
2.本年资金来源合计	**3 520 721**	**2 491 390**	**111 626**	**186 377**	**720 627**
(1)国家预算内资金	47 840	44 670	3 110	60	
(2)国内贷款	727 135	528 285	42 497	87 043	66 680
(3)债　券	22 200	21 300		900	
(4)利用外资	742 516	231 968	718	9 787	500 043
＃对外商直接投资	447 493	17 789		3 448	426 256
对外借款	272 263	214 179	718	6 339	51 027
＃统借统还	26 438	16 993			9 445
(5)自筹资金	1 562 029	1 396 390	42 064	48 966	68 336
中央各部门自筹	84 996	84 781		215	
市自筹	146 410	146 372	36	2	
区自筹	217 578	206 931	20	5 000	5 609
县自筹	30 315	29 823	492		
企、事业单位自有资金	1 082 730	928 483	41 516	43 749	62 727
＃发行股票	12 946			12 946	
(6)其他资金来源	419 001	268 777	23 237	39 621	85 568
＃集　资	72 510	70 217	1 043	71	1 070

3-20 施工和竣工房屋建筑面积

（不含农村集体和个人投资）

单位:万平方米

项目	施工面积			竣工面积		
	1995年	1996年	1996比1995年增长%	1995年	1996年	1996比1995年增长%
一、房屋建筑面积	**1 826.09**	**1 712.00**	**-6.2**	**736.45**	**725.13**	**-1.5**
基本建设	399.87	399.79	-0.02	193.16	195.29	1.1
更新改造	391.72	304.58	-22.2	138.11	155.33	12.5
其他投资	17.55	18.97	8.1	10.43	8.00	-23.3
房地产开发	1 016.95	988.66	-2.8	394.75	366.51	-7.2
#国有经济	1 333.86	1 167.24	-12.5	574.72	567.23	-1.3
基本建设	334.36	350.11	4.7	168.62	188.25	11.6
更新改造	359.23	277.97	-22.6	128.55	146.16	13.7
其他投资	2.95	1.62	-45.1	2.58	1.17	-54.7
房地产开发	637.32	537.54	-15.7	274.97	231.65	-15.8
集体经济	130.22	114.14	-12.3	50.01	54.88	9.7
#房地产开发	115.63	96.79	-16.3	42.16	48.04	13.9
二、住宅建筑面积	**1 162.22**	**1 016.52**	**-12.5**	**486.93**	**494.73**	**1.6**
基本建设	106.34	126.06	18.5	55.58	87.91	58.2
更新改造	262.59	172.10	-34.5	84.98	85.22	0.3
其他投资	5.07	5.60	10.5	1.79	3.10	73.2
房地产开发	788.22	712.76	-9.6	344.58	318.50	-7.6
#国有经济	881.54	741.68	-15.9	378.23	378.35	0.03
基本建设	98.87	126.06	27.5	54.40	87.91	61.6
更新改造	256.13	171.60	-33.0	84.92	84.72	-0.2
房地产开发	526.54	444.02	-15.7	238.91	205.72	13.9
集体经济	96.90	82.12	-15.3	40.11	47.90	19.4
#房地产开发	91.83	76.52	-16.7	38.32	44.80	16.9

3－21　1996年建设项目主要新增生产能力

生产能力(或效益)名称	单位	合计	#基本建设	更新改造
原油开采	万吨/年	38	38	
炼钢	万吨/年	60		60
金属丝及其制品	吨/年	5 000		5 000
发电机组容量	万千瓦	51	50	1
变电设备能力(11万伏及以上)	万千伏安	27	27	
乙烯	吨/年	140 000	140 000	
油漆	吨/年	3 000		3 000
炭黑	吨/年	12 000		12 000
合成纤维聚合物	吨/年	4 000		4 000
中成药	吨/年	40		40
铸钢件能力	吨/年	1 000	1 000	
汽车制造	辆/年	100 000	100 000	
酒	吨/年	1 900	100	1 800
合成洗涤剂原料	吨/年	30 000		30 000
汽车、挂车购置	辆	137		111
新建公路	公里	61	61	
新建独立公路桥梁	延长米	788	788	
	座	2	2	
新(扩)建港口码头	吞吐量:万吨	50		50
	泊位:个	2		2
长途电缆	延长公里	247	105	142
市内电话自动交换机	门	237 288	15 000	222 288
商业饮食服务网点	处	22	1	12
	平方米	24 251	11 000	6 220
高等学校:学生席位	个	1 600	1 600	
建筑面积	平方米	27 765	27 765	
中等学校:学生席位	个	17 840	16 990	850
建筑面积	平方米	93 394	90 051	3 343
小学校:学生席位	个	2 700	2 160	540
建筑面积	平方米	16 856	15 500	1 356
其他学校:学生席位	个	600	600	
建筑面积	平方米	3 300	3 300	
医院病床	张	1 366	866	300
城市道路扩建长度	公里	48	29	19
城市排水管道铺设长度	公里	41	28	13
城市永久性桥梁	座	3	2	1

3－22 1996年重点

单位名称	项目名称	开工时间	投产时间	计划总投资(万元)
一、基本建设大中型项目(47)个				
热电一厂	热电一厂大代小工程	1993.06		43 163
热电公司	陈热热网	1994.04		13 100
华能杨柳青发电有限公司	杨柳青电厂扩建工程	1995.12		469 214
基建工程承包公司	红旗路220KV工程	1994.05	1996.12	13 529
基建工程承包公司	勤俭道220KV工程	1995.02	1996.12	7 798
基建工程承包公司	南郊500KV变电站	1996.12		32 000
基建工程承包公司	延吉道220KV工程	1996.12		9 262
陈塘热电有限公司	陈塘庄热电厂工程	1991.05	1996.12	62 981
大港油田	扩建工程	1996.01		70 595
中国海洋石油渤海公司	天然原油开采业	1996.01		174 784
天津石油化工公司工程管理处	炼油扩建工程(聚酯一阶段工程)	1993.10		187 794
天津石油化工公司工程管理处	延迟焦化工程	1995.07		29 861
天津市盘山电厂	盘山电厂一期工程	1991.10	1996.05	526 307
中国联通天津移动电话营业厅	天津GSM二期工程	1996.02		12 955
天津市邮电管理局	天津电信枢纽	1993.06	1996.12	4 535
天津市邮电管理局	长途通信楼	1993.06	1996.12	16 355
天津市邮电管理局	大港电信机房楼	1994.12	1996.12	3 886
天津邮电管理局	塘沽邮政综合楼	1994.12		8 776
天津联合化学有限公司	天津十四万吨/年乙烯工程	1992.12	1996.12	555 544
天津市第三煤气厂	天津市第三煤气厂	1996.05		99 741
东方红化工厂	五水偏硅酸纳2万吨/年工程	1993.12	1996.12	11 905
天津阿尔斯通水电设备有限公司	新建重型铆焊车间	1993.12		6 480
天津广电通信公司	通信传输及终端设备扩建	1994.02		10 732
天津三星电机有限公司	电子元件扩能	1994.06		24 833
天津三星电管有限公司	彩色显示器件合资项目			306 400
天津松下电子部品有限公司	松下电子部品合资项目	1996.03		63 209
天津市振兴水泥厂	新建项目	1996.12		71 506
天津汽车工业(集团)有限公司	夏利十五万辆扩建项目	1994.05		215 259
天津无缝钢管工程指挥部	天津钢管公司续建直接还原铁厂	1994.07		100 008
自来水公司	新开河水厂第五出厂干管	1994.04	1996.12	6 450
液化气公司	一灌站 混气站工程	1993.03	1996.12	6 041
公交公司	天津站公交枢纽站	1995.11	1996.10	5 030
天津港务局	天津港扩建	1996.01		261 243
天津邮电管理局	天津卫星通信地球站工程收尾	1994.03		8 061

建设项目完成情况

累计完成投资（万元）	#本年完成投资	累计新增固定资产（万元）	新增生产能力（或工程效益）名称	建设规模和新增生产能力			
				计量单位	建设规模	累计新增生产能力	其中：本年新增
43 163	10 094	43 163	火力发电	万千瓦	10.00	10.00	
5 913	2 333						
136 360	128 360		火力发电	万千瓦	60.00		
13 529	6 085	13 529	输电线路长度(11 万伏及以上)	公里	34.00	34.00	12.00
			变电设备能力(11 万伏及以上)	万千伏安	24.00	24.00	12.00
7 798	2 030	7 798	输电线路长度(11 万伏及以上)	公里	26.00	26.00	13.00
			变电设备能力(11 万伏及以上)	万千伏安	24.00	24.00	12.00
6 000	6 000		变电设备能力(11 万伏及以上)	万千伏安	75.00		
3 903	3 903		输电线路长度(11 万伏及以上)	公里	15.00		
62 981	6 276	62 981	变电设备能力(11 万伏及以上)	万千伏安	12.00		
70 595	70 595	68 116	火力发电	万千瓦	10.00	10.00	
126 914	126 914	10 787	其中：天然原油	万吨/年	38.42	38.42	38.42
84 207	42 360	47 454	其中：天然原油	万吨/年	83.00		
			石油加工：蒸馏设备	万吨/年	250.00		
			裂化设备	万吨/年	80.00		
20 715	14 040	220	加氢精制设备	万吨/年	40.00		
472 200	100 500	468 232	焦化设备	万吨/年	100.00		
1 277	1 277		火力发电	万千瓦	100.00	100.00	50.00
			长途电缆	延长公里	105.00	105.00	105.00
			新建微波电路	公里	213.20	213.20	213.20
7 310	1 000	1 000	市内电话自动交换机	门	15 000.00	15 000.00	15 000.00
16 355	5 455	5 455					
3 326	2 226	2 226					
8 000	4 000						
523 554	113 575	510 459					
23 008	21 146	553	乙 烯	吨/年	40 000.00	140 000.00	40 000.00
12 979	1 865	11 688	城市煤气生产能力	万立方米/日	100.00		
1 614	474		合成洗涤剂原料	吨/年	20 000.00	20 000.00	
9 050	6 418						
61 141	26 180	60 048					
29 071	29 071	985					
11 577	10 624						
211 270	23 897	189 674	水 泥	万吨/年	70.00		
99 598	45 861	99 000	轿车制造	辆/年		100 000.00	
6 450	345	6 450	城市自来水管道长度	公里	11.00	11.00	
6 041	706	5 506					
5 030	529	4 967					
112 173	46 751	55 281					
8 061	206	8 061					

3-22续表1

单位名称	项目名称	开工时间	投产时间	计划总投资（万元）
天津市邮电管理局	市话通信管道	1996.04	1996.12	5 983
天津市邮电管理局	邵兴道电话局			6 000
天津市邮电管理局	芥园电话局	1996.10		3 150
天津市邮电管理局	天津邮电管网中心大厦	1994.11		23 756
天津经济技术开发区总公司自来水公司	开发区源水二期管线工程	1996.01		18 600
摩托罗拉(中国)电子有限公司	半导体芯片厂	1995.11		500 000
诺和诺德(中国)生物技术有限公司	基建工程	1996.01		201 690
天津标准国际建材工业有限公司	基建工程	1996.09		17 696
天津比埃菲制药有限公司	比埃菲制药公司厂房	1996.08		7 902
天津市广播电视局	天津市广播电视国际新闻中心	1993.05		29 875
天津经济建设投资集团总公司	南疆油库	1995.05		9 964
天津国际石油储运有限公司	晉由库工程	1994.10		22 550
天津市汉沽区引滦入汉工程指挥部	天津市汉沽区引滦入汉工程指挥部	1995.12		14 957
二、更新改造限额以上项目(59)个				
天津卷烟厂	“八五”技术改造	1994.10		16 274
天津石化公司化工厂	DMT装置技术改造	1995.08	1996.09	18 308
中国联通天津分公司	联通天津通信网建设项目	1995.10		45 530
北辰区水利局	永定新河深槽蓄水工程	1996.04		4 383
伯克气体工业有限公司	开发区高纯气体中心	1995.05		6 979
阿克苏诺贝尔过氧化物有限公司	过氧化物	1996.04		8 558
科莱恩(天津)有限公司	高档染料	1996.12		36 437
天津动力机厂	利用世行贷款技改项目	1994.10		59 790
天津市锻压机床总厂	利用世界银行贷款技改项目	1994.05		17 000
天津市天工工程机械有限公司	利用世界银行贷款技改项目	1994.12		19 994
天津第一机床总厂	天津市机床股份有限公司利用世界银	1994.12		19 627
天津液压机械(集团)有限公司	天津“八五”液压件补充专项	1993.12	1996.06	9 420
扎努西电气机械天津压缩机有限公司	300万台无氟冰箱压缩机	1996.10		62 770
天津阿尔斯通水电设备有限公司	固定资产投资	1995.01		5 700
天津天龙纸业有限责任公司	4万吨/年高级美术铜版纸3万吨/年高	1993.11		121 389
天津造纸厂	胶印书刊纸技改工程	1991.12		19 973
天助精细化学公司	3万吨表面活性剂	1993.10	1996.12	3 194
天津环球磁卡股份有限公司	ic卡生产设备扩建	1995.12	1996.12	3 982
天津宝洁有限公司	技术改造	1994.01		44 490
天津市康美林食品有限公司	技术改造	1994.08	1996.10	4 000
天津万华股份有限公司	引进双向拉伸聚丙烯塑料生产设备			18 170
ACI(天津)模具有限公司	技术改造	1995.03	1996.12	7 806

累计完成投资(万元)	#本年完成投资	累计新增固定资产(万元)	新增生产能力(或工程效益)名　称	建设规模和新增生产能力 计量单位	建设规模	累计新增生产能力	其中:本年新增
5 983	5 983	5 983					
800	800						
2 000	2 000						
19 300	10 000						
16 308	16 308	390					
480 773	186 314	362 634					
27 556	10 521						
1 370	1 370						
2 959	2 959						
32 444	822						
7 308	5 114		商业石油库	万立米	8.00		
17 760	8 297		商业石油库	万立米	16.30		
12 024	12 024		城市自来水供水能力	万吨/日	5.00		
15 530	4 023						
18 308	12 308	17 000					
21 088	15 558	1 158	长途电缆	延长公里	165.00	165.00	142.00
			新建微波电路	公里	30.00	30.00	30.00
			市内电话自动交换机	门	80 000.00		
			长途自动电话交换设备	路端	3 000.00		
457	457		有效灌溉面积	万亩	5.00		
6 281	6 066	700					
7 358	7 038						
13 550	10 127	500	染　料	吨/年	4 000.00		
8 053	2 716	231	柴油机制造	台/年	42 000.00		
				万千瓦/年	446.40		
2 059	1 459	800	金属切削机床制造	台/年	230.00		
3 518	2 597	89	建筑机械制造	台(套)/年	800.00		
3 146	1 649	1 193	金属切削机床制造	台/年	280.00		
8 712	1 925	8 434					
3 178	3 178						
3 063	2 280	1 336					
120 097	88 949	14 658	机制纸及纸板	万吨/年	7.00		
21 451	1 746	947	机制纸及纸板	万吨/年	2.50		
2 678	149	2 678	合成洗涤剂原料	吨/年	30 000.00	30 000.00	30 000.00
2 580	2 580	2 460					
23 356	16 710	23 356					
5 481	1 011	5 425	饼　干	吨/年	15 000.00	15 000.00	15 000.00
10	10						
7 806	5 019	7 502					

3－22 续表 2

单位名称	项目名称	开工时间	投产时间	计划总投资（万元）
天津市铝品总厂	铝锰合金材及制品生产技改	1995.11		6 998
第二棉纺织厂	更新FA系列及配套设备	1995.07	1996.12	2 970
三星毛纺织有限公司	技改项目	1995.08		17 976
合成纤维厂	2 000吨/年锦纶长丝	1995.03		21 494
渤海化工集团股份有限公司天津碱厂	合成氨节能技术改造工程	1996.12		19 042
渤海化工集团股份有限公司天津碱厂	氨碱生产装置节能技改工程	1996.12		11 795
渤海化工集团股份有限公司天津碱厂	低盐份优质重质纯碱节能技改工程	1996.12		15 906
渤海化工集团股份有限公司天津化工厂	氯碱技术改造工程	1996.12		100 504
渤海化工集团股份有限公司大沽化工厂	8万吨/年氯乙烯装置2万吨/年聚氯乙	1994.12		80 423
渤海化工集团股份有限公司大沽化工厂	4万吨/年离子膜烧碱技术改造项目	1995.11		19 842
天津市微型汽车厂	夏利局部换型	1996.11		4 108
天津汽车齿轮有限公司	一期工程填平补齐项目	1991.05	1996.04	8 294
天津汽车齿轮有限公司	利用世行贷款项目	1994.10		19 974
天津华狮汽车仪表有限公司	合资项目	1996.01		13 852
天津市内燃机电机厂	发电机、起动机项目	1992.09	1996.10	3 184
天津电装汽车电机有限公司	合资项目	1996.02		13 800
天津市汽车装饰公司	夏利座椅总成技改	1995.04	1996.06	7 113
天津弹簧制造有限公司	夏利配套悬挂簧技改	1995.04	1996.06	5 069
天津汽车暖风机有限公司	夏利暖风机装置技改	1995.02	1996.06	6 039
天津爱三汽车附件有限公司	合资项目	1996.11		7 318
天津华利汽车有限公司	合资项目	1995.04		50 000
天津汽车电器有限公司	夏利轿车分电器技改	1995.05	1996.06	6 420
天津阿斯莫汽车微电机有限公司	合资项目	1996.06		6 884
天津丰田合成汽车软管有限公司	合资项目	1996.03		4 100
自来水公司	宜兴埠泵站改造	1996.03		4 400
天津市长途电信局	96GSM移动电话扩容	1996.01	1996.12	13 300
天津市长途电信局	GSM移动电话四万门	1996.12		15 358
天津市长途电信局	GSM移动电话扩容工程	1996.12		11 452
天津市市内电话局	利用加拿大贷款扩建市话网	1995.07		62 208
天津市市内电话局	市话通信线路工程	1996.04	1996.12	13 793
天津市市内电话局	网管监控系统工程	1996.12		6 192
天津市市内电话局	市话业务计算机管理系统	1996.01		6 717
天津市市内电话局	同步传输网工程(SDH)	1996.05		6 162
天津百货大楼CO.LTD	百货大楼改扩建工程	1994.04		36 000
天津市石油总公司	更新改造	1996.04		27 000
天津市河北区百货公司	中山商厦	1993.07		15 600
天津市政建设开发公司	黄纬路改造	1996.04	1996.12	19 957

累计完成投资(万元)	#本年完成投资	累计新增固定资产(万元)	新增生产能力(或工程效益)名　称	建设规模和新增生产能力			
				计量单位	建设规模	累计新增生产能力	其中:本年新增
3 600	3 300		铝加工	吨/年	12 000.00		
3 159	2 159	3 159					
17 176	17 176						
19 923	13 344	19 700					
200	200		合成氨	吨/年	8 000.00		
200	200						
200	200						
500	500		烧碱(又称:氢氧化钠)	吨/年	27 000.00		
			塑料树脂及共聚物	吨/年	24 000.00		
79 720	58 202	570	塑料树脂及共聚物	吨/年			
15 342	13 595	948	烧碱(又称:氢氧化钠)	吨/年	40 000.00		
17	17						
9 176	289	8 500					
16 272	14 643						
8 002	8 002	5 480					
3 872	488	3 727					
543	543	543					
6 996	937	6 996					
5 069	686	5 069					
6 039	949	6 039					
1 089	1 089	1 089					
10 359	9 915	695					
6 330	679	5 970					
4 086	4 086	60					
1 328	1 328	134					
4 206	4 206		城市自来水供水能力	万吨/日	55.00		
13 300	13 300	7 880					
8 000	8 000						
7 000	7 000						
62 208	5 976	52 053	市内电话自动交换机	门	40 000.00	210 000.00	10 000.00
13 793	13 793	12 000					
1 500	1 500						
3 868	3 868						
4 000	4 000						
27 076	9 000						
4 275	4 275						
11 407	2 000						
17 216	17 216	17 216	城市道路扩建长度	公里	1.34	1.34	1.34
			城市道路扩建面积	万平方米	4.23	4.23	4.23
			城市排水管道铺设长度	公里	6.30	6.30	6.30

3-23 国有经济其他固定资产投资完成情况

(1992-1996年)

项　目	单　位	1992年	1993年	1994年	1995年	1996年
一、施工项目个数	**个**	**3**	**3**	**1**	**1**	**1**
二、固定资产投资	**万元**	**73 603**	**78 581**	**91 082**	**84 146**	**99 405**
1.按隶属关系分						
中　央	万元	71 782	72 513	91 082	84 146	99 405
地　方	万元	1 821	6 068			
2.按行业分						
工　业	万元	71 782	72 513	91 082	84 146	99 405
交通运输邮电通信业	万元	1 821	6 068			
三、新增固定资产	**万元**	**52 647**	**61 618**	**88 331**	**72 366**	**96 820**
工　业	万元	52 647	58 108	88 331	72 366	96 820
交通运输邮电通信业	万元		3 510			
四、固定资产交付使用率	**%**	**71.5**	**78.4**	**97.0**	**86.0**	**97.4**
五、房屋建筑面积						
施工面积	万平方米	1.1	0.9		2.95	1.62
竣工面积	万平方米	0.8	0.3		2.58	1.17

3-24 房地产开发建设情况

(1992-1996年)

项　目	单　位	1992年	1993年	1994年	1995年	1996年
一、商品房屋开发情况						
本年完成投资额	万元	45 842	180 957	256 571	694 364	715 103
本年房屋施工面积	万平方米	185.29	377.66	418.46	1 016.95	988.66
#住　宅	万平方米	157.66	296.42	313.11	788.22	712.76
本年房屋竣工面积	万平方米	64.81	89.03	128.08	394.75	366.51
#住　宅	万平方米	55.71	80.13	111.43	344.58	318.50
竣工房屋价值	万元	27 949	64 053	144 210	444 606	483 917
#住　宅	万元	21 255	54 291	124 114	351 450	371 777
二、商品房屋销售情况						
本年实际销售商品房屋面积	万平方米	47.58	53.11	60.01	146.58	129.39
本年商品房屋销售额	万元	50 546	101 601	112 640	279 895	310 282

3-25　1996年按经济类型分房地产开发建设情况

项　　目	单　位	合　计	国有经济	集体经济	联营经济
一、商品房屋开发情况					
本年完成投资额	万元	715 103	333 938	72 637	6 206
本年房屋施工面积	万平方米	988.66	537.54	96.79	8.16
#住　宅	万平方米	712.76	444.02	76.52	6.26
本年房屋竣工面积	万平方米	366.51	231.65	48.04	3.34
#住　宅	万平方米	318.50	205.72	44.80	3.34
竣工房屋价值	万元	483 917	253 368	49 754	3 087
#住　宅	万元	371 777	215 535	41 171	3 087
二、商品房屋销售情况					
本年实际销售商品房屋面积	万平方米	129.39	73.82	21.46	0.76
本年商品房屋销售额	万元	310 282	159 077	43 664	2 104

项　　目	单　位	股份制经济	外商投资	港澳台投资	其他经济
一、商品房屋开发情况					
本年完成投资额	万元	83 747	94 429	120 507	3 639
本年房屋施工面积	万平方米	106.42	139.26	95.11	5.38
#住　宅	万平方米	82.56	61.97	38.84	2.59
本年房屋竣工面积	万平方米	36.31	29.56	17.61	
#住　宅	万平方米	30.90	23.01	10.73	
竣工房屋价值	万元	34 673	71 516	71 519	
#住　宅	万元	30 965	42 046	38 973	
二、商品房屋销售情况					
本年实际销售商品房屋面积	万平方米	18.04	5.36	9.95	
本年商品房屋销售额	万元	31 680	22 946	50 811	

3-26　1996年按用途分房地产开发建设情况

项　　目	单　位	合　计	住　宅	#别墅、高档公寓	办公楼	商业营业用房	其　他
一、商品房屋开发情况							
本年完成投资额	万元	715 103	428 672	61 509	66 798	124 930	94 703
本年房屋施工面积	万平方米	988.66	712.76	52.56	77.33	129.21	69.36
本年房屋竣工面积	万平方米	366.51	318.50	18.27	12.28	22.26	13.47
竣工房屋价值	万元	483 917	371 777	60 480	28 699	66 521	16 920
二、商品房屋销售情况							
本年实际销售商品房屋面积	万平方米	129.39	114.42	6.16	5.85	5.97	3.15
本年商品房屋销售额	万元	310 282	248 065	23 096	24 804	31 877	5 536

3-27 1996年天津

序号	受让单位	出让方式	出让地块位置
1	天津市河东林产品公司	协议	河东区卫国道南、万东小马路东
2	天津亚中房地产开发有限公司	协议	和平区营口道三东里
3	大宇宙信息创造(中国)有限公司	协议	西青区外环线东侧复康路南侧
4	天津火柴厂	协议	和平区多伦道北
5	天津迎宾广场有限公司	协议	河西区紫金山路喜来登酒店东
6	天津市长康房地产开发公司	协议	和平区沙市道46号
7	天津市色织一厂	协议	南开区六马路西侧
8	天津市福通房地产开发公司	协议	和平区成都道新建村64-68号
9	天津市骨科医疗器械厂	协议	河东区十经路北八纬路东
10	天津万科兴业(集团)有限公司	协议	和平区南京路南民航大楼西
11	天津钟表厂	协议	和平区西藏路2号
12	开发集团第二经营公司	协议	南开区红旗剧场南侧
13	北辰房地产开发有限责任公司	协议	北辰区津坝路北
14	杏华房地产公司	协议	河北区真理道与江都路转角
15	天津市小提琴厂	协议	河东区红星路东
16	摩托罗拉(中国)电子有限公司	协议	河西区解放南路475号
17	天津市第五染整厂	协议	河北区雅安西道2号
18	天津市染料化学九厂	协议	东丽区程林庄工业区崂山路西
19	民生置业有限公司	协议	河北区民生路与博爱道交口
20	天津市自动化仪表六厂	协议	和平区汉口道与营口道交口
21	天津亚富物业投资有限公司	协议	河西区友谊路围堤道交口
22	天津国民大厦	协议	和平区哈尔滨道
23	天津新型建筑材料房地产开发公司	协议	和平区贵州路
24	天津伊都锦商厦有限公司	协议	和平区滨江道
25	天津外贸华益公司	协议	河北区中山路
26	天津兴粤物业发展有限公司	协议	河西区宾西路西
27	天津市染料化学八厂	协议	东丽区张贵庄路南、吉安道东
28	天津市三峡房地产开发公司	协议	和平区睦南道1.3.5号
29	扎努西电气机械天津压缩机有限公司	协议	河东区八纬路东骨科医院北
30	天津市电子仪表工业物资供应总公司	协议	南开区北草坝金坪路3号
31	天津市凯兴房地产开发公司	协议	南开区长江道102号
32	天津市东方房地产实业公司	协议	河西区台湾路10号
33	天津市河东建设开发公司	协议	东丽区程林庄路南、月牙河东
34	天津市福顺房地产开发有限责任公司	协议	和平区鞍山道与卫津路交口
35	天津市利英房地产开发公司	协议	和平区四川路4-6号
36	天津经济技术开发区垠源房地产公司	协议	南开区宁家房子
37	天津申润置业发展有限公司	协议	南开区鞍山西道玉泉路东
38	大韩民国仁川广域市	协议	和平区南京路
39	广州市星江投资管理有限公司	协议	南开区黄河道南
40	铁道部第十八工程局	协议	津南区津沽公路北
41	中国联合通信有限公司天津公司	协议	南开区津盐公路西侧
42	宁发房地产开发公司	协议	河西区气象台路气象局

市区土地出让一览

土地用途	出让面积(平方米)	出让年限(年)	容积率	楼面地价(元/平方米)
办公楼、公寓、文化娱乐	15 880.7	50	1.0	479.00
商贸、办公、住宅	9 452.0	50	6.67	105.00
工业	8 608.9	50	1.5	720.00
商住	8 898.0	商业40年、住宅70年	2.7	83.33
写字楼、公寓、别墅	27 776.9	50		
商住	2 269.3	70	2.6	160.00
商住	3 290.7	50	1.86	73.12
住宅	3 146.27	70	2.4	61.05
工业	6 202.9	50	1.4	47.50
商贸、写字楼、饭店、停车场	15 256.7	50	8.0	306.00
住宅、公建	26 969.3	50	0.5	450.00
综合	6 079.8	50	3.0	213.00
住宅	17 024.0	70	1.5	56.83
住宅	1 302.0	70	2.0	90.00
住宅	4 449.3	70	2.0	32.87
住宅	1 245.1	70	2.20	15.00
住宅	8 888.1	70	2.10	36.59
工业	38 678.5	50	7.79	75.00
商贸、住宅	2 898.7	50	5.24	464.50
综合	2 949.3	50	7.79	75.00
商贸、综合写字楼	3 269.0	50	11.28	225.10
商场、娱乐、餐饮、旅馆	2 978.5	50	6.5	
综合	1 276.0	50	1.6	579.73
商贸、娱乐、写字楼	4 171.3	50	6.00	3 529.37
住宅	16 142.7	70	2.00	68.85
住宅	4 700.00	70	2.5	52.10
工业	9 727.30	50	1.24	22.86
综合	1 049.6	50	1.5	1 407.33
工业	7 427	50	1.4	47.50
工业	12 563.7	50	0.98	26.29
住宅	4 300.7	70	2.4	110.00
住宅	840.0	70	3.20	65.00
工业	10 358.7	50	1.2	23.80
住宅	3 784.4	70		135.00
住宅	826.4	70		160.00
住宅	18 184.0	70	1.08	135.00
商业、住宅	2 111.0	70	1.6	110.00
写字楼、饭店、文化娱乐、公寓	15 760.0	50	9.00	1 844.00
住宅	1 194.80	70	5.00	146.51
住宅	3 009.3	70	1.76	40.00
办公、写字楼	3 809.1	50	0.85	672.35
住宅	20 349.3	70	2.5	160.00

3－28 农村集体固定资产投资完成情况

(1992－1996年)

项目	1992年	1993年	1994年	1995年	1996年
一、固定资产投资合计(万元)	**235 893**	**273 400**	**369 750**	**465 220**	**573 483**
乡	85 132	93 202	188 624	200 969	247 171
村	150 761	180 198	181 126	264 251	326 312
按用途分					
生产性	229 753	263 960	354 904	412 804	475 990
非生产性	6 140	9 440	14 846	52 416	97 493
按主要行业分					
农、林、牧、渔业	18 520	24 977	39 303	9 228	30 719
工业	210 974	235 281	309 745	405 581	504 061
交通运输业	3 935	2 577	4 080	10 581	695
建筑业	127	606	960	1 457	
文教卫生社会福利业	1 360	4 951	7 800	9 238	16 872
二、新增固定资产(万元)	**212 647**	**241 130**	**323 649**	**401 935**	**416 123**
三、房屋面积(万平方米)					
施工面积	362	230.11	353.47	336.4	368.2
竣工面积	219	213.37	320.76	301.9	288.3

3－29 城镇和农村个人建房情况

(1992－1996年)

项目	单位	1992年	1993年	1994年	1995年	1996年
一、城　镇						
建房户数	户	6 761	6 956	8 236	7 425	6 509
竣工房屋面积	平方米	317 388	318 032	440 771	340 706	419 058
#住　宅	平方米	275 767	303 050	438 552	323 543	400 215
竣工房屋价值	万元	7 375	18 634	19 968	9 699	22 669
#住　宅	万元	6 605	17 634	19 961	8 806	21 783
竣工房屋造价	元/平方米	232	586	453	285	541
#住　宅	元/平方米	240	582	455	272	544
二、农　村						
投资总额	万元	60 765	63 636	85 099	93 578	152 838
#生产性固定资产	万元	13 800	19 078	30 983	35 327	8 733
竣工房屋面积	万平方米	258.0	225.9	238.0	191.4	414.7
#住　宅	万平方米	238.0	209.2	163.0	142.1	385.7
竣工住宅价值	万元	43 203	36 684	54 116	57 630	113 319
竣工住宅造价	元/平方米	181.5	175.4	332.0	405.6	293.8

四、能源和原材料

ENERGY AND RAW MATERIAL

1996 年能源消费总量	2 500.22 万吨标准煤
其中:县以上单位消费量	1 611.27 万吨标准煤
1996 年亿元工业产值耗能源	0.95 万吨标准煤
1996 年全市用水量	233 538 万立方米

全市能源消费总量(万吨标准煤)

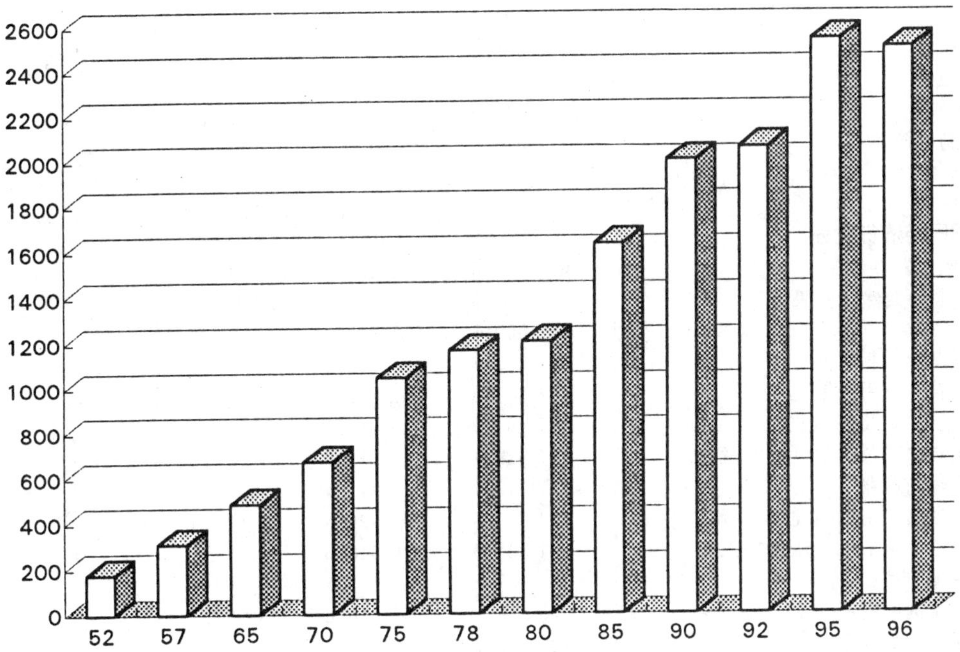

4－1 1996年原材料和能源消费总值

（县及县以上）

单位：万元

项目	合计	工业生产消费	建筑施工消费	运输邮电消费	其他
全市总计	**8 280 034.6**	**7 544 160.9**	**590 515.0**	**114 133.4**	**31 225.3**
一、按类值分					
能源类	1 357 097.6	1 251 339.1	20 983.0	78 691.6	6 083.9
原材料类	6 922 937.0	6 292 821.8	569 532.0	35 441.8	25 141.4
#黑色金属材料类	1 239 667.9	1 035 274.9	192 515.3	8 446.1	3 431.6
有色金属材料类	184 260.4	178 684.4	1 039.7	982.4	3 553.9
化工类	867 735.7	850 569.2	13 591.7	2 424.4	1 150.4
建材类	295 153.1	89 944.8	204 538.4	482.4	187.5
木材类	122 324.8	103 913.4	16 835.2	1 399.5	176.7
金属制品类	60 929.1	54 400.8	5 341.8	995.6	190.9
一次转移价值的机电产品	1 200 000.7	1 141 490.5	45 751.8	10 343.8	2 414.6
其他类	2 952 865.3	2 838 543.8	89 918.1	10 367.6	14 035.8
二、按隶属关系分					
中　央	1 419 049.4	1 073 183.7	248 566.2	89 590.2	7 709.3
地　方	6 860 985.2	6 470 977.2	341 948.8	24 543.2	23 516.0
三、按经济类型分					
国有经济	4 308 291.8	3 638 629.9	548 911.9	108 386.3	12 363.7
集体经济	303 305.3	265 552.2	32 229.7	3 167.4	2 356.0
私营经济					
联营经济	42 843.3	41 900.5	22.1	60.9	859.8
股份制经济	347 572.5	345 977.5	463.9	1 025.4	105.7
“三资”经济	3 278 021.7	3 252 100.8	887.4	493.4	15 540.1
其他经济					
四、按国民经济行业分					
工　业	7 629 674.6	7 535 592.1	59 061.4	4 439.2	30 581.9
#石油和天然气开采业	270 350.5	235 782.4	26 143.9	2 130.0	6 294.2
纺织业	325 860.3	325 437.1	8.8	3.1	411.3
造纸及纸制品业	81 713.8	81 585.9			127.9
文教体育用品制造业	52 348.8	52 258.5		3.7	86.6
石油加工及炼焦业	521 431.9	514 331.9	7 096.0		4.0
化学原料及化学制品制造业	547 529.4	540 511.0	5 826.9	618.5	573.0
医药制造业	111 543.1	111 111.4	9.1	38.0	384.6
非金属矿物制品业	104 035.5	92 696.6	4 603.4	826.1	5 909.4
黑色金属冶炼及压延加工业	691 531.0	690 640.5		3.3	887.2
金属制品业	261 305.5	258 573.1	101.5	13.8	2 617.1
普通机械制造业	265 829.7	265 346.6	0.4	34.9	447.8
专用设备制造业	127 147.7	126 798.1	5.8	14.3	329.5
电气机械及器材制造业	194 837.8	194 488.6		15.4	333.8
电子及通信设备制造业	1 967 201.1	1 967 060.6		39.4	101.1
电力、蒸汽、热水的生产和供应业	191 035.3	175 416.4	14 366.2	216.3	1 036.4
建筑业	532 123.6	4 332.2	527 079.6	97	614.8
#土木工程建筑业	478 072.2	1 552.2	475 852.1	62.2	605.7
交通运输业	118 236.4	4 236.6	4 374	109 597.2	28.6
#铁路运输业	56 225.6	4 150.7	1 751.7	50 323.2	
公路运输业	6 628.5	4.7		6 614.8	9.0
水上运输业	33 682.2	81.2	2 622.3	30 959.1	19.6
航空运输业	8 982.6			8 982.6	

4－2　1996年主要原材料消费量

（县及县以上）

名　　称	单　位	合　计	工业生产消　　费	建筑施工消　　费	运输邮电消　　费
生　铁	吨	1 202 231	1 201 459	772	
钢　材	吨	1 621 637	1 037 578	559 444	12 077
#铁道用钢材	吨	11 637	1 014	4 488	6 135
普通大型钢材	吨	22 408	14 819	7 503	65
普通中型钢材	吨	63 874	36 627	26 496	678
普通小型钢材	吨	362 815	46 343	313 489	1 793
钢　带	吨	28 712	28 534	175	
线　材	吨	403 201	291 900	105 036	526
特厚钢板	吨	5 695	5 576	114	
中厚钢板	吨	139 997	99 290	39 321	1 184
薄钢板	吨	214 929	208 486	5 306	903
硅钢片	吨	10 909	10 874	35	
优质钢型材	吨	66 013	65 063	721	174
无缝钢管	吨	95 845	78 114	17 232	97
焊接钢管	吨	54 769	27 894	25 938	488
铜	吨	14 057.4	14 032.5	0.1	0.1
铝	吨	23 438.8	22 967.7	75.1	
铅	吨	16 951.8	16 943.7	0.1	8.0
锌	吨	7 588.0	7 581.2	3.0	3.8
锡	吨	260.2	260.1		
铜　材	吨	11 655.6	11 594.7	19.8	4.7
铝　材	吨	2 436.5	2 397.1	28.6	3.2
硫　酸	吨	111 376	111 231	2	38
烧　碱	吨	81 917	81 889		26
纯　碱	吨	109 370	109 279	20	11
天然橡胶	吨	21 228	21 033		1
合成橡胶	吨	20 991	20 585		
水　泥	吨	2 161 543	305 915	1 834 395	10 904
平板玻璃	平方米	120 654	66 925	48 088	5 339
原　木	立方米	516 194	490 509	25 469	74
#直接消费	立方米	337 896	335 383	2 439	74
锯　材	立方米	211 124	130 728	78 406	580
润滑油	吨	34 949	22 416	1 528	10 878

4-3 1996 年主要能源按国民经济行业分组消费量

（县及县以上）

行　　业	煤　炭（万吨）	焦　炭（万吨）	原　油（万吨）	汽　油（万吨）	柴　油（万吨）	燃料油（万吨）
总　　计	**500.75**	**104.59**	**26.93**	**10.61**	**43.19**	**67.14**
工　业	**471.55**	**104.45**	**26.92**	**7.25**	**17.08**	**53.58**
#石油和天然气开采业	16.59		14.23	1.58	9.82	6.88
非金属矿采选业	14.95			0.17	0.08	
食品加工业	7.89			0.11	0.37	
食品制造业	9.35			0.16	1.23	1.28
饮料制造业	16.98			0.15	0.08	
烟草加工业	5.28			0.02	0.01	
纺织业	49.73			0.14	0.10	
服装及其他纤维制品制造业	2.65			0.06	0.02	
皮革、毛皮、羽绒及其制品业	4.01			0.03	0.07	
木材加工及竹、藤、棕、草制品	7.97			0.04	0.16	
家具制造业	0.97	0.37		0.01	0.01	0.02
造纸及纸制品业	31.05			0.07	0.07	
印刷业、记录媒介的复制	1.14			0.04		
文教体育用品制造业	1.58			0.04		
石油加工及炼焦业	2.32			0.25	0.32	13.98
化学原料及化学制品制造业	89.73	5.87	11.46	0.90	0.62	8.73
医药制造业	13.05			0.08	0.03	
化学纤维制造业	4.39					
橡胶制品业	13.31			0.16		
塑料制品业	4.80			0.15		
非金属矿物制品业	43.16	0.42	1.01	0.15	0.52	4.22
黑色金属冶炼及压延加工业	52.83	18.97	0.09	0.36	2.40	16.15
有色金属冶炼及压延加工业	2.17	0.06		0.02		0.53
金属制品业	16.47	1.93	0.01	0.21	0.20	1.03
普通机械制造业	16.03	7.41		0.34	0.08	0.01
专用设备制造业	10.04	1.06		0.22	0.08	0.02
交通运输设备制造业	22.49	0.12		0.59	0.20	
电气机械及器材制造业	14.76	0.07	0.12	0.20	0.03	
电子及通信设备制造业	7.59	0.02		0.27	0.09	1.02
仪器仪表及文化、办公用机械制	3.26	0.08		0.06	0.01	
其他制造业	7.53	1.30		0.03	0.01	
电力、蒸汽、热水的生产和供应	8.29	0.26		0.51	0.40	0.29
煤气生产和供应业	4.43	66.50		0.07	0.06	
自来水的生产和供应业	1.38			0.14	0.01	
建筑业						
#土木工程建筑业	6.32	0.03		1.06	3.6	
线路、管道和设备安装业	3.56	0.01		0.19	0.47	
装修装饰业						
交通运输业	**18.31**	**0.10**	**0.01**	**2.15**	**22.06**	**13.58**
#铁路运输业	17.31	0.06		0.28	16.68	
公路运输业	0.51	0.04	0.01	1.58	0.99	0.02
水上运输业	0.03			0.05	3.27	13.45
航空运输业	0.31			0.05	0.01	

4－3续表

行　　业	天然气（亿立方米）	煤制气（亿立方米）	热　力（万百万千焦）	电　力（亿千瓦时）	其他石油制品（吨）
总　　计	**1.34**	**4.58**	**2 764.42**	**152.22**	**13.03**
工　业					
#石油和天然气开采业	1.07			12.18	
非金属矿采选业				0.80	
食品加工业			9.78	3.09	0.21
食品制造业			6.76	1.01	
饮料制造业			6.05	0.77	
烟草加工业			42.77	0.14	
纺织业			144.23	5.53	
服装及其他纤维制品制造业			0.14	0.66	
皮革、毛皮、羽绒及其制品业			0.01	0.20	
木材加工及竹、藤、棕、草制品业			1.13	0.64	
家具制造业			0.96	0.15	
造纸及纸制品业			14.12	1.63	0.02
印刷业、记录媒介的复制			2.14	0.12	
文教体育用品制造业			2.89	0.19	
石油加工及炼焦业			742.98	7.67	9.44
化学原料及化学制品制造业	0.02	0.08	1 456.46	21.21	0.06
医药制造业			31.02	1.02	0.01
化学纤维制造业				0.51	
橡胶制品业			47.67	0.96	0.02
塑料制品业			7.43	0.66	0.02
非金属矿物制品业			8.17	3.44	3.06
黑色金属冶炼及压延加工业	0.07	0.36	120.84	10.45	0.02
有色金属冶炼及压延加工业			0.02	0.49	
金属制品业	0.05	0.04	30.25	2.44	0.01
普通机械制造业	0.02		15.89	1.67	0.05
专用设备制造业		1.12	11.10	1.85	0.01
交通运输设备制造业			27.93	7.92	0.01
电气机械及器材制造业			7.29	2.24	
电子及通信设备制造业		0.04	10.25	2.85	0.01
仪器仪表及文化、办公用机械制造业			5.90	0.34	0.01
其他制造业	0.03	0.01	2.76	0.86	
电力、蒸汽、热水的生产和供应业			7.46	6.37	0.01
煤气生产和供应业	0.08	2.93		0.66	
自来水的生产和供应业				1.94	
建筑业					
#土木工程建筑业				45.87	0.05
线路、管道和设备安装业				0.88	
装修装饰业					
交通运输业					
#铁路运输业				2.12	
公路运输业				0.07	
水上运输业					
航空运输业				0.02	

4－4　分行业能源消费量及构成

（折标准煤）

行　业	能源消费总量(万吨)		构　成(%)		1996年万元产值	
	1995年	1996年	1995年	1996年	耗能源(吨标准煤)	耗电力(万千瓦小时)
总　计	**1 504.77**	**1 611.27**	**100.00**	**100.00**		
工　业	**1 227.75**	**1 322.22**	**81.59**	**82.06**	**0.95**	**0.07**
#石油和天然气开采业	105.27	176.87	7.00	10.98	2.10	0.14
非金属矿采选业	13.00	14.40	0.86	0.89	2.83	0.16
食品加工业	12.11	19.45	0.80	1.21	0.41	0.06
食品制造业	24.03	14.98	1.60	0.93	0.42	0.03
饮料制造业	17.14	15.77	1.14	0.98	0.70	0.03
烟草加工业	2.12	5.83	0.14	0.36	2.07	0.05
纺织业	80.12	63.27	5.32	3.93	1.07	0.09
服装及其他纤维制品制造业	9.30	4.69	0.62	0.29	0.24	0.03
皮革、毛皮、羽绒及其制品业	5.00	3.82	0.33	0.24	0.37	0.02
木材加工及竹、藤、棕、草制品业	9.60	8.61	0.64	0.53	0.73	0.05
家具制造业	1.13	1.73	0.08	0.11	0.53	0.05
造纸及纸制品业	27.44	29.50	1.82	1.83	2.49	0.14
印刷业、记录媒介的复制	3.39	1.50	0.23	0.09	0.26	0.02
文教体育用品制造业	1.78	2.07	0.12	0.13	0.10	0.01
石油加工及炼焦业	103.74	136.07	6.89	8.44	1.83	0.10
化学原料及化学制品制造业	230.12	254.03	15.29	15.77	1.69	0.14
医药制造业	15.22	14.68	1.01	0.91	0.49	0.03
化学纤维制造业	6.02	5.20	0.40	0.32	1.55	0.15
橡胶制品业	15.68	15.26	1.04	0.95	1.03	0.07
塑料制品业	11.74	6.62	0.78	0.41	0.31	0.03
非金属矿物制品业	69.38	58.81	4.61	3.65	2.83	0.17
黑色金属冶炼及压延加工业	241.87	236.00	16.07	14.65	2.78	0.12
有色金属冶炼及压延加工业	6.80	5.19	0.45	0.32	0.76	0.07
金属制品业	33.92	27.34	2.25	1.70	0.69	0.06
普通机械制造业	20.43	18.57	1.36	1.15	0.31	0.03
专用设备制造业	29.59	19.99	1.97	1.24	0.74	0.07
交通运输设备制造业	31.34	50.35	2.08	3.12	0.37	0.06
电气机械及器材制造业	16.41	20.59	1.09	1.28	0.50	0.05
电子及通信设备制造业	16.55	20.33	1.10	1.26	0.07	0.01
仪器仪表及文化、办公用机械制造业	4.70	4.12	0.31	0.26	0.31	0.03
其他制造业	5.74	10.69	0.38	0.66	1.94	0.16
电力、蒸汽、热水的生产和供应业	27.14	13.88	1.80	0.86	0.46	0.21
煤气生产和供应业	20.99	33.10	1.39	2.05	5.96	0.12
自来水的生产和供应业	8.94	8.91	0.59	0.55	3.09	0.67
建筑业	**185.34**	**203.93**	**12.32**	**12.66**	**1.17**	**0.27**
#土木工程建筑业	178.05	196.86	11.83	12.22	1.38	0.32
线路、管道和设备安装业	6.94	7.07	0.46	0.44	0.25	0.03
装修装饰业	0.35		0.02			
交通运输业	**86.08**	**85.12**	**5.72**	**5.28**	**0.75**	**0.02**
#铁路运输业	23.35	45.69	1.55	2.84	1.91	0.09
公路运输业	13.32	4.65	0.89	0.29	0.69	0.01
水上运输业	43.78	24.09	2.91	1.50	0.62	
航空运输业	5.63	5.49	0.37	0.34	0.77	

注：本表统计范围为县及县以上。

4－5 天津市用水情况

(1991－1996 年)

单位:万立方米

地 区	1991 年			1992 年			1993 年		
	小 计	地表水	地下水	小 计	地表水	地下水	小 计	地表水	地下水
总 计	**220 105**	**150 101**	**70 004**	**233 127**	**160 135**	**72 992**	**212 924**	**141 311**	**71 613**
市内六区	63 128	59 053	4 075	65 708	59 063	6 645	65 731	60 361	5 370
塘沽区	10 269	8 267	2 002	7 973	6 030	1 943	9 221	7 275	1 946
汉沽区	6 010	2 298	3 712	6 459	2 065	4 394	5 558	750	4 808
大港区	2 132	14	2 118	4 240	924	3 316	2 724	80	2 644
东丽区	6 953	3 355	3 598	4 843	2 759	2 084	4 829	2 418	2 411
西青区	7 823	4 417	3 406	8 583	5 912	2 671	5 971	3 310	2 661
津南区	14 485	9 115	5 370	11 215	6 869	4 346	6 699	2 859	3 840
北辰区	8 247	4 820	3 427	7 962	5 262	2 700	5 277	3 069	2 209
宁河县	24 959	21 865	3 094	30 266	26 087	4 179	58 353	24 156	4 197
武清县	22 843	12 398	10 445	22 715	11 145	11 570	21 619	11 323	10 296
静海县	13 272	8 300	4 972	14 029	8 924	5 105	5 418		5 418
宝坻县	25 119	12 686	12 433	32 560	20 095	12 465	34 302	20 838	13 464
蓟 县	14 865	3 513	11 352	16 574	5 000	11 574	17 222	4 873	12 349

地 区	1994 年			1995 年			1996 年		
	小 计	地表水	地下水	小 计	地表水	地下水	小 计	地表水	地下水
总 计	**213 868**	**144 671**	**69 197**	**222 724**	**153 418**	**69 306**	**233 538**	**167 956**	**65 582**
市内六区	65 376	59 576	5 800	67 032	63 232	3 800	59 856	56 056	3 800
塘沽区	8 571	6 553	2 018	8 604	6 936	1 668	14 540	13 088	1 452
汉沽区	6 910	2 129	4 781	8 182	3 310	4 872	7 745	2 105	5 640
大港区	2 935		2 935	3 540	344	3 196	3 356	40	3 316
东丽区	5 771	3 052	2 719	4 123	1 530	2 593	5 542	2 997	2 545
西青区	5 698	2 711	2 987	3 743	432	3 311	7 034	3 981	3 053
津南区	6 137	2 130	4 007	8 826	4 855	3 971	9 342	5 476	3 866
北辰区	5 300	3 000	2 300	6 032	3 710	2 332	6 865	4 650	2 215
宁河县	28 698	23 310	5 388	27 122	20 432	6 690	29 625	23 641	5 984
武清县	21 361	10 887	10 474	24 348	12 484	11 864	24 701	13 378	11 323
静海县	3 622	750	2 872	10 467	7 600	2 867	15 902	13 200	2 702
宝坻县	37 474	25 616	11 858	35 681	24 200	11 481	32 426	24 036	8 390
蓟 县	16 015	4 957	11 058	15 024	4 363	10 661	15 024	4 228	10 796

注:本表数据由天津市水利局提供。

4-6　天津市大型水库基本情况

项　　目	单　位	于桥水库	团泊洼水库	北大港水库
建设地点		蓟　县	静海县	大港区
所属河系		海　河	海　河	大清河
总库容	万立方米	155 900	18 000	50 000
设计灌溉面积	万公顷	4.2	6	
有效灌溉面积	万公顷	3	2.76	
年灌溉供水	万立方米	8 050	7 000	

4-7　天津市中型水库基本情况

名　称	座落地点	所在流域	总库容(万立方米)	灌溉面积(万亩)		年灌溉用水(万立方米)
				设　计	有　效	
七里海水库	宁河县	潮白新河	8 000	5.00	6.00	1 800
新地河水库	东丽区	金 钟 河	2 200	4.00	4.00	1 600
鸭淀水库	西青区	津港运河	3 200	7.00	10.00	2 500
黄港一库	塘沽区	黑 猪 河	1 100	1.30	0.83	800
黄港二库	塘沽区	黑 猪 河	4 800	3.10	2.67	400
北塘水库	塘沽区	永淀新河	1 700	1.40	2.00	1 400
营城水库	汉沽区	蓟 运 河	1 100	1.00	0.60	700
钱圈水库	大港区	马厂碱河	2 700	3.00	1.50	
沙井子水库	大港区	青 静 黄	2 000	2.00	2.00	
尔王庄水库	宝坻县	潮白新河	4 600			
上马台水库	武清县	北 运 河	2 680	12.90	12.90	2 390

五、财政和物价

PUBLIC FINANCE AND PRICE

1996 年地方财政收入	79.04 亿元
1996 年地方财政支出	113.21 亿元
其中:教育费支出	16.62 亿元
1996 年城市居民消费价格指数	109.0%
1996 年城市商品零售价格指数	105.1%

全市财政收入(亿元)

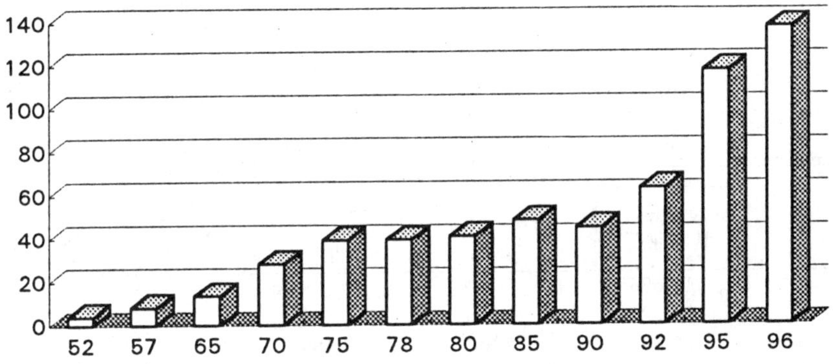

城市商品零售价格指数(%)

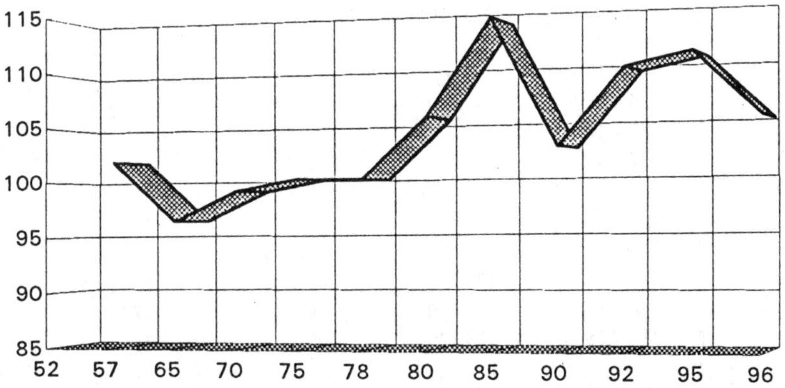

5－1　改革开放以来地方财政收支额

单位:万元

年　份	地方财政收　入	＃各项税收	地方财政支　出	＃基本建设	农业生产和农业事业费
1978	392 512	183 739	145 142	60 036	4 994
1979	376 428	190 903	152 053	68 251	7 164
1980	409 427	206 815	146 690	45 835	6 523
1981－1985	2 063 257	1 328 218	1 021 020	451 999	36 050
1981	401 991	220 370	144 806	49 592	6 655
1982	387 096	229 509	213 816	110 575	6 450
1983	387 439	244 933	204 885	99 732	7 307
1984	404 594	279 625	187 855	79 410	7 518
1985	482 137	353 781	269 658	112 690	8 120
1986－1990	2 465 573	2 281 734	1 804 573	263 981	74 485
1986	545 000	394 032	348 509	73 859	11 860
1987	558 715	422 370	311 631	51 963	12 394
1988	448 116	460 955	349 862	46 451	14 490
1989	464 918	507 071	392 618	48 930	16 834
1990	448 824	497 306	401 953	42 778	18 907
1991－1995	3 081 565	2 793 250	3 109 177	428 357	101 135
1991	580 916	509 179	474 742	39 148	18 828
1992	630 548	587 042	465 235	43 018	16 380
1993	749 605	725 170	512 658	69 849	19 972
1994	501 519	426 185	723 229	96 868	22 926
1995	618 977	545 674	933 313	179 474	28 132
1996	790 403	673 876	1 132 066	232 021	31 112

年　份	文教科卫事业费	＃教　育事业费	科　学事业费	预算外资金收入	预算外资金支出
1978	17 596	10 277	378		
1979	20 638	12 142	434		
1980	23 863	13 835	438		
1981－1985	176 115	97 197	3 825		
1981	26 266	14 732	457		
1982	29 749	16 644	542	172 291	157 109
1983	33 564	18 442	617	215 255	211 631
1984	38 214	20 704	1 092	270 939	250 889
1985	48 322	26 675	1 117	308 505	286 220
1986－1990	382 015	211 940	10 607	1 969 650	1 960 514
1986	60 934	34 184	1 131	349 258	335 558
1987	61 472	33 706	1 943	396 125	375 609
1988	74 731	41 746	2 422	453 966	402 764
1989	87 540	48 169	2 287	352 101	442 537
1990	97 338	54 135	2 824	418 200	404 046
1991－1995	762 498	452 866	22 960	1 819 672	1 741 566
1991	106 749	59 006	2 884	465 841	459 788
1992	116 551	66 388	3 289	514 366	499 958
1993	134 325	79 210	3 801	191 094	167 761
1994	185 469	114 138	5 982	279 673	260 278
1995	219 404	134 124	7 004	368 698	353 781
1996	201 669	166 214	8 187	739 028	697 139

注:1996 年预算外资金收支中增加了乡镇自筹统筹资金和社会保障基金收支数。

5－2 地方财政收入和支出

单位:万元

项目	1995年	1996年	项目	1995年	1996年
地方财政收入合计	**618 977**	**790 403**	**地方财政支出合计**	**933 313**	**1 132 066**
1.工商税收类	537 283	665 775	1.基本建设支出类	179 474	232 021
增值税(25%)	166 564	172 482	2.企业挖潜改造资金类	102 997	94 689
营业税	198 640	246 714	3.简易建筑费类	100	350
个人所得税	37 715	52 963	4.科技三项费用类	9 919	11 649
外商投资企业和外国企业所得税	37 744	85 822	5.支援农村生产支出类	9 510	12 199
城市维护建设税	47 765	50 961	6.农林水利气象等部门的事业费类	13 519	15 065
房产税	15 971	22 917	7.工业交通等部门的事业费类	9 123	10 510
城镇土地使用税	7 825	7 301	8.商业部门事业费类	1 203	779
其他工商税	25 059	26 615	9.城市维护费类	78 221	103 307
2.农牧业税和耕地占用税类	8 391	8 101	10.文教卫生事业费类	212 400	258 261
3.企业所得税类	101 781	111 764	11.科学事业费类	7 004	8 187
#国有企业所得税	27 834	33 183	12.其他部门的事业费类	22 530	35 341
集体企业所得税	35 575	49 227	13.抚恤和社会福利救济费类	15 651	18 392
私营企业所得税	1 294	2 466	14.国防支出类	542	916
地方股份制企业所得税	12 980	10 518	15.行政管理费类	57 248	62 898
4.国有企业计划亏损补贴类	－92 304	－87 900	16.公检法支出类	46 824	59 714
5.国家能源交通重点建设基金收入类	191	668	17.价格补贴支出类	25 550	55 026
6.国家预算调节基金类	280	927	18.其他支出类	83 927	87 640
7.所得税退税类	－12 793	－6 945	19.专项支出类	52 468	57 914
8.专项收入类	55 048	57 276	20.农业综合开发支出类	5 103	3 848
征收排污费收入	5 217	5 621	21.行政事业离退休经费类		3 360
征收城市水资源费收入	426	493			
下放港口以港养港收入	29 601	30 171	**上解中央财政支出**	**287 733**	**287 353**
教育费附加收入	19 804	20 991	原体制上解数	268 917	268 917
9.其他收入类	6 334	17 514	专项上解数	18 816	18 436
10.罚没收入、行政性收费收入类	14 766	23 223			

注:本表为地方财政收支决算数,全市财政收入数为1 374 521万元,比1995年增长15.8%。

5-3 1996年区县级财政收入

单位:万元

项 目	合 计	和平区	河东区	河西区	南开区	河北区	红桥区
区县级财政收入	**430 700**	**26 228**	**12 459**	**13 900**	**14 372**	**12 746**	**8 018**
工商税收类	327 853	19 302	9 258	10 532	11 190	10 367	5 954
#增值税	83 474	3 701	2 816	2 551	3 054	2 550	1 814
营业税	119 427	9 579	5 295	6 146	5 501	5 784	2 964
城建税	10 921						
农牧业税	7 052						
企业收入	66 478	5 035	2 145	1 817	1 916	1 045	1 098
其他收入	29 317	1 891	1 056	1 551	1 266	1 334	966

项 目	塘沽区	汉沽区	大港区	东丽区	西青区	津南区	北辰区
区县级财政收入	**27 055**	**6 524**	**15 738**	**20 082**	**16 426**	**14 363**	**15 099**
工商税收类	21 239	4 697	11 158	15 272	10 110	8 282	10 118
#增值税	2 507	1 143	2 786	4 170	2 943	2 672	2 871
营业税	10 710	1 405	5 419	8 171	4 128	3 089	4 233
城建税	3 631	1 270	1 369				
农牧业税	274	81	254	723	218	454	732
企业收入	3 526	911	2 441	2 822	5 412	4 846	3 245
其他收入	2 016	835	1 885	1 265	686	781	1 004

项 目	宁河县	武清县	静海县	宝坻县	蓟 县	开发区	保税区	科技园区
区县级财政收入	**9 108**	**15 759**	**15 402**	**15 628**	**11 853**	**141 607**	**13 332**	**5 001**
工商税收类	5 410	10 894	10 141	6 275	8 199	124 304	10 840	4 311
#增值税	2 067	2 873	4 442	2 528	1 668	31 891	1 013	1 414
营业税	1 481	3 734	3 246	1 750	3 488	26 066	4 503	2 735
城建税	664	598	788	359	708	1 348	186	
农牧业税	783	1 147	422	982	982			
企业收入	1 752	2 645	3 409	2 823	1 747	16 452	961	430
其他收入	1 163	1 073	1 430	5 548	925	851	1 531	260

5－4　1996年区县级财政支出

单位:万元

项　　目	合　计	和平区	河东区	河西区	南开区	河北区	红桥区
区县级财政支出	**611 864**	**27 029**	**25 346**	**23 095**	**23 681**	**22 492**	**20 653**
基本建设支出	179 135	2 175	7	113	1 296	2	6
支援农村生产支出	3 154						
农林水气事业费支出	6 890						
文教卫生事业费	137 977	9 783	9 138	9 802	9 347	9 376	8 359
行政管理费	40 161	2 300	2 067	2 265	2 047	1 758	1 441
公检法支出	27 052	2 033	1 894	1 873	2 191	1 959	1 694
其他支出	217 495	10 738	12 240	9 042	8 800	9 397	9 153

项　　目	塘沽区	汉沽区	大港区	东丽区	西青区	津南区	北辰区
区县级财政支出	**35 671**	**11 079**	**22 523**	**20 032**	**18 861**	**14 857**	**17 047**
基本建设支出	100	526	1 803	1 428	2 982	1 071	881
支援农村生产支出	232	70	616	456	268	371	243
农林水气事业费支出	880	266	562	516	207	396	323
文教卫生事业费	10 411	3 564	4 516	6 536	5 085	5 512	5 887
行政管理费	3 681	1 612	2 235	1 633	2 234	1 543	1 795
公检法支出	2 742	949	1 236	1 277	1 217	854	870
其他支出	17 625	4 092	11 555	8 186	6 868	5 110	7 048

项　　目	宁河县	武清县	静海县	宝坻县	蓟　县	开发区	保税区	科技园区
区县级财政支出	**13 921**	**20 540**	**21 452**	**22 775**	**19 633**	**212 477**	**15 329**	**3 371**
基本建设支出	19	10	414	3 860	42	151 976	8 132	2 292
支援农村生产支出	56	109	410	158	165			
农林水气事业费支出	437	970	885	646	802			
文教卫生事业费	4 615	9 184	8 305	8 920	8 230	1 403		4
行政管理费	2 355	2 788	2 563	2 432	2 232	721	388	71
公检法支出	734	1 047	1 300	874	924	1 274	110	
其他支出	5 705	6 432	7 575	5 885	7 238	57 103	6 699	1 004

5-5　天津市国家税务局各项税收情况

单位:万元

项　　目	1995年	1996年	项　　目	1995年	1996年
总　　计	**1 213 459**	**1 302 329**	固定资产投资		
一、工商税合计	**1 159 456**	**1 242 121**	方向调节税	126	71
增值税	920 557	918 841	工商税收税款滞		
营业税	29 451	46 054	纳金、罚款收入	5 991	3 501
消费税	97 467	103 885	**二、企业所得税**	**28 363**	**32 649**
专项调节税	137		国有企业	15 979	17 393
个人所得税	25 628	34 308	集体企业	11 631	14 893
外商投资企业和			私营企业	10.9	32
外国企业所得税	38 521	88 753	股份制企业	728	204
城市维护建设税	37 021	38 048	联营企业	13.7	127
车船使用税	170	201	**三、教育费附加**	**14 953**	**15 227**
房产税	2 568	5 830	**四、国家能源交通重点**		
屠宰税	178	252	**建设基金**	**2 553**	**1 386**
城镇土地使用税	3.4	4.1	**五、国家预算调节基金**	**3 348**	**1 864**
印花税	1 639	2 373	**六、其他收入**	**4 787**	**9 082**

5-6　改革开放以来各种物价总指数

年　份	以上年为100		以1991年为100		以1978年为100	
	城市商品零售价格总指数	城市居民消费价格总指数	城市商品零售价格总指数	城市居民消费价格总指数	城市商品零售价格总指数	城市居民消费价格总指数
1978	100.0	100.0			100.0	100.0
1979	101.1	101.0			101.1	101.0
1980	105.5	105.1			106.7	106.1
1981	101.5	101.3			108.3	107.5
1982	100.5	100.5			108.8	108.0
1983	100.5	100.5			109.3	108.5
1984	101.8	101.8			111.3	110.5
1985	113.9	113.1			126.8	125.0
1986	107.2	106.8			135.9	133.5
1987	106.9	106.8			145.3	142.6
1988	117.7	116.9			171.0	166.7
1989	115.1	114.7			196.8	191.2
1990	102.7	103.0			202.1	196.9
1991	108.0	110.2	100.0	100.0	218.3	217.0
1992	109.4	111.4	109.4	111.4	238.8	241.7
1993	114.3	117.6	125.0	131.0	272.9	284.2
1994	115.6	124.0	144.6	162.4	315.5	352.4
1995	110.6	115.3	159.9	187.3	348.9	406.3
1996	105.1	109.0	168.1	204.2	366.7	442.9

5-7 城市居民消费价格分类指数

(以上年为100)

项　目	1995年	1996年
居民消费价格总指数	**115.3**	**109.0**
1.食　品	121.5	106.7
粮　食	139.8	106.1
淀粉及薯类	149.0	99.7
干豆类及豆制品	108.5	132.5
油脂类	118.9	90.4
肉禽及其制品	129.6	100.0
蛋　类	116.5	119.7
水产品	113.7	105.3
菜　类	121.1	109.5
调味品	118.3	117.3
糖　类	114.1	101.9
烟草类	106.9	101.5
酒和饮料	106.3	104.3
干鲜瓜果类	123.9	109.5
糕点类	112.0	111.8
奶及奶制品	123.2	110.5
其他食品	110.7	116.6
饮食业	118.1	110.2
2.衣着类	107.2	104.8
3.家庭设备及用品	104.4	103.4
4.医疗保健	115.5	106.6
5.交通和通讯工具	98.4	100.8
6.娱乐教育文化用品	102.0	107.8
7.居　住	116.0	137.1
8.服务项目	112.8	117.4
电讯费	100.0	100.1
邮　费	100.0	108.5
交通费	103.3	115.7
洗理美容费	124.0	136.7
文娱费	129.9	125.4
学杂保育费	105.9	120.8
修理及其他服务费	116.7	107.9
医疗保健服务费	164.5	151.2

5-8 城市商品零售价格分类指数

(以上年为100)

项　目	1995年	1996年
商品零售价格总指数	**110.6**	**105.1**
1.食　品	121.5	107.9
粮　食	134.4	115.4
油脂类	114.4	90.9
肉禽蛋	125.2	105.9
水产品	113.8	106.1
鲜　菜	124.3	109.4
干　菜	114.8	107.8
鲜　果	122.2	109.7
干　果	123.7	113.7
其他食品	117.2	113.2
饮食业	114.4	107.2
2.饮料烟酒	106.3	103.9
3.服装鞋帽	106.8	104.7
4.纺织品	108.3	101.5
5.中西药品	111.6	104.0
6.化妆品	111.2	105.6
7.书报杂志	110.4	130.9
8.文化体育用品	111.7	107.5
9.日用品	109.1	105.6
10.家用电器	102.2	100.2
11.首　饰	97.8	99.4
12.燃　料	102.7	116.5
13.建筑装璜材料	100.8	101.4
14.机电产品	95.3	96.9

5-9 城市农贸市场农产品成交价格分类指数

(以上年为100)

项　目	1995年	1996年
农产品成交价格总指数	**118.2**	**101.9**
1.粮　食	124.0	107.5
2.油脂类	129.3	93.3
3.肉禽蛋	125.2	99.2
4.水产品	115.2	106.6
5.鲜　菜	120.7	101.3
6.干　菜	100.3	104.0
7.鲜　果	121.1	108.7
8.干　果	110.4	107.9

5－10 固定资产投资价格指数

(以上年为100)

项 目	1995年	1996年
社会投资总额	**107.6**	**102.5**
建筑安装工程	108.3	102.9
设备工器具购置	104.4	100.9
其他费用	111.6	103.4

5－11 工业主要原材料、燃料及动力购进价格指数

(以上年为100)

项 目	1995年	1996年
全部原材料	**112.8**	**99.0**
燃料、动力类	103.8	108.5
黑色金属材料类	91.6	100.2
有色金属材料类	129.2	88.2
化工原料类	132.4	92.8
木材及纸浆类	97.6	99.4
建筑材料类	103.0	103.9
非金属矿类	103.2	92.0
农副产品类	132.7	105.5
纺织原料类	122.0	92.2

5－12 主要工业产品出厂价格指数

(以上年为100)

项 目	1995年	1996年
全部工业品	**110.2**	**100.9**
轻工业	116.7	101.3
以农产品为原料	120.9	102.6
以非农产品为原料	111.3	99.4
重工业	105.7	100.7
采掘业	132.9	102.7
原料工业	101.6	99.7
加工工业	106.7	101.5
生产资料	110.2	100.3
采掘业	132.9	102.7
原料工业	106.9	99.0
加工工业	111.6	101.7
生活资料	110.1	102.0
食 品	118.5	107.1
衣 着	114.5	99.9
一般日用品	108.3	103.9
耐用消费品	101.5	99.5

六、城市建设和环境保护

URBAN CONSTRUCTION AND ENVIRONMENT PROTECTION

1996 年铺装道路长度	3 234 公里
1996 年公共电汽车线路条数	251 条
1996 年人均绿地	3.5 平方米
1996 年全市气化率	92.8%

年末住宅建筑面积(万平方米)

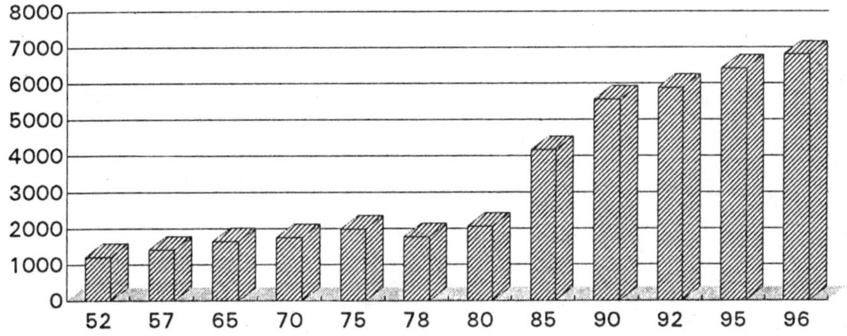

城市铺装道路长度(公里)

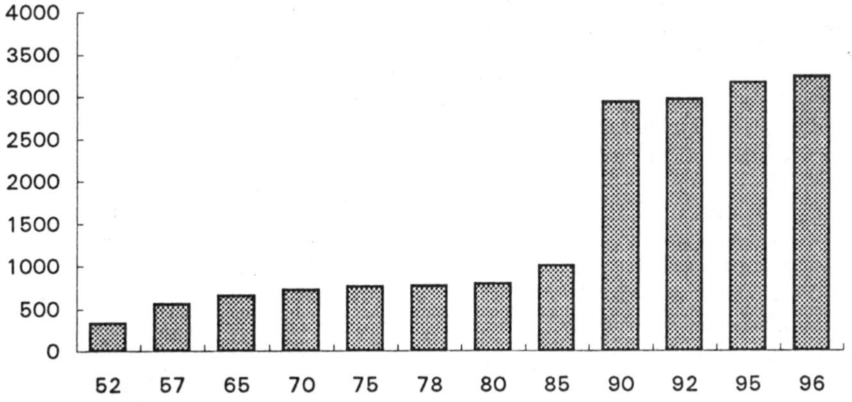

6－1　市政公用设施水平

指　　标	单　位	1990年	1992年	1995年	1996年
人均日生活用水量	公斤	117.5	124.0	127.9	128.1
用水普及率	%	100.0	100.0	100.0	100.0
每万人拥有公共交通车辆	标台	4.8	5.7	5.4	6.0
气化率	%	83.0	87.6	92.2	92.8
人均拥有道路面积	平方米	6.2	7.0	7.4	7.5
排水管道密度	公里/平方公里	7.9	8.1	14.7	14.5
污水处理率	%	18.4	35.0	58.0	58.1
人均公共绿地面积	平方米	2.2	2.4	3.2	3.5
建城区绿化覆盖率	%	11.5	13.5	17.6	19.3
垃圾粪便无害化处理率	%	18.7	48.2	54.4	57.6

注:1995年部分数据为市政公用设施普查数。1995年以后统计的地域范围包括了市辖区内建制镇的设施。

6－2　主要年份城市房屋建筑面积

单位:万平方米

年　份	年末实有房屋建筑面积	#本年新建	年末实有住宅建筑面积	#本年新建	人均住宅居住面积(平方米)
1952	2 202.6		1 226.1		3.7
1957	2 631.5	137.9	1 407.0	65.4	3.3
1962	3 050.0	43.5	1 572.3	13.3	3.1
1965	3 299.0	86.9	1 652.0	26.6	3.0
1970	3 566.4	89.9	1 750.0	21.4	3.7
1975	4 135.0	156.8	1 989.0	55.7	4.2
1980	4 509.0	265.6	2 049.0	176.1	3.6
1985	8 914.0	579.0	4 166.9	323.0	5.6
1986	9 541.0	660.0	4 524.0	369.0	6.0
1987	9 881.0	424.0	4 699.0	213.3	6.1
1988	10 437.3	528.6	5 085.0	322.0	6.4
1989	10 875.6	485.9	5 368.6	309.3	6.6
1990	11 189.8	363.2	5 553.3	203.1	6.7
1991	11 476.0	344.5	5 722.9	194.5	6.8
1992	11 768.4	395.7	5 872.0	214.7	6.9
1993	12 056.1	492.0	6 021.0	302.2	6.9
1994	12 509.5	614.6	6 349.1	448.4	7.1
1995	13 085.3	688.3	6 404.4	487.7	7.5
1996	13 608.0	657.2	6 804.0	483.4	7.7

注:1950－1996年城市累计新建房屋11 758.8万平方米,新建住宅6 601.1万平方米。

6-3 城市房屋建筑面积

单位:万平方米

分 组	年末实有房屋建筑面积			#住宅建筑面积		
	1992年	1995年	1996年	1992年	1995年	1996年
年末实有城市房屋建筑面积	**11 768.44**	**13 085.30**	**13 608**	**5 871.97**	**6 404.40**	**6 803.60**
#房管部门直管产	3 917.67	3 807.00	4 009	2 602.03	3 025.00	3 108.10
私 产	817.92	2 045.10	2 318	818.40	2 045.10	2 317.30
#本年新建	**395.73**	**688.30**	**657.19**	**214.74**	**487.70**	**483.38**
#房管部门直管产	304.70	264.75	276.71	133.70	114.32	156.86
私 产	26.20	215.00	12.80	25.30	215.00	12.24

注:本表包括城区和各系统座落在郊区的房屋,不包括郊区、乡村和农民自建的房屋。

6-4 城市燃气设备能力

项 目	单 位	1990年	1992年	1995年	1996年	1996比1995年增长%
1.液化石油气						
储 罐	个	39	39	37	47	27.0
储气能力	吨	4 712	4 712	4 782	6 064	26.8
2.天然气						
储气能力	万立方米	53.8	53.8	53.8	53.8	
管道长度	公里	2 259	2 299	2 407	2 407	
3.煤制气						
储气能力	万立方米	50	60	73.6	73.6	
管道长度	公里	1 599	1 632	2 031	2 260	11.3

6-5 城市燃气销售量和用气户数

项 目	销售量(吨;万立方米)			用气户数(户)		
	1992年	1995年	1996年	1992年	1995年	1996年
1.液化石油气	**45 935**	**86 522**	**67 031**	**394 690**	**408 393**	**443 680**
#工业用	6 712	5 622	4 407	233	329	336
福利用	305	2 109	1 738	1 557	3 508	3 741
民 用	35 008	62 526	42 213	392 900	404 556	430 464
2.天然气	**15 058**	**14 155**	**13 442**	**521 978**	**563 674**	**576 032**
#工业用	4 659	2 794	2 317	59	59	57
福利用	2 014	1 818	1 713	2 437	2 553	2 594
民 用	7 655	8 494	8 082	519 482	561 062	573 381
3.煤制气	**17 286**	**19 664**	**20 099**	**345 909**	**408 111**	**455 705**
#工业用	3 537	2 860	1 978	24	27	27
福利用	426	515	878	861	1 003	1 047
民 用	12 215	15 190	16 198	345 024	407 081	454 631

6－6 城市自来水

指标	单位	1990年	1992年	1995年	1996年	1996比1995年增长%
综合生产能力	万吨/日	199.1	218.7	221.2	266.8	20.6
供水管道	公里	3 485	3 578	4 005	4 403	9.9
供水总量	万吨	63 203	63 331	67 669	71 821	6.1
售水总量	万吨	59 628	59 579	60 242	64 171	6.5
#生活用水	万吨	24 566	24 363	23 726	23 812	0.4
生产用水	万吨	34 104	35 216	36 516	40 359	10.5
市内最高一日供水	万吨	170.5	162.2	169.7	172.24	1.5
用水人口	万人	572.6	538.3	508.1	509.3	0.2

6－7 城市市政设施情况

指标	单位	1990年	1992年	1995年	1996年
1.道 路					
铺装道路长度	公里	2 932	2 693	3 157	3 234
#高级、次高级	公里	2 699	2 869	3 033	3 117
铺装道路面积	万平方米	2 825	3 130	3 453	3 539
#高级、次高级	万平方米	2 781	3 240	3 378	3 459
人行道面积	万平方米	371	390	474	485
2.桥 梁					
桥梁座数	座	148	153	456	458
#永久性	座	139	150	455	457
#立交桥	座	18	24	35	36
3.路灯盏数	**盏**	**66 884**	**74 961**	**81 641**	**79 551**
4.排泄污水能力					
污水年排放量	万吨	53 218	57 002	69 911	78 773
工业废水	万吨	26 828	34 994	47 882	55 984
生活污水	万吨	26 390	22 008	22 029	22 789
排水管道	公里	2 645	2 748	5 284	5 446
排水泵站	座	183	188	285	299
排水能力	立方米/秒	575	586	733	789
污水处理厂	座	1	1	2	2
污水处理厂能力	万吨/日	26.9	26.9	66.9	66.9

6-8 城市公共交通

指　标	单 位	1990年	1992年	1995年	1996年
一、公共汽车					
营运车辆	辆	1 857	1 976	2 117	2 524
线路条数	条	158	161	227	251
线路长度	公里	2 989	3 105	5 171	5 592
乘客人数	万人次	70 377	61 121	55 798	51 122
平均每日乘客人数	万人次	193	167	153	140
平均每日每车乘客人数	人次	1 027	848	863	795
二、出租汽车					
全社会营运出租汽车	辆	2 942	3 062	26 268	27 565
#公交系统内	辆	531	541	1 667	2 621
三、地　铁					
电动客车	辆	22	22	21	21
行驶里程	万公里	102	91	68	74
乘客人数	万人次	1 088	927	777	523

6-9 城市园林绿化情况

指　标	单 位	1990年	1992年	1995年	1996年
公 园(含动物园)	个	115	127	143	150
花　圃	个	11	10	13	15
园林绿地总面积	公顷	1 851.56	1 992.59	3 017	3 150.78
#公共绿地	公顷	993.19	1 108.77	1 468	1 618.40
公园面积	公顷	599.08	651.12	700	728.40
街道绿地	公顷	394.11	457.65	655	771.51
花圃面积	公顷	28.52	28.56	39.32	54.83
专用绿地	公顷	309.09	332.34	766	903.85
年末实有树木	万株	932.61	1 125.18	1 382	1 483.44
#行道树	万株	86.41	120.70	165.12	170.05
全年植树	万株	91.73	120.11	113	89.92

6－10　1996年公园分布

地　区	公园个数	公园面积（公顷）	地　区	公园个数	公园面积（公顷）
合　计	**150**	**728.40**	塘沽区	6	50.83
和平区	14	12.72	开发区	3	3.03
河东区	16	62.18	汉沽区	5	33.20
河西区	25	119.92	大港区	4	42.34
南开区	16	257.99	东丽区	5	9.74
河北区	23	75.68	西青区	3	3.74
红桥区	24	46.60	津南区	3	4.27
			北辰区	3	6.15

6－11　城市集中供热

项　　目	单　　位	1990年	1992年	1995年	1996年
供热能力:蒸汽	吨/小时	160	190	9 022	10 932
热水	兆瓦/小时	259	627	1 630	1 763
供热总量:蒸汽	万吨/年	34	37	2 367	2 771
热水	百亿千焦/年	51	673	1 114	1 348
供热面积	万平方米	767	914	2 645	3 114

6－12　城市环境卫生事业发展情况

指　　标	单　位	1990年	1992年	1995年	1996年
一、清运垃圾粪便工作量					
清扫街道面积	万平方米	4 298	4 524	4 694	4 278
清运垃圾	万吨	217	230	180	185
清运粪便	万吨	24.9	52	19	16
处理垃圾粪便	万吨	61.4	136	199	201
二、大中型环卫机械					
扫路吸尘车	辆	46	36	22	27
洒水车	辆	51	51	47	43
垃圾车	辆	607	555	540	500
吸粪车	辆	77	70	65	73
三、环境卫生设施					
公共厕所	座	2 389	2 302	3 087	3 033
垃圾转运站	座	194	208	222	210
无害化处理厂	座	7	7	9	9
无害化处理厂能力	吨/日	1 677	2 673	3 341	2 917
四、环卫职工人数	**人**	**11 179**	**11 141**	**10 918**	**10 943**

6－13　环境保护系统基本情况

指　　标	单　位	1990 年	1992 年	1995 年	1996 年	1996 比 1995 年增长数
一、年末实有人数	**人**	**1 258**	**1 314**	**1 505**	**1 532**	**27**
科技人员	人	778	843	855	1 041	186
#科研人员	人	145	164	198	185	－13
监测人员	人	386	400	412	446	34
行政干部	人	279	253	265	265	
工　人	人	201	218	212	226	14
科技业务人员占全部人员比重	%	62	64.2	57	68	11
二、仪器设备总数	**台.套**	**1 242**	**1 986**	**1 881**		
三、机动车(船)拥有量	**辆.艘**	**185**	**154**	**118**		
#监测车	辆	18	32	35		
监测船	艘	4	2	2		

6－14　废气排放及处理情况

指　　标	单　位	1990 年	1992 年	1995 年	1996 年	1996 比 1995 年增长数
工业废气排放总量	**亿标立方米**	**1 336**	**1 328**	**1 705**	**1 536**	**－169**
1. 生产工艺过程中废气排放量	亿标立方米	245	220	376	333	－43
#经过净化处理	亿标立方米	147	174	336	291	－45
2. 燃料燃烧过程中废气排放量	亿标立方米	1 091	1 110	1 329	1 203	－126
#经过消烟除尘	亿标立方米	785	799	1 244	1 151	－93
废气中:二氧化硫	万吨	22	23	26	20	－6

6－15　城市环境噪声情况

指　　标	单　位	1990 年	1992 年	1995 年	1996 年	1996 比 1995 年增长数
城市交通噪声等效声级	分贝	71	70	71	59	－12
城市环境噪声达标面积	平方公里			112	129	17

6－16　工业粉尘、工业废渣排放及处理利用情况

指　　标	单　位	1990 年	1992 年	1995 年	1996 年	1996 比 1995 年增长数
一、工业粉尘产生量	**万吨**	**22**	**20**	**27**	**26**	**－1**
工业粉尘排放量	万吨	6	4	3	3	
工业粉尘回收量	万吨	16	16	24	23	－1
工业粉尘回收率	%	73	80	88	88	
二、工业废渣产生量	**万吨**	**419**	**417**	**554**	**594**	**40**
#已处理量	万吨	27	82	153		
处理率	%	6	20	27		
已综合利用量	万吨	261	331	409	454	45
综合利用率	%	62	72	73	76	3
历年工业废渣堆存总量	**万吨**	**1 080**	**1 200**	**1 281**	**1 254**	**－27**

6－17　工业废水排放及处理量

指　　标	单　位	1990 年	1992 年	1995 年	1996 年	1996 比 1995 年增长数
工业废水排放量	**万吨**	**22 865**	**21 084**	**21 897**	**20 446**	**－1 451**
#经过处理的	万吨	6 480	6 567	6 291	7 921	1 630
符合排放标准的	万吨	12 186	12 137	15 985	15 157	－828
#通过处理达标的	万吨	3 396	5 077	4 770	4 798	28
工业废水处理率	**%**	**46**	**75.1**	**90**	**95**	**5**
工业废水达标率	**%**	**53**	**57.6**	**73**	**74**	**1**
工业废水中有害物质						
汞	吨	1.27	1.13	0.71	0.20	－0.51
镉	吨	0.14	0.02	0.38	0.28	－0.10
六价铬	吨	18.28	4.52	2.24	2.30	0.06
铅	吨	0.20	0.85	3.78	0.47	－3.31
砷	吨	2.56	0.77	3.43	0.31	－3.12
酚	吨	161.22	89.96	136.34	128.09	－8.25
氰化物	吨	21.47	12.74	4.05	1.01	－3.04
石油类	吨	1 790	1 411	1 239	879	－360
化学耗氧量	万吨	12.47	9.68	8.94	6.15	－2.79
悬浮物	万吨		4.19	4.26	4.25	－0.01
硫化物	吨		555.00	352.00	172.15	－179.85

6－18 “三废”综合利用及污染事故处理情况

指 标	单 位	1990年	1992年	1995年	1996年	1996比1995年增长数
“三废”综合利用产品产值	万元	8 506	8 856	12 534	18 668	6 134
“三废”综合利用利润	万元	2 031	1 946	297	3 314	3 017
污染事故	次	174	6		81	
污染赔款总额	万元	300	230		263	
污染罚款总额	万元	233	2		14	

6－19 排污费征收、使用和企事业污染治理情况

指 标	单 位	1990年	1992年	1995年	1996年	1996比1995年增长数
一、排污费交纳单位	个	**2 809**	**4 308**	**5 987**		
排污费征收额	万元	2 858	4 497	5 217	5 106	－111
排污费支出额	万元	2 863	4 317	6 264	6 644	380
二、企事业单位污染治理						
1.资金合计	万元	6 170	12 077	25 375	17 266	－8 109
治理废水	万元	3 309	5 060	10 183	6 633	－3 550
治理废气	万元	1 966	4 381	7 906	2 860	－5 046
治理废渣	万元	66	991	4 224	489	－3 735
治理噪声	万元	276	438	747	1 249	502
其 他	万元	553	1 207	2 316	6 035	3 719
2.当年安排治理项目	个	632	482	429	254	－175
3.当年竣工项目	个	566	453	382	238	－144
治理废水	个	151	102	88	47	－41
治理废气	个	284	251	193	126	－67
治理废渣	个	8	23	21	16	－5
治理噪声	个	101	58	58	26	－32
其 他	个	22	19	22	23	1

七、人民生活和社会福利

PEOPLE'S LIVEHOOD AND SOCIAL WELFARE

1996 年城市居民人均年生活费收入	5 525 元
1996 年农民人均年纯收入	3 142 元
1996 年末城乡居民储蓄存款余额	724 亿元
1996 年城市人均居住面积	7.7 平方米

城乡居民储蓄存款余额（亿元）

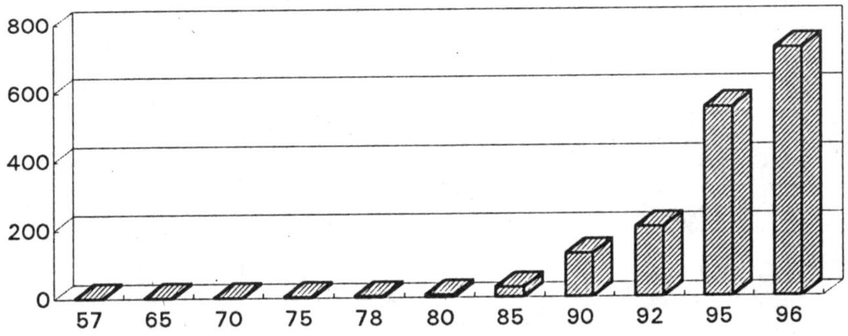

城市居民人均年生活费收入（元）

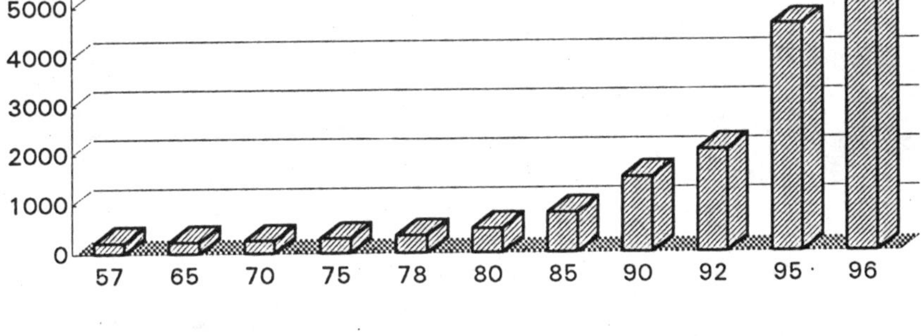

7－1　城乡居民物质文化生活水平提高情况

指　　标	单　位	1991年	1992年	1993年	1994年	1995年	1996年
一、居民收入支出							
职工年平均工资	元	2 724	3 118	4 080	5 364	6 501	7 643
城市居民家庭							
平均每人年生活费收入	元	1 699	2 080	2 579	3 725	4 626	5 525
平均每人年消费性支出	元	1 586	1 907	2 322	3 301	4 064	4 680
农民人均年纯收入	元	1 168	1 410	1 593	1 956	2 531	3 142
农民人均年生活消费支出	元	796	923	1 011	1 274	1 717	2 101
二、居民年平均消费水平							
全市居民	元	1 453	1 689	2 111	2 720	3 380	4 129
农业居民	元	883	1 007	1 224	1 444	1 852	2 381
非农业居民	元	1 902	2 219	2 799	3 701	4 546	5 441
三、储　蓄							
城乡居民人均年末储蓄余额	元	1 877	2 306	3 044	4 430	6 147	8 058
四、住　房							
城市平均每人居住面积	平方米	6.8	6.9	6.9	7.1	7.5	7.7
农村平均每人居住面积	平方米	17.16	17.48	18.68	19.06	19.43	21.83
五、交通和通信							
城市每万人公共电汽车拥有量	标台	5.0	5.7	6.0	5.6	5.4	6.0
城市每万人铺装道路长度	公里	5.12	5.11	5.38	6.85	6.78	6.89
每人每年函件交寄	件	7.2	7.8	9.6	12.1	13.6	12.3
全市每百人拥有电话	部	4.04	4.93	7.35	10.78	15.16	19.4
#市内每百人拥有电话	部	6.22	8.16	12.34	18.02	25.02	31.7
六、人均用煤、气、水、电							
全市人均生活用电量	千瓦小时	102	116	127	151	161	189
全市人均生活用煤量	公斤	449	387	356	352	352	364
城市煤气普及率	%	82.5	87.6	89.0	90.8	92.2	92.8
城市人均生活用水量	吨	46	45	45	45	47	47

注：1.居民年平均消费水平，1991年按国民收入计算，1992年以后按国内生产总值计算。2.人均生活用煤为零售量。

7－1续表

指　　标	单　位	1991年	1992年	1993年	1994年	1995年	1996年
七、每万人拥有零售商业、饮食业网点数	**个**	**118**	**113**	**134**	**154**	**176**	**197**
八、平均每人消费品零售总额	**元**	**1 834**	**2 069**	**2 577**	**3 415**	**4 208**	**5 243**
食品类	元	761	856	985	1 455	1 895	2 295
衣着类	元	318	349	454	562	703	852
用品类	元	720	813	1 073	1 337	1 536	2 007
九、文　化							
每百户城市居民家庭拥有							
电视机	台	127.6	130.2	133.4	138.0	131.6	135.8
录音机	台	77.6	81.6	83.8	82.4	79.0	75.4
每百户农民居民家庭拥有							
电视机	台	98	105	113	115	120	120
录音机	台	33	45	49	46	52	53
平均每人每年有图书	册	15.6	15.9	12.9	11.0	7.8	9.3
平均每百人每天有报纸	份	13.0	14.7	13.9	16.6	16.5	17.1
十、教　育							
每万人中有各级学校学生	人	1 581	1 607	1 605	1 673	1 649	1 766
#大学生	人	57	60	68	75	76	79
学龄儿童入学率	%	99.3	99.2	98.0	99.6	99.7	99.8
十一、卫　生							
每万人拥有医院床位	张	40.3	41.0	41.6	41.7	41.8	42.7
每万人拥有医生	人	37.1	36.5	37.4	37.6	37.7	36.8
平均期望寿命	岁	73.33	73.33	73.33	73.33	74.26	74.26
男	岁	72.07	72.07	72.07	72.07	72.92	72.92
女	岁	74.80	74.80	74.80	74.80	75.74	75.74
十二、赡养人口							
城市每一就业者赡养人口	人	0.45	0.44	0.48	0.37	0.37	0.36
农村每一劳动力负担人口	人	0.6	0.5	0.44	0.42	0.43	0.45
十三、城市绿化							
城市绿化覆盖率	%	13.0	13.5	15.5	16.5	17.6	19.3
城市每人占有公共绿地	平方米	2.3	2.5	2.6	2.8	3.2	3.5

注：1993年以后每万人拥有商、饮、服网点数，不包括服务业。赡养人口不含劳动者本人。

7－2　城市居民家庭基本情况

（1992－1996年）

指　　标	单　位	1992年	1993年	1994年	1995年	1996年
调查户数	户	500	500	500	500	500
平均每户人口	人	3.23	3.19	3.15	3.14	3.11
平均每户就业人口	人	1.89	1.86	1.75	1.74	1.73
平均每户就业面	%	58.51	58.31	55.56	55.41	55.63
平均每户就业者负担人口	人	1.71	1.72	1.79	1.80	1.80
平均每人年实际收入	元	2 238.76	2 769.46	3 982.37	4 931.41	5 975.94
平均每人年生活费收入	元	2 080.08	2 579.06	3 724.75	4 626.40	5 525.48
平均每人年消费性支出	元	1 907.17	2 322.19	3 301.37	4 064.10	4 679.61

7－3　1996年城市不同收入水平居民家庭基本情况

（按平均每人每月生活费收入分组）

项　　目	调查户数（户）	平均每户人　口（人）	平均每户就业人口（人）	平均每一就业者负担人口（人）	平均每人年实际收入（元）	平均每人年生活费收入（元）	平均每人年消费性支出（元）
全　　市	**500**	**3.11**	**1.73**	**1.80**	**5 975.94**	**5 525.48**	**4 679.61**
1.最低收入户（251.05元以下）	50	3.21	1.70	1.89	2 848.86	2 536.32	2 799.45
#更低收入户（216.58元以下）	25	3.09	1.65	1.87	2 728.29	2 223.59	2 828.77
2.低收入户（253.46－294.09元）	50	3.32	1.76	1.89	3 608.66	3 299.72	3 358.65
3.中等偏下收入户（294.42－380.65元）	100	3.30	1.70	1.94	4 368.02	4 076.85	3 764.52
4.中等收入户（380.80－477.97元）	100	3.03	1.64	1.85	5 478.07	5 101.69	4 570.62
5.中等偏上收入户（478.70－596.33元）	100	3.00	1.70	1.76	6 779.66	6 333.08	5 310.37
6.高收入户（599.29－743.11元）	50	2.99	1.83	1.63	8 564.95	7 922.25	5 783.68
7.最高收入户（744.20元以上）	50	2.87	1.96	1.46	12 574.22	11 473.26	8 168.58

7－4 城市居民家庭平均每人全年消费性支出分类

(1992－1996年)

单位:元

项 目	1992年	1993年	1994年	1995年	1996年	1996比1995年增长％
消费性支出	**1 907.17**	**2 322.19**	**3 301.37**	**4 064.10**	**4 679.61**	**15.1**
1.食 品	**1 097.79**	**1 268.32**	**1 719.18**	**2 117.14**	**2 398.47**	**13.3**
#粮 食	183.90	214.88	315.90	407.05	457.68	12.4
淀粉及薯类	13.67	16.28	21.00	25.17	30.70	22.0
干豆类及豆制品	15.14	23.62	32.97	34.42	44.00	27.8
油脂类	45.54	51.64	81.58	84.21	81.73	－2.9
肉禽及制品	218.75	267.25	372.78	453.26	493.18	8.8
蛋 类	75.10	86.91	102.81	125.21	145.83	16.5
水产品类	99.24	106.79	140.57	178.87	196.38	9.8
菜 类	110.76	126.66	164.15	191.11	220.82	15.5
2.衣 着	**245.03**	**310.82**	**424.04**	**499.69**	**572.41**	**14.6**
(1)服 装	138.20	175.94	256.29	296.11	349.24	17.9
#男士服装	51.24	70.35	95.90	111.73	141.05	26.2
女士服装	68.67	87.72	134.99	155.11	169.79	9.5
(2)衣着材料	38.72	51.81	59.13	61.94	60.48	－2.4
#棉 布	2.84	2.93	3.37	4.83	4.50	－6.8
棉花化纤混纺布	0.84	0.98	1.29	1.47	1.78	21.1
化纤布	9.64	8.83	8.56	9.43	12.63	33.9
绸 缎	4.59	6.82	11.79	9.67	5.81	－39.9
毛 线	9.04	17.12	17.81	16.28	15.95	－2.0
(3)鞋、袜、帽及其他衣着	62.33	76.47	98.91	127.83	146.34	14.5
#鞋 类	52.86	63.99	82.58	107.03	124.08	15.9
(4)衣着加工服务费	5.79	6.60	9.70	13.83	16.34	18.1
3.家庭设备、用品及服务	**146.91**	**171.94**	**333.94**	**376.40**	**372.27**	**－1.1**
#耐用消费品	82.41	99.92	225.91	261.42	228.21	－12.7
室内装饰品	10.29	7.18	15.42	11.08	13.99	26.3
家庭服务	8.32	12.98	34.77	28.19	35.09	24.5
4.医疗保健	**27.10**	**59.83**	**68.90**	**97.36**	**141.00**	**44.8**
5.交通与通讯	**44.12**	**88.58**	**169.16**	**221.49**	**247.15**	**11.6**
6.娱乐、教育、文化服务	**170.09**	**209.86**	**268.20**	**336.14**	**435.56**	**29.6**
#娱乐用耐用消费品	80.76	61.50	80.01	68.97	96.12	39.4
7.居 住	**109.26**	**133.92**	**165.35**	**231.74**	**320.88**	**38.5**
#燃 料	41.15	49.91	45.36	55.58	76.61	37.8
8.杂项商品与服务	**66.87**	**78.92**	**152.61**	**184.14**	**191.89**	**4.2**
#个人消费	52.97	64.80	125.66	139.01	147.18	5.9

7－5　1996年城市居民家庭平均每人全年消费性支出

(按水平组分类)

单位:元

项　目	最低收入户	#更低收入户	低收入户	中等偏下收入户
消费性支出	**2 799.45**	**2 828.77**	**3 358.65**	**3 764.52**
1.食　品	**1 708.83**	**1 621.06**	**1 982.92**	**2 152.56**
#粮　食	277.99	273.96	315.89	304.91
淀粉及薯类	25.28	25.37	29.76	30.76
干豆类及豆制品	34.07	29.32	37.52	42.20
油脂类	82.13	91.31	83.69	80.82
肉禽及制品	346.86	331.05	390.87	454.85
蛋　类	104.17	110.00	137.81	141.08
水产品类	103.47	90.49	129.20	174.97
菜　类	176.85	178.45	188.89	199.19
2.衣　着	**237.61**	**260.10**	**248.41**	**402.84**
(1)服　装	139.23	158.32	135.09	238.71
#男士服装	51.52	59.70	51.73	99.53
女士服装	67.67	84.46	61.05	112.99
(2)衣着材料	25.92	31.92	24.29	41.92
#棉　布	3.35	6.34	3.54	3.32
棉花化纤混纺布	1.01	1.09	0.74	1.95
化纤布	4.98	6.72	3.77	7.45
绸　缎	1.04	1.29	2.57	3.53
毛　线	11.50	11.13	5.90	13.24
(3)鞋、袜、帽及其他	65.93	64.84	82.20	114.05
#鞋　类	55.44	54.34	69.66	96.35
(4)衣着加工服务费	6.52	5.01	6.82	8.16
3.家庭设备、用品及服务	**86.06**	**78.15**	**227.98**	**210.84**
#耐用消费品	22.87	17.19	127.28	109.69
室内装饰品	1.05	0.66	1.91	5.45
家庭服务	14.56	12.81	29.80	18.70
4.医疗保健	**82.66**	**80.79**	**64.46**	**107.30**
5.交通与通讯	**104.39**	**118.80**	**129.35**	**174.93**
6.娱乐、教育、文化服务	**271.63**	**335.27**	**333.21**	**300.76**
#娱乐用耐用消费品	25.78	43.62	26.84	31.14
7.居　住	**208.02**	**222.52**	**252.18**	**285.65**
#燃　料	64.67	76.88	73.68	73.78
8.杂项商品与服务	**100.25**	**112.09**	**120.15**	**129.65**
#个人消费	58.75	59.92	76.10	84.51

7-5续表

单位:元

项目	中等收入户	中等偏上收入户	高收入户	最高收入户
消费性支出	**4 570.62**	**5 310.37**	**5 783.68**	**8 168.58**
1.食　品	**2 399.89**	**2 749.47**	**2 621.53**	**3 243.99**
#粮　食	276.21	310.44	293.26	292.72
淀粉及薯类	28.36	32.35	32.38	32.40
干豆类及豆制品	40.96	51.04	47.59	47.38
油脂类	76.86	91.24	73.15	66.97
肉禽及制品	522.67	572.25	520.90	524.89
蛋　类	142.90	161.99	155.67	150.57
水产品类	190.36	231.80	214.07	314.66
菜　类	214.95	250.86	238.67	250.98
2.衣　着	**513.80**	**721.99**	**729.87**	**1 356.87**
(1)服　装	322.15	415.36	456.01	892.75
#男士服装	124.89	159.52	190.05	383.99
女士服装	169.46	204.74	217.02	418.26
(2)衣着材料	49.24	91.84	80.11	121.21
#棉　布	2.67	6.33	7.99	5.97
棉花化纤混纺布	1.03	2.96	2.20	2.15
化纤布	6.72	20.64	13.54	38.04
绸　缎	5.88	8.87	5.17	14.18
毛　线	16.97	22.65	18.62	19.86
(3)鞋、袜、帽及其他	130.14	192.45	169.25	298.31
#鞋　类	109.09	166.27	139.45	254.66
(4)衣着加工服务费	12.28	22.33	24.51	44.60
3.家庭设备、用品及服务	**391.65**	**336.36**	**703.53**	**918.97**
#耐用消费品	251.59	198.21	440.34	639.10
室内装饰品	18.08	10.46	38.54	35.26
家庭服务	32.50	25.54	73.86	86.87
4.医疗保健	**154.97**	**160.48**	**185.09**	**255.87**
5.交通与通讯	**220.17**	**299.63**	**348.28**	**550.45**
6.娱乐、教育、文化服务	**383.71**	**472.34**	**586.36**	**922.00**
#娱乐用耐用消费品	39.83	121.35	150.71	413.09
7.居　住	**325.26**	**362.51**	**337.03**	**493.98**
#燃　料	75.52	83.88	81.25	82.05
8.杂项商品与服务	**181.16**	**207.60**	**272.00**	**426.44**
#个人消费	146.12	162.96	220.84	364.62

7-6 城市居民家庭平均每人主要消费品全年购买量

(1992-1996年)

商品名称	单位	1992年	1993年	1994年	1995年	1996年	1996比1995年增长%
粮食	公斤	122.5	104.9	110.8	109.3	113.5	3.8
食用植物油	公斤	8.8	8.9	9.0	8.4	9.0	7.1
鲜菜	公斤	143.7	127.9	129.4	119.0	136.1	14.4
猪肉	公斤	17.1	16.6	15.5	15.6	16.4	5.1
牛羊肉	公斤	5.2	5.9	5.0	4.8	6.8	41.7
家禽	公斤	3.4	3.9	4.4	2.7	2.9	7.4
鲜蛋	公斤	17.0	16.3	18.0	18.5	18.2	-1.6
鱼	公斤	9.8	9.0	9.4	9.7	9.8	1.0
食糖	公斤	1.4	1.5	1.6	1.7	1.8	5.9
卷烟	公斤	46.4	41.4	41.9	43.3	41.3	-4.6
白酒	公斤	2.6	2.4	2.7	2.8	2.8	
啤酒	公斤	7.7	8.8	10.9	10.1	10.1	
汽水可乐	公斤	2.3	2.0	2.8	3.2	2.9	-9.4
茶叶	公斤	0.2	0.2	0.2	0.2	0.3	50.0
干鲜瓜果	公斤	61.2	59.4	60.0	55.3	65.7	18.8
服装	件	5.7	5.5	5.9	5.8	6.4	10.3
#男士服装	件	1.8	1.9	2.0	2.0	2.3	15.0
女士服装	件	2.5	2.5	2.7	2.7	2.9	7.4
各式童装	件	1.4	1.2	1.2	1.1	1.2	9.1
棉布	米	0.9	0.8	0.6	0.7	0.7	
化纤布	米	1.3	1.1	0.8	0.7	0.8	14.3
呢绒	米	0.3	0.4	0.3	0.3	0.2	-33.3
绸缎	米	0.4	0.5	0.5	0.4	0.2	-50.0
毛线	公斤	0.2	0.4	0.3	0.3	0.2	-33.3
鞋类	双	2.5	2.5	2.4	2.5	2.5	
#皮鞋	双	0.8	0.8	0.8	0.8	0.9	12.5
洗衣粉	公斤	0.5	0.5	0.6	0.7	0.8	14.3
肥皂	块	5.7	6.5	6.5	6.1	6.0	-1.6

7-7 城市居民家庭平均每百户耐用消费品全年购买量

(1992-1996年)

商品名称	单 位	1992年	1993年	1994年	1995年	1996年	1996比1995年增长%
地 毯	平方米	6.5	10.8	10.5	2.5		
组合家具	套	4.2	2.4	2.6	2.2	1.6	-27.3
沙发床	个	1.8	2.6	3.0	1.6	3.2	100.0
沙 发	个	11.6	6.2	10.0	5.2	5.8	11.5
大衣柜	个	0.4	0.6	0.2	0.2		
写字台	张	0.6	0.4	1.0	0.4	2.0	400.0
摩托车	辆	0.8	1.0	0.8	0.4	0.4	
自行车	辆	11.4	12.8	14.4	15.4	12.4	-19.5
缝纫机	台			0.2			
电风扇	台	6.4	2.2	4.2	3.6	2.2	-38.9
洗衣机	台	1.6	2.6	2.8	1.0	2.4	140.0
电冰箱	台	1.4	2.6	2.0	2.0	3.2	60.0
冰 柜	台	1.0	1.4	2.2	1.4	1.4	
彩色电视机	台	4.4	3.0	1.8	1.8	2.8	55.6
黑白电视机	台	0.2		0.2		0.2	
录放像机	台	3.8	0.8	1.8	1.4	1.0	-28.6
游戏机	台	5.4	2.6	2.2	0.6	0.2	-66.7
组合音响	台	0.8	1.2	1.8	1.4	1.4	
立体收录机	台	0.6	1.4	1.2	0.8	1.6	100.0
普通收录机	台	3.0	2.4	4.8	2.8	3.8	35.7
照像机	架	1.4	1.2	1.4	1.4	2.0	42.9
钢 琴	架	0.4	0.2				
空调器	台	0.6	1.2	3.4	6.0	1.6	-73.3
电炊具	台	1.6	2.4	2.8	2.6	4.8	84.6
淋浴热水器	台	0.6	3.6	6.8	4.2	4.6	9.5
抽油烟机	台	3.4	2.8	3.2	2.8	2.2	-21.4

7－8　城市居民家庭平均每百户耐用消费品年末拥有量

(1992－1996年)

商品名称	单　位	1992年	1993年	1994年	1995年	1996年
毛皮大衣	件	35.0	41.6	44.2	47.4	49.2
呢大衣	件	267.0	287.8	301.6	294.0	286.0
地　毯	平方米	59.6	78.0	91.0	116.2	81.2
组合家具	套	46.4	50.8	57.4	67.6	65.0
沙发床	个	20.6	30.4	37.6	43.6	39.8
沙　发	个	137.6	139.0	146.6	131.4	118.6
大衣柜	个	88.6	86.0	86.2	73.8	72.6
写字台	张	53.6	60.2	61.0	58.0	62.0
摩托车	辆	2.0	4.2	8.0	7.8	8.2
自行车	辆	216.8	229.4	233.8	231.0	232.0
缝纫机	台	77.6	77.4	75.8	76.4	75.8
电风扇	台	114.6	119.4	124.0	122.2	122.6
洗衣机	台	85.0	87.4	90.6	93.6	96.8
电冰箱	台	85.8	89.2	95.2	97.6	98.2
冰　柜	台	3.6	6.6	8.6	9.0	10.0
彩色电视机	台	90.4	94.0	100.6	101.8	107.4
黑白电视机	台	39.8	39.4	37.4	29.8	28.4
录放像机	台	20.2	23.4	31.4	33.0	35.4
游戏机	台	28.8	31.4	38.2	39.8	39.4
组合音响	台	3.8	4.2	9.8	12.8	13.4
立体收录机	台	42.6	43.6	43.6	43.6	39.4
普通收录机	台	39.0	40.2	38.8	35.4	36.0
照像机	架	43.4	48.4	52.4	52.4	55.0
钢　琴	架	0.8	0.8	0.8	0.6	0.4
空调器	台	1.0	2.2	6.6	13.4	15.2
电炊具	台	4.2	9.6	15.6	21.0	28.2
淋浴热水器	台	8.8	14.0	24.0	30.2	39.4
抽油烟机	台	18.2	26.2	35.8	43.0	43.6

7－9　城市居民家庭分水平组每百户耐用消费品年末拥有量

商品名称	单位	最低收入户		#更低收入户		低收入户		中等偏下收入户	
		1995 年	1996 年	1995 年	1996 年	1995 年	1996 年	1995 年	1996 年
毛皮大衣	件	38.0	28.0	28.0	32.0	40.0	44.0	29.0	36.0
呢大衣	件	260.0	240.0	224.0	208.0	278.0	236.0	297.0	276.0
地　毯	平方米	58.0	6.0	108.0	8.0	38.0	54.0	105.0	80.0
组合家具	套	54.0	56.0	56.0	52.0	70.0	56.0	63.0	66.0
沙发床	个	32.0	34.0	36.0	36.0	36.0	36.0	39.0	32.0
沙　发	个	74.0	86.0	80.0	92.0	130.0	122.0	117.0	108.0
大衣柜	个	70.0	72.0	68.0	80.0	72.0	80.0	78.0	71.0
写字台	张	40.0	38.0	48.0	36.0	46.0	62.0	54.0	59.0
摩托车	辆	8.0	4.0	12.0	8.0	6.0	8.0	9.0	6.0
自行车	辆	204.0	202.0	180.0	196.0	222.0	250.0	251.0	245.0
缝纫机	台	76.0	78.0	56.0	84.0	74.0	72.0	81.0	75.0
电风扇	台	108.0	110.0	100.0	108.0	132.0	122.0	122.0	122.0
洗衣机	台	78.0	86.0	68.0	88.0	94.0	96.0	92.0	91.0
电冰箱	台	86.0	88.0	84.0	88.0	104.0	96.0	97.0	95.0
冰　柜	台	4.0	2.0		4.0	2.0	8.0	4.0	3.0
彩色电视机	台	82.0	92.0	72.0	88.0	100.0	106.0	106.0	103.0
黑白电视机	台	40.0	32.0	36.0	40.0	24.0	32.0	27.0	30.0
录放像机	台	22.0	24.0	12.0	16.0	28.0	32.0	38.0	30.0
游戏机	台	40.0	42.0	36.0	28.0	34.0	32.0	45.0	36.0
组合音响	台	2.0	4.0			8.0	4.0	11.0	5.0
立体收录机	台	40.0	36.0	40.0	40.0	40.0	40.0	45.0	41.0
普通收录机	台	22.0	26.0	16.0	32.0	34.0	32.0	32.0	34.0
照像机	架	34.0	34.0	24.0	32.0	38.0	36.0	53.0	49.0
钢　琴	架								
空调器	台		2.0		4.0	10.0	6.0	8.0	7.0
电炊具	台	6.0	6.0		8.0	6.0	10.0	12.0	9.0
淋浴热水器	台	4.0	18.0	4.0	20.0	16.0	24.0	24.0	23.0
抽油烟机	台	20.0	16.0	20.0	20.0	22.0	22.0	37.0	38.0

7－9续表

商品名称	单位	中等收入户		中等偏上收入户		高收入户		最高收入户	
		1995年	1996年	1995年	1996年	1995年	1996年	1995年	1996年
毛皮大衣	件	49.0	43.0	55.0	50.0	48.0	54.0	82.0	108.0
呢大衣	件	270.0	297.0	313.0	279.0	350.0	344.0	292.0	336.0
地毯	平方米	22.0	59.0	153.0	68.0	224.0	70.0	282.0	268.0
组合家具	套	63.0	58.0	72.0	63.0	84.0	76.0	72.0	88.0
沙发床	个	35.0	29.0	53.0	37.0	68.0	60.0	46.0	72.0
沙发	个	120.0	105.0	154.0	124.0	160.0	118.0	168.0	186.0
大衣柜	个	79.0	79.0	77.0	71.0	50.0	72.0	78.0	60.0
写字台	张	57.0	58.0	63.0	66.0	72.0	74.0	74.0	80.0
摩托车	辆	4.0	9.0	13.0	11.0	8.0	12.0	4.0	6.0
自行车	辆	221.0	226.0	252.0	233.0	244.0	232.0	192.0	228.0
缝纫机	台	75.0	81.0	77.0	71.0	72.0	80.0	76.0	74.0
电风扇	台	119.0	121.0	132.0	125.0	108.0	126.0	128.0	132.0
洗衣机	台	92.0	104.0	97.0	98.0	100.0	98.0	102.0	102.0
电冰箱	台	95.0	97.0	95.0	101.0	110.0	104.0	102.0	108.0
冰柜	台	3.0	5.0	17.0	10.0	14.0	16.0	22.0	38.0
彩色电视机	台	104.0	107.0	103.0	107.0	108.0	112.0	102.0	130.0
黑白电视机	台	37.0	26.0	30.0	28.0	24.0	28.0	22.0	24.0
录放像机	台	29.0	33.0	35.0	38.0	38.0	30.0	38.0	66.0
游戏机	台	33.0	36.0	48.0	51.0	36.0	34.0	36.0	40.0
组合音响	台	7.0	11.0	15.0	16.0	18.0	16.0	34.0	46.0
立体收录机	台	43.0	45.0	44.0	36.0	46.0	36.0	46.0	38.0
普通收录机	台	39.0	39.0	40.0	40.0	48.0	40.0	28.0	36.0
照像机	架	44.0	51.0	62.0	53.0	58.0	94.0	76.0	80.0
钢琴	架			1.0		2.0	2.0	2.0	2.0
空调器	台	16.0	11.0	11.0	15.0	24.0	24.0	30.0	54.0
电炊具	台	13.0	26.0	30.0	27.0	30.0	52.0	58.0	90.0
淋浴热水器	台	28.0	33.0	44.0	53.0	40.0	70.0	50.0	64.0
抽油烟机	台	42.0	34.0	53.0	55.0	52.0	60.0	72.0	84.0

7-10 农民家庭基本情况

项　　目	单位	1995年	1996年
一、调查户数	户	1 000	1 000
二、调查户常住人口	人	3 905	3 848
三、平均每户常住人口	人	3.91	3.85
四、整半劳动力	人	2 731	2 648
户均整半劳动力	人	2.73	2.65
整半劳动力占人口比重	%	70	69
五、平均每个劳动力负担人口	人	0.43	0.45
六、年末户均生产性固定资产	元	2 285	4 566
七、户均经营耕地面积	亩	6.03	5.34
八、年末人均住房面积	m^2	19.43	21.83
九、平均每人全年总收入	元	3 286	4 000
十、平均每人全年纯收入	元	2 531	3 142
十一、按人均年纯收入分组的户结构			
500元以下	%	0.6	0.2
500-1000元	%	2.8	1.3
1000-1500元	%	10.8	6.1
1500-2000元	%	17.4	11.8
2000-2500元	%	21.6	16.2
2500-3000元	%	17.1	12.6
3000-3500元	%	12.9	14.6
3500-4000元	%	6.4	13.7
4000元以上	%	10.4	23.5
十二、平均每人生活消费支出	元	1 717	2 101
十三、户均职工人数	人	0.13	0.13
十四、户均乡镇企业人数	人	0.86	0.67

7-11 农民家庭劳动力文化程度

单位:人

项　　目	1995年	1996年
每百个劳动力中:		
1.文盲或半文盲	2.82	3.40
2.小　学	30.65	26.51
3.初　中	52.58	54.46
4.高　中	10.55	11.18
5.中　专	3.00	3.40
6.大　专	0.45	1.05

7-12 农民家庭平均每人年纯收入

单位:元

项　　目	1995年	1996年
人均纯收入	**2 531**	**3 142**
一、基本收入	2 436	3 015
1.劳动者的报酬收入	1 278	1 545
从集体组织中得到	351	403
在企业劳动得到	900	1 091
#从集体企业中得到	709	815
2.家庭经营收入	1 158	1 470
#种植业收入	927	979
牧业收入	77	110
工业收入	11	10
建筑业收入	18	47
运输业收入	30	93
商业收入	29	33
饮食业收入	2	12
服务业收入	25	33
二、转移性收入	49	75
三、财产性收入	46	52

7-13　农民家庭平均每人年生活费支出

项　　目	支出额(元)			构　成(%)	
	1995年	1996年	1996比1995年增长%	1995年	1996年
平均每人年生活费支出	**1 717.28**	**2 100.64**	**22.3**	**100.0**	**100.0**
一、食　品	979.62	1 099.42	12.2	57.0	52.3
#1.主　食	430.33	425.86	-1.0	43.9	38.7
2.副　食	362.45	440.31	21.9	37.0	40.0
3.其他食品	158.09	191.97	21.4	16.1	17.5
4.在外饮食	24.69	37.95	53.7	2.5	3.5
二、衣　着	188.13	252.80	34.4	11.0	12.0
三、居　住	194.49	262.50	35.0	11.3	12.5
#住　房	96.31	163.26	69.5	49.5	62.2
四、家庭设备用品及服务	82.46	112.71	36.7	4.8	5.4
#耐用消费品	35.38	50.74	43.4	42.9	45.0
室内装饰品	1.74	2.95	69.5	2.1	2.6
床上用品	5.57	8.58	54.0	6.8	7.6
家庭日用杂品	35.77	46.32	29.5	43.4	41.1
五、医疗保健	78.72	102.87	30.7	4.6	4.9
六、交通和通讯	43.05	53.03	23.2	2.5	2.5
七、文教娱乐用品及服务	116.28	152.43	31.1	6.8	7.3
#文化教育娱乐用品	30.39	37.86	24.6	26.1	24.8
文化教育娱乐服务	85.90	114.56	33.4	73.9	75.2
八、其他商品和服务	34.53	64.88	87.9	2.0	3.1

7-14　1996年农民家庭人均生活消费各项支出

(按收入水平分组)

单位:元

项　　目	食　品	衣　着	居　住	家庭设备	医疗保健	交　通和通讯	文教娱乐用品及服　务	其他商品及服务
500元以下	1 064.00	390.83	51.00	84.67	108.67	98.33	82.50	35.17
500-1000元	853.25	215.75	65.66	24.42	55.17	92.26	121.53	6.72
1000-1500元	791.54	144.86	141.49	56.06	56.52	13.24	111.43	27.52
1500-2000元	924.32	170.81	193.47	82.02	55.03	47.17	88.27	30.82
2000-2500元	974.32	187.28	173.49	70.28	124.14	37.74	146.75	34.31
2500-3000元	1 043.80	188.01	271.75	106.63	148.63	48.00	137.16	52.95
3000-3500元	1 108.02	261.65	185.01	124.50	82.31	34.17	104.82	64.46
3500-4000元	1 267.14	361.47	349.47	109.99	99.25	92.52	179.29	83.82
4000元以上	1 353.53	361.68	425.07	188.16	121.06	71.13	237.30	123.17

7－15 农民家庭平均每人食品及衣着消费量

项　目	单 位	1990年	1992年	1995年	1996年	1996比1995年增长％
粮　食	公斤	238.00	240.15	221.83	208.01	－6.2
蔬　菜	公斤	109.00	120.92	91.76	93.36	1.7
植物油	公斤	4.66	6.98	5.35	6.28	17.4
动物油	公斤	2.16	2.68	1.01	1.15	13.9
猪　肉	公斤	7.14	8.66	6.59	8.42	27.8
牛　肉	公斤	0.60		0.56	0.73	30.9
羊　肉	公斤	0.84		0.61	1.09	78.7
家　禽	公斤	0.72	0.70	0.37	0.38	2.7
肉禽制品	公斤			0.95	1.17	23.2
水产品	公斤	4.76	6.15	7.13	8.52	19.5
食　糖	公斤	1.35	1.57	0.79	0.81	2.5
白　酒	公斤			3.10	3.26	5.2
啤　酒	公斤			6.25	7.03	12.5
糕　点	公斤	2.25		2.04	2.08	2.0
蛋　类	公斤	6.81	7.24	8.50	8.76	3.1
干鲜瓜果	公斤			17.24	24.73	43.5
棉　布	米	2.41	2.51	0.55	0.71	29.1
化纤布	米	2.14	2.13	1.71	1.46	－14.6
呢　绒	米	0.18	0.20	0.11	0.10	－9.1
绸　缎	米	0.05	0.08	0.05	0.20	300.0
毛　线	公斤	0.18	0.24	0.24	0.29	20.8
皮　鞋	双	0.26	0.32	0.51	0.62	21.6
布　鞋	双			0.57	0.52	－8.8
塑料鞋	双			0.14	0.16	14.3
球　鞋	双			0.12	0.13	8.3
毛皮制品	件			0.02	0.02	

7-16 1996年农民家庭主要食品及衣着消费量

(按收入水平分组)

项 目	单 位	500元以下	500-1000元	1000-1500元	1500-2000元	2000-2500元	2500-3000元	3000-3500元	3500-4000元	4000元以上
粮 食	公斤	113.67	186.02	192.65	196.38	203.19	224.94	196.33	206.86	224.37
蔬 菜	公斤	33.67	71.57	86.56	94.56	90.63	97.97	94.81	88.71	97.97
植物油	公斤	6.33	4.13	4.64	4.89	5.29	5.42	6.87	8.01	7.70
动物油	公斤	1.67	1.09	1.03	2.04	1.41	1.25	0.83	0.42	1.04
猪 肉	公斤	8.33	5.13	5.95	7.72	6.90	7.85	8.88	9.07	10.75
牛 肉	公斤	2.17	0.19	0.48	0.76	0.87	0.71	0.61	0.59	0.86
羊 肉	公斤	2.33	0.62	0.50	0.65	0.92	1.02	1.04	1.46	1.56
家 禽	公斤		0.21	0.24	0.40	0.47	0.30	0.32	0.45	0.42
肉禽制品	公斤	1.67	0.58	0.71	0.89	0.90	0.96	1.18	1.23	1.83
水产品	公斤	10.67	6.98	4.46	6.52	7.86	8.21	9.44	8.87	11.06
食 糖	公斤	0.83	0.45	0.48	0.74	0.85	0.72	0.93	0.97	0.84
白 酒	公斤	2.33	2.19	2.03	3.31	2.77	3.31	3.05	3.79	3.90
啤 酒	公斤	1.33	3.94	2.99	5.44	6.25	5.85	7.66	8.71	9.48
糕 点	公斤	2.33	2.23	1.13	2.73	1.71	2.05	1.72	2.35	2.40
蛋 类	公斤	5.00	6.28	6.07	5.96	7.83	6.89	9.88	12.59	10.39
干鲜瓜果	公斤	13.00	13.02	14.67	22.46	22.53	21.65	24.82	26.94	32.00
棉 布	米	0.17	0.34	0.22	0.30	0.82	0.41	0.66	0.49	1.39
化纤布	米	3.83	0.68	1.09	1.09	1.20	1.42	1.30	1.82	1.97
呢 绒	米	0.17	0.04	0.03	0.05	0.09	0.09	0.09	0.16	0.13
绸 缎	米		0.23	0.15	0.26	0.16	0.16	0.25	0.19	0.21
毛 线	公斤	0.70	0.23	0.17	0.25	0.21	0.21	0.29	0.41	0.40
皮 鞋	双	1.00	0.58	0.33	0.42	0.59	0.43	0.75	0.83	0.78
布 鞋	双	0.33	0.58	0.39	0.48	0.57	0.52	0.51	0.59	0.48
塑料鞋	双	0.67	0.21	0.09	0.17	0.19	0.17	0.16	0.10	0.17
球 鞋	双		0.21	0.17	0.10	0.09	0.10	0.15	0.10	0.17
毛皮制品	件			0.01	0.01	0.02	0.01	0.01	0.02	0.05

7－17　年末每百户农民家庭耐用物品拥有量

项　目	单 位	1990年	1992年	1995年	1996年	1996比1995年增长%
自行车	辆	241	232	238	226	-5.0
缝纫机	架	84	83	93	88	-5.4
钟	只	98	98	100	89	-11.0
手　表	只	242	223	241	221	-8.3
电风扇	台	77	88	131	139	6.1
洗衣机	台	38	49	74	76	2.7
电冰箱	台	10	14	45	52	15.6
摩托车	辆	1	3	12	19	58.3
大型家具	件	311		664	678	21.1
#沙　发	个	78	77	158	157	-0.7
写字台	张	51	37	68	63	-7.4
组合家具	件			55	60	9.1
大衣柜	个	83	119	88	75	-14.8
收音机	台	97	67	57	59	3.5
黑白电视机	台	77	74	57	46	-19.3
彩色电视机	台	18	31	63	74	17.5
录像机	台			7	9	28.6
录音机	台	33	44	52	53	1.9
照相机	架	4	3	7	12	71.4
吸尘器	台			2	2	
空调器	台			1	2	100.0

7－18　1996年农民家庭耐用物品每百户拥有量

（按收入水平分组）

项　目	单　位	500元以　下	500－1000元	1000－1500元	1500－2000元	2000－2500元	2500－3000元	3000－3500元	3500－4000元	4000元以上
自行车	辆	150	192	211	217	225	216	238	238	229
缝纫机	架	50	77	87	88	91	87	83	83	88
钟	只	100	115	89	86	86	79	90	90	98
手　表	只	200	154	172	214	220	212	222	222	231
电风扇	台	50	108	133	129	141	135	148	148	139
洗衣机	台	50	69	69	72	76	72	84	84	78
电冰箱	台	50	46	51	42	49	41	58	58	59
摩托车	辆	50	15	28	14	18	21	18	18	23
大型家具	件	750	554	533	601	696	627	667	667	771
#沙　发	个	150	146	141	142	165	130	149	149	173
写字台	张	100	38	62	66	66	60	57	57	66
组合家具	个	100	69	46	57	61	54	61	61	68
大衣柜	个	50	38	70	63	75	70	77	77	84
收音机	台	50	54	54	60	65	59	61	61	54
黑白电视机	台		23	51	61	52	46	39	39	36
彩色电视机	台	100	85	70	53	73	75	80	80	81
录像机	台		8	8	8	8	7	8	8	11
录音机	台	50	54	59	53	49	52	54	54	52
照相机	架		38	8	11	12	13	12	12	10
抽油烟机	台			7	1	3	3	8	8	9
吸尘器	台		8	2	1	2	2	2	2	1
空调器	台		8	3		3	2	2	2	1

7-19 优抚对象及优抚事业单位情况

指　　标	1990年	1992年	1995年	1996年	1996比1995年增长数
优抚人数(人)	**275 182**	**282 885**	**268 954**	**272 105**	**3 151**
烈　属	12 040	12 219	11 682	11 637	-45
牺牲病故军人家属	1 715	1 710	1 649	1 621	-28
现役军人家属	151 382	152 116	135 065	137 233	2 618
革命伤残人员	8 100	7 958	7 917	7 888	-29
在乡复员军人	11 196	11 076	10 114	9 965	-149
在乡退伍军人	90 745	97 802	102 524	103 758	1 234
在乡退伍老红军战士	4	4	3	3	
优抚事业单位					
单位数(个)	**9**	**10**	**9**	**9**	
残废军人休养院	1	1	1	1	
复退军人精神病院	1	1	1	1	
光荣院	7	8	7	7	
床位数(张)	**670**	**718**	**718**	**796**	**78**
残废军人休养院	50	50	50	50	
复退军人精神病院	130	130	130	130	
光荣院	490	538	538	616	78
收养人员数(人)	**581**	**518**	**563**	**634**	**71**
残废军人休养院	36	33	31	31	
复退军人精神病院	120	89	81	83	2
光荣院	425	396	451	520	69
职工人数(人)	**338**	**358**	**392**	**395**	**3**
#医护人员	151	148	147	141	-6

7-20 社会福利事业、企业单位及工作人员数

指　　标	机　构(个)			工作人员(人)		
	1990年	1995年	1996年	1990年	1995年	1996年
福利事业单位						
民政部门办	9	12	12	665	838	856
社会集体办	267	242	252	1 087	1 013	1 059
福利企业单位						
民政部门办	137	270	284	9 827	13 120	11 352
社会集体办	705	1 336	1 385	27 127	57 159	58 867
烈士纪念建筑物管理单位	**9**	**12**	**10**	**129**	**145**	**147**
收容遣送单位	**7**	**6**	**6**	**254**	**158**	**161**
殡葬管理单位	**6**	**5**	**5**	**168**	**160**	**172**

7-21 1996年社会福利事业单位基本情况

指标	单位数(个)	床位数(张)	职工人数(人)	#医护人员	收养人员(人)
总计	**264**	**7 011**	**1 915**	**350**	**5 187**
民政部门办	**12**	**1 772**	**856**	**350**	**1 510**
社会福利院	9	857	424	115	663
儿童福利院	2	415	151	46	398
#SOS儿童村	1	200	27	13	183
精神病人福利院	1	500	281	189	449
社会办敬老院	**252**	**5 239**	**1 059**		**3 677**
城镇办敬老院	102	2 372	536		1 667
农村办敬老院	150	2 867	523		2 010

7-22 社会福利企业情况

指标	单位	1990年	1992年	1995年	1996年	1996比1995年增长数
工业						
单位数	个	709	1 060	1 382	1 435	53
国有经济	个	19	25	22	29	7
集体经济	个	65	85	136	150	14
社会办		625	950	1 224	1 256	32
职工人数	人	35 025	46 783	67 292	67 259	-33
#盲聋哑残人数	人	14 029	19 775	30 191	31 745	1 554
增加值	万元			137 970	100 603	-37 367
国有经济	万元			7 927	6 847	-1 080
集体经济	万元			15 293	6 843	-8 450
社会办	万元			114 750	86 913	-27 837
盈利金额	万元	8 344	18 048	36 635	40 170	3 535
亏损金额	万元	37	493	1 001	1 476	475
商业服务业						
单位数	个	133	169	224	234	10
国有经济	个	6	9	10	15	5
集体经济	个	47	67	102	90	-12
社会办		80	93	112	129	17
职工人数	人	2 197	2 137	2 987	2 960	-27
#盲聋哑残人数	人	854	774	1 161	1 162	1
营业收入	万元	12 168	7 941	21 751	15 022	-6 729
盈利金额	万元	653	661	786	2 192	1 406
亏损金额	万元	3	9	119	334	215

注:商业企业营业收入中不包括社会办商业企业。

7－23　抚恤、社会救济事业费及集体优待供给补助金额

单位:万元

指　　标	1990年	1992年	1995年	1996年	1996 比1995年 增长数
地方财政支付金额					
抚恤事业费	**1 814**	**2 331**	**4 420**	**4 580**	**160**
社会救济费	**780**	**2 048**	**1 834**	**5 913**	**4 079**
农村社会救济费	220	173	605	810	205
城镇社会救济费	149	188	502	4 383	3 881
精减退职老职工救济费	411	559	727	720	－7
自然灾害救济费	**439**	**243**	**72**	**495**	**423**
集体优待供给补助金额					
优待烈军属总金额	870	1 182	1 606	2 019	413
社会散居孤老残幼供给金额	224	245	345	411	66
供给敬老院金额	251	276	449	584	135
社会困难户补助金额	68	70	319	330	11

7－24　享受补助和救济人员情况

指　　标	单　位	1992年	1995年	1996年	1996 比1995年 增长数
社会散居孤老残幼情况					
社会散居孤老残幼	人	6 489	7 092	7 143	51
集体供养人数	人	3 092	2 936	2 883	－53
非农业人口	人		100	108	8
农业人口	人	836	2 836	2 775	－61
国家定期定量救济人数	人		914	889	－25
非农业人口	人		710	699	－11
农业人口	人		204	190	－14
困难户救济情况					
临时救济人次数	人次	62 970	55 139	61 315	6 176
非农业人口	人次		12 139	21 358	9 219
农业人口	人次		43 000	39 957	－3 043
定期定量救济人数	人	3 175	3 670	3 905	235
非农业人口	人		976	1 011	35
农业人口	人		2 694	2 894	200
精减退职老职工救济情况					
救济人数	人	9 584	9 107	8 828	－279
非农业人口	人		2 066	2 042	－24
农业人口	人		7 041	6 786	－255
享受40%救济	人	4 898	4 454	4 363	91
非农业人口	人		1 144	1 143	－1
农业人口	人		3 310	3 220	－90
享受定期定量救济	人	4 686	4 653	4 465	－188
非农业人口	人		922	899	－23
农业人口	人		3 731	3 566	－165

7-25 城镇社区服务和残疾人分散就业情况

指　标	单位	1990年	1992年	1995年	1996年	1996比1995年增长数
城镇社区服务设施数	个	2 294	2 960	1 538	1 768	230
#城镇社区服务中心	个			94	106	12
便民利民服务网点	个			4 038	4 735	697
分散安置"四残"人数	人	2 526	8 017	9 710	9 224	-486
#个体从业者	人	1 172	1 315	2 396	2 491	95

7-26 农村社会保障、养老保险及扶贫情况

项　目	单　位	1990年	1992年	1995年	1996年	1996比1995年增长数
社会保障						
建立社会保障网络的乡镇数	个	20	19	53	59	6
社会保障基金会合计	个	52	59	98	152	54
#扶贫基金会	个	14	25	57	26	-31
互助基金会	个		9	9	94	85
社会保障基金会资金额	万元	138	562	912	957	45
农村养老保险						
参加养老保险人数	人			80 000	80 000	
领取保险金人数	人			676	1 600	924
本年保险金总收入	万元			243	300	57
本年支付保险金总额	万元			40	53	13
扶贫情况						
上年末在扶户数	户	771	2 285	4 314	4 217	-97
本年新增扶贫户数	户	5 171	2 166	2 157	1 639	-518
本年新增脱贫户数	户	4 873	1 118	2 254	3 048	794
年末在扶户数	户	1 069	3 333	4 217	2 808	-1 409

7-27 农村自然灾害救济情况

指　标	单　位	1990年	1992年	1995年	1996年	1996比1995年增长数
自然灾害受灾人口	人	450 350	83 996	267 963	405 721	137 758
特重灾民	人	46 495	48	7 832	52 397	44 565
重灾民	人	94 246	5 885	87 030	112 527	25 497
轻灾民	人	309 609	78 063	173 101	240 797	67 696
得到国家救济人次数	人次	98 542	40 126	60 198	100 628	40 430

八、农村经济

RURAL ECONOMY

1996 年末农村劳动力	167.92 万人
1996 年农业总产值	142.29 亿元
1996 年粮食总产量	207 万吨

农业总产值（亿元）

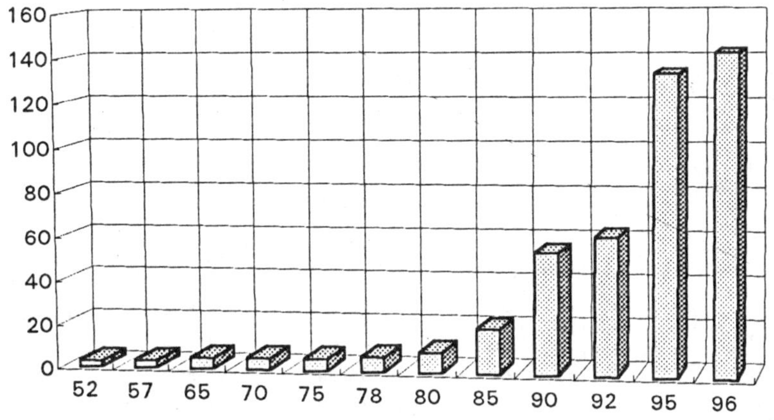

粮食总产量（万吨）

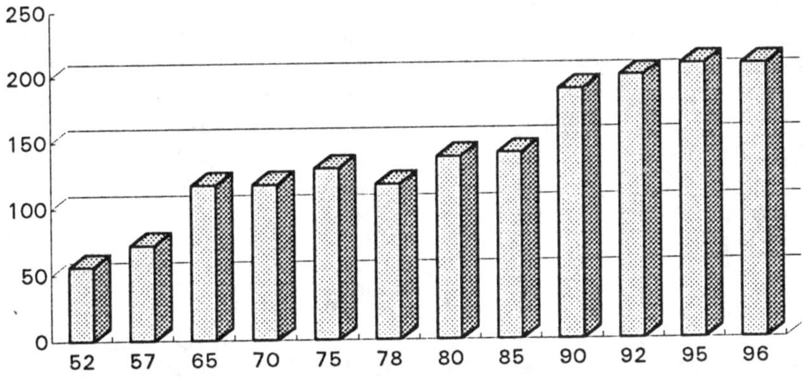

8－1　天津市农工商总公司主要指标

项　　目	单　位	1990年	1994年	1995年	1996年
一、直属企事业单位	**个**	**34**	**45**	**45**	**47**
#农场个数	个	17	17	17	17
工业企业个数	个	8	7	8	13
商业企业个数	个	4	11	11	9
二、土地面积	**亩**	**180 360**	**176 598**	**176 876**	**176 546**
#耕地面积	亩	65 547	62 213	62 380	64 113
三、工农业总产值(现价)	**万元**	**44 846**	**92 220**	**108 119**	**113 148**
工业总产值	万元	28 914	73 166	86 917	93 111
农业总产值	万元	15 932	19 054	21 202	20 037
#农　业	万元	1 633	2 006	3 425	3 408
畜牧业	万元	14 008	16 432	16 582	14 920
渔　业	万元	280	495	971	1 703
四、国内生产总值(现价)	**万元**	**13 606**	**27 109**	**31 177**	**36 535**
第一产业	万元	4 258	3 123	2 500	2 927
第二产业	万元	6 688	19 043	24 245	29 741
第三产业	万元	2 660	4 943	4 532	3 867
五、农作物播种面积	**亩**	**61 372**	**56 466**	**56 503**	**56 950**
#粮食作物	亩	25 261	36 985	38 368	39 856
青饲料作物	亩	30 727	16 777	14 824	11 244
商品蔬菜	亩	2 715	1 815	1 245	2 662
粮食总产量	吨	5 863	6 848	10 542	12 765
青饲料总产量	吨	69 171	38 997	24 221	21 529
商品菜产量	吨	8 823	3 506	1 812	2 517
六、果园面积	**亩**	**15 716**	**13 986**	**13 108**	**11 039**
水果总产量	吨	5 661	4 659	5 065	3 500
七、奶牛年末存栏	**头**	**13 156**	**12 809**	**13 323**	**13 294**
#成母牛	头	7 222	7 751	8 210	7 912
牛奶总产量	吨	45 470	49 674	52 426	53 028
鸡年末存栏	万只	275.91	143.34	73.97	54.27
#产蛋鸡	万只	168.30	92.12	56.63	40.25
鸡蛋总产量	吨	21 042	15 079	8 988	5 913
肉类总产量	吨	2 430	1 754	1 474	1 139
养殖水面	亩	6 281	5 952	7 679	8 941
水产品产量	吨	908	1 117	2 271	2 815
八、农业机械总动力	**万千瓦**	**3.83**	**2.27**	**2.17**	**2.07**
大中型拖拉机	台	166	112	101	90
小型拖拉机	台	94	61	52	56
农场用电量	万千瓦小时	4 059	4 884	5 319	5 096
化肥施用量(折纯)	吨	592	447	512	681
农垦全部汽车拥有量	辆	633	636	617	574
#载重汽车	辆	418	412	357	316
九、主要工业产品产量					
葡萄酒	吨	5 157	9 158	10 365	14 698
淀　粉	吨	23 606	35 645	30 446	17 027
奶　粉	吨	4 969	7 543	8 115	7 852
消毒牛奶	吨	41 010	19 466	17 316	17 139
饲料添加剂	吨	5 748	9 652	6 544	3 933
鸡　笼	组	16 606	6 798	9 444	12 916
金属门窗	万平方米	3.33	4.84	2.38	0.88

8－1续表

项　　目	单　位	1990年	1994年	1995年	1996年
十、固定资产投资总额	**万元**	**2 209**	**3 059**	**7 316**	**7 469**
新增固定资产	万元	2 081	2 914	6 947	6 752
十一、外贸出口产品总值	**万元**	**665**	**10 149**	**12 604**	**10 257**
十二、利润总额	**万元**	**1 204**	**3 275**	**3 057**	**3 227**
十三、年末职工人数	**人**	**25 266**	**20 433**	**18 363**	**16 786**
全年平均职工人数	人	25 233	20 141	18 028	16 948
工资总额	万元	4 616	6 722	7 828	9 380
职工年平均工资	元	1 856	3 337	4 342	5 535
十四、商业营业单位数	**个**	**135**	**145**	**107**	**102**
商业从业人员	人	2 681	2 449	2 430	2 359
商业营业额	万元	25 333	34 345	43 608	31 223
十五、年末固定资产原值	**万元**	**34 055**	**53 259**	**72 995**	**104 963**
年末固定资产净值	万元	24 639	36 377	55 750	81 058
十六、学校数	**所**	**23**	**22**	**19**	**19**
在校学生人数	人	2 519	2 203	1 803	1 903
十七、医疗单位数	**个**	**31**	**23**	**21**	**22**
医务人员	人	174	137	119	111
#医生	人	123	91	84	77

8－2　1996年各区县农村基层组织和乡村建设

地　区	乡政府（个）	镇政府（个）	村民委员会（个）	乡村户数（户）	乡村人口（人）	自来水受益村（个）	通汽车的村（个）	通电话的村（个）
合　计	**148**	**78**	**3 878**	**1 131 946**	**3 948 438**	**3 039**	**3 711**	**3 379**
塘沽区	10	1	47	26 695	77 912	47	47	47
汉沽区	6	1	58	17 334	59 177	58	58	55
大港区	4	3	74	29 174	102 588	66	74	74
东丽区	1	8	114	70 061	213 698	114	114	114
西青区	5	4	160	75 341	240 922	160	160	160
津南区	4	7	173	88 602	290 240	173	145	173
北辰区	4	8	127	69 245	216 243	127	127	127
宁河县	17	5	285	75 168	291 557	285	285	285
武清县	22	12	741	200 438	708 754	741	741	741
静海县	18	10	384	121 741	426 814	384	306	383
宝坻县	27	8	766	148 831	558 630	498	705	685
蓟　县	30	11	949	209 316	764 903	386	949	535

8-3 改革开放以来农业发展情况

年份	农林牧渔业劳动力（万人）	年末实有耕地面积（万公顷）	当年减少耕地面积（万公顷）	造林面积（万公顷）	受灾面积（万公顷）	成灾面积（万公顷）
1978	103.37	46.94	0.58	0.07	21.18	15.63
1979	105.93	46.84	0.52	0.17	9.39	6.23
1980	105.04	46.41	0.43	0.13	13.21	7.72
1981	107.42	46.29	0.13	0.09	22.35	15.25
1982	107.57	46.10	0.39	0.30	12.90	7.89
1983	111.72	45.86	0.27	0.28	28.04	19.59
1984	105.46	45.41	0.45	0.35	23.76	13.35
1985	95.16	44.70	0.74	0.28	11.67	8.22
1986	91.55	44.14	0.58	0.02	8.29	6.42
1987	89.87	43.85	0.33	0.19	13.27	8.48
1988	86.89	43.33	0.56	0.26	18.00	14.29
1989	89.23	43.23	0.12	0.37	14.70	8.40
1990	89.53	43.15	0.11	0.73	11.03	6.08
1991	89.93	43.16	0.05	0.55	8.58	5.29
1992	88.43	42.95	0.22	0.72	13.14	8.15
1993	86.47	42.87	0.11	0.79	10.71	6.88
1994	83.33	42.74	0.14	0.75	13.17	8.40
1995	80.90	42.61	0.15	0.48	5.48	3.12
1996	80.22	42.58	0.05	0.62	10.97	7.24

年份	农用机械总动力（万千瓦）	农用大中型拖拉机（台）	小型拖拉机（台）	灌溉面积（千公顷）	化肥施用量（万吨）	农村用电量（万千瓦小时）	农村居民家庭每户生产性固定资产（元）
1978	176.84	9 622	6 712	370.86	29.03	53 087	
1979	189.71	11 574	8 044	380.92	32.36	61 067	
1980	213.32	12 819	9 175	379.27	27.62	67 281	
1981	220.24	13 175	8 375	379.53	21.17	67 368	
1982	254.44	12 795	7 243	370.73	21.52	68 783	
1983	276.33	12 654	7 855	365.23	23.77	82 032	
1984	310.68	11 870	9 137	360.91	25.56	96 800	
1985	331.25	12 525	11 336	349.43	27.12	103 093	
1986	360.39	12 860	14 557	340.61	27.56	112 929	
1987	382.52	12 523	18 660	340.84	28.04	115 850	
1988	418.30	11 435	22 105	342.62	34.18	132 128	
1989	428.62	10 422	24 571	342.17	39.53	154 286	
1990	439.99	9 504	26 553	345.86	40.99	165 331	950
1991	447.80	8 973	29 585	347.11	42.53	180 834	1 410
1992	449.02	8 552	32 000	346.46	41.19	218 273	1 490
1993	470.05	8 341	31 700	347.46	40.13	231 072	1 970
1994	504.34	8 147	32 400	348.52	41.06	250 611	2 315
1995	532.45	8 156	30 000	354.66	45.29	325 482	2 285
1996	558.02	8 330	34 500	351.57	48.82	358 184	2 330

8－4　改革开放以来农业总产值和播种面积

年　份	农林牧渔业总产值(现价)(亿元)	农业	林业	牧业	渔业
1978	6.72	5.39	0.04	1.06	0.23
1979	8.88	7.10	0.04	1.48	0.26
1980	9.25	7.24	0.05	1.63	0.33
1981－1985	70.71	51.8	0.84	15.19	2.88
1981	8.35	6.10	0.05	1.97	0.23
1982	12.56	10.16	0.11	1.92	0.37
1983	12.68	9.57	0.16	2.48	0.47
1984	16.68	12.17	0.25	3.70	0.56
1985	20.44	13.80	0.27	5.12	1.25
1986－1990	211.03	140.07	2.18	50.52	18.27
1986	26.93	18.79	0.31	5.69	2.14
1987	32.93	22.47	0.37	7.22	2.87
1988	44.49	29.39	0.72	10.09	4.29
1989	51.82	34.71	0.33	12.83	3.95
1990	54.86	34.71	0.45	14.69	5.02
1991－1995	419.04	263.15	2.68	119.32	33.9
1991	58.05	36.67	0.34	16.39	4.65
1992	62.15	39.24	0.45	17.09	5.37
1993	70.62	44.28	0.44	20.12	5.78
1994	94.97	57.71	0.60	29.14	7.52
1995	133.25	85.25	0.85	36.58	10.58
1996	142.29	90.17	0.96	39.03	12.13

年　份	播种面积(万公顷)	#粮食作物	蔬菜	每公顷面积产量(公斤)		
				粮食	棉花	油料
1978	70.04	60.10	3.81	1 950	120	518
1979	68.80	58.51	3.88	2 370	105	615
1980	66.90	56.35	3.70	2 445	195	930
1981－1985						
1981	63.70	52.14	3.68	2 055	225	1 028
1982	60.99	50.11	3.88	2 445	435	1 118
1983	60.76	50.45	3.57	2 197	623	953
1984	62.34	48.67	3.85	2 700	863	1 328
1985	59.62	44.59	3.77	3 150	825	1 125
1986－1990						
1986	58.21	45.74	4.43	3 435	735	1 425
1987	57.36	45.77	4.45	3 660	795	1 455
1988	57.65	45.05	5.17	3 540	555	990
1989	57.30	45.47	5.47	3 735	735	1 425
1990	57.32	45.79	5.49	4 122	855	1 575
1991－1995						
1991	58.15	45.78	5.66	4 336	855	1 740
1992	57.35	44.61	6.17	4 455	566	1 597
1993	56.57	45.16	6.61	4 425	776	1 809
1994	55.51	42.27	7.59	4 503	408	1 765
1995	57.27	44.33	8.10	4 680	645	1 770
1996	57.35	45.15	8.73	4 584	776	1 700

8-5 改革开放以来主要农产品产量

年 份	主要农产品产量(万吨)							
	粮食	棉花	油料	肉类	蛋类	奶类	蔬菜	水产品
1978	117.14	0.23	1.00	6.51	1.64	1.72	122.37	4.49
1979	138.69	0.11	1.51	6.63	1.94	1.96	127.32	3.28
1980	137.76	0.16	2.79	6.46	1.27	2.24	111.72	3.21
1981-1985	615.20	7.49	24.38	32.2	26.84	17.1	667.9	19.71
1981	110.00	0.23	4.50	7.14	1.91	2.61	111.25	2.69
1982	122.51	0.45	4.43	5.90	2.63	2.92	129.29	3.59
1983	110.87	1.14	3.09	5.50	4.49	3.37	128.07	4.11
1984	131.30	3.29	5.52	6.54	7.19	3.90	147.77	4.45
1985	140.52	2.38	6.84	7.12	10.62	4.30	151.52	4.87
1986-1990	842.12	6.25	23.63	46.11	73.45	30.56	1 140.52	45.22
1986	157.60	1.33	5.86	7.57	10.65	4.71	193.95	6.73
1987	167.67	1.28	5.22	7.40	11.20	5.31	202.48	8.13
1988	158.30	1.01	3.45	8.51	15.52	6.18	215.44	9.15
1989	169.80	1.10	4.42	10.74	17.44	6.75	260.51	10.38
1990	188.75	1.53	4.68	11.89	18.64	7.61	268.14	10.83
1991-1995	994.86	6.99	20.95	83.19	113.23	48.84	1 789.34	61.48
1991	198.51	2.55	4.50	13.05	21.40	8.79	282.56	10.81
1992	198.74	1.63	3.96	15.05	21.34	9.51	310.41	11.10
1993	199.82	0.76	4.45	15.43	21.49	9.55	354.34	11.39
1994	190.33	0.93	4.03	18.43	24.93	9.86	407.86	12.83
1995	207.46	1.12	4.01	21.23	24.07	11.13	434.17	15.35
1996	207.00	0.51	3.13	22.68	24.44	11.36	452.71	16.99

年 份	每一农林牧渔业从业者农业生产量(公斤)							
	粮食	棉花	油料	肉类	蛋类	奶类	蔬菜	水产品
1978	1 133.21	2.23	9.67	62.98	15.87	16.64	1 183.81	43.44
1979	1 309.26	1.04	14.25	62.59	18.31	18.50	1 201.93	30.96
1980	1 311.50	1.52	26.56	61.50	12.09	21.33	1 063.59	30.56
1981	1 024.02	2.14	41.89	66.47	17.78	24.30	1 035.65	25.04
1982	1 138.89	4.18	41.18	54.85	24.45	27.15	1 201.92	33.37
1983	992.39	10.20	27.66	49.23	40.19	30.16	1 146.35	36.79
1984	1 245.02	31.20	52.34	62.01	68.18	36.98	1 401.19	42.20
1985	1 476.67	25.01	71.88	74.82	111.60	45.19	1 592.27	51.18
1986	1 721.46	14.53	64.01	82.69	116.33	51.45	2 118.51	73.51
1987	1 865.69	14.24	58.08	82.34	124.62	59.09	2 253.03	90.46
1988	1 821.84	11.62	39.71	97.94	178.62	71.12	2 479.46	105.31
1989	1 902.95	12.33	49.53	120.36	195.45	75.65	2 919.53	116.33
1990	2 108.23	17.09	52.27	132.80	208.20	85.00	2 994.97	120.97
1991	2 207.38	28.36	50.04	145.11	237.96	97.74	3 142.00	120.20
1992	2 247.43	18.43	44.78	170.19	241.32	107.54	3 510.23	125.52
1993	2 310.86	8.79	51.46	178.44	248.53	110.44	4 097.84	131.72
1994	2 284.05	11.16	48.36	221.17	299.17	118.32	4 894.52	153.97
1995	2 564.40	13.84	49.57	262.42	297.53	137.58	5 366.75	189.74
1996	2 580.32	6.33	38.98	282.66	304.67	141.56	5 643.17	211.83

8－6　1996年各区县农村劳动力

单位:人

地区	乡村劳动力资源总数	乡村实有劳动力合计	#农林牧渔业劳动力	工业劳动力	建筑业劳动力	交通运输业和邮电业劳动力	仓储业劳动力	批发、零售贸易、饮食业劳动力
合计	**1 816 585**	**1 679 200**	**802 216**	**508 226**	**95 715**	**84 355**	**8 127**	**76 351**
塘沽区	35 118	29 923	9 773	9 820	1 418	3 231	1 211	1 372
汉沽区	28 396	25 362	12 733	6 499	1 772	1 942	4	699
大港区	42 424	40 731	12 677	20 613	1 022	2 734		1 417
东丽区	98 221	90 417	22 803	36 895	3 276	8 889	3 610	5 417
西青区	120 480	111 092	35 995	59 706	1 371	3 259	794	3 839
津南区	163 435	146 752	38 524	66 414	11 832	8 438	1 111	7 656
北辰区	88 242	81 997	27 682	37 310	1 255	3 553	157	3 501
宁河县	128 348	110 609	66 085	21 224	7 307	4 552		3 878
武清县	372 842	358 796	197 885	94 453	20 452	17 837	793	15 752
静海县	168 725	152 818	71 315	54 648	5 437	5 023	387	4 964
宝坻县	247 299	220 852	124 811	60 893	13 746	6 885	39	7 357
蓟　县	323 055	309 851	181 933	39 751	26 827	18 012	21	20 499

8－7　1996年各区县农村固定资产构成

单位:万元

地区	年末固定资产原值	#农林牧渔业	工业	建筑业	运输业	商业饮食业	#住宅
合计	**4 469 065**	**297 180**	**1 927 328**	**30 437**	**282 679**	**99 429**	**1 672 722**
塘沽区	132 912	15 625	38 323	2 965	30 864	2 670	36 097
汉沽区	53 817	8 612	20 709	345	4 557	313	17 607
大港区	141 945	10 087	73 358	680	9 545	2 531	43 594
东丽区	371 687	17 360	101 995	2 599	43 809	12 453	182 691
西青区	570 071	30 998	329 861	819	21 681	13 715	143 915
津南区	476 646	16 972	202 006	7 936	26 116	14 941	191 849
北辰区	307 937	11 722	162 198	540	17 026	4 568	100 838
宁河县	194 429	17 959	75 894	1 521	8 866	2 177	75 559
武清县	700 041	46 828	316 760	4 123	38 827	9 218	263 212
静海县	668 510	41 297	381 652	3 907	32 545	27 424	170 463
宝坻县	511 018	45 665	138 291	2 312	20 174	3 150	282 463
蓟　县	340 052	34 055	86 281	2 690	28 669	6 269	164 434

8-8 农民家庭每户生产性固定资产原值

单位:元

项目	1990年	1991年	1992年	1993年	1994年	1995年	1996年
年末生产性固定资产原值	**950**	**1 410**	**1 490**	**1 970**	**2 315**	**2 285**	**4 566**
役畜、产品畜	238	382	380	326	498	508	428
大中型铁木农具	61	135	150	178	161	180	124
农林牧渔业机械	136	237	261	333	306	389	1 117
工业机械	3	9	20	11	11	47	29
运输机械	247	241	300	630	562	503	1 626
生产用房	173	377	327	442	778	652	1 242
其他	91	30	55	48		4	

注:本表数据为农村住户抽样调查数。

8-9 农民家庭每百户拥有生产性固定资产数量

项目	单位	1990年	1991年	1992年	1993年	1994年	1995年	1996年
汽车	辆	0.20	1.05	0.30	1.00	1.00	1.00	2.00
大中型拖拉机	台	1.07	1.08	0.83	1.28	1.55	1.20	2.00
小型和手扶拖拉机	台	4.64	5.95	6.47	7.69	8.04	10.14	15.00
机动脱粒机	台	3.75	3.33	5.12	3.55	3.92	4.58	7.00
胶轮大车	辆	14.96	27.35	26.52	20.75	16.90	21.27	19.00
胶轮手推车	辆	67.13	40.52	43.33	45.50	50.20	40.56	33.00
抽水机	台	4.36	3.92	5.17	3.19	3.49	2.75	4.00
水泵	台	5.95	3.38	5.42	4.91	11.57	6.81	12.00
役畜	头	38.63	50.37	51.50	35.53	33.52	31.62	26.00
产品畜	头	9.61	16.28	13.98	14.85	18.55	18.44	13.00

注:本表数据为农村住户抽样调查数。

8－10　1996年各区县耕地面积

单位：公顷

地　区	年末实有耕地	水　田	旱　地	#水浇地	在总计中：粮食占用耕　地	在总计中：蔬菜占用耕　地
合　计	**425 752**	**59 180**	**366 572**	**277 044**	**309 205**	**43 096**
塘沽区	5 232	3 554	1 678	1 678	3 850	1 100
汉沽区	4 523	2 371	2 152	2 152	2 682	332
大港区	13 179	776	12 403	3 593	11 907	398
东丽区	14 062	7 279	6 783	6 670	11 097	2 352
西青区	16 271	3 143	13 128	12 851	9 695	3 690
津南区	15 025	4 572	10 453	9 604	11 236	2 254
北辰区	18 656	1 593	17 063	10 608	11 618	2 979
宁河县	39 547	19 876	19 671	18 112	30 392	5 153
武清县	91 734	726	91 008	73 898	58 725	11 632
静海县	69 354	693	68 661	48 320	60 582	3 236
宝坻县	77 543	10 501	67 042	46 689	62 410	4 396
蓟　县	54 511	2 728	51 783	39 697	31 094	5 392

8－11　1996年各区县农业现代化情况

地　区	农业机械总动力（万千瓦）	#排灌机械	当年实际机播面积（千公顷）	当年实际机耕面积（千公顷）	农　村用电量（万千瓦时）	化肥施用量（实物量）（吨）	农用塑料薄膜使用量（吨）	农药使用量（吨）
合　计	**558.02**	**114.91**	**222.82**	**398.45**	**358 184**	**488 179**	**6 189**	**3 158**
塘沽区	28.03	4.62	0.12	5.14	9 881	4 271	236	50
汉沽区	15.19	3.68	0.21	3.33	10 794	5 806	100	160
大港区	31.14	2.87	6.60	12.53	12 012	5 305	35	57
东丽区	70.08	5.85	1.90	13.72	20 265	9 599	459	219
西青区	43.88	5.61	6.45	15.71	43 569	16 096	1 726	321
津南区	44.94	5.75	4.94	14.79	24 045	13 064	606	119
北辰区	59.01	4.39	7.54	18.25	21 614	15 047	657	339
宁河县	42.14	15.60	6.12	38.12	16 406	52 249	532	515
武清县	81.11	20.61	73.40	89.00	52 275	132 295	783	323
静海县	53.87	14.91	53.00	63.10	85 754	61 763	339	173
宝坻县	40.13	16.02	34.01	72.34	33 033	71 749	359	304
蓟　县	46.43	14.13	26.54	48.54	22 256	98 861	333	517

8－12　1996 年各区县农业总产值和农业商品产值

地区	农林牧渔业总产值(现价)(万元)	#农业产值	农林牧渔业商品产值(万元)	农业	林业	牧业	渔业	农林牧渔业产品商品率(%)
合计	**1 422 900**	**901 720**	**1 126 279**	**643 817**	**2 669**	**364 384**	**115 409**	**79.2**
塘沽区	31 786	12 251	26 432	7 183	2	6 989	12 258	83.2
汉沽区	40 455	12 400	36 799	9 316	37	4 500	22 946	91.0
大港区	21 868	12 485	17 719	8 860	26	6 613	2 220	81.0
东丽区	54 712	37 177	46 375	29 192	238	11 707	5 238	84.8
西青区	75 501	38 995	68 052	32 926		20 118	15 008	90.1
津南区	39 611	25 807	36 228	23 851		8 245	4 132	91.5
北辰区	90 779	54 578	79 485	45 623	55	30 251	3 556	87.6
宁河县	142 496	102 122	116 039	78 153	304	23 830	13 752	81.4
武清县	321 251	220 671	273 778	179 932	600	86 301	6 945	85.2
静海县	166 671	130 696	96 034	67 866	527	22 519	5 120	57.6
宝坻县	221 678	149 020	173 884	104 334	59	60 427	9 064	78.4
蓟　县	184 967	101 154	125 722	52 368	820	65 197	7 337	68.0

8－13　1996 年各区县农业增加值情况

单位:万元

地　区	总产出	中间消耗	增加值合计	固定资产折旧	劳动者报酬	生产税	营业盈余
合　计	**1 422 900**	**717 567**	**705 333**	**25 688**	**567 024**	**9 780**	**102 841**
塘沽区	31 786	17 539	14 247	833	10 229	194	2 991
汉沽区	40 455	23 392	17 063	1 292	15 431	340	
大港区	21 868	11 777	10 091	1 392	7 565	215	919
东丽区	54 712	35 652	19 060	230	18 430	400	
西青区	75 501	39 076	36 425	3 500	22 848	218	9 859
津南区	39 611	17 614	21 997	968	12 142	484	8 403
北辰区	90 779	47 945	42 834	1 806	36 724	332	3 972
宁河县	142 496	71 488	71 008	861	60 802	694	8 651
武清县	321 251	190 593	130 658	2 818	112 284	1 147	14 409
静海县	166 671	60 471	106 200	2 892	95 735	1 153	6 420
宝坻县	221 678	89 875	131 803	4 438	98 565	1 726	27 074
蓟　县	184 967	87 200	97 767	3 008	70 835	2 604	21 320

8－14　1996年各区县主要农作物播种面积

单位:公顷

地　　区	粮食作物合计	谷类作物	#夏收谷物	稻　谷	玉　米	豆　类	薯　类
合　计	**451 525**	**402 674**	**147 561**	**61 741**	**162 854**	**45 924**	**2 927**
塘沽区	3 850	3 832	63	3 462	84	13	5
汉沽区	2 772	2 708	90	2 173	322	64	
大港区	15 132	11 571	3 670	1 247	3 160	3 547	14
东丽区	11 097	10 986		7 323	1 425	111	
西青区	12 695	11 453	3 000	3 015	4 008	1 242	
津南区	11 236	11 030		4 344	2 628	206	
北辰区	14 882	12 230	3 347	2 014	6 208	2 444	208
宁河县	37 338	36 311	6 669	20 054	7 260	1 025	2
武清县	100 344	93 426	41 613	1 338	48 405	6 168	750
静海县	83 560	65 334	28 185	693	29 014	17 824	402
宝坻县	96 519	84 574	34 109	10 419	35 940	11 075	870
蓟　县	57 681	54 892	26 680	4 257	23 260	2 112	677

地　　区	油料作物总计	#花　生	棉　花	蔬菜总计	#大白菜	瓜类总计	#西　瓜
合　计	**18 399**	**6 348**	**6 542**	**87 330**	**15 739**	**3 963**	**2 603**
塘沽区				2 069	275	18	18
汉沽区			82	492	137	18	18
大港区	857	24		390	276	18	12
东丽区				3 337	494	41	41
西青区	93	22		6 398	787		
津南区				4 258	317		
北辰区	1 469	275	6	6 861	1 097	175	156
宁河县	501	169	1 278	8 299	563	362	354
武清县	6 600	2 867	2 165	30 553	5 002	1 174	352
静海县	4 552	478	341	5 800	1 794	552	414
宝坻县	3 217	1 561	2 500	7 808	1 562	766	611
蓟　县	1 031	952	170	10 885	3 427	754	542

8－15　1996 年各区县主要农产品产量

单位:吨

地　区	粮食作物合　计	谷　类作　物	#夏收谷物	稻　谷	玉　米	豆　类	薯　类
合　计	**2 069 971**	**1 991 769**	**673 497**	**474 208**	**754 096**	**65 634**	**12 568**
塘沽区	28 319	28 249	222	26 370	356	39	31
汉沽区	19 329	18 896	411	16 358	1 540	433	
大港区	47 710	43 174	13 054	5 998	11 289	4 507	29
东丽区	76 933	76 658		59 156	5 400	275	
西青区	69 205	67 603	15 700	23 727	19 591	1 602	
津南区	63 863	63 376		29 546	11 753	487	
北辰区	67 181	62 016	16 346	13 724	28 448	4 103	1 062
宁河县	231 759	260 067	25 334	158 229	33 795	1 685	7
武清县	515 000	501 324	249 680	9 175	235 324	10 297	3 379
静海县	322 891	295 912	149 090	4 380	122 350	25 465	1 514
宝坻县	473 859	454 799	185 210	79 717	179 194	15 034	4 026
蓟　县	323 467	317 314	160 631	28 794	126 815	3 150	3 003

地　区	油料作物总　计	#花　生	棉　花	蔬　菜总　计	#大白菜	瓜　类总　计	#西　瓜
合　计	**31 270**	**14 479**	**5 077**	**4 527 079**	**1 187 908**	**197 284**	**123 454**
塘沽区				70 131	16 525	1 239	1 239
汉沽区			77	36 276	8 577	700	700
大港区	784	36		31 262	20 281	986	720
东丽区				212 991	31 311	912	912
西青区	61	16		357 606	39 390		
津南区				169 547	16 500		
北辰区	2 365	530	4	371 005	74 315	4 327	3 963
宁河县	813	294	1 263	285 250	35 874	19 942	19 532
武清县	13 720	7 620	1 917	1 500 000	386 302	62 830	19 514
静海县	5 727	741	234	347 418	119 017	20 749	17 697
宝坻县	5 349	3 036	1 495	435 514	116 081	39 099	21 506
蓟　县	2 283	2 206	87	707 562	323 083	45 456	36 627

8-16 1996年各区县主要农作物单位面积产量

单位:公斤/公顷

地区	粮食作物合计	谷类作物	#夏收谷物	稻谷	玉米	豆类	薯类
合计	**4 584**	**4 946**	**4 564**	**7 681**	**4 631**	**1 429**	**4 293**
塘沽区	7 355	7 373	3 505	7 617	4 238	2 910	5 962
汉沽区	6 973	6 977	4 574	7 526	4 780	6 801	
大港区	3 153	3 731	3 557	4 811	3 572	1 271	2 122
东丽区	6 933	6 978		8 078	3 788	2 476	
西青区	5 452	5 903	5 233	7 870	4 888	1 290	
津南区	5 684	5 746		6 802	4 472	2 361	
北辰区	4 514	5 071	4 883	6 813	4 582	1 679	5 106
宁河县	6 207	6 336	3 799	7 890	4 655	1 644	4 200
武清县	5 132	5 366	6 000	6 856	4 862	1 669	4 508
静海县	3 864	4 529	5 290	6 317	4 217	1 429	3 767
宝坻县	4 910	5 378	5 430	7 651	4 986	1 358	4 628
蓟县	70 369	5 781	6 021	6 764	5 452	1 492	4 433

地区	油料作物总计	#花生	棉花	蔬菜总计	#大白菜	瓜类总计	#西瓜
合计	**1 700**	**2 281**	**776**	**51 839**	**75 477**	**49 783**	**47 430**
塘沽区				33 894	60 004	67 829	67 829
汉沽区			941	73 692	62 789	38 889	38 889
大港区	914	1 508		80 077	73 571	55 393	61 714
东丽区				63 825	63 443	22 463	22 463
西青区	654	729		55 895	50 072		
津南区				39 815	52 105		
北辰区	1 610	1 927	706	54 076	67 773	24 773	25 404
宁河县	1 623	1 741	988	34 370	63 757	55 129	55 113
武清县	2 079	2 658	885	49 095	77 237	53 512	55 469
静海县	1 258	1 550	686	59 900	66 337	37 598	42 767
宝坻县	1 663	1 945	598	55 777	74 309	51 070	35 221
蓟县	2 214	2 316	511	65 001	94 279	60 270	67 611

8－17　1996年各区县畜牧业生产情况

地　区	大牲畜头数总计（头）	#牛	#乳　牛	猪存栏头数（万头）	全年出栏肉猪（万头）	羊存栏只数（万只）	年内羊只出栏（万只）	家禽存栏（万只）	年内家禽出栏（万只）
合　计	**403 940**	**235 739**	**28 547**	**87.78**	**173.07**	**69.84**	**90.69**	**2 353.23**	**3 019.53**
塘沽区	941	700		1.25	3.30	0.15	0.39	36.75	34.84
汉沽区	486	251	131	0.56	1.41	0.19	0.27	35.59	27.19
大港区	9 422	1 087	126	1.04	2.67	2.17	2.17	57.37	50.91
东丽区	3 759	1 868	1 284	3.02	5.39	2.78	3.92	58.11	67.80
西青区	5 177	2 034	843	4.39	11.41	1.54	3.27	150.57	256.89
津南区	3 361	1 288	487	1.44	3.68	1.77	2.75	61.88	185.84
北辰区	11 419	4 946	4 115	3.22	6.80	4.37	5.47	211.36	238.50
宁河县	22 269	8 670	1 450	5.56	11.38	2.29	2.97	161.49	90.06
武清县	97 483	64 229	3 005	12.00	38.00	21.56	36.40	499.46	1 440.65
静海县	40 749	6 836	2 713	3.62	7.20	6.94	7.59	146.04	100.03
宝坻县	97 757	57 783	398	24.03	34.87	13.56	12.94	472.31	215.44
蓟　县	97 083	72 020	8	27.61	6.91	12.53	12.55	367.77	223.66

地　区	肉类总产量（吨）	#猪　肉	牛　肉	羊　肉	禽　肉	#鸡　肉	禽蛋产量（吨）	奶类产量（吨）
合　计	**226 757**	**130 892**	**29 563**	**17 187**	**46 002**	**38 761**	**244 411**	**113 559**
塘沽区	3 406	2 308	279	129	686	681	5 016	
汉沽区	1 575	1 082	30	38	425	422	4 430	53
大港区	3 116	2 002	95	396	616	613	5 877	560
东丽区	6 050	4 044	414	575	1 017	1 016	6 340	4 752
西青区	15 675	9 128	669	498	5 369	2 206	14 305	2 691
津南区	6 436	3 300	203	596	2 329	2 312	5 142	2 969
北辰区	10 725	4 760	1 023	1 419	3 134	3 078	24 490	16 209
宁河县	11 570	7 966	2 008	505	943	880	18 086	3 789
武清县	69 428	26 600	12 938	7 281	21 691	19 712	49 661	16 568
静海县	11 612	6 328	540	2 248	2 075	1 628	16 731	11 384
宝坻县	41 247	28 620	6 740	1 850	3 318	3 127	46 585	1 500
蓟　县	43 798	34 706	3 951	1 652	3 001	2 537	37 583	56

8－18　林业生产、果园面积及产量

项　　目	单　位	1990年	1992年	1995年	1996年	1996比1995年增长%
一、年末实有林地面积	**万公顷**	**4.47**	**7.12**	**8.70**	**9.26**	**6.4**
#当年造林面积	万公顷	0.73	0.72	0.48	0.62	29.2
二、年末实有四旁零星植树	**万株**	**10 599.47**	**5 256.82**	**7 000.62**	**7 369.49**	**5.3**
#当年植树	万株	885.48	993.45	944.39	582.58	－38.3
三、年末实有果园面积	**万公顷**	**2.93**	**2.82**	**3.43**	**3.34**	**－2.6**
四、干果产量	**吨**	**529**	**731**	**683**	**826**	**20.9**
#核　桃	吨	362	412	449	540	20.3
栗　子	吨	87	153	153	183	19.6
五、鲜果产量	**吨**	**101 032**	**141 169**	**199 227**	**212 078**	**6.5**
#苹　果	吨	31 108	39 204	62 790	71 164	13.3
梨	吨	12 274	16 567	17 618	18 271	3.7
桃	吨	26 565	40 744	58 596	58 166	－0.7
鲜　枣	吨	3 622	3 644	5 217	4 365	－16.3
葡　萄	吨	17 433	20 389	34 083	37 980	11.4
柿　子	吨	4 489	12 685	10 723	12 377	15.4
其　他	吨	796	1 221	1 168	9 755	735.2

8－19　1996年各区县渔业生产情况

地　　区	水产品总产量（吨）	海水产品	#养　殖	淡水产品	#养　殖	水产养殖面　积（公顷）	#海水养殖
合　计	**169 936**	**29 420**	**2 086**	**140 516**	**123 392**	**34 062**	**5 055**
塘沽区	15 608	12 075	722	3 533	3 533	4 116	1 893
汉沽区	20 162	10 817	947	9 345	9 183	2 192	1 003
大港区	5 770	1 664	293	4 106	1 785	4 243	1 812
东丽区	8 708	1	1	8 707	8 151	2 409	37
西青区	28 865			28 865	28 595	4 689	
津南区	7 185			7 185	6 999	1 659	
北辰区	6 549	50		6 499	6 010	1 646	
宁河县	11 298	118	118	11 180	10 524	2 821	256
武清县	19 500			19 500	19 000	4 089	
静海县	8 692			8 692	5 112	1 178	
宝坻县	17 404			17 404	14 465	2 500	
蓟　县	12 685			12 685	7 200	1 871	

8－20 1996年乡镇企业基本情况

项　目	合　计	乡　办	村　办	联　户	个　体
一、企业个数(个)	**96 599**	**2 819**	**9 401**	**7 995**	**76 384**
农　业	29	11	18		
工　业	28 573	1 999	6 947	3 704	15 923
建筑业	1 781	126	168	269	1 218
交　通	24 981	180	482	2 550	21 769
商　业	27 510	364	1 321	902	24 923
餐饮业	6 495	45	253	313	5 884
房地产	35	20	14		1
服务业	7 195	74	198	257	6 666
二、年末人数(人)	**1 137 176**	**275 261**	**560 342**	**67 466**	**234 107**
农　业	1 105	355	750		
工　业	866 282	228 194	493 902	51 902	92 284
建筑业	72 101	30 512	16 704	4 124	20 761
交　通	76 725	7 047	21 753	6 446	41 479
商　业	71 679	5 626	16 326	3 037	46 690
餐饮业	25 059	1 190	3 629	1 184	19 056
房地产	1 017	507	505		5
服务业	23 208	1 830	6 773	773	13 832
三、营业收入(万元)	**11 509 467**	**2 459 114**	**6 548 457**	**603 689**	**1 898 207**
农　业	9 418	2 777	6 641		
工　业	9 248 379	2 086 972	5 616 535	515 762	1 029 110
建筑业	253 732	85 321	71 602	18 764	78 045
交　通	479 392	96 601	98 727	40 039	244 025
商　业	1 186 131	147 522	641 594	18 847	378 168
餐饮业	141 769	6 792	22 678	5 233	107 066
房地产	70 938	15 290	55 568		80
服务业	119 708	17 839	35 112	5 044	61 713
四、利润总额(万元)	**1 087 241**	**242 904**	**596 119**	**58 918**	**189 300**
农　业	397	131	266		
工　业	887 158	207 216	532 893	48 853	98 196
建筑业	30 334	9 780	11 066	1 430	8 058
交　通	66 016	14 353	14 405	4 281	32 977
商　业	60 044	7 394	22 486	2 789	27 375
餐饮业	18 544	595	3 866	744	13 339
房地产	8 541	2 244	6 287		10
服务业	16 207	1 191	4 850	821	9 345

8－20 续表

项　目	合　计	乡　办	村　办	联　户	个　体
五、固定资产原值(万元)	**2 748 547**	**802 024**	**1 605 077**	**80 551**	**260 895**
农　业	3 696	1 467	2 229		
工　业	2 208 782	712 081	1 340 695	64 972	91 034
建筑业	40 121	19 049	9 906	1 845	9 321
交　通	209 649	24 194	84 861	7 861	92 733
商　业	108 916	21 977	50 666	3 544	32 729
餐饮业	48 840	10 916	14 212	1 669	22 043
房地产	94 821	3 528	91 283		10
服务业	33 722	8 812	11 225	660	13 025
六、流动资产合计(万元)	**3 463 855**	**1 021 974**	**2 132 726**	**72 862**	**236 293**
农　业	4 795	1 046	3 749		
工　业	3 053 156	926 561	1 954 042	63 800	108 753
建筑业	53 229	24 601	19 211	1 233	8 184
交　通	98 787	13 569	35 670	4 078	45 470
商　业	169 188	33 640	82 219	2 870	50 459
餐饮业	22 215	1 438	5 793	485	14 499
房地产	37 874	15 885	21 985		4
服务业	24 611	5 234	10 057	396	8 924
七、实交各种税金(万元)	**201 881**	**55 147**	**115 001**	**10 468**	**21 265**
农　业	46	16	30		
工　业	167 460	46 001	104 352	9 058	8 049
建筑业	7 063	3 300	2 256	186	1 321
交　通	10 702	2 624	2 217	615	5 246
商　业	10 627	2 137	4 397	392	3 701
餐饮业	2 900	208	598	149	1 945
房地产	898	388	507		3
服务业	2 185	473	644	68	1 000
八、应付工资总额(万元)	**638 814**	**143 996**	**292 284**	**35 747**	**166 787**
农　业	519	230	289		
工　业	456 050	117 153	255 690	27 623	55 584
建筑业	35 189	13 828	9 569	1 667	10 125
交　通	56 303	5 518	10 926	3 337	36 522
商　业	51 360	5 146	8 663	2 026	35 525
餐饮业	21 602	535	2 011	470	18 586
房地产	1 453	489	960		4
服务业	16 338	1 097	4 176	624	10 441
九、出口产品交货值(万元)	**1 419 711**	**600 218**	**819 493**		
#工　业	1 419 711	600 218	819 493		

8-21 1996年各区县乡镇企业主要指标

单位:万元

地 区	企业个数(个)	平均人数(人)	工资总额	总产值(90价)	出口产品交货值(现价)	营业收入
总 计	**96 599**	**1 140 978**	**638 814**	**11 987 207**	**1 419 711**	**11 509 467**
塘沽区	3 436	28 799	13 924	167 404	11 701	171 534
汉沽区	164	15 055	6 374	91 978	15 560	88 917
大港区	3 136	48 128	25 891	402 107	36 780	378 643
东丽区	1 102	52 809	39 932	547 626	78 086	825 746
西青区	8 350	123 993	84 018	1 757 522	136 302	1 607 865
津南区	9 851	134 795	69 477	1 473 028	166 454	1 363 130
北辰区	10 245	99 392	49 367	1 110 088	107 602	1 140 005
宁河县	12 028	75 175	56 155	1 079 151	59 064	945 718
武清县	12 021	181 146	77 312	1 611 586	263 791	1 235 524
静海县	4 236	127 507	72 529	1 957 713	173 948	2 052 429
宝坻县	15 996	153 718	98 634	1 206 395	273 437	1 258 937
蓟 县	16 034	100 461	45 201	582 609	96 986	441 019

地 区	利润总额	实交税金	固定资产原值	流动资产合计	百元固定资产原值实现利润	百元收入实现利润
总 计	**1 087 241**	**201 881**	**2 748 547**	**3 463 855**	**39.56**	**9.45**
塘沽区	20 594	6 172	77 979	80 840	26.41	12.01
汉沽区	3 696	1 993	25 836	54 963	14.31	4.16
大港区	20 039	11 912	95 652	142 217	20.95	5.29
东丽区	38 497	13 295	167 615	237 126	22.97	4.66
西青区	169 366	18 958	545 603	485 709	31.04	10.53
津南区	157 784	29 907	303 341	444 262	52.02	11.58
北辰区	101 241	16 044	272 093	436 139	37.21	8.88
宁河县	80 476	8 106	154 248	171 826	52.17	8.51
武清县	162 095	24 046	324 255	421 272	49.99	13.12
静海县	157 111	47 151	474 690	587 176	33.10	7.65
宝坻县	145 623	14 578	188 033	266 438	77.45	11.57
蓟 县	30 719	9 719	119 202	135 887	25.77	6.97

九、工 业

INDUSTRY

1996 年街、乡以上工业企业单位数	11 073 个
1996 年全部工业总产值	2 522.42 亿元
其中:轻工业占比重	46.6%
重工业占比重	53.4%

工业总产值（亿元）

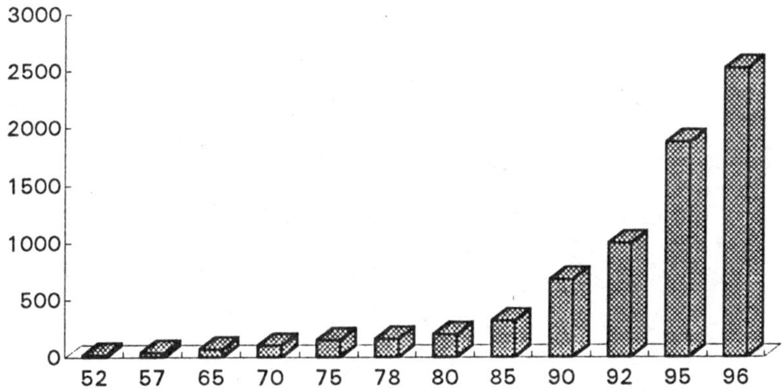

乡及乡以上工业增加值构成

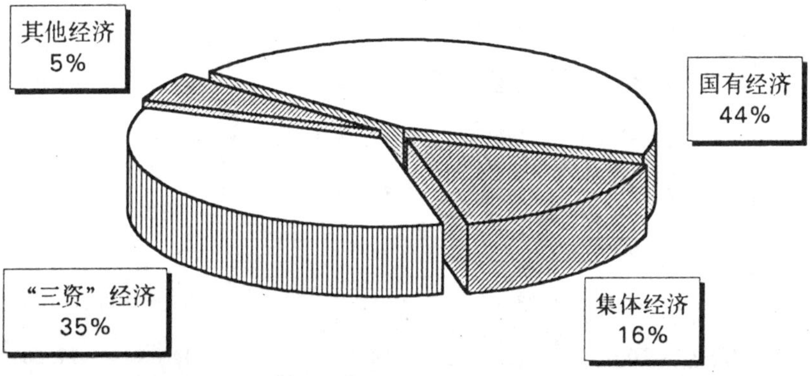

9－1　全部工业总产值和增长速度

(1985－1996 年)

年　　份	全部工业总产值	轻工业	重工业	街道、乡及以上工业总产值	轻工业	重工业
绝对数(亿元)						
1985	319.47	164.22	155.25	290.99	147.86	143.13
1986	344.73	174.84	169.89	318.97	162.42	156.55
1987	405.49	205.51	199.98	360.59	182.93	177.66
1988	521.10	267.48	253.62	443.08	226.55	216.53
1989	634.24	317.43	316.81	508.39	254.13	254.26
1990	679.94	354.50	325.44	543.47	266.27	277.20
1991	786.60	392.29	394.31	599.31	274.65	324.66
1992	997.91	465.48	532.43	722.35	308.34	414.01
1993	1 401.84	530.05	871.79	1 068.09	354.79	713.30
1994	1 754.30	760.80	993.50	1 293.80	504.40	789.40
1995(原规定)	2 230.69	901.54	1 329.15	1 594.26	625.10	969.16
1995(新规定)	1 879.65	752.03	1 127.62	1 382.43	536.06	846.37
1996	2 522.42	1 175.17	1 347.25	1 666.26	678.68	987.58
比上年增长%						
1985	15.88	12.84	20.05	13.60	9.28	19.22
1986	6.54	7.27	5.58	5.13	5.44	4.76
1987	11.83	7.05	18.11	8.53	6.67	10.76
1988	18.40	19.67	16.89	11.26	12.54	9.79
1989	9.03	12.32	5.04	3.05	2.71	3.45
1990	7.82	5.27	11.15	3.69	3.08	4.40
1991	12.18	7.05	17.73	5.87	2.32	12.32
1992	24.23	22.49	26.33	16.68	12.91	20.05
1993	25.06	8.92	40.46	27.62	8.51	43.63
1994	19.06	33.77	8.17	13.85	30.75	3.11
1995	23.50	11.15	34.80	16.44	11.63	20.32
1996	24.66	31.76	19.50	19.34	20.02	18.75

注:工业总产值指标 1995 年以前为现价原规定,以后为现价新规定,增长速度按可比价计算。以下各表同。

9－2　改革开放以来工业发展情况

（街、乡及以上独立核算工业）

年　份	企　业单位数（个）	年平均职工人数（万人）	工　业总产值（亿元）	工　业增加值（亿元）	固定资产原　值（亿元）	固定资产净　值（亿元）	流动资产平均余额（亿元）
1978	3 981	121.31	151.01		88.75	54.45	46.51
1979	4 001	121.85	163.87		97.39	60.93	45.30
1980	4 171	127.30	183.45		106.71	67.55	46.14
1981	4 333	134.76	190.76		117.75	74.77	49.03
1982	4 411	141.96	201.04		124.22	77.87	52.36
1983	4 422	138.01	214.73		132.50	82.64	54.94
1984	4 649	144.21	234.95		156.68	101.72	61.42
1985	5 278	149.18	285.29		183.01	119.09	66.91
1986	5 831	152.08	309.14		203.55	132.18	80.72
1987	5 852	157.81	352.61		229.71	150.86	89.12
1988	6 154	157.21	431.14		264.70	174.58	100.56
1989	6 495	157.35	493.58		310.87	195.30	123.71
1990	6 698	159.31	524.53		329.93	217.17	148.83
1991	6 819	155.64	578.66	133.45	379.97	252.86	173.89
1992	7 418	160.30	697.91	158.12	458.50	298.42	207.99
1993	12 454	178.08	1 065.83	210.38	611.67	397.33	559.47
1994	11 280	177.93	1 293.80	270.71	852.75	549.75	756.09
1995	10 671	173.58	1 382.43	348.62	1 273.46	905.27	888.92
1996	10 490	165.56	1 635.96	347.56	1 338.28	976.96	1 044.83

年　份	利税总额（亿元）	产品销售收　入（亿元）	资　金利税率（%）	产　值利税率（%）	百元销售收入实现利润（元）	增加值率（%）	万元工业总产值耗能源（吨标准煤）
1978	38.10	141.56	37.7	25.2	17.29	32.3	
1979	41.29	160.28	38.4	25.2	17.14		
1980	44.48	173.94	39.1	24.3	14.74	33.1	
1981	47.33	186.44	38.2	24.8	16.65		
1982	46.37	195.79	36.8	23.1	15.07		3.88
1983	47.95	209.79	35.7	22.3	14.61		3.81
1984	51.54	230.99	31.6	21.9	13.94		3.71
1985	65.41	280.08	35.2	22.9	13.74	31.2	3.44
1986	65.04	306.38	30.6	21.0	12.24		3.13
1987	67.82	347.11	28.3	19.2	11.17		2.91
1988	69.63	423.08	25.3	16.2	8.85		2.43
1989	59.75	454.76	18.7	12.1	5.77		2.29
1990	48.30	465.55	10.7	9.2	3.68	24.7	2.15
1991	52.61	538.91	9.6	9.1	3.77	22.5	1.88
1992	59.40	646.91	9.2	8.5	3.66	22.7	1.68
1993	84.32	1 040.49	9.6	7.9	3.23	20.8	1.36
1994	109.86	1 101.71	9.3	8.5	3.94	20.9	0.86
1995	133.51	1 376.70	8.8	8.4	4.33	21.9	1.00
1996	139.73	1 498.67	7.2	8.5	4.51	21.3	0.95

注：1.流动资金平均余额1991年以前为定额流动资金。2.增加值率1991年以前为净产值率。3.计算资金利税率所用全部资金，1990年以后为固定资产净值平均余额和全部流动资金平均余额之和。1990年以前为年末固定资产净值和定额流动资金平均余额之和。4.1995年万元工业总产值耗能源指标中现价产值用新规定计算。

9－3　改革开放以来国有工业发展情况

（街、乡及以上独立核算工业）

年　份	企　业 单位数 （个）	年平均职 工 人 数 （万人）	工　业 总产值 （亿元）	工　业 增加值 （亿元）	固定资产 原　值 （亿元）	固定资产 净　值 （亿元）
1978	1 224	81.13	127.58		79.47	47.87
1979	1 179	80.59			86.83	53.37
1980	1 180	83.51	153.87		94.64	58.87
1981	1 148	87.03	159.64		103.83	64.62
1982	1 192	91.57	166.06		108.52	66.51
1983	1 192	88.03	177.15		115.06	70.25
1984	1 156	90.51	193.29		136.56	87.68
1985	1 267	94.27	229.92		159.35	102.07
1986	1 962	94.90	244.84		174.96	111.83
1987	1 850	97.35	275.27		196.15	126.57
1988	1 923	97.73	330.74		223.16	144.22
1989			373.78		258.69	160.37
1990	1 109		387.00		273.52	176.86
1991	1 094		436.43		314.71	207.30
1992	1 028	96.08	492.15	109.25	376.34	245.69
1993	2 165	117.79	628.76	127.37	467.63	292.18
1994	1 629	93.50	648.10	148.76	612.46	363.96
1995	1 927	90.70	682.02	186.27	942.91	644.15
1996	1 918	83.05	558.84	152.52	910.56	647.65

年　份	流动资产 平均余额 （亿元）	利税总额 （亿元）	产品销售 收　　入 （亿元）	资　金 利税率 （%）	产　值 利税率 （%）	百元销售 收入实现 利润（元）
1978	38.24	32.09		37.3	25.2	
1979	36.23	35.75		39.1		
1980	37.05	38.17	146.58	39.8	24.8	17.07
1981	39.18	41.40	156.59	39.9	25.9	17.20
1982	41.08	39.73	162.09	36.8	23.9	15.41
1983	43.72	40.69	173.37	35.7	22.9	14.74
1984	49.26	41.31	190.86	32.4	21.4	14.35
1985	51.58	54.51	225.75	35.5	23.7	13.81
1986	61.81	53.19	244.76	30.6	21.3	12.11
1987	69.58	55.63	275.53	28.4	20.2	11.24
1988	76.64	56.03	331.61	25.4	16.9	8.62
1989	93.85	46.77	352.99	18.4	12.5	5.41
1990	112.41	37.35	356.60	10.7	9.6	3.04
1991	129.89	39.01	407.79	9.3	8.9	3.01
1992	255.46	37.32	459.59	7.9	7.6	2.18
1993	345.77	37.91	663.86	6.7	6.0	0.62
1994	444.30	44.50	584.78	6.3	6.9	0.47
1995	474.69	44.91	625.98	5.6	6.6	0.54
1996	518.45	37.06	594.08	3.3	6.6	0.34

9－4　工业企业单位数和工业总产值

(街、乡及以上工业)

项　　目	企业单位数(个)		工业总产值(亿元)		
	1995 年	1996 年	1995 年	1996 年	1996 比 1995 年增长％
全市总计	**10 671**	**11 073**	**1 382.43**	**1 666.26**	**19.3**
一、按经济类型分					
国有经济	1 927	2 069	582.51	587.86	4.9
集体经济	6 727	6 962	208.92	287.61	20.0
联营经济	143	191	19.06	30.28	69.5
股份制经济	44	17	50.38	41.74	－11.2
“三资”经济	1 830	1 834	521.57	718.77	34.5
外商投资经济	1 089	1 123	383.07	579.57	35.3
港、澳、台投资经济	741	711	138.50	139.20	－0.4
二、按隶属关系分					
中央工业	132	169	199.83	204.84	0.7
地方工业	10 539	10 904	1 182.60	1 461.41	21.1
市属工业	5 504	5 814	960.64	1 113.59	18.1
#工业系统	3 539	3 575	616.89	653.40	9.8
县属工业	357	411	29.98	38.96	11.7
区属工业	1 782	1 686	33.94	41.09	39.7
街属工业	806	997	6.18	15.29	36.5
乡、镇属工业	2 090	1 996	151.86	252.48	32.7
三、按轻重分					
轻工业	5 599	5 623	536.06	678.68	20.0
以农产品为原料	3 284	3 269	308.99	407.27	32.0
以非农产品为原料	2 315	2 354	227.07	271.41	6.9
重工业	5 072	5 450	846.37	987.58	18.8
采掘业	29	40	79.34	84.57	4.8
原料工业	791	903	291.28	300.15	10.6
加工工业	4 252	4 507	475.75	602.86	19.7
四、按规模分					
大　型	255	260	837.43	914.75	8.1
中　型	447	480	161.09	151.39	－3.8
小　型	9 969	10 333	383.91	600.12	53.3

9－5　地方工业企业单位数和工业总产值

（街、乡及以上工业）

项　目	企业单位数(个)		工业总产值(亿元)		
	1995年	1996年	1995年	1996年	1996比1995年增长%
全市总计	**10 539**	**10 904**	**1 182.60**	**1 461.41**	**21.1**
一、按经济类型分					
国有经济	1 795	1 934	382.68	384.79	2.9
集体经济	6 727	6 938	208.92	286.60	20.0
联营经济	143	189	19.06	30.26	69.3
股份制经济	44	17	50.38	41.74	-11.2
"三资"经济	1 830	1 826	521.58	718.02	34.5
外商投资经济	1 089	1 119	383.07	578.91	35.1
港、澳、台投资经济	741	707	138.51	139.11	平
二、按隶属关系分					
市属工业	5 504	5 814	960.64	1 113.59	18.1
#工业系统	3 539	3 575	616.89	653.40	9.8
县属工业	357	411	29.98	38.96	11.7
区属工业	1 782	1 686	33.94	41.09	39.7
街属工业	806	997	6.18	15.29	36.5
乡、镇属工业	2 090	1 996	151.86	252.48	32.7
三、按轻重分					
轻工业	5 548	5 586	528.82	671.04	22.1
以农产品为原料	3 255	3 248	304.30	402.24	36.0
以非农产品为原料	2 293	2 338	224.52	268.80	7.0
重工业	4 991	5 318	653.78	790.37	18.0
采掘业	27	32	0.30	0.31	7.1
原料工业	767	857	197.49	208.64	10.3
加工工业	4 197	4 429	455.99	581.42	20.4
四、按规模分					
大　型	235	241	653.77	752.09	9.9
中　型	430	454	152.37	142.11	-4.9
小　型	9 874	10 209	376.46	567.21	51.2

9-6 分行业工业企业单位数和工业总产值

(街、乡及以上工业)

行 业	企业单位数(个)		工业总产值(亿元)		
	1995年	1996年	1995年	1996年	1996比1995年增长%
总 计	**10 671**	**11 073**	**1 382.43**	**1 666.26**	**19.3**
#石油天燃气开采业	2	15	79.04	84.26	4.7
非金属矿采选业	28	28	5.44	5.35	-0.5
食品加工业	295	313	56.97	57.79	-2.1
食品制造业	357	392	41.66	41.18	29.7
饮料制造业	122	115	22.82	24.48	19.3
烟草加工业	1	1	2.90	2.82	-2.5
纺织业	553	545	77.87	82.47	13.9
服装及其他纤维制品制造业	660	671	36.82	50.72	40.6
皮革、毛皮、羽绒及其制品业	210	203	16.59	20.99	35.1
木材加工及竹、藤、棕、草制品业	160	160	12.23	13.29	26.8
家具制造业	115	121	5.61	5.63	13.3
造纸及纸制品业	278	269	17.36	18.67	5.4
印刷业、记录媒介的复制	351	320	6.24	8.52	40.1
文教体育用品制造业	210	225	12.54	24.71	16.9
石油加工及炼焦业	38	48	71.58	82.31	24.5
化学原料及化学制品制造业	804	837	105.17	176.67	68.9
医药制造业	118	106	27.53	39.57	60.1
化学纤维制造业	37	39	8.03	7.13	5.9
橡胶制品业	152	151	16.23	19.68	15.4
塑料制品业	501	505	20.16	26.28	32.6
非金属矿物制品业	528	556	25.58	33.02	38.3
黑色金属冶炼及压延加工业	112	120	92.55	93.19	9.1
有色金属冶炼及压延加工业	101	101	11.04	14.15	41.1
金属制品业	961	975	54.69	64.81	17.6
普通机械制造业	844	843	59.78	67.72	0.4
专用设备制造业	521	618	30.51	31.39	-4.9
交通运输设备制造业	867	933	142.27	160.83	7.6
电气机械及器材制造业	699	740	41.39	52.02	16.6
电子及通信设备制造业	338	341	212.27	288.35	20.9
仪器仪表及文化、办公用机械制造业	284	304	12.91	13.87	-0.8
其他制造业	362	356	12.14	15.11	24.9
电力、蒸汽、热水的生产和供应业	42	97	35.02	30.01	-8.0
煤气生产和供应业	7	12	6.82	6.36	6.2
自来水的生产和供应业	8	10	2.54	2.88	-0.7

9－7 分行业国有工业企业单位数和工业总产值

（街、乡及以上工业）

行　业	企业单位数(个)		工业总产值(亿元)		
	1995年	1996年	1995年	1996年	1996比1995年增长%
总　计	**1 927**	**2 069**	**582.51**	**587.86**	**4.9**
石油天燃气开采业	2	8	79.04	84.26	4.7
非金属矿采选业	6	7	5.24	5.05	－2.5
食品加工业	93	95	12.29	8.30	－32.9
食品制造业	80	85	4.75	4.84	－10.8
饮料制造业	19	21	9.61	7.80	－11.2
烟草加工业	1	1	2.90	2.82	－2.5
纺织业	116	109	48.36	43.11	－6.2
服装及其他纤维制品制造业	37	44	1.15	0.95	－19.0
皮革、毛皮、羽绒及其制品业	20	25	2.01	1.14	－40.0
木材加工及竹、藤、棕、草制品业	21	20	0.56	0.46	－22.2
家具制造业	17	21	0.35	0.37	9.4
造纸及纸制品业	49	47	9.45	8.50	－15.4
印刷业、记录媒介的复制	99	89	2.51	2.53	1.6
文教体育用品制造业	32	37	1.59	2.09	17.8
石油加工及炼焦业	2	7	64.99	73.74	22.3
化学原料及化学制品制造业	163	148	24.12	22.11	－9.4
医药制造业	27	21	9.77	9.46	7.1
化学纤维制造业	5	4	1.44	0.98	－39.2
橡胶制品业	26	27	6.31	7.69	21.5
塑料制品业	81	90	4.84	5.16	13.9
非金属矿物制品业	94	108	12.78	12.64	3.4
黑色金属冶炼及压延加工业	23	23	78.81	77.77	4.4
有色金属冶炼及压延加工业	12	13	3.11	1.20	－60.1
金属制品业	141	137	14.79	14.37	－0.9
普通机械制造业	131	147	21.88	28.47	29.7
专用设备制造业	123	139	19.27	18.31	－9.0
交通运输设备制造业	176	193	65.75	75.67	19.2
电气机械及器材制造业	117	102	13.40	13.12	－5.9
电子及通信设备制造业	68	79	14.26	12.37	－11.0
仪器仪表及文化、办公用机械制造业	71	67	5.74	4.72	－21.3
其他制造业	31	55	0.46	0.38	－26.1
电力、蒸汽、热水的生产和供应业	33	83	31.68	28.25	－6.4
煤气生产和供应业	6	8	6.78	6.33	6.6
自来水的生产和供应业	5	9	2.52	2.88	－2.9

9－8 分行业“三资”工业企业单位数和工业总产值

（街、乡及以上工业）

行业	企业单位数(个)		工业总产值(亿元)		
	1995年	1996年	1995年	1996年	1996比1995年增长%
总　计	**1 830**	**1 834**	**521.57**	**718.77**	**34.5**
#食品加工业	63	57	38.91	39.67	－6.8
食品制造业	91	89	31.95	24.02	8.4
饮料制造业	51	45	11.87	14.86	34.8
纺织业	97	95	12.98	17.46	47.0
服装及其他纤维制品制造业	189	183	16.88	20.18	24.7
皮革、毛皮、羽绒及其制品业	84	68	12.01	15.43	38.8
木材加工及竹、藤、棕、草制品业	39	33	10.06	10.92	30.4
家具制造业	23	26	4.28	3.96	8.2
造纸及纸制品业	19	15	1.61	1.85	1.3
印刷业、记录媒介的复制	21	17	0.93	0.62	－29.0
文教体育用品制造业	34	46	8.32	18.99	14.1
石油加工及炼焦业	9	6	0.26	0.49	180.0
化学原料及化学制品制造业	129	135	20.30	87.66	306.7
医药制造业	48	47	15.06	23.54	92.7
化学纤维制造业	19	16	2.97	2.35	－16.8
橡胶制品业	21	20	3.08	4.34	7.8
塑料制品业	95	83	8.16	6.93	－21.4
非金属矿物制品业	58	64	4.29	7.50	91.7
黑色金属冶炼及压延加工业	9	9	3.41	3.84	57.4
有色金属冶炼及压延加工业	18	15	1.99	3.85	189.6
金属制品业	107	103	18.14	21.28	3.9
普通机械制造业	58	68	24.47	25.23	－23.2
专用设备制造业	71	79	4.67	4.81	－22.6
交通运输设备制造业	100	100	50.11	51.75	－16.2
电气机械及器材制造业	95	122	15.78	24.38	32.0
电子及通信设备制造业	140	143	190.71	272.19	26.1
仪器仪表及文化、办公用机械制造业	60	64	5.05	6.58	17.4
其他制造业	78	80	3.22	3.94	20.6

9-9 分行业地方工业企业单位数和工业总产值

（街、乡及以上工业）

行业	企业单位数(个)		工业总产值(亿元)		
	1995年	1996年	1995年	1996年	1996比1995年增长%
总计	**10 539**	**10 904**	**1 182.60**	**1 464.41**	**21.1**
#非金属矿采选业	27	28	5.37	5.35	1.7
食品加工业	294	310	56.97	57.68	-2.3
食品制造业	355	390	41.64	41.15	29.7
饮料制造业	120	114	22.81	24.47	19.3
纺织业	552	545	77.75	82.47	15.0
服装及其他纤维制品制造业	658	670	36.81	50.72	40.6
皮革、毛皮、羽绒及其制品业	210	202	16.59	20.99	35.1
木材加工及竹、藤、棕、草制品业	157	159	11.95	13.15	28.9
家具制造业	115	121	5.61	5.63	13.3
造纸及纸制品业	277	267	16.69	17.78	5.1
印刷业、记录媒介的复制	338	312	5.79	8.06	43.2
文教体育用品制造业	209	225	12.53	24.71	16.9
石油加工及炼焦业	37	42	6.59	17.65	153.0
化学原料及化学制品制造业	788	824	104.25	175.56	68.9
医药制造业	113	105	26.37	38.26	62.1
化学纤维制造业	36	37	7.57	7.13	4.0
橡胶制品业	152	151	16.23	19.68	15.4
塑料制品业	498	503	20.07	26.23	33.0
非金属矿物制品业	526	548	25.50	32.68	36.8
黑色金属冶炼及压延加工业	112	119	92.55	93.19	9.1
有色金属冶炼及压延加工业	101	101	11.04	14.15	41.1
金属制品业	953	965	53.30	62.90	17.0
普通机械制造业	840	839	59.75	68.47	1.0
专用设备制造业	508	598	25.91	27.52	-2.4
交通运输设备制造业	846	905	131.94	148.70	8.1
电气机械及器材制造业	693	730	41.01	51.08	15.5
电子及通信设备制造业	336	339	208.72	284.93	21.1
仪器仪表及文化、办公用机械制造业	279	303	12.51	13.87	2.0
其他制造业	360	355	12.12	15.11	25.0
电力、蒸汽、热水的生产和供应业	29	68	7.21	3.68	-22.7
煤气生产和供应业	7	11	6.82	5.57	-3.2
自来水的生产和供应业	8	8	2.54	2.88	-3.6

9－10 改革开放以来主要工业产品产量

年 份	布（万米）	纱（万吨）	机制纸及纸板（万吨）	合成洗涤剂（万吨）	饮料酒（万吨）	家用电冰箱（万台）	家用洗衣机（万台）	电视机（万台）	#彩色电视机
1978	33 727	8.30	19.26	2.38	2.88	0.50		2.54	
1979	36 067	9.20	21.46	2.70	3.66	0.55	0.01	8.11	
1980	39 215	9.96	22.75	2.95	4.49	0.40	1.06	15.28	0.60
1981	42 427	10.73	21.25	3.19	5.86	0.14	7.14	36.70	
1982	45 831	11.50	22.82	3.53	5.76	0.23	11.90	36.11	
1983	46 803	11.95		3.70	6.75	0.51	8.24	43.62	
1984	44 865	11.67		4.12	7.46	2.01	10.53	61.59	
1985	44 043	11.95	24.60	5.04	8.40	6.89	16.48	90.22	34.02
1986	43 798	12.22	26.45	5.39	9.79	9.79	9.99	89.85	33.54
1987	43 885	12.57	27.92	5.56	10.60	14.53	15.40	100.02	55.46
1988	43 410	12.67	27.10	5.88	10.96	33.32	33.96	135.25	62.07
1989	41 729	11.30	28.31	7.36	9.47	40.41	36.74	137.85	57.32
1990	49 194	11.69	26.75	8.54	9.28	23.34	33.40	143.93	62.46
1991	46 790	11.23	27.18	9.34	10.75	6.71	38.09	140.27	72.63
1992	43 031	10.86	33.32	10.56	10.88	9.27	50.48	140.99	68.29
1993	39 259	11.59	36.84	10.00	11.40	2.71	57.99	134.88	73.30
1994	41 437	13.19	31.01	9.68	11.09	3.95	64.83	124.00	80.37
1995	49 803	12.35	41.42	11.95	12.34	3.70	64.30	160.82	109.54
1996	39 662	10.51	45.89	12.07	10.72	0.29	60.02	157.34	117.80

年 份	原油（万吨）	发电量（亿千瓦小时）	钢（万吨）	水泥（万吨）	硫酸（万吨）	烧碱（万吨）	农用化肥（万吨）	化学农药（万吨）
1978	316.90	51.68	101.75	47.34	10.52	17.02	4.67	7.31
1979	307.30	52.56	109.53	56.52	11.86	19.26	5.39	7.50
1980	307.41	63.20	124.94	62.55	12.38	19.93	6.22	7.82
1981	303.84	72.96	125.15	75.71	12.41	19.19	4.78	7.32
1982	302.24	75.01	124.56	81.80	13.53	21.21	5.85	6.91
1983	310.41	77.34	133.86	82.68	13.22	21.27	7.05	3.65
1984	320.81	79.57	132.49	90.52	12.00	21.97	7.66	2.69
1985	374.63	80.65	111.93	105.11	11.72	23.36	5.56	2.31
1986	413.33	78.38	150.32	112.41	10.33	23.97	4.09	2.14
1987	453.01	81.09	162.96	120.19	11.30	24.73	6.56	1.67
1988	462.79	91.07	156.44	129.37	8.32	25.18	7.61	1.75
1989	470.43	96.60	151.57	127.84	8.09	24.90	7.79	1.75
1990	469.50	94.85	166.74	122.14	7.70	25.23	7.21	1.97
1991	474.90	90.27	175.43	137.24	8.31	27.25	7.85	2.12
1992	491.76	98.62	183.45	144.58	8.15	27.99	7.84	2.01
1993	517.00	126.65	221.98	152.39	7.36	28.27	10.61	2.37
1994	589.00	122.47	188.55	177.00	7.79	29.28	15.75	2.81
1995	620.82	133.65	171.57	200.62	5.58	32.57	9.74	1.69
1996	646.60	146.04	200.99	207.88	8.11	50.75	11.31	2.95

9-11 主要工业产品产量

产品名称	单 位	1995年	1996年	产品名称	单 位	1995年	1996年
钢	万吨	171.57	200.99	汽 车	辆	131 113	152 686
钢 材	万吨	430.38	440.89	＃轿 车	辆	65 170	88 000
生 铁	万吨	168.85	169.04	内燃机商品量	万千瓦	531	778
焦 碳	万吨	174.78	183.53	金属切削机床	台	1 448	1 193
水 泥	万吨	200.62	207.88	电视机	万部	160.82	157.34
平板玻璃	万重量箱	196.09	211.14	＃彩色电视机	万部	109.54	117.80
发电量	亿千瓦小时	133.65	146.04	录像机	万台	40.65	63.74
原 油	万吨	620.82	646.60	化学纤维	万吨	10.25	8.82
原油加工量	万吨	443.16	368.06	纱(混合)	万吨	12.35	10.51
天然气	亿立方米	7.57	7.58	布(混合)	万米	49 803	39 662
液化气	万吨	18.98	18.19	印染布	万米	28 554	39 447
硫 酸	万吨	5.58	8.11	针棉织品折纱	万吨	1.04	1.26
纯 碱	万吨	63.16	66.69	毛 线	吨	7 861	9 297
烧 碱	万吨	32.57	50.75	呢 绒	万米	1 103	802
合成氨	万吨	10.82	11.90	合成洗涤剂	万吨	11.95	12.07
农用化肥	万吨	9.74	11.31	原 盐	万吨	220.39	226.71
化学农药	吨	16 863	29 545	机制纸及纸板	万吨	41.42	45.89
农用塑料薄膜	吨	17 838	14 571	手持机	万部	78.70	144.14
电 石	万吨	5.65	5.24	饮料酒	万吨	12.34	10.72
油 漆	吨	192 059	92 380	＃啤 酒	万吨	2.07	4.83
染 料	吨	48 616	62 072	服 装	万件	24 558	29 676
轮胎外胎	万条	159.82	133.66	家用电冰箱	万台	3.70	0.29
化学原料药	吨	5 302	4 432	家用洗衣机	万台	64.30	60.02
电 梯	台	4 007	3 692	电风扇	万台	5.65	8.37
交流电动机	万千瓦	113.43	78.56	自行车	万辆	576.36	381.52
变压器	万千伏安	375.38	128.95	手 表	万只	205.78	493.77
电焊条	万吨	15.86	16.88	微型计算机	万部	6.18	11.97
卷 烟	万箱	17.01	16.02	摩托车	万辆	40.49	40.42
人造板	万立方米	21.43	24.46	吸尘器	万台	0.37	1.16
中成药	万吨	0.49	0.33	空气调节器	万台	5.90	5.60
食用植物油	万吨	8.06	9.63	照相机	万只	36.56	79.28
燃气用具	万台	55.55	107.02	家 具	万件	188.59	216.64

9－12　工业企业主要产品销售量和产销率

（街、乡及以上工业）

产品名称	单 位	1995年		1996年	
		销售量	产销率%	销售量	产销率%
生 铁	万吨	146.17	86.69	104.11	61.59
钢 材	万吨	428.57	99.88	148.97	74.12
硫 酸	万吨	5.43	97.31	7.05	86.93
烧 碱	万吨	31.04	95.30	37.53	73.95
纯 碱	万吨	58.58	92.75	61.12	91.65
轮胎外胎	万条	159.56	100.66	110.84	82.93
水 泥	万吨	201.18	100.99	188.30	90.58
平板玻璃	万重量箱	183.21	93.43	190.15	90.06
焦 碳	万吨	74.71	42.75	87.36	47.60
原 油	万吨	595.86	95.98	624.14	96.53
汽 车	万辆	131 312	100.15	151 954	99.52
电视机	万台	162.01	100.74	154.87	98.43
#彩色电视机	万台	111.51	101.80	113.29	96.17
家用洗衣机	万台	59.00	97.84	59.88	99.77
电风扇	万台	2.73	79.13	2.29	27.30
家用电冰箱(柜)	万台	3.67	99.19	0.27	93.95
纱(混合)	万吨	6.70	96.54	5.68	54.04
布(混合)	万米	47 381	97.77	28 987	73.09
毛 线	吨	4 615	59.07	8 366	90.02
呢 绒	万米	830	100.36	599	74.69
合成洗涤剂	万吨	10.52	89.38	11.63	96.35
录像机	万米	37.46	92.19	62.37	97.85
服 装	万件	21 352	93.55	19 035	64.14
自行车	万辆	567.65	100.60	212.68	55.75
手 表	万只	192.83	93.71	151.82	30.75
微型计算机	万台	6.64	107.44	11.99	100.17
人造板	万立方米	18.75	87.51	22.19	90.70
中成药	万吨	0.50	102.29	0.20	59.70
食用植物油	万吨	6.81	84.58	5.24	54.45
燃气用具	万台	55.38	99.69	14.31	13.37
摩托车	万辆	38.88	96.02	26.89	66.52
吸尘器	万台	0.27	73.78	1.25	107.97
空气调节器	万台	5.48	92.98	1.71	30.48
照相机	万架	33.96	92.89	78.43	98.93
家 具	万件	180.25	95.58	143.14	66.07

9－13 1996年独立核算工业企业主要财务指标

(街、乡及以上工业)

项　　目	企业单位数(个)	年平均职工人数(人)	工业总产值(万元)	工业增加值(万元)	资本金合计(万元)	资产总计(万元)
全市总计	**10 490**	**1 655 556**	**16 359 556**	**3 475 646**	**5 986 493**	**24 029 358**
一、按隶属关系分						
中　央	128	158 186	1 759 682	598 433	874 150	3 008 155
地　方	10 362	1 497 370	14 599 874	2 877 213	5 112 343	21 021 203
二、按经济类型分						
国有经济	1 918	830 537	5 588 406	1 525 177	2 931 488	13 552 165
集体经济	6 534	504 490	2 863 473	563 796	545 967	2 348 613
联营经济	189	39 129	302 602	60 972	93 626	441 414
股份制经济	17	38 387	417 394	125 767	162 367	888 750
"三资"经济	1 832	243 013	7 187 681	1 199 934	2 253 045	6 798 416
外商投资经济	1 123	161 701	5 795 722	965 997	1 656 162	5 087 304
港、澳、台投资经济	709	81 312	1 391 959	233 937	596 883	1 711 112
三、按轻重分						
轻工业	5 339	781 489	6 777 392	1 138 645	2 096 445	8 541 710
以农产品为原料	3 093	461 575	4 065 321	624 375	997 827	4 515 147
以非农产品为原料	2 246	319 914	2 712 071	514 270	1 098 618	4 026 563
重工业	5 151	874 067	9 582 164	2 337 001	3 890 048	15 487 648
采掘工业	29	81 219	613 740	266 127	357 945	1 126 282
原料工业	820	219 729	2 944 070	659 018	1 568 974	6 573 169
加工工业	4 302	573 119	6 024 354	1 411 856	1 963 129	7 788 197
四、按规模分						
大　型	260	574 999	9 147 480	2 174 708	3 508 666	14 168 223
中　型	480	304 338	1 513 900	366 424	840 208	3 532 626
小　型	9 750	776 219	5 698 176	934 514	1 637 619	6 328 509

注:1996年独立核算工业企业财务指标中均未包含中国海洋石油渤海公司,而1995年均包含。

9－13 续表 1

单位:万元

项 目	流动资产合计	#存货	#产成品	流动资产年平均余额	固定资产合计	固定资产原价
全市总计	**11 185 471**	**3 790 505**	**1 470 370**	**10 448 332**	**10 796 891**	**13 382 784**
一、按隶属关系分						
中 央	1 101 124	343 710	81 753	1 060 285	1 816 773	2 958 041
地 方	10 084 347	3 446 795	1 388 617	9 388 047	8 980 118	10 424 743
二、按经济类型分						
国有经济	5 457 872	1 655 012	636 755	5 184 538	7 205 000	9 105 586
集体经济	1 458 963	591 189	304 609	1 343 440	711 413	901 457
联营经济	179 938	62 992	30 672	171 644	202 009	216 851
股份制经济	381 921	98 920	38 423	343 333	425 300	451 682
“三资”经济	3 706 777	1 382 392	459 911	3 405 377	2 253 169	2 707 208
外商投资经济	2 812 218	1 015 234	312 735	2 463 064	1 576 484	1 904 723
港、澳、台投资经济	894 559	367 158	147 176	942 313	676 685	802 485
三、按轻重分						
轻工业	4 308 125	1 615 059	749 268	4 013 158	3 324 208	4 074 397
以农产品为原料	2 168 080	840 058	384 585	2 068 542	1 924 143	2 337 797
以非农产品为原料	2 140 045	775 001	364 683	1 944 616	1 400 065	1 736 600
重工业	6 877 346	2 175 446	721 102	6 435 174	7 472 683	9 308 387
采掘工业	425 284	84 986	14 552	388 400	674 381	1 192 554
原料工业	2 246 084	652 240	228 088	2 218 745	4 012 899	4 746 415
加工工业	4 205 978	1 438 220	478 462	3 828 029	2 785 403	3 369 418
四、按规模分						
大 型	6 135 190	2 008 178	622 173	5 831 899	7 074 478	8 975 238
中 型	1 554 351	524 911	249 672	1 429 874	1 624 406	1 996 141
小 型	3 495 930	1 257 416	598 525	3 186 559	2 098 007	2 411 405

9-13续表2

单位:万元

项目	固定资产净值年平均余额	产品销售收入	#产品销售成本	产品销售税金及附加	利税总额	#利润总额
全市总计	**8 921 357**	**14 986 662**	**12 425 425**	**149 362**	**1 397 324**	**675 965**
一、按隶属关系分						
中　央	1 542 814	1 964 027	1 748 043	66 951	193 972	21 737
地　方	7 378 543	12 932 635	10 677 382	82 411	1 203 352	654 228
二、按经济类型分						
国有经济	5 999 635	5 940 842	4 986 454	108 907	370 601	20 402
集体经济	605 175	2 423 283	2 005 073	13 263	231 424	146 212
联营经济	109 229	264 432	217 041	1 030	28 974	18 405
股份制经济	284 791	431 316	351 837	2 484	46 805	20 404
"三资"经济	1 922 527	5 926 789	4 865 020	23 678	719 520	470 542
外商投资经济	1 330 891	4 492 024	3 642 491	20 798	604 055	414 398
港、澳、台投资经济	591 636	1 434 765	1 222 529	2 880	115 465	56 144
三、按轻重分						
轻工业	2 832 278	5 741 805	4 761 172	51 716	410 202	169 948
以农产品为原料	1 668 880	3 310 490	2 783 324	33 975	222 655	83 408
以非农产品为原料	1 163 398	2 431 315	1 977 848	17 741	187 547	86 540
重工业	6 089 079	9 244 857	7 664 253	97 646	987 122	506 017
采掘工业	565 619	602 352	508 208	13 712	57 287	5 528
原料工业	3 327 917	3 302 095	2 894 598	43 604	230 355	60 999
加工工业	2 195 543	5 340 410	4 261 447	40 330	699 480	439 490
四、按规模分						
大　型	6 014 972	8 727 399	7 210 200	118 590	1 008 181	518 726
中　型	1 272 529	1 803 053	1 547 273	9 228	52 558	-24 585
小　型	1 633 856	4 456 210	3 667 952	21 544	336 585	181 824

9－14　1996年地方独立核算工业企业主要财务指标

（街、乡及以上工业）

项　　目	企　业单位数（个）	年平均职工人数（人）	工　业总产值（万元）	工　业增加值（万元）	资本金合　计（万元）	资产总计（万元）
全市总计	**10 362**	**1 497 370**	**14 599 874**	**2 877 213**	**5 112 343**	**21 021 203**
一、按经济类型分						
国有经济	1 822	674 654	3 846 494	928 401	2 080 290	10 580 688
集体经济	6 511	503 579	2 853 405	563 223	545 277	2 347 044
联营经济	188	39 089	302 336	60 966	93 186	440 815
股份制经济	17	38 387	417 394	125 767	162 367	888 750
“三资”经济	1 824	241 661	7 180 242	1 198 856	2 231 223	6 763 906
外商投资经济	1 119	160 564	5 789 142	964 601	1 636 590	5 056 671
港、澳、台投资经济	705	81 097	1 391 100	234 255	594 633	1 707 235
二、按轻重分						
轻工业	5 312	771 779	6 700 983	1 110 957	2 054 891	8 401 234
以农产品为原料	3 076	455 995	4 015 029	602 708	972 666	4 421 337
以非农产品为原料	2 236	315 784	2 685 954	508 249	1 082 225	3 979 897
重工业	5 050	725 591	7 898 891	1 766 256	3 057 452	12 619 969
采掘业	28	9 280	3 069	832	2 370	5 979
原料工业	784	182 853	2 085 807	407 529	1 204 261	5 252 089
加工工业	4 238	533 458	5 810 015	1 357 895	1 850 821	7 361 901
三、按规模分						
大　型	241	436 744	7 520 862	1 636 438	2 777 204	11 566 469
中　型	454	291 839	1 421 065	314 992	711 268	3 160 694
小　型	9 667	768 787	5 657 947	925 783	1 623 871	6 294 040

9－14续表1

单位:万元

项　目	流动资产合计	#存货	#产成品	流动资产年平均余额	固定资产合计	固定资产原价
全市总计	**10 084 347**	**3 446 795**	**1 388 617**	**9 388 047**	**8 980 118**	**10 424 743**
一、按经济类型分						
国有经济	4 373 172	1 316 663	557 793	4 134 581	5 398 315	6 160 315
集体经济	1 457 830	590 776	304 447	1 342 494	711 073	901 012
联营经济	179 617	62 714	30 479	171 325	201 780	216 592
股份制经济	381 921	98 920	38 423	343 333	425 300	451 682
"三资"经济	3 691 807	1 377 722	457 475	3 396 314	2 243 650	2 695 142
外商投资经济	2 799 002	1 011 190	310 415	2 455 799	1 568 645	1 895 892
港、澳、台投资经济	892 805	366 532	147 060	940 515	675 005	799 250
二、按轻重分						
轻工业	4 226 047	1 599 599	746 088	3 928 014	3 270 178	4 007 894
以农产品为原料	2 103 816	829 714	383 616	1 999 703	1 897 048	2 303 291
以非农产品为原料	2 122 231	769 885	362 472	1 928 311	1 373 130	1 704 603
重工业	5 858 300	1 847 196	642 529	5 460 033	5 709 940	6 416 849
采掘业	1 881	542	436	2 079	1 986	3 619
原料工业	1 890 287	539 216	187 537	1 851 102	3 070 662	3 260 977
加工工业	3 966 132	1 307 438	454 556	3 606 852	2 637 292	3 152 235
三、按规模分						
大　型	5 122 729	1 686 953	550 684	4 850 512	5 550 826	6 429 005
中　型	1 486 959	510 226	243 028	1 370 119	1 343 286	1 601 536
小　型	3 474 659	1 249 616	594 905	3 167 416	2 086 006	2 394 202

9－14 续表 2

单位:万元

项　　目	固定资产净值年平均余额	产品销售收入	#产品销售成本	产品销售税金及附加	利税总额	#利润
全市总计	**7 378 543**	**12 932 635**	**10 677 382**	**82 411**	**1 203 352**	**654 228**
一、按经济类型分						
国有经济	4 466 313	3 894 551	3 246 278	41 974	178 503	－48
集体经济	604 837	2 421 893	2 004 007	13 245	231 317	146 215
联营经济	108 994	264 109	216 734	1 030	29 019	18 464
股份制经济	284 791	431 316	351 837	2 484	46 805	20 404
“三资”经济	1 913 608	5 920 766	4 858 526	23 678	717 708	469 193
外商投资经济	1 323 298	4 486 493	3 636 934	20 798	601 473	412 260
港、澳、台投资经济	590 310	1 434 273	1 221 592	2 880	116 235	56 933
二、按轻重分						
轻工业	2 793 427	5 668 997	4 703 647	37 541	393 637	171 712
以农产品为原料	1 645 198	3 266 735	2 748 630	19 985	206 172	83 929
以非农产品为原料	1 148 229	2 402 262	1 955 017	17 556	187 465	87 783
重工业	4 585 116	7 263 638	5 973 735	44 870	809 715	482 516
采掘业	1 748	2 173	1 804	25	4	－108
原料工业	2 515 591	2 123 643	1 879 069	5 752	118 017	41 216
加工工业	2 067 777	5 137 822	4 092 862	39 093	691 694	441 408
三、按规模分						
大　型	4 686 025	7 040 068	5 797 081	53 116	837 367	504 185
中　型	1 069 169	1 461 771	1 233 338	7 985	31 475	－30 997
小　型	1 623 349	4 430 796	3 646 963	21 310	334 510	181 040

9－15　1996年分行业独立核算工业企业主要财务指标

（街、乡及以上工业）

行　业	企　业单位数（个）	年平均职工人数（人）	工　业总产值（万元）	工　业增加值（万元）	资本金合　计（万元）	资产总计（万元）
总　计	**10 490**	**1 655 556**	**16 359 556**	**3 475 646**	**5 986 493**	**24 029 358**
＃石油和天然气开采业	4	71 939	610 671	265 295	355 575	1 120 303
非金属矿采选业	27	24 602	53 458	35 064	41 421	174 271
食品加工业	288	25 839	577 685	33 086	105 936	520 123
食品制造业	351	40 748	411 583	106 473	172 841	685 718
饮料制造业	109	11 967	244 655	58 044	89 759	312 496
烟草加工业	1	3 757	28 174	18 991	16 084	78 387
纺织业	532	167 982	822 711	134 078	221 775	1 297 585
服装及其他纤维制品制造业	639	88 975	503 866	95 582	104 200	368 164
皮革、毛皮、羽绒及其制品业	198	26 801	209 888	24 433	61 093	214 718
木材加工及竹、藤、棕、草制品业	150	10 489	132 841	22 193	63 831	187 390
家具制造业	115	7 690	56 273	13 938	20 308	65 743
造纸及纸制品业	257	29 585	185 767	43 061	62 605	456 061
印刷业，记录媒介的复制	294	17 511	84 961	26 785	31 064	126 925
文教体育用品制造业	219	21 055	247 055	29 624	43 815	142 380
石油加工及炼焦业	40	28 584	823 132	173 783	176 103	660 747
化学原料及化学制品制造业	796	109 468	1 765 968	254 514	443 609	1 881 557
医药制造业	104	25 474	395 720	146 883	99 872	511 354
化学纤维制造业	37	8 603	71 290	16 740	26 146	102 585
橡胶制品业	144	30 717	196 007	42 757	63 122	308 193
塑料制品业	479	35 586	262 489	38 691	99 145	327 120
非金属矿物制品业	521	75 976	329 846	90 739	154 420	661 265
黑色金属冶炼及压延加工业	113	75 547	931 872	162 822	712 203	3 141 364
有色金属冶炼及压延加工业	99	12 170	141 460	17 679	23 813	152 754
金属制品业	936	106 192	647 296	99 904	235 638	1 096 346
普通机械制造业	821	106 936	676 702	204 196	467 714	1 218 585
专用设备制造业	574	83 652	313 767	92 254	146 572	630 131
交通运输设备制造业	873	132 079	1 605 913	393 862	414 015	2 237 304
电气机械及器材制造业	718	85 940	520 130	98 654	331 371	1 060 383
电子及通信设备制造业	335	77 281	2 883 535	532 332	557 794	2 422 595
仪器仪表及文化、办公用机械制造业	298	40 955	138 740	39 400	83 549	296 403
其他制造业	334	39 803	150 421	28 341	51 162	168 538
电力、蒸汽、热水的生产和供应业	61	16 688	243 205	124 171	269 776	1 000 611
煤气生产和供应业	12	10 448	63 642	－362	117 423	182 325
自来水的生产和供应业	8	4 506	28 833	11 646	122 074	218 464

9－15 续表 1

单位:万元

行 业	流动资产合 计	#存 货	#产成品	流动资产年平均余额	固定资产合 计	固定资产原 价
总 计	**11 185 471**	**3 790 505**	**1 470 370**	**10 448 332**	**10 796 891**	**13 382 784**
#石油和天然气开采业	423 403	84 444	14 116	386 322	672 395	1 188 935
非金属矿采选业	71 977	28 474	26 589	72 105	84 457	108 798
食品加工业	297 145	122 725	51 770	318 388	185 462	236 461
食品制造业	287 507	73 594	25 428	259 601	329 943	393 472
饮料制造业	143 139	54 180	19 718	138 966	120 560	141 380
烟草加工业	58 713	8 246	14	63 700	17 781	21 939
纺织业	597 992	263 918	137 578	569 250	592 378	750 216
服装及其他纤维制品制造业	220 610	100 369	50 355	203 013	114 028	142 328
皮革、毛皮、羽绒及其制品业	127 404	59 895	28 007	114 474	62 478	78 593
木材加工及竹、藤、棕、草制品业	87 643	35 069	13 575	72 119	72 028	82 619
家具制造业	39 379	14 600	4 914	37 625	21 749	27 309
造纸及纸制品业	121 678	36 183	21 818	113 195	309 908	332 887
印刷业，记录媒介的复制	57 407	18 789	8 236	51 652	53 736	70 504
文教体育用品制造业	88 245	36 797	14 732	84 823	42 820	61 303
石油加工及炼焦业	211 138	107 291	42 891	225 006	433 700	771 195
化学原料及化学制品制造业	798 637	266 284	110 750	725 577	892 142	922 940
医药制造业	304 407	81 038	36 481	251 319	155 923	195 836
化学纤维制造业	40 839	15 745	6 298	33 108	49 546	64 989
橡胶制品业	136 747	38 819	18 384	125 127	89 403	109 282
塑料制品业	138 337	58 631	24 418	134 081	157 633	167 707
非金属矿物制品业	249 427	90 780	48 471	227 112	359 255	402 051
黑色金属冶炼及压延加工业	1 106 545	330 347	111 722	1 137 225	1 894 337	2 013 370
有色金属冶炼及压延加工业	89 942	32 210	14 329	83 346	48 581	51 472
金属制品业	607 308	216 297	102 542	589 418	417 429	464 978
普通机械制造业	587 426	255 581	74 481	571 553	511 161	603 504
专用设备制造业	346 610	155 760	50 590	334 149	246 080	346 319
交通运输设备制造业	1 479 957	339 399	112 265	1 286 643	639 909	742 680
电气机械及器材制造业	563 101	233 874	92 669	528 699	345 880	417 511
电子及通信设备制造业	1 286 997	473 399	147 362	1 133 607	717 197	913 641
仪器仪表及文化、办公用机械制造业	175 456	73 097	33 344	161 353	89 404	123 247
其他制造业	109 824	52 142	24 012	104 074	47 803	60 489
电力、蒸汽、热水的生产和供应业	255 759	14 468	1	246 312	714 284	954 318
煤气生产和供应业	56 948	16 912	2 231	48 381	120 876	190 485
自来水的生产和供应业	17 672	1 102	240	16 728	186 353	229 723

9－15 续表 2

单位:万元

行　　业	固定资产净值年平均余额	产品销售收入	#产品销售成本	产品销售税金及附加	利税总额	#利　润
总　　计	**8 921 357**	**14 986 662**	**12 425 425**	**149 362**	**1 397 324**	**675 965**
#石油和天然气开采业	563 871	600 179	506 404	13 687	57 283	5 636
非金属矿采选业	72 236	46 700	27 365	2 438	7 406	－22
食品加工业	169 698	636 624	587 467	491	－4 370	－8 642
食品制造业	295 280	431 941	331 657	581	57 370	31 655
饮料制造业	111 979	210 004	144 895	10 760	46 793	22 542
烟草加工业	14 921	31 669	24 034	13 888	16 359	
纺织业	474 060	762 859	668 166	2 127	6 119	－15 001
服装及其他纤维制品制造业	102 091	442 009	379 758	883	33 188	21 611
皮革、毛皮、羽绒及其制品业	54 680	188 259	166 524	263	6 023	2 346
木材加工及竹、藤、棕、草制品业	60 030	130 255	114 012	206	16 057	7 629
家具制造业	18 921	58 830	47 433	146	6 960	4 915
造纸及纸制品业	281 463	170 198	144 382	663	11 251	4 468
印刷业，记录媒介的复制	45 155	65 737	49 586	466	12 275	7 754
文教体育用品制造业	37 253	162 549	136 265	274	9 603	5 579
石油加工及炼焦业	349 299	795 322	664 156	36 132	84 183	13 236
化学原料及化学制品制造业	608 169	1 174 735	959 732	12 925	93 514	33 868
医药制造业	129 823	358 926	204 772	875	107 785	76 618
化学纤维制造业	28 340	63 897	54 231	146	6 861	4 241
橡胶制品业	66 110	182 104	151 255	5 113	14 773	3 173
塑料制品业	115 776	180 757	150 011	884	9 663	2 192
非金属矿物制品业	284 066	296 387	235 248	2 013	22 172	8 574
黑色金属冶炼及压延加工业	1 665 335	947 550	850 689	994	27 152	7 220
有色金属冶炼及压延加工业	35 185	131 634	115 457	219	8 372	5 868
金属制品业	325 272	583 264	507 691	1 238	12 700	－3 300
普通机械制造业	422 888	735 958	596 212	3 047	80 297	33 104
专用设备制造业	199 210	328 109	269 811	1 413	2 556	－8 305
交通运输设备制造业	436 859	1 616 216	1 258 318	31 495	212 396	118 290
电气机械及器材制造业	308 556	475 723	387 203	1 052	12 212	－6 525
电子及通信设备制造业	592 734	2 219 696	1 825 985	968	371 815	292 447
仪器仪表及文化、办公用机械制造业	75 936	130 758	103 789	454	4 357	－827
其他制造业	41 846	132 026	110 276	314	6 559	3 239
电力、蒸汽、热水的生产和供应业	637 623	592 583	533 135	2 842	53 717	21 791
煤气生产和供应业	121 943	67 627	81 805	218	－12 247	－13 996
自来水的生产和供应业	174 745	35 577	37 702	150	－3 797	－5 380

9-16 1996年分行业独立核算国有大中型工业企业主要财务指标

(街、乡及以上工业)

行 业	企业单位数(个)	年平均职工人数(人)	工业总产值(万元)	工业增加值(万元)	资本金合计(万元)	资产总计(万元)
总 计	**480**	**677 702**	**5 090 575**	**1 388 689**	**2 669 114**	**11 721 016**
石油和天然气开采业	1	71 939	610 671	265 295	355 575	1 120 303
非金属矿采选业	3	15 704	50 504	34 252	40 825	172 895
食品加工业	21	8 547	42 042	13 860	33 653	127 340
食品制造业	13	8 020	23 832	6 951	11 809	83 458
饮料制造业	8	5 168	75 012	16 513	8 024	94 891
烟草加工业	1	3 757	28 174	18 991	16 084	78 387
纺织业	63	98 355	393 158	67 998	84 793	780 384
服装及其他纤维制品制造业	4	1 351	3 266	1 346	1 910	12 804
皮革、毛皮、羽绒及其制品业	4	2 943	5 156	-1 154	14 837	46 480
木材加工及竹、藤、棕、草制品业	2			742	3 853	12 303
家具制造业	3	1 059	1 988	1 078	2 011	8 913
造纸及纸制品业	8	12 359	64 577	15 650	12 387	300 873
印刷业，记录媒介的复制	10	4 555	15 076	6 606	10 477	42 485
文教体育用品制造业	5	2 687	11 218	4 395	2 058	20 079
石油加工及炼焦业	3	26 725	737 354	162 316	166 079	634 767
化学原料及化学制品制造业	31	26 273	171 476	44 199	34 245	352 370
医药制造业	11	12 256	92 754	26 262	28 801	130 007
化学纤维制造业	1	1 486	8 948	1 801	2 177	29 803
橡胶制品业	6	8 282	62 034	14 115	8 314	71 502
塑料制品业	11	6 869	40 620	6 121	7 055	86 145
非金属矿物制品业	20	26 203	86 802	26 221	48 516	269 330
黑色金属冶炼及压延加工业	13	62 719	732 294	135 734	658 138	2 777 922
有色金属冶炼及压延加工业	7	3 854	11 354	1 581	2 521	33 477
金属制品业	31	29 621	120 081	22 501	47 831	390 506
普通机械制造业	29	43 144	263 319	75 800	273 894	619 611
专用设备制造业	33	41 944	148 805	42 555	72 179	390 202
交通运输设备制造业	28	50 887	716 173	184 142	116 104	877 463
电气机械及器材制造业	27	26 109	115 257	30 902	42 913	341 665
电子及通信设备制造业	28	26 116	108 406	28 645	61 221	383 414
仪器仪表及文化、办公用机械制造业	17	18 236	34 919	14 021	24 199	139 615
其他制造业	2	1 582	976	-413	5 772	7 023
电力、蒸汽、热水的生产和供应业	28	14 397	223 203	110 280	235 007	894 238
煤气生产和供应业	6	10 269	63 304	-624	114 725	178 053
自来水的生产和供应业	2	4 286	27 823	10 009	121 128	212 310

9－16续表1

单位:万元

行　业	流动资产合　计	#存　货	#产成品	流动资产年平均余额	固定资产合　计	固定资产原　价
总　计	**4 475 015**	**1 426 126**	**512 131**	**4 336 258**	**6 519 837**	**8 412 088**
石油和天然气开采业	423 403	84 444	14 116	386 322	672 395	1 188 935
非金属矿采选业	71 112	28 201	26 401	71 279	83 989	108 083
食品加工业	58 981	19 957	10 204	62 350	55 247	76 495
食品制造业	36 187	6 869	2 323	36 832	36 922	46 324
饮料制造业	32 075	13 649	7 405	30 752	43 127	47 034
烟草加工业	58 713	8 246	14	63 700	17 781	21 939
纺织业	323 192	129 639	73 613	314 442	392 842	514 516
服装及其他纤维制品制造业	6 019	2 297	1 744	5 730	6 092	8 034
皮革、毛皮、羽绒及其制品业	21 805	8 419	4 196	21 574	11 032	15 135
木材加工及竹、藤、棕、草制品业	4 126	711	8	3 961	7 735	10 007
家具制造业	2 668	1 243	935	2 625	5 042	5 964
造纸及纸制品业	53 167	14 740	11 604	50 926	245 862	256 393
印刷业，记录媒介的复制	16 592	4 981	1 859	16 027	22 635	32 061
文教体育用品制造业	10 545	3 942	1 110	11 661	5 884	8 294
石油加工及炼焦业	196 963	102 100	40 415	215 180	423 412	759 014
化学原料及化学制品制造业	140 958	62 576	27 628	130 042	162 018	200 423
医药制造业	63 581	22 148	8 169	55 162	46 517	63 559
化学纤维制造业	5 995	3 129	1 573	4 431	23 447	27 830
橡胶制品业	36 571	12 065	4 345	32 326	24 178	36 415
塑料制品业	26 513	11 321	5 090	27 211	49 798	35 949
非金属矿物制品业	80 529	27 007	15 071	78 449	172 868	173 404
黑色金属冶炼及压延加工业	951 230	262 094	63 759	921 142	1 713 776	1 827 836
有色金属冶炼及压延加工业	16 439	4 667	812	16 191	14 946	18 520
金属制品业	205 015	55 071	31 567	205 896	164 493	173 464
普通机械制造业	223 931	89 042	27 794	217 168	351 962	407 461
专用设备制造业	192 064	90 957	27 912	200 043	175 339	247 508
交通运输设备制造业	463 562	143 030	17 259	421 705	377 823	442 134
电气机械及器材制造业	168 692	86 299	31 540	158 811	106 768	144 850
电子及通信设备制造业	207 524	66 523	35 526	215 654	111 713	159 171
仪器仪表及文化、办公用机械制造业	71 801	29 325	14 918	71 016	50 581	68 359
其他制造业	3 779	2 299	1 134	4 154	2 908	4 014
电力、蒸汽、热水的生产和供应业	233 838	12 545		223 655	636 605	865 920
煤气生产和供应业	53 206	16 298	2 088	45 643	120 471	189 949
自来水的生产和供应业	14 242	292	1	14 198	183 630	227 095

9－16 续表 2

单位:万元

行　　业	固定资产净值年平均余额	产品销售收入	#产品销售成本	产品销售税金及附加	利税总额	#利　润
总　计	**5 503 512**	**5 402 584**	**4 579 487**	**105 268**	**342 511**	**20 613**
石油和天然气开采业	563 871	600 179	506 404	13 687	57 283	5 636
非金属矿采选业	71 800	44 619	25 673	2 420	7 119	－235
食品加工业	53 182	60 692	53 486	205	－775	－2 434
食品制造业	34 182	24 820	20 687	116	1 024	－194
饮料制造业	34 429	57 960	45 365	6 144	16 212	6 728
烟草加工业	14 921	31 669	24 034	13 888	16 359	
纺织业	304 958	377 283	344 702	1 208	－13 108	－26 307
服装及其他纤维制品制造业	5 950	2 870	2 421	13	178	25
皮革、毛皮、羽绒及其制品业	10 817	6 514	6 437	34	－2 271	－2 621
木材加工及竹、藤、棕、草制品业	7 786	1 432	1 391	2	490	457
家具制造业	4 298	2 198	1 728	19	239	51
造纸及纸制品业	231 090	57 738	50 784	222	386	－1 649
印刷业、记录媒介的复制	21 534	15 585	12 682	76	1 107	184
文教体育用品制造业	4 892	13 494	10 516	43	699	90
石油加工及炼焦业	343 688	721 715	599 690	35 718	76 304	7 453
化学原料及化学制品制造业	131 916	193 069	153 937	920	7 292	－794
医药制造业	37 455	91 543	64 288	549	10 265	4 844
化学纤维制造业	4 481	7 462	6 807	20	270	50
橡胶制品业	20 018	59 678	50 683	3 438	5 455	－574
塑料制品业	23 340	32 543	27 907	83	263	－650
非金属矿物制品业	127 821	83 298	69 360	446	4 115	－804
黑色金属冶炼及压延加工业	1 565 737	728 888	647 030	524	18 756	7 235
有色金属冶炼及压延加工业	13 814	11 654	10 875	5	－1 227	－1 367
金属制品业	106 555	141 379	126 581	295	－7 258	－10 898
普通机械制造业	288 766	265 554	211 724	1 287	11 990	－2 189
专用设备制造业	138 336	155 074	132 929	603	－10 592	－14 977
交通运输设备制造业	237 295	707 467	553 817	19 479	105 673	59 381
电气机械及器材制造业	95 125	110 779	85 620	334	2 226	－1 823
电子及通信设备制造业	94 300	111 934	90 300	508	3 899	－1 391
仪器仪表及文化、办公用机械制造业	42 064	33 250	26 257	219	786	－986
其他制造业	2 899	1 573	1 705	20	－841	－864
电力、蒸汽、热水的生产和供应业	574 788	552 570	499 833	2 452	47 179	19 292
煤气生产和供应业	118 903	66 154	80 629	200	－12 277	－14 007
自来水的生产和供应业	172 500	29 945	33 211	95	－4 708	－6 050

9－17　独立核算工业企业主要经济效益指标

（街、乡及以上工业）

项　目	单　位	全　市		#地　方	
		1995年	1996年	1995年	1996年
全　市					
资金利税率	%	8.8	7.2	9.4	7.2
增加值率	%	21.9	21.3	18.5	18.9
工业全员劳动生产率(以增加值表示)	元/人	20 084	20 993	16 208	19 235
流动资产周转次数	次	1.6	1.4	1.5	1.4
亏损企业个数	个	3 133	3 386	3 097	3 354
亏损企业亏损额	万元	345 072	419 283	275 877	396 793
国有经济					
资金利税率	%	5.6	3.3	4.3	2.1
增加值率	%	27.3	27.3	19.99	24.6
工业全员劳动生产率(以增加值表示)	元/人	20 536	18 365	10 026	13 793
流动资产周转次数	次	1.3	1.2	1.0	0.9
亏损企业个数	个	525	669	489	646
亏损企业亏损额	万元	179 022	185 092	109 827	164 309
集体经济					
资金利税率	%	11.0	11.9	11.0	11.9
增加值率	%	17.7	19.7	17.7	19.7
工业全员劳动生产率(以增加值表示)	元/人	8 809	11 175	30 627	11 183
流动资产周转次数	次	1.7	1.8	1.7	1.8
亏损企业个数	个	1 673	1 713	1 673	1 707
亏损企业亏损额	万元	44 670	49 626	44 670	49 576
“三资”经济					
资金利税率	%	16.5	13.5	16.5	13.5
增加值率	%	17.2	16.7	17.2	15.2
工业全员劳动生产率(以增加值表示)	元/人	42 775	49 379	42 794	49 603
流动资产周转次数	次	2.0	1.7	2.0	1.7
亏损企业个数	个	897	962	897	960
亏损企业亏损额	万元	119 207	179 493	119 207	177 895
股份制经济					
资金利税率	%	9.3	7.5	9.3	7.5
增加值率	%	24.8	30.1	24.8	30.1
工业全员劳动生产率(以增加值表示)	元/人	34 759	32 760	34 759	32 760
流动资产周转次数	次	1.3	1.3	1.3	1.3
亏损企业个数	个	4	5	4	5
亏损企业亏损额	万元	357	2 340	357	2 340

9－18 地方预算内国有工业企业主要财务和经济效益指标

指 标	单 位	1995年	1996年	1996比1995年增长%
企业单位数	个	642	648	0.9
职工平均人数	人	646 740	644 308	－0.4
工业总产值(当年价格)	亿元	432.58	365.08	－15.6
国家资本	亿元	112.05	148.30	32.4
法人资本	亿元	1.99	3.58	79.9
工业增加值	亿元	88.22	85.55	－3.0
资产总计	亿元	766.05	1 005.77	31.3
#流动资产	亿元	350.94	418.97	19.4
#存货	亿元	108.97	125.50	15.2
#产成品	亿元		50.40	
固定资产合计	亿元		488.96	
#固定资产原价	亿元	374.77	553.78	47.8
固定资产净值	亿元	266.25	435.06	63.4
产品销售收入	亿元	380.31	373.84	－1.7
#产品销售成本	亿元	314.87	306.49	－2.7
产品销售税金及附加	亿元	4.33	4.26	－1.6
实现利税总额	亿元		20.14	
#利润	亿元	6.42	2.10	－67.3
增加值率	%	20.39	23.4	3.0
全员劳动生产率	元/人	13 641	13 278	－2.7
亏损企业数	个	263	279	6.1
企业亏损额	亿元	6.41	10.26	60.1

注：此表为财政局口径。

9－19 新产品试制和投产情况

指 标	1995年	1996年	1996比1995年增长%
一、新产品			
试成数	1 430	1 882	31.6
投产数	1 386	1 608	16.0
投产数占试成数%	96.9	85.4	－11.5
二、轻纺产品新规格新花样			
试成数	13 054	8 505	－34.9
投产数	13 548	9 289	－31.4
投产数占试成数%	103.8	109.2	5.4
在投产产品中			
达到国内先进水平的	642	925	44.1
达到国际先进水平的	162	164	1.2
三、投产产品成效			
创产值（亿元）	110.64	146.7	32.6

9－20　1996年分地区独立核算工业企业主要财务指标

（街、乡及以上工业）

地　区	企业个数（个）	资产总计（亿元）	固定资产原　价（亿元）	固定资产净值年平均余额（亿元）	流动资产年平均余额（亿元）	销售收入（亿元）
全市合计	**10 490**	**2 402.94**	**1 338.28**	**892.14**	**1 044.83**	**1 498.67**
和平区	370	59.64	39.31	26.94	22.35	26.42
河东区	1 105	204.13	105.77	61.86	104.76	113.82
河西区	992	297.36	122.84	85.25	143.90	150.88
南开区	1 257	213.48	98.21	60.75	107.72	107.91
河北区	948	161.16	69.22	51.68	86.46	76.33
红桥区	723	51.56	22.70	14.89	22.69	27.21
塘沽区	741	350.72	177.24	123.34	153.46	306.32
汉沽区	268	53.33	27.74	19.28	17.55	29.20
大港区	330	210.70	205.54	97.39	70.51	149.20
东丽区	534	277.54	193.39	170.06	79.50	97.41
西青区	525	151.52	85.55	55.10	56.46	117.34
津南区	344	37.56	22.16	10.50	15.47	29.96
北辰区	594	151.10	73.04	48.64	67.29	84.98
宁河县	232	19.45	9.61	6.92	9.25	23.91
武清县	521	55.32	26.71	20.09	28.44	53.53
静海县	298	24.15	11.47	8.15	12.43	24.75
宝坻县	363	30.75	12.59	9.42	17.93	40.46
蓟　县	344	22.05	13.55	9.04	10.37	19.03
天津铁厂	1	31.42	21.63	12.83	18.28	20.02

地　区	销售税金及附加（亿元）	利税总额（亿元）	#利润总额（亿元）	工　业总产值（亿元）	工业总产值1996比1995年增长%（可比价格）	工业增加值（亿元）
全市合计	**14.94**	**139.73**	**67.60**	**1 635.96**	**19.3**	**347.56**
和平区	0.15	0.43	－0.86	26.28	－3.6	6.00
河东区	0.29	0.35	－3.18	176.08	84.2	19.42
河西区	1.55	12.71	3.96	135.38	－7.1	31.83
南开区	0.49	6.28	1.35	104.53	－11.0	25.71
河北区	0.23	0.28	－2.46	78.16	－5.7	15.93
红桥区	0.45	1.62	－0.07	22.87	－12.2	6.85
塘沽区	0.81	47.23	34.51	347.06	20.6	70.83
汉沽区	0.22	2.35	0.48	29.03	16.2	7.87
大港区	5.01	13.86	1.36	150.78	3.8	44.99
东丽区	1.62	12.70	7.34	103.04	8.0	24.39
西青区	2.21	13.50	7.60	126.70	31.7	26.09
津南区	0.08	1.96	1.25	30.15	18.6	5.56
北辰区	0.96	7.57	3.40	87.20	9.8	20.28
宁河县	0.20	2.24	1.55	27.60	32.8	4.07
武清县	0.11	7.23	5.78	76.01	127.0	12.98
静海县	0.19	2.17	1.35	25.83	27.8	5.04
宝坻县	0.15	4.65	3.41	45.34	88.2	9.50
蓟　县	0.16	1.41	0.62	24.14	41.1	4.33
天津铁厂	0.07	1.21	0.20	19.76	8.9	5.90

9－21 大中型工业企业主要经济指标和占全市比重

(街、乡及以上工业)

指 标	单 位	全市工业	大中型		国有大中型	
			绝对数	占全市%	绝对数	占全市%
1995 年						
企业单位数	个	10 671	702	6.6	464	4.4
全部职工年平均人数	万人	173.58	92.27	53.2	71.84	41.4
工业总产值(现价)	亿元	1 382.43	1 001.73	72.5	528.06	38.2
工业增加值(现价)	亿元	348.62	273.28	78.4	173.49	49.8
资本金合计	亿元	637.97	380.26	59.6	229.11	35.9
资产总计	亿元	2 164.96	1 669.47	77.1	1 170.10	54.1
#流动资产年平均余额	亿元	888.92	637.75	71.7	411.31	46.3
固定资产净值年平均余额	亿元	628.11	516.45	82.2	379.83	60.5
产品销售收入	亿元	1 376.70	1 010.68	73.4	567.73	41.2
#产品销售成本	亿元	1 134.79	833.19	73.4	473.25	41.7
产品销售税金及附加	亿元	14.66	12.17	83.0	10.06	68.6
利税总额	亿元	133.51	108.32	81.1	42.75	32.0
资金利税率	%	8.8	9.4		5.4	
全员劳动生产率	元/人	20 084	29 617		24 999	
亏损企业个数	个	3 133	264	8.4	168	5.4
亏损企业亏损额	亿元	34.51	22.36	64.8	14.88	43.1
1996 年						
企业单位数	个	11 073	740	6.7	480	4.3
全部职工年平均人数	万人	165.56	87.93	53.1	67.77	40.9
工业总产值(现价)	亿元	1 666.26	1 066.14	64.0	509.06	30.6
工业增加值(现价)	亿元	347.56	254.11	73.1	138.87	34.0
资本金合计	亿元	598.65	434.89	72.7	266.91	44.6
资产总计	亿元	2 402.94	1 770.08	73.7	1 172.10	48.8
#流动资产年平均余额	亿元	1 044.83	726.18	69.5	433.63	41.5
固定资产净值年平均余额	亿元	892.14	728.75	81.7	550.35	61.7
产品销售收入	亿元	1 498.67	1 053.05	70.3	540.26	36.1
#产品销售成本	亿元	1 242.54	875.75	70.5	457.95	36.9
产品销售税金及附加	亿元	14.94	12.78	85.5	10.53	70.5
利税总额	亿元	139.73	106.07	75.9	34.25	24.5
资金利税率	%	7.2	7.3		3.5	
全员劳动生产率	元/人	20 993	28 899		20 491	
亏损企业个数	个	3 386	364	10.8	231	6.8
亏损企业亏损额	亿元	41.93	26.02	62.1	15.21	36.3

9－22 乡镇属独立核算工业企业主要经济指标

指　　标	单 位	合 计	轻工业	重工业	大 型	中 型	小 型
1995 年							
工业企业单位数	个	2 090	1 184	906	1	16	2 073
全部职工年平均人数	人	211 733	133 060	78 673	413	8 831	202 489
工业总产值	万元	1 518 551	899 471	619 080	7 533	86 470	1 424 548
工业增加值	万元	286 125	164 890	121 235	1 928	15 542	268 655
固定资产原价	万元	517 176	289 632	227 544	5 596	36 269	475 311
固定资产净值平均余额	万元	357 865	197 714	160 151	4 831	26 713	326 321
流动资产年平均余额	万元	686 651	424 985	261 666	1 425	49 964	635 262
产品销售收入	万元	1 349 198	800 860	548 338	7 350	84 588	1 257 260
＃产品销售成本	万元	1 104 018	651 043	452 975	5 285	71 759	1 026 975
产品销售税金及附加	万元	6 421	3 014	3 407		401	6 020
利税总额	万元	204 893	108 997	95 896	1 044	8 726	195 123
资金利税率	%	19.6	17.5	22.7	16.7	11.4	20.3
全员劳动生产率	元/人	13 513	12 392	15 410	46 683	17 599	13 268
流动资产周转次数	次	2.0	1.9	2.1	5.2	1.7	2.0
亏损企业个数	个	270	116	154		1	269
企业亏损额	万元	12 443	5 200	7 243		59	12 384
1996 年							
工业企业单位数	个	1 996	1 120	876		14	1 982
全部职工年平均人数	人	230 768	187 719	122 099		5 441	225 327
工业总产值	万元	2 524 835	1 605 884	918 951		85 190	2 439 645
工业增加值	万元	463 882	286 338	177 544		16 107	447 775
固定资产原价	万元	711 081	379 865	331 216		35 992	675 089
固定资产净值平均余额	万元	468 034	279 406	188 629		24 879	443 155
流动资产年平均余额	万元	870 590	524 390	346 200		40 551	830 039
产品销售收入	万元	2 086 972	1 287 125	799 847		70 183	2 016 789
＃产品销售成本	万元	1 722 027	1 065 261	656 766		56 156	1 665 871
产品销售税金及附加	万元	7 847	4 017	3 830		126	7 721
利税总额	万元	262 258	158 511	103 747		10 232	252 026
资金利税率	%	19.6	19.7	19.4		15.6	19.8
全员劳动生产率	元/人	20 102	15 254	14 541		29 603	19 872
流动资产周转次数	次	2.4	2.5	2.3		1.7	2.4
亏损企业个数	个	114	67	47		2	112
企业亏损额	万元	5 275	3 643	1 632		922	4 353

9-23 乡镇属分行业工业企业单位数和工业总产值

行　业	企业单位数(个)		工业总产值(亿元)		
	1995年	1996年	1995年	1996年	1996比1995年增长%
总　计	**2 090**	**1 996**	**151.86**	**252.48**	**32.7**
#非金属矿采选业	19	19	0.16	0.26	65.7
食品加工业	99	95	4.49	9.96	45.7
食品制造业	55	45	2.42	5.00	43.1
饮料制造业	25	22	1.00	1.50	14.3
纺织业	140	132	11.01	23.17	31.7
服装及其他纤维制品制造业	204	177	18.29	30.23	34.9
皮革、毛皮、羽绒及其制品业	51	53	4.01	10.21	2.6
木材加工及竹、藤、棕、草制品业	29	24	1.00	1.35	51.5
家具制造业	17	20	0.81	2.27	197.0
造纸及纸制品业	57	64	4.56	6.60	18.0
印刷业、记录媒介的复制	30	27	0.43	1.24	84.4
文教体育用品制造业	24	23	1.46	3.60	84.3
石油加工及炼焦业	7	7	3.49	7.97	59.7
化学原料及化学制品制造业	184	185	18.55	25.39	25.8
医药制造业	17	18	1.93	5.64	77.5
化学纤维制造业	19	13	3.63	3.77	3.6
橡胶制品业	26	31	3.42	4.84	43.2
塑料制品业	97	80	3.93	5.03	6.0
非金属矿物制品业	224	218	7.79	12.18	22.3
黑色金属冶炼及压延加工业	41	41	6.53	8.17	24.3
有色金属冶炼及压延加工业	30	33	4.08	7.22	11.0
金属制品业	197	184	14.44	21.34	20.3
普通机械制造业	131	118	7.48	7.32	21.2
专用设备制造业	44	46	1.53	4.34	30.2
交通运输设备制造业	148	129	12.59	23.28	29.1
电气机械及器材制造业	71	80	5.06	9.86	22.4
电子及通信设备制造业	11	9	0.96	0.63	-13.8
仪器仪表及文化、办公用机械制造业	12	12	0.30	0.57	18.6
其他制造业	79	90	6.38	9.53	-2.8
煤气生产和供应业	1	1	0.04	0.02	

9-24 冶金工业总公司主要经济指标

项 目	单 位	1995年	1996年	1996比1995年增长%
全部工业企业				
企业单位数	个	212	199	-6.1
工业总产值	万元	851 157	783 882	-3.9
独立核算工业企业				
企业单位数	个	208	193	-7.2
职工年平均人数	人	93 618	76 140	-18.7
工资总额	万元	77 269	75 501	-2.3
工业总产值	万元	846 575	780 379	-3.6
工业增加值(分配法)	万元	167 852	128 394	-21.6
资产总额	万元	1 633 271	1 725 291	5.6
固定资产原价	万元	648 516	769 380	18.6
固定资产净值年平均余额	万元	352 754	455 154	29.0
流动资产合计	万元	987 502	1 020 733	3.4
#产成品	万元	116 820	110 163	-5.7
产品销售收入	万元	925 914	795 679	-14.1
#产品销售成本	万元	855 741	746 678	-12.7
利税总额	万元	36 470	-7 591	
资金利税率	%	2.23		
产销率	%	108.19	97.83	
亏损企业个数	个	89	113	27.0
亏损企业亏损额	万元	12 216	31 267	156.0
地方预算内国有企业				
企业单位数	个	38	38	
工业总产值	万元	583 265	501 362	-13.2
固定资产原价	万元	381 521	534 132	40.0
固定资产净值	万元	249 004	386 526	55.2
流动资产合计	万元	678 168	796 146	17.4
#产成品	万元	80 557	85 913	6.7
产品销售收入	万元	653 322	495 500	-24.2
#产品销售成本	万元	637 124	478 063	-25.0
利税总额	万元	29 412	-22 597	
#利润总额	万元	-1 728	-27 469	
亏损企业个数	个	18	29	61.1
亏损企业亏损额	万元	7 390	27 502	272.2

9－25 化学工业总公司主要经济指标

项　目	单　位	1995年	1996年	1996比1995年增长％
全部工业企业				
企业单位数	个	294	295	0.3
工业总产值	万元	426 791	422 991	1.0
独立核算工业企业				
企业单位数	个	288	290	0.7
职工年平均人数	人	72 167	63 417	－12.1
工资总额	万元	41 545	43 468	4.6
工业总产值	万元	425 022	427 570	0.9
工业增加值(分配法)	万元	79 378	90 899	14.5
资产总额	万元	611 328	719 984	17.8
固定资产原价	万元	287 774	330 607	14.9
固定资产净值年平均余额	万元	147 893	198 320	34.1
流动资产合计	万元	296 839	340 140	14.6
＃产成品	万元	45 499	53 747	18.1
产品销售收入	万元	426 608	427 253	0.2
＃产品销售成本	万元	365 428	358 433	－1.9
利税总额	万元	14 824	22 413	51.2
资金利税率	％	3.62	4.49	
产销率	％	86.37	97.71	
亏损企业个数	个	89	123	38.2
亏损企业亏损额	万元	8 608	8 101	－5.9
地方预算内国有企业				
企业单位数	个	53	53	
工业总产值	万元	212 948	219 909	7.8
固定资产原价	万元	190 969	221 244	15.9
固定资产净值	万元	121 293	130 778	7.8
流动资产合计	万元	136 293	169 377	24.3
＃产成品	万元	21 746	24 734	13.7
产品销售收入	万元	214 448	220 103	2.6
＃产品销售成本	万元	186 116	185 644	0.3
利税总额	万元	7 576	10 093	33.2
＃利润总额	万元	－2 889	－2 692	
亏损企业个数	个	17	20	17.6
亏损企业亏损额	万元	4 204	3 869	－8.0

9－26　机电工业总公司主要经济指标

项　　目	单　位	1995年	1996年	1996比1995年增长%
全部工业企业				
企业单位数	个	528	526	－0.4
工业总产值	万元	753 542	692 611	－8.1
独立核算工业企业				
企业单位数	个	525	522	－0.6
职工年平均人数	人	132 197	129 430	－2.1
工资总额	万元	82 146	85 301	3.8
工业总产值	万元	753 242	692 312	－8.1
工业增加值(分配法)	万元	243 880	205 269	－15.8
资产总额	万元	1 424 481	1 615 007	13.3
固定资产原价	万元	576 784	618 444	7.2
固定资产净值年平均余额	万元	324 457	348 475	7.4
流动资产合计	万元	778 478	902 820	15.9
＃产成品	万元	94 824	114 868	21.1
产品销售收入	万元	807 621	788 480	－2.4
＃产品销售成本	万元	620 152	645 353	4.1
利税总额	万元	127 807	78 133	－38.9
资金利税率	%	12.4	6.04	
产销率	%	99.4	97.43	
亏损企业个数	个	236	255	8.0
亏损企业亏损额	万元	18 999	27 723	45.9
地方预算内国有企业				
企业单位数	个	93	91	－2.2
工业总产值	万元	255 274	240 600	－5.7
固定资产原价	万元	410 382	420 769	2.5
固定资产净值	万元	255 663	268 402	1.0
流动资产合计	万元	384 832	411 342	6.8
＃产成品	万元	52 665	69 836	32.6
产品销售收入	万元	282 594	257 299	－9.0
＃产品销售成本	万元	215 057	203 486	－5.4
利税总额	万元	23 124	5 007	－78.4
＃利润总额	万元	3 430	－7 986	
亏损企业个数	个	49	49	
亏损企业亏损额	万元	6 978	13 134	88.2

9－27 电子仪表工业总公司主要经济指标

项 目	单 位	1995年	1996年	1996比1995年增长%
全部工业企业				
企业单位数	个	467	467	
工业总产值	万元	807 915	944 350	16.9
独立核算工业企业				
企业单位数	个	451	467	3.5
职工年平均人数	人	101 905	94 759	－7.0
工资总额	万元	541 518	58 315	7.7
工业总产值	万元	806 881	944 350	17.0
工业增加值(分配法)	万元	143 965	134 630	－6.5
资产总额	万元	1 371 483	1 505 177	9.7
固定资产原价	万元	479 811	556 549	16.0
固定资产净值年平均余额	万元	266 902	341 111	27.8
流动资产合计	万元	848 354	911 710	7.5
#产成品	万元	133 525	153 218	14.7
产品销售收入	万元	793 122	868 394	9.5
#产品销售成本	万元	665 568	750 801	12.8
利税总额	万元	48 216	17 164	－62.9
资金利税率	%	5.9	1.9	
产销率	%	99.6	94.8	
亏损企业个数	个	183	240	31.1
亏损企业亏损额	万元	11 019	23 544	113.7
地方预算内国有企业				
企业单位数	个	104	109	4.8
工业总产值	万元	154 981	136 073	－12.2
固定资产原价	万元	246 622	257 562	4.4
固定资产净值	万元	158 321	157 854	－0.3
流动资产合计	万元	333 017	306 413	－8.0
#产成品	万元	48 169	46 877	－2.7
产品销售收入	万元	161 340	138 082	－14.4
#产品销售成本	万元	127 992	111 775	－12.7
利税总额	万元	5 200	9 385	80.5
#利润总额	万元	－2 439	－3 389	
亏损企业个数	个	35	49	40.0
亏损企业亏损额	万元	4 240	4 379	3.3

9－28 纺织工业总公司主要经济指标

项　　目	单　位	1995年	1996年	1996比1995年增长％
全部工业企业				
企业单位数	个	391	345	－11.8
工业总产值	万元	609 647	530 393	－13.0
独立核算工业企业				
企业单位数	个	173	166	－4
职工年平均人数	人	146 457	129 110	－11.8
工资总额	万元	67 246	67 423	0.3
工业总产值	万元	568 303	511 814	－9.9
工业增加值(分配法)	万元	88 676	92 349	4.1
资产总额	万元	1 079 913	1 048 611	－2.9
固定资产原价	万元	583 998	669 257	14.6
固定资产净值年平均余额	万元	330 141	385 967	16.9
流动资产合计	万元	424 435	434 016	2.3
＃产成品	万元	72 896	99 807	36.9
产品销售收入	万元	586 436	498 148	－15.1
＃产品销售成本	万元	515 842	451 705	－12.4
利税总额	万元	11 344	－13 107	
资金利税率	%	1.67		
产销率	%	100.3	98.14	
亏损企业个数	个	86	115	33.7
亏损企业亏损额	万元	19 975	36 422	82.3
地方预算内国有企业				
企业单位数	个	105	98	－0.1
工业总产值	万元	482 456	411 269	－14.8
固定资产原价	万元	493 822	573 176	16.1
固定资产净值	万元	334 958	319 688	－4.6
流动资产合计	万元	352 852	356 107	0.9
＃产成品	万元	61 568	83 971	36.4
产品销售收入	万元	478 317	399 075	－16.6
＃产品销售成本	万元	421 534	364 562	－13.5
利税总额	万元	12 637	－13 566	
＃利润总额	万元	－6 890	－27 983	
亏损企业个数	个	49	65	32.7
亏损企业亏损额	万元	11 749	29 835	153.9

9-29 一轻总公司主要经济指标

项 目	单 位	1995年	1996年	1996比1995年增长%
全部工业企业				
企业单位数	个	436	464	6.4
工业总产值	万元	574 585	637 979	11.0
独立核算工业企业				
企业单位数	个	436	464	6.4
职工年平均人数	人	103 874	93 930	-9.6
工资总额	万元	57 989	61 834	6.6
工业总产值	万元	571 360	636 214	11.4
工业增加值(分配法)	万元	133 718	153 010	14.4
资产总额	万元	1 235 746	1 414 220	14.4
固定资产原价	万元	675 975	755 349	11.7
固定资产净值年平均余额	万元	319 031	572 528	79.5
流动资产合计	万元	519 691	589 110	13.4
#产成品	万元	71 817	85 490	19.0
产品销售收入	万元	585 755	622 901	6.3
#产品销售成本	万元	461 033	482 575	4.7
利税总额	万元	42 867	45 243	5.5
资金利税率	%	5.31	4.02	
产销率	%	96.6	96.4	
亏损企业个数	个	152	189	24.3
亏损企业亏损额	万元	17 672	22 814	29.1
地方预算内国有企业				
企业单位数	个	109	109	
工业总产值	万元	217 467	204 702	-5.9
固定资产原价	万元	491 222	506 772	3.2
固定资产净值	万元	398 776	393 545	-1.3
流动资产合计	万元	302 732	324 019	7.0
#产成品	万元	46 886	53 527	14.2
产品销售收入	万元	264 883	241 039	-9.0
#产品销售成本	万元	201 459	183 456	-8.9
利税总额	万元	21 365	16 437	-23.1
#利润总额	万元	2 893	-53	
亏损企业个数	个	32	42	31.3
亏损企业亏损额	万元	6 196	7 991	29.0

9-30 二轻局主要经济指标

项　　目	单　位	1995年	1996年	1996比1995年增长%
全部工业企业				
企业单位数	个	571	586	2.6
工业总产值	万元	280 844	294 729	7.1
独立核算工业企业				
企业单位数	个	571	586	2.6
职工年平均人数	人	109 755	103 198	-6.0
工资总额	万元	35 070	34 647	-1.2
工业总产值	万元	280 844	294 729	4.5
工业增加值(分配法)	万元	48 339	44 040	-8.9
资产总额	万元	659 415	715 584	8.5
固定资产原价	万元	237 978	281 340	18.2
固定资产净值年平均余额	万元	135 324	206 707	52.8
流动资产合计	万元	387 877	384 749	-0.8
＃产成品	万元	64 263	67 016	4.3
产品销售收入	万元	292 498	284 343	-2.8
＃产品销售成本	万元	254 681	243 676	-4.3
利税总额	万元	-14 711	-12 690	
资金利税率	%			
产销率	%	93.15	92.66	
亏损企业个数	个	317	346	9.2
亏损企业亏损额	万元	25 963	29 906	15.2
地方预算内国有企业				
企业单位数	个	66	74	12.1
工业总产值	万元	70 161	76 452	9.0
固定资产原价	万元	96 304	89 424	-7.1
固定资产净值	万元	68 207	61 703	-9.5
流动资产合计	万元	112 196	103 618	-7.7
＃产成品	万元	20 043	19 984	-0.3
产品销售收入	万元	85 743	78 349	-8.6
＃产品销售成本	万元	73 190	67 733	-1.5
利税总额	万元	-3 757	-3 749	
＃利润总额	万元	-4 587	-7 485	
亏损企业个数	个	38	47	23.7
亏损企业亏损额	万元	6 840	7 941	6.1

9－31 医药集团有限公司主要经济指标

项 目	单 位	1995年	1996年	1996比1995年增长％
全部工业企业				
企业单位数	个	104	67	－35.6
工业总产值	万元	249 814	282 347	13.0
独立核算工业企业				
企业单位数	个	104	61	－41.4
职工年平均人数	人	28 131	25 240	－10.3
工资总额	万元	22 432	25 427	13.4
工业总产值	万元	249 814	280 649	12.3
工业增加值(分配法)	万元	111 573	123 156	10.4
资产总额	万元	327 951	414 720	26.5
固定资产原价	万元	139 976	154 590	10.4
固定资产净值年平均余额	万元	87 189	109 511	25.6
流动资产合计	万元	171 436	248 974	45.2
＃产成品	万元	26 771	28 406	6.1
产品销售收入	万元	245 045	278 236	13.5
＃产品销售成本	万元	148 272	146 289	－1.3
利税总额	万元	59 592	87 003	46.0
资金利税率	％	18.17	20.98	
产销率	％	97	100.36	
亏损企业个数	个	23	25	8.7
亏损企业亏损额	万元	4 200	7 239	73.6
地方预算内国有企业				
企业单位数	个	25	16	－36.0
工业总产值	万元	90 052	83 137	－7.7
固定资产原价	万元	59 970	62 976	5.0
固定资产净值	万元	39 920	42 011	5.2
流动资产合计	万元	22 658	63 522	180.4
＃产成品	万元	8 582	7 700	－10.3
产品销售收入	万元	88 164	81 703	－7.3
＃产品销售成本	万元	64 604	55 560	－14.0
利税总额	万元	10 197	9 550	－6.4
＃利润总额	万元	3 825	3 820	－0.1
亏损企业个数	个	5	6	20.0
亏损企业亏损额	万元	2 411	635	－73.7

9－32 建筑材料集团总公司主要经济指标

项　　目	单　位	1995年	1996年	1996比1995年增长%
全部工业企业				
企业单位数	个	106	96	－9.4
工业总产值	万元	70 374	76 477	8.7
独立核算工业企业				
企业单位数	个	105	96	－8.6
职工年平均人数	人	25 494	23 830	－6.5
工资总额	万元	12 783	12 761	－0.2
工业总产值	万元	70 220	76 477	8.9
工业增加值(分配法)	万元	20 221	20 599	1.9
资产总额	万元	272 483	309 352	13.5
固定资产原价	万元	199 044	218 828	9.9
固定资产净值年平均余额	万元	77 487	173 523	124
流动资产合计	万元	55 370	61 754	11.5
＃产成品	万元	8 076	7 036	－12.9
产品销售收入	万元	69 986	79 996	14.3
＃产品销售成本	万元	58 781	68 031	15.7
利税总额	万元	5 160	－3	
资金利税率	%	4		
产销率	%	96.2	97.2	
亏损企业个数	个	52	61	17.3
亏损企业亏损额	万元	4 304	5 281	22.7
地方预算内国有企业				
企业单位数	个	39	38	－2.6
工业总产值	万元	57 640	52 974	－8.1
固定资产原价	万元	174 248	185 031	6.1
固定资产净值	万元	142 210	150 293	5.7
流动资产合计	万元	43 168	45 384	5.1
＃产成品	万元	6 718	5 074	－24.5
产品销售收入	万元	57 202	53 181	－7.0
＃产品销售成本	万元	47 261	44 886	－5.0
利税总额	万元	5 101	1 969	－61.4
＃利润总额	万元	1 326	－959	
亏损企业个数	个	20	26	30.0
亏损企业亏损额	万元	1 763	2 110	19.7

9－33 汽车工业(集团)有限公司主要经济指标

项 目	单 位	1995 年	1996 年	1996 比 1995 年 增长%
全部工业企业				
企业单位数	个	1	1	
工业总产值	万元	1 020 134	1 289 132	26.4
独立核算工业企业				
企业单位数	个	1	1	
职工年平均人数	人	55 479	55 556	0.1
工资总额	万元	62 222	71 550	15.0
工业总产值	万元	1 020 134	1 289 132	26.4
工业增加值(分配法)	万元	260 813	295 502	13.3
资产总额	万元	1 233 578	1 672 197	35.6
固定资产原价	万元	361 462	677 975	87.6
固定资产净值年平均余额	万元	187 872	446 699	137.8
流动资产合计	万元	673 920	846 847	25.7
＃产成品	万元	49 473	56 770	14.7
产品销售收入	万元	984 443	1 206 628	22.6
＃产品销售成本	万元	767 270	916 200	19.4
利税总额	万元	134 659	134 270	－0.3
资金利税率	%	18.4	11.4	
产销率	%	115.6	105.3	
亏损企业个数	个			
亏损企业亏损额	万元			
地方预算内国有企业				
企业单位数	个			
工业总产值	万元	670 599	883 126	31.7
固定资产原价	万元	288 424	477 287	65.5
固定资产净值	万元	221 199	398 432	80.1
流动资产合计	万元	500 387	626 693	25.2
＃产成品	万元	32 502	35 675	9.8
产品销售收入	万元	732 673	870 060	18.8
＃产品销售成本	万元	555 839	637 175	14.6
利税总额	万元	114 252	115 603	1.2
＃利润总额	万元	56 061	58 701	4.7
亏损企业个数	个			
亏损企业亏损额	万元			

9－34 飞鸽自行车集团公司主要经济指标

项　　目	单　位	1995年	1996年	1996比1995年增长％
全部工业企业				
企业单位数	个	125	123	－1.6
工业总产值	万元	103 645	55 500	－47.7
独立核算工业企业				
企业单位数	个	125	123	－1.6
职工年平均人数	人	29 469	26 606	－9.7
工资总额	万元	13 822	11 525	－16.6
工业总产值	万元	103 645	55 500	－47.7
工业增加值(分配法)	万元	22 546	11 981	－46.9
资产总额	万元	198 392	197 432	－0.5
固定资产原价	万元	86 996	88 821	2.1
固定资产净值年平均余额	万元	50 115	58 140	16.0
流动资产合计	万元	115 498	110 948	－3.9
＃产成品	万元	18 100	13 582	－25.0
产品销售收入	万元	104 675	62 454	－40.3
＃产品销售成本	万元	93 449	58 357	－37.6
利税总额	万元	210	－5 187	
资金利税率	%	0.13		
产销率	%	102.06	103.2	
亏损企业个数	个	69	81	17.4
亏损企业亏损额	万元	6 862	8 597	25.3
地方预算内国有企业				
企业单位数	个	15	15	
工业总产值	万元	60 417	25 145	－57.9
固定资产原价	万元	72 577	72 383	－0.3
固定资产净值	万元	48 064	46 831	－2.6
流动资产合计	万元	79 986	73 281	－8.4
＃产成品	万元	11 015	8 622	－21.7
产品销售收入	万元	61 588	31 066	－49.6
＃产品销售成本	万元	53 931	29 660	－45.0
利税总额	万元	245	－4 039	
＃利润总额	万元	－3 583	－5 451	
亏损企业个数	个	11	13	18.2
亏损企业亏损额	万元	4 088	5 681	39.0

9－35　服装联合总公司主要经济指标

项　　目	单　位	1995 年	1996 年	1996 比 1995 年 增长%
全部工业企业				
企业单位数	个	61	56	－8.2
工业总产值	万元	42 812	36 268	－8.3
独立核算工业企业				
企业单位数	个	61	56	－8.2
职工年平均人数	人	16 863	16 793	－0.4
工资总额	万元	5 187	5 672	9.3
工业总产值	万元	42 812	39 248	－8.3
工业增加值(分配法)	万元	14 872	12 977	－12.7
资产总额	万元	70 248	82 786	17.8
固定资产原价	万元	31 577	37 511	18.8
固定资产净值年平均余额	万元	23 737	26 517	11.7
流动资产合计	万元	39 723	44 051	10.9
#产成品	万元	13 993	13 213	－5.6
产品销售收入	万元	42 196	39 921	－5.4
#产品销售成本		34 508	31 391	－9.0
利税总额		6 052	1 273	－78.9
资金利税率		9.5	3.17	
产销率	%	77.6	89.8	
亏损企业个数	个	24	29	20.8
亏损企业亏损额	万元	1 929	1 113	－42.3
地方预算内国有企业				
企业单位数	个	7	7	
工业总产值	万元	3 976	4 189	5.4
固定资产原价	万元	3 464	9 287	168.1
固定资产净值	万元	2 264	6 755	198.4
流动资产合计	万元	3 380	6 878	103.5
#产成品	万元	1 304	2 197	68.5
产品销售收入	万元	4 194	3 711	－11.5
#产品销售成本	万元	3 703	3 251	－12.2
利税总额	万元	9	246	2 633.3
#利润总额	万元	－203	65	
亏损企业个数	个	2		
亏损企业亏损额	万元	208		

9－36　渤海化工集团工业总公司主要经济指标

项　　目	单　位	1995年	1996年	1996 比1995年 增长％
全部工业企业				
企业单位数	个	53	125	135.8
工业总产值	万元	308 876	361 931	17.2
独立核算工业企业				
企业单位数	个	53	103	94.3
职工年平均人数	人	30 118	45 270	50.3
工资总额	万元	32 772	54 882	67.5
工业总产值	万元	308 876	361 931	17.2
工业增加值(分配法)	万元	99 225	132 061	33.1
资产总额	万元	687 175	1 140 428	66.0
固定资产原价	万元	362 399	525 315	45.0
固定资产净值年平均余额	万元	221 072	359 583	62.7
流动资产合计	万元	212 949	339 966	59.6
＃产成品	万元	20 241	42 721	111.1
产品销售收入	万元	311 068	379 568	22.0
＃产品销售成本	万元	245 145	310 641	26.7
利税总额	万元	38 915	36 839	－5.3
资金利税率	％	9.33	6.9	
产销率	％	98.6	97.5	
亏损企业个数	个	17	30	76.5
亏损企业亏损额	万元	444	3 551	699.8
地方预算内国有企业				
企业单位数	个		9	
工业总产值	万元		51 365	
固定资产原价	万元		191 205	
固定资产净值	万元		146 254	
流动资产合计	万元		89 136	
＃产成品	万元		26 423	
产品销售收入	万元		46 356	
＃产品销售成本	万元		27 738	
利税总额	万元		4 784	
＃利润总额	万元		－2 664	
亏损企业个数	个		3	
亏损企业亏损额	万元		2 682	

9－37　天津钢管公司主要经济指标

项　　目	单　位	1995年	1996年	1996比1995年增长％
全部工业企业				
企业单位数	个	1	1	
工业总产值	万元	125 162	183 599	48.3
独立核算工业企业				
企业单位数	个	1	1	
职工年平均人数	人	7 150	7 187	0.5
工资总额	万元	7 849	9 757	24.3
工业总产值	万元	125 162	183 599	46.7
工业增加值(分配法)	万元	19 132	39 400	105.9
资产总额	万元	1 644 609	1 643 440	－0.1
固定资产原价	万元	1 298 130	1 298 731	0.1
固定资产净值年平均余额	万元	54 346	1 286 066	2 266.4
流动资产合计	万元	283 480	246 932	－12.9
＃产成品	万元	4 099	23 223	466.6
产品销售收入	万元	138 218	181 051	31.0
＃产品销售成本	万元	114 075	136 749	19.9
利税总额	万元	7 096	15 545	119.1
资金利税率	%	2.68	0.99	
产销率	%	105.69	97.73	

9－38　村办及村以下工业主要指标

指　　标	单　位	1995年	＃轻工业	1996年	＃轻工业
村办及村以下工业					
户数	户	24 318	16 717	30 702	27 107
从业人员	人	596 347	333 613	630 039	403 756
工业总产值	万元	4 972 158	2 073 322	8 561 653	4 961 313
上缴税金	万元	134 106	57 070	168 693	105 522
自有资金	万元	722 901	346 485	3 453 859	1 768 436
＃村办工业					
企业单位数	个	7 640	3 315	6 947	3 352
工业总产值	万元	4 367 279	1 661 182	6 529 218	2 931 578
年末全部从业人员	人	471 031	242 180	493 902	267 619
产品销售收入	万元	3 657 691	1 414 546	5 616 535	2 447 384
产品销售税金及附加	万元			34 168	14 322
应交所得税	万元			104 582	49 259
利润总额	万元	323 971	129 507	532 893	254 670
固定资产原价	万元	959 328	413 640	1 340 695	635 911
流动资产年末数	万元	1 433 022	631 084	1 954 042	973 403

注:1995年为工业普查数据,1996年村办自有资金为固定资产原价与流动资产年末数之和。

9－39 大中型工业企业主要工业技术经济指标

(1995年)

指标名称	单位	技术水平
电力工业		
发电标准煤耗	克/千瓦·时	377.73
火电厂用电率	%	9.33
线路损失率	%	2.72
石油开采业		
油田原油商品率	%	96.28
原油(气)生产用电单耗	千瓦·时/吨	167.74
天然气商品率	%	95.48
炼铁		
高炉有效容积利用系数	吨/立方米.日	1.78
生铁合格率	%	99.82
入炉焦比	千克/吨	463.76
转炉炼钢		
转炉日历利用系数	吨/公称吨·昼夜	33.02
钢锭合格率	%	99.67
转炉钢金属料消耗	千克/吨	1 178.40
转炉日历作业率	%	58.55
电炉日历利用系数	吨/百万伏安·昼夜	6.05
钢锭合格率	%	98.15
轧钢		
钢材合格率	%	96.81
轧钢机日历作业率	%	42.75
炼焦		
冶金焦合格率	%	99.45
结焦率	%	77.32
耐火材料生产		
耐火砖合格率	%	92.13
粘土砖原料消耗	千克/吨	1 215.83
铜冶练		
铜电解回收率	%	99.90
铜冶炼综合能耗(折标准煤)	千克/吨	1 460.48
石油加工业		
汽、煤、柴、润总收率	%	47.92
石油产品综合商品收率	%	92.80
石油产品产量合格率	%	100.00
加工一吨原油综合能耗(标油)	千克/吨	59.52
硫酸		
合格率	%	100.00
耗硫磺(实物)	千克/吨	335.29
隔膜固碱		
一级品率	%	100.00
耗原盐(折100%)	千克/吨	1 564.93
耗交流电	千瓦·时/吨	2 711.09
水银固碱		
一级品率	%	100.00
耗原盐(折100%)	千克/吨	1 491.37
耗交流电	千瓦·时/吨	3 587.90
隔膜液碱		
合格率	%	100.00
耗原盐(折100%)	千克/吨	1 553.30
耗交流电	千瓦·时/吨	2 631.12
苛化液碱		
合格率	%	100.00
耗纯碱(100%)	千克/吨	1 427.16
水银液碱		
合格率	%	100.00
耗原盐(折100%)	千克/吨	1 477.08
耗交流电	千瓦·时/吨	3 552.38
纯碱(联碱法)		
一级品率	%	100.00
耗洗盐(100%)	千克/吨	1 163.05
耗氨	千克/吨	341.94
耗电	千瓦·时/吨	214.65
碳化塔容积利用系数	吨/立方米×日	0.71
纯碱(氨碱法)		
一级品率	%	100.00
耗原盐(100%)	千克/吨	1 464.82
耗氨(100%)	千克/吨	5.19
耗电	千瓦·时/吨	80.04
碳化塔容积利用系数	吨/立方米×日	0.92
小苏达		
合格率	%	100.00
耗纯碱(100%)	千克/吨	643.67
耗电	千瓦·时/吨	33.13
敌敌畏		
原油平均含量	%	83.71
耗敌百虫(100%)	千克/吨	1 571.80
甲基1 605		
原油平均含量	%	81.64
耗三氯硫磷(实物)	千克/吨	1 135.66
耗甲醇(实物)	千克/吨	647.55
乙基1 605		
原油平均含量	%	87.07
耗五硫化二磷	千克/吨	796.48
耗乙醇	千克/吨	687.38
氯化苯		
合格率	%	100.00
耗纯苯	千克/吨	735.03
耗氯气	千克/吨	709.95
苯酚		
一级品率	%	100.00
耗纯苯	千克/吨	1 028.13
耗硫酸(100%)	千克/吨	1 398.78
聚氯乙烯		
一级品率	%	90.18
耗电石(300升/千克)	千克/吨	1 386.05
耗氯气	千克/吨	773.02
综合能耗(标油)	千克/吨	5 950.28
轮外胎		
合格率	%	99.86
耗生胶	千克/条	16.32
布面胶鞋合格率(综合)	%	98.51

注:表9－39至9－44为1995年工业普查资料。

9-39 表续

指标名称	单 位	技术水平	指标名称	单 位	技术水平
每吨粘胶短纤维用浆粕	千克	1 005.67	每百千克毛线净用毛条量	千克	108.12
每吨粘胶短纤维用标准煤量	千克	1 859.37	毛线精纺锭千锭时产量	千克	112.24
合成纤维一等品率(混合)	%	90.97	精梳毛织品入库一等品率	%	93.97
每吨锦纶用原料量	千克	1 082.34	每百米精梳毛织品净用毛条量		
每吨锦纶用标准煤量	千克	1 315.27	(包括羊毛及化纤)	千克	41.40
每吨涤纶长丝用原料量	千克	1 080.75	精梳毛织机每台时产量	米	1.70
每吨涤纶长丝用标准煤量	千克	611.60	出口服装合格率	%	99.27
水泥			布鞋合格率	%	100.00
出厂水泥合格率	%	100.00	轻工业		
通用水泥一等品率	%	27.18	机制纸及纸板成品率	%	121.57
回转窑熟料平均标号	号	644.24	每辆710MM载重自行车耗用钢材	千克	29.65
立窑熟料平均标号	号	412.59	机械手表成品返修率	%	23.32
每吨熟料烧成耗标准煤	千克	190.17	每万只闹钟(指铜夹板钟)耗用铜及铜材	千克	1 609.71
每吨水泥综合能耗	千克	165.82	每吨日用玻璃制品耗用标准煤	吨	1.15
回转窑运转率	%	86.33	每吨日用玻璃制品耗用纯碱	千克	62.89
立窑运转率	%	73.28	2升保温瓶胆一等品率	%	89.21
平板玻璃			每万个2升保温瓶胆耗用标准煤	吨	24.72
总成品率	%	77.87	每万支铅笔耗用原木	立方米	0.32
每重量箱平板玻璃综合能耗	千克/重量箱	28.31	普通灯泡综合合格率	%	85.57
每重量箱平板玻璃消耗纯碱	千克/重量箱	10.34	每万只15-40瓦普灯耗用钨丝	万米	1.38
玻璃纤维			出口硬包装罐头合格率	%	98.27
商品玻璃纤维纱合格率	%	100.00	啤酒合格率	%	100.00
拉丝成品率	%	86.70	每吨啤酒耗用标准煤(11-12度)	千克	105.22
每吨玻璃纤维纱耗玻璃球	千克	1 308.34	轻革一级品率	%	81.82
每吨玻璃纤维纱耗电量	千瓦·时/吨	1 741.23	每吨重革耗用牛皮	吨	1.90
砖瓦			每平方米轻革耗用牛皮	千克	4.20
粘土砖合格率	%	92.53	出口皮鞋合格率	%	99.21
每万块砖综合耗用标准煤	千克/万块	956.80	木家具一次合格率	%	96.43
每万块砖综合耗电	千瓦·时/万块	331.93	木家具板材利用率	%	50.73
油毡			全钢家具合格率	%	100.00
油毡合格率	%	99.50	全钢家具钢材利用率	%	93.75
每卷油毡消耗沥青	千克/卷	18.11	皮制篮球合格率	%	100.00
每卷油毡消耗原纸	千克/卷	7.15	每平方米羊毛手工地毯耗用色毛纱	千克	6.74
每卷油毡消耗标准煤	千克/卷	4.85	聚氯乙烯压延薄膜一级品率	%	99.14
机械工业			每吨聚氯乙烯压延薄膜耗用树脂	吨	0.67
铸铁件综合废品率	%	12.17	聚乙烯吹塑薄膜合格率	%	98.26
铸钢件综合废品率	%	3.67	聚乙烯地膜合格率	%	97.07
机械加工件综合废品率	%	1.60	聚丙烯编织袋一级品率	%	98.47
金属切削机床利用率	%	65.53	精铝锅一级品率	%	63.37
钢材利用率	%	68.00	每个24厘米精铝锅耗用铝材	千克	0.48
每吨锻锤能力产量	吨	150.54	铸铁锅合格率	%	88.89
每千吨锻造水压机能力产量	吨	809.88	每吨铸铁锅耗用生铁(包括铁屑和废铁)	吨	1.11
热处理件废品率	%	0.32	家用电冰箱一次合格率	%	94.97
纺织工业			每台150-200升双门电冰箱耗用薄钢板	千克	18.93
棉纱(纯棉)一等品率	%	99.16	空气调节器一次合格率	%	93.18
棉纺绽每千锭时平均产纱量(混合数)	千克	18.91	每台空气调节器耗用薄钢板	千克	24.41
棉布(纯棉)入库一等品率	%	97.00	双桶洗衣机一次合格率	%	85.64
每百米布用纱量(包括化纤)	千克	17.89	每台双桶洗衣机(洗衣容量		
每百米布用电量(混合)	千瓦·时	25.91	2.5-3.5公斤)壳耗用薄钢板	千克	8.00
棉布织机每台时产量(混合数)	米	3.44	每台30吨地上衡、地中衡耗用生铁	吨	1.60
每百米印染布用碱量(折100%)	千克	2.15	每台30吨地上衡、地中衡耗用钢材	吨	7.33
			棉(纯棉)印染布入库一等品率	%	91.67

9-40　街、乡及以上工业主要产品生产能力

(1995年)

产品名称	单　位	年初生产能　力	年末生产能　力	产品名称	单　位	年初生产能　力	年末生产能　力
天然原油	万吨	612	599	化学农药原药(折 100%)	吨	38 341	38 569
天然气	万立方米	25 004	24 904	油　漆	吨	97 579	96 070
原　盐	吨	2 101 258	2 134 258	油　墨	吨	11 842	9 349
大　米	吨	188 600	190 665	染　料	吨	36 611	36 048
小麦粉	吨	945 931	937 711	合成纤维单体	吨	90 005	90 011
食用植物油	吨	109 970	111 138	炭　黑	吨	54 848	54 850
畜类屠宰	吨	67 988	67 988	肥　皂	吨	70 301	69 301
机制糖(年产糖量)	吨	3 458	4 110	合成洗涤剂	吨	457 293	465 203
饲　料	吨	832 080	837 494	化学原料药	吨	11 387	12 715
味　精	吨	6 700	9 700	中成药	吨	8 354	9 860
白　酒	吨	56 081	60 079	轮胎外胎	万条	192	155
啤　酒	吨	75 000	35 000	自行车外胎	万条	1 842	1 842
卷　烟	箱	488 841	463 352	塑料制品	吨	14 196 232	14 293 305
化学纤维合计	吨	216 273	218 280	(按两班生产计算)			
印染布	万米	259 781	259 767	水　泥	吨	2 191 426	2 196951
梭织面料服装	万件	328 676	334 083	油毡油纸	卷	3 130 070	3130 070
(机织面料服装)				平板玻璃	重量箱	2 475 164	2 482 964
锯　材	立方米	77 232	102 985	日用玻璃制品	吨	106 559	98 223
家　具	件	2 824 119	2 733 700	卫生陶瓷	件	439 941	439941
机制纸	吨	124 717	124 552	日用陶瓷	件	3 239 500	3 146 000
机制纸板	吨	242 051	477 651	耐火材料制品	吨	231 672	244 457
蒸馏设备能力	处理吨	4 517 329	7 020 306	生　铁	吨	1 665 560	1 659 122
裂化设备能力	处理吨	1 770 266	2 370 592	钢	吨	2 330 510	2 550 819
机械化焦炉生产的焦炭	吨	1 787 954	1 816916	初轧处理钢锭能力	吨	1 252 500	1 254 920
硫　酸(折 100%)	吨	115 000	115 000	成品钢材	吨	9 468851	10 037 136
合成氨	吨	107 000	107 000	铜电解能力	吨	23 600	23 600
农用化学肥料	吨	114 012	118 648	金属集装箱	件	41 600	41 600

9－40 续表

产品名称	单 位	年初生产能 力	年末生产能 力	产品名称	单 位	年初生产能 力	年末生产能 力
钢丝绳	吨	24 774	38 774	汽 车	辆	155 550	163 550
日用精铝制品	吨	684 277	684 283	自行车(按两班生产)	辆	8 596 963	9 035 676
燃气灶	台	222 010	222 010	民用钢质船舶	艘	30	33
燃气热水器	台	60 002	60 015	民用钢质船舶	综合万吨	13	13
电焊条	吨	188 910	243 910	水轮发电机	千瓦	408 000	808 000
工业锅炉	台	1 505	1 905	水轮发电机	组	21	42
工业锅炉	蒸吨	1 205 806	1 206 913	交、直流电动机	台	1 118 675	1 128 987
内燃机	千瓦	7 389 000	8 980 280	交、直流电动机	千瓦	614 620	620 370
金属切削机床	台	3 256	3 178	变压器	千伏安	3 635 565	4 509 455
锻压机械	台	1 490	1 664	电力电缆	公里	1 089 941	1 094 941
锻压机械	吨	13 452	14 522	蓄电池	千伏安时	593 259	665 648
起重机械	台	96 915	100 948	普通灯泡	万只	5 300	5 300
电 梯	台	7 603	7 603	荧光灯	万只	1 924	1 922
泵	台	48 617	49 731	洗衣机	台	800 000	800 000
风 机	台	9 080	12 283	吸尘器	台	400 000	400 000
减速机	台	57 988	58 855	家用电冰箱	台	374 000	374 000
轴 承	万套	510	520	电风扇	台	24 022	24 022
矿山设备	台	10 653	12 654	房间空气调节器	台	120 009	120 011
卷烟加工机械	台	59	51	程控交换机	线	1 320 310	1 320 330
纺织机械	台	6 074	6 027	电子计算机	部	75 678	80 683
纺织机械	吨	16 014	15 863	大规模半导体集成电路	万块	40 693	55 677
缝纫机(按两班生产)	架	487 562	517 362	彩色电视机	部	1 680 000	1 948 000
造纸机械	台	4 422	7 274	衡 器	台	70 897	80 043
化工设备	台	1 037	1 127	照像机	台	491 384	492 502
水泥设备	吨	2 500	2 500	复印机	台	20 000	20 000
包装机械	台	3 132	3 254	钟	只	2 839 633	2 791 633
大中型拖拉机	台	10 000	10 000	手 表	只	5 030 000	5 030 000
医疗仪器设备	台	72 091	77 837				

9-41 大中型工业企业主要产品质量

(1995年)

产品名称	单 位	产品数量			
		合 计	优等品	一等品	合格品
窄钢带	吨	459 993	42 390	169 047	248 556
焊 管	吨	776 102	363 060	301 324	111 718
预应力钢丝	吨	33 520		30 985	2 535
电解铜	吨	12 873		12 873	
纯铜板	吨	3 060		1 951	1 109
车用汽油	吨	860 268	412 837	277 893	169 538
柴 油	吨	1 151 607	78 595	616 480	456 532
燃料油	吨	1 031 268			1 031 268
硫 酸	吨	49 800		49 800	
尿 素	吨	42 150	7 587	19 747	14 816
甲 醛	吨	35 933	6 310	29 623	
聚氯乙烯树脂	吨	97 202	16 285	72 202	8 715
聚 酯	吨	21 642	19 171	2 471	
力车胎	条	17 200 000			17 200 000
胶 鞋	双	590 000		590 000	
六味地黄丸	丸	102 650 543		143	102 650 400
银翘解毒片	片	16 580 000			16 580 000
藿香正气水	瓶	4 890 000	3 800 000	990 000	100 000
普通硅酸盐水泥	吨	250 976	142 672	94 868	13 436
普通平板玻璃	重量箱	1 937 000	420 174	1 405 348	111 478
烧结普通砖	块	56 188 200			56 188 200
石油沥清纸胎油毡	卷	1 661 694		1 661 694	
柴油机	千瓦	138 800		17 800	121 000
汽油机	千瓦	1 134 364	17 190	1 056 215	60 959
电动葫芦	台	2 368	342	1 604	422
离心泵	台	2 693		45	2 648
螺杆泵	台	5 106		85	5 021
罗茨鼓风机	台	1 339			1 339
摆线减速机	台	32 528	11 700	18 769	2 059
向心球轴承	套	2 430 000	390 000	730 000	1 310 000
轮式拖拉机	台	7 810		7 810	
交流电机	千瓦	79 205		57 088	22 117
电力变压器	千伏安	683 776	24 825	375 846	283 105
互感器	台	11 439			11 439
电力电缆	公里	102 119	1 610	81 733	18 776
电焊条及焊丝	吨	36 668	33 033	589	3 046
流量仪表	台	338 768		274 509	64 259
电度表	只	1 140 653			1 140 653

9-41 续表 1

产品名称	单 位	产品数量			
		合 计	优等品	一等品	合格品
照相机	台	363 928			363 928
静电复印机	台	1 145			1 145
录音机电机	只	5 225 000		5 225 000	
起动用铅酸蓄电池	只	2 955 738	2 955 738		
黑白显象管(35CM,44CM)	只	325 500		316 039	9 461
黑白电视机	部	512 492	228 200		284 292
彩色电视机	部	1 095 405	11 533		1 083 872
电子琴(37 键以上娱乐琴)	架	1 005 822			1 005 822
录音机芯	台	566 924	363 594	179 428	23 902
电视机高频头(调频器)	只	913 020	913 020		
无线电话机(便携台,车载台,基地台)(150MC,450MC)	部	1 000			1 000
自动电话机	部	53 593	2 850	15 473	35 270
数字用户程控交换机	台	62 645			62 645
传真机	部	9 300			9 300
微型数字电子计算机	部	1 453			1 453
电讯电缆	米	104 817 190	4 356 000	58 777 000	41 684 190
印刷电路板	块	1 144 239			1 144 239
粘胶短纤维	吨	7 054		7 044	10
涤纶短纤维	吨	66 671	54 014	12 277	380
棉 纱	吨	57 882	598	53 889	3 395
棉 布	万米	12 018	843	9 692	1 483
棉印染布	万米	11 051		6 903	4 148
精梳毛织品	万米	420	234	159	27
粗梳毛织品	万米	119		69	50
毛 毯	万条	5			5
毛 线	吨	5 773		5 686	87
凸版印刷纸	吨	9 770			9 770
自行车	辆	1 593 487			1 593 487
指针式石英手表	只	3 613 177		218 000	3 395 177
普通照明管形荧光灯	只	2 914 025		2 914 025	
食用盐	吨	114 869	90 082	10 682	14 105
食用酒精	吨	22 480		10 549	11 931
家用电冰箱	台	5 506		5 131	375

9－41 续表 2

产品名称	产品价值(现价、千元)			
	合　计	优等品	一等品	合格品
窄钢带	1 277 108	141 276	465 839	669 993
焊　管	1 698 888	610 389	710 016	378 483
预应力钢丝	151 270		139 692	11 578
电解铜	81 843		81 843	
纯铜板	83 648		55 965	27 683
车用汽油	1 661 378	803 332	544 243	313 803
柴　油	1 873 232	127 299	1 002 487	743 446
燃料油	747 215			747 215
硫　酸	24 620		24 620	
尿　素	77 301	14 459	36 174	26 668
甲　醛	44 378	8 209	36 169	
聚氯乙烯树脂	688 492	113 158	514 055	61 279
聚　酯	187 398	166 002	21 396	
力车胎	51 164			51 164
胶　鞋	12 000		12 000	
六味地黄丸	3 289		903	2 386
银翘解毒片	994			994
藿香正气水	3 912	3 040	792	80
普通硅酸盐水泥	69 527	39 479	27 358	2 690
普通平板玻璃	155 334	40 559	106 409	8 366
烧结普通砖	7 243			7 243
石油沥清纸胎油毡	56 282		56 282	
柴油机	37 230		4 880	32 350
汽油机	136 677	7 564	116 569	12 544
电动葫芦	30 077	9 382	12 686	8 009
离心泵	22 320		260	22 060
螺杆泵	42 872		1 256	41 616
罗茨鼓风机	3 963			3 963
摆线减速机	114 550	37 800	64 150	12 600
向心球轴承	5 950	952	1 785	3 213
轮式拖拉机	329 550		329 550	
交流电机	6 806		3 235	3 571
电力变压器	43 175	1 933	20 687	20 555
互感器	11 710			11 710
电力电缆	455 295	38 368	294 956	121 971
电焊条及焊丝	190 590	185 694	2 262	2 634
流量仪表	16 178		9 462	6 716
电度表	67 446			67 446

9－41 续表 3

产品名称	产品价值(现价、千元)			
	合 计	优等品	一等品	合格品
照相机	122 600			122 600
静电复印机	23 070			23 070
录音机电机	292 109		292 109	
起动用铅酸蓄电池	229 644	229 644		
黑白显象管(35CM,44CM)	4 867		4 736	131
黑白电视机	111 536	8 192		103 344
彩色电视机	1 851 393	25 445		1 825 948
电子琴(37 键以上娱乐琴)	633 150			633 150
录音机芯	23 870	17 370	6 160	340
电视机高频头(调频器)	12 740	12 740		
无线电话机(便携台,车载台,基地台)(150MC,450MC)	9 444			9 444
自动电话机	237 264	211	231 605	5 448
数字用户程控交换机	62 511			62 511
传真机	39 687			39 687
微型数字电子计算机	6 103			6 103
电讯电缆	151 990	12 870	13 360	125 760
印刷电路板	74 747			74 747
粘胶短纤维	113 267		113 100	167
涤纶短纤维	1 006 465	815 395	185 334	5 736
棉 纱	1 082 774	7 590	1 008 331	66 853
棉 布	647 814	43 995	490 699	113 120
棉印染布	550 168		349 974	200 194
精梳毛织品	233 488	128 771	89 683	15 034
粗梳毛织品	44 554		27 245	17 309
毛 毯	8 738			8 738
毛 线	375		370	5
凸版印刷纸	43 972			43 972
自行车	414 484			414 484
指针式石英手表	52 879		4 508	48 371
普通照明管形荧光灯	12 535		12 535	
食用盐	37 140	31 709	2 243	3 188
食用酒精	143 745		67 382	76 363
家用电冰箱	8 497		7 984	513

9－42　电子计算机、机械手等设备拥有量和动力机械总能力

（1995年街、乡及以上工业）

设备名称	单　位	年末设备数量总计	国产设备合　计	按出厂年限分		
				90年代	80年代	70年代及以前
大中型电子计算机(包括巨型计算机)	台	13	1	1		
小型电子计算机	台	117	24	17	6	1
微型电子计算机	台	13 852	5 481	4 297	1 147	37
自动化生产线	条	349	77	48	27	2
机电控制自动化生产线	条	159	45	28	15	2
电子计算机控制自动化生产线	条	145	24	16	8	
半自动化生产线	条	1 110	473	217	230	26
机电控制半自动化生产线	条	721	283	141	130	12
电子计算机控制半自动化生产线	条	127	30	15	15	
机械手	台	294	127	31	89	7
气动机械手	台	182	66	11	52	3
液压机械手	台	14	4	1	3	
电工机械手	台	29	12	8		4
工业机器人	台	30	1		1	
可变程序控制机器人	台	26				
示教模拟再现机器人	台	1	1		1	
动力机械总能力	千瓦	16 111 212				
原动机	千瓦	6 564 749				
#用于推动发电机的原动机	千瓦	2 320 705				
发电机	千瓦	2 137 385				
电动机	千瓦	10 440 791				
电气器械	千瓦	1 426 377				

设备名称	单　位	进口设备合　计	按出厂年限分			在总计中：闲置设备
			90年代	80年代	70年代及以前	
大中型电子计算机(包括巨型计算机)	台	12	9	3		
小型电子计算机	台	93	60	28	5	5
微型电子计算机	台	8 371	7 392	948	31	49
自动化生产线	条	272	187	82	3	1
机电控制自动化生产线	条	114	76	36	2	
电子计算机控制自动化生产线	条	121	93	27	1	
半自动化生产线	条	637	299	314	24	27
机电控制半自动化生产线	条	438	185	236	17	25
电子计算机控制半自动化生产线	条	97	69	28		
机械手	台	167	70	91	6	5
气动机械手	台	116	56	54	6	2
液压机械手	台	10	1	9		
电工机械手	台	17	4	13		
工业机器人	台	29	19	10		2
可变程序控制机器人	台	26	19	7		2
示教模拟再现机器人	台					

9－43　街、乡及以上工业主要生产设备及其新旧程度

（已安装设备1995年末价值量）　　单位：万元

项　　目	国产设备合　　计	按出厂年限分		
		90年代	80年代	70年代及以前
总　　计	**1 929 221**	**763 248**	**854 518**	**311 455**
一、按隶属关系分				
中央企业	538 998	229 861	217 955	91 182
市属企业	1 128 549	394 383	540 765	193 401
区属企业	28 173	20 009	6 427	1 737
县属企业	42 868	18 576	20 103	4 189
街道企业	3 787	1 591	1 567	629
镇属企业	41 093	22 747	16 388	1 958
乡属企业	101 983	51 245	41 479	9 259
其　他	43 770	24 836	9 834	9 100
二、按经济类型分				
国有经济	1 327 055	482 673	601 572	242 810
集体经济	220 690	92 941	98 036	29 713
联营经济	25 561	11 016	12 125	2 420
股份制经济	166 729	65 004	81 458	20 267
中外合资经营企业	96 290	47 348	37 159	11 783
中外合作经营企业	6 991	2 778	2 736	1 477
外资企业	12 592	11 503	983	106
港澳台与大陆合资经营	55 871	38 624	15 030	2 217
港澳台与大陆合作经营	8 713	3 100	4 974	639
港澳台独资企业	8 729	8 261	445	23
三、按轻重分				
轻工业	463 312	176 201	228 326	58 785
重工业	1 465 909	587 047	626 192	252 670
四、按规模分				
大型企业	1 209 708	449 197	560 897	199 614
中型企业	335 726	129 383	140 001	66 342
小型企业	383 787	184 668	153 620	45 499
五、按行业大类分				
煤炭采选业	150	150		
石油和天然气开采业	150 920	69 890	67 994	13 036
非金属矿采选业	10 328	4 138	4 121	2 070

9－43续表1

单位:万元

项　　目	国产设备合　计	按出厂年限分		
		90年代	80年代	70年代及以前
食品加工业	26 055	10 320	14 352	1 383
食品制造业	28 944	12 325	15 356	1 263
饮料制造业	15 891	8 651	6 634	606
烟草加工业	3 942	1 814	1 914	214
纺织业	101 079	24 185	58 892	18 002
服装及其他纤维制品制造业	20 148	11 078	8 433	638
皮革、毛皮、羽绒及其制品业	11 601	5 920	4 663	1 018
木材加工及竹、藤、棕、草品业	7 356	2 558	3 751	1 047
家具制造业	6 141	4 940	695	505
造纸及纸制品业	32 907	9 221	15 734	7 953
印刷业、记录媒介的复制	8 881	4 200	3 500	1 181
文教体育用品制造业	4 785	1 437	2 481	868
石油加工及炼焦业	63 471	28 730	25 385	9 356
化学原料及化学制品制造业	213 256	70 462	113 761	29 033
医药制造业	22 987	11 192	10 300	1 495
化学纤维制造业	6 329	3 283	2 773	273
橡胶制品业	22 849	6 388	13 349	3 112
塑料制品业	26 079	13 434	10 986	1 659
非金属矿物制品业	54 975	24 417	21 216	9 342
黑色金属冶炼及压延加工业	218 860	78 555	102 789	37 516
有色金属冶炼及压延加工业	13 922	6 054	6 364	1 504
金属制品业	73 522	32 717	30 492	10 313
普通机械制造业	121 643	48 060	48 389	25 194
专用设备制造业	84 646	20 932	28 341	35 373
交通运输设备制造业	120 706	37 614	54 233	28 860
电气机械及器材制造业	62 996	27 010	24 322	11 664
电子及通信设备制造业	25 946	9 236	12 856	3 854
仪器仪表及文化、办公用机械制造业	17 808	2 638	9 922	5 248
其他制造业	7 494	3 577	3 464	453
电力、蒸汽、热水的生产和供应业	328 437	163 184	118 454	46 799
煤气生产和供应业	8 699	1 962	6 494	244
自来水的生产和供应业	5 469	2 978	2 109	382

9－43 续表 2

单位:万元

项 目	进口设备合 计	按出厂年限			闲 置设 备
		90 年代	80 年代	70 年代及以前	
总 计	**2 278 982**	**614 210**	**1 460 124**	**204 648**	**18 624**
一、按隶属关系分					
中央企业	505 297	58 721	297 062	149 514	3 871
市属企业	1 466 335	297 333	1 124 794	44 208	13 677
区属企业	15 807	8 883	6 345	579	91
县属企业	9 066	6 585	2 437	44	82
街道企业	217	61	33	123	2
镇属企业	13 509	11 686	1 806	17	90
乡属企业	25 619	20 481	4 691	447	43
其 他	243 132	210 460	22 956	9 716	768
二、按经济类型分					
国有经济	1 621 083	194 351	1 249 099	177 633	10 383
集体经济	33 832	11 703	14 936	7 193	730
联营经济	15 000	8 304	6 316	379	55
股份制经济	79 938	24 747	54 605	586	4 652
中外合资经营企业	194 537	114 698	71 916	7 923	1 281
中外合作经营企业	3 094	1 139	625	1 331	5
外资企业	99 963	78 096	19 108	2 759	224
港澳台与大陆合资经营	90 277	43 758	41 227	5 292	488
港澳台与大陆合作经营	5 636	3 502	2 069	64	404
港澳台独资企业	135 623	133 913	223	1 488	403
三、按轻重分					
轻工业	537 637	314 002	200 718	22 917	5 660
重工业	1 741 345	300 208	1 259 406	181 731	12 964
四、按规模分					
大型企业	1 907 779	418 239	1 307 720	181 820	11 733
中型企业	168 476	80 036	74 710	13 730	4 051
小型企业	202 727	115 935	77 694	9 098	2 840
五、按行业大类分					
煤炭采选业					
石油和天然气开采业	78 598	26 268	47 428	4 902	2 210
非金属矿采选业	118		67	51	200

9－43续3

单位:万元

项　目	进口设备合计	按出厂年限			闲置设备
		90年代	80年代	70年代及以前	
食品加工业	27 632	20 096	7 441	95	28
食品制造业	109 387	106 303	2 688	396	233
饮料制造业	26 376	7 364	19 011	2	
烟草加工业	6 334	1 675	4 660		
纺织业	113 211	45 365	59 655	8 190	868
服装及其他纤维制品制造业	20 462	14 471	5 757	233	564
皮革、毛皮、羽绒及其制品业	15 596	10 663	4 585	348	
木材加工及竹、藤、棕、草品业	17 630	13 022	4 195	413	17
家具制造业	2 749	994	1 755		114
造纸及纸制品业	19 181	7 040	11 318	822	404
印刷业、记录媒介的复制	14 506	8 807	4 617	1 082	343
文教体育用品制造业	4 970	2 637	2 272	61	
石油加工及炼焦业	155 144	20 700	34 698	99 745	933
化学原料及化学制品制造业	63 809	39 918	22 555	1 336	5 403
医药制造业	11 261	6 479	4 778	4	307
化学纤维制造业	11 034	6 506	4 528		
橡胶制品业	14 785	2 539	8 949	3 297	465
塑料制品业	64 422	46 150	16 234	2 038	104
非金属矿物制品业	23 193	16 546	6 597	49	509
黑色金属冶炼及压延加工业	807 301	5 046	799 877	2 378	101
有色金属冶炼及压延加工业	5 463	635	4 802	26	188
金属制品业	46 441	23 541	19 477	3 423	737
普通机械制造业	65 568	34 380	24 977	6 212	554
专用设备制造业	25 605	11 172	7 691	6 742	1 838
交通运输设备制造业	39 670	16 812	15 635	7 223	847
电气机械及器材制造业	47 833	22 714	22 356	2 763	177
电子及通信设备制造业	169 252	83 713	81 940	3 599	929
仪器仪表及文化、办公用机械制造业	14 361	3 987	6 333	4 042	439
其他制造业	4 795	2 717	1 575	503	36
电力、蒸汽、热水的生产和供应业	252 140	5 866	201 605	44 669	79
煤气生产和供应业	139	71	68		
自来水的生产和供应业	19	14		5	

9－44　街乡及以上工业主要生产设备及新旧程度

（已安装设备 1995 年末实物量）

设备名称	单　位	国产设备合　计	按出厂年限分			进口设备合　计	按出厂年限分			闲　置设　备
			90 年代	80 年代	70 年代及以前		90 年代	80 年代	70 年代及以前	
工业锅炉	台	19 168	2 239	12 538	4 391	5 193	21	5 168	4	61
金属切削机床	台	82 946	15 154	31 597	36 195	4 718	1 013	2 042	1 663	941
锻压设备	台	21 308	4 319	10 774	6 215	1 127	411	549	167	197
起重设备	台	15 735	4 095	7 435	4 205	414	115	209	90	120
输送设备	台	5 594	1 696	2 802	1 096	361	166	165	30	129
焊接设备	台	21 180	7 534	9 714	3 932	1 144	491	549	104	99
切割设备	台	2 239	1 439	674	126	158	100	57	1	4
滚镀设备	台	253	68	148	37	13		13		1
电镀槽	台	828	169	518	141	6	3	2	1	4
内燃机车	台	83	21	45	17	4			4	
蒸汽机车	台	27	5	4	18					
货　车	台	1 685	607	698	380	6	6			
汽　车	辆	22 847	13 556	8 913	378	3 288	1 772	1 357	159	50
船　舶	艘	309	88	28	193	116	114		2	
包装机械	台	2 409	1 509	797	103	424	334	75	15	66
除尘设备	台	2 892	810	1 791	291	68	15	47	6	40
有害气体处理设备	台	338	103	225	10	14	8	6		8
污水处理设备	台	1 190	361	690	139	84	65	18	1	38
发电机组	台	990	370	490	130	81	38	30	13	9
电站锅炉设备总计	台	68	19	29	20	5		2	3	
注采设备	台(套)	2 333	960	956	417	10		5	5	25
屠宰设备	台	174	55	115	4	6	6			
畜肉制品生产专用设备	台(条)	671	432	239		102	23	79		
炼制设备	台	55	18	37						
饲料粉碎机	台	136	51	81	4	6	1	5		2
饲料加工成套设备	套	167	25	141	1	6	1	5		1
饼干生产线设备	条	16	6	10		5	3	2		1
卷接机组	条	30		30		27	5	22		
棉布织机合计	台	16 803	2 891	8 029	5 883	1 140	510	397	233	212
毛纺锭	锭	36 521	5 217	23 496	7 808	51 504	9 076	14 860	27 568	
聚烯烃编织袋织机	台	295	150	112	33					16
帽子加工设备	台	1 022	378	306	338	4		4		
胶合板成套设备	套	31	7	23	1	11	4	6	1	
造纸机	台	1 032	936	62	34	1		1		
织毯机	台	260		108	152	1			1	
无纺针刺地毯机	台	272	12	260		4	1	3		

9－44 续表 1

设备名称	单位	国产设备合计	按出厂年限分			进口设备合计	按出厂年限分			闲置设备
			90年代	80年代	70年代及以前		90年代	80年代	70年代及以前	
炼油生产设备(装置)	套	34	9	24	1	3		3		
硫酸生产专用设备	套	3		3						
盐酸生产设备	套	25	9	15	1	1		1		
烧碱生产设备	套	24	18	5	1	3	1	2		
纯碱生产专用设备	套	1		1						
电石生产设备	套	7	2	1	4					
合成氨生产设备	套	2	1		1					
尿素生产设备	套	1	1							
碳铵生产设备	套	2		1	1					
磷肥生产设备	套	7	3	3	1					
钾肥生产设备	套					1	1			
复合肥生产专用设备	套	26	20	6						
化学农药生产设备	套	30	13	16	1	1	1			2
有机化工原料生产设备(装置)	套	69	15	40	14	2		1	1	2
油漆生产专用设备	套	202	92	110		1			1	
油墨加工设备	套	1 274	599	586	89	22	6	16		
染料生产设备	套	983	606	357	20					2
合成树脂生产设备(装置)	套	67	28	33	6	6		3	3	2
合成橡胶生产设备(装置)	套	27	13	13	1					
合成纤维单体及聚合物生产设备(装置)	套	26	13	10	3	14	1	12	1	
感光材料生产及加工设备	套	116	36	80						
香精加工机械	台	106	28	74	4					
香料加工机械	台	801	322	255	224	8			8	
饮片设备	台	46	16	10	20					
中药提取设备	台	96	39	47	10	2	2			
口服液设备	台	58	48	10		1	1			
轮胎加工设备	套	330	84	245	1					
力车胎加工设备	套	30	27	3						
橡胶管带加工设备	套	39	9	20	10					
胶鞋加工设备	套	178	158	14	6	10	10			2
乳胶制品成型机	套	8	3	5						
人造革生产线设备	条	3		3		3	1	2		
合成革生产线设备	条	8		8						
塑料鞋生产专用设备	台	2		2						

9－44 续表 2

设备名称	单　位	国产设备合　计	按出厂年限分			进口设备合　计	按出厂年限分			闲　置设　备
			90 年代	80 年代	70 年代及以前		90 年代	80 年代	70 年代及以前	
机械化焦炉	座	4	2	2						
炼铁高炉	套(座)	65	35	26	4					
高炉风机	台	17	6	10	1					
铸铁机	台	6		3	3					
平　炉	套(座)	17	5	9	3					
电　炉	套(座)	105	62	33	10	2		1	1	2
转　炉	套(座)	9	4		5					
连铸机	套(台)	4		2	2	3		2	1	
轧钢设备	套	766	360	306	100	9	4	4	1	1
镀层设备	套	53	33	15	5	1		1		
铁合金生产设备	座	10	5	4	1					
鼓风炉	座	11	4	4	3					
反射炉	座	48	24	18	6					1
重冶电炉	座	18		17	1					1
电解槽	台	388	317	67	4					
板、带、箔材轧机	列	221	96	73	52	15		8	7	1
制管机	台	16	3	13		2		2		
拉伸机(冷拔机)	台	421	126	224	71	2	2			1
拉丝机	台	4 748	1 463	2 462	823	2 778	20	2 758		20
木螺丝圆钉专用设备	台	1 416	630	677	109					
日用不锈钢制品生产专用机械	台	402	335	55	12	28	1	27		
燃气用具制造专用设备	台	271	271							
电焊条生产专用设备	条	31	16	15		1		1		
弹簧生产线设备	条	123	14	97	12	3	2	1		1
轴承生产线设备	条	4		2	2					
紧固件生产线设备	条	71	18	49	4	2		2		
机车车辆修理专用设备	台	64	33	28	3					
船　坞	座	4			4					
船　台	座	6		1	5					
灯泡加工设备	条	3	3			2			2	
家用空调器加工装配生产线	条	5	1	4		6	5	1		
电话机组装线	条	14	11	3		4		4		
计算机组装线	条	80	80							
磁性材料及元件生产线	条	5		4	1	22	21	1		
电子案秤加工装配生产线	条	31	31							1
专用自动车床	台	285	15	239	31	233	4	61	168	
多工位钻孔攻丝机	台	24		16	8	12		2	10	
机械表装配线设备	条	13	13							

天津市第三次工业普查公报

天津市第三次工业普查办公室、天津市统计局

1996年12月

根据国务院关于开展第三次全国工业普查的部署,天津市的工业普查工作,在各级政府的正确领导下,经过各级工业普查办公室的充分准备和精心组织,以及全市近十万名普查人员的共同努力,圆满地完成了普查登记、数据审核、质量抽查、数据处理、汇总上报等任务。工业普查数据达到了预期的质量控制目标。

通过工业普查,天津市获得了1995年全市范围内全部工业企业和工业生产单位的大量信息。这些信息反映了工业企业在社会主义市场经济条件下生产经营和业务活动的基本面貌,包括企业生产要素指标,企业生产、消费、交换、分配指标,企业基本经营状况指标,企业技术进步指标等,为摸清工业底数,制定长远发展规划和政策提供了重要的依据,对保持工业经济的持续、快速、健康发展,加快社会主义市场经济建设,具有十分重要的意义。现将天津市第三次工业普查的主要结果公布如下:

一、工业经济规模与实力

自1985年第二次全国工业普查以来,天津工业经济总体规模显著扩大,发展水平明显提高,工业实力进一步增强。到1995年底,全市工业企业和生产单位共有34 989个,比1985年增加7 679个。其中街乡及以上企业10 671个,增加5 393个;村办和合作经营工业单位9 946个,增加428个;城乡个体工业户14 372个,增加1 858个。

近10年来,天津工业获得了较快的发展。从反映工业生产最终成果的工业增加值来看,1995年为451.84亿元,比1985年增加1.16倍,年均增长8%,(增长速度按可比价格计算,下同)占全市国内生产总值的49.11%,在全市国民经济中占主导地位。全市工业产出额(即现价工业总产值[原规定],下同)为2 230.69亿元,比1985年增长3.27倍,年均增长15.62%。(增长速度按可比价格计算,下同)其中街乡及以上工业产出额为1 594.26亿元,增长1.83倍,年均增长11.0%。工业产品的国际市场竞争力不断提高,1995年天津市街乡及以上工业企业的工业产品出口交货值达215.49亿元,比1985年增长3.64倍,年均增长16.6%,出口交货值占同口径工业产出额的比重由8.9%上升到15.6%。

随着工业投资规模的不断扩大,工业经济的物质基础不断增强。1995年,街乡及以上独立核算工业企业拥有固定资产原价1 273.46亿元,比1985年增长5.96倍,年均增长21.41%。主要工业产品生产能力明显提高,产量大幅度增加。1995年主要工业产品产量比1985年增长情况见下表:

产品名称	计量单位	1995年	比1985年增长%
钢	万吨	171.57	53.28
钢材	万吨	430.38	1.93倍
生铁	万吨	168.85	1.07倍
发电量	亿千瓦小时	133.65	65.72
原油	万吨	620.82	65.72

原油加工量	万 吨	443.16	40.50
天燃气	亿立方米	7.57	32.81
水 泥	万 吨	200.62	90.87
平板玻璃	万重量箱	196.09	1.18 倍
纯 碱	万 吨	63.16	22.93
烧 碱	万 吨	32.57	39.43
油 漆	万 吨	19.20	3.02 倍
农用化肥	万 吨	9.74	75.18
汽 车	万 辆	13.11	5.31 倍
电 梯	台	4 007	2.77 倍
交流电动机	万千瓦	113.43	56.84
电焊条	万 吨	15.86	1.08 倍
微型计算机	万 部	6.18	285 倍
纱(混合)	万 吨	12.35	3.35
布(混合)	万 米	49 803	13.08
自行车	万 辆	576.36	2.34
家用洗衣机	万 台	64.30	2.90 倍
家用电视机	万 台	160.82	78.25
其中:彩色电视机	万 台	109.54	2.22 倍
化学纤维	万 吨	10.25	66.31
原 盐	万 吨	220.39	24.18
机制纸及纸板	万 吨	41.42	68.37
服 装	万 件	24 558	5.42 倍
合成洗涤剂	万 吨	11.95	1.37 倍

天津工业的迅速发展,使不少产品形成了一定生产规模,一些产品产量在全国占一定的地位。1995 年,一些主要产品占全国产量的比重为:原油占 4.2%,天燃气占 4.3%,化学农药占 4.7%,汽车占 8.7%,自行车占 15.5%,家用洗衣机占 6.8%,家用电视机占 4.6%,化学纤维占 3.6%等。

二、工业所有制结构

随着改革开放的深入发展,全市工业所有制结构呈现出以公有制为 主体的多种经济成份并存的格局。普查结果显示,国有工业比重下降,非国有工业比重显著上升,主要指标比重变化如下:

	按企业单位个数计算的比重(%)		按从业人员计算的比重(%)	
	1985 年	1995 年	1985 年	1995 年
全市工业	100	100	100	100
国有工业	5.08	5.51	59.99	39.09

集体工业	34.20	40.72	36.61	41.54
联营工业	0.20	0.54	1.72	1.62
股份制工业		0.13		1.80
三资工业	0.09	5.57	0.22	10.75
私营工业		6.45		1.93
个体工业	60.43	41.08	1.46	3.27
全市工业中:				
乡镇工业(注1)	64.27	69.25	12.42	33.44

	按资产总额计算的比重(%)		按工业产出额计算的比重(%)	
	1985年	**1995年**	**1985年**	**1995年**
全市工业	100	100	100	100
国有工业	80.21	54.00	79.04	30.99
集体工业	17.82	17.36	18.89	33.10
联营工业	1.42	1.24	1.41	1.08
股份制工业		4.14		2.87
三资工业	0.44	22.42	0.45	28.81
私营工业		0.64		1.33
个体工业	0.11	0.20	0.21	1.82
全市工业中:				
乡镇工业	3.51	15.52	3.78	33.96

1995年,天津市国有工业企业有1 927个,资产总额达到1 309.55亿元,占全市工业的54%;增加值为186.27亿元,占41.2%;产品销售收入625.98亿元,占35.85%;利税总额44.91亿元,占33.64%。在能源、原材料等基础产业中,国有工业仍占主导地位。如在产出额中,石油天然气业占100%,非金属矿采选业占83.89%,石油加工及炼焦业占89.30%,电力、蒸气热水的生产和供应业占89.90%,煤气生产和供应业占96.23%,自来水的生产和供应业占96.30%。

1995年底,天津市"三资"工业企业为1 948个(已投产企业,下同),比1985年增加1 930个。其中在街乡及以上"三资"企业中:合资企业1 077个,占58.85%,合作企业58个,占3.17%,外商及港澳台独资企业695个,占37.98%。

从"三资"企业产出额的行业构成来看,1995年,轻工业占49.87%,重工业占50.13%,主要分布在电子及通讯设备制造业,交通运输设备制造业,食品加工业,食品制造业,普通机械制造业,金属制品业。

1995年,街乡及以上"三资"企业工业增加值为98.12亿元,占全部街乡及以上工业增加值的28.15%,工业产出额571.28亿元,占35.83%,比1985年增长408倍,年均增长82.46%,销售收入484.22亿元,占全部工业的35.17%,利税总额62.78亿元,占47.02%,上交税金23.61亿元,占27.52%。

乡镇工业发展加快。1995年底,天津市共有乡镇企业和生产单位24 231个,比1985年增加5 002个,拥有资产总额376.38亿元,从业人员79.19万人。1995年乡镇工业产出额638.32亿元,比1985年增长15.92倍,年均增长32.7%;产品销售收入548.0亿元,增长17.75倍,年均增长34.06%;利润总额48.84亿元,增长10.85倍,年均增长28.05%;实际上交税金110.67亿元(注2),增长56.66倍,年均增长50.0%。

乡办和村办工业的规模和技术水平有了很大提高。1995年,在乡办和村办工业中,达到大中型标准的企业62个,主要工业生产设备中,90年代出厂的占55.68 %,80年代出厂的占36.74%,70年代以前出厂的占7.58%。

1995年,天津市有私营工业2 256户,从业人员4.57万人,年产出额25.09亿元,自有资金4.05亿元;个体工业14 372户,自有资金5.17亿元,年产出额达34.18亿元。

三、工业企业规模结构

1995年,天津市拥有大中型工业企业747个,其中特大型工业企业7个,大型工业企业253个,中型工业企业487个,大中型工业企业个数占全部工业企业数的3.62%;大中型工业企业拥有从业人员96.40万人,占全部工业企业的42.08 %;拥有资产总额1 713.83亿元,占全部工业企业的70.82%;工业增加值250.46亿元,占全部工业企业的55.43%;销售收入1 094.46亿元,占62.02%;利税总额116.60亿元,占68.48%。

在大中型工业企业中国有企业仍占主体地位。1995年,国有大中型工业企业在全部大中型工业企业中的比重,企业数占62.12%,职工人数占74.52%,资产总额占68.27%,增加值占69.27%,销售收入占51.87%,利税总额占36.66 %。

1995年与1985年相比,大中型工业的规模迅速扩大,企业个数增加了433个,资产总额增加13.6倍,实现利税增长1.9倍。在主要行业中,大中型工业企业占主体地位。如黑色金属冶练及压延加工业、化学工业、化学纤维工业、医药工业、橡胶制品业、交通运输设备制造业、电子及通讯设备制造业中,大中型工业企业所占生产份额为70%至90%以上,塑料制品业、纺织业、机械工业、电气器械及器材制造业中,大中型工业企业生产份额占50%至70%左右。国计民生的一些骨干产品绝大多数都集中在大中型企业,如原油、天然气、原盐、电力、煤气、原油加工产品、卷烟等。

1995年,大中型工业企业拥有工程技术人员6.92万人,占职工总数的3.92%,高于小型企业2.26%的比重;大专以上文化程度的占7.95%,中专、技工及高中文化的占39.82%,具有高中级技术职务的8.08万人,占4.58%,均高于小型工业企业。1995年大中型工业企业的主要经济效益指标好于小型企业。

1995年末,天津市小型工业企业有19 870个,占全市工业企业的96.38%,资产总额为706.25亿元,占29.18%,从业人员人数132.68万人,占57.92%。1995年,小型工业企业工业增加值为201.38亿元,占全市工业企业的44.57%。小型企业多数集中在服装及其他纤维制品制造业,皮革、皮毛、羽绒及其制品业,木材加工及竹、藤、棕草制品业,家具制造业,造纸及纸制品业,印刷业、记录媒介的复制业,文教体育用品制造业,化学原料及化学制品制造业,化学纤维制造业,橡胶制品业,塑料制品业,非金属矿物制品业,金属制品业,专用设备制造业,电气机械及器材制造业,仪器仪表及文化、办公用机械制造业,其他制造业。1995年,小型企业产品销售收入668.82亿元,占全市工业企业的37.98%,比1985年增长4.66倍,年均增长18.93%;利税总额53.66亿元,占全市工业企业的31.52%,比1985年增长1.15倍。

四、工业企业地区分布结构

第三次工业普查资料,不仅能看出天津市工业按行政区划(坐落地点)的分布情况,还可以反映出经济技术开发区、保税区、新技术产业园区的工业分布状况。1995年,主要指标地区分布比重(%)见下表:

	企业单位个数	从业人员人数	资产总额	工业产出额
全市工业	100	100	100	100
中心六个区	20.25	40.68	38.67	27.17

滨海三个区	8.36	14.45	24.69	26.47
其他四个区	21.27	23.74	26.56	27.25
五个县	50.12	21.13	10.08	19.11
在全市工业中:				
开发区	1.71	3.81	12.22	15.79
保税区	0.09	0.05	0.22	0.26
新技术产业园区	0.51	0.65	2.12	0.23

从1995年天津市工业企业和工业生产单位个数分布情况看,一半在各区,一半在各县,其中中心六个区和其他四个区工业企业较多,滨海三个区大中型企业较多,各县主要是乡镇企业、小型企业较多。1995年,天津市工业的经济总量80%以上集中在各区,工业产出额超百亿元的区县有:河东区、河西区、南开区、塘沽区、大港区、东丽区、西青区、北辰区、静海县。

滨海新区的大型工业基地已初步形成。据统计,1995年滨海新区工业产出额590.74亿元,比1994年增长39.4%,占全市工业的26.5%。1995年全市规模最大的100家企业中有19家坐落在滨海新区。大港油田、钢管公司、渤海化工集团、天津石化公司等7家企业1995年工业产出额占全区的27%。

五、工业产业结构

1995年,在全市工业中轻工业产出额达901.54亿元,占全市工业的40.42%,比1985年增长4.10倍,年均增长17.69 %;重工业工业产出额达1 329.16亿元,占59.58%,增长7.05倍,年均增长23.19%。

“八五”时期,天津市工业在充分发挥地区优势的前提下重点发展了冶金、化工、汽车机械、电子四大支柱产业。按天津市特定的口径计算,1995年工业四大支柱产业的资产总额在街乡及以上工业中的比重已达49.44%,其中冶金行业占15.83%,化工行业占9.5%,汽车机械行业占14.66%,电子行业占9.45%;工业产出额在街乡及以上工业中的比重达53.02%,其中冶金行业占8.44%,化工行业占11.7%,汽车机械行业占16.32%,电子行业占16.56%。全市街乡及以上工业产业结构1995年与1985年相比发生了较大的变化。主要行业(按统一标准归类)情况见下表:

	资产总额比重(%)		产出额比重(%)	
	1985年	1995年	1985年	1995年
街乡及以上工业中:				
石油和天然气开采业	5.68	7.22	1.94	2.04
食品饮料制造、烟草加工业	3.70	6.81	6.14	8.62
纺织业	10.49	5.82	14.59	5.59
造纸及纸制品业	0.11	1.91	1.78	1.18
石油加工及炼焦煤气业	1.52	3.60	2.71	3.56
化学原料及化学制品制造业	8.44	7.72	8.21	7.76
医药制造业	1.84	2.86	1.26	1.67
金属矿物制品业	3.39	2.63	2.37	1.72

黑色金属冶炼及压延加工业	6.78	13.90	5.73	4.66
金属制品业	4.24	4.49	4.86	4.20
普通机械及专用设备制造业	13.59	7.62	12.34	7.68
交通运输设备制造业	4.47	6.99	3.65	12.28
电气机械及器材制造业	4.23	3.97	5.01	3.59
电子及通信设备制造业	4.47	8.38	5.40	18.01
仪器仪表及文化办公用机械制造业	1.38	1.23	1.05	1.11
电力、蒸气、热水的生产和供应业	4.77	5.13	1.93	1.37

按工业普查行业分类标准共 40 个大类，197 个中类，607 个小类。天津市工业分布在 35 个大类，180 个中类和 519 个小类行业中，天津市工业行业小类占行业分类标准小类的 85.50 %。在街乡及以上工业中，1995 年比 1985 年工业产出额年均增长速度超过 10%的有 11 个行业，其中电子及通信设备制造业增长 30.43 %，交通设备制造业增长 27.41%，饮料制造业增长 18.68%，医药制造业增长 18.70%，文教体育用品制造业增长 17.19%，木材加工业增长 14.15%，服装业增长 13.89%，仪器仪表业增长 13.78%，石油加工、炼焦及煤气业增长 13.21%，家具制造业增长 12.61%。

六、工业劳动者状况

天津市工业劳动者队伍进一步扩大。1995 年，全市工业企业和生产单位的从业人员为 236.81 万人，比 1985 年增长 20.21%，占全社会劳动者比重，1985 年为 43.20%，1995 年为 45.96%，上升了 2.76 个百分点。街乡及以上工业中的女性从业人员为 81.23 万人，占从业人员总数的45.85%。

按经济类型划分，1995 年，在全市工业从业人员中，国有工业从业人员 92.56 万人，占 39.09%；集体工业 98.37 万人，占 41.54%；联营工业 3.84 万人，占 1.62%；股份制工业 4.27 万人，占 1.80%；“三资”工业 25.46 万人，占 10.75%；私营工业 4.57 万人，占 1.93%；个体工业7.74万人，占 3.27%。在全市工业从业人员中，乡镇工业有 79.19 万人，占 33.44%。

按从业人员的岗位分，1995 年，在街乡及以上工业企业中工人和学徒 107.57 万人，占 60.72%，工程技术人员 10.94 万人，占6.17%，管理人员 18.70 万人，占 10.55%。

从职工年龄构成看，中青年是工业生产的生力军。1995 年，街乡及以上工业企业中 20 及 20 岁以下的 9.52 万人，占 5.49%；21 - 35 岁的 77.92 万人，占 44.91%；36 - 50 岁的 75.67万人，占 43.62%；51 岁以上的 10.38 万人，占 5.98%。

职工的文化技术素质明显提高。1995 年，在街乡及以上工业企业中，大专以上文化程度的 13.92 万人，占 8.02%；中专、技工及高中文化程度的 69.18 万人，占 39.88%；初中及以下文化程度的 90.39 万人，占 52.10%。1995 年与 1985 年比较，大专以上文化程度的职工比例提高 3.26 个百分点，中专及高中文化程度提高 0.53 个百分点，初中及以下文化程度下降 15.17个百分点。在街乡及以上工业企业已评定技术职称的专业技术人员中，高级技术职务的 1.82 万人，占7.91%，中级 6.09 万人，占 26.45%，初级 15.11 万人，占 65.64%。

1995 年工业企业从业人员平均工资为 5 958元，比 1985 年增长 4.49 倍，平均每年递增18.57%，扣除物价影响，实际增长 5.38%。

七、工业技术装备水平

通过技术改造和技术引进，天津工业的技术装备水平有了较大提高。1995年末，街乡及以上工业企业固定资产原价1 273.46亿元，比1985年增长5.96倍，从业人员人均装备71 878元，比1985年增长4.60倍，固定资产净值905.27亿元，占原价的71.09％。工业机器设备原价601.79亿元，占全部固定资产的57.52％，机器设备净值429.76亿元，占机器设备原价的71.41％。

1995年末，在街乡及以上工业已安装使用的设备中，90年代出厂的占32.73％，80年代出厂的占55.0％，70年代及以前出厂的占12.27％，进口设备占54.16％，国产设备占45.84％。在大中型工业企业中，达到国际先进水平的设备占7.47％，国内先进水平的设备占26.88％。

八、工业科技活动情况

第三次工业普查资料显示，1995年，全市大中型工业企业拥有技术开发机构371个，技术开发人员2.94万人，占企业技术人员的42.59％；当年投入技术开发及技术活动经费10.34亿元，完成技术开发和研究发展项目(课题)2 223个。科技的投入，带来了可喜的产出成果。1995年，大中型工业企业全部技术性收入达9.71亿元，其中高技术性收入8.78亿元，占90.42％；高技术产品销售收入67.75亿元，新产品销售收入114.67亿元，分别占全部产品销售收入的6.19％和10.48％。

随着工业技术水平的提高，工业技术经济指标得到了明显的改善。一些主要产品质量指标，单位产品原材料、燃料、动力消耗指标，单位产品综合能源消耗指标，实物劳动生产率，设备利用情况等指标，都达到了较好水平。据272种主要产品质量指标统计1995年优等品率为12.5％，一等品率为21.1％，均超过1985年；据171项物资消耗、劳动效率、设备利用率等主要技术经济指标统计，1995年水平好于1985年的占64％。

九、企业生产经营状况

据对街乡及以上独立核算工业企业普查统计，1995年产品销售收入达1 376.70亿元，比上年增长24.96％，产销率达99.6％，一些主要产品如轮胎外胎、水泥、汽车、电视机、呢绒、自行车、微型计算机等产品的产销率均超过100％。1995年，在大中型企业中销售收入超过10亿元以上的产品有：天然原油、供电量、售电量、方便面、合成纤维、汽油、柴油、燃料油、塑料树脂及共聚物、塑料管材、炼钢生铁、钢锭、钢坯、成品钢材、汽油机、载货汽车、轿车、摩托车、移动通讯手持机、彩色电视机等；销售利税达亿元以上的主要产品有：原油、原盐、发电量、方便面、合成纤维、汽油、柴油、纯碱、塑料树脂及共聚物、合成纤维单体、塑料管材、生铁、成品钢材、汽油机、载货汽车、轿车、摩托车、移动通讯手持机、程控交换机、半导体集成电路等。

1995年，街乡及以上工业企业由于产销衔接的较好，流动资金周转速度比上年有所加快；按增加值计算的全员劳动生产率达20 084元，比上年增长24.91％；实现利润59.64亿元，比上年增长24.85％。但有些经济效益指标不够理想，经济运行质量有待提高。

以上公布的是第三次工业普查的主要基本数据，全部普查资料还有待于进一步开发分析，市工业普查办公室将继续进行加工整理分析，陆续提出汇编资料和专题报告，并欢迎社会各界开发利用。

注①：乡镇工业包括乡办、村办、农村合作经营、农村私营、农村个体工业。

注②：实际上交税金包括产品销售税金及附加、增值税、所得税以及房产税、印花税、车船使用税、土地使用税等。

(1997年2月6日在《天津日报》发表)

十、建筑业

CONSTRUCTION

1996年建筑企业单位数	461个
1996年建筑企业职工平均人数	29.06万人
1996年建筑企业施工产值	173.57亿元
1996年建筑企业利税	6.28亿元

建筑施工产值（亿元）

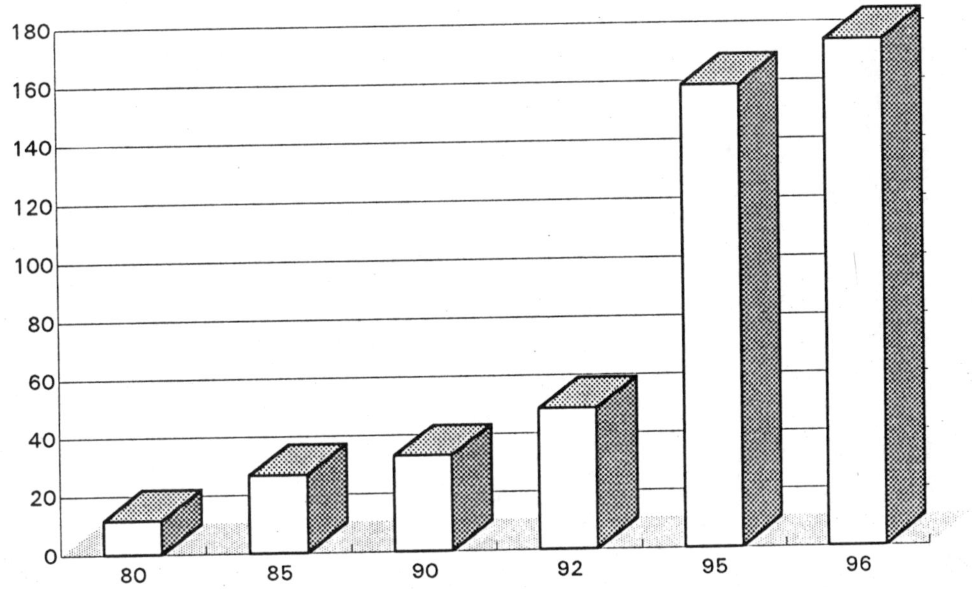

10－1　建筑企业基本情况

（按经济类型分）

指　标	单　位	全　市		#国有经济		#地　方	
		1995年	1996年	1995年	1996年	1995年	1996年
企业个数	个	693	461	164	140	126	104
全部职工平均人数	万人	31.53	29.06	24.79	23.29	14.08	12.89
从业人员报酬	万元	223 268	206 482	181 319	176 058	62 974	69 336
增加值	万元	488 827	524 536	406 008	451 252	150 293	177 915
自行完成的施工产值	万元	1 656 748	1 735 679	1 353 329	1 466 280	611 777	674 987
竣工产值	万元	948 267	1 075 203	765 937	877 877	344 369	370 022
房屋建筑施工面积	万平方米	1 604.10	1 579.53	1 330.87	1 276.39	803.28	818.11
房屋建筑竣工面积	万平方米	640.25	567.98	453.70	380.33	298.60	261.66
#住　宅	万平方米	328.40	285.82	242.91	189.33	178.12	141.01

指　标	单　位	城镇集体经济		联营经济		港澳台投资经济		外商投资经济	
		1995年	1996年	1995年	1996年	1995年	1996年	1995年	1996年
企业个数	个	441	290	4	5	17	7	12	12
全部职工平均人数	万人	3.58	5.38	0.09	0.07	0.08	0.04	0.09	0.09
从业人员报酬	万元	26 717	28 595	1 524	61	408	238	769	326
增加值	万元	49 652	67 026	2 552	222	2 591	1 219	2 470	2 340
自行完成的施工产值	万元	206 828	247 823	7 012	681	7 483	2 971	8 597	7 182
竣工产值	万元	104 491	180 727	8 325	1 780	5 158	2 742	6 243	3 774
房屋建筑施工面积	万平方米	161.41	294.25		3.08	1.81	0.83	17.97	4.98
房屋建筑竣工面积	万平方米	93.10	180.55		3.08	1.84	0.83	13.19	3.18
#住　宅	万平方米	38.96	45.13				0.18	8.13	

注：自1996年起建筑业统计范围为企业资质等级四级以上企业。

10－2　建筑企业基本情况

(按专业类型分)

指　标	单　位	土木工程		设备安装		装修装饰	
		1995年	1996年	1995年	1996年	1995年	1996年
企业个数	个	349	268	182	120	162	73
全部职工平均人数	万人	26.52	24.57	4.27	4.08	0.74	0.42
从业人员报酬	万元	177 459	161 945	41 083	42 574	4 727	1 964
增加值	万元	390 984	418 800	86 803	99 370	11 039	6 366
自行完成的施工产值	万元	1 320 006	1 424 964	308 215	287 239	28 527	23 475
竣工产值	万元	739 395	892 667	187 543	165 231	21 328	17 306
房屋建筑施工面积	万平方米	1 545.64	1 545.89	28.27	20.59	30.19	13.05
房屋建筑竣工面积	万平方米	599.15	543.23	13.85	15.19	27.24	9.56
#住　宅	万平方米	315.90	274.88	8.40	10.42	4.10	0.52

10－3　建筑企业基本情况

(按企业资质等级分)

指　标	单　位	资质一、二级企业		资质三级以下企业	
		1996年	占全市比重%	1996年	占全市比重%
企业个数	个	130	28.2	331	71.8
全部职工平均人数	万人	25.07	86.3	3.99	13.7
增加值	万元	424 997	81.1	99 539	18.9
自行完成的施工产值	万元	1 556 356	89.7	179 323	10.3
竣工产值	万元	941 106	87.5	134 097	12.5
房屋建筑施工面积	万平方米	1 401.99	88.8	177.54	11.2
房屋建筑竣工面积	万平方米	439.35	77.4	128.63	22.6
#住　宅	万平方米	203.22	71.1	82.60	28.9

10－4 改革开放以来建筑企业基本情况

年份	企业个数（个）	全部职工平均人数（万人）	施工产值（万元）	房屋建筑施工面积（万平方米）	房屋建筑竣工面积（万平方米）
1978	45	16.71	87 817		
1979	47	20.20	122 110	650.56	290.46
1980	77	21.40	116 448	693.43	332.80
1981	70	19.60	101 540	703.36	336.20
1982	72	20.20	125 518	782.66	421.20
1983	77	18.40	143 691	818.17	397.40
1984	84	20.90	203 376	921.23	464.40
1985	88	21.76	261 710	1 040.02	505.50
1986	88	22.23	275 938	902.13	483.00
1987	85	21.85	295 390	917.42	451.90
1988	83	20.20	310 770	865.15	409.80
1989	81	19.70	323 534	774.30	399.10
1990	82	18.71	317 009	675.46	333.60
1991	83	18.95	361 739	582.73	295.41
1992	96	18.76	484 293	721.50	344.70
1993	237	25.87	826 585	1 210.94	505.02
1994	482	36.28	1 305 160	1 359.96	600.15
1995	693	31.53	1 656 748	1 604.10	640.25
1996	461	29.06	1 735 679	1 579.53	567.98

注:1993 年以后含乡镇企业数。

10－5 建筑企业劳动生产率

项目	自行完成的施工产值(万元)		职工年平均人数(万人)		劳动生产率(元/人)	
	1995 年	1996 年	1995 年	1996 年	1995 年	1996 年
总计	**1 656 748**	**1 735 679**	**31.53**	**29.06**	**52 545**	**59 724**
一、按经济类型分						
#国有经济	1 353 329	1 466 280	24.79	23.29	54 592	62 961
中央	741 552	791 293	10.71	10.40	69 239	76 086
地方	611 777	674 987	14.08	12.89	43 450	52 365
城镇集体经济	206 828	247 823	3.58	5.40	57 773	45 893
联营经济	7 012	681	0.09	0.07	77 911	9 729
港澳台经济	7 483	2 971	0.08	0.04	93 538	74 275
外商投资经济	8 597	7 182	0.09	0.09	95 522	79 789
二、按行业类别分						
土木工程	1 320 006	1 424 964	26.52	24.57	49 774	57 996
房屋	790 272	816 652	14.46	16.00	45 549	51 041
矿山	5 700	6 020	0.08	0.08	71 256	75 250
铁路公路	343 890	412 898	5.20	5.42	66 133	76 179
堤坝电站	113 554	159 831	1.78	2.38	63 794	67 156
其他土木	66 590	29 563	2.12	0.69	31 410	42 845
设备安装	308 215	287 239	4.27	4.08	72 181	70 402
线路管道安装	207 441	168 032	2.52	2.28	82 317	73 698
设备安装	100 774	119 207	1.75	1.80	57 585	66 226
装修装饰	28 527	23 475	0.74	0.41	38 551	57 256

10－6　建筑企业主要财务指标

单位:万元

指　标	全市总计		#国有经济		#地　方	
	1995年	1996年	1995年	1996年	1995年	1996年
资本金合计	334 465	393 621	269 711	321 758	123 279	151 113
流动资产合计	1 162 489	1 429 552	945 140	1 181 620	476 822	562 884
#存　货	248 249	295 263	179 463	221 622	76 783	86 330
固定资产合计	399 103	457 047	358 699	413 201	143 022	159 802
固定资产原价	607 011	725 956	555 429	667 787	198 380	221 249
#生产经营用	415 883	565 273	383 143	517 782	111 415	156 366
累计折旧	209 177	273 041	197 443	257 513	55 990	62 905
#本年折旧	33 742	43 404	30 708	40 255	8 413	9 678
专项工程	23 082	21 541	20 113	19 117	4 088	3 886
无形及递延资产合计	9 753	11 129	7 396	9 451	2 269	4 402
资产总计	1 657 327	2 001 217	1 383 167	1 694 429	659 229	771 911
工程结算收入	1 533 800	1 712 610	1 297 969	1 458 047	582 152	669 529
工程结算成本	1 307 860	1 468 846	1 112 626	1 253 490	506 949	586 334
工程结算税金及附加	46 719	43 714	35 625	34 570	15 257	12 983
工程结算利润	179 220	200 050	149 719	169 987	59 947	70 212
其他业务收入	59 250	176 523	54 487	153 541	17 318	49 147
其他业务利润	6 360	57 340	5 119	51 180	1 831	12 285
管理费用	114 707	125 380	96 991	106 771	45 143	48 948
#税　金	2 760	2 575	1 821	2 064	646	915
利润总额	16 036	16 523	4 518	6 139	3 125	3 776
应交所得税	5 022	5 287	2 960	3 063	1 307	1 567
转作奖金的利润	1 085	1 205	277	111	264	111
应付利润	2 507	2 949	1 140	1 037	375	735
利税总额	65 515	62 812	41 964	42 773	19 028	17 674
本年应付工资总额	202 381	185 600	163 926	158 301	55 720	61 665
本年应付福利费总额	20 887	20 882	17 393	17 757	7 254	7 671

10－6续表

单位:万元

指　标	城镇集体经济		联营经济		港澳台投资经济		外商投资经济	
	1995年	1996年	1995年	1996年	1995年	1996年	1995年	1996年
资本金合计	34 485	58 402	998	1 537	3 483	5 126	4 208	3 826
流动资产合计	165 084	226 320	2 951	1 197	13 271	6 664	8 623	7 164
#存　货	58 592	69 429	805	391	1 774	856	1 458	681
固定资产合计	22 100	38 422	1 333	961	1 076	797	1 142	766
固定资产原价	28 625	51 418	2 040	948	1 369	1 001	1 581	990
#生产经营用	16 855	43 385	1 985	557	783	883	1 112	807
累计折旧	7 010	14 028	710	133	315	219	485	237
#本年折旧	1 717	2 659	261	41	182	104	187	98
专项工程	2 323	2 418	15					
无形及递延资产合计	1 722	1 482	18		63	83	73	89
资产总计	199 953	278 055	5 756	2 164	14 545	7 550	10 620	8 528
工程结算收入	137 372	234 979	7 817	688	7 844	2 757	7 835	7 632
工程结算成本	114 767	199 684	7 050	569	5 879	1 882	6 345	5 750
工程结算税金及附加	5 028	8 749	253	20	668	78	163	129
工程结算利润	17 577	26 546	514	99	1 297	797	1 327	1 753
其他业务收入	4 479	19 446	43	322	189	2 710	10	21
其他业务利润	1 204	5 556	－2	15	－3	542	2	5
管理费用	12 458	15 849	590	127	1 205	688	932	1 271
#税　金	278	502		1	9	3	2	2
利润总额	5 233	9 445	11	－30	114	110	433	579
应交所得税	1 525	1 908	4	1	49	43	34	161
转作奖金的利润	396	1 074			14	2		
应付利润	642	1 834	4		114	66	67	
利税总额	10 539	10 195	264	－9	791	191	598	710
本年应付工资总额	24 032	25 676	1 401	56	346	199	718	280
本年应付福利费总额	2 685	2 919	123	5	62	39	52	46

10－7 建筑企业工程质量、机械设备及经济效益指标

指　　标	单　位	全　市		#国有经济		#地　方	
		1995年	1996年	1995年	1996年	1995年	1996年
一、建筑企业工程质量							
房屋竣工率	%	37.2	36.0	34.1	29.8	37.2	32.0
单位工程竣工个数	个	8 891	7 980	3 330	3 187	1 590	1 634
#优良工程个数	个	3 958	2 458	1 692	1 496	433	395
房屋建筑竣工面积	万平方米	561.83	567.98	453.70	380.33	298.60	261.66
#优良工程面积	万平方米	259.46	224.52	238.50	171.32	127.09	114.27
工程优良品率							
按项目个数计算	%	44.5	30.8	50.8	46.9	27.2	24.2
按竣工面积计算	%	46.2	39.5	52.6	45.0	42.6	43.7
二、建筑企业机械设备情况							
自有机械设备年末总台数	台	54 482	53 471	41 914	36 230	23 895	17 824
自有机械设备年末总功率	万千瓦	138.36	137.98	110.17	109.22	43.77	40.47
#施工机械功率	万千瓦	86.23	97.66	74.19	73.46	25.83	24.54
自有机械设备净值	万元	179 888	384 677	164 162	178 790	60 526	47 006
技术装备率	元/人	6 281	13 237	6 622	7 677	4 299	3 647
动力装备率	千瓦/人	4.83	4.75	4.44	4.69	3.11	3.14
三、建筑企业经济效益指标							
全员劳动生产率	元/人	52 545	59 724	54 592	62 961	43 450	52 365
平均每一职工竣工面积	平方米	19.6	19.5	18.3	16.3	21.2	20.3
每百元产值实现利税	元	3.4	3.6	3.1	2.9	3.1	2.6
每百元产值占用流动资产	元	71.7	82.4	69.8	80.6	77.9	83.4
每百元工资实现利税	元	25.7	33.8	23.1	27.0	30.2	28.7
全员资金占有率	元/人	53 079	75 253	52 595	68 477	44 023	56 065

十一、交通运输和邮电通信

TRANSPORTATION, POST AND TELECOMMUNICATION

1996 年港口泊位	75 个	其中:万吨级以上	48 个
1996 年社会货运量	24 133 万吨		
1996 年邮电业务总量	256 978 万元		

港口货物吞吐量（万吨）

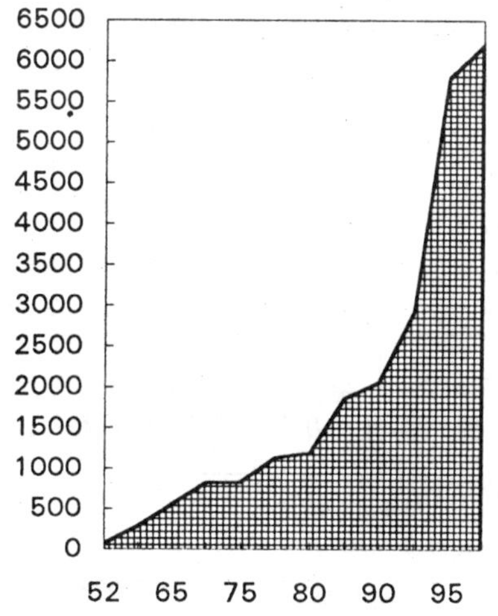

社会货运量（万吨）

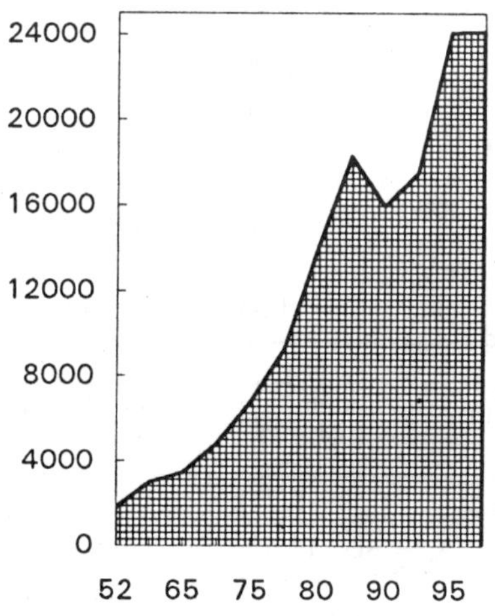

邮电业务总量（万元）

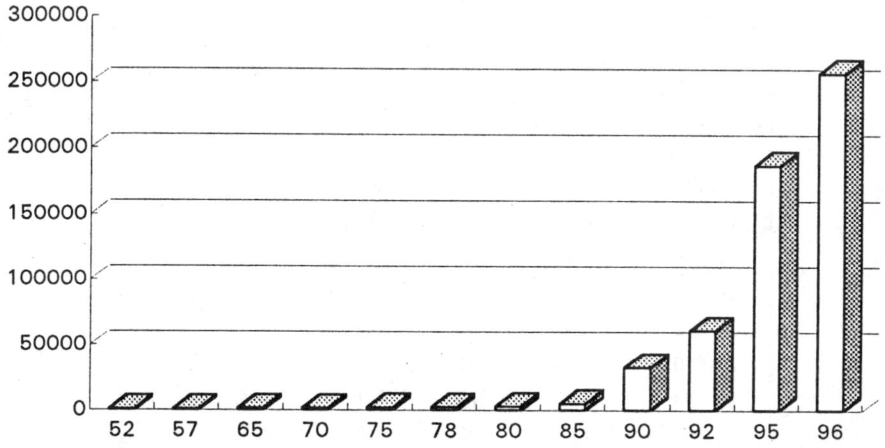

11－1　改革开放以来运输邮电业基本情况

年　份	铁路里程(公里)	公路里程(公里)	内河航道里程(公里)	客运量(万人)	#铁　路	公　路	水　运
1978						533	
1979						602	
1980				2 216	1 567	646	
1981						712	
1982						740	
1983						796	
1984						860	
1985	3 392	3 792	458	2 984	2 192	788	
1986	3 428	3 825	386	2 873	2 088	779	
1987	3 428	3 918	386	2 838	2 111	718	
1988	3 577	3 940	103	2 601	1 976	616	
1989	3 667	3 983	90	2 550	2 047	496	
1990	3 679	4 007	90	2 175	1 722	447	
1991	3 702	4 068	90	2 922	1 718	1 196	
1992	3 758	4 088	90	2 662	1 731	897	
1993	3 789	4 117	90	3 225	1 812	1 380	4
1994	4 033	4 156	90	3 373	1 863	1 463	6
1995	4 064	4 243	90	3 308	1 802	1 464	5
1996	4 230	4 264	90	3 125	1 580	1 496	5

年　份	货运量(万吨)	#铁　路	公　路	水　运	旅客周转量(百万人公里)	#铁　路	公　路	水　运
1978	9 241	1 877	6 417	701			243.1	
1979	13 522	1 976	10 511	811			264.8	
1980	13 949	1 785	11 065	789		3 028	288.7	
1981	15 017	1 612	12 455	734			320.7	
1982	16 332	1 692	13 670	751			347.9	
1983	16 829	1 910	14 000	650			401.2	
1984	17 781	2 063	14 628	799			449.9	
1985	18 249	2 242	14 500	818		5 234	455.8	
1986	18 525	2 063	14 935	882		5 558	467.1	
1987	18 400	2 150	14 618	896		5 960	448.3	
1988	16 693	2 088	12 829	975		6 745	423.8	
1989	15 543	2 723	11 426	1 014		6 214	329.2	
1990	15 929	2 228	12 329	1 046		5 409	306.9	
1991	18 308	2 290	14 537	1 163		4 974	940.5	
1992	17 522	2 392	13 562	1 248		6 242	819.0	
1993	21 640	2 618	17 244	1 347	8 824.8	6 584	1 462.8	91.6
1994	23 783	2 634	19 270	1 421	8 298.5	5 778	1 639.1	49.2
1995	24 040	2 722	19 323	1 517	7 927.0	5 437	1 679.5	40.7
1996	24 133	2 668	19 491	1 489	7 598.6	4 917	1 771.8	43.1

11－1 续表

年份	货物周转量(亿吨公里)	＃铁路	公路	水运	民用汽车拥有量(辆)	＃公路部门
1978			8.4	392.1	35 716	3 416
1979			13.8	489.8	40 948	3 835
1980	666.9	144.3	17.7	504.9	41 749	3 987
1981			21.2	470.5	47 053	4 213
1982			24.6	468.7	52 695	4 490
1983			26.6	463.3	58 956	4 664
1984			29.3	521.7	66 417	4 959
1985	765.4	190.0	33.8	539.8	79 860	4 939
1986	881.1	203.8	34.2	641.1	90 777	4 978
1987	930.4	222.1	35.2	671.1	100 090	5 069
1988	1 022.0	230.0	43.9	746.0	102 198	5 247
1989	1 035.0	235.0	42.3	755.5		
1990	1 139.3	234.1	52.2	852.3	124 292	
1991	1 215.5	204.1	37.2	973.4	140 484	
1992	1 321.2	216.5	37.2	1 066.6	160 909	
1993	1 340.9	264.2	45.6	1 030	203 287	
1994	1 324.6	224.9	45.9	1 052.6	232 802	
1995	1 412.3	230.0	41.3	1 139.2	267 951	
1996	1 051.5	223.7	41.2	783.8	323 383	

年份	邮电业务总量(不变价)(万元)	邮电局所(处)	市话交换机容量(门)	农话交换机容量(门)	电话机拥有量(部)	城市	农村
1978	2 710	217	45 370			74 234	
1979	2 901	220	46 270			84 756	
1980	3 163	223	48 670		99 781	89 931	9 850
1981	3 441	230	50 720			101 152	
1982	3 642	240	58 350			108 984	
1983	3 890	249	64 900			113 473	
1984	4 478	249	78 150			124 253	
1985	5 290	268	96 850		161 647	149 771	11 876
1986	6 158	272	108 490		200 252	187 505	12 747
1987	7 244	274	127 040		203 636	188 213	15 423
1988	10 061	273	192 060		233 189	215 584	17 605
1989	12 538	278			248 981		18 463
1990	32 735	281	227 156		317 824	297 662	20 162
1991	44 527	280			351 281	328 283	22 998
1992	61 063	273			428 608	399 174	29 434
1993	97 062	277	521 212	44 927	639 101	608 521	29 278
1994	132 465	297	1 006 588	131 160	960 309	881 548	46 434
1995	187 195	300	1 376 300	146 200	1 356 092	1 202 200	73 600
1996	256 978	314	1 487 300	206 800	1 746 500	1 484 500	111 600

注：邮电业务总量1989年以前为80年不变价，1990年以后为90年不变价。

11-2 港口设施

指 标	单 位	1990年	1992年	1995年	1996年	1996比1995年增长%
码头长度	米	10 356	12 032	12 252	12 463	1.7
港口泊位	个	61	70	73	75	2.7
#万吨级泊位	个	33	48	48	48	
铁路专用线长度	米		72 375	77 055	77 055	
仓库总面积	平方米	216 122	201 766	198 385	194 951	-1.7
堆场总面积	平方米	1 200 703	1 749 470	2 214 377	2 207 900	-0.3
集装箱堆场堆存能力	TEU	20 406	22 426	31 466	31 466	
装卸机械台数	台		1 377	1 409	1 432	1.6

11-3 港口货物吞吐量

单位:万吨

指 标	出口量				进口量			
	1992年	1995年	1996年	1996比1995年增长%	1992年	1995年	1996年	1996比1995年增长%
港口吞吐量合计	**1 915**	**4 551**	**4 839.1**	**6.3**	**1 014**	**1 236**	**1 349.2**	**9.2**
国 外	1 120	2 547	2 119.9	-16.8	799	987	1 033.8	4.7
国 内	795	2 004	2 719.2	35.7	215	249	315.4	26.7
分品种货物吞吐量								
煤 炭	788.0	2 826	3 236.8	14.5	37.4		0.1	
石 油	55.8	40	201.0	402.5	61.0	59	105.1	78.1
金属矿石	8.5	22	13.8	-37.3	116.3	250	201.6	-19.4
钢 铁	218.8	501	367.8	-26.6	130.9	76	131.0	72.4
矿建材料	20.6	26	26.1	0.4	0.5	69	98.6	42.9
水 泥	14.6	8	0.9	-88.8	13.0			
木 材	7.9	7	5.6	-20.0	7.2	11	12.2	10.9
非金属矿石	138.7	252	162.6	-35.5		2	8.8	340.0
化肥农药		17	13.2	-22.4		185	163.4	-11.7
盐	62.5	30	30.5	1.7	34.5	5	4.6	-8.0
粮 食	108.8	68	41.6	-38.8	195.3	201	172.7	-14.1

11－4　民用运输船舶拥有量

指　　标	单　位	1990年	1992年	1995年	1996年	1996比1995年增长%
一、机动船艘数	**艘**	**175**	**193**	**254**	**254**	
载客量	客位	9	9	2 071	2 000	－3.4
净载重量	吨位	79 091	88 590	1 891 799	1 822 180	－3.7
总功率	千瓦	123 081	96 676	872 119	870 227	－0.2
客船艘数	艘			11	10	－9.1
载客量	客位			998	927	－7.1
客货船艘数	艘	2	2	2	2	
载客量	客位	9	9	1 073	1 073	
净载重量	吨位	10	10	5 886	5 886	
货船艘数	艘	45	52	146	142	－2.7
净载重量	吨位	79 081	88 580	1 885 913	1 816 294	－3.7
拖船艘数	艘	128	139	95	100	5.3
二、驳船艘数	**艘**	**490**	**466**	**451**	**432**	**－4.2**
净载重量	吨位	69 809	57 649	51 623	46 228	－10.5

11－5　民用车辆拥有量

单位:辆

指　　标	1990年	1992年	1995年	1996年	1996比1995年增长%
一、民用汽车	**124 292**	**160 909**	**267 951**	**323 383**	**20.7**
载客汽车	30 180	44 805	89 388	122 829	37.4
#大　型	6 495	7 619	8 947	9 108	1.8
普通载货汽车	84 344	104 716	166 394	186 175	11.9
专用载货汽车	4 955	5 970	4 126	5 337	29.4
其他专用汽车	3 482	3 923	5 181	5 369	3.6
特种汽车	1 331	1 495	2 862	3 673	28.3
二、轮胎式拖拉机	**31 258**	**36 343**	**38 300**	**39 656**	**3.5**
三、摩托车	**124 492**	**174 446**	**286 272**	**284 653**	**－0.6**
四、其他机动车	**715**	**723**	**29 936**	**45 711**	**52.7**
五、载货挂车	**8 009**	**9 494**	**11 666**	**12 303**	**5.5**

11－6　运输线路长度

单位:公里

指　　标	1990年	1992年	1995年	1996年	1996比1995年增长%
一、铁　路					
总延展里程	3 679	3 758	4 064	4 230	4.1
通车里程	2 172	2 172	2 308	2 444	5.9
营业里程	1 192	1 212	1 258	1 321	5.0
二、公　路					
通车里程	4 007	4 088	4 243	4 264	0.5
#晴雨通车里程	3 571	3 661	3 833	3 858	0.7
#高级及次高级路面	3 542	3 548	3 734	3 759	0.7
三、内河航道					
航运里程	90	90	90	90	
#水深一米以上	90	90	90	90	
四、管　道					
输油管道长度(管线在一千米以上)	93	93	105	108	2.9

11－7　民用航空航线里程

单位:公里

航线名称	计价距离	航线名称	计价距离
天津－广州	1 910	天津－南京－桂林	1 800
天津－深圳	2 021	天津－宁波	1 260
天津－黄山－海口	2 535	天津－黄山	1 070
天津－汕头	1 918	天津－上海－温州	1 551
天津－海口	2 370	天津－长沙－昆明－大理	2 744
天津－西安－成都	1 640	天津－南京－深圳	2 206
天津－重庆	1 530	天津－昆明－西双版纳	2 660
天津－上海	1 131	天津－昆明－思茅	2 531
天津－福州	1 622	天津－大连－哈尔滨	1 265
天津－温州	1 545	天津－大连－牡丹江	1 398
天津－厦门	1 729	天津－香港	2 095

11－8 社会货物运输量和周转量

项 目	货运量(万吨)				周转量(亿吨公里)			
	1992 年	1995 年	1996 年	1996 比 1995 年 增长%	1992 年	1995 年	1996 年	1996 比 1995 年 增长%
总 计	**17 522**	**24 040**	**24 133**	**0.4**	**1 321.20**	**1 412.3**	**1 051.54**	**－25.5**
铁 路(天津地区)	2 392	2 722	2 668	－2.0	216.5	230.0	223.67	－2.8
公 路	13 562	19 323	19 491	0.9	37.19	41.3	41.23	－0.2
＃交通部门		1 715	1 491	－13.1		4.9	4.19	－14.5
水 运	1 248	1 517	1 489	－1.8	1 066.59	1 139.2	783.83	－31.2
民 航	0.78	5	11	120.0	0.16	0.87	1.87	114.9
管道输油量	319	473	474	0.2	0.76	0.9	0.94	4.4

11－9 社会客运量和周转量

项 目	客运量(万人次)				旅客周转量(百万人公里)			
	1992 年	1995 年	1996 年	1996 比 1995 年 增长%	1992 年	1995 年	1996 年	1996 比 1995 年 增长%
总 计	**2 662**	**3 308**	**3 125**	**－5.5**		**7 927.0**	**7 598.55**	**－4.1**
铁 路(天津地区)	1 731	1 802	1 580	－12.3	6 242	5 437.2	4 917.47	－9.6
公 路	897	1 464	1 496	2.2	819	1 679.5	1 771.82	5.5
＃交通部门		334	308	－7.8		447.8	476.90	6.5
水 运		5	5			40.7	43.09	5.9
民 航	34	37	44	18.9		769.6	866.17	12.5

11－10 通信网络和设备能力情况

指 标	单 位	1992 年	1995 年	1996 年	1996 比 1995 年 增长%
一、通信网络情况					
邮电局所总数	处	273	300	314	4.7
邮路总长度(单程)	公里	36 629	43 410	58 354	34.4
＃一级邮路	公里		37 037	51 684	39.5
二级邮路	公里		1 281	1 215	－5.2
＃铁路邮路	公里	5 763	5 264	5 360	1.8
自办汽车邮路	公里	4 312	7 255	7 307	0.7
长话业务电路总数	路	4 529	24 392	32 132	31.7
二、通信设备能力情况					
邮运汽车	辆	162	250	302	20.8
长途自动交换机容量	路端		75 600	76 680	1.4
局用交换机容量	万门	34.99	152.25	169.41	11.3
全市话机总数	万部	42.86	135.61	174.65	28.8
＃市内电话	万部	39.92	120.22	148.45	23.5
无线寻呼系统容量	户		390 000	590 000	51.3
模拟移动通信交换机容量	户		75 000	100 000	33.3
数字移动通信交换机容量	户		30 000	80 000	166.7

11－11　邮电业务量

指　　标	单　位	1992年	1995年	1996年	1996比1995年增长%
一、邮电业务总量	**万元**	**61 063**	**187 195**	**256 978.37**	**37.3**
二、主要业务分类情况					
函　件	万件	6 830	12 176	10 991.70	－9.7
包　裹	万件	131	147	162.27	10.4
汇　票	万张	217	247	264.85	7.2
邮政快件	万件		499	466.62	－6.5
机要文件	万件		65	60.40	－7.1
特快专递	万件		93	125.42	34.9
订销报纸累计份数	万份	26 833	28 054	26 290.95	－6.3
订销杂志累计份数	万份	1 767	1 555	1 409.83	－9.3
报纸期发份数	万份	230	159	165.76	4.3
杂志期发份数	万份	152	98	99.81	1.8
邮政储蓄收储余额	万元		357 682	490 565.01	37.2
集邮业务	万枚		6 586	6 165.74	－6.4
公众电报	万份		105	74.01	－29.5
用户电报	万次		17	14.47	－14.9
国内长途电话	万次	4 128	12 847	17 210.72	34.0
国际电话	万次		410	489.06	19.3
港澳台电话	万次		217	232.42	7.1
本地电话用户到达数	万户	19.76	83	107.85	29.9
本地计次制电话通话量	万次		323 180	344 177.13	6.5
住宅电话用户	户	84 555	584 985	818 281	39.9
公用电话部数	部		16 172	22 362	38.3
无线寻呼用户	户		227 930	333 807	46.5
移动电话用户	户		80 273	150 397	87.4

11－12　分地区邮电局所数

单位:处

地　　区	1992年	1995年	1996年	地　　区	1992年	1995年	1996年
全市总计	**273**	**300**	**314**	津南区	5	9	11
一、市辖区	**187**	**211**	**218**	北辰区	10	9	9
和平区	21	20	20	**二、市辖县**	**86**	**89**	**96**
河东区	19	21	23	宁河县	9	10	18
河西区	16	18	23	武清县	21	23	20
南开区	16	23	25	静海县	19	18	29
河北区	17	19	26	宝坻县	19	21	19
红桥区	13	16	9	蓟　县	18	17	10
塘沽区	24	27	27	每一局所服务面积			
汉沽区	6	5	5	（平方公里）	42.98	39.73	37.96
大港区	21	21	22	每一局所服务人口			
东丽区	10	11	8	（万　人）	3.34	2.97	2.86
西青区	9	12	10				

十二、批发零售贸易和餐饮业

WHOLESALE & RETAIL TRADE AND CATERING TRADE

1996 年批发零售网点数	161 070 个
1996 年餐饮业网点数	25 785 个
1996 年社会消费品零售总额	470.04 亿元
1996 年批发零售贸易业商品购进总额	980.73 亿元
1996 年批发零售贸易业商品销售总额	1 035.88 亿元

社会消费品零售总额(亿元)

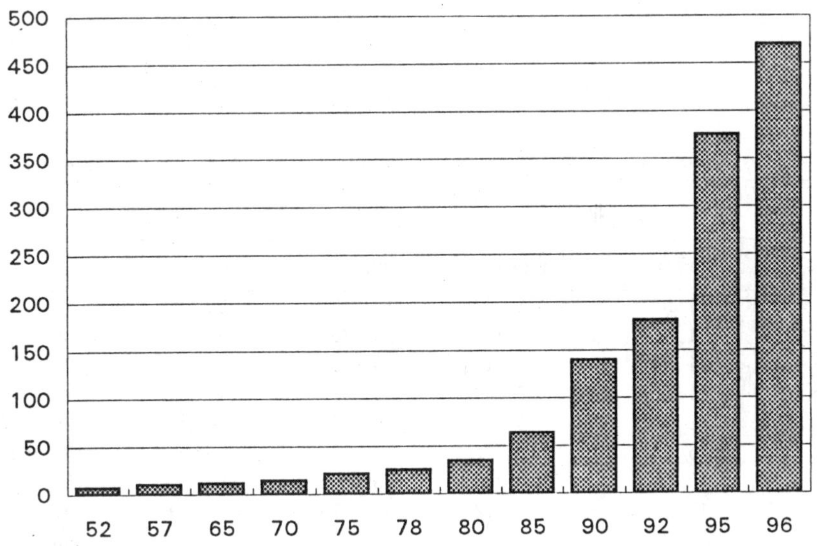

12-1 改革开放以来社会商业发展情况

单位:万元

年份	社会消费品零售总额	按经济类型分			按行业分	
		国有	集体	其他	批发零售贸易业	餐饮业
1978	252 049	205 093	77 766		255 941	12 021
1979	290 837	234 828	84 706		287 271	13 868
1980	346 414	261 306	108 376		322 555	15 566
1981-1985	2 387 235	1 648 044	783 599		2 144 085	107 938
1981	380 427	274 209	127 149		345 396	16 406
1982	397 624	291 871	126 895		359 353	17 180
1983	446 277	314 208	143 543		401 918	18 332
1984	521 738	365 178	168 653		470 288	25 143
1985	641 169	402 578	217 359		567 130	30 877
1986-1990	5 724 290	2 827 606	1 923 724		5 040 424	323 508
1986	813 933	438 003	290 192		720 674	41 973
1987	955 671	503 113	327 064		844 202	49 616
1988	1 212 831	605 854	423 263		1 077 290	62 589
1989	1 343 010	625 616	451 054		1 171 777	79 188
1990	1 398 845	655 020	432 151		1 226 481	90 142
1991-1995	12 470 655	3 749 330	2 369 270		8 998 662	853 651
1991	1 594 432	748 758	454 722		1 377 565	113 262
1992	1 811 969	612 502	423 681		1 422 957	125 997
1993	2 274 197	704 178	457 575	1 112 444	1 738 624	145 885
1994	3 033 695	788 098	480 306	1 765 291	2 087 661	210 081
1995	3 756 362	895 794	552 986	2 307 582	2 371 855	258 426
1996	4 700 449	1 156 852	998 016	2 545 581	2 671 350	364 726

年份	按行业分		按类别分			
	制造业	其他行业	吃	穿	用	烧
1978	11 260	3 637	121 373	50 620	71 045	9 011
1979	14 523	3 904	134 289	60 715	86 718	9 115
1980	24 080	7 747	151 791	76 209	108 894	9 520
1981-1985	214 081	53 672	999 626	444 598	882 614	60 397
1981	32 812	8 393	162 955	82 161	125 225	10 086
1982	36 327	10 097	172 521	76 785	137 668	10 650
1983	40 934	10 080	189 395	86 021	159 640	11 221
1984	47 214	11 042	223 179	86 396	199 238	12 925
1985	56 794	14 060	251 576	113 235	260 843	15 515
1986-1990	417 356	86 700	2 227 297	1 022 321	2 380 713	93 959
1986	64 308	18 577	317 896	150 212	329 515	16 310
1987	73 747	23 607	372 388	170 854	396 448	15 981
1988	92 650	19 893	443 703	225 913	521 879	21 336
1989	105 855	15 681	534 771	234 834	554 567	18 838
1990	80 796	8 942	558 539	240 508	578 304	21 494
1991-1995	535 286	2 180 534	5 263 703	2 109 623	4 843 225	254 104
1991	69 741	131 342	662 047	276 846	626 243	29 296
1992	74 653	188 362	748 510	305 706	711 774	45 979
1993	94 755	294 933	869 432	400 857	946 526	57 382
1994	113 927	622 026	1 292 145	499 044	1 187 194	55 312
1995	182 210	943 871	1 691 569	627 170	1 371 488	66 135
1996	376 036	1 288 337	2 057 810	763 542	1 799 534	79 563

注:1992年以前的经济类型和行业分组为社会商品零售总额。

12－2　1996年批发贸易业机构、网点及人员

项　　目	合　计			#市辖区		
	机　构（个）	网　点（个）	人　员（人）	机　构（个）	网　点（个）	人　员（人）
总　　计	**7 699**	**9 806**	**183 988**	**6 213**	**7 635**	**152 604**
一、按经济类型分						
国有经济	1 656	2 633	81 434	1 334	2 045	71 527
集体经济	4 802	5 754	85 985	3 884	4 471	67 320
私营经济	764	841	7 447	548	615	5 620
个体经济						
联营经济	55	78	904	41	43	450
股份制经济	77	122	3 188	66	88	2 696
“三资”经济	326	359	4 809	324	357	4 795
外商投资经营	171	202	3 720	170	201	3 710
港澳台投资经济	155	157	1 089	154	156	1 085
其他经济	19	19	221	16	16	196
二、按国民经济行业分						
食品饮料烟草和家庭用品批发业	**3 455**	**4 512**	**80 561**	**2 841**	**3 580**	**68 017**
食品、饮料、烟草批发业	900	1 427	23 137	648	971	17 140
棉、麻、土畜产品批发业	69	113	2 217	52	82	1 724
纺织品、服装和鞋帽批发业	514	574	9 953	474	531	9 526
日用百货批发业	434	507	12 035	394	454	10 526
日用杂品批发业	76	136	2 207	62	107	1 783
五金、交电、化工批发业	1 320	1 508	23 137	1 081	1 237	20 062
药品及医疗器械批发业	142	247	7 875	130	198	7 256
能源、材料和机械电子设备批发业	**3 766**	**4 659**	**87 599**	**3 004**	**3 633**	**72 190**
能源批发业	309	487	15 519	178	267	11 213
化工材料批发业	441	491	8 735	391	436	8 014
木材批发业	98	119	2 232	77	96	1 820
建筑材料批发业	645	818	10 388	472	539	7 991
矿产品批发业	28	29	271	21	22	209
金属材料批发业	625	729	14 752	451	526	11 535
机械、电子设备批发业	1 113	1 247	18 266	1 027	1 158	16 779
汽车、摩托车及零配件批发业	372	417	7 420	283	321	5 908
再生物资回收批发业	135	322	10 016	104	268	8 721
其他批发业	**478**	**635**	**15 828**	**368**	**422**	**12 397**
工艺美术品批发业	45	48	1 305	39	41	1 201
图书报刊批发业	18	19	613	16	17	321
农业生产资料批发业	113	206	3 970	34	40	2 056
其他类未包括的批发业	302	362	9 940	279	324	8 819
三、按企业规模分						
大　型	55	243	18 608	52	226	18 395
中　型	480	1 009	45 440	353	678	36 170
小　型	7 164	8 554	119 940	5 808	6 731	98 039

12－3　1996 年零售贸易餐饮业机构、网点及人员

项　　目	合　　计			#市辖区		
	机　构（个）	网　点（个）	人　员（人）	机　构（个）	网　点（个）	人　员（人）
零售贸易业总计	**6 412**	**151 264**	**321 856**	**5 148**	**74 962**	**203 125**
一、按经济类型分						
国有经济	1 282	3 128	58 090	1 125	2 743	54 073
集体经济	4 198	6 613	74 026	3 271	4 190	53 654
私营经济	763	808	7 180	595	639	5 757
个体经济		140 508	167 924		67 197	75 179
联营经济	24	28	2 333	19	21	2 255
股份制经济	123	149	10 385	119	145	10 338
“三资”经济	12	14	1 710	11	13	1 692
外商投资经营	5	7	732	5	7	732
港澳台投资经济	7	7	978	6	6	960
其他经济	10	16	208	8	14	177
二、按国民经济行业分						
食品、饮料和烟草零售业	1 150	56 985	102 488	965	28 259	62 316
日用百货零售业	1 012	30 688	82 988	772	14 401	52 229
纺织品、服装和鞋帽零售业	287	350	7 167	270	324	6 988
日用杂品零售业	173	343	4 191	151	320	3 948
五金、交电、化工零售业	2 160	5 607	33 171	1 814	3 541	27 570
药品及医疗器械零售业	187	222	2 614	178	213	2 521
图书报刊零售业	70	1 113	3 615	63	585	2 773
其他零售业	1 373	55 956	85 622	935	27 319	44 780
三、按企业规模分						
大　型	15	42	16 111	14	40	14 444
中　型	586	3 227	52 636	413	1 962	40 880
小　型	5 811	147 995	253 109	4 721	72 960	147 801
餐饮业总计	**1 162**	**25 785**	**78 015**	**1 001**	**15 287**	**52 865**
一、按经济类型分						
国有经济	266	559	12 627	256	540	12 324
集体经济	795	1 051	14 394	651	835	11 840
私营经济	29	32	537	25	28	508
个体经济		24 052	45 676		13 798	23 547
联营经济	8	9	346	6	7	328
股份制经济	2	3	123	1	1	13
“三资”经济	60	76	4 293	60	76	4 293
外商投资经营	40	54	3 112	40	54	3 112
港澳台投资经济	20	22	1 181	20	22	1 181
其他经济	2	3	19	2	2	12
二、按国民经济行业分						
正　餐	939	1 641	25 506	784	1 275	22 410
快　餐	39	50	1 956	35	46	1 901
其他餐饮业	184	24 094	50 553	182	13 966	28 554
三、按企业规模分						
大　型	24	216	7 118	24	216	7 118
中　型	57	143	4 415	53	135	4 258
小　型	1 081	25 426	66 482	924	14 936	41 489

12－4　按地区分的批发零售贸易餐饮业机构、网点及人员情况

(1996 年)

地　区	批发贸易业			零售贸易业			餐饮业		
	机　构（个）	网　点（个）	人　员（人）	机　构（个）	网　点（个）	人　员（人）	机　构（个）	网　点（个）	人　员（人）
全市总计	**7 699**	**9 806**	**183 988**	**6 412**	**10 756**	**153 932**	**1 162**	**1 733**	**32 339**
一、市辖区	**7 139**	**8 701**	**168 917**	**5 825**	**9 150**	**140 136**	**1 080**	**1 598**	**30 497**
和平区	1 107	1 496	43 557	939	1 382	31 316	298	337	9 274
河东区	755	880	21 266	509	805	12 102	77	170	1 954
河西区	999	1 170	20 358	649	935	15 715	106	165	4 029
南开区	1 038	1 296	22 623	961	1 366	20 843	157	176	3 574
河北区	747	862	15 236	638	944	14 760	75	190	3 435
红桥区	607	731	12 802	586	977	13 699	52	140	2 550
塘沽区	477	577	8 354	470	727	10 324	144	168	2 413
汉沽区	109	139	2 321	151	222	3 194	45	50	555
大港区	153	203	2 611	194	332	4 637	21	50	852
东丽区	416	484	5 538	151	281	2 598	32	34	366
西青区	294	349	4 986	194	332	3 327	30	43	643
津南区	80	125	2 125	110	316	3 059	9	16	132
北辰区	357	389	7 140	273	531	4 562	34	59	720
二、市辖县	**560**	**1 105**	**15 071**	**587**	**1 606**	**13 796**	**82**	**135**	**1 842**
宁河县	79	155	2 890	57	162	1 475	6	11	223
武清县	159	201	2 727	300	659	4 819	39	39	434
静海县	131	202	3 027	81	245	2 738	15	24	514
宝坻县	76	142	2 868	77	186	1 908	6	14	257
蓟　县	115	405	3 559	72	354	2 856	16	47	414

注：本表不含个体。

12－5　按主管部门分的批发零售贸易业主要经济指标

(1996年)

项　目	机构(个)	网点(个)	人员(人)	资产总额(万元)	商品销售总额(万元)	增加值(万元)
全市总计	**14 111**	**20 125**	**331 781**	**1 465 098**	**10 237 426**	**260 408**
中央单位	526	812	18 050	314 123	1 583 396	27 159
农林水利气象系统	133	253	5 731	17 102	87 528	2 531
工业系统	3 174	3 398	56 145	203 560	2 262 217	62 005
城建系统	406	437	4 902	22 811	65 869	6 779
运输邮电系统	526	561	5 551	102 902	132 645	8 222
商业系统	1 485	4 830	86 127	295 677	2 271 489	－6 787
外经外贸系统	276	335	12 881	108 516	1 056 903	－11 616
科学研究系统	9	17	315	2 126	10 714	541
教育卫生系统	61	61	688	2 219	7 982	1 647
文化体育系统	85	142	2 756	6 118	69 872	5 857
计委系统	364	753	16 219	66 130	555 341	16 720
政法系统	79	108	1 397	5 915	42 251	2 483
党政机关	66	67	833	8 399	13 706	441
民主党派和人民团体	392	412	5 740	14 251	72 325	4 391
其他市直系统	5	5	52	85	200	35
和平区	682	839	15 950	28 685	227 477	30 377
河东区	462	588	8 574	14 948	97 757	7 056
河西区	584	686	11 417	28 119	147 968	16 782
南开区	806	1 029	16 079	32 502	175 685	13 894
河北区	585	706	10 839	34 344	120 048	9 554
红桥区	567	774	10 709	14 200	93 252	8 410
塘沽区	463	555	9 084	23 374	118 133	12 957
汉沽区	175	190	3 145	5 437	43 870	2 099
大港区	192	228	2 995	9 464	81 228	3 271
东丽区	370	410	3 941	23 213	187 820	5 438
西青区	334	345	4 245	13 729	83 204	6 467
津南区	135	140	1 676	5 795	25 441	1 986
北辰区	435	472	5 074	19 992	129 541	7 576
宁河县	58	66	1 206	1 679	12 692	193
武清县	348	361	3 715	9 062	105 918	5 255
静海县	129	148	1 918	9 230	118 519	4 545
宝坻县	39	50	989	4 267	29 414	1 515
蓟　县	117	300	2 194	7 403	72 008	1 458
外省市在津企业	40	44	505	9 181	131 554	1 070
地方其他单位	3	3	139	540	3 459	97

12－6　社会消费品零售总额

指　　标	绝对数(万元)			构　　成(%)	
	1995 年	1996 年	1996 比 1995 年 增长%	1995 年	1996 年
社会消费品零售总额	**3 756 362**	**4 700 449**	**25.1**	**100.0**	**100.0**
一、按销售地区分					
市	3 147 286	3 913 621	24.4	83.8	83.3
县	240 912	300 840	24.9	6.4	6.4
县以下	368 164	485 988	32.0	9.8	10.3
二、按经济类型分					
国有经济	1 046 048	1 156 852	10.6	27.8	24.6
集体经济	660 461	998 016	51.1	17.6	21.2
私营经济	59 055	107 462	82.0	1.6	2.3
个体经济	501 435	716 448	42.9	13.3	15.2
联营经济	10 552	51 274	385.9	0.3	1.1
股份制经济	243 702	258 240	6.0	6.5	5.5
“三资”经济	56 331	114 910	104.0	1.5	2.4
外商投资经营	42 883	89 671	109.1	76.1	78.0
港澳台投资经济	13 448	25 239	87.7	23.9	22.0
其他经济	1 178 778	1 297 247	10.1	31.4	27.6
三、按行业分					
批发零售贸易业	2 221 601	2 671 350	20.2	59.1	56.8
餐饮业	258 426	364 726	41.1	6.9	7.8
制造业	332 464	376 036	13.1	8.9	8.0
其他行业	943 871	1 288 337	36.5	25.1	27.4
#农民对非农业居民零售	935 022	1 276 535	36.5	99.1	99.1
四、按用途分					
吃	1 691 569	2 057 810	21.7	45.0	43.8
穿	627 170	763 542	21.7	16.7	16.2
用	1 371 488	1 799 534	31.2	36.5	38.3
烧	66 135	79 563	20.3	1.8	1.7

注:本表个体零售额为市工商局”城乡个体工商业基本情况统计”年报数据,1995 年相关数字做了调整。

12－7　批发零售贸易业商品购进、销售及库存总额

指　标	合计		#大　型		中　型	
	1995年	1996年	1995年	1996年	1995年	1996年
绝对数(万元)						
一、商品购进总额	**8 665 001**	**9 807 272**	**3 771 895**	**4 319 965**	**3 158 457**	**3 425 179**
1.从生产者购进	4 836 433	5 518 883	2 421 381	2 736 692	1 527 717	1 730 026
#农副产品购进	143 654	173 713	21 515	33 096	50 195	63 798
2.从批发零售贸易业购进	3 176 439	3 344 820	870 089	924 005	1 510 183	1 484 244
3.进口额	574 273	616 260	479 761	434 920	82 799	145 647
4.其　他	77 857	327 309	665	224 348	37 759	65 263
二、商品销售总额	**9 352 900**	**10 358 847**	**4 009 911**	**4 613 275**	**3 481 599**	**3 570 289**
1.批发小计	7 773 352	8 519 989	3 540 764	4 123 355	2 803 698	2 771 758
#对生产经营单位批发	2 493 540	3 230 233	820 863	966 228	1 013 831	1 352 000
#对农民农业生产资料批发	93 113	81 978	10 657	6 140	53 466	50 082
对批发零售贸易业批发	3 865 210	4 006 381	2 061 133	2 092 780	1 232 652	1 238 163
出口额	1 414 602	1 283 374	658 768	1 064 346	557 215	181 594
2.对居民和社会集团零售	1 579 548	1 838 859	469 148	489 920	677 901	798 531
三、年末库存总额	**1 339 498**	**1 615 240**	**399 669**	**606 762**	**590 961**	**537 300**
构　成(%)						
一、商品购进总额	**100.0**	**100.0**	**43.5**	**44.1**	**36.5**	**34.9**
1.从生产者购进	100.0	100.0	50.1	49.6	31.6	31.4
#农副产品购进	100.0	100.0	15.0	19.1	34.9	36.7
2.从批发零售贸易业购进	100.0	100.0	27.4	27.6	47.5	44.4
3.进口额	100.0	100.0	83.5	70.6	14.4	23.6
4.其　他	100.0	100.0	0.9	68.5	48.5	19.9
二、商品销售总额	**100.0**	**100.0**	**42.9**	**44.5**	**37.2**	**34.5**
1.批发小计	100.0	100.0	45.6	48.4	36.1	32.5
#对生产经营单位批发	100.0	100.0	32.9	29.9	40.7	41.9
#对农民农业生产资料批发	100.0	100.0	11.5	7.5	57.4	61.1
对批发零售贸易业批发	100.0	100.0	53.3	52.2	31.9	30.9
出口额	100.0	100.0	46.6	82.9	39.4	14.2
2.对居民和社会集团零售	100.0	100.0	29.7	26.6	42.9	43.4
三、年末库存总额	**100.0**	**100.0**	**29.8**	**37.6**	**44.1**	**33.3**

注:本表数据不含个体,包含汽车销售公司数据,以下相关表同。

12－8　批发零售贸易业商品购进总额

单位:万元

项　　目	商品购进总额		#从生产者购进		#农副产品购进	
	1995 年	1996 年	1995 年	1996 年	1995 年	1996 年
总　　计	**8 665 001**	**9 807 272**	**4 836 433**	**5 518 883**	**143 654**	**173 713**
一、按经济类型分						
国有经济	6 239 285	6 364 917	3 693 099	3 726 925	107 547	96 420
集体经济	1 845 038	2 459 272	823 420	1 213 671	35 504	46 992
私营经济		161 302		93 582		7 609
联营经济	38 391	127 181	8 547	66 701	57	826
股份制经济	444 920	458 699	264 156	258 425	271	21 133
“三资”经济	97 015	217 432	47 025	155 009	275	734
外商投资经营	53 664	160 087	26 319	115 152	267	493
港澳台投资经济	43 352	57 345	20 705	39 857	8	241
其他经济	353	18 469	186	4 569		
二、按国民经济行业分						
食品饮料烟草和家庭用品批发业	**2 733 466**	**2 510 962**	**1 401 505**	**1 074 375**	**113 841**	**80 158**
食品、饮料、烟草批发业	1 098 770	1 118 134	306 673	257 618	92 066	67 647
棉、麻、土畜产品批发业	170 994	186 401	88 856	49 309	17 024	5 731
纺织品、服装和鞋帽批发业	596 529	330 593	492 219	237 491	663	653
日用百货批发业	345 238	225 428	204 440	132 586	609	1 150
日用杂品批发业	25 854	23 654	13 488	12 042	858	937
五金、交电、化工批发业	322 504	410 237	178 332	253 621	342	1 778
药品及医疗器械批发业	173 578	216 515	117 498	131 710	2 279	2 263
能源、材料和机械电子设备批发业	**3 556 373**	**4 656 699**	**2 442 050**	**3 092 281**	**1 320**	**8 402**
能源批发业	493 953	954 082	325 325	476 538	207	1 076
化工材料批发业	359 880	401 764	246 119	243 218	829	
木材批发业	32 801	36 629	16 116	17 100		2 054
建筑材料批发业	89 186	144 122	63 937	108 473	14	1 458
矿产品批发业	92 837	14 148	60 882	7 088		213
金属材料批发业	903 754	1 348 078	521 162	987 069	10	3 126
机械、电子设备批发业	514 573	399 308	319 561	235 931	260	477
汽车、摩托车及零配件批发业	986 916	1 277 047	875 787	1 007 209		
再生物资回收批发业	82 473	81 521	13 161	9 655		
其他批发业	**589 345**	**896 423**	**305 866**	**607 274**	**2 241**	**17 101**
工艺美术品批发业	53 633	37 094	52 346	35 068		387
图书报刊批发业	25 216	33 828	22 582	29 358		
农业生产资料批发业	261 898	280 989	121 517	148 223	374	2 418
其他类未包括的批发业	248 597	544 512	109 421	394 624	1 868	14 296
零售业	**1 785 817**	**1 743 188**	**687 011**	**744 953**	**26 252**	**68 052**
食品、饮料和烟草零售业	285 020	306 718	77 114	93 762	15 148	34 577
日用百货零售业	778 338	771 961	359 519	358 833	10 375	29 754
纺织品、服装和鞋帽零售业	58 293	40 319	26 529	24 130		129
日用杂品零售业	18 799	21 964	7 851	10 586	118	75
五金、交电、化工零售业	203 883	274 576	105 210	125 418	308	993
药品及医疗器械零售业	17 257	24 196	2 242	4 409	29	30
图书报刊零售业	28 962	37 020	14 870	19 061		10
其他零售业	395 267	266 433	93 676	108 754	274	2 485

12-9 批发零售贸易业商品销售和库存总额

单位:万元

项目	商品销售总额		#批发		年末库存总额	
	1995年	1996年	1995年	1996年	1995年	1996年
总计	**9 352 900**	**10 358 847**	**7 773 352**	**8 519 989**	**1 339 498**	**1 615 240**
一、按经济类型分						
国有经济	6 678 580	6 662 891	5 871 995	5 878 818	887 764	1 053 940
集体经济	1 998 971	2 594 989	1 523 273	1 965 883	362 670	392 414
私营经济		167 236		137 377		32 197
联营经济	43 217	130 267	33 301	78 412	4 256	16 581
股份制经济	506 935	539 832	263 233	281 104	48 149	67 732
"三资"经济	124 849	245 867	81 202	161 666	36 572	50 578
外商投资经营	83 541	188 958	48 057	116 552	30 589	43 980
港澳台投资经济	41 308	56 909	33 145	45 114	5 983	6 598
其他经济	348	17 765	348	16 729	87	1 799
二、按国民经济行业分						
食品饮料烟草和家庭用品批发业	**2 925 707**	**2 539 265**	**2 643 509**	**2 255 752**	**590 500**	**537 672**
食品、饮料、烟草批发业	1 064 545	890 779	964 504	808 422	199 084	255 694
棉、麻、土畜产品批发业	198 834	182 079	196 135	179 610	35 885	25 635
纺织品、服装和鞋帽批发业	715 829	448 747	702 143	441 244	135 290	44 282
日用百货批发业	382 267	251 492	353 091	223 608	75 466	40 783
日用杂品批发业	30 071	28 073	22 891	21 163	5 411	7 121
五金、交电、化工批发业	331 715	489 874	282 012	428 030	70 200	91 524
药品及医疗器械批发业	202 446	248 221	122 733	153 674	69 165	72 634
能源、材料和机械电子设备批发业	**3 904 692**	**4 755 107**	**3 708 372**	**4 498 118**	**429 184**	**651 098**
能源批发业	607 584	988 725	582 050	911 404	41 587	69 539
化工材料批发业	380 341	410 355	377 197	399 866	48 315	58 213
木材批发业	34 008	38 160	31 107	34 808	4 241	6 517
建筑材料批发业	103 287	157 941	87 733	130 452	14 473	31 492
矿产品批发业	61 766	18 940	61 216	17 907	7 562	1 199
金属材料批发业	1 002 298	1 350 311	985 452	1 321 854	135 200	308 015
机械、电子设备批发业	555 894	470 887	516 507	441 007	88 256	61 657
汽车、摩托车及零配件批发业	1 063 656	1 225 590	973 340	1 148 669	68 739	92 871
再生物资回收批发业	95 858	94 200	93 771	92 151	20 812	21 595
其他批发业	**638 384**	**1 068 063**	**624 767**	**1 045 416**	**77 244**	**127 929**
工艺美术品批发业	64 640	40 765	63 813	39 953	10 261	11 454
图书报刊批发业	24 241	34 155	22 916	34 002	1 876	2 022
农业生产资料批发业	279 665	298 012	277 094	288 761	35 507	32 858
其他类未包括的批发业	269 839	695 131	260 945	682 701	29 600	81 595
零售业	**1 884 117**	**1 996 412**	**796 704**	**720 702**	**242 571**	**298 542**
食品、饮料和烟草零售业	322 013	353 873	86 472	93 195	36 440	53 342
日用百货零售业	920 776	908 915	371 875	322 235	106 710	109 537
纺织品、服装和鞋帽零售业	65 287	56 962	33 219	17 417	12 328	13 831
日用杂品零售业	22 131	25 542	9 023	10 203	3 923	4 886
五金、交电、化工零售业	216 194	301 320	146 549	165 022	34 967	53 056
药品及医疗器械零售业	21 579	27 970	3 189	4 960	4 282	4 731
图书报刊零售业	27 131	36 848	2 791	3 737	6 826	6 476
其他零售业	289 007	284 983	143 586	103 935	37 094	52 684

12－10　1996年国有批发零售贸易业主要经济指标

项　　目	机　构（个）	网　点（个）	人　员（人）	商品购进总　额（万元）	商品销售总　额（万元）	年末库存总　额（万元）
总　　计	**2 938**	**5 761**	**139 524**	**6 364 917**	**6 662 891**	**1 053 940**
一、按国民经济行业分						
食品饮料烟草和家庭用品批发业	**793**	**1 371**	**36 213**	**1 645 413**	**1 635 624**	**349 876**
食品、饮料、烟草批发业	413	821	15 331	936 149	699 142	232 199
棉、麻、土畜产品批发业	17	22	799	98 259	123 861	17 249
纺织品、服装和鞋帽批发业	114	142	4 756	235 615	349 485	19 622
日用百货批发业	73	118	6 144	141 006	162 156	20 296
日用杂品批发业	5	6	77	695	1 065	316
五金、交电、化工批发业	137	199	6 941	148 211	205 067	42 977
药品及医疗器械批发业	34	63	2 165	85 479	94 849	17 217
能源、材料和机械电子设备批发业	**743**	**1 051**	**35 944**	**3 395 991**	**3 436 027**	**477 534**
能源批发业	85	212	11 380	733 087	773 930	56 195
化工材料批发业	92	126	4 156	264 022	267 366	41 887
木材批发业	40	60	1 480	31 845	33 051	5 208
建筑材料批发业	137	176	3 537	69 720	79 221	15 630
矿产品批发业	7	7	114	8 662	13 702	506
金属材料批发业	215	267	8 068	876 272	864 626	265 419
机械、电子设备批发业	101	118	3 836	218 136	262 040	33 024
汽车、摩托车及零配件批发业	60	79	3 248	1 186 390	1 133 800	58 536
再生物资回收批发业	6	6	125	7 859	8 291	1 130
其他批发业	**120**	**211**	**9 277**	**665 022**	**806 748**	**99 417**
工艺美术品批发业	8	11	843	32 970	36 526	10 453
图书报刊批发业	9	10	499	32 506	32 779	1 938
农业生产资料批发业	24	75	1 679	151 514	160 409	19 870
其他类未包括的批发业	79	115	6 256	448 032	577 034	67 156
零售业	**1 282**	**3 128**	**58 090**	**658 491**	**784 492**	**127 113**
食品、饮料和烟草零售业	563	1 831	25 478	216 912	250 302	43 288
日用百货零售业	174	211	16 384	245 666	306 264	40 014
纺织品、服装和鞋帽零售业	49	67	2 966	16 091	29 972	6 345
日用杂品零售业	6	6	70	606	766	46
五金、交电、化工零售业	211	247	4 436	49 180	56 868	10 077
药品及医疗器械零售业	34	37	470	7 110	7 521	1 641
图书报刊零售业	49	109	1 778	32 218	32 046	6 294
其他零售业	196	620	6 508	90 710	100 754	19 408
二、按企业规模分						
大　型	56	222	21 881	3 715 488	3 912 634	520 819
中　型	536	2 006	59 829	1 973 695	2 056 943	352 696
小　型	2 346	3 533	57 814	675 734	693 314	180 425

12－11 1996年批发零售贸易业主要商品销售数量

品名	单位	批发	#对生产经营单位批发	出口	零售
粮食	吨	1 124 464	144 217	31 600	498 535
食用植物油	吨	70 030	6 475	6 413	70 576
猪和猪肉	吨	55 997	1 964	1 310	7 317
牛和牛肉	吨	5 776	24	1 235	1 703
羊和羊肉	吨	149	4	42	729
鲜蛋	吨	15 267	2 652		4 626
家禽	吨	5 731	778	177	2 380
水产品	吨	134 269	4 495	1 645	7 243
鲜菜	吨	15 668	632	14 671	4 452
牛奶	吨	2 198	76		14 851
奶粉	吨	4 048	2 305		1 599
糕点	吨	3 836	123		11 963
盐	吨	304 696	80 570	71	5 688
食糖	吨	91 202	28 593	1 060	5 988
卷烟	箱	274 634	540		50 941
酒	吨	78 348	5 910	1 074	13 525
#白酒	吨	29 530	1 570	233	5 289
啤酒	吨	44 794	4 206		6 016
茶叶	吨	1 145	12	10	1 180
棉花	吨	64 326	53 624		
布	百米	1 507 813	509 741	547 923	73 031
#棉布	百米	783 523	146 250	428 760	35 067
呢绒	百米	87 464	23 084	25 150	12 962
绸缎	百米	82 352	24 152	3 446	13 776
各种服装	百件	727 573	4 407	417 125	183 639
#西装	百件	3 346	637	2 473	10 900
牛仔装	百件	1 623		1 283	27 680
男女衬衣	百件	53 183	495	44 380	30 109
防寒服	百件	3 888	830	2 298	15 242
皮革服装	百件	6 361	6	5 874	4 320
裘皮服装	百件	76		59	940
童装	百件	81 636	43	55 328	16 097
针织内衣裤	百件	697 904	302 335	263 525	64 894
毛线	百公斤	15 506	6 230		35 935
鞋	百双	367 655	3 484	201 340	116 440
#皮鞋	百双	85 449	265	78 485	34 814
合成洗衣粉	吨	7 614	394	170	3 079
钟	百个	9 569	6 377	191	14 230
#石英钟	百个	9 183	6 240		6 626
手表	百只	2 352	85		20 794
#进口手表	百只	222			1 445
电子表	百只	729	80		9 743
黄金饰品	万元	15 642			41 870

注：本表数据不含个体。

12－11 续表 1

品　　名	单　位	批　发	#对生产经营单位批发	出　口	零　售
照相机	架	22 231			51 006
自行车	辆	326 084	32 704	23 499	233 027
摩托车	辆	109 728	8 829	8	39 479
电视机	台	364 447	32 221	14 626	166 149
#彩色电视机	台	267 046	23 048	64	139 809
25 英寸以上彩电	台	92 348	10 897		32 734
半导体收音机	台	68 399	952		86 283
录音机	台	94 071	4 853		196 268
#组合音响	台	22 009	142		35 001
摄像机	台	1 094	24		3 035
录像机	台	29 395	121		29 628
家用电脑	台	831	355		15 767
游戏机	台	1 107			10 773
家用电风扇	台	198 708	39 114		127 320
家用洗衣机	台	138 428	1 393	300	93 805
家用电冰箱	台	149 160	4 497	223	107 811
#家用冰柜	台	10 905	3 415		17 347
房间空调器	台	57 739	13 069		43 084
抽油烟机	台	19 052	3 916		59 413
吸尘器	台	7 247	256		15 893
电暖器	台	27 674	2 110	31	55 516
淋浴器	个	7 446	2 846	2 063	35 595
电熨斗	个	2 912	246		27 778
电话机	部	250 392	74 818		224 656
传真机	台	3 924	3 334		1 685
打字机	台	6 476	5 516		9 553
钢　琴	架	38			409
电子琴	架	4 729	14		2 507
彩色胶卷	个	200 575	10 220		202 193
食品加工机	台	7 159	2 382		29 170
#微波炉	台	4 427	1 432		15 787
家　俱	万元	8 909	1 064	6 891	6 589
化学肥料	吨	609 348	198 828	23 197	
化学农药	吨	15 710	6 833	6 761	
农用塑料薄膜	吨	26 821	12 302		
农用动力机械	台	16 530	8 767	2 448	
拖拉机	台	3 304	2 178	3	
手扶拖拉机	台	1 439	1 339		
半机械化农具	部	2 282	1 770		
汽　车	辆	217 633	19 927	209	16 003
#载货汽车	辆	85 514	2 914	55	
轿　车	辆	109 127	11 371	3	6 485

12－11续表2

品　名	单　位	批　发	#对生产经营单位批发	出　口	零　售
生　铁	吨	63 924	51 459	5 764	
钢　材	吨	3 754 327	2 671 027	26 998	78 935
#铁道用钢材	吨	38 020	32 612		
普通大型钢材	吨	37 837	32 927		
普通中型钢材	吨	122 254	69 381	2 206	7 177
普通小型钢材	吨	586 797	330 547	9 516	15 071
钢　带	吨	110 366	87 211	4 971	
线　材	吨	573 221	382 746		14 971
特厚钢板	吨	18 800	17 083		
中厚钢板	吨	426 592	344 630	180	
薄钢板	吨	1 065 929	813 880	2 447	
硅钢片	吨	20 574	18 511		
优质型材	吨	25 965	15 421		896
无缝钢管	吨	126 693	73 776	1 097	
焊接钢管	吨	36 039	15 953		5 394
铜	吨	11 022	10 267	340	
铝	吨	15 894	9 660		
铅	吨	7 718	7 136		
锌	吨	20 027	15 203		
锡	吨	182	163		
铜　材	吨	74 722	72 076	95	
铝　材	吨	63 993	63 197	15	
硫　酸	吨	32 158	26 352		
烧　碱	吨	34 291	20 261	11 442	
纯　碱	吨	102 833	25 117	71 279	685
天然橡胶	吨	59 370	47 194		
合成橡胶	吨	28 210	24 151	19	
水　泥	吨	1 122 138	908 306	118 323	226 829
平板玻璃	重量箱	141 891	110 702		51 662
原　木	立方米	82 164	74 586		8 388
锯　材	立方米	79 856	37 757	1 276	9 626
煤　炭	吨	8 169 642	4 315 602		3 259 465
焦　炭	吨	170 517	23 579	114 327	
原　油	吨	6 612	6 412		
汽　油	吨	1 836 437	1 107 737		3 289 299
柴　油	吨	2 886 401	2 112 432	86 528	87 666
煤　油	吨	27 515	15 732		1 919
燃料油	吨	1 377 786	259 491		11 058
润滑油	吨	316 972	277 362		13 402

12－12 1996年批发零售贸易业财务状况

单位:万元

指标	合计	按经济类型分				
		国有经济	集体经济	股份制经济	"三资"经济	其他经济
一、资本金						
资本金合计	1 396 540	741 432	336 875	117 117	126 465	74 651
#国家资本金	822 400	656 236	71 036	47 836	37 090	10 202
外商资本金	86 606	360	138	3 074	82 992	42
二、年末资产负债						
资产总额	6 701 466	4 546 652	1 296 417	396 238	286 038	176 121
流动资产年末合计	5 081 029	3 408 745	1 056 188	266 398	221 601	128 097
#存　货	1 518 359	997 321	355 771	62 527	57 422	45 318
流动资产年平均余额	4 802 786	3 293 272	1 003 482	209 879	185 983	110 170
固定资产合计	1 076 021	786 151	136 351	92 662	31 231	29 626
固定资产原值	1 132 990	838 789	165 073	59 027	38 939	31 162
累计折旧	216 994	149 438	45 112	8 414	11 378	2 652
固定资产净值	915 996	689 351	119 961	50 613	27 561	28 510
固定资产净值平均余额	841 493	638 183	112 473	41 046	24 468	25 323
无形及递延资产合计	97 984	68 923	13 371	7 294	4 883	3 513
负债总额	5 132 106	3 696 424	935 154	192 084	204 110	104 334
流动负债合计	4 736 866	3 453 162	828 821	174 706	183 381	96 796
长期负债合计	254 946	134 137	82 501	16 871	17 885	3 552
所有者权益合计	1 569 359	850 228	361 263	204 153	81 928	71 787
#股　本	175 684	32 008	18 742	110 738	2 670	11 526
三、损益及分配						
商品销售收入(营业收入)	8 699 265	5 344 540	2 334 789	468 461	239 686	311 789
商品销售收入净额	8 662 416	5 316 961	2 330 134	466 756	237 007	311 558
商品销售成本(营业成本)	7 978 700	4 968 430	2 112 305	413 820	202 528	281 617
经营费用(营业费用)	390 095	216 367	119 427	18 927	18 420	16 954
商品销售税金及附加	14 748	6 468	6 656	1 600	－1 185	1 209
商品销售利润	278 873	125 697	91 746	32 408	17 244	11 778
代购代销收入	12 419	7 150	2 294	2	2 884	89
主营业务利润	291 292	132 846	94 040	32 410	20 128	11 868
其他业务利润	65 777	42 773	16 974	3 906	298	1 826
管理费用	321 782	186 298	83 319	20 691	21 235	10 239
财务费用	223 624	186 997	20 133	5 462	8 317	2 715
营业利润	－188 337	－197 676	7 561	10 163	－9 125	740
补贴收入	99 623	96 847	2 677	11	81	7
利润总额	－47 319	－72 421	14 572	18 150	－8 150	530
应交所得税	22 591	12 104	6 471	3 435	222	359
四、经济效益						
商品经营费用率(%)	4.5	4.1	5.1	4.1	7.8	5.4
商品销售利润率(%)	3.2	2.4	3.9	6.9	7.3	3.8
资本金利润率(%)	－3.4	－9.8	4.3	15.5	－6.4	0.7

12－13　1996年批发贸易业财务状况

单位:万元

指　　标	合　计	按经济类型分				
		国有经济	集体经济	股份制经济	"三资"经济	其他经济
一、资本金						
资本金合计	1 093 890	662 194	224 231	44 563	111 633	51 269
#国家资本金	706 856	588 564	49 250	29 392	33 162	6 488
外商资本金	76 205	253	49	3 074	72 828	1
二、年末资产负债						
资产总额	5 507 571	4 052 632	923 112	148 285	262 538	121 004
流动资产年末合计	4 304 804	3 123 266	758 495	121 116	208 936	92 991
#存　货	1 265 354	907 680	246 557	29 310	54 088	27 719
流动资产年平均余额	4 109 120	3 030 998	726 376	102 169	171 222	78 355
固定资产合计	732 345	600 427	80 315	11 717	25 117	14 769
固定资产原值	809 516	648 707	99 424	10 636	34 830	15 919
累计折旧	167 347	126 169	27 963	1 925	9 762	1 528
固定资产净值	642 169	522 538	71 461	8 711	25 068	14 391
固定资产净值平均余额	591 960	486 034	67 046	6 943	20 339	11 598
无形及递延资产合计	65 588	56 098	6 542	262	2 251	435
负债总额	4 411 716	3 384 914	686 187	87 081	184 490	69 044
流动负债合计	4 097 274	3 173 928	601 649	84 845	173 477	63 375
长期负债合计	189 761	109 145	67 484	1 763	8 242	3 127
所有者权益合计	1 095 854	667 719	236 925	61 203	78 048	51 959
#股　本	86 402	23 696	12 178	39 115	2 211	9 202
三、损益及分配						
商品销售收入(营业收入)	7 026 954	4 705 369	1 749 655	165 774	196 658	209 498
商品销售收入净额	6 998 153	4 682 258	1 746 119	164 905	195 602	209 269
商品销售成本(营业成本)	6 527 225	4 409 456	1 605 644	147 417	170 780	193 928
经营费用(营业费用)	273 931	172 595	76 023	8 320	9 148	7 845
商品销售税金及附加	6 920	3 649	3 527	384	－1 247	607
商品销售利润	190 077	96 558	60 924	8 784	16 921	6 890
代购代销收入	9 211	6 959	2 059		121	72
主营业务利润	199 287	103 517	62 983	8 784	17 042	6 961
其他业务利润	42 722	31 216	9 873	923	－302	1 012
管理费用	226 438	145 528	54 368	6 427	14 861	5 254
财务费用	205 870	177 103	15 516	3 497	8 563	1 191
营业利润	－190 300	－187 899	2 972	－216	－6 684	1 527
补贴收入	93 301	90 761	2 443	10	82	5
利润总额	－66 677	－73 632	7 829	1 408	－3 775	1 493
应交所得税	14 410	8 963	4 340	533	218	356
四、经济效益						
商品经营费用率(%)	3.9	3.7	4.4	5.0	4.7	3.7
商品销售利润率(%)	2.7	2.1	3.5	5.3	8.7	3.3
资本金利润率(%)	－6.1	－11.1	3.5	3.2	－3.4	2.9

12－14 1996年零售贸易业财务状况

单位:万元

指标	合计	按经济类型分				
		国有经济	集体经济	股份制经济	“三资”经济	其他经济
一、资本金						
资本金合计	302 650	79 238	112 643	72 554	14 832	23 383
#国家资本金	115 544	67 672	21 786	18 444	3 928	3 714
外商资本金	10 401	107	89		10 164	41
二、年末资产负债						
资产总额	1 193 895	494 019	373 305	247 953	23 500	55 118
流动资产年末合计	776 225	285 479	297 693	145 281	12 666	35 106
#存　货	253 005	89 641	109 215	33 217	3 334	17 598
流动资产年平均余额	693 666	262 274	277 106	107 710	14 761	31 815
固定资产合计	343 676	185 724	56 036	80 945	6 114	14 857
固定资产原值	323 474	190 083	65 649	48 391	4 110	15 241
累计折旧	49 647	23 267	17 150	6 489	1 616	1 125
固定资产净值	273 827	166 814	48 499	41 902	2 494	14 118
固定资产净值平均余额	244 533	152 148	45 427	34 103	4 130	8 725
无形及递延资产合计	32 396	12 825	6 829	7 032	2 632	3 078
负债总额	720 390	311 510	248 967	105 003	19 620	35 290
流动负债合计	639 592	279 234	227 172	89 861	9 904	33 421
长期负债合计	65 185	24 992	15 017	15 108	9 642	426
所有者权益合计	473 505	182 509	124 338	142 950	3 880	19 828
#股　本	89 282	8 312	6 564	71 622	459	2 325
三、损益及分配						
商品销售收入(营业收入)	1 672 311	639 171	585 134	302 687	43 028	102 291
商品销售收入净额	1 664 263	634 703	584 015	301 851	41 405	102 289
商品销售成本(营业成本)	1 451 475	558 974	506 661	266 403	31 748	87 689
经营费用(营业费用)	116 164	43 772	43 404	10 607	9 272	9 109
商品销售税金及附加	7 828	2 819	3 029	1 217	63	600
商品销售利润	88 796	29 138	30 822	23 624	323	4 889
代购代销收入	3 208	191	235	2	2 763	17
主营业务利润	92 005	29 329	31 057	23 626	3 086	4 907
其他业务利润	23 055	11 557	7 101	2 983	599	815
管理费用	95 344	40 769	28 951	14 264	6 374	4 986
财务费用	17 754	9 894	4 618	1 966	－247	1 523
营业利润	1 962	－9 777	4 589	10 379	－2 441	－788
补贴收入	6 322	6 086	234	1	－1	2
利润总额	19 358	1 211	6 744	16 741	－4 376	－962
应交所得税	8 181	3 141	2 131	2 902	4	3
四、经济效益						
商品经营费用率(%)	7.0	6.9	7.4	3.5	22.4	8.9
商品销售利润率(%)	5.3	4.6	5.3	7.8	0.8	4.8
资本金利润率(%)	6.4	1.5	6.0	23.0	－29.5	－4.1

12-15 1996 年餐饮业财务状况

单位:万元

指 标	合 计	#国有经济	集体经济	"三资"经济	外商投资	港澳台投资
一、资本金						
资本金合计	68 558	7 674	11 154	44 508	33 490	11 018
#国家资本金	11 841	5 359	1 972	2 776	1 413	1 363
外商资本金	31 075	45		31 026	23 634	7 392
二、年末资产负债						
资产总额	153 206	46 772	29 334	70 105	57 639	12 466
流动资产年末合计	63 020	18 812	13 493	28 333	24 891	3 442
#存 货	6 504	2 484	2 348	1 318	987	331
流动资产年平均余额	17 773	5 486	6 545	4 285	2 462	1 823
固定资产合计	45 906	20 799	11 413	10 657	7 314	3 343
固定资产原值	46 844	15 683	14 299	13 559	9 057	4 502
累计折旧	10 202	2 990	3 537	3 343	2 127	1 216
固定资产净值	36 642	12 693	10 762	10 216	6 930	3 286
固定资产净值平均余额	32 237	11 079	9 958	9 309	6 257	3 052
无形及递延资产合计	22 714	2 761	2 733	16 685	12 495	4 190
负债总额	90 518	30 829	16 927	39 142	30 167	8 975
流动负债合计	62 056	19 201	14 896	24 504	15 670	8 834
长期负债合计	27 365	11 254	1 747	14 331	14 220	111
所有者权益合计	62 688	15 942	12 407	30 963	27 472	3 491
#股 本	21 600	168	346	20 637	20 637	
三、损益及分配						
商品销售收入(营业收入)	118 508	51 782	37 798	25 765	20 893	4 872
商品销售成本(营业成本)	66 274	29 970	22 248	12 139	9 717	2 422
经营费用(营业费用)	33 268	13 012	9 445	9 938	7 580	2 358
商品销售税金及附加	5 824	2 359	1 914	1 407	1 127	280
主营业务利润	11 634	6 028	3 581	1 810	2 013	-203
其他业务利润	862	569	120	178	47	131
管理费用	13 887	5 064	3 010	5 299	3 234	2 065
财务费用	1 969	828	260	713	604	109
营业利润	-3 359	705	432	-4 022	-1 777	-2 245
利润总额	-2 093	1 683	589	-3 883	-1 691	-2 192
应交所得税	962	653	341	63	63	
四、经济效益						
商品经营费用率(%)	28.1	25.1	25.0	38.6	36.3	48.4
资本金利润率(%)	-3.1	21.9	5.3	-8.7	-5.0	-19.9

12－16 批发和零售贸易餐饮业实行体制改革企业情况

(1996 年)

项目	企业数		商品销售收入(营业收入)		增加值	
	个数(个)	占所属行业比重(%)	金额(万元)	占所属行业比重(%)	金额(万元)	占所属行业比重(%)
一、批发贸易业	**2 728**	**35.4**	**3 152 454**	**45.0**	**67 550**	**96.0**
租赁经营	122	1.6	15 520	0.2	1 072	1.5
承包经营	1 362	17.7	890 259	12.7	29 005	41.2
国有民营	166	2.2	358 027	5.1	5 265	7.5
连锁经营	13	0.2	14 539	0.2	452	0.6
租壳卖瓤	8	0.1	1 769		157	0.2
职工自营	120	1.6	22 222	0.3	1 269	1.8
资产经营	267	3.5	559 773	8.0	9 270	13.2
集团经营	249	3.2	585 016	8.4	524	0.7
有限责任公司	374	4.9	578 000	8.3	14 731	20.9
股份合作	47	0.6	127 329	1.8	5 805	8.2
二、零售贸易业	**2 691**	**42.0**	**744 119**	**44.7**	**71 779**	**44.9**
租赁经营	137	2.1	17 296	1.0	1 931	1.2
承包经营	1 404	21.9	242 732	14.6	21 895	13.7
国有民营	230	3.6	44 392	2.7	3 700	2.3
连锁经营	51	0.8	33 767	2.0	3 365	2.1
租壳卖瓤	67	1.0	25 310	1.5	1 805	1.1
职工自营	129	2.0	11 339	0.7	1 498	0.9
资产经营	106	1.7	11 193	0.7	1 404	0.9
集团经营	134	2.1	55 111	3.3	7 591	4.7
有限责任公司	372	5.8	291 345	17.5	27 296	17.1
股份合作	61	1.0	11 634	0.7	1 294	0.8
三、餐饮业	**658**	**56.6**	**53 074**	**44.8**	**11 649**	**41.2**
租赁经营	37	3.2	1 654	1.4	452	1.6
承包经营	350	30.1	19 862	16.8	5 091	18.0
国有民营	138	11.9	4 876	4.1	1 329	4.7
连锁经营	41	3.5	80	0.1	18	0.1
职工自营	34	2.9	1 108	0.9	9	
资产经营	9	0.8	533	0.4	114	0.4
集团经营	12	1.0	10 284	8.7	3 296	11.7
有限责任公司	33	2.8	13 627	11.5	1 083	3.8
股份合作	4	0.3	1 050	0.9	257	0.9

资料来源:天津市首次批发和零售贸易餐饮业普查资料。

12－17　城乡集市贸易主要指标

项　目	合　计		城　市		乡　村	
	1995 年	1996 年	1995 年	1996 年	1995 年	1996 年
一、城乡集贸市场成交额(万元)	**1 660 823**	**2 350 322**	**1 065 091**	**1 609 424**	**595 732**	**740 898**
#粮食类	46 023	90 041	32 477	65 872	13 546	24 169
油脂油料类	62 608	89 788	44 485	63 874	18 123	25 914
棉烟麻类	11 621	20 011	5 098	7 224	6 523	12 787
肉食禽蛋类	265 210	388 896	172 572	281 896	92 638	107 000
水产品类	251 318	318 110	205 478	258 083	45 840	60 027
蔬菜类	203 994	271 079	94 249	142 101	109 745	128 978
干鲜果类	140 730	172 632	97 738	119 460	42 992	53 172
二、城乡集贸市场成交量(吨)						
粮　食	183 512	291 544	116 734	199 361	66 778	92 183
油脂油料	75 525	116 253	51 463	72 233	24 062	44 020
猪　肉	80 189	104 302	41 292	67 109	38 897	37 193
牛　肉	23 308	35 891	17 657	23 451	5 651	12 440
羊　肉	27 097	33 624	21 467	21 758	5 630	11 866
鲜　蛋	26 166	136 669	7 531	105 983	18 635	30 686
家　禽	5 513	13 832	4 806	9 561	707	4 271
水产品	209 742	212 301	164 300	157 736	45 442	54 565
蔬　菜	1 374 289	1 563 053	582 259	696 403	792 030	866 650

资料来源:《天津市工商行政管理局统计资料》。

12－18　商品交易市场分类情况

单位:个

项　目	市场数		城　市		乡　村	
	1995 年	1996 年	1995 年	1996 年	1995 年	1996 年
合　计	**549**	**638**	**337**	**361**	**212**	**277**
一、消费品市场	**520**	**578**	**319**	**316**	**201**	**262**
消费品综合市场	36	369	14	189	22	180
农副产品市场	407	103	249	51	158	52
工业消费品市场	77	72	56	46	21	26
其　他		34		30		4
二、生产资料市场	**29**	**60**	**18**	**45**	**11**	**15**
生产资料综合市场	6	9	2	7	4	2
工业生产资料市场	14	35	13	27	1	8
农业生产资料市场	9	1	3		6	1
其　他		15		11		4

资料来源:《天津市工商行政管理局统计资料》。

十三、对外经济贸易和旅游

FOREIGN ECONOMY TRADE AND TOURISM

1996 年天津海关进出口商品总值	216.85 亿美元
1996 年外贸出口商品总值	40.49 亿美元
1996 年“三资”企业合同数	1 087 个
1996 年实际利用外资	29.84 亿美元
1996 年接待旅游人数	23.33 万人

外贸出口商品总值(亿美元)

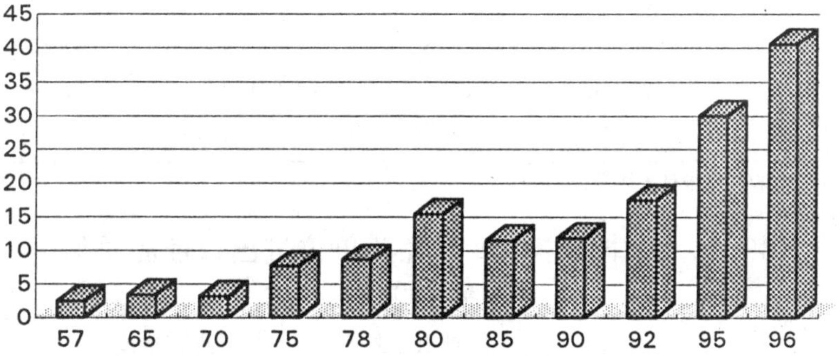

实际利用外资(亿美元)

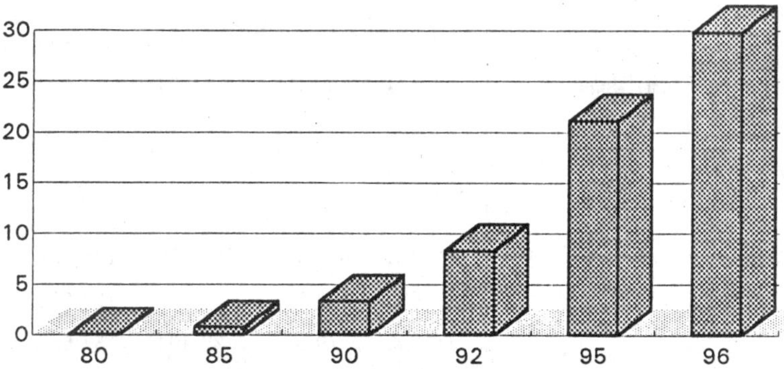

13-1 天津口岸进出口贸易总值

(1981-1996年)

年 份	按美元计算(亿美元)			按人民币计算(亿元)		
	进出口总值	出口总值	进口总值	进出口总值	出口总值	进口总值
1981	57.84	22.74	35.10	96.62	37.99	58.63
1982	58.36	25.80	32.56	108.21	47.84	60.37
1983	60.55	22.92	37.63	119.42	45.19	74.23
1984	69.35	21.77	47.58	154.21	48.06	106.15
1985	96.18	20.07	76.11	283.30	59.13	224.17
1986	96.82	26.37	70.45	338.13	92.11	246.02
1987	89.98	32.85	57.13	334.91	122.27	212.64
1988	102.77	38.78	63.99	388.00	146.00	242.00
1989	106.30	39.70	66.60	399.69	149.27	250.42
1990	85.95	42.53	43.42	410.84	203.29	207.55
1991	91.37	46.48	44.89	486.98	239.59	247.39
1992	104.61	54.60	50.01	572.23	298.68	273.55
1993	125.04	66.03	59.01	726.48	383.63	342.85
1994	161.67	86.81	74.86	1 397.96	750.65	647.31
1995	217.46	127.81	89.65	1 821.23	1 070.41	750.82
1996	216.85	122.89	93.96	1 804.19	1 022.44	781.75

资料来源:13-1至13-5表资料来自天津海关。

13-2 天津口岸中天津经营单位进出口商品总值

(按贸易性质分)

单位:万美元

项 目	进出口总值		进口总值		出口总值	
	1995年	1996年	1995年	1996年	1995年	1996年
合 计	**700 728**	**828 978**	**364 775**	**447 391**	**335 953**	**381 587**
一般贸易	246 393	244 012	85 666	91 253	160 727	152 759
免税外汇商品	991	675	991	675		
寄售、代销贸易	643	118	637	100	6	18
华侨、港澳同胞及外籍华人捐赠品	304	199	304	199		
补偿贸易	263	102	18	2	245	100
对外承包工程货物	9	6		1	9	6
租赁贸易		1		1		
进料加工装配贸易	305 734	371 483	166 470	188 687	139 264	182 796
外商投资企业作为投资进口的设备物品	60 678	103 512	60 678	103 512		
来料加工贸易	60 295	79 917	27 404	37 553	32 891	42 364
易货贸易	772	955	368	483	404	472
国际援赠	1 831	400	1 362	274	469	126
其 他	22 815	27 598	20 877	24 651	1 938	2 946

13－3　天津口岸进出口商品总值

(按系统分)　　单位:万美元

项　　目	进出口总值		进口总值		出口总值	
	1995 年	1996 年	1995 年	1996 年	1995 年	1996 年
总　　计	**2 174 624**	**2 168 480**	**896 556**	**939 602**	**1 278 068**	**1 228 878**
一、天津市经营单位	**700 728**	**828 978**	**364 775**	**447 391**	**335 953**	**381 587**
天津市外贸公司	276 610	230 227	90 133	77 119	186 477	153 108
天津中外合资企业	191 154	262 115	123 885	158 276	67 269	103 839
天津中外合作企业	10 182	11 557	4 979	5 970	5 203	5 588
天津外商独资企业	222 782	325 079	145 778	206 026	77 004	119 052
二、中央、外省市其他经营单位	**1 473 896**	**1 339 502**	**531 781**	**492 211**	**942 115**	**847 291**

13－4　天津口岸中天津经营单位进出口商品总值

(按国别、地区分)　　单位:万美元

国　家 (地区)	进出口总值		进口总值		出口总值	
	1995 年	1996 年	1995 年	1996 年	1995 年	1996 年
合　　计	**700 728**	**828 978**	**364 775**	**447 391**	**335 953**	**381 587**
#日　本	197 108	217 303	119 419	127 143	77 689	90 160
香　港	64 347	67 719	19 755	27 110	44 592	40 609
韩　国	91 825	139 469	60 429	86 674	31 396	52 795
美　国	108 919	125 537	51 720	59 539	57 199	65 998
新加坡	22 242	26 740	15 969	19 114	6 273	7 626
德　国	24 696	32 836	12 387	18 614	12 309	14 222
台　湾	20 635	24 094	16 094	20 588	4 541	3 506
意大利	9 768	15 100	5 000	10 246	4 768	4 854
英　国	14 188	19 976	5 906	9 704	8 282	10 272
澳大利亚	9 723	9 012	3 564	3 918	6 159	5 094
加拿大	10 878	10 153	5 921	6 264	4 957	3 889
法　国	9 989	9 562	2 876	3 881	7 113	5 681
荷　兰	8 398	11 905	2 239	2 736	6 160	9 169
马来西亚	7 244	11 101	4 165	7 386	3 079	3 715
比利时	5 469	6 723	707	2 916	4 762	3 807
埃　及	4 303	3 374	49	29	4 304	3 345
瑞　士	2 059	2 843	1 601	2 387	458	456
泰　国	6 120	4 284	3 110	1 929	3 010	2 355
印　尼	8 764	8 292	4 468	4 247	4 296	4 045
瑞　典	3 428	2 309	1 953	979	1 475	1 330
俄罗斯	7 830	12 769	3 832	8 584	3 998	4 185
西班牙	2 927	3 535	933	1 879	1 994	1 656
巴基斯坦	2 795	2 394	219	155	2 576	2 239
巴　西	8 704	6 238	7 458	4 838	1 245	1 400
伊　朗	2 355	3 275	881	247	1 474	3 028
新西兰	1 856	1 394	1 169	901	687	493

13－5　天津口岸中天津经营单位进出口商品分类

单位:万美元

项　目	进出口总值		进口总值		出口总值	
	1995年	1996年	1995年	1996年	1995年	1996年
合　计	**700 728**	**828 978**	**364 775**	**447 391**	**335 953**	**381 587**
农副产品	63 905	64 031	32 291	30 697	31 613	33 334
矿产品	13 163	18 611	1 195	3 980	11 968	14 631
化工产品	39 780	42 247	14 206	18 517	25 574	23 730
纺织原料及制品	124 161	124 434	33 964	33 222	90 198	91 212
冶金工业产品	55 400	55 598	24 959	29 256	30 441	26 342
机电产品	320 535	423 360	224 194	286 050	96 341	137 300
其他工业产品	83 784	101 227	33 966	45 669	49 818	55 038

13－6　改革开放以来外贸经营单位进出口商品总值

单位:万美元

年　份	进出口总额	进口总额	#中央外汇进口	地方外汇进口	出口总额
1978	98 838	12 364	20	12 344	86 474
1979	138 321	16 240	908	15 332	122 081
1980	182 696	28 474	11 421	17 054	154 222
1981	168 330	14 660	5 774	8 786	153 670
1982	153 729	11 318	5 532	5 612	142 411
1983	157 817	15 083	7 401	7 377	142 734
1984	146 749	23 384	6 466	16 300	123 365
1985	148 603	33 329	6 973	23 106	115 274
1986	166 405	40 911	9 932	30 304	125 494
1987	201 281	49 569	18 048	31 033	151 712
1988	227 846	59 578	18 967	40 204	168 268
1989	221 421	52 817	8 708	44 109	168 604
1990	220 979	42 424	5 415	36 004	178 555
1991	202 013	41 377	2 645	36 557	160 636
1992	237 577	62 343	3 625	56 641	175 234
1993	277 666	83 432	805	82 208	194 234
1994	331 232	91 254	3 582	87 662	239 978
1995	654 556	354 715	5 121	344 860	299 841
1996	829 743	424 830			404 913

13－7　外贸经营单位进出口商品总值

单位:万美元

公　　司	进口总值			出口总值		
	1995 年	1996 年	1996 比 1995 年增长％	1995 年	1996 年	1996 比 1995 年增长％
总　　计	**354 715**	**424 830**	**19.8**	**299 841**	**404 913**	**35.0**
外贸专业公司	24 055	22 834	－5.1	127 539	130 040	2.0
#粮　油	326	454	39.3	2 696	1 445	－46.4
食　品	3 050	3 054	0.1	7 004	8 105	15.7
纺织品	181	348	92.3	12 165	12 201	0.3
丝　绸	980	1 172	19.6	3 203	4 000	24.9
服　装	6 709	6 170	－8.0	19 008	16 704	－12.1
土　产	334	97	－71.0	4 902	6 075	23.9
畜　产	744	1 204	61.8	6 013	7 500	24.7
地　毯	139	565	3.1 倍	3 400	3 205	－5.7
工艺品	77	185	1.4 倍	8 011	4 816	－39.9
轻　工	692	350	－49.4	5 208	3 725	－28.5
文　体	1 133	1 508	33.1	5 122	5 401	5.4
五金矿产	2 713	1 711	－36.9	7 797	10 082	29.3
化　工	1 124	1 298	15.5	8 254	7 355	－10.9
机　械	3 048	1 175	－61.5	8 238	10 012	21.5
设　备	826	966	16.9	10 079	9 046	－10.2
医药保健	648	675	4.2	3 363	3 548	5.5
地方工贸公司	26 188	24 521	－6.4	50 393	45 372	－10.0
客商投资企业	275 940	370 272	34.2	100 175	215 196	114.8
其他单位	28 532	7 203	－74.8	21 734	14 305	－34.2

13－8　外贸经营单位分国别和地区进出口总值

单位:万美元

国　家(地区)	出口总值			进口总值		
	1995 年	1996 年	1996 比 1995 年增长％	1995 年	1996 年	1996 比 1995 年增长％
总　　计	**299 841**	**404 913**	**35.0**	**354 715**	**424 830**	**19.8**
亚　洲	175 454	272 198	55.1	251 623	265 777	5.6
#香　港	54 759	112 068	1.0 倍	37 225	37 372	0.4
澳　门	590	163	－72.4	10	14	40.0
朝　鲜	200	552	1.8 倍	47	182	2.9 倍
韩　国	26 376	26 095	－1.1	56 213	75 134	33.7
日　本	54 790	88 352	61.3	111 849	102 162	－8.7
菲律宾	1 295	1 404	8.4	244	613	1.5 倍
缅　甸	116	138	19.0		173	
泰　国	3 199	2 343	－26.8	2 724	1 530	－43.8
马来西亚	2 636	3 311	25.6	4 120	8 542	1.1 倍
新加坡	7 605	9 662	27.0	15 721	18 157	15.5
巴基斯坦	3 107	3 516	13.2	241	150	－37.8
伊　朗	1 324			880	132	－85.0
叙利亚	383	546	42.6			
黎巴嫩	361	561	55.4			
约　旦	410	317	－22.7			
也　门	318	332	4.4			
伊拉克						
沙　特	922	1 042	13.0	222	258	16.2
科威特	245	804	2.3 倍			
巴　林	20	24	20.0	4		

13-8 续表

国家（地区）	出口总值			进口总值		
	1995年	1996年	1996比1995年增长%	1995年	1996年	1996比1995年增长%
非　洲	7 482	8 388	12.1	1 037	3 940	2.8倍
#埃　及	3 509	3 848	9.7		2	
苏　丹	97	29	-70.1		238	
利比亚	44	280	5.4倍			
肯尼亚	667	278	-58.3		58	
坦桑尼亚	473	194	-59.0		145	
欧　洲	43 084	45 516	5.6	41 161	50 165	21.9
#独联体	2 759			2 020		
波　兰	496	821	65.5	4	2	-50.0
匈牙利	1 211	1 038	-14.3	27	8	-70.4
捷　克	94	220	1.3倍	738	621	-15.9
保加利亚	41	86	1.1倍		5	
阿尔巴尼亚	12	16	33.3		3	
罗马尼亚	334	732	1.2倍	1	9	8倍
德　国	9 319	8 577	-8.0	12 571	12 870	2.4
南斯拉夫	84	35	-58.3			
法　国	2 956	3 175	7.4	3 418	4 447	30.1
意大利	4 357	4 057	-6.9	4 536	8 064	77.8
荷　兰	3 646	4 744	30.1	2 030	2 323	14.4
比利时	2 228	1 601	-28.1	509	2 223	3.4倍
英　国	9 187	8 530	-7.2	5 681	10 207	79.7
爱尔兰	138	114	-17.4	2	46	22倍
丹　麦	779	810	4.0	1 443	676	-53.2
芬　兰	784	1 019	30.0	154	900	4.8倍
瑞　典	1 206	1 627	34.9	844	578	-31.5
挪　威	233	209	-10.3	34	13	-61.8
瑞　士	832	898	7.9	1 795	3 287	83.1
奥地利	232	149	-35.8	4 176	301	-92.8
西班牙	1 494	1 637	9.6	822	1 265	53.9
拉丁美洲及北美洲	62 769	68 964	9.9	56 945	67 800	19.1
#墨西哥	49	152	2.1倍	105	659	5.3倍
古　巴	66	877	12.3倍		3	
智　利	663	1 781	1.7倍	5	269	52.8倍
加拿大	4 733	4 329	-8.5	1 909	4 059	1.1倍
美　国	53 263	59 068	10.9	45 574	56 182	23.3
大洋洲及太平洋地区	5 493	4 845	-11.8	3 895	4 762	22.3
#澳大利亚	4 899	4 180	-14.7	2 930	3 604	23.0
新西兰	454	461	1.5	965	1 159	20.1
其　他	5 559	5 002	-10.0	54	32 386	598.7倍

资料来源：天津市对外经济贸易委员会。

13－9 1996年外贸经营单位大宗商品出口总值

单位:万美元

商品名称	金 额	商品名称	金 额	商品名称	金 额
电子元器件	82 017	化纤布	4 959	录摄相机散件	1 650
服 装	50 610	医药原料	4 669	染料中间体	1 603
无线电通讯设备	21 925	钢 材	4 570	工农具	1 560
有线电通讯设备	19 662	耐火材料	4 321	电工设备	1 498
#电 话	18 192	#矾 土	1 144	农 药	1 405
乐 器	10 085	轻重烧镁	1 140	铁合金	1 383
#电子乐器	9 498	耐火土	845	录像机	1 346
其他汽车、电车		动力机械	4 184	体育用品	1 276
摩托车零件	8 351	水产品	4 020	日用皮制品	1 292
船 舶	7 723	饲 料	3 783	#劳保手套	548
#集装箱	5 552	电视机及散件	3 426	焦 炭	1 200
化工原料	7 279	家 具	3 149	花生仁果	1 200
纺织原料	6 873	肠 衣	2 871	罐 头	1 145
棉 布	6 588	化纤制品	2 783	芸 豆	1 114
食用植物油	5 971	旅游制品	2 765	阀 门	1 111
录音机	5 853	铸铁制品	2 677	速冻食品	1 104
金属制品	5 796	木 材	2 553	苇帘制品	1 079
#钉 丝	1 898	各种染料	2 449	塑 料	1 055
电焊条	1 504	计算机	2 259	水泥设备	1 033
水管零件	617	金属器皿	2 062	建筑材料	1 005
棉制品	5 598	#不锈钢餐具	1 901	#水 泥	540
地 毯	5 413	蔬 菜	2 004	干菜及制品	1 001
各种鞋	5 143	呢 绒	1 903		
汽车零件	5 139	医疗器械	1 650		

13－10 天津口岸进出口商品检验情况

项 目	单 位	1995年	1996年
一、进口商品检验			
批 数	批	2 791	4 277
金 额	万美元	178 016	226 353
#经检验发现不合格商品			
批 数	批	283	368
金 额	万美元	456	1 667
二、出口商品检验			
批 数	批	35 360	38 413
金 额	万美元	229 028	248 917
#经检验发现不合格商品			
批 数	批	357	171
金 额	万美元	2 548	1 074

13－11 利用外资情况

项目	单位	1979－1996年累计	1995年	1996年
一、引进外资新签协议合同数	个	**11 157**	**1 486**	**1 459**
对外借款	个	660	97	372
客商直接投资	个	10 497	1 389	1 087
合资企业	个	4 580	476	366
合作企业	个	318	63	45
独资企业	个	5 599	850	676
二、协议(合同)外资金额	万美元	**1 880 098**	**420 653**	**512 831**
对外借款	万美元	317 139	35 600	120 400
客商直接投资	万美元	1 562 959	385 053	392 431
合资企业	万美元	804 719	184 561	199 083
合作企业	万美元	74 143	16 254	34 534
独资企业	万美元	684 097	184 238	158 814
三、实际利用外资额	万美元	**1 088 662**	**211 010**	**298 358**
对外借款	万美元	506 661	58 924	97 771
客商直接投资	万美元	575 946	152 064	200 587
合资企业	万美元	342 822	86 755	116 586
合作企业	万美元	19 877	7 706	5 534
独资企业	万美元	213 247	57 603	78 467
客商其他投资	万美元	6 055	22	

13－12 实际利用外资情况

单位：万美元

项目	1979－1996年累计	1991－1996年累计	1995年	1996年	1996比1995年增长%
总计	**1 088 662**	**911 778**	**211 010**	**298 358**	**41.4**
1.借用国外资金	**506 661**	**370 425**	**58 924**	**97 771**	**65.9**
外国政府贷款	60 650	55 178	6 612	10 095	52.7
国际金融组织贷款	47 795	32 186	11 210	1 898	－83.1
出口信贷	57 738	54 441	11 151	3 480	－68.8
外国银行商业贷款	294 742	196 974	29 951	71 272	140.0
对外发行债券、股票	45 736	31 646		11 026	
2.客商直接投资	**575 946**	**540 796**	**152 064**	**200 587**	**31.9**
合资企业	342 822	312 797	86 755	116 586	34.4
合作企业	19 877	18 974	7 706	5 534	－28.2
独资企业	213 247	209 025	57 603	78 467	36.2
3.客商其他投资	**6 055**	**557**	**22**		
国际租赁	1 777	240			
补偿贸易中客商作价设备	4 278	317	22		

13－13 1996年借用国外资金情况

单位:万美元

项目	上年结转资金	本年新增借款	偿还本金	外汇汇率差额	期末借款余额	偿还利息
国外贷款合计	**235 990**	**97 771**	**90 205**	**－1 006**	**242 550**	**8 912**
1.按债务期限分						
中长期	229 503	34 606	25 689	－1 006	237 414	8 699
短 期	6 487	63 165	64 516		5 136	213
2.按借款方式分						
外国政府贷款	46 340	10 095	777	－135	55 523	760
国际金融组织贷款	36 147	1 898	2 509		35 536	1 067
出口信贷	53 111	3 480	4 218	－871	51 502	3 385
外国银行商业贷款	65 682	71 272	76 666		60 288	1 908
对外发行债券、股票	34 710	11 026	6 035		39 701	1 792

13－14 客商投资企业协议和实际利用外资情况

项目	签定协议(合同)数(个)		协议总投资(万美元)		#协议外资额(万美元)		实际利用外资金额(万美元)	
	1996年	至1996年底累计	1996年	至1996年底累计	1996年	至1996年底累计	1996年	至1996年底累计
总 计	**1 087**	**10 497**	**501 002**	**2 134 569**	**392 431**	**1 562 959**	**200 587**	**575 946**
一、按投资方式分								
合资企业	366	4 580	297 636	1 343 011	199 083	804 719	116 586	342 822
合作企业	45	318	44 552	107 461	34 534	74 143	5 534	19 877
独资企业	676	5 599	158 814	684 097	158 814	684 097	78 467	213 247
二、按行业分								
农 业	4	41	64	7 935	54	3 905	240	1 966
工业及建筑业	596	6 233	334 569	1 283 099	264 098	928 217	130 936	366 208
交通运输	1	77	1 783	14 435	1 632	9 313	2 397	5 682
商业饮食物资供应业	420	3 377	51 668	303 928	44 557	228 976	21 824	58 989
房地产业公共事业服务业	32	436	95 909	456 105	72 488	344 172	33 918	109 929
其他行业	34	333	17 009	69 067	9 602	48 376	11 272	33 172
三、按国别(地区)分								
#香 港	265	4 313	163 278	800 149	119 857	546 133	57 901	213 625
台 湾	111	1 132	7 783	102 320	6 756	73 615	10 454	26 112
韩 国	136	717	33 571	126 503	29 253	101 222	14 636	30 711
日 本	116	1 004	73 931	208 574	51 262	145 896	31 478	72 846
美 国	197	1 502	54 236	313 230	49 207	253 013	23 305	65 968
新加坡	43	293	10 271	50 551	7 231	35 416	11 107	29 984
英 国	16	90	6 954	35 745	5 436	23 976	15 138	37 381
德 国	13	85	2 589	26 897	2 088	16 115	12 318	19 533
澳 门	3	111	1 562	16 494	1 562	9 415	609	2 908

13-15 1996年客商投资企业签约和投资情况

（按主管系统分）

单 位	个数（个）	协议总投资（万美元）	#协议外资额	单 位	个数（个）	协议总投资（万美元）	#协议外资额
总 计	**1 087**	**501 002**	**392 431**				
开发区	187	104 894	83 012	二轻局	7	7 293	5 295
保税区	384	45 974	41 051	机电工业总公司	2	339	213
新技术产业园区	55	880	6 144	电子仪表总公司	3	530	413
市内各系统	516	186 961	138 819	冶金工业总公司	5	10 562	5 766
六个中心区	97	8 067	6 618	汽车工业集团有限公司	8	35 680	19 325
和平区	19	3 240	3 025	服装联合公司	1	76	47
南开区	25	1 257	922	计委系统	2	740	493
河东区	11	494	433	物资集团	2	740	493
河西区	17	1 669	1 292	建委系统	15	20 514	12 400
河北区	14	1 081	684	建工集团总公司	2	375	292
红桥区	11	326	262	市政工程局	5	11 962	6 603
农委系统	283	71 135	62 820	房管局	1	482	241
其他四个区	165	45 457	41 866	规划局	1	10	5
东丽区	51	2 798	2 225	建材集团	3	7 180	4 898
西青区	35	17 911	16 296	公用局	1	361	217
津南区	36	18 154	17 625	园林局	1	130	130
北辰区	43	6 594	5 720	其 他	1	14	14
市辖县	81	11 548	8 003	交委系统	4	6 488	5 993
蓟 县	7	982	714	港务局	3	6 460	5 970
静 海	20	3 720	2 201	邮电局	1	28	23
武 清	24	3 357	2 635	商委系统	2	883	698
宝 坻	9	910	601	天津食品工贸集团总公司	1	483	338
宁 河	21	2 579	1 852	供销社	1	400	360
滨海三个区	32	11 006	10 441	外经贸委系统	5	1 979	954
塘沽区	16	3 578	3 305	外经贸委	2	160	80
汉沽区	2	292	148	旅游局	2	1 771	853
大港区	14	7 136	6 988	外贸总公司	1	48	21
农场局	4	127	52	其他归属	18	8 866	8 152
其他	1	2 997	2 457	驻津单位	2	1 298	1 258
经委系统	32	57 603	33 230	机关局	4	235	149
纺织工业总公司	2	164	81	体 委	1	13	10
一轻总公司	4	2 959	2 090	其 他	11	7 320	6 735

注：1.协议总投资、协议外资额按主管系统分不包括增资部分。2.新技术产业园区与市内各系统数有交叉。

13－16　1996年客商投资企业生产经营情况

单位:万元

项　　目	企业数(个)	全部从业人员数(人)	全部从业人员劳动报酬	销售(营业)收入	销售(营业)成本	应交税金	利润总额
合　　计	**3 377**	**323 210**	**309 182**	**7 358 472**	**5 561 156**	**258 499**	**439 337**
一、按投资方式分							
中外合资	859	116 990	128 312	2 556 416	1 999 841	127 179	103 412
中外合作	70	6 437	4 972	48 387	37 245	1 080	－4 089
外商独资	743	70 983	71 785	2 727 585	1 849 706	66 207	302 757
港澳台合资	1 051	94 996	71 071	1 355 891	1 136 083	35 332	3 875
港澳台合作	53	5 550	4 701	73 574	60 279	5 880	－1 179
港澳台独资	601	28 254	28 340	596 620	478 004	22 821	34 561
二、按国民经济行业分							
农、林、牧、渔业	14	359	176	2 586	2 064	8	－375
采掘业	1	55	89	7 918	8 157		－611
制造业	2 450	291 849	273 174	6 845 362	5 223 282	244 778	466 708
＃食品加工业	93	8 246	7 263	498 930	462 835	－2 062	－14 256
食品制造业	133	17 711	19 245	410 418	296 847	22 725	48 675
饮料制造业	68	6 343	6 109	153 297	108 252	13 992	13 559
纺织业	126	11 279	8 120	176 058	146 301	1 569	6 722
服装及其他纤维品制造业	287	36 555	19 496	228 534	194 595	3 419	6 113
家具制造业	36	5 144	3 418	56 957	46 626	1 184	－4 910
石油加工及炼焦业	6	191	163	4 534	3 774	－22	－212
化学原料及制品制造业	176	13 798	13 855	308 375	238 237	16 343	7 230
医药制造业	52	8 124	11 360	188 777	83 036	18 592	54 576
塑料制品业	117	7 172	5 529	89 258	68 577	3 101	3 987
非金属矿物制品业	95	8 232	7 859	210 005	185 169	7 810	－796
黑色金属冶炼及压延	23	2 027	1 528	52 277	46 976	260	1 042
普通机械制造业	72	13 102	18 259	303 359	254 920	21 957	22 910
交通运输设备制造业	145	28 597	34 404	568 132	472 760	34 471	20 844
电气机械及器材制造业	120	17 531	15 420	264 683	205 946	10 206	723
电子及通信设备制造业	181	37 616	50 744	2 490 830	1 685 932	70 628	290 777
建筑业	115	3 927	4 120	44 391	35 668	678	－1 456
地质勘查业、水利管理业	2	68	54	81	85	4	－61
交通运输、仓储及邮电通信业	122	4 115	5 425	56 154	34 339	2 104	4 840
＃公路运输业	15	845	1 055	10 104	5 544	331	2 051
邮电通信业	3	50	41	342	259	8	－40
批发和零售贸易、餐饮业	367	9 613	8 235	243 518	200 406	3 059	－11 546
＃食品饮料烟草批发业	249	4 231	4 040	182 331	162 562	1 378	－5 574
餐饮业	55	3 438	2 780	25 282	11 733	1 337	－3 800
金融、保险业	1	8	38	349		2	－777
＃金融业	1	8	38	349		2	－777
房地产业	128	2 782	3 378	34 720	16 244	2 511	－13 672
＃房地产开发与经营业	118	2 489	3 085	33 427	14 049	2 460	－12 119
社会服务业	154	10 024	14 175	119 682	37 538	5 297	－3 354
＃旅馆业	19	5 307	7 275	69 972	10 604	3 478	1 885
信息咨询服务业	25	646	460	3 133	1 328	115	－357

13－16续表

单位:万元

项　　目	企业数(个)	全部从业人员数(人)	全部从业人员劳动报酬	销售(营业)收入	销售(营业)成本	应交税金	利润总额
卫生、体育和社会福利业	1	12	20				
教育、文化艺术及广播电影业	2	4	13	29	1	2	－53
#文化艺术业	2	4	13	29	1	2	－53
科学研究和综合技术服务业	9	238	133	1 478	1 390	13	－145
其他行业	11	156	155	2 206	1 984	44	－161
三、按坐落地点分							
市辖区	3 029	278 656	284 453	6 952 998	5 212 851	251 196	432 800
五　县	348	44 554	24 729	405 475	348 305	7 304	6 537
四、按主管系统分							
#外经贸委	19	1 660	1 659	29 551	26 275	181	－1 596
一轻总公司	73	11 460	14 512	329 635	248 905	24 043	1 606
二轻总公司	75	15 420	8 493	123 333	99 853	3 721	－3 686
电子仪表工业总公司	58	16 892	21 890	642 156	574 424	8 859	3 609
纺织工业总公司	29	3 408	2 661	48 904	41 695	314	2 911
化学工业总公司	36	6 658	5 806	99 936	81 537	3 439	570
机关行政管理局	8	1 474	2 060	22 112	4 186	1 418	3 911
机电工业总公司	53	16 224	23 700	468 263	387 215	41 554	38 176
建筑材料集团总公司	14	2 241	2 804	23 516	20 914	227	－2 177
建筑工程集团总公司	35	1 642	1 838	31 717	10 874	1 156	2 443
旅游局	10	1 743	3 061	29 280	7 021	1 344	－999
水产局	4	270	237	17 289	10 531	－11	3 870
物资集团总公司	9	2 271	2 685	70 567	62 812	5 932	5 258
医药总公司	18	7 901	11 536	210 736	101 713	18 909	49 855
邮电管理局	15	638	1 324	15 881	11 936	394	－2 022
和 平 区	127	3 873	3 637	30 309	19 887	1 148	－3 626
河 西 区	78	3 458	3 028	35 578	24 668	1 566	74
南 开 区	140	6 057	4 034	78 003	53 763	3 937	8 508
塘 沽 区	119	4 940	3 701	47 133	35 001	919	－6 004
汉 沽 区	23	1 279	867	16 974	14 612	226	－583
东 丽 区	198	19 352	11 978	222 715	202 524	2 436	－4 344
西 青 区	137	11 435	7 621	174 327	131 927	3 382	8 674
津 南 区	67	8 345	4 100	52 354	45 047	804	341
北 辰 区	151	8 955	4 296	92 392	83 735	1 145	1 721
宁 河 县	35	3 675	1 540	25 826	21 802	848	－47
武 清 县	126	14 591	8 828	127 721	108 129	2 545	1 114
静 海 县	82	10 828	6 145	170 588	148 123	1 995	6 652
宝 坻 县	69	11 166	6 161	61 018	52 728	1 036	－631
蓟　　县	30	3 948	1 881	17 430	14 594	703	16
汽车工业公司	17	16 636	19 586	240 868	199 814	14 563	4 562
海运公司	12	811	855	10 214	8 304	302	－638
服装联合总公司	23	4 079	2 530	26 074	21 987	2 118	1 086
农工商总公司	21	1 072	835	48 003	26 342	6 895	14 063
飞鸽自行车集团公司	29	1 233	952	22 170	20 100	608	－774

13－17　1996年新批准重点客商投资企业名单

（协议外资额在1000万美元以上）

企业名称	投资方式	投资国别（地　区）	经营范围	协议外资额（万美元）
天津三星电管有限公司	合资企业	香　　港	电气机械器材制造	30 640
天津丰田汽车发动机有限公司	合资企业	日　　本	交通运输设备制造	13 343
天津松下电子部品有限公司	合资企业	日　　本	电子通信设备制造	6 438
天津华新津威冷轧板材有限公司	合资企业	英属维尔京	金属制品业	5 392
罗纳普朗克渤海(天津)蛋氨酸有限公司	合资企业	法　　国	化学工业	4 337
天津百事食品有限公司	独资企业	美　　国	食品制造业	3 005
天津维信(集团)有限公司	独资企业	香　　港	商业	3 000
大宇空调(天津)有限公司	独资企业	南 朝 鲜	其他工业	3 000
埃佩克(天津)包装材料设备有限	独资企业	澳大利亚	商业	2 999
天津新世界房地产开发有限公司	合作企业	英属维尔京	房地产管理业	2 998
天津宝洁工业有限公司	独资企业	香　　港	化学工业	2 995
天津宝洁工业纸制品有限公司	独资企业	香　　港	造纸及纸制品业	2 995
哈沃斯(天津)家具有限公司	独资企业	美　　国	家具制造业	2 990
天津顶好油脂有限公司	独资企业	凯曼群岛	食品制造业	2 980
埃索(天津)有限公司	独资企业	美　　国	石油加工业	2 980
北方空气产品(天津)有限公司	独资企业	美　　国	其他行业	2 950
天津华新津华实业有限公司	独资企业	英属维尔京	金属制品业	2 950
天津香岛旅游村开发有限公司	合作企业	英属维尔京	其他行业	2 920
天津宝洁工业洗涤剂有限公司	独资企业	香　　港	化学工业	2 910
家福(天津)国际贸易有限公司	独资企业	荷　　兰	商业	2 900
液化空气(天津)有限公司	独资企业	法　　国	其他工业	2 900
壳牌天津沥青有限公司	独资企业	荷　　兰	化学工业	2 890
奥科亚制瓶(天津)有限公司	合资企业	美　　国	化学工业	2 803
天津华新天友实业有限公司	独资企业	英属维尔京	金属制品业	2 800
天津港保税区宜荣国际货物配送	独资企业	香　　港	商业	2 800
天津华新津广实业有限公司	独资企业	英属维尔京	金属制品业	2 700
天津丰津汽车传动部件有限公司	合资企业	日　　本	其他工业	2 695
天津伊都锦商厦有限公司	合资企业	日　　本	其他行业	2 660
天津佳辰造纸有限公司	合资企业	印　　尼	造纸及纸制品业	2 649
天津阳光塑料有限公司	合资企业	日　　本	塑料制品业	2 542
欧加华(天津)国际贸易有限公司	独资企业	荷　　兰	商业	2 500
菲仕兰(天津)乳制品有限公司	合资企业	荷　　兰	食品制造业	2 460
新宝企业(天津)有限公司	合资企业	英属维尔京	电气机械器材制造	2 398
天津三星电子显示器有限公司	合资企业	南 朝 鲜	电子通信设备制造	2 384
天津华新津兴实业有限公司	独资企业	英属维尔京	金属制品业	2 300
天津日板安全玻璃有限公司	合资企业	日　　本	其他工业	2 243

13－17 续表

企业名称	投资方式	投资国别（地　区）	经营范围	协议外资额（万美元）
天津兴明泰石膏制品有限公司	合资企业	新加坡	化学工业	2 120
天津顶津食品有限公司	独资企业	英　国	食品制造业	2 000
天津东都石油化工有限公司	独资企业	日　本	化学工业	2 000
劲量电池(天津)有限公司	独资企业	美　国	其他工业	2 000
天津华新津泰标准件有限公司	独资企业	英属维尔京	金属制品业	2 000
攀缘(天津)高科国际有限公司	合资企业	美　国	商业	1 980
天津华新津友铜熔炼有限公司	合资企业	英属维尔京	金属制品业	1 788
天津华新津友电解铜有限公司	合资企业	英属维尔京	化学工业	1 776
天津快速(集团)交通发展有限公司	合资企业	新加坡	土木工程建筑业	1 649
天津天旭高速公路有限公司	合作企业	英属维尔京	其他行业	1 641
天津天永高速公路有限公司	合作企业	英属维尔京	公用事业	1 637
海马(天津)发展有限公司	独资企业	泰　国	食品制造业	1 600
天津天富高速公路有限公司	合作企业	英属维尔京	公用事业	1 571
天津新伟祥工业有限公司	独资企业	香　港	金属制品业	1 500
天津港保税区腾达(集团)有限公司	独资企业	澳大利亚	商业	1 500
天津港保税区宜荣实业有限公司	独资企业	香　港	化学工业	1 500
陶氏房地产(天津)开发有限公司	独资企业	澳　门	房地产管理业	1 500
天津天显高速公路有限公司	合作企业	英属维尔京	公用事业	1 465
天津乐金塑料制品有限公司	合资企业	南朝鲜	塑料制品业	1 403
天津九河国际村有限公司	合资企业	日　本	房地产管理业	1 350
天津乐金精密化工有限公司	合资企业	南朝鲜	化学工业	1 350
天津乐山地毯有限公司	合资企业	新加坡	纺织工业	1 344
天津泰达国际酒店集团有限公司	合资企业	新加坡	房地产管理业	1 325
天津国际康复中心有限公司	合资企业	英属维尔京	卫生事业	1 265
东海橡塑(天津)有限公司	合资企业	日　本	橡胶制品业	1 260
大宇微波炉(天津)有限公司	独资企业	南朝鲜	其他工业	1 250
精密不锈钢工程(天津)有限公司	独资企业	日　本	商业	1 250
天津百氏可乐饮料有限公司	合资企业	美　国	饮料制造业	1 200
天津顶峰淀粉开发有限公司	独资企业	英　国	食品制造业	1 200
天津华狮汽车仪表有限公司	合资企业	马来西亚	仪器仪表计量器具	1 089
天津兴源包装机械有限公司	合资企业	香　港	机械工业	1 083
天津亚洲钢管有限公司	合资企业	英属维尔京	金属制品业	1 080
艾默生电气(天津)有限公司	独资企业	美　国	电气机械器材制造	1 000
天津金斯利化工有限公司	合资企业	美　国	化学工业	1 000

13－18　接待国际旅游人数和居住天数

（1990－1996年）

单位:人次;天

项　目	1990年	1991年	1992年	1993年	1994年	1995年	1996年
一、接待人数(含不过夜)	**65 404**	**98 538**	**109 292**	**135 014**	**165 891**	**200 629**	**233 258**
接待人数(过夜)	56 013	62 715	87 513	109 358	128 105	130 769	121 137
1.外国人	35 542	38 399	55 274	73 038	95 469	97 695	91 886
#日　本	17 954	18 369	22 468	25 461	40 641	33 569	32 125
菲律宾	184	332	518	609	460	737	507
新加坡	1 195	1 253	1 822	2 665	6 085	4 260	4 642
泰　国	423	930	814	715	1 409	893	674
印　尼	116	195	352	576	714	822	850
美　国	2 854	3 245	4 775	5 540	17 080	8 922	8 512
加拿大	614	605	1 007	1 361	1 813	1 727	1 733
英　国	1 213	1 406	1 357	1 957	2 520	3 376	2 876
法　国	245	694	1 423	1 302	1 254	1 562	1 568
德　国	1 129	1 090	1 591	1 989	7 221	3 022	2 733
意大利	671	841	1 100	1 136	1 127	1 007	1 164
独联体	814	667	1 302	3 376	2 286	1 996	1 076
澳大利亚	954	793	872	1 137	1 624	2 428	1 556
2.华　侨	577	282	793	298	455	966	1 305
3.港澳台同胞	19 894	24 034	31 446	36 022	32 181	32 108	27 946
二、平均每人居住天数	**5.0**	**4.9**	**5.0**	**5.3**	**5.3**	**6.1**	**6.7**

13－19　国际旅游外汇收入和构成情况

单位:万美元

项　目	1995年	1996年	项　目	1995年	1996年
合　计	**13 275**	**15 191**			
长途交通	2 523	6 208	住　宿	5 394	2 392
飞　机	2 347	5 024	餐　饮	1 828	1 222
火　车	114	350	娱　乐	157	363
汽　车	32	308	购　物	1 578	2 375
海　运	30	526	邮电通讯	380	590
其　他			市内交通	215	365
游　览	587	277	其　他	613	1 399

13－20 天津接待国内旅游情况

(1996年)

项　　目	人数 (万人)	消费额 (亿元)
总　　计	**2 453**	**199.65**
1.接待北京一日游	267	8.88
2.宾馆、饭店接待国内过夜游客	1 982	182.76
3.居民家庭接待过夜游客	204	8.01

资料来源:13－20至13－22表取自天津首次国内旅游抽样调查结果。

13－21 天津市居民外出旅游情况

(1996年)

项　　目	人数 (万人)	消费额 (亿元)
总　　计	**336.67**	**39.99**
一、按出游方式分		
随旅行团出游	16.73	0.79
非游行团出游	319.94	39.20
二、按出游目的地分		
出游本市	88.01	5.15
出游外埠	245.87	30.37
出　国	2.79	4.47

13－22 天津接待国内游客和天津居民外出旅游消费额构成

(1996年)

单位:亿元

项　　目	天津接待国内游客				天津居民外出旅游			
	合　计	一日游	宾馆接待	居民家庭接待	合　计	出游本市	出游外埠	出　国
合　　计	**199.65**	**8.88**	**182.76**	**8.01**	**39.99**	**5.15**	**30.37**	**4.47**
#餐饮费	48.38	2.05	45.10	1.23	5.17	1.00	3.47	0.70
住宿费	30.01		29.63	0.38	4.59	0.16	4.36	0.07
游览费	4.64	0.23	4.24	0.17	0.84	0.03	0.81	
购物费	40.89	4.93	33.80	2.16	6.01	1.67	3.92	0.42
娱乐费	8.19	0.41	7.60	0.18	0.94	0.07	0.66	0.21
交通费	33.54	0.90	31.18	1.46	10.32	0.18	7.49	2.65

13-23 天津市因公出国人员

(1992-1996年)

单位:人次

年份	总计	友好访问	经济贸易	科学技术	文化体育	培训留学	劳务及其他	国际会议
1992	10 741	485	5 838	804	445	1 866	1 303	
1993	16 479	343	8 896	2 144	955	2 573	1 568	
1994	14 685	388	7 744	402	650	3 130	2 371	
1995	15 494	535	7 881	187	857	2 904	2 331	799
1996	16 432	594	8 067	17	680	3 123	2 560	1 391

13-24 天津市涉外宾馆一览表

宾馆名称	星级	客房数	床位数	地址
喜来登大酒店	五星	281	295	河西区紫金山路
凯悦饭店	四星	440	588	和平区解放北路219号
水晶宫饭店	四星	292	584	河西区友谊路28号
利顺德大饭店	四星	208	400	和平区台儿庄路33号
津利华大酒店	四星	270	489	河西区友谊路32号
友谊宾馆	三星	287	574	和平区南京路94号
北方宾馆	三星	177	354	塘沽区东沽闸北路1号
胜利宾馆	三星	273	439	塘沽区津塘公路11号
乐园宾馆	三星	229	453	河西区乐园路1号
天津宾馆	三星	544	1 157	河西区宾水道1号
金帆大厦	三星	70	120	开发区第一大街49号
先达大酒店	三星	180	360	河西区环湖中路
龙凤酒店	三星	146	292	河东区光华路甲1号
体育宾馆	三星	106	200	河西区宾水道延长线
皇宫饭店	三星	76	121	和平区解放北路117号
凯撒皇宫酒店	三星	84	158	河西区气象台路4号
天华宾馆	三星	38	38	塘沽区津港公路南
富利华大酒店	二星	62	124	河东区七纬路104号
金珠大酒店	二星	45	95	河西区尖山路2-3号
惠中饭店	二星	75	153	和平区华中路2号
华城宾馆	二星	120	265	南开区红旗路南路253号
金都宾馆	二星	58	118	南开区红旗路169号
津华饭店	二星	97	177	和平区解放北路158号
新港国际海员俱乐部	二星	95	185	塘沽区新港六米
科技大厦	二星	72	144	河西区友谊路25号
王朝大酒店	二星	81	162	河北区建国道142号
钢管宾馆	二星	51	117	河西区尖山路2号
津海大酒店	二星	100	230	静海县大邱庄镇
津东饭店	二星	147	346	河东区六纬路99号
雍阳宾馆	二星	130	360	武清县杨村镇
渤海大楼饭店	二星	69	145	和平区和平路277号
天馨宾馆	二星	144	288	河东区六纬路122号
中冀宾馆	二星	150	300	河西区围堤道1号路
会宾园饭店	一星	188	350	南开区水上公园路
红楼影都	一星	47	98	南开区津淄公路28号
国际大厦		116	116	和平区南京路75号
三泽新住宅有限公司		15	35	南开区水上公园路
宾侨新村有限公司		30	120	南开区津淄公路46号
天北别墅		70	60	南开区津淄公路46号
温泉宾馆		190	380	河西区小围堤道
渤海宾馆		245	667	塘沽区新北公路21号
夏日酒店		78	144	塘沽区滨海游乐城内
立达宾馆		59	118	南开区南门外大街406号
裕城大酒店		43	96	和平区岳阳道35号
金禧大酒店		313	323	南开区南开三马路
富蓝特大酒店		58	114	和平区新华路231号
津门饭店		120	281	河东区津塘公路184号

13－25　对外承包工程和劳务合作

（1990－1996年）

项　　目	单　位	1990年	1991年	1992年	1993年	1994年	1995年	1996年
签订合同份数	个	198	218	318	134	521	1 019	1 320
＃对外承包工程	个	2	10	7	47	10	8	9
劳务合作	个	196	208	311	87	500	990	1 285
签订合同金额	万美元	5 739	11 515	11 310	19 026	9 426	11 917	15 824
＃对外承包工程	万美元	2 050	4 203	5 810	937	2 376	6 717	7 956
劳务合作	万美元	3 689	7 312	5 500	18 089	6 929	5 079	7 439
实际营业额	万美元	2 801	3 885	5 600	10 249	6 029	8 128	8 809
＃对外承包工程	万美元	607	637	2 185	3 284	1 749	1 976	1 978
劳务合作	万美元	2 194	3 248	3 415	6 965	4 065	6 025	6 538
年末在外劳动人数	人	3 176	4 116	5 284	6 115	7 380	9 202	10 033
＃对外承包工程	人	230	281	826	819	771	527	515
劳务合作	人	2 946	3 835	4 458	5 296	6 609	8 675	9 518

13－26　1996年对外承包工程和劳务合作

（分国别、地区）

国别地区	合同份数（份）	合同额（万美元）	营业额（万美元）	派出人次（人次）	年末在国外人数（人）
合　　计	**1 320**	**15 824**	**8 809**	**5 458**	**10 033**
香　港	81	625	1 557	391	482
澳　门			5		11
台湾省	90	946	325	316	207
越　南			2		
老　挝	3	1 894	1 870	80	506
柬埔寨	1	13	24	8	19
日　本	9	273	168	258	397
菲律宾			4		4
泰　国	14	36	47	31	63
新加坡	36	1 681	1 256	544	759
文　莱				1	
印度尼西亚	1	1		1	1
斯里兰卡	1	1	10	2	16
伊　朗	2	5 200		12	6
土耳其	1			1	1
阿联酋	4	40	47	13	46
韩　国	14	1 825	788	1 372	1 818
以色列	5	554	148	60	95
埃　及				11	
科特迪瓦	1	1			2
尼日利亚	1	49	65	27	10
加　蓬				1	2
坦桑尼亚			1	2	2
毛里求斯			1		2
马达加斯加			2		7
纳米比亚				12	3
波　兰	1	1	1	1	1
保加利亚	1	3		2	2
罗马尼亚	1			1	1
德　国	1	515	87		
英　国	2	9	9	1	7
瑞　士	1	6	6		
美　国	46	767	209	365	656
斐　济	4	108	116	3	60
其　他	978	961	1 943	1 944	4 847
国境内	21	315	118		

十四、金融和保险业

BANKING AND INSURANCE

1996 年金融系统存款余额	1 391.62 亿元
1996 年金融系统贷款余额	1 325.49 亿元
1996 年银行现金收入	1 696.42 亿元
1996 年银行现金支出	1 704.67 亿元
1996 年保费收入	17.18 亿元

金融系统存贷款余额（亿元）

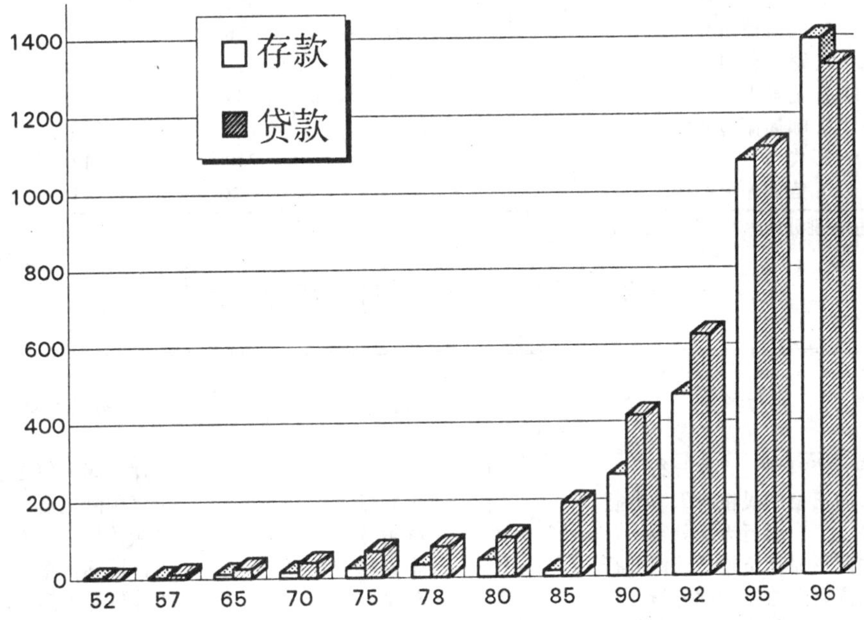

14－1　各类金融机构和人员

项　目	1995年		1996年	
	机构(个)	人员(人)	机构(个)	人员(人)
各类金融机构	**2 333**	**41 170**	**2 578**	**41 366**
一、银行类机构	**1 482**	**26 102**	**1 768**	**30 421**
中央银行	2	630	3	604
商业银行	1 468	25 226	1 746	29 392
政策性银行	1	50	7	195
外资银行	11	196	12	230
按级别分组				
各银行省级分行	12	3 831	15	3 821
各银行区县支行	101	9 187	176	13 096
各银行区县分理处	433	8 188	538	8 294
各银行区县储蓄所	925	4 700	1 027	4 980
#城　市	738	3 847	820	4 160
郊　县	187	853	207	820
二、非银行类机构	**851**	**15 068**	**810**	**10 945**
1.保险公司	161	2 247	172	2 300
2.信托投资公司	5	342	4	762
3.证券经营公司	94	2 800	98	2 123
4.城市信用社	66	3 868		
5.农村信用社	234	4 716	233	4 716
6.财务公司	1	15	1	22
7.金融市场	1	34	1	20
8.邮局储蓄所	276	798	286	790
9.典当行	12	240	14	204
10.信誉评级机构	1	8	1	8

注:银行机构按级别分组中不含外资银行。

14－2　1996年外资银行在津分行一览

银行名称	行　长	办公地址
英国渣打银行天津分行	何家荣	天津国际大厦1层
法国巴黎国民银行天津分行	柏狄雄	天津国际大厦16层
香港汇丰银行天津分行	陈美芬	利顺德饭店地面层
法国里昂信贷银行天津分行	张家麟	天津国际大厦710
法国兴业银行天津分行	黄家驹	天津国际大厦1309
新加坡华侨银行天津分行	林亚弟	天津国际大厦702
美国大通银行天津分行	温守诺	天津国际大厦14层
韩国外换银行天津分行	权五辰	利顺德饭店地面层
韩国朝兴银行天津分行	金永杓	天津国际大厦1901
日本樱花银行天津分行	熊木敬悦	天津国际大厦1210
日本东海银行天津分行	大森茂延	天津国际大厦811
韩国新韩银行	廉泰明	天津国际大厦507

注:截至1996年末,日本三和银行、瑞士丰泰保险、香港道亨银行、韩国企业银行、日本富士银行、美国全美人寿保险、美国恒康人寿保险、日本三井火灾保险、荷兰银行、日本东京海上火灾保险、日本千代田火灾海上保险、香港东亚银行有限公司等24家外资金融机构在天津设有代表处。

14－3　改革开放以来银行系统各项存贷款余额

单位:万元

年份	存款合计	企业存款	财政性存款	机关团体存款	城镇储蓄存款	农业存款	信托及其他类存款	贷款合计
1978	328 532	157 998	57 359	52 827	36 370	23 978		801 425
1979	403 012	193 438	66 643	59 617	52 345	30 969		887 379
1980	440 545	238 293	44 786	45 068	71 012	35 480	5 906	1 026 605
1981	519 341	250 763	47 513	54 777	83 871	46 984	35 433	1 077 256
1982	661 185	329 725	53 678	63 587	105 717	61 819	46 659	1 126 068
1983	727 035	356 228	45 534	70 260	135 447	78 452	41 114	1 253 786
1984	913 802	457 587	43 294	66 487	180 556	68 676	97 202	1 389 920
1985	1 111 409	584 787	73 735	64 489	237 691	70 250	80 457	1 810 044
1986	1 225 523	633 114	35 211	75 625	324 802	95 812	60 959	2 177 719
1987	1 433 616	698 441	43 435	80 390	438 135	106 140	67 075	2 473 904
1988	1 575 473	707 069	66 112	82 121	498 300	128 333	93 538	2 770 777
1989	1 800 323	681 128	66 170	95 784	722 971	117 975	116 295	3 205 920
1990	2 363 051	837 796	84 812	106 661	1 018 805	185 849	129 198	3 877 242
1991	2 976 489	1 049 817	102 742	144 522	1 303 122	212 009	164 277	4 499 526
1992	3 761 858	1 419 863	235 025		1 604 707	242 685	259 578	5 395 304
1993	4 615 158	1 584 229	237 729		2 152 816	287 442	352 942	6 559 907
1994	5 969 590	2 507 467	242 582		3 174 608	23 107	21 826	7 885 143
1995	8 124 462	3 219 872	375 943		4 451 446	28 852	48 349	9 423 664
1996	10 574 676	4 302 363	285 788		5 924 418	25 910	36 197	11 087 762

年份	#工业贷款	商业贷款	建筑企业贷款	个体工商业贷款	乡镇企业贷款	农业贷款	固定资产贷款	信托及其他类贷款
1978	342 740	451 606	80			4 224	2 775	
1979	387 086	491 364	30			4 586	4 256	57
1980	386 027	600 721	2 256	5	3 263	4 441	28 203	1 689
1981	370 883	635 737	2 528	13	6 033	4 924	56 364	1 689
1982	368 884	651 406	2 577	7	8 068	5 444	86 957	2 725
1983	390 099	723 824	3 844	17	11 499	6 365	106 957	11 181
1984	467 612	640 706	26 620	206	30 013	13 735	142 052	68 976
1985	659 905	767 221	54 630	114	34 996	15 757	196 313	70 848
1986	778 823	907 247	63 921	106	56 824	20 781	265 853	64 609
1987	832 581	1 018 187	69 990	137	75 166	29 801	323 548	73 902
1988	912 852	1 171 558	73 681	317	88 956	41 114	354 663	69 801
1989	1 090 721	1 374 445	75 388	403	92 403	57 046	375 468	140 046
1990	1 344 222	1 609 881	82 267	375	107 548	78 606	500 005	154 338
1991	1 556 912	1 712 158	88 565	287	122 037	97 397	738 769	183 401
1992	1 783 208	1 900 099	97 453	315	135 017	111 578	1 056 719	310 916
1993	2 188 959	2 107 337	107 606	508	161 787	142 031	1 439 340	412 339
1994	2 434 655	2 144 773	130 586	1 436	209 979	123 097	2 039 655	188 244
1995	2 832 591	2 375 171	161 792	1 041	254 194	163 724	2 570 014	212 750
1996	3 274 138	2 704 530	227 112	2 757	297 813	224 617	2 865 438	381 726

注:从 1993 年起存款合计中含“中央财政存款”。

14－4 银行现金收入和支出

单位:万元

项　目	1990年	1995年	1996年	1996比1995年增长%
一、现金收入总计	**2 399 209**	**12 854 640**	**16 964 187**	**32.0**
商品销售收入	905 206	2 579 310	3 025 276	17.3
＃县以下	308 602	594 998	691 921	16.3
服务事业收入	191 732	660 691	856 745	29.7
税款收入	13 113	32 874	42 764	30.1
农村信用社收入	38 665	242 407	240 919	－0.6
乡镇企事业收入	56 487	474 070	629 107	32.7
城乡个体经营收入	12 151	124 539	222 370	78.6
储蓄存款收入	937 180	6 272 203	8 344 150	33.0
其他金融机构收入	68 077	664 759	819 433	23.3
汇兑收入	17 420	90 879	135 426	49.0
债券收入	38 405	158 889	95 680	－39.8
其他收入	120 773	1 554 019	2 552 317	64.2
二、现金支出总计	**2 420 002**	**12 754 602**	**17 046 710**	**33.7**
工资及对个人其他支出	968 958	2 548 784	2 929 396	14.9
＃国家职工工资奖金	519 722	1 353 088	1 508 620	11.5
城镇集体单位工资奖金	119 781	272 724	274 518	0.7
国家和集体对个人其他支出	329 455	886 322	1 103 424	24.5
农副产品采购支出	92 470	165 498	150 677	－9.0
工矿产品收购支出	10 130	50 554	86 652	71.4
行政企事业管理费支出	153 066	731 572	941 434	28.7
农村信用社支出	165 321	616 401	716 628	16.3
乡镇企事业支出	126 926	536 809	647 187	20.6
城乡个体经营支出	24 670	176 389	254 007	44.0
储蓄存款支出	676 127	5 471 418	7 403 222	35.3
其他金融机构支出	13 076	482 937	716 424	48.4
汇兑支出	28 785	83 408	119 796	43.6
债券支出	36 608	121 608	138 956	14.3
其他支出	123 865	1 769 224	2 942 331	66.3
三、货币投放(＋)或回笼(－)	**＋20 793**	**－100 038**	**＋82 523**	

14－5　金融系统信贷收支情况

单位:万元

项　　目	金融系统			#银行系统		
	1995年	1996年	1996比1995年增长%	1995年	1996年	1996比1995年增长%
一、各项存款总计	**10 777 549**	**13 916 163**	**29.1**	**8 100 857**	**10 574 676**	**30.5**
1.企业存款	3 850 466	5 145 741	33.6	3 218 236	4 302 363	33.7
#工业存款	723 666	755 101	4.3	723 666	755 101	4.3
商业存款	364 814	375 951	3.1	364 814	375 951	3.1
建筑企业存款	219 554	233 591	6.4	219 554	233 591	6.4
2.地方财政性存款	404 481	318 965	－21.1	404 481	318 965	－21.1
3.城乡储蓄存款	5 501 931	7 240 011	31.6	4 453 723	5 924 418	33.0
#定期储蓄	4 810 364	6 331 226	31.6	3 930 418	5 226 077	33.0
4.农业存款	228 097	258 239	13.2	28 241	25 910	－8.3
5.信托类存款	598 837	605 572	1.1	21 988	30 962	40.8
6.其他类存款	222 195	380 812	71.4	2 646	5 235	97.8
二、各项贷款总计	**11 139 647**	**13 254 852**	**19.0**	**9 423 676**	**11 087 762**	**17.7**
1.短期贷款	7 665 135	9 198 074	20.0	6 643 467	7 840 598	18.0
#工业贷款	2 899 683	3 356 773	15.8	2 837 250	3 274 138	15.4
工业企业贷款	2 236 934	2 621 338	17.2	2 227 321	2 609 847	17.2
物资供销企业贷款	401 826	408 338	1.6	401 826	408 338	1.6
集体工业贷款	191 175	249 662	30.6	138 355	178 518	29.0
科技开发贷款	69 748	77 435	11.0	69 748	77 435	11.0
商业贷款	2 427 085	2 775 485	14.4	2 375 178	2 704 530	13.9
#商业内贸贷款	788 253	871 978	10.6	788 253	871 978	10.6
外贸贷款	953 126	925 316	－2.9	953 126	925 316	－2.9
建筑业贷款	161 791	227 112	40.4	161 791	227 112	40.4
私营及个体贷款	34 707	114 634	230.3	1 041	2 757	164.8
乡镇企业贷款	857 106	1 001 177	16.8	254 137	297 813	17.2
农业贷款	224 346	294 550	31.3	163 730	224 617	37.2
三资企业贷款	515 437	670 350	30.1	515 437	670 350	30.1
其他短期贷款	544 980	757 993	39.1	334 903	439 281	31.2
2.中长期贷款	2 617 532	2 894 619	10.6	2 567 459	2 865 438	11.6
#技术改造贷款	937 324	984 294	5.0	937 324	984 294	5.0
基本建设贷款	1 432 514	1 665 687	16.3	1 432 514	1 665 687	16.3
地方经济开发贷款	71 680	70 536	－1.6	71 680	70 536	－1.6
3.信托类贷款	479 712	498 060	3.8	9 195	20 367	121.5
4.其他类贷款	377 268	664 099	76.0	203 555	361 359	77.5

注:1.本表已含投资银行和代理开发银行数据。2.各项存款总计中"中央财政存款",其中:1995年为－28458万元;1996年为－33177万元。3.1995年数据调整为与1996年同口径。

14－6　1996年银行结汇售汇情况

单位:万美元

项　目	全　市	#中国银行	项　目	全　市	#中国银行
结汇收入合计	**311 294**	**197 247**	**售汇支出合计**	**115 590**	**53 117**
一、贸易收入	245 726	143 821	一、贸易支出	88 315	37 789
1.国内企业	164 772	124 566	1.国内企业	67 270	31 021
2.外商投资企业	80 954	19 255	2.外商投资企业	21 045	6 768
二、非贸易收入	55 655	53 101	二、非贸易支出	4 184	3 817
#运输及港口	6 376	5 899	#运输及港口	1 432	1 390
劳务及承包工程	2 221	1 650	劳务及承包工程	36	3
国内及居民外汇	6 807	6 512	国内及居民外汇	438	438
房地产租赁	504	185	政府机构交往	1 081	1 081
利润、利息	164		外国驻华商务机构		
外国驻华商务机构	526	573	外商投资企业	152	121
外商投资企业	29 048	28 950	其他非贸易支出	660	480
其他非贸易收入	9 778	9 263	三、资本支出	23 080	11 511
三、资本收入	9 909	325	#偿还外债	9 793	7 624
#借入外债	1 324		偿还国内外汇贷款	13 157	3 887
出售有价证券			境外投资	15	
外商投资	8 441	325	其他资本支出	59	
其他资本收入	1		四、其他支出	11	
四、其他收入	4				
外汇交易买入	**103 889**	**5 083**	**外汇交易卖出**	**262 112**	**148 445**
1.银行间市场买入	88 040		1.银行间市场卖出	96 178	
2.总分行间买入	15 849	5 083	2.总分行间卖出	165 934	148 445

14－7　1996年天津市保险业务情况

项　目	承保额(亿元)	保费收入(万元)	赔款支出(万元)
总　计	**2 488.21**	**171 768.01**	**62 613.00**
#市人民保险公司	1 591.69	93 328.10	47 230.60
1.国内业务小计	1 482.23	137 771.88	43 443.02
#市人民保险公司	720.51	45 457.00	22 055.80
#人身险业务小计	199.16	63 373.15	10 185.99
#市人民保险公司	97.99	19 008.60	6 813.90
2.涉外业务小计	1 005.99	33 996.13	19 169.98
#市人民保险公司	774.69	28 862.50	18 360.90

注:本表包括市人民保险公司、太平洋保险公司、平安保险公司。

14－8 储蓄存款和单位存款利率表

(1990－1996年)

单位:年利率%

项目	1990年4月15日	1990年8月21日	1991年4月21日	1993年5月15日	1993年7月11日	1996年5月1日	1996年8月23日
一、活期	**2.88**	**2.16**	**1.80(注2)**	**2.16(注3)**	**3.15**	**2.97**	**1.98**
二、整存整取三个月	**6.30**	**4.32**	**3.24**	**4.86**	**6.66**	**4.86**	**3.33**
半年	7.74	6.48	5.40	7.20	9.00	7.20	5.40
一年	10.08	8.64	7.56	9.18	10.98	9.18	7.47
二年	10.98	9.36	7.92	9.90	11.70	9.90	7.92
三年	11.88	10.08	8.28	10.80	12.24	10.80	8.28
五年	13.68	11.52	9.00	12.06	13.86	12.06	9.00
八年及以上	16.20	13.68	10.08	14.58	17.10	17.10	17.10
三、存本取息、零存整取、整存零取							
一年	8.28	7.2	6.12	7.20	9.0	7.20	5.40
三年	10.08	8.64	6.84	9.18	10.98	9.18	7.47
五年	11.88	10.08	7.56	10.80	12.24	10.80	8.28
四、定活两便							
不满三个月	2.88	2.16	1.80	2.16	3.15	2.97	1.98
三个月	5.67	3.888	2.916	2.916	3.996	2.916	1.998
半年	6.966	5.832	4.86	4.32	5.40	4.32	3.24
一年及一年以上	9.072	7.776	6.804	5.508	6.588	5.508	4.482
五、华侨人民币储蓄存款							
一年		10.08	8.28	10.80	12.24	停办新存款	停办新存款
三年		11.52	9.00	12.06	13.86	老存款仍	老存款仍
五年		13.68	9.90	14.58	17.10	执行老利率	执行老利率

注:1.本利率表为法定存款利率表。2.城乡居民储蓄活期存款从1991年7月1日起执行;企业活期存款从1991年4月21日起执行。3.活期存款利率从1993年7月1日起执行。

14－9　流动资金和固定资产贷款利率表

（1990－1996年）　　单位:年利率%

项　目	1990年3月21日	1990年8月21日	1991年4月21日	1993年5月15日	1993年7月11日
一、流动资金贷款					
1.一般流动资金					
半　年	9.00	8.64	8.10	8.82	9.00
一　年	10.08	9.36	8.64	9.36	10.98
2.个体工商户贷款	在10.08%基础上上浮20%	在9.36%基础上上浮20%	在8.64%基础上上浮20%	在9.36%基础上上浮20%	在10.98%基础上上浮20%
二、固定资产贷款					
1.技术改造贷款	10.08	9.36	8.46	9.18	10.98
2.基本建设贷款					
一年以内	10.08	9.36	8.46	9.18	10.98
一年以上至三年	10.80	10.08	9.00	10.80	12.24
三年以上至五年	11.52	10.80	9.54	12.06	13.86
五年以上至十年	11.88	11.16	9.72	12.24	14.04
十年以上	11.88	11.16	（注2）		

项　目	1995年1月1日	1995年7月1日	1996年5月1日	1996年8月23日
一、流动资金贷款				
1.一般流动资金				
半　年	9.00	10.08	9.72	9.18
一　年	10.98	12.06	10.98	10.08
2.个体工商户贷款	在10.98%基础上上浮20%	在12.06%基础上上浮20%	在10.98%基础上上浮10%	在10.08%基础上上浮10%
二、固定资产贷款				
1.技术改造贷款	11.70	（注3）		
2.基本建设贷款				
一年以内	11.70	12.24	11.52	10.08
一年以上至三年	12.96	13.50	13.14	10.98
三年以上至五年	14.58	15.12	14.94	11.70
五年以上至十年	14.76	15.30	15.12	12.42
十年以上				

注:1.本利率表为法定贷款利率表。2.自1991年4月21日以后,固定资产贷款五年期以上的利率均按五年期以上档次利率执行。3.从1995年7月1日起,技术改造贷款利率和基本建设贷款利率合并为固定资产贷款利率,执行统一期限档次。

十五、教育和科学技术

EDUCATION AND SCIENCE & TECHNOLOGY

1996 年高等学校在校学生	7.14 万人
1996 年专业技术人员	59.04 万人
1996 年取得重大科技成果数	936 项
1996 年大中型工业企业中从事科技活动的人员	3.52 万人
1996 年大中型建筑企业中从事科技活动的人员	0.47 万人

各类学校在校学生数（万人）

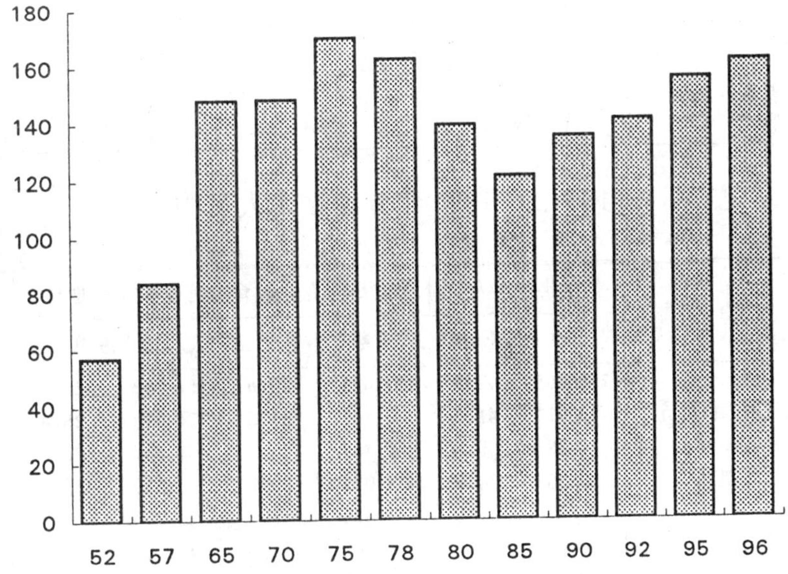

15-1 专业技术人员

单位:人

项目	全市		#国有		平均每万人口有科技人员(1996年)	平均每万职工有科技人员(1996年)
	1995年	1996年	1995年	1996年		
合计	**601 936**	**590 397**	**570 366**	**566 728**	**657**	**2 079**
一、自然科学专业技术人员	**259 737**	**275 628**	**248 739**	**265 924**	**307**	**971**
工程技术人员	162 607	164 145	154 450	157 115	183	579
农业技术人员	3 417	3 481	3 183	3 283	3	12
科学研究人员	2 769	2 679	2 766	2 675	2	9
卫生技术人员	71 420	72 308	68 840	69 859	81	255
教学人员	13 248	26 634	13 244	26 611	30	93
其他	6 276	6 381	6 256	6 381	8	22
二、社会科学专业技术人员	**342 199**	**314 769**	**321 627**	**300 804**	**350**	**1 108**
科学研究人员	1 272	1 343	1 244	1 329	2	4
教学人员	128 552	114 406	128 261	114 139	127	403
财会人员	60 434	56 203	54 812	52 286	63	198
统计人员	12 695	12 189	10 986	10 817	14	43
编辑、记者、播音员	2 401	2 472	2 397	2 470	3	9
翻译人员	1 618	1 637	1 593	1 598	1	6
经济人员	87 816	79 261	78 414	73 726	88	279
图书、档案、资料人员	8 302	8 250	7 889	7 875	9	29
工艺美术人员	1 146	956	907	708	1	3
其他	37 963	38 052	35 124	35 856	42	134

15-2 1996年专业技术人员构成

单位:人

项目	女专业技术人员		受过高等专业教育		受过中等专业教育		高级职称人数	中级职称人数
	人数	占总计%	人数	占总计%	人数	占总计%		
合计	**279 465**	**47.3**	**121 621**	**20.6**	**156 193**	**26.5**	**45 054**	**161 035**
一、自然科学专业技术人员	**113 917**	**41.3**	**87 155**	**31.6**	**70 078**	**25.4**	**31 528**	**78 659**
工程技术人员	48 891	29.8	57 457	35.0	46 887	28.6	20 285	48 006
农业技术人员	868	24.9	1 072	29.5	539	15.5	291	976
科学研究人员	986	36.8	2 339	87.3	250	9.3	1 046	1 022
卫生技术人员	50 271	69.5	11 503	15.9	11 304	15.6	4 113	16 050
教学人员	12 899	48.4	13 605	51.1	9 944	37.3	5 656	9 998
其他	2		1 179	18.5	1 154	18.1	137	2 607
二、社会科学专业技术人员	**165 548**	**52.6**	**34 466**	**10.9**	**86 115**	**27.4**	**13 526**	**82 376**
科学研究人员	586	43.6	763	56.8	460	34.3	343	650
教学人员	71 347	62.3	17 844	15.6	29 974	26.2	6 481	36 926
财会人员	38 485	68.4	2 996	5.3	14 978	26.6	700	7 867
统计人员	9 661	79.2	487	4.0	2 926	24.0	204	1 749
编辑、记者、播音员	917	37.0	1 116	45.1	882	35.7	478	1 047
翻译人员	893	54.6	998	61.0	547	33.4	176	624
经济人员	24 575	31.0	6 706	0.9	19 069	24.1	1 640	13 797
图书、档案、资料人员	6 269	75.9	1 232	2.8	3 350	40.6	390	2 689
工艺美术人员	306	32.0	78	8.2	294	30.8	89	263
其他	12 509	1.3	2 246	0.6	13 635	35.8	3 025	16 764

15－3　国民经济各行业专业技术人员

单位：人

行　业	1995年			1996年		
	合　计	自然科学	社会科学	合　计	自然科学	社会科学
总　计	**601 936**	**259 737**	**342 199**	**590 397**	**275 628**	**314 769**
农、林、牧、渔、水利业	11 350	7 488	3 862	9 380	6 611	2 769
工　业	168 988	90 397	78 591	184 741	100 020	84 721
地质普查和勘探业	17 073	9 479	7 594	964	704	260
建筑业	43 125	28 957	14 168	41 700	28 244	13 456
交通运输、邮电通讯业	32 196	18 240	13 956	31 184	17 730	13 454
商业、公共饮食业、物资供销和仓储业	49 514	6 937	42 577	43 778	6 471	37 307
房地产管理、公共事业、居民服务和咨询服务业	13 568	5 589	7 979	13 798	5 888	7 910
卫生、体育和社会福利业	55 624	50 736	4 888	57 352	52 189	5 163
教育、文化艺术及广播电视业	153 049	19 017	134 032	153 375	33 165	120 210
科学研究和综合技术服务业	20 493	16 771	3 722	20 709	16 876	3 833
金融、保险业	24 441	1 048	23 393	17 834	918	16 916
国家政党机关和社会团体	7 879	3 357	4 522	10 401	4 812	5 589
其　他	4 636	1 721	2 915	5 181	2 000	3 181

15－4　1996年自然科学专业技术人员

单位：人

行　业	合　计	#工　程技术人员	农业技术人员	科学研究人员	卫生技术人员	教学人员
总　计	**275 628**	**164 145**	**3 481**	**2 679**	**72 308**	**26 634**
农、林、牧、渔、水利业	6 611	3 717	2 557	2	293	25
工　业	100 020	88 653	192	14	9 308	1 522
地质普查和勘探业	704	670			28	6
建筑业	28 244	26 332	10		1 711	152
交通运输、邮电通讯业	17 730	8 677	1	77	2 927	471
商业、公共饮食业、物资供销和仓储业	6 471	3 581	19	4	2 568	15
房地产管理、公共事业、居民服务和咨询服务业	5 888	5 219	24	6	569	69
卫生、体育和社会福利业	52 189	542	7	174	51 253	206
教育、文化艺术及广播电视业	33 165	6 577	37	701	1 723	24 126
科学研究和综合技术服务业	16 876	13 941	141	1 667	1 109	18
金融、保险业	918	873		3	40	1
国家政党机关和社会团体	4 812	3 602	465	26	701	11
其　他	2 000	1 761	28	5	78	12

15－5　1996年社会科学专业技术人员

单位:人

行业	合计	科学研究人员	教学人员	财会人员	统计人员	编辑、记者、播音员
总计	**314 769**	**1 343**	**114 406**	**56 203**	**12 189**	**2 472**
农、林、牧、渔、水利业	2 769	1	314	107	123	10
工业	84 721	70	7 277	17 848	7 546	155
地质普查和勘探业	260		21	86	14	1
建筑业	13 456		502	4 112	763	25
交通运输、邮电通讯业	13 454		1 678	2 802	506	24
商业、公共饮食业、物资供销和仓储业	37 307	2	260	9 573	1 431	21
房地产管理、公共事业、居民服务和咨询服务业	7 910	3	263	2 712	562	10
卫生、体育和社会福利业	5 163	6	522	2 798	211	30
教育、文化艺术及广播电视业	120 210	1 015	102 858	4 526	142	1 973
科学研究和综合技术服务业	3 833	224	119	1 230	156	131
金融、保险业	16 916	10	27	6 878	62	
国家政党机关和社会团体	5 589	10	468	1 540	339	79
其他	3 181	2	97	1 991	334	13

行业	翻译人员	经济人员	体育教练人员	图书、档案、资料人员	工艺美术人员	其他
总计	**1 637**	**79 261**	**606**	**8 250**	**956**	**37 446**
农、林、牧、渔、水利业	24	585	1	84		548
工业	650	31 546	17	2 317	470	16 825
地质普查和勘探业		83		6		49
建筑业	92	4 509	1	262	24	3 166
交通运输、邮电通讯业	54	5 336	1	177	4	2 872
商业、公共饮食业、物资供销和仓储业	161	21 858		349	148	3 504
房地产管理、公共事业、居民服务和咨询服务业	177	2 343	1	168	25	1 646
卫生、体育和社会福利业	22	58	538	234	8	738
教育、文化艺术及广播电视业	177	716	17	3 812	216	4 758
科学研究和综合技术服务业	172	710		433	51	607
金融、保险业	23	9 252		50		614
国家政党机关和社会团体	41	1 165	28	289	5	1 625
其他	44	1 100	2	69	5	494

15－6　独立科学研究和技术开发机构情况

指　　标	自然科学研究与技术开发机构		社会、人文科研与开发机构		科学技术情报和文献机构	
	1995年	1996年	1995年	1996年	1995年	1996年
机构数(个)	**140**	**139**	**5**	**5**	**11**	**11**
专业技术干部(人)	17 917	17 002	325	344	904	899
高级职称	4 025	3 821	111	121	220	234
中级职称	6 578	5 683	129	125	445	425
初级职称	6 331	4 297	78	75	204	180
其　　他	983	1 952	7	25	35	21
经费支出总额(万元)	**147 094**	**111 732**	**1 178**	**1 370**	**3 508**	**3 141**

15－7　独立自然科学研究机构课题开展和投入

课题类型	课题数(项)		投入人力(人年)		投入经费(万元)	
	1995年	1996年	1995年	1996年	1995年	1996年
合　　计	**2 338**	**2 428**	**6 264**	**7 334**	**15 232**	**23 108**
按课题类型分						
基础研究	28	21	82	45	39	115
应用研究	174	180	475	485	796	672
试验发展	521	480	1 480	1 575	3 344	3 009
研究与试验发展成果应用	1 045	1 122	2 679	3 653	7 460	14 338
科技服务	424	495	1 084	1 143	2 073	3 357
生产性活动	146	130	464	433	1 520	1 617

15－8　三项专利申请受理量和批准量

单位：项

项　　目	申请量			批准量		
	1990年	1995年	1996年	1990年	1995年	1996年
合　　计	**975**	**1 648**	**1 743**	**637**	**1 034**	**899**
一、按种类分						
发　明	161	239	285	49	63	51
实用新型	736	1 151	1 111	554	785	666
外观设计	78	258	347	34	186	182
二、按对象分						
工矿企业		234	388		99	161
大专院校		63	70		41	45
科研单位		61	52		46	41
机关团体		121	25		137	68
个　　人		1 169	1 208		711	584

15-9 天津市重大科技研究成果和获奖成果

(1990-1996年)

单位:项

项目	1990年	1991年	1992年	1993年	1995年	1996年
重大科学技术研究成果数	662	820	942	694	552	936
获奖成果						
#国家发明奖	10	6	8	8	5	5
国家科技进步奖	22	29	14	11	12	11

15-10 1996年天津市获国家发明奖科技成果一览

序号	项目名称	发明单位	奖励等级
1	液膜结晶技术分离高纯对二氯苯	天津大学	三等
2	隔声防火玻璃	公安部天津消防科学研究所	三等
3	八字型螺旋槽端面密封气系统试验装置	天津市机械密封件厂、天津市克兰密封有限公司	四等
4	动态设定型变刚度厚控方法	机械部天津电气传动设计研究所	三等
5	S14系列转子混砂机	天津大学等	三等

15-11 1996年天津市获国家科技进步奖科技成果一览

序号	项目名称	发明单位	奖励等级
1	王朝全汁干型葡萄酒规模化生产工艺技术	中法公营王朝酿酒有限公司	三等
2	中浓度高稳型烟草专用肥及其应用技术	中国农业生产资料天津公司、天津土壤肥料研究所	三等
3	青霉素结晶新型技术与设备	天津大学、华北制药厂	二等
4	塔里木沙漠石油公路工程技术研究	塔里木石油勘探开发指挥部天津大学等	一等
5	<CS>催化裂化剂研制与应用和RH2200.CC14重油催化裂化催化剂	天津石化公司炼油厂等	二等
6	年产24万吨磷铵国产化装置	天津橡胶制品一厂等	一等
7	105M2燃油蓄热式显像管玻壳玻璃池炉	天津津京玻壳股份有限公司	二等
8	高坝地基处理技术研究	中国水利水电基础工程局科研所、天津大学自动化系等	三等
9	ABT生根粉系列的推广	天津市农林局等	特等
10	微机重力坝CAD系统	水利部电力工业部天津勘测设计研究院	二等
11	ZR-881抗燃油的研制及工业应用	天津市滨海化工厂	三等

15－12　高等学校科研课题开展与投入

（理、工、农、医类）

项　　目	课题数（项）		投入人力（人）		投入经费（万元）	
	1995 年	1996 年	1995 年	1996 年	1995 年	1996 年
合　　计	**3 356**	**3 243**	**5 753**	**5 840**	**11 491**	**14 446**
按课题类型分						
基础研究	781	606	1 430	930	1 243	1 217
应用研究	1 652	1 667	3 035	3 304	5 226	6 291
试验发展	655	578	865	1 119	3 628	3 928
科技服务	268	392	423	487	1 394	3 010
按社会经济目标分						
陆地、海洋与大气的开发与估价	9	26	17	32	22	92
民用宇宙空间	6	1	15	1	45	5
农业、林业与渔业的发展	148	156	260	176	229	334
促进工业的发展	1 253	1 450	1 991	2 320	5 266	8 776
能源生产储存和分配	175	87	272	166	852	327
交通、通讯事业的发展	247	178	336	268	1 059	658
教育事业的发展	92	63	129	68	277	123
卫生事业的发展	782	707	1 754	1 767	742	933
社会发展和社会经济服务	128	114	127	174	814	985
环境保护	122	83	154	176	434	473
知识的全面发展	246	267	457	476	580	559
其他民用目标	101	59	113	104	384	486
国　防	47	52	128	112	787	695

15－13　高等学校研究发展机构科技专著和论文

（理、工、农、医类）

（1991－1996 年）

项　　目	单　位	1991 年	1992 年	1993 年	1994 年	1995 年	1996 年
科技专著	**部**	**197**	**133**	**139**	**202**	**126**	**151**
	万字	3 460	4 216	4 528	3 037	4 676	4 223
自然科学	部	31	29	14	56	43	35
	万字	941	979	425	1 281	1 113	673
工程科学	部	59	49	54	60	47	64
	万字	1 190	868	1 067	1 193	1 564	2 144
医学科学	部	60	31	31	35	33	48
	万字	662	974	2 286	538	1 992	1 376
农业科学	部	2	5	6	51	3	4
	万字	53	32	22	25	7	30
其他科学	部	45	19	34			
	万字	614	1 363	728			
科学论文	**篇**	**4 358**	**4 572**	**4 822**	**4 799**	**5 215**	**5 565**
#国外发表	篇	607	679	611	627	770	783

15－14　1996年技术监督机构人员、行政执法及科技成果情况

项　　目	单　位	合　计	市级单位	#市技术监督局	市计量技术研究所	县级单位
一、机构人员情况						
机构数	个	51	8	1	1	43
职工人数	人	1 645	669	120	221	976
行政机构人员	人	742	142	120		600
事业机构人员	人	903	527		221	376
#执法人员	人	551	69	69		482
二、行政案件情况						
行政受理案件	件	2 424	239	239		2 185
行政处罚案件	件	1 590	196	196		1 394
结案案件	件	2 173	196	196		1 977
罚没金额	万元	743	205	205		538
三、科技项目情况						
项目总数	项	50	50	22	25	
#市　级	项	18	18	1	17	
经费金额	万元	104	104	28	75	
#市　级	万元	50	50		50	
四、科技成果情况						
成果鉴定	项	10	10	10		
成果推广	项	10	10		10	
五、科技成果获奖情况						
获奖项目数	项	6	6	3	2	
省部级二等奖	项	1	1		1	
省部级三等奖	项	2	2		1	
地方级二等奖	项	1	1	1		
地方级三等奖	项	2	2	2		

15－15　计量仪器检定情况

（1991－1996年）

单位:台;件

计量仪器分类	1991年	1992年	1993年	1994年	1995年	1996年
总　计	**449 656**	**480 944**	**447 866**	**465 444**	**499 477**	**508 922**
长　度	35 965	43 367	20 102	14 349	20 224	41 736
温　度	4 796	3 947	2 975	4 121	5 711	9 832
力　学	391 979	399 455	405 455	424 721	457 887	428 400
#衡　器	113 709	115 151	140 270	142 384	117 226	141 345
电　磁	3 862	14 235	5 139	7 709	7 186	17 855
光　学	289	343	329	224	567	1 753
声　学	55	127	134	183	233	370
化　学	2 731	3 061	2 100	5 321	4 829	4 512
电离辐射		8	45	59	49	158
无线电	603	606	581	559	912	1 652
时间频率	581	652	442	399	463	596
其　他	8 795	15 143	10 564	7 799	1 413	2 058

15－16　1996年大中型工业和建筑业科技活动情况

项　目	单　位	合　计	按经济类型分				按大中型分	
			国有经济	集体经济	“三资”经济	其他经济	大型	中型
一、工　业								
1.有科技活动企业数	个	337	251	16	49	21	144	193
企业办科技机构数	个	278	198	15	47	18	143	135
2.从事科技活动人员	人	35 209	28 004	372	4 036	2 797	25 383	9 826
#科学家和工程师	人	21 988	17 839	218	2 426	1 505	16 612	5 376
企业办科技机构人员	人	8 158	6 305	79	1 050	724	6 364	1 794
#科学家和工程师	人	5 215	3 971	42	700	502	4 151	1 064
研究与发展人员	人	12 313	9 746	164	1 624	779	8 897	3 416
#科学家和工程师	人	8 323	6 560	106	1 175	482	6 325	1 998
3.企业科技活动经费筹集	万元	117 698	86 744	594	17 510	12 850	84 638	33 059
#政府财政拨款	万元	1 957	1 647		20	290	1 128	829
企业自筹资金	万元	82 604	62 063	393	14 123	6 025	67 170	15 434
4.企业科技活动经费支出	万元	108 889	80 734	617	14 310	13 228	87 014	21 875
#企业内部支出	万元	101 727	77 859	617	10 058	13 193	80 067	21 660
#开发新产品用款	万元	35 806	22 858	366	6 197	6 385	27 608	8 198
研究与发展经费支出	万元	53 691	37 247	111	6 496	9 837	47 005	6 686
5.企业科技活动项目数	项	1 878	1 447	39	294	98	1 180	698
新产品项目数	项	1 774	1 293	39	348	94	945	829
当年已完成项目数	项	1 177	858	38	215	66	653	524
6.新产品销售收入	万元	889 384	334 023	16 592	471 522	67 247	744 021	145 363
新产品实现利税	万元	123 247	60 515	1 306	55 093	6 333	88 398	34 849
企业对外转让成果收入	万元	2 492	2 185		307		2 492	
#出口收入	万元	674	374		300		674	
7.获奖成果数	项	196	170	3	12	11	163	33
#国家级	项	15	11		2	2	12	3
8.专利申请数	件	96	50	2	39	5	63	33
专利授权数	件	49	22	1	22	4	42	7
9.技术改造经费支出	万元	238 021	135 022	1 319	26 507	75 173	217 015	21 006
技术引进经费支出	万元	85 271	30 089	66	12 822	42 294	74 934	10 337
用于消化吸收经费支出	万元	1 217	342		801	74	806	411
购买国内技术经费支出	万元	5 333	801		2 739	1 793	5 109	224
二、建筑业								
有科技活动企业数	个	18	18				15	3
从事科技活动人员	人	4 683	4 683				4 598	85
#科学家和工程师	人	2 965	2 965				2 896	69
研究与发展人员	人	870	870				836	34
#科学家和工程师	人	546	546				532	14
企业科技活动经费筹集	万元	5 312	5 312				5 300	12
#政府财政拨款	万元	323	323				323	
企业自筹资金	万元	4 255	4 255				4 244	11
企业科技活动经费支出	万元	4 906	4 906				4 877	29
#企业内部支出	万元	4 817	4 817				4 793	24

15-17 天津市科学技术协会和所属学会科技活动

项 目	单 位	1995年			1996年		
		合 计	市科协	市级学会	合 计	市科协	市级学会
一、机构与人员							
机 构	个	167	1	166	121	1	120
人 员	人	120 466	70	120 396	117 786	64	117 722
二、学术交流情况							
1.学术会议	次	494	8	486	600	28	572
国 内	次	470	5	465	578	28	550
国 际	次	24	3	21	22		22
参加人数	人次	40 741	1 650	39 091	55 139	6 245	48 894
国 内	人次	38 643	1 300	37 343	52 990	6 245	46 745
国 际	人次	2 098	350	1 748	2 149		2 149
交流论文	篇	7 723	566	7 157	5 188	170	5 018
国 内	篇	6 928	396	6 532	5 112	170	4 942
国 际	篇	795	170	625	76		76
2.科学考察	次	85		85			
国 内	次	71		71			
国 际	次	14		14			
参加人数	人次	767		767			
国 内	人次	719		719			
国 际	人次	48		48			
三、科学普及							
科普讲座	次	839	7	832	557	3	554
参加人数	人次	114 447	2 650	111 797	64 949	1 500	63 449
科普展览	次	292	1	291	130	18	112
参加人数	人次	302 902	10 000	292 902	487 467	180 000	307 467
四、科技培训							
培训班数	个(期)	305	18	287	391	200	191
培训人数	人次	23 974	975	22 999	50 567	10 000	40 567
五、科技咨询服务							
无偿咨询项目	项	945		945	440		440
完成技术合同数	项	1 334	109	1 225	835	241	594
决策咨询数	项				1 863	993	870
六、青少年科技活动							
科技夏(冬)令营	次	21	4	17	11	1	10
参加人数	人次	11 691	4 000	7 691	6 094	2 000	4 094
青少年科技竞赛	次	36	6	30	21	2	19
科技竞赛获奖	项	3 294	1 405	1 889			

15－18　主要年份各类学校在校学生数和专任教师数

年份	学校数(所)			在校学生数(万人)			专任教师数(人)		
	高等学校	中等学校	小学	高等学校	中等学校	小学	高等学校	中等学校	小学
1952	7	84	2 989	1	6	51	1 211	2 499	13 097
1957	6	181	2 470	2	17	65	2 341	7 793	16 329
1962	17	256	2 777	3	18	85	5 572	10 889	24 299
1965	16	520	3 070	3	32	113	5 330	16 439	31 692
1970	9	820	3 502		36	112	3 919	19 085	33 473
1975	10	1 066	3 637	2	76	92	5 174	36 371	42 391
1978	22	1 191	3 357	2	81	79	6 327	45 632	40 550
1980	28	1 217	3 399	3	57	79	8 312	46 447	40 720
1985	28	1 085	3 302	5	43	73	10 527	42 634	39 871
1986	28	1 089	3 274	5	45	73	11 108	44 499	40 948
1987	28	1 073	3 261	5	46	73	11 474	47 353	42 872
1988	28	1 053	3 277	5	44	76	11 143	48 252	44 309
1989	28	1 041	3 275	5	43	81	11 124	46 446	43 241
1990	28	1 013	3 259	5	44	86	11 121	47 056	47 110
1991	27	1 003	3 232	5	46	87	10 704	46 460	47 762
1992	26	981	3 238	5	48	87	10 391	46 935	49 030
1993	26	975	3 243	6	50	89	10 160	46 688	50 448
1994	26	991	3 219	7	53	90	10 170	46 591	51 616
1995	25	1 059	3 216	7	60	88	10 490	47 196	51 401
1996	20	1 098	3 185	7	66	88	9 811	48 771	51 202

注:1996 年高等学校中不包括分校数。

15－19　1996 年各类学校数、学生数及教职工数

学校类别	学校数(所)	毕业生数(人)	招生数(人)	在校学生数(人)	教职工数(人)	#专任教师数
合　计	**4 303**	**321 058**	**395 020**	**1 613 999**	**165 050**	**109 784**
高等学校	20	18 429	22 664	71 354	26 203	9 811
中等专业学校	78	13 259	21 168	67 033	10 440	4 767
技工学校	143	10 653	15 590	39 191	9 277	4 437
农业、职业中学	143	12 333	21 765	63 098	6 555	4 123
高　中	129	11 167	20 065	61 398		4 069
初　中	4	1 166	1 700	1 700		54
完　中	10					
普通中学	734	120 679	169 395	493 551	50 368	35 444
高　中	190	18 331	28 215	77 361		6 576
初　中	544	102 348	141 180	416 190		28 868
小　学	3 185	145 705	144 438	879 772	62 207	51 202

15－20　平均每万人口中有在校学生数

单位:人

项　目	平均每万人口中有在校学生			平均每一教师负担学生数		
	1992年	1995年	1996年	1992年	1995年	1996年
合　计	**1 607**	**1 649**	**1 766**	**13**	**14**	**14**
高等学校	60	76	79	5	6	7
中等学校	552	637	708	10	13	13
中等专业学校	44	63	75	8	13	14
技工学校	39	33	44	7	7	9
农业、职业中学	33	56	70	11	15	15
普通中学	436	484	549	11	13	14
高　中	74	73	86	9	11	12
初　中	362	412	463	11	14	14
小　学	996	939	979	18	17	17

15－21　各级学校女学生和女教师比重

单位:%

项　目	女学生占学生总数比重			女教师占教师总数比重		
	1992年	1995年	1996年	1992年	1995年	1996年
合　计	**48.35**	**48.54**	**49.40**	**60.25**	**62.11**	**62.63**
高等学校	40.04	40.68	41.09	33.82	36.62	36.84
中等学校	49.32	48.99	51.62	54.49	57.17	58.16
中等专业学校	52.14	53.64	53.68	49.46	51.27	51.79
技工学校	38.60	44.07	36.00			
农业、职业中学	58.38	58.32	57.90	57.69	60.16	59.64
普通中学	49.32	48.81	48.95	54.92	57.68	58.84
高　中	49.34	48.46	48.68	45.12	47.12	48.92
初　中	49.32	48.87	49.00	57.41	60.03	61.10
小　学	48.31	48.40	48.78	70.81	71.43	71.44

15－22　各级学校学生升学率

单位:%

项　目	1990年	1992年	1995年	1996年	1996比1995年增长数
高中毕业生升学率	44.30	47.2	60.84	66.38	5.54
初中毕业生升学率	68.40	74.4	78.80	83.09	4.29
学龄儿童入学率	99.80	99.2	99.66	99.76	0.10

15－23 各级学校毕业生数

单位:人

项目	1950－1996年 47年合计	1981－1990年 10年合计	1981－1985年 5年合计	1986－1990年 5年合计	1991－1996年 6年合计
高等学校	298 718	105 513	39 432	66 081	96 703
中等专业学校	280 040	76 560	32 077	44 483	69 818
技工学校	274 781	72 798	28 502	44 296	63 815
农、职业中学	108 930	47 495	13 433	34 062	61 435

15－24 1996年普通高等学校分科学生数

单位:人

学科	毕业生数			招生数			在校学生数		
	合计	本科	专科	合计	本科	专科	合计	本科	专科
总计	**18 429**	**10 030**	**8 399**	**22 664**	**14 340**	**8 324**	**71 354**	**49 899**	**21 455**
哲学	26	26		40	40		105	105	
经济学	2 922	1 428	1 494	3 382	2 144	1 238	10 845	7 944	2 901
法学	373	149	224	534	391	152	1 623	1 168	455
教育学	646	94	552	910	371	539	2 154	962	1 192
文学	1 949	926	1 023	2 782	1 430	1 352	7 927	4 942	2 985
历史学	306	157	149	251	129	122	766	472	294
理学	1 606	896	710	1 747	980	767	5 195	3 659	1 536
工学	8 995	5 467	3 528	11 547	8 022	3 525	36 775	26 515	10 260
农学	414	180	234	390	151	239	990	496	494
医学	1 192	707	485	1 072	682	390	4 974	3 636	1 338
总计中:师范	1 818	480	1 338	2 425	846	1 579	5 799	2 555	3 244

15-25　分学科研究生人数

单位:人

科　别	1995 年			1996 年		
	合　计	博士生	硕士生	合　计	博士生	硕士生
在校学生数	**6 060**	**964**	**5 096**	**6 278**	**1 119**	**5 159**
哲　学	64	23	41	81	32	49
经济学	1 515	127	1 388	1 441	220	1 221
法　学	137		137	153		153
教育学	36		36	42		15
＃体育学	10		10	11		11
文　学	226	8	218	249	13	236
＃艺术学	11		11	15		15
历史学	193	54	139	213	75	138
理　学	860	204	656	857	199	658
工　学	2 658	466	2 192	2 837	479	2 358
＃力　学	64	29	35	47	21	26
医　学	348	68	280	387	89	298
农　学	23	14	9	18	12	6
毕业生数	**1 198**	**167**	**1 031**	**1 756**	**239**	**1 517**
哲　学	14	2	12	20	7	13
经济学	180	17	163	387	27	360
法　学	36		36	37		37
教育学	6		6	8		8
＃体育学	2		2	3		3
文　学	63	4	59	76		76
＃艺术学	2		2	3		3
历史学	37	6	31	86	5	81
理　学	229	38	191	236	55	181
工　学	576	82	494	819	132	687
＃力　学	26	7	19	29	12	17
医　学	53	16	37	85	13	72
农　学	4	2	2	2		2
招生数	**1 792**	**393**	**1 399**	**2 129**	**440**	**1 689**
哲　学	23	7	16	39	22	17
经济学	312	72	240	422	101	321
法　学	51		51	60		60
教育学	14		14	15		15
＃体育学	3		3	5		5
文　学	75	3	72	102	8	94
＃艺术学	7		7	6		6
历史学	59	25	34	86	30	36
理　学	301	81	220	298	68	230
工　学	847	167	680	996	169	827
＃力　学	10	7	3	13	5	8
医　学	100	28	72	123	35	88
农　学	10	10		8	7	1

15－26　研究生在学、毕业、招生及指导教师人数

单位:人

指　标	合　计		攻读博士学位		攻读硕士学位	
	1995年	1996年	1995年	1996年	1995年	1996年
在校生数	6 060	6 278	964	1 119	5 096	5 159
毕业生数	1 198	1 756	167	239	1 031	1 517
招生人数	1 792	2 129	393	440	1 399	1 689
指导教师	1 650	1 971	21		1 629	

15－27　1996年高等学校基本情况

项　目	学校数（所）	在　校学生数（人）	毕　业生　数（人）	招生数（人）	教　职工　数（人）	#专任教师
合　计	**20**	**71 354**	**18 429**	**22 664**	**20 816**	**9 811**
综合大学	1	8 100	2 135	2 099	3 475	1 688
理工院校	6	32 736	7 943	10 308	8 580	4 116
农林院校	1	1 150	472	480	351	163
医药院校	2	4 959	1 199	1 073	1 889	855
师范院校	3	10 013	2 892	3 944	2 553	1 179
语文院校	1	1 707	325	512	520	274
财经院校	2	9 122	2 402	2 938	2 061	888
体育院校	1	1 089	385	420	434	171
艺术院校	2	1 183	235	390	619	332
职业大学	1	1 295	441	500	334	145

15－28　1996年高等学校分科专任教师数

单位:人

学　科	合　计	教　授	副教授	讲　师	助　教	教　员
合　计	**9 811**	**1 062**	**3 117**	**3 983**	**1 217**	**432**
哲　学	261	35	90	107	21	8
经济学	939	84	267	453	91	44
法　学	132	14	34	65	11	8
教育学	716	35	160	379	121	21
文　学	1 557	151	366	681	263	96
历史学	171	25	50	69	21	6
理　学	1 875	217	748	620	175	115
工　学	3 352	400	1 142	1 304	385	121
农　学	97	11	34	43	6	3
医　学	711	90	226	262	123	10

15－29　高等学校分科学生数

单位:人

学科	在校生数		毕业生数		招生数	
	1995年	1996年	1995年	1996年	1995年	1996年
合计	**68 080**	**71 354**	**20 203**	**18 429**	**22 055**	**22 664**
哲学	95	105	25	26	18	40
经济学	10 608	10 845	3 311	2 922	3 479	3 382
法学	1 575	1 623	485	373	716	543
教育学	1 868	2 154	713	646	708	910
文学	7 177	7 927	2 175	1 949	2 677	2 782
历史学	983	766	429	306	262	251
理学	5 191	5 195	1 739	1 606	1 621	1 747
工学	34 290	36 775	10 051	8 995	10 871	11 547
农学	1 017	990	399	414	373	390
医学	5 276	4 974	876	1 192	1 330	1 072

15－30　中等专业学校分科学生数

单位:人

学科	在校生数		毕业生数		招生数	
	1995年	1996年	1995年	1996年	1995年	1996年
合计	**59 731**	**67 033**	**10 718**	**13 259**	**20 532**	**21 168**
工科	29 480	28 990	5 162	4 674	9 294	9 576
农林	3 016	654	370	314	995	225
医药	5 323	4 731	1 226	1 226	1 715	1 430
财经	6 939	13 028	1 169	1 817	2 259	3 842
政法	2 129	2 205	459	556	986	687
体育	736	871	198	167	170	277
艺术	1 182	2 048	193	241	318	606
师范	7 864	7 970	1 854	2 466	2 673	2 386
#幼师	1 833	884	446	290	674	249
其他	3 062	6 536	88	1 798	2 122	2 139

15－31　技工学校分行业学生数

单位:人

行　业	在校学生人数		毕业生人数		招生人数	
	1995年	1996年	1995年	1996年	1995年	1996年
总　计	**31 509**	**39 191**	**11 356**	**10 653**	**11 369**	**15 590**
农、林、牧、渔、水利业	201	61	87	21	78	
机械制造、加工业	8 087	7 178	4 040	3 000	2 371	2 048
地质矿产业		207				104
冶金工业	935	605	549	454	337	236
电力工业		146				126
石油工业	1 158	1 001	680	553	411	315
化学工业	1 540	2 411	748	657	399	994
有色金属工业		22	17	23		22
轻工业	1 639	2 589	749	548	513	1 206
纺织工业	1 654	1 606	159	237	279	983
电子、仪器、仪表业	2 368	2 290	244	557	766	889
电工、电气业	3 902	4 502	1 064	1 378	1 252	1 477
医药、医疗业	259	420	128	187	92	147
建材、建工、城建业	1 754	2 862	720	619	662	1 293
交通运输业	1 387	2 814	661	823	546	1 153
邮电通讯业	371	453	104	138	51	95
商业、饮食、旅游、服务业	2 054	2 570	346	578	996	1 222
其　他	4 200	7 454	1 060	880	2 616	3 280

15－32　1996年按部门分普通中学和小学生基本情况

单位:人

指　标	小　学			普通中学		
	在校生数	毕业生数	招生数	在校生数	毕业生数	招生数
总　计	**879 772**	**145 705**	**144 438**	**493 551**	**120 679**	**169 395**
教育部门及集体办	833 812	139 220	133 528	441 344	112 370	147 083
其他部门办	36 614	6 251	6 017	26 124	7 417	8 591
民　办	9 346	234	4 893	26 083	892	13 721

15－33　1996年普通中小学分布情况

地　区	学校数(所)		在校学生数(人)		专任教师数(人)	
	普通中学	小　学	普通中学	小　学	普通中学	小　学
全市总计	**734**	**3 185**	**493 551**	**879 772**	**35 014**	**51 036**
一、市辖区	**466**	**795**	**335 685**	**511 211**	**23 505**	**32 819**
和平区	39	63	36 043	47 876	2 429	2 849
河东区	42	65	32 124	51 673	2 119	2 997
河西区	51	78	41 742	55 329	2 520	3 034
南开区	47	74	36 128	56 331	2 373	3 220
河北区	53	78	39 647	54 681	2 427	3 119
红桥区	46	70	32 572	49 574	2 049	3 041
塘沽区	35	61	26 796	40 931	1 878	2 746
汉沽区	18	30	10 930	14 891	896	1 330
大港区	44	48	21 274	28 090	2 163	2 282
东丽区	22	79	14 466	26 934	1 066	2 153
西青区	19	45	14 771	24 509	1 195	1 967
津南区	25	49	14 929	31 090	1 162	1 988
北辰区	21	49	12 782	27 295	1 064	1 900
天津铁厂	4	6	1 481	2 007	164	193
二、市辖县	**268**	**2 390**	**157 866**	**368 561**	**11 509**	**18 217**
宁河县	32	228	18 046	41 640	1 333	2 036
武清县	68	487	42 610	78 852	3 059	4 072
静海县	43	276	25 707	45 735	1 955	3 207
宝坻县	53	671	30 419	81 534	2 351	4 403
蓟　县	72	728	41 084	120 800	2 811	4 499

15－34　1996年普通中学、职业中学及小学校舍情况

单位:平方米

地　　区	占地面积	校舍建筑面积			学生人均建筑面积	
		普通中学	职业中学	小　学	普中、职中	小　学
全市总计	**32 715 324**	**3 199 388**	**564 823**	**3 359 411**	**6.74**	**3.82**
一、市辖区						
和平区	388 455	140 003	40 523	129 666	4.44	2.92
河东区	1 010 114	213 713	17 537	191 279	6.25	3.70
河西区	975 146	249 394	29 038	214 597	5.92	3.88
南开区	1 007 584	189 681	81 384	205 103	6.46	3.64
河北区	1 147 939	291 400	28 903	203 196	7.05	3.72
红桥区	805 716	172 685	45 253	175 949	5.79	3.55
直属校	413 239	99 530		8 452	12.89	2.45
塘沽区	1 734 818	190 740	66 492	201 418	7.84	4.92
汉沽区	628 097	71 744	8 154	61 033	6.63	4.10
大港区	2 508 778	259 623	65 680	165 450	13.94	5.89
东丽区	1 354 345	108 618	17 408	150 987	7.53	5.61
西青区	1 012 312	86 188	21 479	110 951	6.30	4.53
津南区	1 285 835	98 015	9 966	127 465	6.68	4.10
北辰区	1 264 129	126 630	23 951	135 918	10.42	4.98
天津铁厂	61 399	13 967		10 552	9.43	4.32
二、市辖县						
宁河县	1 570 642		5 925	131 303	5.90	3.15
武清县	4 449 423		17 642	312 961	5.14	3.97
静海县	2 494 700		29 948	216 978	6.52	4.74
宝坻县	3 897 224		31 363	253 379	6.62	3.11
蓟　县	4 705 429		24 177	352 774	6.02	2.92

注:占地面积包括中等师范学校、幼儿园、教师进修学校、特殊教育学校及其他。

15－35　1996 年普通中学分课程专任教师学历情况

单位:人

项　　目	合　计	#政　治	语　文	数　学	物　理	化　学	生　物	外　语	历史地理
总　　计	**35 444**	**2 607**	**5 742**	**6 633**	**2 995**	**1 968**	**1 315**	**5 233**	**2 947**
初　中	**28 868**	**2 138**	**4 809**	**5 545**	**2 248**	**1 237**	**1 109**	**4 358**	**2 300**
大学本科毕业及以上	5 879	352	895	1 080	445	275	387	662	673
#师范院校毕业	4 754	315	819	895	335	222	331	530	608
大学专科毕业	17 978	1 461	3 312	3 552	1 471	776	549	3 068	1 311
#师范院校毕业	15 667	1 265	2 903	3 189	1 348	702	496	2 656	1 167
中专毕业	4 014	256	503	677	261	142	144	559	252
#师范院校毕业	3 596	236	475	631	242	134	128	468	248
高中毕业及以下的	997	69	99	236	71	44	29	65	64
高　中	**6 576**	**469**	**933**	**1 088**	**747**	**731**	**206**	**875**	**647**
大学本科毕业及以上	4 133	273	615	759	465	495	151	451	433
#师范院校毕业	3 632	254	567	680	403	452	133	392	406
大学专科毕业	2 294	187	311	319	271	223	53	409	212
#师范院校毕业	2 123	174	297	305	257	217	51	380	205
中专毕业	109	7	3	7	6	8	2	15	1
#师范院校毕业	93	7	2	7	6	7	2	13	1
高中毕业及以下的	40	2	4	3	5	5			1

15－36　1996 年小学分课程专任教师学历情况

单位:人

项　　目	合　计	#思想品德课	语　文	数　学	语文数学	外　语	自　然	历史地理	音体美
总　　计	**51 202**	**1 096**	**13 256**	**10 311**	**10 213**	**3 529**	**1 583**	**1 108**	**5 957**
大学本科毕业及以上	130	2	21	23	9	24	4	4	23
#师范院校毕业	62	1	14	8	6	10	3	1	10
大学专科毕业	6 548	128	1 873	1 330	964	981	165	102	490
#师范院校毕业	3 314	65	920	648	676	432	88	52	224
中专毕业	38 073	696	9 745	7 685	8 206	2 371	1 055	786	4 712
#师范院校毕业	34 649	615	9 011	7 072	7 688	2 162	902	683	4 150
高中毕业	4 248	165	1 047	936	697	136	225	115	497
高中毕业及以下的	2 203	105	570	337	337	17	134	101	235

15－37　成人教育学校校数和学生情况

项　　目	学校数(所)			在校学生数(人)		
	1995年	1996年	1996比1995年增长数	1995年	1996年	1996比1995年增长数
成人高等学校	**44**	**44**		**59 449**	**61 980**	**2 531**
广播电视大学	1	1		12 557	12 470	－87
职工大学	34	34		17 430	18 041	611
管理干部学院	8	8		4 947	4 870	－77
教育学院	1	1		2 392	3 127	735
普通高校办函授部、夜大学				22 123	23 472	1 349
成人中等学校	**96**	**101**	**5**	**47 694**	**45 834**	**－1 860**
中等技术学校	80	84	4	47 130	45 426	－1 704
电视中专	2	2		9 342	6 389	－2 953
职工中专	54	58	4	23 769	24 023	254
干部中专	14	15	1	6 471	8 826	2 355
农民中专	10	9	－1	7 548	6 188	－1 360
中小学教师进修学校	16	17	1	564	408	－156

项　　目	招生数(人)			毕业生数(人)		
	1995年	1996年	1996比1995年增长数	1995年	1996年	1996比1995年增长数
成人高等学校	**21 578**	**21 856**	**278**	**17 182**	**16 578**	**－604**
广播电视大学	4 095	4 616	521	4 186	4 448	262
职工大学	5 546	5 605	59	5 200	5 205	5
管理干部学院	1 892	2 020	128	2 258	1 930	－328
教育学院	908	1 150	242	642	546	－96
普通高校办函授部.夜大学	9 137	8 465	－672	4 896	4 449	－447
成人中等学校	**20 407**	**18 176**	**－2 231**	**16 201**	**16 328**	**127**
中等技术学校	20 133	18 064	－2 069	14 372	16 176	1 804
电视中专	2 689	2 236	－453	2 883	4 835	1 952
职工中专	10 295	9 367	－928	7 086	6 315	－771
干部中专	3 096	4 750	1 654	3 177	2 990	－187
农民中专	4 053	1 711	－2 342	1 226	2 036	810
中小学教师进修学校	274	112	－162	1 829	152	－1 677

15－38　1996年其他专项成人教育学生数

单位:人

项目	合计	单科班	专业证书班	岗位培训班			文化补习班	其他
				资格培训	适应培训	工人技术等级培训		
毕业生	61 011	2 956	1 601	27 752	10 189	8 318	1 681	8 514
招　生	63 040	3 707	1 056	28 384	12 325	2 171	3 055	12 342
在校生	30 431	4 974	1 301	10 979	5 497	479	1 725	5 476

15－39　特殊教育基本情况

指　标	盲聋哑学校		弱智学校		工读学校	
	1995年	1996年	1995年	1996年	1995年	1996年
学校数(所)	7	8	17	13	3	2
在校学生人数(人)	684	741	3 421	2 569	473	
初　中	124	207	37	14		
小　学	560	534	3 384	2 555		
教职工人数(人)	394	455	356	335	217	137
＃专任教师数	272	315	266	256	109	71

15－40　1996年技工学校培训多种人员情况

单位:人

项　目	在职工人培训		军地两用人才培训结业人数	就业前训练结业人数	乡镇人员培训结业人数
	招收人数	结(毕)业人数			
总　计	**56 648**	**29 261**	**351**	**2 752**	**5 385**
地方国有单位办校	**49 962**	**25 932**	**351**	**2 625**	**5 385**
劳动部门办校	9 697	916	146	1 706	3 035
主管局(公司)办校	24 333	15 354	205	469	2 350
工厂(企业性公司)办校	15 932	9 662		450	
国务院部委技校	**6 686**	**3 329**		**127**	

15－41　托幼园所基本情况

指　标	单位	1990年	1992年	1995年	1996年	1996比1995年增长数
托幼园所数	所	7 329	5 920	4 695	4 286	－409
＃幼儿园	所	1 422	2 007	1 531	1 859	328
入托儿童数	人	319 877	295 907	250 895	242 145	－8 750
三岁以上儿童	人	264 246	260 178	233 043	229 690	－3 353
三岁以下儿童	人	55 631	35 729	17 852	12 455	－5 397
教职工数	人	39 774	35 268	24 259	23 055	－1 204
＃教养员	人	14 956	15 109	13 275	12 896	－379

15－42　档案事业基本情况

项　　目	单　位	1990年	1992年	1995年	1996年	1996比1995年增长数
机　构　数	**个**	**425**	**584**	**620**	**604**	**－16**
#档案馆	个	27	30	31	31	
机关事业单位档案馆	个	181	202	240	320	80
大型工业企业档案馆	个	217	352	330	234	－90
专职工作人员	**人**	**1 832**	**2 110**	**2 049**	**2 043**	**－6**
#档案馆	人	374	570	405	393	－12
机关事业单位档案馆	人	405	522	486	680	194
大型工业企业档案馆	人	1 053	1 018	956	768	－188
兼职工作人员	**人**	**4 127**	**5 551**	**4 161**	**4 426**	**265**
#机关事业单位档案馆	人	408	819	1 271	1 888	617
大型工业企业档案馆	人	3 719	4 732	2 890	2 538	－352

15－43　档案馆档案资料馆藏和开发利用情况

项　　目	单　位	1990年	1992年	1995年	1996年	1996比1995年增长数
馆藏档案						
全　宗	个	1 833	1 895	2 070	2 144	74
案　卷	万卷	245	264	309	303	－6
录音、录像、影片	盘	683	2 838	1 728	1 845	117
照　片	张	82 218	99 231	116 716	119 597	2 881
馆藏资料						
资料数量	万册	26	23	33	25	－8
利用档案资料						
利用人次	万人次	4	3.8	3	4	1
利用档案	万卷次	13	14	26	20	－6
利用资料	册次	13 772	13 950	15 926	13 502	－2 424
复制档案资料	万页	11	7	19	115	96
编研档案资料						
公开出版	种	8	6	4	6	2
	万字	182	418	36	255	219
内部参考	种	43	68	44	43	－1
	万字	451	280	247	93	－154

15-44 机关事业单位档案资料保存和开发利用情况

项 目	单 位	1990年	1992年	1995年	1996年	1996比1995年增长数
保存档案						
全 宗	个	440	557	529	520	-9
案 卷	万卷	95	147	185	257	72
底 图	万张	6	267	342	522	180
录音、录像、影片	万盘	1	1	1	1	
照 片	万张	3	5	15	21	6
保存资料						
保存数量	万册	4	30	33	22	-11
借阅利用档案资料						
利用人次	万人次	6	8	7	9	2
利用档案资料数量	万卷册数	12	29	21	31	10
编研档案资料						
公开出版	种	14	20	11	11	
	万字	269	390	149	105	-44
内部参考	种	149	184	181	213	32
	万字	745	4 019	263	971	708

15-45 大型工业企业档案资料保存和开发利用情况

项 目	单 位	1990年	1992年	1995年	1996年	1996比1995年增长数
保存档案						
全 宗	个		371	388	306	-82
案 卷	万卷	165	250	211	192	-19
底 图	万张	344	1 087	345	328	-17
缩微胶片	万张	10	9	6	5	-1
保存资料						
保存数量	万册	24	15	18	16	-2
借阅利用档案资料						
利用人次	万人次	22	20	15	11	-4
利用档案资料数量	万卷册数	44	63	54	36	-18
编研档案资料						
公开出版	种	11	22	5	7	2
	万字	213	167	27	30	3
内部参考	种	755	675	336	278	-58
	万字	680	7 182	149 747	66 863	-82 884

十六、文化、体育、卫生及其他

CULTURE, SPORTS, PUBLIC HEALTH AND OTHERS

1996 年图书总印数	8 333 万册
1996 年卫生技术人员数	7.10 万人
其中:医生	3.30 万人
1996 年医院床位数	3.83 万张

图书总印数（万册）

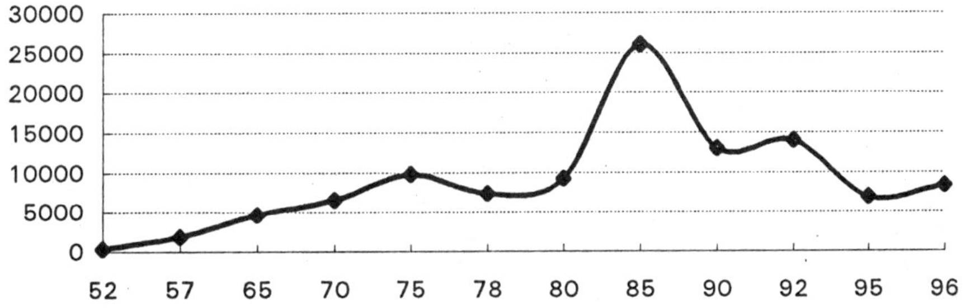

卫生技术人员数（万人）

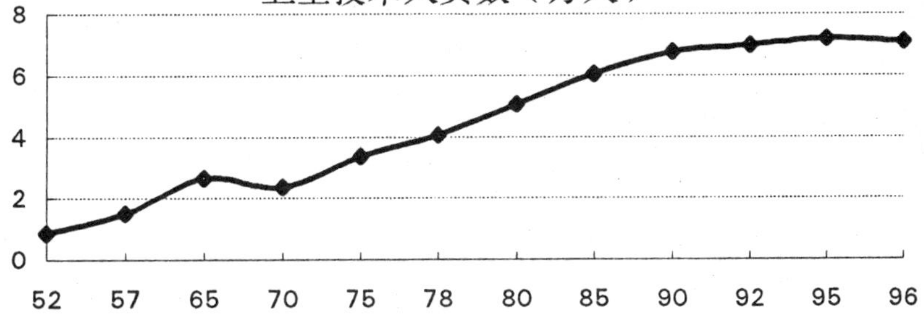

医院床位数（万张）

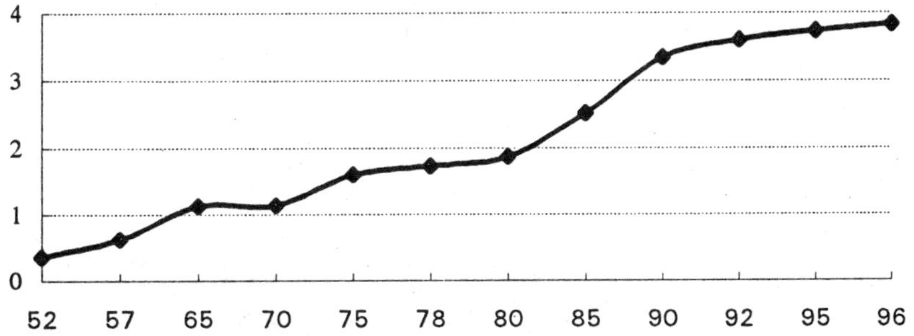

16－1　1996年文化事业活动单位机构和人员

单位:个;人

项　　目	总　　计		文化部门		其他部门	
	机构数	人　数	机构数	人　数	机构数	人　数
电影事业	662	4 003	94	2 116	568	1 887
艺术事业	47	2 817	47	2 817		
出版事业	13	1 142	9	949	4	193
文物事业	22	722				
图书馆事业	31	1 156	31	1 084		
群众文化事业	347	1 687	19	1 687	328	819
其他文化事业	31	1 387	31	1 387		

16－2　电影事业基本情况

项　　目	1990年	1992年	1995年	1996年
机　构(个)	**668**	**659**	**662**	**662**
电影制片厂	1	1	1	1
电影发行放映管理机构	20	19	19	19
电影放映单位	647	639	642	642
电影院	55	54	54	54
影剧院	26	28	28	28
开放礼堂俱乐部	46	44	45	45
电影放映队	372	366	366	366
对内俱乐部	148	147	149	149
电影放映单位拥有座席(个)	**132 162**	**116 547**	**130 432**	**130 432**
工作人员(人)	**4 521**	**4 107**	**4 003**	**4 003**

16－3　电影放映情况

项　　目	单位数(个)		放映场次(场次)		观众人次(万人次)	
	1995年	1996年	1995年	1996年	1995年	1996年
35m/m电影放映单位						
专业电影院	54	54	33 620	32 827	298	211
影剧院	28	28	15 160	17 841	162	133
礼　堂	45	45	10 508	10 229	141	109
放映队	33	33	2			
对内俱乐部	133	133	1 912	1 778	108	144
16m/m电影放映单位						
放映队	333	333	270	189	220	2
对内俱乐部	16	16	1 183	422	54	4

16－4　艺术事业基本情况

指　　标	单　位	1990年	1992年	1995年	1996年	1996比1995年增长数
一、艺术表演团体						
机构数	**个**	**23**	**21**	**19**	**17**	**－2**
话剧团、儿童剧团	个	2	2	2	2	
歌舞剧团	个	1	1	1	1	
文工团、文宣队	个	2	2	2	1	－1
戏曲剧团	个	12	11	9	7	－2
#京　剧	个	3	3	3	2	－1
曲剧团、杂技团、木偶团	个	3	3	3	3	
乐团、合唱团	个	3	2	1	1	
工作人员数	**人**	**2 248**	**2 234**	**2 787**	**1 964**	**－723**
二、艺术表演场所						
机构数	**个**	**16**	**16**	**30**	**30**	
剧场、音乐厅	个	14	14	27	27	
书场、曲艺厅	个	2	2	2	2	
座席数	**个**	**13 221**	**12 202**	**25 400**	**24 616**	**－784**
工作人员数	**人**	**481**	**483**	**765**	**853**	**88**

16－5　艺术表演活动情况

指　　标	单　位	1990年	1992年	1995年	1996年	1996比1995年增长数
艺术表演团体						
演出场次	场	3 600	2 236	2 900	2 530	－370
#到农村演出	场	700	600	700	642	－58
观众人次	万人次	425	201	277	361	84
艺术表演场所						
演出场次	场	1 544	3 308	500	392	－108
观众人次	万人次	133	30.9	130	43	－87

16－6　群众文化事业基本情况

指　　标	单　位	1990年	1992年	1995年	1996年	1996比1995年增长数
单位数	**个**	**19**	**20**	**19**	**19**	
群众艺术馆	个	1	1	1	1	
文化馆	个	18	19	18	18	
工作人员数	**人**	**955**	**955**	**847**	**868**	**21**
文化活动情况						
举办展览	次	153	105	76	130	54
举办讲作、报告会	次	118				
组织文艺活动次数	次	1 503	664	3 883	1 231	－2 652
举办训练班　班次	班	733	942	656	473	－153
结业人数	人	31 858	34 000	26 900	11 691	－12 209
放映录像　场次	场		20 200	9 800	5 900	－3 900
观众人次	万人次		130	28	1 703	1 675

16－7　公共图书馆、博物馆和文物保护单位基本情况

指　　标	单　位	1990年	1992年	1995年	1996年	1996比1995年增长数
公共图书馆数						
单位数	个	30	31	31	31	
工作人员数	人	1 182	1 081	1 084	1 156	72
藏　书	万册	665	645	677	659	－18
阅览室座席	个	4 996	4 800	4 800	4 876	76
建筑面积	平方米	46 251	47 000	76 900	76 421	－469
#阅览室	平方米	9 123	9 123	13 100	21 228	8 128
书　库	平方米	14 259	14 259	20 000	21 428	1 428
借阅人次	万人次	245	201	265	148	－117
借阅册次	万册次	468	273	237	190	－47
博物馆						
单位数	个	10	13	14	14	
工作人员数	人	482	490	456	512	56
文物藏品	万件	54	54	54	54	
举办陈列	个	54	42	51	42	－9
举办展览	个	43	38	46	46	
参观人次	万人次	74	100	56	64	8
文物保护单位						
单位数	个	6	7	7	7	
工作人员数	人	80	72	93	97	4
藏　品	件	2 700	2 131	2 234	2 142	－92

16－8　图　书　出　版

指　　标	种　类（种）			总印数(万册)		
	1990年	1995年	1996年	1990年	1995年	1996年
总　　计	**2 972**	**2 376**	**2 779**	**13 048**	**6 921**	**8 333**
#本　版	2 772	2 282	2 639	12 098	5 932	7 062
书　籍	1 555	1 489	1 699	8 065	2 887	3 788
#本　版	1 549	1 484	1 695	8 052	2 834	
课　本	495	592	839	2 179	3 465	4 311
图　片	922	295	241	2 804	569	234

16-9 1996年书籍和课本分类

类别	种类(种)	总印数(万册)	类别	种类(种)	总印数(万册)
总计	**2 538**	**8 099**			
马列主义、毛泽东思想			自然科学总论	19	18
哲学	12	9	数理科学、化学	40	17
社会科学总论	9	5	天文学、地球科学	1	
政治、法律	22	23	生物科学	1	
军事			医药、卫生	144	64
经济	138	73	农业科学	13	5
文化、科学、教育、体育	1 286	7 190	工业技术	197	130
语言、文字	78	78	交通运输	8	8
文学	232	151	航天、航空	1	4
艺术	170	207	环境科学		
历史、地理	136	99	综合性图书	31	18

16-10 杂志出版

指标	种类(种)			总印数(万册)		
	1990年	1995年	1996年	1990年	1995年	1996年
总计	**165**	**206**	**215**	**4 379**	**4 790**	**4 919**
综合	1	12	14	200	501	413
哲学、社会科学	18	20	21	422	624	625
自然科学、技术	116	147	150	864	989	1 129
文化、教育	11	11	13	1 851	1 802	1 894
文学、艺术	13	12	12	527	610	688
少年儿童读物	4	3	4	503	258	164
画刊	2	1	1	12	6	6

16-11 报纸出版

项目	种类(种)			总印数(万份)		
	1990年	1995年	1996年	1990年	1995年	1996年
总计	**18**	**28**	**29**	**38 400**	**53 706**	**55 962**
综合报	7	9	8	28 414	36 648	39 345
专业报	11	19	21	9 986	17 058	16 617
省、自治区、直辖市级报纸合计	18	9	25	38 400	35 771	55 477
综合报	7	6	5	28 414	35 202	38 958
专业报	11	3	20	9 986	569	16 519
专区(市)级报纸合计		19	4		17 935	485
综合报		3	3		1 446	387
专业报		16	1		16 489	98

16－12　广播电台情况

指　　标	单　位	1990年	1995年	1996年	1996比1995年增长数
一、广播电台和广播情况					
广播电台	座	1	1	1	
发射机	架	5	5	6	1
发射机功率	千瓦	123.5	130.0	140.0	10.0
节目套数	套	5	6	6	
平均每日播音时间	时:分	68:50	87:10	96:22	9.12
平均每日自办节目	时:分	58:50	84:48	93:52	9.04
广播覆盖率(%)	%	95	100	100	
二、广播节目制作情况					
合　计	时:分/年	6 588:56	27 715:40	26 132	－1 584:20
新　闻	时:分/年	425:50	3 589:10	4 017	427:50
文　艺	时:分/年	3 787:26	12 896:40	11 756	－1 141:20
专　题	时:分/年	1 997:40	6 113:45	2 313	－3 801:15
教　育	时:分/年	180:00	851:40	1 585	730:20
服务性	时:分/年	198:00	4 264:25	6 461	2 196:35

16－13　电视台情况

指　　标	单　位	1990年	1995年	1996年	1996比1995年增长数
一、基本情况					
电视台(座)	座	2	9	9	
发射机	架	28	31	31	
发射机功率	千瓦	74.5	135.9	135.9	
节目套数	套	3	11	11	
平均每周播出时间	时:分	162:23	373:46	428:54	55:08
平均每周自办节目播出时间	时:分	103:46	360:28	416:03	55:35
电视覆盖率	%	89	95	95	
自制节目时间	时:分	1 115:59	4 739:10	4 358	－382:50
二、电视每周播出自办节目情况					
合　计	时:分	103:46	360:28	416:03	55:35
新　闻	时:分	11:13	24:57	22:48	－3:51
专　题	时:分	13:01	71:38	86:30	14:52
教　育	时:分	17:33	37:09	42:00	4:51
文　艺	时:分	57:21	210:14	221:18	11:04
服务性	时:分	4:38	16:30	43:27	26:57

16－14　1996年广播和电视节目制作情况

单位:小时

项　　目	自制节目时间	新　闻	专　题	教　育	文　艺	服务性
一、广　播						
天津人民广播电台	25 766	4 017	2 313	1 219	11 756	6 461
二、电　视						
合　计	4 358	861	860	45	1 838	754
天津电视台	1 778	405	770	31	482	90
塘沽区电视台	216	26	8			182
汉沽区电视台	56	41	4	2	5	4
大港区电视台	121	91				30
宁河县电视台	455	67	18	12	259	99
武清县电视台	160	32	8		35	85
静海县电视台	456	78	18		247	113
宝坻县电视台	170	61	18			91
蓟县电视台	946	60	16		810	60

16－15　1996年各区县有线广播基本情况

项　　目	广播机构		农村有线广播普及情况				广播喇叭合计(万只)
	县市广播台站(个)	乡广播台站(个)	通广播村(个)	村通广播率(%)	已装喇叭农户(万户)	喇叭入户率(%)	
合　计	**12**	**220**	**3 324**	**86.00**	**0.44**	**0.40**	**378.16**
塘沽区	1	9	47	100.00			
汉沽区	1	7	54	100.00			
大港区	1	7	71	95.95			
东丽区	1	9	108	97.30	0.02	0.30	0.16
西青区	1	8	140	95.89	0.42	7.32	0.56
津南区	1	10	170	100.00			0.12
北辰区	1	12	127	100.00			0.13
宁河县	1	21	292	100.00			0.13
武清县	1	34	716	96.63			0.50
静海县	1	28	383	99.22			0.28
宝坻县	1	34	313	40.86			376.00
蓟　县	1	41	903	94.95			0.28

16－16　1996年区县电视台基本情况

项　　目	电视台(座)	节目套数(套)	平均每周播出时间(时:分)	转中央台	转省级台	自办节目	#新闻
塘沽区电视台	1	1	8:20			8:20	1:00
汉沽区电视台	1	1	21:41			21:41	0:45
大港区电视台	1	1	35:40			35:40	1:45
宁河县电视台	1	1	27:15			27:15	1:81
武清县电视台	1	1	35:00	3:30		31:30	2:15
静海县电视台	1	1	49:00	4:05	1:45	43:10	4:30
宝坻县电视台	1	1	11:35			11:35	1:10
蓟县电视台	1	1	16:55			16:55	1:10

16－17　1996年有线电视基本情况

项　　目	有线电视台 系统内 座数(个)	终端(万个)	传输线路 电缆(公里)	光缆(公里)
一、系统内合计	**2**	**73.00**	**181**	**128**
天津有线电视台	1	70.00	50	80
塘沽区有线电视台	1	3.00	100	30
二、系统外合计	**6**	**4.75**	**31**	**18**
天津港务局有线电视台	1	1.20	2	
天津碱厂有线电视台	1	0.80	3	3
天津石化公司有线电视台	1	1.38	3	
大港石油管理局有线电视台	1	0.40	20	10
中石化四公司有线电视台	1	0.50	3	
渤海石油公司有线电视台	1	0.47		5

16－18　1996年系统内有线电视宣传和节目制作情况

项　　目	台数(座)	节目套数(套)	平均每周播出时间(时:分) 合计	转中央台节目	自办节目 小计	新闻	其他	全年制作节目时间(小时)
合　　计	**2**	**3**	**289:39**	**3:30**	**286:09**	**1:00**	**285:09**	**469**
天津有线电视台	1	2	289:39	3:30	236:09		236:09	104
第1套节目		1	77:12	3:30	73:42		73:42	104
第2套节目		1	162:27		162:27		162:27	
塘沽区有线电视台	1	1	50:00		50:00	1:00	49:00	365

16-19　1996年广播电视覆盖情况

类　别	合　计		#中央台第一套节目		省级台第一套节目	
	覆盖人口数（万人）	覆盖率（%）	覆盖人口数（万人）	覆盖率（%）	覆盖人口数（万人）	覆盖率（%）
一、广　播						
全　市	**894.67**	**100.00**	**894.67**	**100.00**	**890.77**	**99.56**
市内六区	370.67	100.00	370.67	100.00	370.67	100.00
塘沽区	44.80	100.00	44.80	100.00	44.80	100.00
汉沽区	16.70	100.00	16.70	100.00	16.70	100.00
大港区	31.20	100.00	31.20	100.00	31.20	100.00
东丽区	29.71	100.00	29.71	100.00	29.71	100.00
西青区	30.76	100.00	30.76	100.00	30.76	100.00
津南区	36.23	100.00	36.23	100.00	36.23	100.00
北辰区	31.00	100.00	31.00	100.00	31.00	100.00
宁河县	34.61	100.00	34.61	100.00	34.61	100.00
武清县	78.50	100.00	78.50	100.00	78.50	100.00
静海县	49.39	100.00	49.39	100.00	49.39	100.00
宝坻县	64.00	100.00	64.00	100.00	64.00	100.00
蓟　县	77.10	100.00	77.10	100.00	73.20	94.94
二、电　视						
全　市	**894.93**	**95.00**	**894.93**	**95.00**	**848.39**	**94.83**
市内六区	354.43	95.62	354.43	95.62	354.43	95.62
塘沽区	42.56	95.00	42.56	95.00	42.56	95.00
汉沽区	15.87	95.03	15.87	95.03	15.87	95.03
大港区	29.64	95.00	29.64	95.00	29.64	95.00
东丽区	28.23	95.02	28.23	95.02	28.23	95.02
西青区	29.22	94.99	29.22	94.99	29.22	94.99
津南区	34.42	95.00	34.42	95.00	34.42	95.00
北辰区	29.45	95.00	29.45	95.00	29.45	95.00
宁河县	32.88	95.00	32.88	95.00	32.88	95.00
武清县	74.58	95.01	74.58	95.01	74.58	95.01
静海县	46.92	95.00	46.92	95.00	46.92	95.00
宝坻县	60.80	95.00	60.80	95.00	60.80	95.00
蓟　县	70.93	92.00	70.93	92.00	69.39	90.00

16－20　1996年体育场地情况

单位:个

项　　目	合　计	#体育场	体育馆	游泳池	有看台的灯光球场	小运动场	足球场
全　　市	**4 721**	**17**	**18**	**76**	**10**	**446**	**33**
#体委系统	215	9	11	19	7	3	9

16－21　体委系统体育工作者

单位:人

年　　份	体育工作者人数	专　职教练员	国家级教练员	每十万人口中体育工作者
1994	3 150	558	9	36
1995	3 416	570	9	38
1996	3 363	553	9	37

16－22　《国家体育锻炼标准》达标情况

年　　份	达标人数合　计(万人)	中　　学		小　　学	
		达标人数(万人)	达标率(%)	达标人数(万人)	达标率(%)
1994	78.2	29.5	93.7	48.3	91.0
1995	89.6	34.8	92.4	54.5	89.4
1996	93.5	37.2	94.7	55.7	92.9
1996比1995年增长数	3.9	2.4	2.3	1.2	3.5

16－23　等级裁判员和运动员发展人数

单位:人

年　　份	合　　计		#一　　级		二　　级		三　　级	
	总人数	#女　性	总人数	#女　性	总人数	#女　性	总人数	#女　性
裁判员								
1994	298	70	110	27	87	18	87	20
1995	428	70	81	17	175	17	158	33
1996	405	87	119	27	168	31	110	25
运动员								
1994	1 711	618	84	15	850	259	475	188
1995	1 833	726	112	57	1 003	331	415	168
1996	2 454	1 051	87	47	945	343	718	331

16－24 天津市举办运动竞赛情况

（县及县以上）

年份	举办运动会次数（次）	参加运动会人数（万人）	体委系统		其他系统	
			运动会次数(次)	参加人数（万人）	运动会次数(次)	参加人数（万人）
1994	369	101	230	78	139	23
1995	356	97	237	71	119	26
1996	235	23	132	17	103	6
1996比1995年增长数	－121	－74	－105	－54	－16	－20

16－25 改革开放以来卫生机构、床位及技术人员数

年份	卫生事业机构（个）	#医院	卫生机构床位数（张）	#医院	卫生技术人员数（人）	#医生	护理人员
1978	3 065	310	18 974	17 288	40 653	15 776	12 629
1979	3 342	327	19 937	17 929	46 099	17 489	14 287
1980	3 535	332	20 911	18 753	50 662	20 474	15 839
1981	3 610	332	21 987	20 301	54 535	22 941	16 555
1982	3 548	337	23 332	21 503	56 152	23 765	16 929
1983	3 582	344	24 351	22 658	58 645	25 033	17 745
1984	3 592	353	25 611	23 906	59 405	25 517	17 762
1985	3 550	285	27 402	25 191	60 412	25 555	18 520
1986	3 631	282	29 218	27 247	62 897	26 750	19 463
1987	3 465	282	30 786	28 371	63 067	27 222	19 303
1988	3 363	285	33 245	30 640	63 924	29 968	19 372
1989	3 420	291	34 122	32 224	65 766	31 619	20 264
1990	3 392	293	35 581	33 382	67 485	32 034	21 228
1991	3 397	300	37 504	35 124	68 887	32 385	22 086
1992	3 287	301	38 137	36 035	69 815	32 320	22 804
1993	3 182	304	39 023	36 724	70 920	33 026	22 884
1994	3 182	419	38 986	37 157	71 217	33 373	22 936
1995	3 182	416	39 092	37 280	71 806	33 693	23 177
1996	4 171	476	39 612	38 284	71 014	32 975	23 156

16－26　卫生事业机构

单位:个

名　　称	1990 年	1995 年	1996 年	1996 比 1995 年增长数
总　　计	**3 392**	**3 182**	**4 171**	**989**
医　院	293	416	476	60
#县及县以上医院	125	130	132	2
疗养院、所	3	3	3	
门诊部、所	2 960	2 623	3 549	926
专科防治所、站	20	21	20	－1
卫生防疫站	24	26	26	
妇幼保健站、所	18	17	18	1
药品检验所、站	8	8	9	1
医学科学研究机构	15	16	16	
高等医学教育机构	3	2	3	1
其他卫生事业机构	42	44	51	7
平均每个医院负担人口(人)	29 565	21 507	18 875	－2 632

16－27　卫生机构的床位数

单位:张

名　　称	1990 年	1995 年	1996 年	1996 比 1995 年增长数
总　　计	**35 581**	**39 092**	**39 612**	**520**
医　院	33 382	37 280	38 284	1 004
#县及县以上医院	27 427	31 009	31 199	190
疗养院、所	685	710	590	－120
门诊部、所	522	592	132	－460
专科防治所、站	337	340	340	
其他卫生机构	655	130	266	136
平均每千人口有医院床位	3.85	4.17	4.26	0.09

16－28　1996 年分科医师数

项　　目	总　计	内　科	外　科	妇产科	儿　科	眼　科	耳鼻喉科	皮肤科	传染科
合　计	**23 886**	**5 879**	**3 172**	**1 966**	**1 246**	**473**	**422**	**267**	**315**
中医师	4 642	934		142	125	50	39	39	3
西医师	19 244	4 945	3 172	1 824	1 121	423	383	228	312

项　　目	精神科	结核科	口腔科	职业病科	肿瘤科	检验科	中医科	骨伤科	其　他
合　计	**294**	**214**	**784**	**174**	**472**	**208**	**2 393**	**214**	**5 393**
中医师	3		31		12		2 393	129	742
西医师	291	214	753	174	460	208		85	4 651

16－29 卫生技术人员数

单位:人

项目	1990年	1995年	1996年	1996比1995年增长数
总计	**67 458**	**71 806**	**71 014**	**－792**
医生	32 034	33 693	32 975	－718
西医	26 313	27 886	27 117	－769
西医师	23 695	24 429	23 707	－722
西医士	2 618	3 457	3 410	－47
中医	5 680	5 774	5 806	32
中医师	5 060	5 224	5 301	77
中医士	298	377	397	20
其他中医	322	173	108	－65
中西医结合高级医师	41	33	52	19
护理人员	21 228	23 177	23 156	－21
护师	10 676	11 251	12 279	1 028
护士	7 358	9 908	9 193	－715
助产士	424	520	377	－143
护理员	2 470	1 498	1 307	－191
药剂人员	5 687	5 877	6 048	171
中药剂师	926	900	936	36
西药剂师	2 466	2 433	2 606	173
中药剂士	663	708	721	13
西药剂士	1 006	1 203	1 265	62
中药剂员	172	195	165	－30
西药剂员	454	438	355	－83
检验人员	3 483	3 655	3 933	278
检验师	2 372	2 417	2 748	331
检验士	856	1 063	1 029	－34
检验员	246	175	156	－19
其他	5 053	5 404	4 902	－502

16－30 1996年按管理部门和性质分的卫生事业基本情况

部门	卫生机构(个)	机构床位数(张)	卫生技术人员(人)					
			合计	医生	护理人员	药剂人员	检验人员	其他人员
总计	**4 171**	**39 612**	**71 014**	**32 975**	**23 156**	**6 048**	**3 933**	**4 902**
卫生部门	426	30 389	49 654	20 361	18 308	4 374	3 022	3 589
工业及其他部门	1 642	6 942	15 915	8 946	4 198	1 253	774	744
集体单位	500	1 871	3 560	2 299	488	383	116	274
私人开业	1 574	360	1 678	1 237	111	22	17	291
其他	29	50	207	132	51	16	4	4

16－31　1996 年各类医院机构、床位及人员数

类　别	医院数（个）	床位数（张）	人员数（人）	#卫生技术人员	#医　生	护理人员
全市医院总计	**476**	**38 284**	**69 191**	**54 235**	**22 037**	**21 280**
县及县以上医院	132	31 199	55 417	42 860	16 163	18 555
市	120	28 643	51 066	39 261	14 590	17 313
县	12	2 556	4 351	3 599	1 573	1 242
在县及县以上医院中						
综合医院	72	16 305	30 110	23 198	8 886	9 894
中医医院	16	1 887	3 261	2 648	1 250	805
传染病院	3	510	726	555	166	268
精神病院	4	2 288	1 725	1 292	258	906
结核病院	2	740	678	469	118	225
妇幼保健院	5	574	1 018	805	270	384
儿童医院	1	521	1 226	966	292	483
肿瘤医院	1	600	1 203	923	339	419
口腔医院	1	100	475	351	156	136

16－32　县及县以上医院诊疗和病床使用情况

项　目	单　位	1990 年	1995 年	1996 年	1996 比 1995 年增长数
诊疗情况					
诊疗人数	万人次	2 737	1 846	1 860	14
#门诊	万人次	2 318	1 532	1 543	11
入院人数	万人次	35	32	33	1
平均每月诊疗人数					
门诊诊疗人数	万人次	190	128	129	1
入院诊疗人数	万人次	3	3	3	
病床使用情况					
病人治愈率	%	64	58	56	－2
病床周转次数	次	13	11	11	
病床使用率	%	89	65	60	－5
病床工作日	日	324	236	220	－16
出院者平均住院日数	日	23	21	20	－1

16－33　1996 年医院和卫生院医疗情况

类　　别	机构数（个）	总诊疗人数（人）	#门诊人数（人）	健康检查人数（人）	入院人数（人）	出院人数（人）
县及县以上医院	129	18 602 854	15 429 776	437 507	326 558	327 864
乡(镇)卫生院	230	5 845 095	5 603 510	53 883	53 883	53 894
其他医院	62	3 433 908	2 878 566	15 574	15 574	15 749

16－34　农村村级卫生组织情况

指　　标	单　位	1990 年	1995 年	1996 年	1996 比 1995 年增长数
医药费实行减免的村数	**个**	**245**	**453**	**579**	**126**
无医疗点的村数	**个**	**247**	**229**	**237**	**8**
村设置的医疗点数	**个**	**4 304**	**5 027**	**4 704**	**－323**
村或群众集体办	个	1 692	1 966	1 757	－209
乡村医生和卫生员联合办	个	586	263	251	－12
乡卫生院设点	个	22	78	67	－11
个体办	个	1 908	2 506	2 248	－258
其　他	个	96	214	381	167
乡村医生和卫生员人数	**人**	**7 738**	**8 337**	**7 957**	**－380**
乡村医生	人	6 850	7 724	7 461	－263
卫生员	人	888	613	496	－117
农村接生员	**人**	**1 834**	**1 571**	**987**	**－584**
平均每千农业人口中有乡村医生	**人**	**2**	**2**	**2**	

16－35　1996 年 7 岁以下儿童保健工作情况

单位：人

地　区	7 岁以下儿童保健服务						5 岁以下儿童营养评价	
	新生儿访视数	保健管理人数	3 岁以下系统管理人数	眼保健人　数	听力保健人数	口腔保健人数	实　查人　数	体重低于营养评价标准人数
全　市	**53 702**	**533 726**	**178 149**	**134 171**	**93 584**	**441 940**	**340 158**	**2 168**
市辖区	27 905	273 059	101 450	93 445	83 960	211 588	174 642	1 470
市辖县	25 797	260 667	76 699	40 726	9 624	230 352	165 516	698
宁河县	2 589	25 903	6 973	450		25 903	17 572	70
武清县	5 307	63 811	18 949	5 882	4 862	54 197	35 618	205
静海县	4 925	40 660	15 343	4 131	4 131	38 251	27 188	3
宝坻县	6 485	48 091	17 828	30 263	631	30 263	28 032	220
蓟　县	6 491	82 202	17 606			81 738	57 106	200

注：5 岁以下儿童营养评价标准为“体重中位数两个标准差”。

16－36　适龄儿童疫苗接种情况

（1991－1996年）　　单位：%

疫苗种类	1991年	1992年	1993年	1994年	1995年	1996年
麻　疹	98.50	98.49	96.03	98.81	98.33	99.17
脊髓灰质炎	99.40	99.12	99.50	99.48	99.19	99.05
百白破	98.69	98.86	98.51	98.78	97.55	99.34
卡介苗	98.90	97.30	97.80	94.60	99.03	99.35

16－37　妇幼保健情况

（1991－1996年）　　单位：%

指　　标	1991年	1992年	1993年	1994年	1995年	1996年
孕妇保健覆盖率	98.64	97.83	97.06	97.24	96.75	95.83
七岁以下儿童保健覆盖率	68.00	84.37	88.52	91.18	90.87	96.60
农村孕妇住院分娩率	65.48	70.03	72.85	76.02	80.14	84.96

16－38　1996年居民前十位死亡原因和死亡专率

序位及死因	死亡专率（1/10万）	占全部死亡人数的%
1.心脏病	143.39	23.90
2.脑血管病	137.69	22.95
3.恶性肿瘤	96.27	16.25
4.呼吸系病	82.78	13.80
5.损伤和中毒	30.23	5.04
6.消化系病	22.52	3.75
7.泌尿、生殖系统病	14.90	2.48
8.内分泌、营养和代谢及免疫疾病	12.21	2.04
9.新生儿病	871.38	1.28
10.神经系病	6.49	1.08

注：新生儿病的死亡专率＝新生儿死亡人数/1995年出生人数。

16－39　1996年卫生机构技术人员技术职称状况

单位:人

项　　目	卫生技术人员中获得技术职称人员合计	主任医、药、护、技师	副主任医、药、护、技师	主治(主管)医、药、护、技师
总　　计	**18 248**	**1 141**	**3 382**	**13 725**
卫生部门合计	**14 068**	**836**	**2 403**	**10 829**
#医　院	12 175	712	2 035	9 428
门诊部、所	63	5	11	47
专科防治所、站	141	2	12	127
卫生防疫机构	479	8	61	410
妇幼保健机构	153	7	23	123
药品检验机构	111	8	25	78
医学科学研究机构	625	86	158	381
高等医学教育机构	76	8	23	45
中等医药卫生学校	101		32	69
工业及其他部门合计	**3 084**	**135**	**657**	**2 292**
#医　院	1 947	21	330	1 596
卫生防疫机构	50		2	48
集体单位合计	**977**	**154**	**285**	**538**
私人开业合计	**41**		**9**	**32**
其他合计	**78**	**16**	**28**	**34**

项　　目	其他技术人员及管理人员中获得技术职称的人员	主任医、药、护、技师	副主任医、药、护、技师	主治(主管)医、药、护、技师	高级会计、统计、经济师及其他	会计、统计、经济师及其他
总　　计	**3 171**	**123**	**432**	**1 230**	**262**	**1 124**
卫生部门合计	**2 215**	**89**	**317**	**922**	**130**	**757**
#医　院	1 484	61	212	714	69	428
门诊部、所	1			1		
专科防治所、站	27	2	5	11	1	8
卫生防疫机构	83	3	14	35		31
妇幼保健机构	18	1	3	8		6
药品检验机构	17	2	4	6		5
医学科学研究机构	302	19	53	83	43	104
高等医学教育机构	61		3	11	5	42
中等医药卫生学校	89		17	31	8	33
工业及其他部门合计	**892**	**29**	**108**	**295**	**127**	**333**
#医　院	334	7	50	158	8	111
卫生防疫机构	9		1	8		
集体单位合计	**57**	**5**	**6**	**10**	**5**	**31**
私人开业合计	**5**		**1**	**1**		**3**
其他合计	**2**			**2**		

16－40 1996年检察机关立案侦查经济案件情况

项目	侦查经济案件	#贪污	受贿	行贿	挪用公款	偷税抗税	假冒商标
一、受案(件)	**1 438**	**594**	**418**	**3**	**169**	**124**	**19**
二、立案(件)	**713**	**222**	**179**	**3**	**107**	**102**	**21**
#5万元至10万元	114	38	13		34	11	3
10万元至50万元	115	14	7		48	19	7
50万元至100万元	19	4	2		4	2	1
100万元以上	20	6			2	7	1
三、立案案犯构成(人)	**777**	**253**	**182**	**4**	**113**	**108**	**26**
机关工作人员	39	15	14		9	1	
国营企事业工作人员	379	151	130	1	48	26	
基层群众组织工作人员	26	13	3	2	2	4	2
集体经济组织工作人员	219	61	32		51	28	10
个体劳动者	62	4				46	8
其他	52	9	3	1	3	3	6
四、结案							
件数(件)	714	219	193	2	114	94	19
人数(人)	780	249	197	2	122	102	24
1.移送起诉							
件数(件)	456	177	141		73	16	5
人数(人)	510	205	145		80	21	8
2.移送免予起诉							
件数(件)	198	21	41	2	32	71	7
人数(人)	209	23	41	2	32	74	9
3.撤销案件							
件数(件)	60	21	11		9	7	7
人数(人)	61	21	11		10	7	7
五、造成直接经济损失(万元)	**11 382**	**1 582**	**510**	**1**	**3 623**	**1 153**	**105**
六、挽回直接经济损失(万元)	**5 538**	**1 245**	**529**	**1**	**1 454**	**1 159**	**101**

16－41 1996年法院经济纠纷案件收案和结案情况

单位:件

项目	收案	结案	#调解	判决
合计	**12 709**	**12 488**	**4 532**	**4 408**
经济合同纠纷(国内)	11 949	11 745	4 301	4 194
涉外经济纠纷	23	51	4	12
经济损害赔偿纠纷	80	61	17	20
经济权属纠纷	6	8	2	4
企业破产	35	29	6	4
交通运输经济纠纷	208	196	72	59
海事海商经济纠纷	262	244	70	65
其他经济纠纷	146	154	60	50

16－42 1996年法院民事案件收案和结案情况

单位:件

项目	收案	结案	#调解	判决
合计	**32 941**	**33 207**	**15 004**	**11 027**
婚姻家庭	16 989	17 194	9 108	4 415
#离婚	14 400	14 584	7 969	3 423
抚育	1 062	1 069	564	340
赡养	943	948	400	345
继承	350	335	115	147
房屋	3 818	3 871	1 250	1 556
人身财产赔偿	3 315	3 372	1 350	1 588
债务	6 776	6 716	2 691	2 576
知识产权	15	24	11	6
人身权	86	85	28	34
其他	1 592	1 610	451	705

16－43 1996年法院行政案件收案和结案情况

单位:件

项目	收案	结案					
			维持	撤消	变更	撤诉	其他
合计	**306**	**313**	**158**	**28**	**2**	**77**	**48**
公安	92	89	45	7		19	18
工商	8	8	3	2		3	
卫生	3	1				1	
文化		1	1				
土地	45	43	9	14		11	9
城建	66	58	32	2		18	6
环保							
专利	1	1	1				
民政							
税务	1	1				1	
其他	90	111	67	3	2	24	15

16－44 调解工作

项目	单位	1990年	1995年	1996年	1996年比1995年增长数
司法助理员	人	370	411	410	－1
人民调解委员会	个	8 270	7 759	7 901	142
调解人员	人	186 764	155 827	173 593	17 766
调解民间纠纷	件	45 317	35 018	39 079	4 061
调解成功	件	39 856	32 790	37 205	4 415
防止民事案件转化为刑事案件	件		387	402	15
	人		561	848	287
防止非正常死亡案件	件	281	265	252	－13
	人	365	291	294	3

16－45 律 师 工 作

项 目	单 位	1990年	1995年	1996年	1996比1995年增长数
律师事务所	所	45	127	144	17
律师工作人员	人	1 032	1 580	1 489	－91
#专职律师	人	449	688	763	75
兼职律师	人	322	449	411	－38
特邀律师	人		443	315	－128
聘请常年法律顾问的单位	家	2 500	4 551	3 884	－667
民事代理	件	8 433	6 732	5 590	－1 142
经济案件	件	2 437	5 495	4 775	－720
刑事辩论	件	4 111	3 699	3 279	－420
行政代理	件		111	124	13
非诉讼事务	件	377	16 228	8 655	－7 573
解答法律咨询	人次	28 764	32 502	25 444	－7 058
代写法律文书	件	11 666	9 852	7 932	－1 920

16－46 公 证 工 作

项 目	单 位	1990年	1995年	1996年	1996比1995年增长数
公证机构	个	20	20	20	
公证员	人	145	286	288	2
办理公证	件	36 380	111 801	140 234	28 433
国内公证	件	26 644	82 326	103 750	21 424
#经济公证	件	11 420	47 271	53 711	6 440
涉外公证	件	9 736	29 475	36 484	7 009
#经济公证	件	269	953	1 594	641

16－47 妇联组织情况

项 目	单 位	1990年	1995年	1996年	1996比1995年增长数
妇联组织机构	**个**	**369**	**374**	**366**	**－8**
区妇联	个	13	13	13	
县妇联	个	5	5	5	
乡妇联	个	224	225	220	－5
街妇联	个	127	131	128	－3
妇联干部总数	**人**	**666**	**623**	**609**	**－14**
市妇联	人	73	74	72	－2
区妇联	人	134	118	116	－2
县妇联	人	46	37	36	－1
乡镇、街道妇联	人	413	394	385	－9

16－48 妇联工作情况

项目	单位	总计	市级	区级	县级
双学双比活动					
实用技术培训情况					
接受技术培训的妇女数	人	271 880	367	89 132	182 381
女农民技术员	人	9 543	182	2 903	6 458
妇女技术示范户	个	14 269	168	2 505	11 596
扶贫情况					
被帮扶妇女数	人	13 335	311	362	12 662
脱贫妇女数	人	9 997	311	302	9 384
巾帼建功活动					
岗位建功成材					
参加建功活动人数	万人	86	40	37	9
表彰标兵数	人	345	290	54	1
下岗女工再就业情况					
培训下岗女工人数	人	15 353		15 283	70
介绍下岗女工就业人数	人	25 000	10 117	14 823	
三八红旗手	人	1 260	290	758	212
三八红旗集体	个	213	49	131	33
五好文明家庭	户	1 496	100	986	410
家庭教育场所					
家长学校	个	3 864	2 687	2 016	671
广播父母学校	个	22	2	20	
实施春蕾计划					
资助女童入学或返校数	人	751	440	227	84
社会捐资总额	万元	43	15	18	10

16－49 1996年基层工会组织基本情况

单位:个;人

项目	机构数(个)	项目	人员数(人)	项目	人员数(人)
基层工会组织	8 799	工会会员总数	2 316 583	专职干部文化构成	
车间工会委员会	21 057	＃女会员	1 061 022	大学本科	1 176
工会小组	127 844	工会专职工作人员	15 403	大专	3 960
验收合格职工之家	6 324	＃专职干部	12 408	中专、中技	3 049
女职工委员会	3 803	工会专职正副主席	6 061	高中及以下	4 223
		＃女正副主席	2 183		

十七、改革开放和滨海新区

REFORM, OPENING AND NEW COASTLINE AREA

1996年新组建企业集团63个　　　　累计已达　231个

滨海新区1996年完成国内生产总值　320.29亿元　　占全市的29.1%

天津经济技术开发区至1996年底已投产的"三资"企业达1 785家

天津港保税区1996年通关货物总值为6.95亿美元

天津与国外结成友好城市一览

友好城市	友城所在国家和省(州、县、区)	缔结时间	签约地点
神户市	日本兵库县	1973年6月24日	天　津
费　城	美国宾夕法尼亚州	1980年2月10日	寄　签
墨尔本市	澳大利亚维多利亚州	1980年5月5日	天　津
四日市市	日本三重县	1980年10月28日	天　津
萨拉耶沃市	波黑共和国	1981年5月28日	天　津
北家莱海峡大区	法国北家莱海峡大区	1984年10月10日	天　津
伦巴第大区	意大利伦巴第大区	1985年5月9日	寄　签
格罗宁根市	荷　兰	1985年9月12日	格罗宁根
千叶市	日本千叶市	1986年5月7日	天　津
普罗夫迪夫大区	保加利亚普罗夫迪夫大区	1989年10月15日	普罗夫迪夫大区
伊兹密尔市	土尔其伊兹密尔市	1991年9月25日	伊兹密尔
阿比让市	科特迪瓦	1992年9月26日	天　津
乌兰巴托市	蒙　古	1992年9月27日	天　津
哈尔科夫市	乌克兰	1993年6月14日	天　津
延雪坪市	瑞　典	1993年9月23日	天　津
仁川市	韩　国	1993年12月7日	仁　川
萨尔州	德　国	1996年9月27日	天　津
罗兹市	波　兰	1996年10月11日	罗　兹

1996年经济体制改革进展情况

1996年，天津市认真贯彻执行党的十四届五中全会和江泽民总书记关于加快国有企业改革步伐的重要讲话精神，按照全国体改会议的部署，遵循市委、市政府提出的“工作创一流、‘九五’高起步、实现翻两番”的总体要求和有关改革工作的部署安排，围绕实现两个根本性转变，结合学习上海等地经验，以深化国有企业改革为中心，全面推进各项改革，在许多方面加快了步伐，加大了力度，取得了重要进展，促进了国民经济持续快速健康发展和社会全面进步。

一、现代企业制度试点步伐加快

1996年新批准试点企业108户，累计214户，其中国有大中型骨干企业175户，占骨干企业总数的41.2%，达到了市委、市政府确定的目标要求。列入试点的国有企业资产总额超过1 000亿元，占全部国有企业资产总额的60%以上。1995年批准的106户试点企业，经过一年左右的实施运作，初步建立了新的财产组织形式、公司治理结构和内部运行机制。1996年的108户试点企业，基本完成了试点方案的论证和审批，相继转入实施运作阶段。汽车集团公司、大港油田集团公司、建工集团总公司、公交总公司、金牛面粉公司等一批试点企业，以试点为契机，理顺关系，调整结构，深化改革，转换机制，企业面貌发生了可喜变化。同时，对原有72家股份有限公司和有限责任公司进行了规范，并组织了几家公司的股票上市。

二、国有大中型企业嫁接改造调整取得新成果

全市国有大中型企业已分别实行嫁接、改造、调整的，累计达总数的60%以上；其中工业系统1996年完成65户，累计195户，占总数的62%。通过嫁、改、调，发展了一批高技术、高水平的产品，使一批老企业焕发了生机。

三、抓大放小、兼并破产、资产重组迈出了较大步伐

新组建企业集团63个，累计已达231个。采取多种途径和形式放开放活国有小企业和集体企业，工业系统实行不同形式改制的国有小企业累计达514户，占总数的73%；在已完成改制的125户国有小企业中，有45%的企业实现了减亏或扭亏为盈。市区国有、集体企业改组为股份合作制的已达600多户。乡村集体企业实行不同形式改制的已过半数，其中实行股份合作制的已达3 500多家，实行风险抵押的达6 300多家，分别占总数的39%和79%。企业兼并、破产步伐明显加快，工业系统去年兼并、破产80户，累计已达280户(其中破产20户)，盘活资产存量27亿多元，预计可冲销呆帐准备金9亿多元，不少企业开始出现转机。继续实施“双优化工程”，全年共计52个项目，盘活土地683万平方米，支持企业资金26亿元。

四、加大了对企业改革的政策扶持力度

1996年相继下发了10多个文件规定，在财税、信贷、安置富余职工、盘活存量资产、放开放活小企业、支持科技进步、推动兼并破产、发展企业集团、减轻企业负担等方面，出台了一系列政策措施，支持企业的改革与发展。通过多元投资、贷改投等形式，帮助企业增资减债，使国有工业企业的资产负债率由1994年的79%下降到70%。

五、市场体系的培育和建设取得新进展

各类商品市场和要素市场继续发展，初步形成多层次的市场体系框架。期货市场和主要批发市场成交额实现3 648亿元，同比增长2.7倍；其中1996年新开业的12个批发市场新增交易额20亿元。商业连锁经营进一步发展。金融改革和发展迈出新的步伐。

六、社会保障制度改革继续推进

城镇企业职工养老保险和失业保险，按照市人大通过的两个《条例》组织实施，扩大了社会统筹覆盖面，参保职工分别占全市职工总数的80%和94%，并且提高了保障水平。继续多渠道安排就业和实施再就业工程，下岗职工实现再就业累计20万人。塘沽区医疗保险制度改革试点进展顺利，取得重要经验。结合大规模危陋平房改造和“安居工程”建设，城填住房制度改革进一步深化，公房出售力度加大，全年出售公房136.6万平方米，收回资金3.15亿元。

在肯定1996年天津市改革工作取得重要进展的同时，必须清醒地看到存在的问题和差距，主要是：经济结构的许多方面不尽合理，调整改组的步伐较慢；一些国有企业生产经营困难，效益下滑，亏损增加，在市场竞争面前茫无所措；思想解放不够，市场观念和开拓创新意识不强，特别是在解决重点难点问题上缺乏创造性的实招和突破性的进展；有些改革措施和政策措施的落实力度不够，进展迟缓。这些问题和差距，都需要深刻认识，认真反思，高度重视，在新的一年里，采取有力措施，切实加以改进，走出新路子，开创新局面。

(天津市经济体制改革委员会)

17－1　1996年新批企业集团一览

集团名称	子企业数	母公司名称	母公司性质	母公司注册资本（万元）	主要经营范围	审批部门
天津永盛集团	10	天津永盛集团公司	有限责任	2 100	针织坯布成衣内衣漂染	体改委、农委
天津惠利集团	5	天津惠利集团公司	有限责任	2 000	制鞋服装加工制造商业	体改委、农委
天津大北海集团	7	大北海集团公司	有限责任	2 018	服装生产加工机械制造	体改委、农委
天津海翔集团	14	天津海翔集团公司	有限责任	3 800	钢轧延、橡胶制品、商业	体改委、农委
天津海青集团	9	天津海青集团公司	有限责任	2 008	有色黑色金属加工制造	体改委、农委
天津市油脂集团	6	油脂集团公司	国有独资	25 307	食油生产加工销售	体改委、商委
天津益商集团	25	天津益商集团公司	国有独资	61 000	商业物资供销	市委、市政府
天津畜产进出口集团	12	畜产进出口集团公司	国有独资	2 110	绒毛皮毛畜产品进出口	体改委、经贸委
天津三岔口集团	5	三岔口集团公司	有限责任	2 616	服装、塑料、丝带织染	体改委、农委
天津达盛集团	5	天津达盛集团公司	有限责任	2 745	服装、绣花、纸包装品	体改委、农委
天津大来集团	5	天津大来集团公司	有限责任	2 703	织布内衣服装纸包装品	体改委、农委
天津凯瑞集团	5	天津凯瑞集团公司	有限责任	2 422	各种服装卫生材料化工	体改委、农委
天津建宇集团	5	天津建宇集团公司	有限责任	3 100	铁路运输煤炭运输销售	体改委、农委
天津万达集团	5	天津万达集团公司	有限责任	4 500	自行车、摩托车内外胎	体改委、农委
天津石油集团	22	天津石油集团公司	国有独资	7 130	成品油经营、仓储运输	体改委、商委
天津银燕集团	5	天津银燕集团公司	有限责任	2 010	地毯系列、服装、皮革	体改委、农委
天津食品工贸集团	16	食品工贸集团公司	国有独资	41 300	食品加工营销资产经营	市委、市政府
天津经济建设投资集团		经投集团公司	国有独资	200 000	资产经营	市政府
天津水电工程集团	7	振津管道集团公司	有限责任	3 038	水利水电工程设备安装	体改委、农委
天津市金鸵集团	6	金鸵集团公司	有限责任	2 000	农用三轮车农机具	体改委、农委
天津和平海湾电源集团		海湾电源集团公司	有限责任		高能电池系列产品	经委
天津野采王集团	5	野采王集团公司	有限责任	2 005	山野菜、农、林、牧、渔	体改委、农委
天津再兴集团	16	天津再兴集团公司	有限责任	2 640	钢材、建材、化工、造纸	体改委、农委
天津纺织进出口集团	8	纺织进出口集团公司	国有独资	6 648	商品进出口、易货贸易	体改委、经贸委
天津练达集团	5	天津练达集团公司	有限责任	2 050	原油生产加工工程设计	体改委
天津星河集团	5	天津星河集团公司	有限责任	3 000	金属制品商业物资批发	体改委、农委
天津华泰集团	10	天津华泰集团公司	股份有限	10 500	基础设施开发勘察设计	体改委
天津迅达摩托车集团		迅达摩托车集团公司	有限责任		摩托车及零配件	经委
天津天狮集团	5	天津天狮集团有限公司	有限责任	5 000	营养高钙素系列产品	体改委
天津光辉集团	5	天津光辉集团有限公司	有限责任	4 500	农药、化工产品	体改委、农委
天津赛达橡塑集团	5	赛达橡塑集团有限公司	有限责任	4 000	模具铸件自行车内外胎	体改委、农委
天津市大华雁发集团	5	大华雁发集团有限公司	有限责任	4 307	汽车配件制造汽车货运	体改委、农委

17－1续表

集团名称	子企业数	母公司名称	母公司性质	母公司注册资本(万元)	主要经营范围	审批部门
天津德塔科技集团	5	德塔科技集团有限公司	有限责任	4 500	成套控制系统仪器仪表	体改委、农委
天津自强集团	5	天津自强集团有限公司	有限责任	4 017	汽车装具配件物资批发	体改委、农委
天津井田集团	5	天津井田集团有限公司	有限责任	6 000	电器设备服装、纺织品	体改委、农委
天津川野集团	5	天津川野集团有限公司	有限责任	5 000	二、三轮摩托车系列	体改委、农委
天津市钛铁集团	18	天津市钛铁集团公司	有限责任	5 300	钛铁粉化工建材电焊条	体改委、农委
天津市腾达集团	10	天津市腾达集团公司	有限责任	5 800	自行车文教用品水暖	体改委、农委
天津市鑫城集团	10	天津市鑫城集团公司	有限责任	5 400	纺织印染服装电线化工	体改委、农委
天津市精武集团	12	天津市精武集团公司	有限责任	5 200	各种水产养殖畜牧食品	体改委、农委
天津市百灵集团	5	天津市百灵集团公司	有限责任	5 500	生产加工各种打火机轮	体改委、农委
天津星都集团	6	天津星都集团有限公司	有限责任	5 600	服装针棉织品地毯商业	体改委、农委
天津亚中集团	8	天津亚中集团有限公司	有限责任	5 580	塑料制品地毯制造服装	体改委、农委
天津弘扬鑫鑫集团	8	弘扬鑫鑫集团有限公司	有限责任	5 018	各种纸制品、金属制品	体改委、农委
天津双利集团	5	天津双利集团有限公司	有限责任	5 080	羊毛地毯化工助剂钢材	体改委、农委
天津亚华集团	5	天津亚华集团有限公司	有限责任	5 060	地毯皮革制品旅游包	体改委、农委
天津大发集团	5	天津大发集团有限公司	有限责任	5 180	纺纱布坯制造商业物资	体改委、农委
天津公交集团		天津公交集团有限公司	有限责任		公共交通运输	体改委、建委
天津五矿进出口集团	5	五矿进出口集团公司	有限责任	10 189	商品进出口、边贸	体改委、经贸委
天津自来水工程集团		自来水工程集团公司	有限责任		自来水工程设计、施工	体改委、建委
天津林营集团	5	天津林营集团有限公司	有限责任	5 192	各种色布服装制作纸张	体改委、农委
天津振宇集团	5	天津振宇集团有限公司	有限责任	5 325	各种服装、缝纫机零件	体改委、农委
天津天航摩托车集团	5	天航摩托车集团公司	有限责任	4 960	摩托车及发动机制造	体改委、农委
天津利和集团	18	天津利和集团有限公司	有限责任	3 183.76		体改委、经贸委
天津天尊集团	5	天津天尊集团有限公司	有限责任	4 859	白酒啤酒保健酒汽车运输	体改委、农委
天津久安集团	5	天津久安集团有限公司	有限责任	4 682	低压电器系列、配电箱	体改委、农委
天津冠达集团	5	天津冠达集团有限公司	有限责任	4 000	化工、建材、汽车运输	体改委、农委
天津圣罗科工贸集团	5	圣罗科工贸集团公司	有限责任	3 709	各种中高档衬衣、内衣	体改委、农委
天津南开允公集团	33	南开允公集团有限公司	有限责任	8 000	科技产品开发研制电子	体改委
天津液化气集团	5	液化气集团有限公司	国有独资	9 569	液化气及相关产品	体改委、建委
天津天仪集团						经委
天津重型机械集团						经委
天津塑料集团						经委

（市体改委提供）

17－2　1996年现代企业制度试点企业概况

单位:万元

项　目	企业数(个)	职工人数(人)	工资总额	工业总产值(现价)	工业增加值	资产总额
总　计	**198**	**581 216**	**515 439**	**4 334 950**	**2 053 023**	**12 536 311**
一、按经济形式分						
国有经济	140	487 764	427 369	3 514 049	1 788 651	9 982 170
国家控股经济	39	68 292	72 333	538 349	154 758	2 004 929
集体控股经济	11	13 979	6 715	209 018	76 831	272 656
其他经济	8	11 181	9 022	73 534	32 783	276 556
二、按企业规模分						
特大型	4	129 971	162 020	2 233 573	1 573 322	4 840 554
大　型	107	374 167	299 995	1 745 561	423 560	6 428 859
中　型	70	69 214	47 633	318 960	50 422	1 138 764
小　型	17	7 864	5 791	36 856	5 719	128 134
三、按主管行业类别分						
采掘业	3	87 089	95 516	661 175	314 282	1 309 381
制造业	112	315 690	277 396	3 638 497	1 714 983	8 171 410
电力、煤气及水的生产和供应业	3	7 165	7 917	5 124	1 636	162 574
建筑业	10	78 587	59 008			793 428
运输邮电业	9	35 604	28 774	2 457	392	369 020
批发和零售贸易餐饮业	45	47 143	40 108	13 086	10 630	1 123 703
#餐饮业	2	438	771			2 947
房地产业	5	2 809	2 596			461 436
其他行业	11	7 129	4 124	14 611	11 100	145 359
四、按财产组织形式分						
股份有限公司	22	51 388	57 422	493 356	164 638	1 782 016
有限责任公司	65	94 466	75 834	822 551	124 166	2 103 915
国有独资公司	87	387 775	344 823	2 879 627	1 709 038	7 928 315
尚未实行公司制的国有独资企业	17	35 399	29 848	77 003	20 342	572 426
其　他	7	12 188	7 512	62 413	34 839	149 639
五、按企业改革工作的主管部门分						
国家经贸委	1	491	800			57 699
国家体改委	9	131 301	163 476	2 244 218	1 574 777	4 926 557
市经(贸)委	15	33 732	28 874	122 188	26 566	630 317
市体改委	110	284 196	224 780	1 202 320	208 376	4 994 688
企业主管部门	63	131 496	97 509	766 224	243 304	1 927 050
六、按确定试点企业时间分						
1994年	34	267 644	276 998	2 881 761	1 696 362	7 616 049
1995年	70	133 986	105 694	813 645	263 531	1 922 068
1996年	94	179 586	132 747	639 544	93 130	2 998 194

资料来源:截止1996年底已运行的198家现代企业制度试点企业专项调查资料。

17-2续表

单位:万元

项　目	固定资产原　价	固定资产净　值	流动资产	销售收入	利税总额	#利润总额
总　计	**6 976 693**	**5 347 367**	**5 578 654**	**6 412 748**	**388 676**	**94 307**
一、按经济形式分						
国有经济	6 170 021	4 748 904	4 336 604	5 020 796	269 719	27 515
国家控股经济	641 118	455 631	946 813	943 557	82 002	40 395
集体控股经济	90 437	71 178	135 873	272 536	30 793	23 934
其他经济	75 117	71 654	159 364	175 859	6 162	2 463
二、按企业规模分						
特大型	3 303 333	2 539 168	1 604 025	1 961 854	222 883	96 286
大　型	3 189 871	2 476 527	3 295 916	3 574 835	130 119	-15 069
中　型	440 917	301 158	611 419	810 139	32 958	12 298
小　型	42 572	30 514	67 294	65 920	2 716	792
三、按主管行业类别分						
采掘业	1 314 684	696 605	493 681	644 763	64 641	5 649
制造业	4 664 108	3 895 471	3 221 649	3 360 927	245 775	50 596
电力、煤气及水的生产和供应业	185 223	135 458	12 182	32 043	-5 145	-7 036
建筑业	195 078	136 913	617 584	755 142	20 367	3 903
运输邮电业	244 035	179 525	140 143	118 231	21 042	19 042
批发和零售贸易餐饮业	315 307	260 243	686 687	1 398 176	22 254	6 170
#餐饮业	620	470	1 617	6 299	784	451
房地产业	14 503	11 204	351 902	62 356	17 197	14 583
其他行业	43 755	31 948	54 826	41 110	2 545	1 400
四、按财产组织形式分						
股份有限公司	555 632	408 201	814 560	747 134	74 584	43 350
有限责任公司	1 224 473	1 012 616	894 835	1 052 414	55 126	-24 739
国有独资公司	4 888 742	3 702 149	3 359 910	4 096 635	237 925	67 974
尚未实行公司制的国有独资企业	265 838	196 474	431 423	323 033	17 552	6 000
其　他	42 008	27 927	77 926	193 532	3 489	1 722
五、按企业改革工作的主管部门分						
国家经贸委	13 710	11 488	45 815	79 914	-979	-1 068
国家体改委	3 310 898	2 543 803	1 638 259	1 979 954	223 844	96 492
市经(贸)委	259 921	204 566	346 226	487 362	9 800	-1 393
市体改委	2 407 529	1 852 409	2 542 005	2 437 354	98 297	-16 966
企业主管部门	984 635	735 101	1 006 349	1 428 164	57 714	17 242
六、按确定试点企业时间分						
1994年	4 360 195	3 282 501	3 336 417	3 354 702	273 317	106 655
1995年	872 512	636 039	983 589	1 263 372	55 543	17 684
1996年	1 743 987	1 428 827	1 258 648	1 794 674	59 816	-30 032

17－3　滨海新区主要经济指标

项　　目	单　位	1995年	1996年	1996比1995年增长％	占全市比重％	
					1995年	1996年
户籍户数	户	33.83	34.11	0.8	12.2	12.2
户籍人口	万人	100.24	100.79	0.5	11.2	11.2
按农业非农业分:						
农业人口	万人	29.96	28.48	－4.9	7.7	7.4
非农业人口	万人	70.28	72.31	2.9	13.8	14.1
按性别分:						
男性	万人	52.28	52.51	0.4	11.5	11.5
女性	万人	47.96	48.28	0.7	10.9	10.9
职工人数	万人	55.81	58.31	4.5	19.3	20.5
职工工资总额	亿元	46.25	55.54	20.1	25.0	26.2
职工年平均工资	元	8 287	9 525	14.9		
国内生产总值	亿元	241.64	320.29	28.3	26.3	29.1
第一产业	亿元	4.74	4.84	－4.8	7.5	6.9
第二产业	亿元	166.90	224.78	31.9	33.3	38.5
第三产业	亿元	70.00	90.67	20.4	19.7	20.3
工农业总产值	亿元	520.60	713.41	39.8	24.2	26.8
＃工业总产值	亿元	510.34	701.44	40.2	25.3	27.8
社会固定资产投资	亿元	152.40	157.05	3.1	38.8	36.0
＃基础设施	亿元	20.60	26.30	27.7		
＃市重点项目	亿元	29.30	26.80	－8.5	33.5	29.8
区级财政收入	亿元	12.77	20.43	60.0	10.9	14.9
区级财政支出	亿元	23.17	29.71	28.2	24.8	26.2
社会消费品零售额	亿元	35.25	46.90	33.0	9.4	10.0
外贸出口总值	亿美元	10.10	17.46	72.9	33.7	43.0
新批三资企业项目	个	761	606	－20.4	54.8	55.7
新批三资企业协议外资金额	亿美元	18.41	18.67	1.4	47.9	47.6

17－4　滨海新区基础设施投资完成情况

单位:万元

项　　目	1995年	1996年	1996比1995年增长％	构　成(％)	
				1995年	1996年
合　　计	**206 157**	**262 860**	**27.5**	**100.0**	**100.0**
道路桥梁	27 680	73 773	166.5	13.4	28.1
港口	34 793	4 590	－86.8	16.9	1.7
排水	14 548	14 816	1.8	7.1	5.6
供水	7 800	27 611	254.0	3.8	10.5
供电供热	2 619	15 068	475.3	1.3	5.7
通讯	22 211	19 811	－10.8	10.8	7.5
其他	96 508	72 795	－24.6	46.8	27.7

17－5 滨海新区区级财政收支情况

单位:万元

项 目	1995年	1996年	1996比1995年增长%	占全市同级比重(%)
地方财政收入	127 680	204 256	60.0	47.4
#工商税收入类	105 192	172 238	63.7	52.5
#增值税	34 409	39 340	14.3	47.1
营业税	34 138	48 103	40.9	40.3
城建税	6 974	7 804	11.9	71.5
农牧业税	469	609	29.9	8.6
企业收入	16 672	24 291	45.7	36.5
其他收入	5 347	7 118	33.1	24.3
地方财政支出	231 726	297 099	28.2	48.6
基本建设支出	134 675	162 537	20.7	90.7
农林水气事业费支出	1 124	1 708	52.0	24.8
支援农村生产支出	776	918	18.3	29.1
文教卫生事业费	21 436	19 894	-7.2	14.4
行政管理费	10 387	8 637	-16.8	21.5
公检法支出	4 387	6 311	43.9	23.3
其他支出	58 941	97 074	64.7	44.6

注:本表包括范围为塘沽、汉沽、大港区、开发区和保税区。

17－6 经济技术开发区城市建设情况

(截至1996年底)

项 目	合 计(万平方米)	厂 房	住宅及公建	项 目	数 量	项 目	数 量
累计房屋开工面积	339.80	183.90	155.90	规划区域面积	33平方公里	绿化覆盖面积	120公顷
#1996年	61.10	18.70	42.40	#已开发面积	20平方公里	公交客运车辆	164标台
累计房屋竣工面积	232.50	157.20	75.30	桥 梁	2座	出租车辆	2 269辆
#1996年	33.20	19.50	13.70	路 灯	2 536盏	客运总量	504万人次

17－7 经济技术开发区国民经济主要指标

项目	单位	1995 年	1996 年	1996 比 1995 年增长%
1.国内生产总值	万元	801 102	1 310 135	60.6
第二产业	万元	674 871	1 106 599	62.2
工　业	万元	672 141	1 100 836	62.1
建筑业	万元	2 730	5 763	102.6
第三产业	万元	126 231	203 536	49.1
交通、仓储及邮电通信业	万元	4 500	10 862	129.2
批发和零售贸易、餐饮业	万元	53 292	86 915	55.2
金融、保险业	万元	36 663	52 850	37.1
房地产业	万元	8 405	12 777	18.8
其他行业	万元	23 371	40 132	46.3
2.工业产品销售收入	万元	2 158 984	3 617 960	67.6
#外商投资企业	万元	2 122 588	3 563 872	67.9
3.工业总产值(现价)	万元	2 277 394	3 701 106	62.5
客商投资企业	万元	2 240 479	3 646 558	62.8
内资企业	万元	36 915	54 548	47.8
按轻重工业分				
轻工业	万元	1 098 838	1 627 377	48.1
重工业	万元	1 178 556	2 073 729	76.0
4.出口总额	万美元	90 103	145 020	60.9
5.利润总额	万元	347 791	511 420	47.0
6.财政收入	万元	165 571	216 065	30.5
7.财政支出	万元	165 654	217 486	31.3
8.当年批准客商投资企业	个	361	187	－48.2
9.当年批准客商投资企业协议投资额	万美元	181 129	191 604	5.8
10.从业人员	人	112 874	140 150	24.2
客商投资企业	人	79 682	99 853	25.3
内资企业	人	33 192	40 297	21.4
按产业分组				
第二产业	人	86 348	102 131	18.3
第三产业	人	26 526	38 019	43.3
按文化程度分组				
大专以上	人	30 550	35 810	17.2
高中至大专	人	70 984	78 552	10.7
高中以下	人	11 340	25 788	127.4
按劳动岗位分组				
管理人员	人	11 503	18 920	64.5
工程技术人员	人	19 575	22 417	14.5
其　他	人	81 796	98 813	20.8
11.客商投资企业主要经济效益指标				
利润总额	万元	297 427	427 868	43.9
每百元产值实现利润	元	11	12	9.1
产销率	%	94.7	97.7	3.0

注:国内生产总值及其构成项绝对数按现价计算,速度按可比价计算。

17－8　经济技术开发区基础设施完成投资和形成能力

项　目	1996 年基础设施实际完成投资（万元）	#建筑工程	项　目	单　位	1996 年年末基础设施形成能力
总　计	**119 411**	**84 005**	道路:长度	公里	65.1
1.道　路	16 771	12 863	面积	万平方米	185.6
2.排　水	21 301	14 071	给水管网	公里	151.2
3.给　水	22 191	17 930	排水管网	公里	292.5
4.电　力	4 397	1 227	供自来水	万吨/日	10.5
5.热　电	8 613	4 552	供　热	吨/小时	445
6.通　讯	930	400	发电厂	千瓦	2×9 800
7.燃　气	3 241	225	供　电	兆伏安	2×50
8.绿　化	4 406	4 260	供燃气	万立方米/日	10
9.填　土	9 577	9 577	供气管网	公里	22.2
10.其　他	27 984	18 900	程控电话	门	10 000
			通信管道	孔公里	558
			有线电视网线	公里	40
			铁路专用线	公里	8.2

17－9　经济技术开发区已批准客商投资企业情况

年　份	批准客商投资企业(家)	协议投资额（万美元）	注册资本（万美元）	开业投产企业（家）
1985－1996 年累计	**2 744**	**778 475**	**428 525**	**1 785**
1985	14	3 192	2 073	
1986	27	4 342	3 487	20
1987	34	2 280	2 181	28
1988	48	8 482	6 895	30
1989	40	10 569	7 087	12
1990	54	12 237	6 377	30
1991	121	18 565	13 451	55
1992	462	70 261	40 576	92
1993	909	123 536	90 022	278
1994	487	152 278	89 153	469
1995	361	181 129	78 156	543
1996	187	191 604	89 067	228

注:表中数字以核发批准证书为准。

17－10 经济技术开发区客商投资企业情况

(截止 1996 年底)

国别(地区)	企业个数(个)	协议投资总额(万美元)	#协议外资额	国别(地区)	企业个数(个)	协议投资总额(万美元)	#协议外资额
合计	**2 699**	**753 056**	**592 923**	越南	1	200	50
1.按投资方式分				罗马尼亚	9	314	301
合资企业	1 164	378 803		捷克	5	239	225
合作企业	48	12 111		瑞典	2	130	70
独资企业	1 487	362 142	362 142	西班牙	5	134	119
2.按国别、地区分				阿根廷	5	603	387
香港	1 155	169 327	112 903	俄罗斯	3	103	80
美国	402	188 748	167 185	巴哈马	1	600	600
台湾	257	39 917	32 431	挪威	3	108	90
丹麦	3	26 430	26 215	塞浦路斯	5	77	65
韩国	123	102 396	79 084	玻利维亚	2	58	58
日本	244	47 769	36 081	阿联酋	1	57	14
英国	41	67 207	56 291	巴基斯坦	2	64	42
德国	23	14 218	12 601	尼日利亚	1	50	50
新加坡	99	27 515	19 245	约旦	1	42	13
瑞士	9	12 802	8 989	南非	1	40	40
澳大利亚	39	5 153	2 769	奥地利	2	40	40
加拿大	71	11 822	9 296	拉脱维亚	1	30	30
西萨摩亚	1	2 927	2 634	秘鲁	1	30	30
泰国	26	5 769	4 611	以色列	1	556	272
澳门	40	5 337	3 563	新西兰	3	84	84
荷兰	9	5 533	4 579	斯威士兰	1	28	28
意大利	4	824	370	印度	1	28	17
蒙古	2	380	300	孟加拉国	1	12	4
法国	20	3 970	2 488	乍得	1	20	20
印尼	9	2 118	1 220	巴勒斯坦	1	17	9
马来西亚	13	1 397	1 141	百慕大	1	14	14
巴拿马	6	357	239	墨西哥	1	14	14
比利时	14	1 447	1 106	乌拉圭	1	10	10
匈牙利	12	386	358	叙利亚	1	10	3
菲律宾	3	392	200	也门	1	10	10
波兰	2	300	230	英属维尔京	2	3 588	2 662
芬兰	2	1 288	1 288				

注:表中数据以核发营业执照的企业为准。

17－11　经济技术开发区客商投资企业按行业分类

（截至1996年底）

行　业	企业数（个）	协议投资总额（万美元）	＃协议外资额	行　业	企业数（个）	协议投资总额（万美元）	＃协议外资额
合　　计	**2 699**	**753 056**	**592 923**	文教体育用品制造业	42	4 114	3 714
＃电子及通讯设备制造业	183	203 907	182 043	电力蒸汽热水的生产及供应业	1	2 988	2 092
房地产开发与经营业	203	77 475	52 240	石油加工及炼焦业	10	2 938	2 117
化工原料及化学品制造业	131	51 589	35 006	土木工程建筑业	6	2 828	2 370
食品加工业	122	43 724	35 870	化学纤维制造业	10	2 641	2 280
医药制造业	33	36 438	31 524	综合技术服务业	42	2 567	2 144
食品制造业	62	34 601	32 186	地质勘察业	4	1 425	714
电子机械及器材制造业	88	34 472	25 082	餐饮业	15	1 365	956
专用设备制造业	142	21 911	16 582	公路运输业	8	1 137	633
饮料制造业	45	19 422	12 269	水上运输业	7	1 117	615
塑料制品业	58	17 747	14 440	造纸及纸制品业	18	1 006	718
金属制品业	88	17 715	10 944	房地产管理业	14	975	812
交通运输设备制造业	91	17 310	10 731	有色金属冶练及压延加工业	3	763	522
普通机械制造业	62	15 315	11 062	居民服务业	14	665	509
服装及其他纤维制品制造业	310	15 256	12 369	公共设施服务业	6	638	575
家具制造业	32	14 971	14 344	其他社会服务业	12	561	462
橡胶制品业	21	13 064	10 813	能源材料和机械电子设备批发业	7	445	304
非金属矿物制品	96	11 830	7 980	农　业	3	441	174
娱乐服务业	17	11 626	9 292	零售业	3	370	138
皮革毛皮羽绒及其制品业	60	7 925	5 205	渔　业	1	366	179
纺织业	55	7 041	5 454	煤炭采选业	4	195	97
印刷业、记录媒介的复制业	36	6 531	6 149	铁路运输业	1	168	101
黑色金属冶练及压延加工业	9	5 554	2 855	线路管道和设备安装业	7	161	146
其他制造业	69	5 130	4 104	其他行业	4	136	95
建筑物的装修装饰业	109	5 127	4 101	其他交通运输业	2	70	70
仓储业	21	4 955	2 487	其他矿采选业	1	45	32
信息、咨询服务业	117	4 590	4 171	畜牧业	2	30	30
交通运输辅助业	24	4 557	2 411	水利管理业	1	28	7
木材加工及竹藤棕草制品业	29	4 520	3 470	林　业	1	12	12
计算机应用服务业	74	4 388	3 420	科学研究业	1	5	5
仪器仪表及文化办公用机械制造业	62	4 164	2 664				

注：表中数字以核发营业执照的企业为准。

17－12　天津港保税区主要经济指标

项　　目	单　位	1995 年	1996 年	1996 比 1995 年增长％
一、国内生产总值	万元	33 930	77 498	128.4
第二产业	万元	2 549	15 498	508.0
第三产业	万元	31 381	62 000	97.6
二、工业总产值	万元	46 800	70 010	49.6
三、进出区货物总值	亿美元	12.78	27.01	111.3
四、企业进出口额	万美元	31 263	39 281	25.6
＃进　口	万美元	20 473	23 962	17.0
五、通关进出口额	万美元	33 528	69 512	107.3
＃进　口	万美元	21 358	23 956	12.2
六、各项税收总额	万元	45 077	71 230	58.0
＃工商税及所得税	万元	10 207	15 119	48.1
海关关税	万元	23 796	32 410	36.2
海关代征税	万元	11 074	23 701	114.0
七、企业销售(营业)收入	亿元	35.04	49.75	42.0
八、企业利税总额	万元	11 562	21 798	88.5
九、土地出让面积	平方米	32 792	100 642	206.9
十、基础设施投资完成额	万元	10 846	6 758	－37.7
十一、竣工房屋面积	万平方米	10.26	35.79	248.8
＃加工仓储	万平方米	2.95	17.46	491.9

17－13　天津港保税区招商情况

项　　目	单　位	1995 年	1996 年	自建区累计
一、批准企业个数	**个**	**422**	**453**	**3 506**
客商投资企业	个	336	370	2 773
合资企业	个	46	45	545
合作企业	个	3	2	10
独资企业	个	287	323	2 218
国内投资企业	个	86	83	733
二、协议投资总额	**万美元**	**41 695**	**49 355**	**291 473**
客商投资企业投资总额	万美元	30 387	40 726	209 719
合资企业	万美元	6 576	8 999	68 192
合作企业	万美元	757	2 200	3 176
独资企业	万美元	23 054	29 527	138 351
＃协议外方投资总额	万美元	27 362	35 906	174 044
合资企业	万美元	3 553	4 312	32 939
合作企业	万美元	755	2 067	3 006
独资企业	万美元	23 054	29 527	138 305
国内投资企业投资总额	万美元	4 695	3 659	70 170
企业增资额	万美元	6 613	4 970	11 583
＃外方增资额	万美元	5 458	4 317	9 775
三、客商投资企业实际利用外资	**万美元**	**18 027**	**20 310**	**68 740**

17-14 1996年滨海三区概况

指标名称	单位	塘沽区	汉沽区	大港区
常住户数	户	147 284	57 429	96 746
户籍人口	万人	45.05	16.72	31.58
#城镇人口	万人	36.91	12.17	20.74
职　工	万人	20.05	6.00	15.20
乡村劳动力	万人	3.0	2.54	4.50
国内生产总值(现价)	万元	790 603	172 525	736 930
第一产业	万元	14 930	17 063	11 086
第二产业	万元	345 353	102 461	591 992
第三产业	万元	430 320	53 001	133 852
国内生产总值指数(以上年=100,按可比价计算)	%	105.2	115.1	108.7
区县级财政收入	万元	27 055	6 524	15 738
固定资产投资(不含农村集体和个人投资)	万元	633 134	69 655	529 324
房屋施工面积(不含农村集体和个人投资)	万平方米	163.74	13.34	101.32
房屋竣工面积(不含农村集体和个人投资)	万平方米	73.23	9.77	81.65
年末实有耕地面积	万公顷	0.52	0.45	1.56
农林牧渔业总产值(现价)	万元	38 898	40 455	29 128
农林牧渔业总指数(以上年=100,按可比价计算)	%	126.1	112.3	115.0
乡镇企业单位数	个	338	161	453
#工　业	个	194	161	381
乡镇企业人数	万人	2.06	1.50	3.58
#工　业	万人	1.21	1.50	3.47
村以上工业企业单位数	个	598	319	1 233
总产值(现价)	万元	720 076	335 197	1 867 352
资产总额	万元	1 667 576	438 397	2 829 288
固定资产原值	万元	1 139 977	227 558	2 890 530
社会消费品零售总额	万元	222 420	42 455	123 779
批发零售贸易业网点	个	907	340	473
饮食业网点	个	116	43	40
私营工商企业户数	户	838	396	529
注册资本	万元	32 553	7 511	15 564
个体工商业户数	户	13 109	4 795	6 380
资金	万元	28 044	3 565	10 693
直接利用外资协议额	万美元	6 242	2 272	6 816
外贸出口商品总值	万美元	15 077	3 088	4 134
小学校数	所	61	30	48
普通中学校数	所	35	18	44
卫生机构数	个	308	19	95
#医　院	个	21	8	17

注:本表塘沽区数据不含开发区、保税区数。

17-15 新技术产业园区基本情况

(1992-1996年)

项目	单位	1992年	1993年	1994年	1995年	1996年	1996比1995年增长%
年末企业单位数	个	571	1 052	1 573	2 222	2 752	23.9
从业人员数	人	16 958	22 185	36 581	41 617	63 354	52.2
#大专以上学历	人	7 978	8 997	14 703	16 111	20 077	24.6
中级以上职称	人	4 661	5 391	9 431	10 372	13 098	26.3
研究与开发人员	人	3 741	4 293	6 741	7 270	7 883	8.4
总产值	万元	76 245	223 825	397 924	613 604	861 658	40.4
技工贸总收入	万元	90 188	246 781	415 660	670 518	969 563	44.6
#技术收入	万元		20 666	24 736	33 859	64 091	89.3
利润总额	万元	8 602	29 788	36 068	47 543	69 920	31.7
交纳税金总额	万元	4 266	9 365	20 560	22 558	37 583	66.6

17-16 12个开发小区客商投资情况

(截止1996年底)

地区	协议项目个数(个)	#1996年	协议总投资(万美元)	#1996年	在协议总投资中:协议外资额(万美元)	#1996年
总计	**792**	**110**	**93 927**	**30 938**	**74 337**	**27 922**
滨海三区	**276**	**16**	**27 616**	**4 522**	**18 939**	**4 183**
塘沽区	223	9	19 373	378	11 890	218
汉沽区	19	2	1 146	292	583	148
大港区	34	5	7 097	3 852	6 466	3 817
其他四区	**375**	**75**	**52 001**	**22 709**	**44 545**	**21 045**
东丽区	95	16	9 064	1 273	7 226	925
西青区	82	11	16 134	7 151	13 604	6 489
津南区	65	30	17 881	12 945	17 096	12 428
北辰区	133	18	8 742	1 340	6 619	1 203
市辖县	**141**	**19**	**14 310**	**3 707**	**10 853**	**2 694**
宁河县	15	6	2 636	1 137	1 904	698
武清县	37	5	2 753	381	2 262	196
静海县	36	3	2 160	638	1 745	638
宝坻县	40	4	3 607	780	2 611	545
蓟县	13	1	3 154	771	2 331	617

17－17　1996年天津市经济技术协作情况

指　　标	合　计	协进部分	#经济联合	技术合作	协出部分	#经济联合	技术合作
本期签订项目个数(个)	10 449	8 579	1 846	6 733	1 870	187	1 683
执行项目数(个)	9 659	7 880	1 506	6 374	1 779	181	1 598
本　期	9 622	7 853	1 494	6 359	1 769	175	1 594
#省市间	645	516	104	412	129	32	97
结　转	37	27	12	15	10	6	4
#省市间	15	11	1	10	4	2	2
合同计划总投资额(万元)	440 391	372 427	289 833	82 594	67 964	15 741	52 223
#天津市	123 798	120 217	118 337	1 880	3 581	3 521	60
至本期止累计实际投入(万元)	130 265	118 719	114 114	4 605	11 546	10 141	1 406
#天津市	37 080	32 429	32 384	45	4 651	4 591	60
本期实际投入(万元)	114 961	107 653	105 153	2 500	7 308	6 698	610
#省市间	58 721	55 951	54 543	1 408	2 770	2 220	550
#天津市	11 676	10 602	9 951	651	1 074	1 014	60
执行项目本期实现经济效益							
产　值(万元)	164 524	152 362	139 130	13 232	12 162	7 914	4 248
#天津市	18 847	14 828	14 296	532	4 019	4 019	
利　润(万元)	16 195	15 235	13 869	1 366	960	577	383
#天津市	958	813	813		145	122	23
税　金(万元)	4 008	3 461	3 161	300	547	227	320
#天津市	227	206	206		21	21	
创　汇(万美元)	3 161	2 822	1 909	913	339		339
#天津市	1 946	1 946	1 263	683			

17－18　1996年天津市人才协作状况

单位:人

形　　式	合　计	按交流区域分		按技术职级分				代培的学生	
		省市间	市　内	高级技术管理人员	中级技术管理人员	初级技术管理人员	技术工人	大专学生	中专学生
总　　计	**10 611**	**2 845**	**7 505**	**255**	**834**	**1 872**	**5 797**	**3 833**	**5 903**
聘　进	5 357	185	5 173	219	712	360	4 057	1	8
聘　出	749	1	748		2	739	8		
调　入	1 360	23	1 315	36	117	360	802	3	10
调　出	226	15	19		3	39	183		
天津为对方代培	1 308	1 193	115			374		3 650	5 200
对方为天津代培	898	842	7				595	179	124
天津为对方培训	454	446	8				10		444
对方为天津培训	259	140	120				142		117

17－19　1996年天津市内联引资情况

单位名称	新签协议合同数（项）	协议合同金额（万元）	天津投资（万元）	外地投资（万元）	外商投资（万元）	实际利用内资额（万元）
总　　计	**791**	**610 448**	**84 615**	**513 943**	**11 890**	**321 540**
一、市属各局	**23**	**145 970**	**55 263**	**90 707**		**58 492**
冶金工业总公司	2	7 000		7 000		7 000
化学工业总公司	1	400		400		200
机电工业总公司	3	613	330	283		283
电子仪表总公司	3	1 500		1 500		1 500
一轻总公司	1	33 100		33 100		33 100
二轻总公司		2 000		2 000		1 200
纺织工业总公司	1	500		500		500
汽车总公司	1	6 000		6 000		6 000
水利局						1 000
渤海化工公司	1	80 978	52 978	28 000		
港务局	1	3 000		3 000		3 000
交通局	1	905	705	200		200
建工集团总公司	2	4 809	1 050	3 759		1 969
建材集团总公司	1	2 625		2 625		200
益商集团总公司	1	1 050	200	850		850
市供销合作总社		500		500		500
物资集团公司	4	990		990		990
二、"三区"	**188**	**43 558**	**2 121**	**40 698**	**739**	**35 557**
经济技术开发区	70	20 000		20 000		14 859
天津港保税区	27	12 636		12 636		12 636
新技术产业园区	91	10 922	2 121	8 062	739	8 062
三、各区县	**574**	**376 855**	**27 231**	**341 973**	**7 651**	**164 136**
和平区	70	42 500		42 500		21 618
河东区	75	44 306		44 306		17 247
河西区	140	53 046	2 956	50 090		15 040
南开区	5	27 700		27 700		11 300
河北区	65	55 106	48	50 501	4 557	26 380
红桥区	20	39 055	10	39 045		24 735
塘沽区	29	15 695	3 505	12 190		7 990
汉沽区	11	6 250		6 250		3 100
大港区	14	13 584	7 096	6 488		2 717
东丽区	7	7 780		7 780		4 010
西青区	8	10 691	1 200	7 237	2 254	3 920
津南区	15	8 535	1 155	7 080	300	3 930
北辰区	11	8 700	945	7 755		4 576
宁河县	20	6 200		6 200		2 267
武清县	7	7 415	32	7 383		4 588
静海县	15	13 059	5 519	7 000	540	3 753
宝坻县	16	6 980	900	6 080		3 790
蓟　县	46	10 253	3 865	6 388		3 175
四、其　他		**3 500**			**3 500**	**63 355**

17-20　人才和劳务市场情况

项　目	劳务市场			人才市场		
	1995年	1996年	1996比1995年增长数	1995年	1996年	1996比1995年增长数
进场单位数(个)	13 737	13 961	224	4 002	6 327	2 325
进场人次(人)	1 366 000	1 498 000	132 000	235 433	292 128	56 695
达成意向人次(人)	308 400	359 000	50 600	70 677	85 202	14 525
#国有经济	15 420			5 098	8 841	3 743
集体经济	70 932			20 426	9 757	-10 669
"三资"经济	191 208			38 566	52 658	14 092
私营经济	21 588			5 860	7 666	1 806
其他经济	9 252			727	6 280	5 553

17-21　技术市场基本情况

项　目	签定合同数(项)			合同金额(万元)		
	1995年	1996年	1996比1995年增长%	1995年	1996年	1996比1995年增长%
合　计	**10 630**	**8 348**	**-21.5**	**121 199**	**133 475**	**10.1**
一、按技术合同类别分						
技术开发合同	1 533	1 710	11.5	53 790	67 586	25.6
技术转让合同	509	595	16.9	10 960	14 169	33.7
技术咨询合同	1 292	1 181	-8.6	10 777	8 578	-20.4
技术服务合同	7 296	4 862	-33.4	45 672	43 142	-5.5
二、按合同卖方类别分						
#科技机构	1 843	1 935	5.0	34 595	50 031	44.6
高等院校	396	471	18.9	5 572	7 562	35.7
工业企业	2 367	1 902	-19.6	38 185	22 144	-42.0
技术贸易机构	2 345	2 018	-13.9	24 774	30 481	23.0
三、按合同买方类别分						
#工业企业	6 792	4 970	-26.8	66 426	75 299	13.4
科研机构	708	484	-31.6	7 365	5 644	-23.4
各级管理部门	260	349	34.2	18 683	17 699	-5.3
技术贸易机构	260	201	-22.7	1 368	1 944	42.1
四、按社会经济目标分						
#农业、林业与渔业的发展	86	75	-12.8	4 088	3 232	-20.9
促进工业的发展	8 501	6 285	-26.1	78 628	86 521	10.0
能源生产储存和分配	302	389	28.8	10 181	8 087	-20.6
交通、通讯事业的发展	217	303	39.6	4 782	6 386	33.5
教育、卫生事业发展	216	217	0.5	1 957	6 129	213.2
社会发展和社会经济服务		502			8 623	
环境保护	98	102	4.1	487	1 557	219.7
五、按技术流向分类						
天　津	8 194	5 994	-26.8	74 965	74 339	-0.8
外　地	2 436	2 354	-3.4	46 235	59 136	27.9

证券市场概况

1996年全市各类证券(不包括国债)交易总额为663.9亿元,其中在上海、深圳A股的股票交易额为584.5亿元,占深、沪证券市场份额的2.71%,比上年的138.14亿元增加了323%。天津证券经营机构在深、沪两个交易所共拥有153个席位,占深、沪两个交易所席位总数的3.3%,比上年的82个席位增长87%。天津市在上海各类证券交易额达378.11亿元,占上海证券市场份额的4.2%;在深圳各类证券交易额达206.39亿元,占深圳证券市场份额的1.7%。

至1996年底全市上市企业已达7家,既有A、B股,也有H股,共9只股票。各上市企业以其良好的业绩和规范的运作,得到了市场的认可,其中天津磁卡从1995年收盘价4.96元上升到1996年收盘价18.44元,涨幅达271.76%,列沪市1996年涨幅前三名。

1996年,天津证券交易中心在不断完善软、硬件基础上,积极稳妥地发展和规范现有品种,并且成功地引进了秦皇岛和平投资股份公司3 760万元个人股来津上柜交易。1996年天津基金成交金额为37.88亿元,比上年增长251%,天证指数从1995年收盘的104.67点,上升到1996年收盘的132.96点,涨幅为27%,流通市值为12.69亿元,比上年增长103%。天津定向募集股份公司个人股柜台交易也十分活跃,全年交易金额为41.6亿元,比上年增长820%。津股指数年收盘222.76点,比上年收盘上涨90%。

期货市场

1996年天津初步形成了以天津期货联合交易所为龙头,以本地7家经纪公司为骨干,以及16家异地经纪公司营业部和期货兼营机构的多层次期货市场体系。天津联合期货交易所现有3个交易大厅,210个席位,会员单位154家,其中经纪公司61家,流通企业81家,其他机构12家,会员结构合理,遍及全国26个省、市、自治区。天津联合期货交易所挂牌交易的期货品种有:天津红小豆、铝和铜等。1996年成交合约10 567 198手,成交金额3 873.5亿元。天津各期货经纪机构代理的主要期货品种有:橡胶、咖啡、红小豆、绿豆、胶合板等,1996年代理客户成交金额1 200亿元。

17－22　1996年证券市场交易情况

项　　目	上市公司(家)	证券交易总额(亿元)	比上年增长%	流通股本(万股)	比上年增长%	流通市值(亿元)	比上年增长%
合　　计	**7**	**663.90**	**333.0**	**101 851.31**			
天津公司在上海	5	378.11	179.0	25 940.50	31.0	20.30	213.0
天津公司在深圳	2	206.39	757.0	7 796.81	55.0	7.07	452.0
天津证券交易中心		79.40		68 114.00	5.8	27.99	150.0
#内部股		41.60	820.0				
基　金		37.80	251.0				

17－23　上市股份公司情况

(截止1996年12月31日)

公司名称	总股本(万股)	流通股本(万股)	流通市值(亿元)
天津立达国际商场股份有限公司	13 797	5 028	2.7
天津劝业场股份有限公司	14 199	6 061	4.5
天津海运股份有限公司	23 300	12 989	8.0
天津港储运股份有限公司	13 969	3 650	3.6
天津环球磁卡股份有限公司	7 293	2 610	4.6
天津渤海化工(集团)股份有限公司	133 000	45 249	8.1
天津美伦股份有限公司	6 937	2 769	4.4

注:本表含H股。

17－24　外汇调剂市场情况

单位:万美元

项　　目	1994年	1995年	1996年	1996比1995年增长％
外汇调剂额总数	177 341	236 561	222 669	－5.9
调入外汇数	86 978	123 351	109 190	－11.5
调出外汇数	90 363	113 210	113 479	2.4

资料来源:天津市外汇调剂中心。

17－25　城市房产市场交易情况

指　　标	单　位	1992年	1995年	1996年	1996比1995年增长％
一、房产买卖					
房产买卖成交面积	万平方米	14.8	29.1	350.5	1 104.5
#住　宅	万平方米	12.6	27.6	344	1 146.4
办公用房	万平方米	2.2	1.0	0.8	－20.0
商业用房	万平方米		0.4	0.57	42.5
房产交易金额	万元	13 935	39 667	304 572	667.8
#住　宅	万元	9 567	36 723	295 234	703.9
办公用房	万元	4 368	2 760	7 628	176.4
商业用房	万元		184	1 710	829.3
二、房产租赁					
出租面积	万平方米	35.2	161.9	45.29	－72.0
#住　宅	万平方米	31.7	145	38.55	－73.4
办公用房	万平方米	1.0	5.5	3.05	－44.5
商业用房	万平方米	2.5	7.0	3.20	－54.3
租金收入	万元	253	561	66.13	－88.2
#住　宅	万元	118	435	53.97	－87.6
办公用房	万元	15	57	2.56	－95.5
商业用房	万元	120	69	9.6	－86.1
三、向个人出售住宅					
出售住宅面积	万平方米	8.21	186	82.9	－55.4
收回资金	万元	8 292	318 477	16 123	－94.9
出售旧住房	万平方米		45	201.1	346.9
收回资金	万元		11 829	43 695	269.4

17－26 1996年主要商品交易市场基本情况

市场名称	交易场所面积(平方米)	交易席位数(个)	交易商品范围	交易地址
消费品交易市场				
红旗路农贸批发市场服务部	90 000	1 700	疏菜、果品、海鲜产品	南开区王顶堤复康路立交桥两侧
大胡同小百货批发市场	18 950	1 586	服装 小百货 鞋帽	红桥区金钟桥大街金店胡同
何庄子蔬菜批发市场	100 000	5 000	蔬菜 水果 副食品	津南区大沽路何庄子村南
体院北食品批发市场	28 700	525	食品	河西区体北道1号
蓟县城关农贸市场	30 000	1 300	农副产品 工业品	蓟县城内
宝坻城关农贸市场	54 000	850	农副产品	宝坻县城内
西青二经路农贸市场	5 400	320	农副产品 工业品	西青区杨柳青二经路
镇江道洋货市场	9 000	380	服装 面料	河西区大沽路镇江道
东丽温州城服装批发市场	6 000	1 000	服装 日用品	河北区育红路9号
烈士路农贸市场	5 760	500	农副产品 服装 百货	南开区烈士路
塘沽向阳市场	5 000	1 410	服装 食品 水产品 家俱	塘沽区沈阳道增1号
静海县津海商城	52 000	5 500	工业品	静海县东方红路15号
武清县杨村农贸市场	9 300	2 500	农副产品 工业品	武清县杨村
兴业里鞋帽批发市场	6 500	500	鞋	南开区西湖道78号
金钟路蔬菜批发市场	12 900	300	蔬菜 水产品 水果	河北区金钟路158号
中国天津粮油批发交易市场	600	150	粮油	河东区六纬路1号
供销社丁字沽综合批发市场	4 000	430	糖酒食品 副食调料 百货	红桥区丁字沽三号路1号
生产资料交易市场				
北洋(天津)钢材批发交易市场	700	87	金属材料	河东区六纬路4号
天津钢铁炉料交易市场	1 725	65	钢材 铁合金 有色金属等	河西区宾水道1号
中国北方食糖批发市场	1 376	68	粮食 糖	河北区龙门大厦B区三楼
煤炭交易市场	960		煤炭 焦炭	河西区宾水道1号
汽车交易市场	16 000	500	汽车	南开区红旗路楚雄道
金属材料交易市场	600	22	金属材料	河东区六纬路大王庄街11号
东兴汽车交易市场	30 000	82	汽车	河东区东兴立交桥西侧
石化交易中心	280	30	石油 化工	河西区友谊路10号
纺织原材料批发交易市场	240	50	纺织原料 纺织器材	和平区营口道1号
蝶桥旧机动车交易市场	10 800		旧机动车	河东区蝶桥东侧
旧机动车交易中心	3 415		旧机动车	河北区真理道54号
机电产品交易市场	1 000	35	机电产品	河东区九经路8号
宜兴埠木材交易市场	2 400	18	木材 建筑材料	宜兴埠津围公路
汽车工业品交易中心	300	88	汽车 摩托车	河西区贺江道汽配城地区201号
生产资料第一批发交易市场	1 200	28	冶金、机电产品	南开区长江道17号
汽车配件城	21 000	45	汽车及配件 机电产品	河西区解放南路南端
期货交易市场				
天津联合期货交易所	1 200	150	红小豆 铜 铝	河西区宾水道天津宾馆会议楼4楼

17－27　主要消费品交易市场各类商品交易额

单位:万元

年　份	交易额合计	#粮食类	肉　类	干鲜菜类	食品类	衣着类
1995	730 169	59 677	14 230	98 739	109 723	180 053
1996	1 012 174	55 798	18 207	114 410	152 567	271 775
1996比1995年增长%	38.6	－6.5	27.9	15.9	39.0	50.9

17－28　1996年主要消费品交易市场交易额

单位:万元

市场名称	交易额合计	#粮食类	肉　类	干鲜菜类	食品类	衣着类
红旗路农贸批发市场	172 599	1 814		29 553		
大胡同小百货批发市场	171 577					100 499
何庄子蔬菜批发市场	74 475	342		46 446	25 700	
体院北食品批发市场	111 000	957			95 592	
蓟县城关农贸市场	41 417	907	6 378	8 768		
宝坻城关农贸市场	32 329	1 560	1 146	1 582	1 110	12 000
西青二经路农贸市场	38 819		4 418	11 509	8 394	
镇江道洋货市场	54 474					54 474
东丽温州城服装批发市场	29 900					29 900
烈士路农贸市场	23 309	498	1 940	3 308	3 746	60
塘沽向阳市场	27 449		2 586		1 504	17 903
静海县津海商城	78 955	146			4 203	36 196
武清县杨村农贸市场	13 573	2 452	1 547	4 032		1 205
兴业里鞋帽批发市场	19 538					19 538
金钟路蔬菜批发市场	9 389	57		9 092		
中国天津粮油批发交易市场	46 951	46 951				
供销社丁字沽综合批发市场	14 600	114	192	120	12 318	

17－29　主要消费品交易市场主要商品交易量

单位:吨

年　份	粮　食	油及油料	肉	蛋	水产品	蔬　菜	果　品
1995	388 524	10 725	10 720	1 930	53 402	639 780	355 302
1996	295 977	12 802	15 132	5 408	72 711	835 371	372 266
1996比1995年增长%	－23.8	19.4	41.2	180.2	36.2	30.6	4.8

17－30　1996年主要消费品交易市场交易量

单位：吨

市场名称	粮　食	油及油料	肉	蛋	水产品	蔬　菜	果　品
红旗路农贸批发市场	8 833	4 379			54 556	200 640	261 595
大胡同小百货批发市场							
何庄子蔬菜批发市场	3 293	784				396 385	10 092
体院北食品批发市场	3 090	1 050					
蓟县城关农贸市场	10 201	668	2 475	284	2 663	17 202	32 373
宝坻城关农贸市场	6 455	943	2 944	132	249	12 603	3 932
西青二经路农贸市场			3 600		2 112	115 094	10 667
镇江道洋货市场							
东丽温州城服装批发市场							
烈士路农贸市场	1 538	766	1 450	1 037	4 057	12 327	4 679
塘沽向阳市场			1 584		829		
静海县津海商城	423	81					392
武清县杨村农贸市场	4 991	1 800	1 670	1 305	640	1 743	3 491
兴业里鞋帽批发市场							
金钟路蔬菜批发市场	550				249	70 747	304
中国天津粮油批发交易市场	252 308						
供销社丁字沽综合批发市场	380	50	320	1 800	15	200	360

17－31　主要生产资料交易市场各类商品交易额

单位：万元

年　份	交易额合计	#期货交易额	#冶金类	煤炭类	机电产品类	石油化工类	木材类
1995	9 783 322	5 519 881	5 515 792	95 141	333 582	259 722	7 551
1996	39 713 976	38 735 276	847 552	62 842	301 528	306 530	6 104
1996比1995年增长%	305.9	601.7	－84.6	－33.9	－9.6	18.0	－19.2

17－32　主要生产资料交易市场主要商品交易量

年　份	钢　材（吨）	煤　炭（吨）	汽　车（辆）	锯　材（立方米）	成品油（吨）	化工产品（吨）
1995	12 882 939	5 193 688	40 132	83 900	55 524	312 712
1996	778 826	2 842 480	44 295	67 825	155 099	371 395
1996比1995年增长%	－94.0	－45.3	10.4	－19.2	179.3	18.8

1996年市政府批准夏利等五十九个产品为天津名牌产品。天津名牌产品有效期为三年，从1996年6月1日起至1999年6月1日止。

17－33　天津市名牌产品名单

序号	企业名称	注册商标	产品名称
1	天津市汽车工业集团公司	夏利	TJ7100系列轿车
2	天津市汽车工业集团公司	华利	TJ6320、TJ6350系列微型客车
			TJ1010系列微型厢式货车
3	天津市内燃机厂	天内	TJ376Q系列发动机
			TJ370Q系列发动机
4	天津市锻压机床总厂	金星	液压机
5	天津市减速机总厂	天星	行星摆线针轮减速机
6	天津市电线总厂	金山	电气装备用电线电缆
7	天津市电缆总厂	小猫	系列电缆
8	天津市工业泵总厂	CTP	螺杆泵
9	天津市电磁线厂	盾	换位导线
10	天津市大站阀门厂	力	低压阀门系列
11	渤海化工集团股份有限公司天津大沽化工厂	红三晶	环氧丙烷
12	渤海化工集团股份有限公司天津大沽化工厂	红三晶	烧碱
13	渤海化工集团股份有限公司天津碱厂	红三角	纯碱、重质纯碱
14	渤海化工集团股份有限公司天津化工厂	天工	氯化苯、氯化钡、氯仿
15	天津市劳动保护橡胶厂	安全	劳保绝缘制品
16	天津灯塔涂料股份有限公司	灯塔	油漆
17	天津炭黑厂	海豚	橡胶用炭黑
18	天津市中河化工厂	环	顺丁炼二酸酐系列
19	天津市大华胶鞋厂	天宝	全胶雨鞋
20	天津市万达摩托车胎厂	万程	自行车内外胎
21	天津通信广播公司(天津通广三星电子有限公司使用商标)	北京	彩电
22	天津长城电子公司天津长城(集团)有限公司	长城画龙	彩电
23	天津津京玻壳股份有限公司	金牛	黑白显像管玻壳
24	天津市天磁公司	天磁	矿泉壶、磁化杯系列
25	天津通信广播公司	鸿雁	民用电台
26	天津德塔控制系统有限公司	节仪	特种线缆
27	天津中环三津有限公司	三津	单色管
28	天津市东花园仪表厂	东仪	YQY型气体减压器
			YQE型气体减压器

17－33 续表

序号	企业名称	注册商标	产品名称
29	天津电子线缆公司	鸿雁	电线电缆
30	天津市轧钢三厂	众字	热轧带肋钢筋
31	天津市轧钢二厂	双锚	热轧带肋钢筋
32	天津津海钢管集团有限公司	津登	螺旋焊管
33	天津钢管公司	TPCO	石油套管
34	天津顶益国际食品有限公司	康师傅	方便面
35	天津市红星冷食品公司	红星	冰淇淋
36	天津手表厂	海鸥	手表
37	天津市牙膏厂	兰天	兰天六必治牙膏
38	天津感光材料公司	天津	X 光胶片
39	天津郁美净日用化学厂	郁美净	儿童霜
40	天津市洗衣机公司(天津新宝天洋家电有限公司使用商标)	新天洋	洗衣机
41	天津梦乡软体家具有限公司	梦乡	弹簧软床垫
42	天津自行车厂	飞鸽	自行车
43	天津长芦海晶有限公司	海晶	工业盐
44	天津豪爽饮料有限公司	豪爽	无酒精饮料
45	天津食友食品有限公司	乐美思	速冻食品
46	天津津武鞋业有限公司	武波	机制线缝鞋
47	中法合营王朝葡萄酿酒有限公司	王朝	葡萄酒
48	天津六中药制药有限公司	松柏	速效救心丸
49	天津市药业公司	天药	皮质激素类
50	天津市中津制药厂	金世	盐酸硫胺(VBI)
51	天津市东亚毛纺厂	抵羊	毛线系列
52	天津美纶股份有限公司	美纶	涤纶长丝
53	天津仁立毛纺织厂	天马	精纺毛织品
54	天津第一棉纺织厂	天泉	棉布、棉纱
55	天津津达制衣有限公司	津达	男西服
56	天津市水泥厂	骆驼	425＃ 525＃水泥
57	天津市玻璃厂	远洋	平板玻璃
58	天津市雍阳新型建筑材料总厂	豹鸣	膨胀剂系列
59	天津市益中汽车安全带厂	益中	汽车安全带

17－34　1996年产品质量监督检验情况

项　　目	监督检查企业（个）	查出不合格产品企业（个）	不合格产品企业所占比　例（%）	检验批次（批次）	合格批次（批次）	批　次合格率（%）	上　年批　次合格率（%）	批次合格率比上年增减百分点
合　　计	**2 392**	**374**	**16**	**2 683**	**2 302**	**86**	**84.98**	**1**
一、农用产品	**75**	**8**	**11**	**99**	**91**	**92**		
＃农用化肥	24	2	8	25	23	92	69	23
化学农药	13	3	23	32	29	91	65	26
饲料	26	3	12	30	27	90	91	－1
农用薄膜	3			3	3	100	100	
二、加工食品和饮料	**441**	**99**	**22**	**508**	**404**	**80**		
＃白酒	18	4	22	25	21	84	93	－9
啤酒	2			2	2	100	100	
食用植物油	47	6	13	54	47	87	93	－6
糕点、糖果	82	18	22	97	79	81	68	13
冷冻饮料	78	14	18	91	77	85	65	20
乳制品	37	18	49	46	24	52	70	－18
三、家用电器	**68**	**2**	**3**	**79**	**77**	**97**		
＃收录机、音响设备	2			3	3	100		
洗衣机	1			1	1	100	100	
电风扇	2			2	2	100		
吸油烟机	1			2	2	100	100	
空调器	5			5	5	100		
厨房电器具	8	1	13	10	9	90		
电热器具	8			8	8	100	100	
计算机	4	1	25	4	3	75		
四、轻工产品	**743**	**132**	**18**	**784**	**650**	**83**		
＃纸制品	71	15	21	73	58	79	100	－21
玩具	9	2	22	9	7	78	100	－22
家具	231	21	9	233	212	91	94	－3
眼镜（架、片）	2			2	2	100		
灯泡、灯管	51	9	18	53	44	83	100	－17
铝制品、压力锅	15	2	13	15	13	87	50	37
燃气灶具	1			1	1	100	100	
金银首饰	9	5	56	9	4	44		
合成洗涤剂	33	11	33	40	28	70		
化妆品	31	4	13	31	27	87	100	－13
五、纺织、鞋类产品	**167**	**11**	**7**	**199**	**188**	**94**		
＃毛织品	12			13	13	100	91	9
皮革及制品	21	1	5	22	21	95		
鞋	35	4	11	44	40	91	97	－6
六、化工产品	107	10	9	147	137	93		
＃涂料、油漆	31	5	16	52	47	90	77	13
化学试剂	13			16	16	100	100	
七、建材产品	**190**	**28**	**15**	**198**	**170**	**86**		
＃水泥	20			27	27	100	95	5
砖、瓦	61	10	16	61	51	84	88	－4
平板玻璃	1			1	1	100	100	
卫生建筑陶瓷	10			10	10	100		
八、机电产品	**410**	**58**	**14**	**454**	**395**	**87**		
＃电线、电缆	30	5	17	34	28	82	85	－3
低压电器及元件	39	6	15	55	49	89	98	－9
消防器材	9	2	22	9	7	78	100	－22
九、冶金产品、金属制品	**119**	**13**	**11**	**134**	**121**	**90**		
十、能源产品	**20**	**8**	**40**	**26**	**19**	**73**		
十一、医疗器械	**16**			**17**	**17**	**100**		
十二、其他	**36**	**5**	**14**	**38**	**33**	**87**		

资料来源：天津市技术监督局，下表同。

17－35　1996年商品质量监督检验情况

项　　目	检查商业企业（个）	检查商品批次（批次）	合格批次（批次）	批次合格率（%）	上年批次合格率（%）	查出伪劣商品批次（批次）	上年查出伪劣商品批次（批次）
合　　计	**2 641**	**16 632**	**12 039**	**72**	**66**	**1 908**	**1 309**
一、农用产品	**137**	**2 836**	**2 284**	**81**		**14**	
农用化肥	17	45	32	71	72		4
化学农药	51	1 321	1 028	78	82		6
饲料	26	57	45	79	92	12	
种子	15	47	47	100	90		
二、加工食品和饮料	**1 136**	**3 529**	**2 366**	**67**		**641**	
白酒	540	1 798	1 152	64	93	471	12
啤酒	11	33	26	79	94		3
罐头	10	49			82	21	14
糕点、糖果	125	220	133	60	74	21	39
非酒精液体饮料	9	18	9	50	90	2	3
冷冻饮料	93	221	138	62	78	39	96
三、家用电器	**48**	**76**	**61**	**80**		**4**	
厨房电器具	18	20	19	95			
计算机	6	14	11	79			
电话机	3	6	6	100			
四、轻工产品	**365**	**2 937**	**2 196**	**75**		**57**	
家具	27	304	271	89	91	7	4
眼镜(架、片)	32	311	206	66	54	1	18
灯泡、灯管	10	29	13	45		16	6
金银手饰	5	21	5	24			
化妆品	110	1 723	1 457	85	82	18	15
五、纺织、鞋类产品	**67**	**272**	**234**	**86**		**9**	
针织品	15	26	15	58	88		4
皮革制品	10	31	22	71		9	
鞋	39	175	157	90	80		9
六、化工产品	**57**	**106**	**52**	**49**		**28**	
涂料、油漆	21	36	23	64	42	8	29
七、建材产品	**68**	**140**	**96**	**69**		**19**	
水泥	38	68	51	75	43		
油毡、油纸	17	18	14	78	17	4	4
装饰材料	11	39	22	56		15	
八、机电产品	**590**	**5 638**	**4 357**	**77**		**513**	
轴承	28	43	37	86	80	6	5
阀类、泵	17	110	67	61	77		6
电线、电缆	142	2 474	2 085	84	63	57	30
电动工具	4	63	41	65	50		2
低压电器及元件	86	673	510	76	59	48	14
九、冶金产品、金属制品	**1**	**1**	**1**	**100**			
型材	1	1	1	100			2
十、能源产品	**150**	**929**	**242**	**26**		**621**	
汽油、柴油	68	115	69	60		30	
十一、其他	**22**	**168**	**150**	**89**		**2**	

17－36　1996 年受理消费者投诉情况

年　份	总　计	质　量	价　格	虚假广告	假冒商品	计　量	欺诈骗销	其　他
一、受理投诉件数总计(件)	**3 810**	**3 292**	**149**	**16**	**107**	**87**	**31**	**128**
1.家用电子电器类	429	422					1	6
电视机	158	155						3
电冰箱(冰柜)	89	88						1
洗衣机	18	18						
录放相机	17	16					1	
收录音机(音响)	23	22						1
空调器	14	14						
电风扇	12	12						
抽排油烟机	24	24						
其　他	74	73						1
2.家用机械类	350	341	1			1	1	6
照相机	7	7						
自行车(山地车、助力车)	70	66	1					3
摩托车(残疾人车)	125	125						
钟　表	44	44						
燃气热水器	31	29				1		1
其　他	73	70					1	2
3.日用百货类	1 728	1 651	48		2	2	1	24
家　俱	306	290	4				1	11
服　装	542	515	20					7
鞋	764	738	23					3
化妆品	52	51			1			
其　他	64	57	1		1	2		3
4.食品类	303	173	28		16	70	3	13
烟、酒、饮料	101	75	2		14	7		3
鲜肉、禽、鱼	75	29	8			34	2	2
保健食品	20	16			1			3
其　他	107	53	18		1	29	1	5
5.药和医疗用品类	55	40	8		1			6
6.服务类	407	280	35	6	2	11	24	49
美　容	30	18		6				6
邮　电	31	13	3		2			13
餐饮业	27	9	18					
旅游、出租	43	17	1				23	2
修理、装修业	107	93	5					9
其　他	169	130	8			11	1	19
7.农用生产资料类	240	153			85			2
#农药、种子、化肥、饲料	208	121			85			2
8.其他类	298	232	29	10	1	3	1	22
二、解决件数总计(件)	**3 795**							
三、为消费者免受损失(万元)	**629**							

注:本资料为天津市消费者协会系统的统计数据,不含各监测站的统计资料。

中国天津出口商品交易会

1996年中国天津出口商品交易会于1996年3月7日至14日在天津体育展览中心举行，经过各主办单位的共同努力，今年的交易会又取得了圆满成功。为期8天的交易会共有来自世界五大洲73个国家和地区的2 000名客商到会洽谈业务，本届交易会共签订进出口合同6.1亿美元，比上届交易会增长8.9%，其中出口成交5.83亿美元，比上届增长14.3%(外商投资企业签订出口合同2.27亿美元，占大会总成交近4成；会期签订技术出口合同2518万美元，比上届增长了9倍多)。交易会期间，还签订了利用外资项目26个，协议投资总额1.36亿美元；达成利用外资项目意向30多个，意向协议投资额3 000多万美元。此外，内贸业务成交几千万元，零售业务也十分活跃。整体超过上届水平。

本届交易会共有海内外431家工商企业参展。大会共设置展览摊位550个，总面积达13 000平方米，除13个主办省区市的企业参展外，还有来自黑龙江、吉林、辽宁、河南、安徽、山东、江苏、浙江、上海、湖南、云南、贵州、福建和海南等地的外贸企业以及澳大利亚、斯里兰卡、南非、荷兰、韩国和香港的工商企业参加了本届交易会，成为历届参加省市和参展企业最多的一次。

本届交易会得到了各级领导和海内外人士更多的关心与关注。北京、山西、新疆、西藏、新疆生产建设兵团、西安和天津市的领导同志，国家外经贸部、国家科委的领导同志专程来津参加了交易会的开幕式活动并为大会开幕剪彩。以高层人士带队的香港华润集团公司代表团、澳门南光集团公司代表团、台湾两岸商务协调会代表团、香港中华总商会代表团和南非自由省经贸代表团等20多个来自海外的经贸团组，近20个国家的驻华使节及商务官员，以及部分外商投资企业和外资银行的外方代表也参加了交易会的开幕式并入场参观。他们普遍认为本届交易会展览水平有了提高，展出的大部分商品提高了档次。各级领导的关心和海内外各界人士的关注支持，以及交易会本身更加引人注目的业务成果，使中国天津出口商品交易会进一步扩大了在海内外的影响。

(天津市对外经济贸易委员会)

'96天津春季全国商品交易会

由国内贸易部和天津市人民政府共同举办的'96天津春季全国商品交易会，自4月4日开幕，历时4天，于4月7日圆满结束。交易盛况超过前两届，参会客商逾10万人次，会内会外成交额达68.16亿元。客商反映，天交会的影响越来越大，是展示企业的广阔舞台，是拓展生意的理想市场。

天津春季全国商品交易会已经连续办了三届，市场格局已经日趋成熟。天交会的举办，对促进全国新的流通格局形成，推动北方商贸金融中心建设起到越来越重要的作用。

一、增强了集散功能

本届交易会扩大了展地，丰富了交易内容，加大了招商力度，使规模大大超过前两届。一是，通过内挖外扩，展位由1995年的800个增加到1 200个，扩大了50%，适应了日益增多参展企业的要求；二是，交易由以日用工艺品为主，农副产品、食品、保健品为辅，又扩展到房地产、金融服务、现代室内装饰用品等产品。同时设立了服装、自行车、副食品、建材产品专馆，并争取到京、津、沪、穗'96文化预签会在津同期举行，在综合与专业交易结合上迈出可喜的一步。特别是在交易会期间，还举办了厂商座谈会、信息发布会、项目洽谈会，举办了天津投资环境报告会、高科技成果转让洽谈会等活动，充分体现了本届交易会坚持以综合交易为主，又突出专业特色和商流、物流、信息流相结合的特点，使天交会迈上了一个新台阶；三是，主动向全国1 500个县和近2万家工商企业发函直接邀请，并派出5路招商小组，在河北、山西、河南、山东、吉林、哈尔滨等省市召开新闻发布会，分赴7省8市近100个县登门招商，使参会企业超过1 000家，比上届增加30%，采购客商数万人，而且大型采购团日益增多。比如北京、河北采购队伍分别超过2 300人和1 000人。上海、广东、浙江、福建等外地客商反映，本届交易会客流明显多于前两届，认为规模声势之大，成交效果之好，都称得上是一流的，表示今后每届天交会都要参加。天交会经过三年的连续举办，天津作为北方商贸金融中心作用得到发挥，声势越来越大，吸引力越来越强，过去是各地行政部门要企业参加，而现在更多的企业都是主动参加。

二、活跃了流通，扩大了影响

本届天交会为全国工商企业展示自己的形象，开拓国内外市场提供了舞台，给市场带来了活力，给企业带来机遇，给产品带来出路。

天津各参展交易团都把参加天交会作为各局转制、企业亮相、拓展渠道、开拓市场的机遇，精心组织企业参展参会。市经委统一组织由纺织、服装、一轻、二轻、自行车、机械、电子、化工和工业新产品信息中心等单位组成的大型参展交易团，有53个行业，展出4 500种产品，其中新产品、名优产品占63%，取得了较好的交易成果。同时，面对激烈的市场竞争，还把天交会作为学习国内外先进经验的大课堂,组织千余家企业负责人和科技、销售人员到会参观学习,座谈体会收获。市集体经济办公室组织了7个区、局的83家集体企业参展,签定成交合同和协议8 700万元。河西区经委展出180种商品,其中一半以上是高新技术产品,象中央空调、多功能按摩床、远红外保健服、汽车电脑平衡仪,分别与山东、广东等十几个省市签定合同总额达1 860万元。新研制的壁画电暖气、异形车把,造型美观,设计灵巧,与俄罗斯、韩国、马来西亚等国的客商签定了供销合同和合资合作意向,为产品打入国际市场拓宽了渠道。益商集团公司为树立企业整体形象,组织了15个站、司、商场,用81个展位展示3 000多种精选样品,受到各地客商好评,除成交3.06亿元外,还组织2 400人次到会了解市场信息,寻求、洽谈50多个合作意向,开辟了新的市场网络。粮食局展出5大类,近100个产品,各地客商对展出的粮油、食品、保健品、化工产品,不仅积极订货,而且表示会后到厂进一步洽谈,取得满意的交易成果。社会招商企业参展踊跃,应邀和闻讯到会参展企业达400家以上,占本届天交会参展企业的30%多。其中服装行业参展企业为姣姣者,大维、爱之如、斯必得、贵雅等40余家企业交易额在500万元以上的占2/3。市工商联组织13家企业参展,企业各显其能,异常活跃,成交额达2 823万元,比上届参展企业和成交额都翻了一番。

天交会作为全国性大型交易会,辐射面越来越广,影响越来越大,被国内外工商企业所瞩目,业不分工商,货不分南北,同场竞争,吸引着更多客商参展参会。全国各地参展的34个交易团普遍反映良好。特别是百家知名企业展出的"金桥奖"商品在天交会一展风采,海尔集团、长城集团、广电集团、上菱集团等一批在国内外市场具有广泛影响和雄厚实力的企业参展,不仅吸引了众多客商,为企业本身带来良好效益,也为提高天交会的档次和吸引力起到良好作用。河北省石家庄宝石集团公司生产的"环宇"电视机创造了近两年来参加各种交易会最高成交额。邯郸净水器厂在会上推出系列产品,成交量达全年三个季度的产量,他们感动地说,天交会为我们产品打开了销路,给企业提供了做大生意、展示企业产品的好机遇。上海广电集团的产品在会上成交异常活跃,会间成交1.5亿元,称赞天交会客户洽谈实、交易多、效益好。浙江省万能缝纫机有限公司成交5 000多台缝纫机,出乎预料。

三、促进了内外结合

内外结合是天交会发展的必然趋势,本届交易会坚持对外扩大开放,境外企业显著增多,不仅为境内外企业相互了解和学习提供了窗口,还为境内外企业扩大贸易拓宽了通道。应邀参展参会的日本、韩国、俄罗斯、法国、德国、马来西亚、泰国及香港、台湾地区的客商参展展位达100多个,比上届交易会增加了3.5倍。通过天交会的贸易洽谈,境内外企业广泛接触,为进一步加强经贸合作开创了条件。会间,京、津、沪、穗、鲁等省市500多家企业同境外企业洽谈了引资、出口和合作项目,境外企业也主动同参会企业接触,洽谈贸易,都取得了良好效果。天津天宝集团同俄罗斯、韩国、马来西亚的客商签定了供销合同和合资合作意向。天津天翔有限公司同美国客商签定了铝材新型暖气包销合同。台资灿坤电器跨国集团,不惜花重金,以模特表演的形式宣传推销产品,希望通过天交会扩大影响。台湾世贸中心称赞天交会规模大,组织得好,表示明年要组团参加天交会。香港贸发局由上届率6个企业增加到本届率17家企业参会,共设21个展位,虽以展示企业为主,但在会间接签定单110万美元,意向成交62.2万美元,收到有意向的贸易咨询650份,新建立的业务联系超过2 700个,成果大大好于去年。为此,香港贸发局会后专门发电传致谢天交会,并将组团参加天交会作为今年工作重点,表示要组织更多企业参加明年天交会。

(天津春季全国商品交易会组委会)

十八、排名榜

SENIRITY BY MAIN STATISTICAL INDICATORS

1996 年百强工业企业实现销售收入 1 002.96 亿元 占全市乡以上工业的 66.9%

实现利税 127.79 亿元 占全市乡以上工业的 91.5%

1996 年销售额超亿元的批发贸易企业有 125 家

1995 年在全国同行业排序中进前 20 名的天津企业有 208 家

18－1　1996年产品销售收入百强工业企业

名次	企业名称	产品销售收入（千元）	名次	企业名称	产品销售收入（千元）
1	摩托罗拉（中国）电子有限公司	16 334 607	51	天津市富士达摩托车制造有限公司	327 080
2	汽车工业集团公司	12 198 910	52	天津卷烟厂	316 693
3	中国石化天津石油化工公司	7 217 152	53	天津市第二煤气厂	311 089
4	大港油田集团有限责任公司	6 001 790	54	立信集团公司	310 470
5	医药集团公司	4 762 450	55	天津尚赫保健用品有限公司	308 677
6	渤海化工集团公司	4 540 000	56	中法合营王朝葡萄酿酒有限公司	307 517
7	天津奥的斯电梯有限公司	2 293 536	57	天津东亚毛纺厂集团	306 000
8	北海粮油工业（天津）有限公司	2 256 114	58	天津市第四棉纺织厂	300 552
9	天津顶益国际食品有限公司	2 221 675	59	天津长城（集团）有限公司	287 178
10	天津天铁冶金集团有限公司	2 002 140	60	天津市自来水集团有限公司	283 538
11	天津三美电机有限公司	1 978 389	61	大站集团公司	281 000
12	天津天钢集团有限公司	1 865 970	62	天津市双街钢管实业总公司	270 230
13	天津钢管公司	1 810 505	63	天津荣亨台精密集团有限公司	268 570
14	天津通广三星电子有限公司	1 481 536	64	天津三星光电子有限公司	257 549
15	中药集团公司	1 343 790	65	扎努西电气机械天津压缩机有限公司	257 508
16	万全集团公司	1 235 440	66	天津市津西境美综合利用福利化工厂	250 730
17	天津三星电机有限公司	1 198 093	67	天津市天盾有限公司	250 060
18	正大集团（天津）油脂有限公司	1 120 581	68	天津统一工业有限公司	246 122
19	天津本田摩托有限公司	1 071 605	69	天津国际联合轮胎橡胶有限公司	244 218
20	塑料集团公司	775 960	70	天津韩飞鞋业有限公司	243 461
21	天津雅马哈电子乐器有限公司	757 744	71	天津市华丰汽车装饰有限公司	243 374
22	建材集团公司	730 300	72	天津爱普生有限公司	236 833
23	天津造船公司	692 894	73	天津振华纸业有限责任公司	234 632
24	天津天美汽车配件有限公司	680 007	74	天津液压机械（集团）公司	234 349
25	天津三星电子有限公司	625 955	75	天津市第三棉纺织厂	224 418
26	天津宝洁有限公司	602 274	76	天津通信广播公司	221 793
27	天津日电电子通信工业有限公司	583 921	77	天津市冷轧薄板厂	219 460
28	飞鸽集团公司	582 780	78	天津开发区总公司电力公司	217 388
29	恒兴顺集团公司	579 900	79	唐华集团公司	216 620
30	天津福津木业有限公司	575 383	80	天津美特容器有限公司	216 436
31	港田集团公司	566 080	81	天津三峰客车有限公司	207 845
32	天津可口可乐饮料有限公司	547 186	82	天津农药股份有限公司	207 679
33	天津正大饲料科技有限公司	545 169	83	天津海豚炭黑有限公司	205 576
34	天津天鼎纺织集团有限公司	520 910	84	天津市电缆总厂	205 215
35	天一纺织集团有限公司	500 780	85	天津国际海运货柜工程有限公司	204 909
36	高达集团公司	475 350	86	天津市静海县电力局	204 603
37	天津汉高洗涤剂有限公司	453 981	87	津宝通达集团有限公司	203 250
38	天津轧五线材有限公司	423 720	88	大宇（天津）电子有限公司	200 023
39	津海集团公司	420 330	89	天津有机化学工业总公司	198 043
40	北洋集装箱有限公司	394 960	90	维信（天津）工贸有限公司	197 000
41	天津轮胎橡胶工业有限公司	382 579	91	天津天元集团有限公司	195 910
42	天津市华海石油化工总厂	375 100	92	天津大桥集团公司	192 705
43	天津灯塔涂料股份有限公司	372 933	93	三源电力集团公司	190 260
44	天福集团公司	360 540	94	现代精密无缝钢管厂	190 090
45	天津市第二棉纺织厂	356 299	95	天津津京玻壳股份有限公司	188 216
46	天津新宝天洋家电有限公司	342 131	96	天津大通铜业有限公司	187 166
47	天津梅兰日兰有限公司	336 852	97	天津市西青区石油深度加工厂	187 060
48	天津市轧一制钢有限公司	334 850	98	天津东洋油墨（第一）有限公司	185 837
49	邮电部天津设备厂	327 486	99	王顶堤集团公司	183 630
50	皮鞋集团公司	327 110	100	天津美特包装有限公司	181 851

18－2　1996年实现利税百强工业企业

名次	企业名称	利税总额（千元）	名次	企业名称	利税总额（千元）
1	摩托罗拉(中国)电子有限公司	3 560 410	51	天津市津西境美综合利用福利化工厂	26 410
2	汽车集团公司	1 355 420	52	现代精密无缝钢管厂	26 320
3	医药集团公司	893 100	53	立信集团公司	26 090
4	中国石化天津石油化工公司	763 035	54	天津市富士达摩托车制造有限公司	25 510
5	天津顶益国际食品有限公司	580 286	55	下伍旗乡机动车福利配件厂	25 130
6	大港油田集团有限责任公司	572 830	56	大华集团公司	24 760
7	天津奥的斯电梯有限公司	497 363	57	天津市长城化工厂	24 320
8	渤海化工集团公司	423 230	58	艾格福天津有限公司	24 298
9	中法合营王朝葡萄酿酒有限公司	199 913	59	天津市小康川野摩托车厂	24 070
10	万全集团公司	198 350	60	天津三美电机有限公司	23 945
11	天津本田摩托有限公司	196 433	61	天津市德塔控制系统有限公司	23 440
12	天津卷烟厂	163 589	62	天津市大华胶鞋厂	23 250
13	天津尚赫保健用品有限公司	159 935	63	天津安传电子有限公司	23 182
14	天津钢管公司	155 452	64	天津市人造板公司	23 149
15	天津梅兰日兰有限公司	135 452	65	天津天美汽车配件有限公司	22 635
16	天津天铁冶金集团有限公司	121 010	66	天津欧亚床垫家具有限公司	22 388
17	天海集团有限公司	119 110	67	轮船实业发展公司	21 860
18	天津福津木业有限公司	115 131	68	唐华集团公司	21 840
19	天津日电电子通信工业有限公司	83 935	69	津宝通达集团有限公司	21 730
20	津海集团公司	80 400	70	天津国际联合轮胎橡胶有限公司	20 884
21	港田集团公司	77 740	71	天津塘沽瓦特斯阀门有限公司	20 651
22	天津市天宫葡萄酿酒公司	77 114	72	天津新宝天洋家电有限公司	20 457
23	天津宝洁有限公司	67 988	73	天津海豚炭黑有限公司	20 414
24	天津开发区总公司电力公司	64 711	74	天津市汽车货厢厂	20 210
25	天津环球磁卡股份有限公司	64 708	75	天津市华丰汽车装饰有限公司	20 199
26	天津婕妮化妆品有限公司	60 362	76	华明集团公司	19 810
27	天津可口可乐饮料有限公司	57 395	77	恒兴顺集团公司	19 740
28	天津轮胎橡胶工业有限公司	53 852	78	天津市冠达实业总公司	19 071
29	天津努德莱斯巴食品有限公司	53 745	79	PPG汽车涂料(天津)有限公司	19 027
30	天津荣亨台精密集团有限公司	53 320	80	天津东亚毛纺厂集团	18 965
31	王顶堤集团公司	53 090	81	大站集团公司	18 750
32	高达集团公司	50 860	82	天津市天马铝材福利加工厂	18 720
33	天津爱普生有限公司	50 264	83	北洋集装箱有限公司	18 604
34	扎努西电气机械天津压缩机有限公司	46 838	84	亚华集团公司	18 040
35	天津酿酒厂	46 403	85	天津西装厂	17 700
36	天津灯塔涂料股份有限公司	40 700	86	天津市宁河县酒厂	17 497
37	天津市飞鹰集团公司	40 130	87	天津顶信纸业有限公司	17 405
38	天津雅马哈电子乐器有限公司	39 384	88	天津美纶股份有限公司	17 000
39	天津正大饲料科技有限公司	38 148	89	金凯集团公司	16 970
40	天津津京玻壳股份有限公司	38 025	90	天津天宝电子有限公司	16 948
41	天津牧津企业有限公司	37 777	91	天一纺织集团有限公司	16 510
42	天津市西青区石油深度加工厂	37 600	92	天津万力建筑板材有限公司	16 247
43	天津市津达制衣有限公司	35 703	93	天津市艾奇自行车总公司	15 930
44	天津市双街钢管实业总公司	32 030	94	天津市华益家具有限公司	15 830
45	邮电部天津设备厂	31 969	95	天津市静海县电力局	15 781
46	天津市华海石油化工总厂	30 990	96	天津三联工业技术玻璃有限责任公司	15 710
47	富裕注塑制模(天津)有限公司	30 213	97	天津市安琪尔特种线缆有限公司	15 622
48	天福集团公司	30 154	98	天津稳泰化工兴业有限公司	15 514
49	天津轧五线材有限公司	27 290	99	天津市牙膏厂	15 470
50	天津美特容器有限公司	26 732	100	光达集团公司	15 380

18－3 1996年前30名地方建筑施工单位排名榜

单位:千元

名次	单位名称	施工产值	名次	单位名称	利润总额
1	天津市第三建筑工程公司	812 131	1	天津市塘沽区渤海建筑安装工程公司	9 770
2	天津市第二建筑工程公司	740 223	2	天津市津海建筑工程公司	7 363
3	天津市第一建筑工程公司	575 558	3	天津市煤气总公司环球工程技术发展公司	7 351
4	天津市第六建筑工程公司	527 241	4	天津市地方铁路工程公司	7 245
5	天津市第一市政工程公司	456 228	5	天津市第二建筑工程公司	5 480
6	天津第五市政工程公司	310 287	6	天津市第六建筑工程公司	5 419
7	天津市第四建筑工程公司	261 307	7	武清县建筑总公司	5 307
8	天津市第七建筑工程公司	229 497	8	天津市第三建筑工程公司	5 084
9	天津市第二市政工程公司	207 199	9	天津市第一建筑工程公司	5 011
10	天津市第五建筑工程公司	176 360	10	天津石化通达机械工程部	3 658
11	天津第三市政工程公司	162 082	11	天津市塘沽区给水管道建设公司	3 561
12	天津市和平区房屋建筑工程公司	145 998	12	静海县第三建筑总公司	3 334
13	天津市第二房屋建筑工程公司	135 188	13	天津市地方铁路建设公司	3 030
14	天津市自来水工程总公司	135 109	14	天津市自来水公司供水机电设备工程部	2 987
15	天津市河东区房屋建筑工程公司	123 970	15	天津市津电通用电气公司	2 967
16	天津市建材建设工程公司	123 345	16	天津天美室内外装饰有限公司	2 871
17	天津市第三房屋建筑工程公司	118 020	17	天津宝坻县水利建筑公司	2 819
18	天津市津南建筑安装工程总公司	112 283	18	新科(天津)建设工程有限公司	2 746
19	天津市塘沽第一建筑工程总公司	105 530	19	天津第五市政工程公司	2 430
20	天津市盛华建筑工程公司	104 200	20	天津市无瑕建筑安装公司	2 365
21	天津市第一房屋建筑工程公司	100 950	21	天津市南洋装饰工程公司	2 250
22	中国石化四建三合实业总公司	97 737	22	天津市津南区第二建筑工程公司	2 235
23	天津市河北区房屋建筑工程公司	90 887	23	天津汉沽滨海电力工程有限公司	2 222
24	天津市南开区房屋建筑工程公司	89 020	24	天津市津南区南华建筑安装公司	2 110
25	天津市红桥区房屋建筑工程公司	84 540	25	天津市第一市政工程公司	2 103
26	天津市河东区建筑工程公司	75 272	26	天津市津南区北闸口建筑公司	2 100
27	天津市机电设备安装公司	73 724	27	天津市大港光大电气安装公司	1 739
28	天津市汉沽区建筑工程总公司	72 772	28	天津市津南区双港乡建筑工程公司	1 697
29	天津化工厂建筑安装工程总公司	70 000	29	天津市塘沽区第三建筑工程公司	1 604
30	天津市静海县建筑工程总公司	68 000	30	天津化工厂天达工贸总公司天青建安公司	1 589

18－4　1996年销售总额超亿元的批发贸易企业

名次	单位名称	销售额（万元）	名次	单位名称	销售额（万元）
1	天津汽车工业销售公司	782 239	41	天津工艺品进出口(集团)公司	34 386
2	中国石化销售华北公司	180 062	42	天津丝绸进出口集团公司	33 204
3	天津市石油总公司	150 291	43	天津市冶金供销运输总公司	33 099
4	中国烟草总公司天津市公司	143 075	44	天津市丽兴物资公司	32 699
5	天津服装进出口公司(天津市服装联合总公司)	139 123	45	天津市糖业食品总公司	31 283
6	天津宝钢北方贸易有限公司	120 604	46	中国黑色金属材料华北公司	30 924
7	中国农业机械华北公司	110 283	47	天津医药保健品进出口公司	30 577
8	天津纺织品进出口公司	94 967	48	中国水利电力物资天津公司	29 341
9	中国燕兴天津公司	94 630	49	中国包装进出口天津公司	29 336
10	天津亿利达集团有限公司	92 681	50	天津市石油总公司静海公司	28 337
11	中国邮电器材华北公司	86 095	51	天津裕华经济贸易总公司	27 486
12	天津五金矿产进出口公司	83 660	52	中国医药天津采购供应站	26 624
13	天津市粮油购销公司	78 141	53	天津轻工业品进出口公司	26 379
14	天津机械设备进出口公司	75 444	54	天津地毯进出口公司	25 359
15	天津机械进出口集团有限公司	67 707	55	天津市孚洋公司	25 208
16	天津畜产进出口公司	62 367	56	天津渤海化工联合进出口公司	23 956
17	中国钢铁炉料华北公司	60 684	57	天津市食品公司猪肉经营部	21 932
18	天津市对外贸易总公司	58 374	58	中国轻工业原材料华北公司	21 435
19	中国轻工物资供销华北公司	58 357	59	中国汽车贸易天津公司	21 235
20	天津市纺织工业供销公司	57 170	60	天津市大港区港中石油经销联营公司	20 500
21	中化天津进出口公司	56 589	61	天津文化用品供应站天津凯得经济贸易总公司	20 276
22	天津市农业生产资料总公司	51 978	62	天津市商业物资供销总公司	20 175
23	中国化工供销华北公司	51 768	63	天津港保税区祥通国际工贸公司	19 887
24	天津土产进出口集团有限公司	50 878	64	天津市煤业建筑器材三公司	19 753
25	天津市金属材料总公司	50 567	65	天津市正泰实业总公司	19 400
26	天津市石油总公司大港公司	49 488	66	天津百宏进口电器有限公司	18 603
27	天津市物资综合贸易中心	48 841	67	北洋(天津)工贸有限公司	18 313
28	天津市石油总公司销售公司	48 216	68	中石化一霍尼韦尔(天津)有限公司	18 014
29	天津文教体育用品进出口公司	45 097	69	天津市三环石化产品经销公司	17 814
30	天津药材集团有限公司	44 082	70	天津贾源物资供销公司	17 620
31	中国交通物资华北公司	43 950	71	天津家用纺织品进出口公司	17 472
32	天津卷烟厂卷烟物资调拨站	43 723	72	天津市生产资料有限公司	17 076
33	天津市胜克塞斯钢制品有限公司	43 428	73	天津市金泰来贸易有限公司	17 024
34	天津太平(集团)有限公司	42 928	74	天津市津海华兴实业公司	16 800
35	天津汽车工业物资供应公司	41 049	75	中国石油物资天津公司	16 771
36	中国北方工业天津公司	40 742	76	天津市农业机械总公司	16 470
37	天津海豚轮胎销售有限责任公司	37 581	77	天津市明山物资供应站	16 268
38	天津市机电设备总公司汽车经销公司	35 647	78	天津市新华书店发行部	16 165
39	天津百货商务贸易总公司	35 047	79	天津市黑色金属材料公司	15 955
40	天津食品进出口股份有限公司	34 718	80	天津市建筑材料供应总公司	15 909

18－4续表

名次	单位名称	销售额(万元)
81	天津市石油总公司津南公司	15 283
82	中国电子物资华北公司	14 992
83	天津市石油总公司宁河公司	14 984
84	天津市石油总公司加油供应公司	14 870
85	天津东洋油墨印刷物资有限公司	14 714
86	天津市威海轮胎销售有限责任公司	14 592
87	天津市月季花粮油经营部	14 582
88	北洋大宇(天津)国际发展有限公司	14 158
89	天津二塑物资供销有限公司	14 142
90	天津市食品公司	14 022
91	新华书店天津发行所	13 986
92	中国有色金属工业华北供销公司	13 434
93	天津市天马企业发展有限公司	13 143
94	天津橡胶工业供销公司	13 116
95	天津市中糖华丰实业有限公司	12 740
96	天津市煤业建筑器材一公司	12 736
97	天津文化用品商贸总公司	12 715
98	中国船舶工业物资华北公司	12 526
99	天津市华农进出口公司	12 434
100	中国新兴天津进出口公司	12 307
101	天津市南开五金经营公司	12 231
102	天津市石油总公司武清公司	12 149
103	天津市宁河县生产资料公司	12 059
104	天津市石油总公司北辰公司	11 821
105	天津世界商厦有限公司	11 782
106	天津市粮食总公司	11 548
107	天津石化华隆实业公司	11 436
108	天津市煤业建筑器材五公司	11 255
109	天津市五金交电总公司	11 229
110	天津市石油总公司汉沽公司	11 048
111	天津市化轻橡胶经销公司	10 747
112	天津电子仪表进出口公司	10 692
113	中国机械工业供销华北公司	10 680
114	天津市糖业食品第三批发公司	10 643
115	天津市煤业建筑器材二公司	10 598
116	天津市华北轻工供销联营公司	10 538
117	飞鸽自行车集团公司(天津)物资供应公司	10 495
118	天津化工厂材料供销公司	10 416
119	天津市机械工业物资总公司	10 387
120	天津市二轻局供销公司	10 381
121	天津汽车工业交通出租车销售有限公司	10 321
122	中粮天津粮油进出口公司	10 268
123	天津市武清县机电公司	10 107
124	天津市煤业建筑器材六公司	10 095
125	天津市油脂集团有限公司	10 006

18－5　1996年销售总额超五千万元的零售贸易企业

名次	单位名称	销售额(万元)
1	天津市劝业场股份有限公司	146 126
2	天津市和平区滨江商厦	86 094
3	天津百货大楼股份有限公司	83 603
4	天津华联商厦股份有限公司	79 708
5	天津金元宝商厦有限责任公司	43 948
6	天津商场	38 791
7	天津市东方商业大厦有限责任公司	33 515
8	天津立达国际商场股份有限公司	31 492
9	天津伊势丹有限公司	30 688
10	天津市南楼百货商场	20 727
11	天津市宁河县贸易开发区总公司	20 466
12	天津市东海商厦集团有限公司	16 836
13	中国汽车工业天津销售公司	16 835
14	天津市长信国脉通信器材公司	14 777
15	天津市大天津糖酒食品公司	13 156
16	天津永安百货	10 669
17	中国人民银行天津市分行天津金店	10 266
18	天津塘沽商业大厦集团有限公司	10 111
19	天津市大港商厦有限责任公司	8 599
20	天津市佟楼百货商场	8 002
21	天津新中国现代文化用品公司	7 999
22	天津龙门大厦有限公司	7 554
23	天津市东亚澳迪新贸易发展公司	7 300
24	天津市东丽区军粮城供销社	7 101
25	天津市河西百货商场	7 000
26	天津市汉沽区百货大楼	6 751
27	天津市天意(天津)商业公司	6 367
28	天津市武清县物资经销部	6 339
29	天津市和平区百货公司新兴时装商厦	6 265
30	天津大荣国籍贸易有限公司	6 143
31	东海食品商厦	5 779
32	天津市电子仪表销售服务公司经营部	5 668
33	天津市汉沽商厦	5 529
34	天津市路顺储运汽配服务中心	5 504
35	天津市红桥区蔬菜副食品公司大胡同副食基层店	5 078
36	天津市和平百货建新服装皮货商店	5 000

18－6　1996年零售额超五百万元的餐饮企业

名次	单位名称	零售额（万元）
1	天津麦当劳食品有限公司	6 361
2	天津肯德基有限公司	5 261
3	天津市河西区饮食公司鸿起顺饭庄	3 681
4	天津市美膳酒楼	3 144
5	天津市狗不理包子总店	2 894
6	天津市华善餐饮有限公司	2 767
7	天津市宴宾楼饭庄	2 620
8	天津市登瀛楼饭庄	2 526
9	天津市天津烤鸭店	2 226
10	桂发祥麻花饮食集团公司	2 104
11	天津市桂发祥第一麻花公司	1 954
12	天津市和平区康乐饮料公司	1 660
13	天津食为天食品发展有限公司	1 644
14	天津起士林大饭店	1 604
15	天津市华夏饮食业经营总公司	1 554
16	天津市玉华台大酒楼	1 516
17	天津市南市狗不理包子铺	1 429
18	天津市汉沽区天华饮食服务公司	1 412
19	天津市古井大酒家	1 367
20	天津市河北区川鲁饭店	1 331
21	江南春酒家有限公司	1 304
22	天津市和平区饮食公司宏业基层商店	1 287
23	天津市北辰区饮食服务公司	1 157
24	天津市华盛餐饮贸易公司	1 124
25	天津市富利华餐饮总公司新联快餐公司	1 114
26	天津市狗不理集团速冻食品销售中心	1 073
27	天津市和平区康乐饮料公司经营部	959
28	天津台北大圆碗快餐有限公司	926
29	天津艾菲尔大饭店有限公司	879
30	天津市鸭溪大酒楼	784
31	天津市津荷浙江大酒楼有限公司	760
32	天津市桂发祥第二麻花公司	758
33	天津市和平区美伽利快餐厅	729
34	天津百世威餐饮发展有限公司	699
35	天津市华茂餐饮贸易公司	664
36	天津市富利华餐饮总公司新亚快餐公司	657
37	天津市富利华餐饮总公司天味香快餐公司	656
38	天津市宝坻县物资局招待所	638
39	天津市南市食品街桂发祥麻花分店	635
40	天津市耳朵眼炸糕公司	593
41	潮洲城天津美食有限公司	590
42	天津家必得(天津)比萨饼有限公司	581
43	天津市塔园酒楼	569
44	天津新渤海大酒店有限公司	554
45	天津市和平区饮食公司京津餐厅	531
46	天津市苏闽菜馆	522
47	天津市蓬莱春大酒楼	519
48	天津市华鑫餐饮贸易公司	516

18－7　1996年农村经济总收入超过亿元的村

村　名　称	农村经济总收入（亿元）
塘沽区(2个)	
新城镇新城村	1.35
中心庄乡中心庄村	1.19
汉沽区(2个)	
双桥子乡大神塘村	1.60
营城乡五七村	1.49
大港区(6个)	
太平村镇郭庄子村	1.51
太平村镇窦庄子村	2.56
中塘镇大安村	1.32
中塘镇薛卫台村	1.18
中塘镇中塘村	2.63
上古林镇上古林村	2.27
东丽区(20个)	
新立镇四合庄村	1.01
新立镇张贵庄村	1.23
新立镇新兴村	1.24
新立镇东杨场村	3.96
小东庄镇小东庄村	1.47
军粮城镇一村	1.00
军粮城镇山岭村	1.33
军粮城镇苗街村	3.10
军粮城镇东封村	2.97
华明镇范庄村	1.92
华明镇李明庄村	1.37
赤土镇贯庄村	1.41
赤土镇赤土村	1.94
程林街增兴窑村	1.42
程林街南大桥村	1.20
大毕庄镇赵沽里村	1.25
大毕庄镇孙庄子村	1.14
大毕庄镇长青村	1.52
无瑕街新袁村	1.05
西青区(26个)	
西营门乡王顶堤村	1.83
中北斜乡谢庄村	5.86
中北斜乡西马村	1.96
中北斜乡西姜井村	2.21

18－7续表

村名称	农村经济总收入(亿元)	村名称	农村经济总收入(亿元)
中北斜乡大梢口村	1.14	北仓镇北仓村	2.31
中北斜乡芦北口村	1.18	天穆镇刘房子村	2.07
杨柳青镇大柳滩村	1.68	天穆镇王庄村	1.64
杨柳青镇前桑元村	6.50	天穆镇西于庄村	2.45
张沃镇西琉城村	1.46	天穆镇东于庄村	1.20
张沃镇古佛寺村	1.52	天穆镇白庙村	1.88
南河镇小南河村	1.66	天穆镇火咀村	1.14
上辛口乡第六埠村	5.23	天穆镇勤俭村	1.09
上辛口乡水高庄村	4.00	天穆镇柳滩村	3.46
李七庄乡王兰庄村	2.39	天穆镇天穆村	3.13
李七庄乡边村	1.20	天穆镇吴嘴村	1.62
李七庄乡宁家房子村	1.40	天穆镇南仓村	2.87
李七庄乡梨元头村	1.25	天穆镇马庄村	1.29
大寺镇门道口村	3.13	宁河县(6个)	
大寺镇大任庄村	3.50	大北涧沽乡独立村	1.23
大寺镇王村	4.82	大北涧沽乡船沽村	2.13
王稳庄乡王稳庄村	1.48	大北涧沽乡中兴沽村	1.06
王稳庄乡小金庄村	1.18	造甲城乡造甲村	1.02
王稳庄乡大候庄村	1.15	北淮淀乡北淮淀村	1.31
王稳庄乡小孙庄村	1.88	北淮淀乡乐善庄村	1.14
王稳庄乡小韩庄村	1.02	武清县(2个)	
津南区(14个)		南蔡村镇南陈庄村	2.43
八里台镇八里台村	4.03	汊沽港乡一街	6.12
八里台镇大韩庄村	2.78	静海县(17个)	
八里台镇大孙庄村	2.77	大张庄乡赵官屯村	1.20
南洋镇五登房村	1.35	西翟庄乡庞庄子村	1.33
双港乡海河湾村	5.76	蔡公庄乡惠丰东村	1.02
双桥河乡东泥沽村	1.99	梁头乡梁头村	1.96
小站镇黄台村	1.13	东双塘乡西双塘村	4.83
小站镇东花园村	1.91	东双塘乡杨家园村	1.69
小站镇东大站村	2.74	东双塘乡东双塘村	2.73
葛沽镇石闸村	1.24	大丰堆乡崔家庄村	1.29
葛沽镇三合村	1.68	大丰堆乡史家庄村	1.72
葛沽镇殷庄村	1.78	城关乡下三里村	1.00
葛沽镇大滩村	1.99	杨成庄乡双窝村	1.65
咸水沽镇新兴村	1.06	杨成庄乡董庄窠村	1.68
北辰区(21个)		大邱庄镇津美村	25.50
西堤头镇刘快庄村	3.55	大邱庄镇津海村	23.77
西堤头镇西堤头村	3.48	大邱庄镇尧舜村	45.98
西堤头镇东堤头村	1.46	大邱庄镇万全街	14.09
宜兴埠镇一村	5.01	静海镇五村	1.05
宜兴埠镇九村	1.14	宝坻县(3个)	
宜兴埠镇十村	1.18	高家庄乡后西苑村	1.79
青光镇韩墅村	1.85	高家庄乡前西苑村	1.28
青光镇青光村	1.88	大钟庄镇北王村	1.51

18-8　1996年乡村联工业出口创汇百强企业

单位:万元

名次	企业名称	出口交货值	名次	企业名称	出口交货值
1	博克来(天津)建材有限公司	38 630	51	天津市利海食品有限公司	4 754
2	天津环球企业集团公司	28 056	52	天津市桦成木业有限公司	4 686
3	天津市通达集团有限公司	22 855	53	天津市北方制衣总厂一分厂	4 624
4	天津市富强集团公司	19 950	54	天津市津津制药厂	4 557
5	天津瀛海化工集团	19 900	55	天津市亚华地毯厂	4 520
6	天津西装厂	13 500	56	宝坻县三岔口乡工贸服装厂	4 365
7	天津市联星金属制品有限公司	11 921	57	宝坻县亚洲地毯厂	4 338
8	天津市武清县环宇地毯实业公司	10 846	58	天津市天祥丝绸服装厂	4 318
9	天津市天马纺织制品总厂	10 721	59	天津市顺荣食品厂	4 230
10	天津市联合毛纺厂	10 422	60	天津市津武纸制品有限公司	4 200
11	天津市长城化工厂	10 024	61	天津市斯诺特鞋业制造有限公司	4 150
12	天津市兰化染料厂	9 407	62	宝坻县三岔口乡衬衫厂	4 058
13	天津惠利集团有限公司	9 380	63	天津市振兴服装洗水厂	4 057
14	天津市双街钢管实业总公司	9 269	64	天津市耀华冷冻厂	4 048
15	天津市腾达集团公司	8 894	65	天津市津南久兴餐具厂	4 005
16	天津市食友食品厂	8 690	66	天津市南羊食品冷冻厂	4 000
17	天津市金美达针织集团有限公司	8 600	67	宝坻县华荣服装雨衣厂	4 000
18	天津市胜利制衣公司	8 268	68	天津宁河县廉庄乡联合制鞋有限公司	4 000
19	天津津都制衣有限公司	8 123	69	天津市现代化工厂	3 968
20	天津市庆洋土特产有限公司	8 082	70	天津市利昂制衣有限公司	3 950
21	武清县外贸春蕾服装厂	8 045	71	天津市韩飞鞋业有限公司	3 920
22	天津市振兴地毯公司	7 477	72	宝坻县马家店乡雨衣厂	3 837
23	天津朝光革靴有限公司	7 243	73	天津咏友制衣有限公司	3 828
24	天津市东方染料化工厂	7 177	74	武清县崔黄口镇邢窑开源地毯厂	3 800
25	天津市染料厂分厂	7 119	75	天津市津南兴达化工厂	3 792
26	天津市武清县大发针织厂	7 030	76	蓟县蒙鄱乡澳蒙制衣有限公司	3 782
27	天津市华益家具有限公司	7 001	77	天津市染化七厂一分厂	3 740
28	天津惠港不锈钢制品有限公司	6 970	78	天津市河北制药厂第一分厂	3 712
29	天津市北辰区嘉文公司	6 901	79	蓟县东赵乡长虹服装厂	3 700
30	天津市大港联营电焊条厂	6 645	80	天津市光华造纸厂	3 700
31	天津市元通针织服装厂	6 400	81	天津市驰外水暖器材总厂	3 642
32	天津市振宇服装厂	6 270	82	天津市津南工艺品厂	3 614
33	天津市三环染料化学工业总厂	5 984	83	蓟县东塔乡联盛化纤棉有限公司	3 600
34	天津高丽亚那工艺品有限公司	5 970	84	宝坻县环球衬衫厂	3 590
35	蓟县东塔乡服装集团公司	5 950	85	天津市津宝木制品厂	3 570
36	天津市天利粮油食品有限公司	5 590	86	天津志成打火机有限公司	3 537
37	天津津汇制衣有限公司	5 560	87	天津市西青区绗缝绣品厂	3 530
38	天津市后巷乡胶背地毯厂	5 437	88	天津市津南制花厂	3 522
39	天津市光达集团公司	5 350	89	天津大华制衣有限公司	3 510
40	天津市金埠纺织装饰制造厂	5 340	90	天津升阳儿童用品有限公司	3 460
41	天津市三岔口丝绸服装联营厂	5 322	91	天津大钟服装厂	3 451
42	天津太阳毛纺有限公司	5 257	92	天津市天马制衣厂	3 377
43	天津市静海民主针织服装工公司	5 150	93	天津市津京线材厂	3 370
44	天津市渔网厂	5 124	94	天津同和文教用品实业有限公司	3 364
45	天津外贸通达服装厂	5 085	95	天津市北海制衣厂	3 336
46	天津市中津制药厂	5 050	96	武清县大黄堡乡东八里庄双利地毯厂	3 308
47	宝坻县达盛服装厂	5 002	97	天津市东亚地毯集团公司	3 308
48	天津市明春实业有限公司	5 000	98	天津市四立鞋业有限公司	3 307
49	天津天星新马皮革制品有限公司	4 906	99	天津市金猫有限责任公司	3 287
50	天津市登峰旅游用品厂	4 848	100	天津市天福木制品有限公司	3 200

18-9 1996年乡村联工业销售收入百强企业

单位:万元

名次	企业名称	销售收入	名次	企业名称	销售收入
1	天津亚洲钢管企业集团有限公司	161 727	51	天津市华发福利油脂公司	14 875
2	天津尧舜钢管企业集团有限公司	112 750	52	天津市小康川野摩托车厂	14 782
3	天津市大邱庄宏林工业公司	79 098	53	天津津港塑料制品有限公司	14 674
4	天津市胜达工业公司	62 422	54	天津市营城滨海工业公司	14 589
5	天津津海金属集团有限公司	61 420	55	宝坻县后西苑屠宰厂	13 973
6	天津市奥凯钢铁有限公司	54 794	56	天津西装厂	13 371
7	天津市富强集团公司	51 344	57	天津市渔网厂	13 263
8	天津市大邱庄津美钢铁工业公司	50 752	58	天津市大华胶鞋厂	13 123
9	天津尧舜钢铁企业集团有限公司	50 249	59	天津市恒通工业贸易公司	12 947
10	天津津海钢管集团有限公司	47 997	60	天津市西马汽车装焊厂	12 892
11	天津津海钢铁集团有限公司	46 736	61	天津市井田实业公司	12 662
12	天津万通钢管公司	45 869	62	天津大明工业公司	12 582
13	天津万达摩托内胎厂	42 851	63	天津市大港中涤合成化工厂	12 477
14	天津市大邱庄尧舜铜材厂	42 770	64	天津市光达集团公司	12 471
15	博克来(天津)建材有限公司	40 256	65	天津振华集团公司	12 344
16	天津市港田发动机有限公司	38 162	66	天津市建津轧钢工业公司	12 184
17	天津市华海石油化工总厂	37 510	67	天津市先达汽车工贸公司	11 900
18	天津津海机械集团有限公司	35 192	68	宝坻县宏利屠宰加工厂	11 800
19	天津瀛海化工集团	33 345	69	天津市德塔控制系统有限公司	11 669
20	天津市富士达摩托车制造有限公司	32 708	70	天津市金埠纺织装饰制造厂	11 517
21	天津市大邱庄津亚工业公司	30 118	71	天津市津西钢管厂	11 500
22	天津市残联曙光有色金属制品厂	29 952	72	天津市永兴标准件厂	11 495
23	天津市汽车制造冲压分厂	28 206	73	天津市朝阳车胎厂	11 370
24	天津市双街钢管实业总公司	27 023	74	天津市红联橡胶制品厂	11 215
25	天津荣亨精铸集团有限公司	26 857	75	天津市恒兴泰纺织有限公司	11 100
26	天津市芦台线材总厂	26 098	76	天津市天马纺织制品总厂	11 000
27	天津市津西境美综合利用福利化工厂	25 073	77	天津环球企业集团公司	10 941
28	天津市汽车空调器厂	24 770	78	天津市染料厂分厂	10 863
29	天津市芦台电线电缆厂	24 720	79	天津市艾奇自行车总公司	10 574
30	天津市利达钢管厂	22 287	80	天津市华北橡胶厂	10 240
31	天津市金美达针织集团有限公司	20 986	81	天津市西姜井利民钢材厂	10 200
32	天津市津达集团有限公司	20 325	82	天津市港田集团公司	9 974
33	天津市大邱庄尧舜轧钢总厂	19 600	83	天津市武清县环宇地毯实业公司	9 890
34	天津天元集团有限公司	19 591	84	天津市北辰区光辉农药厂	9 872
35	天津市现代精密无缝钢管厂	19 009	85	天津市煤化工厂	9 867
36	天津市西青区石油深度加工厂	18 706	86	天津市金峰五金线材厂	9 805
37	天津市顺成旅游用品有限公司	17 833	87	天津市盛达化工厂	9 780
38	天津天宇有色金属集团公司	16 800	88	天津市航空摩托车发动机制造公司	9 654
39	天津市六埠福利染整厂	16 792	89	天津宝袁化纤棉有限公司	9 506
40	天津市三环染料化学工业总厂	16 684	90	天津市静海县振华针织厂	9 500
41	天津市春蕾福利包装袋厂	16 443	91	天津万兴毛纺(集团)有限公司	9 481
42	天津市海通工贸总公司	16 276	92	天津市亨达鞋业公司	9 312
43	天津市长城化工厂	16 157	93	天津市现代化工厂	9 260
44	天津市兰化染料厂	15 877	94	天津市津南拔丝十一厂	9 182
45	天津市大邱庄尧舜发展股份有限公司	15 637	95	天津市联星金属制品有限公司	9 016
46	天津市东双塘轧钢厂	15 318	96	天津市电焊条公司大寺电焊条厂	8 979
47	天津津海机电集团有限公司	15 300	97	天津市金鑫实业总公司	8 968
48	天津市恒兴微型汽车冲压件厂	15 015	98	天津市中津制药厂	8 845
49	乐金电子(天津)电器有限公司	14 955	99	天津市大沽电石厂	8 777
50	天津市飞鹰集团公司	14 897	100	天津市博克实业总公司	8 703

18-10 1996年乡村联工业实现利税百强企业

单位:万元

名次	企业名称	利税总额	名次	企业名称	利税总额
1	天津亚洲钢管企业集团有限公司	9 648	51	宝坻县宏利屠宰加工厂	1 832
2	天津市胜达工业公司	9 038	52	天津西装厂	1 773
3	天津万达摩托内胎厂	8 156	53	天津市春蕾福利包装袋厂	1 746
4	天津市大邱庄宏林工业公司	7 845	54	天津市朝阳车胎厂	1 738
5	天津津海机械集团有限公司	7 573	55	天津天宇有色金属集团公司	1 736
6	天津市港田发动机有限公司	6 975	56	天津振华集团公司	1 698
7	天津尧舜钢管企业集团有限公司	6 905	57	天津市自强汽车装具厂	1 616
8	天津市富强集团公司	6 386	58	天津市艾奇自行车总公司	1 593
9	天津市大邱庄津美钢铁工业公司	6 010	59	天津市华益家具有限公司	1 585
10	天津市奥凯钢铁有限公司	5 709	60	天津三联工业技术玻璃有限责任公司	1 576
11	天津荣亨精铸集团有限公司	5 335	61	天津市永兴标准件厂	1 542
12	博克来(天津)建材有限公司	5 262	62	天津市光达集团公司	1 541
13	天津津海钢管集团有限公司	5 140	63	天津市天马纺织制品总厂	1 539
14	天津津海金属集团有限公司	4 841	64	天津市光源打火机有限公司	1 528
15	天津津海钢铁集团有限公司	4 440	65	天津市六埠福利染整厂	1 522
16	天津市飞鹰集团公司	4 022	66	天津市田源淀粉制造有限公司	1 493
17	天津市西青区石油深度加工厂	3 760	67	天津市华北橡胶厂	1 468
18	天津万通钢管公司	3 618	68	天津市亨达鞋业公司	1 443
19	天津市汽车空调器厂	3 551	69	天津市腾达集团公司	1 424
20	天津市恒兴微型汽车冲压件厂	3 435	70	天津高丽亚那工艺品有限公司	1 417
21	天津市三环染料化学工业总厂	3 410	71	天津津港塑料制品有限公司	1 406
22	天津市双街钢管实业总公司	3 229	72	天津市津东华明纸箱厂	1 380
23	天津市华海石油化工总厂	3 099	73	天津瀛海化工集团	1 369
24	天津欧亚床垫家具有限公司	2 829	74	天津市博克实业总公司	1 357
25	天津市大邱庄尧舜轧钢总厂	2 796	75	天津市工农化学厂	1 349
26	天津尧舜钢铁企业集团有限公司	2 672	76	天津万兴毛纺(集团)有限公司	1 341
27	天津市境美综合利用福利化工厂	2 641	77	天津宝袁化纤棉有限公司	1 332
28	天津市现代精密无缝钢管厂	2 632	78	天津朝光革靴有限公司	1 308
29	天津市富士达摩托车制造有限公司	2 563	79	天津市武清县环宇地毯实业公司	1 291
30	天津市兰化染料厂	2 519	80	天津市津信塑料制品有限公司	1 288
31	武清县下伍旗乡机动车福利配件厂	2 514	81	天津市津西钢管厂	1 287
32	天津市长城化工厂	2 485	82	天津惠利集团有限公司	1 284
33	三德兴(天津)工业有限公司	2 414	83	天津津华皮业有限公司	1 281
34	天津市小康川野摩托车厂	2 407	84	天津市染化七厂一分厂	1 273
35	天津市大邱庄津亚工业公司	2 389	85	天津市北辰区光辉农药厂	1 269
36	天津市汽车制造冲压分厂	2 382	86	天津市金埠纺织装饰制造厂	1 259
37	天津市德塔控制系统有限公司	2 344	87	天津市振宇服装厂	1 257
38	天津市大华胶鞋厂	2 334	88	天津市大邱庄尧舜发展股份有限公司	1 252
39	天津市东双塘轧钢厂	2 196	89	天津市汽车工贸公司汽车修理厂	1 243
40	天津市利达钢管厂	2 183	90	天津市顺成旅游用品有限公司	1 241
41	天津市通达集团有限公司	2 175	91	天津市胜利化工厂	1 238
42	宝坻县后西苑屠宰厂	2 126	92	天津天元集团有限公司	1 237
43	天津市金美达针织集团有限公司	2 051	93	天津市台湾亿联法朗制品有限公司	1 224
44	天津市汽车货厢厂	2 031	94	天津市有容通迅线缆有限公司	1 206
45	天津市盛达化工厂	1 988	95	天津环球企业集团公司	1 202
46	天津市恒通工业贸易公司	1 979	96	天津市津西北方汽车配件厂	1 198
47	天津津海机电集团有限公司	1 961	97	天津市井田实业公司	1 182
48	天津市残联曙光有色金属制品厂	1 951	98	天津市静海县孟家庄金属制品工业公司	1 180
49	天津市三环化学工业总厂一分厂	1 923	99	天津市大邱庄汽车装配厂	1 175
50	天津市天马铝材福利加工厂	1 923	100	天津市红联橡胶制品厂	1 162

18－11　1996年客商投资企业销售收入百强企业

名次	企业名称	销售收入(万元)	名次	企业名称	销售收入(万元)
1	摩托罗拉(中国)电子有限公司	1 193 484	51	天津美特包装有限公司	18 185
2	中国天津奥的斯电梯有限公司	229 354	52	中石化一霍尼韦尔(天津)有限公司	18 014
3	北海粮油工业(天津)有限公司	225 586	53	天津市顺成旅游用品有限公司	17 833
4	天津顶益国际食品有限公司	222 169	54	虹志电脑(中国)有限公司	17 135
5	天津三美电机有限公司	197 839	55	天津三星康宁有限公司	16 392
6	天津通广三星电子有限公司	148 154	56	天津顶正印刷包材有限公司	16 378
7	天津华利汽车有限公司	140 040	57	第一饭店有限公司	16 014
8	天津三星电机有限公司	119 809	58	天津华士化工有限公司	15 771
9	中美天津史克制药有限公司	117 952	59	天津环美家俱有限公司	15 583
10	正大集团(天津)油脂有限公司	112 007	60	天津津达制衣有限公司	15 456
11	天津本田摩托车有限公司	107 161	61	天津顶园国际食品有限公司	15 453
12	天津雅马哈电子乐器有限公司	75 774	62	天津塘沽瓦特斯阀门有限公司	15 075
13	天津天美汽车配件有限公司	68 001	63	天津牧津纤维有限公司	14 551
14	天津三星电子有限公司	62 596	64	天津喜来登大酒店	14 549
15	天津宝洁有限公司	60 227	65	北洋大宇天津国际发展有限公司	14 158
16	天津日电电子通信工业有限公司	58 392	66	西斯尔(天津)混凝土工业有限公司	14 048
17	天津市福津木业有限公司	57 538	67	天津爱津服装有限公司	13 764
18	天津可口可乐饮料有限公司	54 719	68	卡夫天美食品(天津)有限公司	13 540
19	天津正大饲料科技有限公司	54 517	69	天津世里门服装有限公司	13 540
20	天津汉高洗涤剂有限公司	45 398	70	天津努德莱斯巴食品有限公司	13 377
21	天津轧五线材有限公司	42 372	71	天津金燕焊接材料有限公司	13 105
22	北洋集装箱有限公司	39 496	72	天津统一企业食品有限公司	12 990
23	天津药材集团有限公司	38 126	73	天津中富容器有限公司	12 744
24	天津新宝天洋家电有限公司	34 213	74	天津天马缝纫机制造有限公司	12 676
25	舜丰钢铁有限公司	33 061	75	天津国际大厦有限公司	12 618
26	天津富士达摩托车制造有限公司	32 707	76	天津大明工业公司	12 582
27	天津尚赫保健用品有限公司	30 868	77	天津顶信纸业有限公司	12 571
28	中法合营王朝葡萄酿酒有限公司	30 752	78	光达集团公司	12 471
29	天津长城(集团)有限公司	28 718	79	天津星湖实业有限公司	12 430
30	仙妮蕾德(天津)企业有限公司	27 567	80	浦铁(天津)钢材加工有限公司	12 427
31	天津梅兰日兰有限公司	27 401	81	天津双龙有色金属制品有限公司	12 013
32	天津三星光电子有限公司	25 755	82	大成食品(天津)有限公司	11 789
33	扎努西电气机械天津压缩机有限公司	25 751	83	天津津东汽车空调器有限公司	11 285
34	天津合天钢铁有限公司	25 728	84	天津奇伟日用化学有限公司	11 247
35	天津统一工业有限公司	24 479	85	天津德塔控制系统有限公司	11 186
36	天津国际联合轮胎橡胶有限公司	24 422	86	天津婕妮化妆品有限公司	10 964
37	天津新韩精机有限公司	24 422	87	永安百货有限公司	10 753
38	天津伊势丹有限公司	24 389	88	武清印染有限公司	10 517
39	天津韩飞鞋业有限公司	24 346	89	天津现代电子有限公司	10 414
40	天津华丰汽车装饰有限公司	24 337	90	PPG汽车涂料(天津)有限公司	10 395
41	天津津海金属材料有限公司	24 099	91	天津大真空有限公司	10 072
42	天津爱普生有限公司	23 683	92	康地万达(天津)有限公司	9 951
43	天津美特容器有限公司	21 644	93	乐金电子(天津)电器有限公司	9 944
44	天津三峰客车有限公司	20 785	94	艾格福天津有限公司	9 887
45	天津国际海运货柜工程有限公司	20 491	95	天津津住线束有限公司	9 756
46	大宇电子有限公司	20 002	96	天津南华工具(集团)有限公司	9 729
47	天津皮特斯钢铁有限公司	19 700	97	天津速效制药有限公司	9 703
48	维信(天津)工贸有限公司	19 700	98	李七庄纺纱有限公司	9 697
49	天津大通铜业有限公司	18 717	99	天津万兴毛纺(集团)有限公司	9 480
50	天津东洋油墨(第一)有限公司	18 584	100	天津关西涂料化工有限公司	9 383

18－12　1996年客商投资企业利税总额百强企业

名次	企业名称	利税总额（万元）	名次	企业名称	利税总额（万元）
1	摩托罗拉(中国)电子有限公司	356 041	51	天宝电子有限公司	1 695
2	中美天津史克制药有限公司	71 786	52	天津津信汽车塑料有限公司	1 612
3	天津顶益国际食品有限公司	62 153	53	天津津海金属材料有限公司	1 595
4	中国天津奥的斯电梯有限公司	49 736	54	天津德塔控制系统有限公司	1 594
5	中法合营王朝葡萄酿酒有限公司	19 991	55	天津市华益家具有限公司	1 583
6	天津本田摩托车有限公司	19 643	56	天津港商业保税仓库有限公司	1 576
7	天津尚赫保健用品有限公司	15 944	57	光达集团公司	1 538
8	天津华利汽车有限公司	15 768	58	天津美特包装有限公司	1 522
9	天津梅兰日兰有限公司	13 444	59	天津振华国际货运有限公司	1 516
10	天津市福津木业有限公司	11 513	60	天津稳泰化工兴业有限公司	1 516
11	仙妮蕾德(天津)企业有限公司	8 689	61	天津星光橡塑有限公司	1 513
12	天津日电电子通信工业有限公司	8 394	62	天津乐仁堂制药有限公司	1 513
13	天津宝洁有限公司	6 799	63	天津天马缝纫机制造有限公司	1 486
14	天津婕妮化妆品有限公司	6 036	64	天津东洋油墨(第一)有限公司	1 447
15	天津可口可乐饮料有限公司	5 740	65	天津乐达利印刷制品有限公司	1 440
16	天津努德莱斯巴食品有限公司	5 375	66	天津市阿斯莫汽车微电机有限公司	1 437
17	天津爱普生有限公司	5 026	67	天津汉高洗涤剂有限公司	1 393
18	扎努西电气机械天津压缩机有限公司	4 684	68	天津博康福汽车部辅件有限公司	1 352
19	天津国际大厦有限公司	4 365	69	威特瑞天津食品有限工司	1 342
20	天津津达制衣有限公司	4 230	70	天津万兴毛纺织(集团)有限公司	1 341
21	天津雅马哈电子乐器有限公司	3 938	71	天津福家家具有限公司	1 324
22	天津正大饲料科技有限公司	3 815	72	中国大冢制药有限公司	1 298
23	天津牧津纤维有限公司	3 778	73	绿点(天津)塑胶有限公司	1 268
24	天津华美快速印刷有限公司	3 735	74	天朝酿酒有限公司	1 260
25	天津速效制药有限公司	3 518	75	天津顺成旅游用品有限公司	1 241
26	天津顶正印刷包材有限公司	3 407	76	台湾亿联法郎制品有限公司	1 224
27	天津天利航空机电有限公司	3 153	77	天津双龙有色金属制品有限公司	1 220
28	富裕注塑制模(天津)有限公司	3 021	78	天津大维制衣有限公司	1 192
29	第一饭店有限公司	2 750	79	天津津福汽车塑料件有限公司	1 190
30	天津轧五线材有限公司	2 729	80	天津津裕电业有限公司	1 138
31	天津美特容器有限公司	2 673	81	华峰合成面料制造有限公司	1 136
32	天津富士达摩托车制造有限公司	2 551	82	李七庄纺纱有限公司	1 113
33	PPG汽车涂料(天津)有限公司	2 548	83	天津天海内衣有限公司	1 111
34	天津顶信纸业有限公司	2 432	84	天津李宁皮具有限公司	1 092
35	艾格福天津有限公司	2 430	85	天津华勤通信设备有限公司	1 060
36	天津北方包装有限公司	2 418	86	天津金燕焊接材料有限公司	1 055
37	天津三美电机有限公司	2 395	87	天津亚美保健饮料有限公司	1 052
38	天津安传电子有限公司	2 318	88	天津合天钢铁有限公司	1 051
39	天津欧亚床垫家具有限公司	2 239	89	维信(天津)工贸有限公司	1 047
40	天津皮特斯钢铁有限公司	2 090	90	韩国源进产业有限公司	1 043
41	天津国际联合轮胎橡胶有限公司	2 088	91	台湾乔山金属制品有限公司	1 028
42	天津塘沽瓦特斯阀门有限公司	2 065	92	天津天进涤纶棉有限公司	998
43	天津新宝天洋家电有限公司	2 047	93	天津宝联化纤有限公司	995
44	天津华丰汽车装饰有限公司	2 020	94	橙宝鲜橙汁有限公司	961
45	津华饭店有限公司	2 014	95	天津美登高食品有限公司	961
46	天津太河制药有限公司	1 999	96	天津大明工业公司	934
47	天津津东汽车空调器有限公司	1 994	97	舜丰钢铁有限公司	924
48	北洋集装箱有限公司	1 920	98	天津施莱德照明器材有限公司	902
49	天津天美汽车配件有限公司	1 907	99	天津劳特国际有限公司	876
50	天津万力建筑板材有限公司	1 706	100	雷尼(天津)木业有限公司	861

18－13　1996年客商投资企业出口创汇百强企业

名次	企业名称	出口创汇(万美元)	名次	企业名称	出口创汇(万美元)
1	摩托罗拉(中国)电子有限公司	64 760	51	天津新韩精机有限公司	562
2	天津三美电机有限公司	28 070	52	天津华德温纺织有限公司	549
3	天津三星电机有限公司	13 117	53	天津孚达制衣有限公司	545
4	天津雅马哈电子乐器有限公司	10 278	54	天津佳利福铸铁搪瓷制品有限公司	543
5	天津天美汽车配件有限公司	6 478	55	天津丰韩实业有限公司	542
6	北洋集装箱有限公司	5 453	56	天津高丽亚那工艺品有限公司	525
7	北海粮油工业(天津)有限公司	5 152	57	诺曼地橡胶有限公司	516
8	天津通广三星电子有限公司	4 541	58	亚洲(天津)鞋业有限公司	508
9	天津三星电子有限公司	4 058	59	来福股份有限公司	507
10	天津韩飞鞋业有限公司	2 684	60	天津塘沽瓦特斯阀门有限公司	502
11	大宇电子有限公司	2 665	61	大港通信有限公司	498
12	天津三星光电子有限公司	2 585	62	康地万达(天津)有限公司	491
13	天津国际海运货柜工程有限公司	2 476	63	天津北斗电子有限公司	482
14	天津环美家俱有限公司	2 015	64	天津中环三津有限公司	479
15	天津三星康宁有限公司	1 820	65	天津新宇纺织品有限公司	466
16	中美天津史克制药有限公司	1 796	66	天津华士化工有限公司	429
17	天津爱普生有限公司	1 670	67	天津安传电子有限公司	421
18	天津世里门服装有限公司	1 633	68	关东针织有限公司	418
19	天津星湖实业有限公司	1 408	69	天津天立林产品有限公司	408
20	天津牧津纤维有限公司	1 362	70	天津远洋玻璃制品有限公司	403
21	天津现代电子有限公司	1 253	71	天津漆原服饰有限公司	396
22	天津华愿国际贸易有限公司	1 252	72	天津昭和机电有限公司	395
23	天津惠通达国际贸易有限公司	1 230	73	天津天星时装有限公司	379
24	天津市福津木业有限公司	1 225	74	天津福助工业有限公司	375
25	津英纺纱有限公司	1 153	75	天津汇宇实业有限公司	371
26	李七庄纺纱有限公司	1 143	76	荣汉电子有限公司	366
27	天津国际联合轮胎橡胶有限公司	1 109	77	天津哈娜好医材有限公司	362
28	天津大真空有限公司	1 102	78	天津高鹤工艺品有限公司	342
29	天津新宝天洋家电有限公司	1 077	79	天津三协食品有限公司	340
30	天津长城(集团)有限公司	990	80	天津天神山服装有限公司	339
31	天津关西涂料化工有限公司	969	81	天津万乐毛衫有限公司	337
32	天津博克来家庭用品实业有限公司	962	82	天津圣波矿业有限公司	327
33	天津朝光革靴有限公司	893	83	天津津枫木业有限公司	320
34	天津天马缝纫机制造有限公司	881	84	天津金鑫食品有限公司	315
35	天津美式家具有限公司	875	85	新亚渔具(天津)有限公司	310
36	天津亚真电子有限公司	861	86	天津嘉义实业有限公司	308
37	飞马(天津)缝纫机有限公司	856	87	天津裕昌纺织品有限公司	308
38	天津汇英实业有限公司	814	88	天津津达制衣有限公司	305
39	天津吉利制衣有限公司	800	89	大新电研天津电子有限公司	305
40	天津三和电机有限公司	754	90	英业达(天津)电子技术有限公司	303
41	正大集团(天津)油脂有限公司	728	91	天津真星纺织有限公司	295
42	绵丰毛纺有限公司	711	92	天津雅丽饰工艺品有限公司	292
43	天津津住线束有限公司	690	93	天津中南钟表有限公司	284
44	天津日电电子通信工业有限公司	661	94	天津费加罗电子有限公司	283
45	天津昭和电子有限公司	640	95	天津大陆国际贸易有限公司	281
46	绿点(天津)塑胶有限公司	622	96	天津燕桥焊接材料有限公司	278
47	天津普林电路有限公司	611	97	天津英昌钢琴铸件有限公司	276
48	飞龙畜产制品有限公司	611	98	天津天海内衣有限公司	271
49	天津三达铸造有限公司	607	99	成真化妆用具(天津)有限公司	271
50	天津福家家具有限公司	589	100	天津申达食品有限公司	270

18-14 1995年全国同行业按销售收入排序前20名的天津企业

行业	单位名称	销售收入(万元)	名次
配合及混合饲料制造业	天津正大饲料科技有限公司	38 313.0	15
食用植物油加工业	北海粮油工业(天津)有限公司	224 857.0	2
	天津豫泰实业有限公司	49 422.0	6
屠宰业	天津市肉类联合加工厂	11 414.0	20
肉类副产品加工业	天津华德肠衣有限公司	6 165.9	4
	天津华裕肠衣有限公司	2 806.0	15
	天津畜产进出口公司肠衣加工厂	2 753.9	16
鱼糜及鱼糜制品加工业	天津尚赫保健用品有限公司	7 874.7	2
糖果业	嘉年华(天津)国际有限公司	6 803.0	19
方便主食品业	天津顶益国际食品有限公司	243 036.0	1
肉类罐头制造业	天津市罐头厂	4 129.0	20
调味料制造业	天津市第一调料酿造厂	8 656.0	1
	山东菱花集团总公司静海味精厂	4 255.0	6
冷冻饮品制造业	威特瑞(天津)食品有限公司	5 130.1	13
	天津美登高食品有限公司	4 361.0	17
	天津市华康食品厂	4 155.0	19
酒精制造业	天津市冠达实业总公司	18 824.0	7
	天津酒精厂	12 229.0	15
	天津市挂月酿酒总厂	11 173.2	18
葡萄酒制造业	中法合营王朝葡萄酿酒有限公司	21 416.0	2
碳酸饮料制造业	天津可口可乐饮料有限公司	53 325.0	4
果菜汁饮料制造业	天马企业集团工业总公司	4 692.1	15
固体饮料制造业	卡夫天美食品有限公司	12 584.0	3
	天津努德莱斯巴食品有限公司	8 861.0	6
其他纤维原料初步加工业	天津牧津纤维有限公司	9 390.0	5
棉纺业	天津市第一棉纺织厂	47 344.0	18
毛纺业	天津市东亚毛纺厂	37 978.0	3
工业用呢、工业用毡制造业	天津市工业用呢厂	5 311.0	2
毛针织品业	天津市天福羊毛衫总厂	7 625.8	13
其他毛皮制品业	天津畜产进出口公司皮毛加工厂	6 416.0	1
	天津飞龙畜产制品有限公司	6 269.0	2
羽毛(绒)加工业	维信(天津)工贸有限公司	13 935.8	4
	天津畜产进出口公司绒毛加工厂	6 315.0	8
锯材加工业	天津美式家具有限公司	4 181.0	15
	天津津枫木业有限公司	4 179.4	16
胶合板制造业	天津福津木业有限公司	42 436.0	2
刨花板制造业	天津福家家具有限公司	5 686.0	7
其他人造板制造业	天津劳伦斯装饰材料有限公司	2 968.1	15
生产用木制品业	天津环美地板有限公司	3 690.7	19
木制家具制造业	天津环美家俱有限公司	10 725.0	5
金属家具制造业	天津博克来家庭用品实业有限公司	14 746.4	4
其他家具制造业	天津欧亚床垫家具有限公司	6 182.9	5
机制纸及纸板制造业	天津板纸厂	31 432.0	19
纸制品业	天津市纸箱一厂	10 645.0	14
文具制造业	天津市美术颜料厂	3 659.0	11
笔制造业	天津铅笔厂	4 365.0	15
各种体育器材制造业	宝坻县奥林体育器材厂	3 000.0	17
西乐器制造业	天津市乐器公司	3 393.0	6
电子乐器制造业	天津雅马哈电子乐器有限公司	66 015.0	1
其他文教体育用品制造业	联合化学(天津)有限公司	3 712.6	4
原油加工业	中国石化天津石油化工公司	739 839.0	9
石油制品业	天津市华海石油化工总厂	28 432.0	3

18－14续表1

行业	单位名称	销售收入(万元)	名次
	天津大港油田重油公司	14 364.6	9
	天津市汉沽石油化学厂	13 306.0	10
	天津大港油田炼达实业公司	10 008.7	16
无机酸制造业	天津市长城化工厂	11 512.0	6
	天津市硫酸厂	7 084.0	17
	天津市宏鑫化工厂	6 561.0	18
烧碱制造业	渤海化工(集团)股份有限公司天津化工厂	110 821.0	3
	渤海化工(集团)股份有限公司天津大沽化工厂	86 383.0	4
纯碱制造业	渤海化工(集团)股份有限公司天津碱厂	91 872.0	2
农药原药制造业	天津农药股份有限公司	21 333.0	13
有机化工原料制造业	天津有机化学工业总公司	19 761.0	15
涂料制造业	天津灯塔涂料股份有限公司	39 289.0	5
油墨制造业	天津东洋油墨(第一)有限公司	16 631.0	2
染料制造业	天津华士化工有限公司	15 985.0	10
	天津市染料厂分厂	12 642.0	12
	天津市工农化工厂	8 256.0	18
功能高分子制造业	南开大学化工厂	3 000.0	12
合成纤维单(聚合)体制造业	天津市兴和化工厂	7 978.0	11
化学试剂、助剂制造业	天津炭黑厂	17 097.0	13
	天津溶剂厂	12 729.0	20
专项化学用品制造业	天津市天助精细化学公司	5 578.0	8
信息化学品制造业	天津感光材料公司	12 590.0	8
添加剂制造业	天津北方食品有限公司	6 572.0	5
	天津市津武糖精厂	4 597.0	9
肥皂及皂粉、合成洗涤剂制造业	天津宝洁有限公司	46 413.0	6
	天津汉高洗涤剂有限公司	40 465.0	10
香料、香精制造业	天津瀛海集团公司	10 419.0	5
	天津市第一香料厂	5 292.0	11
牙膏制造业	天津市牙膏厂	13 948.0	6
化学药品原药制造业	天津药业有限公司	31 561.0	15
化学药品制剂制造业	中美天津史克制药有限公司	95 164.0	2
粘胶纤维制造业	天津市人造纤维厂	14 490.0	18
锦纶纤维制造业	天津市合成纤维厂	9 358.0	10
渔网制造业	天津市渔网厂	4 230.0	2
轮胎制造业	天津市轮胎厂	26 318.0	19
力车胎制造业	天津津泰橡胶股份有限公司	21 610.0	3
	天津市朝阳车胎厂	10 840.0	11
日用橡胶制品业	天津市橡胶制品一厂	5 685.0	3
	天津市乳胶厂	5 282.0	4
	天津市橡胶制品三厂	3 459.0	9
塑料板、管、棒材制造业	天津市近代化学厂	10 940.0	12
塑料丝、绳及编织品制造业	天津石化精卫实业总公司	6 478.2	19
塑料包装箱及容器制造业	天津中富容器有限公司	13 631.0	3
日用塑料杂品制造业	天津育新塑料包装有限公司	6 899.0	11
砼结构构件制造业	天津建筑构件公司	9 081.0	7
轻质建筑材料制造业	天津万力建筑板材有限公司	2 772.2	15
防水密封建筑材料制造业	天津市油毡厂	6 123.0	5
工业技术用玻璃制造业	天津市三联工业技术玻璃有限责任公司	4 378.0	15
日用玻璃制品业	天津市玻璃器皿厂	9 569.0	13
建筑、卫生陶瓷制造业	嘉泰陶瓷工业有限公司	9 642.0	20
钢压延加工业	天津钢管公司	138 218.0	13
其他重有色金属冶炼业	天津开发区东方矽钢片厂	5 487.1	3

18-14 续表 2

行　　业	单 位 名 称	销售收入(万元)	名次
有色金属合金业	天津市冶炼厂	3 115.0	19
	天津市津港有色金属材料厂	3 008.9	20
重有色金属压延加工业	天津市津海有色金属轧延工业公司	44 474.0	6
	天津市大邱庄尧舜铜材厂	19 672.0	18
手工具制造业	天津南华工具(集团)有限公司	10 490.0	2
其他工具制造业	中国林业机械总公司天津林业工具厂	3 929.0	6
集装箱制造业	北洋集装箱有限公司	38 550.0	9
	天津国际海运货柜工程有限公司	31 926.0	15
金属包装物品及容器制造业	天津美特包装有限公司	15 439.0	15
金属丝绳及其制品业	天津市第一钢丝绳厂	14 519.0	7
	天津市第二钢丝绳厂	13 458.0	10
	天津市预应力钢丝一厂	13 171.0	11
水暖管道零件制造业	天津市武清县武东玛钢制品总厂	9 254.9	5
	天津市静海县津海制管厂	8 444.3	7
其他建筑用金属制品业	天津来福有限公司	3 713.7	8
铝制品业	天津美特容器有限公司	15 823.0	7
不锈钢制品业	天津市餐具公司	8 432.3	9
	天津市第二餐具厂	6 254.0	15
炊事用具制造业	天津市日用五金制品八厂	3 075.8	10
	天津市佳利福铸铁搪瓷制品有限公司	2 896.7	11
其他日用金属制品业	天津市日用五金电器工业总公司	3 474.0	19
铁制小农具制造业	天津农具厂	4 906.0	5
	天津市同达企业总公司	4 420.0	6
焊条制造业	天津大桥集团公司	13 162.0	6
	天津金燕焊接材料有限公司	12 311.0	8
	天津大桥集团大寺电焊条厂	7 744.6	12
	天津市电焊条公司静海电焊条厂	6 814.0	14
其他类未包括的金属制品业	天津天富软管工业有限公司	5 066.0	16
内燃机制造业	天津市内燃机厂	88 659.0	7
锻压设备制造业	天津市锻压机床总厂	13 028.0	2
机床附件制造业	天津市机床电器总厂	2 876.0	8
起重运输设备制造业	天津奥的斯电梯有限公司	190 731.0	3
泵制造业	天津市芦台精密铸造总厂	13 493.0	5
	天津市工业泵总厂	7 527.0	19
风机制造业	天津市鼓风机总厂	4 270.0	13
冷冻设备制造业	扎努西电气机械天津压缩机有限公司	41 072.0	5
其他通用设备制造业	天津市减速机总厂	11 498.0	8
阀门制造业	天津塘沽瓦特斯阀门有限公司	15 237.0	2
液压件及液力件制造业	天津液压机械集团公司	14 952.0	1
锻件制造业	天津市江兴实业总公司	4 045.0	15
	天津市汽车锻件厂	3 384.0	18
冶金工业专用设备制造业	天津重型机器厂	28 036.0	7
包装工业专用设备制造业	天津天利航空机电有限公司	6 268.0	5
纺织、服装、皮革工业专用设备制造	国营天津纺织机械厂	15 976.0	10
制浆、造纸工业专用设备制造业	天津轻工业机械厂	3 229.0	17
拖拉机制造业	天津拖拉机制造厂	48 096.0	9
畜牧机械制造业	天津正大机械有限公司	2 734.0	3
医用材料及医疗用品制造业	天津哈娜好医材有限公司	4 372.0	11
缝纫机制造业	天马缝纫机制造有限公司	17 809.4	5
邮政机械及器材制造业	邮电部天津通信设备厂	10 007.0	2
机车车辆配件制造业	天津机车车辆机械厂	14 341.0	2
	北京铁路局天津机车车辆配件厂	2 862.7	14

18－14续表3

行　业	单位名称	销售收入(万元)	名次
	天津市宁河县农机修理厂	2 649.4	16
铁路专用器材制造业	铁路信号厂	4 509.0	8
载重汽车制造业	天津华利汽车有限公司	158 981.0	10
客车制造业	天津三峰客车有限公司	24 891.0	12
小轿车制造业	天津市微型汽车厂	392 874.0	3
微型汽车制造业	天津市专用汽车厂	34 717.0	3
汽车零部件及配件制造业	天津天美汽车配件有限公司	38 436.0	8
摩托车整车制造业	天津本田摩托有限公司	147 961.0	6
自行车制造业	天津自行车厂	41 202.0	12
海洋运输船制造业	天津造船公司	58 024.0	8
发电机制造业	天津发电设备总厂	9 367.0	13
开关控制设备制造业	天津梅兰日兰有限公司	22 957.0	8
电线电缆制造业	天津市芦台永兴企业集团	43 000.0	11
蓄电池制造业	天津统一工业有限公司	18 662.0	2
	天津市蓄电池厂	6 603.0	15
洗衣机制造业	天津新宝天洋家电有限公司	33 544.0	9
电焊机制造业	天津市益德电器有限公司	3 750.9	7
交换设备制造业	天津日电电子通信工业有限公司	60 138.0	6
通信终端设备制造业	邮电部天津电话设备厂	32 203.0	6
	天津通信广播公司	22 781.0	11
其他通信设备制造业	摩托罗拉(中国)电子有限公司	1 056 731.0	1
广播电视设备制造业	天津安传电子有限公司	3 935.2	11
电子计算机外部设备制造业	天津爱普生有限公司	22 604.0	14
电真空器件制造业	天津津京玻壳股份有限公司	41 499.0	12
半导体器件制造业	天津市中环半导体公司	6 928.0	12
电子元件制造业	天津三美电机有限公司	252 096.0	1
电视机、录像机、摄像机制造业	天津通广三星电子有限公司	129 582.0	5
	天津长城(集团)有限公司	51 889.0	17
	天津三星电子有限公司	49 083.0	19
收音机、录音机制造业	天津新韩精机有限公司	29 211.0	16
其他电子设备制造业	天津大真空有限公司	7 738.7	13
工业自动化仪表制造业	中石化—霍尼韦尔(天津)有限公司	21 444.7	5
汽车仪器仪表制造业	天津市汽车仪表总厂	5 068.0	6
电子测量仪器制造业	天津费加罗电子有限公司	3 164.0	11
衡器制造业	天津市衡器公司	3 428.0	10
照相机及器材制造业	天津三星光电子有限公司	9 863.0	10
复印机制造业	天津市复印设备公司	6 951.0	6
钟表制造业	天津手表厂	10 885.0	12
地毯制造业	天津环宇集团公司	6 678.8	11
	后巷乡巷虹集团	6 096.4	12
	天津市亚华地毯厂	5 029.1	17
眼镜制造业	天津志成眼镜有限公司	2 852.0	12
生活用其他产品制造业	天津高丽亚那工艺品有限公司	5 374.6	15
电力供应业	天津市电力公司城区供电公司	167 400.0	7
蒸汽、热水生产和供应业	天津市热电公司	10 005.0	10
煤气生产业	天津市第二煤气厂	32 775.0	2
	天津市第一煤气厂	4 214.0	20
煤气供应业	天津市天燃气公司	13 828.0	8
自来水生产业	天津市自来水公司	23 917.0	4
天然原油开采业	大港油田集团有限责任公司	599 294.0	6
	中国海洋石油渤海公司	199 473.0	16
海盐业	天津长芦海晶集团有限公司	20 748.0	4
	天津长芦汉沽盐场	15 013.0	5

十九、区县基本情况

BASIC STATISTICAL OF DISTRICTS AND COUNTIES

1996 年天津有 18 个区县

13 个市辖区有：和平区、河东区、河西区、南开区、河北区、红桥区、塘沽区
汉沽区、大港区、东丽区、西青区、津南区、北辰区

5 个市辖县包括：宁河县、武清县、静海县、宝坻县、蓟县

19－1　和平区基本情况

指标名称	单　位	1990年	1995年	1996年
*常住户数	户	148 236	149 993	149 931
*户籍人口	万人	49.43	47.58	47.18
男	万人	24.10	23.04	22.80
女	万人	25.33	24.54	24.38
*人口出生率	‰	10.00	4.54	4.14
*人口自然增长率	‰	3.30	－1.37	－2.45
国内生产总值(现价)	万元	43 694	111 394	156 025
第二产业	万元	5 113	16 230	19 227
第三产业	万元	38 581	95 164	136 798
国内生产总值指数(以上年＝100,按可比价计算)	%		120.1	130.6
区县级财政收入	万元	18 881	22 794	26 228
区县级财政支出	万元	10 246	22 738	27 029
#教育经费支出	万元	3 881	7 600	9 261
*固定资产投资(不含农村集体和个人投资)	万元		471 479	422 170
#区县属	万元		2 207	5 273
*房屋施工面积(不含农村集体和个人投资)	万平方米		314.27	322.56
#区县属	万平方米		2.00	3.22
*房屋竣工面积(不含农村集体和个人投资)	万平方米		113.69	97.42
#区县属	万平方米		0.47	1.28
乡以上工业企业单位数	个	88	177	146
从业人员	万人	0.45	0.58	0.58
总产值(现价)	万元	4 744	20 885	17 435
产品销售收入	万元	4 645	22 056	18 628
利税总额	万元	808	3 301	1 178
资产总额	万元	4 705	31 996	27 051
固定资产原值	万元	923	5 874	9 007
流动资产合计	万元	3 985	21 223	19 515
社会消费品零售总额	万元	87 238	155 548	190 500
批发零售贸易业网点	个			926
饮食业网点	个			207
*私营工商企业户数	户		659	1 148
雇工人数	人		5 460	7 187
注册资本	万元		20 302	36 995
总产值	万元		360	461
营业收入	万元		7 537	9 156
*个体工商业户数	户		12 315	13 661
从业人员	人		14 152	15 509
资金	万元		7 962	11 780
营业额	万元		32 675	41 193
直接利用外资协议额	万美元		1 505	2 100
外贸出口商品总值	万美元		39.5	124
*小学校数	所	51	60	63
在校学生数	人	52 233	50 606	47 876
*普通中学校数	所	25	39	39
在校学生	人	21 524	33 264	36 043

注:"*"为全区数据,其余为区县属数。1990年工业总产值为现价原口径,1995年和1996年为现价新口径。

19-2 河东区基本情况

指标名称	单位	1990 年	1995 年	1996 年
* 常住户数	户	191 003	207 545	210 637
* 户籍人口	万人	59.80	61.83	62.04
男	万人	30.45	31.27	31.33
女	万人	29.35	30.56	30.71
* 人口出生率	‰	9.48	4.86	4.31
* 人口自然增长率	‰	3.22	-1.29	-2.17
国内生产总值(现价)	万元	20 740	86 317	111 355
第二产业	万元	5 624	15 976	19 377
第三产业	万元	15 116	70 341	91 978
国内生产总值指数(以上年=100,按可比价计算)	%		119.6	119.1
区县级财政收入	万元	10 694	10 024	12 459
区县级财政支出	万元	7 167	17 098	25 346
♯教育经费支出	万元	2 659	6 712	8 784
* 固定资产投资(不含农村集体和个人投资)	万元		157 115	170 266
♯区县属	万元		8 056	20 408
* 房屋施工面积(不含农村集体和个人投资)	万平方米		191.08	167.29
♯区县属	万平方米		16.05	11.83
* 房屋竣工面积(不含农村集体和个人投资)	万平方米		52.40	74.77
♯区县属	万平方米		1.63	1.21
乡以上工业企业单位数	个	205	322	229
从业人员	万人	0.88	0.88	0.64
总产值(现价)	万元	11 970	42 269	37 257
产品销售收入	万元	6 210	40 861	41 172
利税总额	万元	2 146	6 053	4 756
资产总额	万元		14 178	35 480
固定资产原值	万元	2 571	8 157	7 848
流动资产合计	万元		47 250	20 199
社会消费品零售总额	万元	54 772	39 300	48 000
批发零售贸易业网点	个			625
饮食业网点	个			78
* 私营工商企业户数	户		669	741
雇工人数	人		5 826	5 236
注册资本	万元		14 656	16 850
总产值	万元		3 743	5 974
营业收入	万元		25 640	14 498
* 个体工商业户数	户		12 201	13 225
从业人员	人		14 839	16 113
资金	万元		12 930	15 447
营业额	万元		60 466	64 245
直接利用外资协议额	万美元		931	911
外贸出口商品总值	万美元		1 300	3 041
* 小学校数	所	63	66	65
在校学生数	人	51 223	55 915	51 673
* 普通中学校数	所	37	40	42
在校学生	人	16 745	28 165	32 124

注:"*"为全区数据,其余为区县属数。1990 年工业总产值为现价原口径,1995 年和 1996 年为现价新口径。

19-3 河西区基本情况

指标名称	单 位	1990年	1995年	1996年
*常住户数	户	206 958	229 354	232 221
*户籍人口	万人	64.77	68.16	68.52
男	万人	32.61	34.10	34.24
女	万人	32.16	34.06	34.29
*人口出生率	‰	9.82	4.75	4.29
*人口自然增长率	‰	3.60	-0.87	-2.04
国内生产总值(现价)	万元	28 384	96 168	127 869
第二产业	万元	7 228	17 491	20 992
第三产业	万元	21 156	78 677	106 871
国内生产总值指数(以上年=100,按可比价计算)	%		113.2	125.1
区县级财政收入	万元	12 220	11 212	13 900
区县级财政支出	万元	7 943	17 807	23 095
#教育经费支出	万元	3 212	6 960	9 470
*固定资产投资(不含农村集体和个人投资)	万元		288 902	398 018
#区县属	万元		983	1 186
*房屋施工面积(不含农村集体和个人投资)	万平方米		329.84	291.53
#区县属	万平方米		1.48	3.07
*房屋竣工面积(不含农村集体和个人投资)	万平方米		116.44	107.06
#区县属	万平方米		0.95	1.22
乡以上工业企业单位数	个	141	309	302
从业人员	万人	0.42	0.76	0.78
总产值(现价)	万元	7 717	48 857	42 411
产品销售收入	万元	7 483	45 486	37 250
利税总额	万元	1 533	4 973	2 732
资产总额	万元	5 562	64 373	62 615
固定资产原值	万元	1 734	19 442	18 458
流动资产合计	万元	4 430	42 327	39 061
社会消费品零售总额	万元	10 948	56 864	73 398
批发零售贸易业网点	个			747
饮食业网点	个			102
*私营工商企业户数	户		731	1 100
雇工人数	人		5 943	12 195
注册资本	万元		14 172	38 484
总产值	万元			
营业收入	万元		6 481	9 162
*个体工商业户数	户		5 933	8 470
从业人员	人		6 468	8 976
资金	万元			
营业额	万元		81 085	84 540
直接利用外资协议额	万美元		1 024	881
外贸出口商品总值	万美元		1 007	862
*小学校数	所	66	79	78
在校学生数	人	54 786	58 978	55 329
*普通中学校数	所	34	51	51
在校学生	人	22 454	36 833	35 257

注:"*"为全区数据,其余为区县属数。1990年工业总产值为现价原口径,1995年和1996年为现价新口径。

19－4　南开区基本情况

指标名称	单　位	1990年	1995年	1996年
* 常住户数	户	213 213	241 123	244 591
* 户籍人口	万人	68.37	71.95	72.54
男	万人	34.88	36.57	36.81
女	万人	33.49	35.38	35.73
* 人口出生率	‰	9.37	4.28	4.06
* 人口自然增长率	‰	3.09	－0.90	－1.69
国内生产总值(现价)	万元	31 793	82 001	104 174
第二产业	万元	6 837	12 810	32 791
第三产业	万元	24 956	69 191	71 383
国内生产总值指数(以上年＝100,按可比价计算)	%		113.2	129.2
区县级财政收入	万元	15 355	12 612	14 372
区县级财政支出	万元	7 149	18 424	23 681
＃教育经费支出	万元	2 752	7 109	8 988
* 固定资产投资(不含农村集体和个人投资)	万元		225 784	175 394
＃区县属	万元		2 835	1 518
* 房屋施工面积(不含农村集体和个人投资)	万平方米		217.67	222.62
＃区县属	万平方米		9.50	2.24
* 房屋竣工面积(不含农村集体和个人投资)	万平方米		84.36	70.01
＃区县属	万平方米		3.24	0.94
乡以上工业企业单位数	个	174	380	369
从业人员	万人	0.94	1.28	1.21
总产值(现价)	万元	11 278	56 790	93 530
产品销售收入	万元		60 094	96 329
利税总额	万元	2 077	5 043	19 807
资产总额	万元		75 767	112 751
固定资产原值	万元	2 965	15 364	22 156
流动资产合计	万元		52 022	89 879
社会消费品零售总额	万元	24 440	81 759	82 447
批发零售贸易业网点	个			1 061
饮食业网点	个			96
* 私营工商企业户数	户	28	717	835
雇工人数	人		6 345	7 349
注册资本	万元		17 897	20 479
总产值	万元		1 368	1 744
营业收入	万元		11 538	12 597
* 个体工商业户数	户	6 448	12 212	13 647
从业人员	人		13 348	14 847
资金	万元		11 068	12 960
营业额	万元		34 019	47 392
直接利用外资协议额	万美元		1 043	1 102
外贸出口商品总值	万美元		2 809	2 976
* 小学校数	所	69	72	74
在校学生数	人	55 226	59 550	56 331
* 普通中学校数	所	34	38	47
在校学生	人	19 978	32 765	36 128

注:“*”为全区数据,其余为区县属数。1990年工业总产值为现价原口径,1995年和1996年为现价新口径。

19－5　河北区基本情况

指标名称	单　位	1990 年	1995 年	1996 年
*常住户数	户	188 195	206 013	208 039
*户籍人口	万人	60.67	61.61	61.55
男	万人	30.77	31.17	31.14
女	万人	29.90	30.44	30.42
*人口出生率	‰	9.93	4.63	4.22
*人口自然增长率	‰	3.43	－1.50	－1.86
国内生产总值(现价)	万元	22 072	87 543	113 760
第二产业	万元	5 294	14 240	26 957
第三产业	万元	16 778	73 303	86 803
国内生产总值指数(以上年＝100,按可比价计算)	%		124.9	126.5
区县级财政收入	万元	13 018	10 619	12 746
区县级财政支出	万元	8 066	18 177	22 492
#教育经费支出	万元	3 191	6 889	9 151
*固定资产投资(不含农村集体和个人投资)	万元		96 166	134 751
#区县属	万元		2 449	20 433
*房屋施工面积(不含农村集体和个人投资)	万平方米		130.76	122.84
#区县属	万平方米		5.87	6.63
*房屋竣工面积(不含农村集体和个人投资)	万平方米		36.42	53.87
#区县属	万平方米		0.40	0.83
乡以上工业企业单位数	个	156	290	309
从业人员	万人	0.56	0.92	2.08
总产值(现价)	万元	8 114	28 552	42 821
产品销售收入	万元	8 050	29 175	41 916
利税总额	万元	1 345	3 375	3 423
资产总额	万元		35 423	69 951
固定资产原值	万元	1 814	9 656	21 969
流动资产合计	万元		25 050	46 260
社会消费品零售总额	万元	60 455	53 899	69 281
批发零售贸易业网点	个			729
饮食业网点	个			124
*私营工商企业户数	户		622	766
雇工人数	人		5 614	6 795
注册资本	万元		14 247	17 969
总产值	万元		8 364	5 524
营业收入	万元		18 373	14 847
*个体工商业户数	户		12 900	14 314
从业人员	人		16 040	17 555
资金	万元		8 855	10 641
营业额	万元		29 941	30 918
直接利用外资协议额	万美元		2 148	1 090
外贸出口商品总值	万美元		506	540
*小学校数	所	73	74	78
在校学生数	人	54 780	58 226	54 681
*普通中学校数	所	39	48	53
在校学生	人	20 250	34 989	39 647

注:“*”为全区数据,其余为区县属数。1990 年工业总产值为现价原口径,1995 年和 1996 年为现价新口径。

19-6 红桥区基本情况

指标名称	单 位	1990年	1995年	1996年
*常住户数	户	184 067	196 655	197 983
*户籍人口	万人	57.20	57.58	57.48
男	万人	29.10	29.10	29.03
女	万人	28.10	28.48	28.45
*人口出生率	‰	10.35	4.62	4.09
*人口自然增长率	‰	3.41	-1.39	-2.15
国内生产总值(现价)	万元	24 217	78 361	109 798
第二产业	万元	4 714	11 042	12 715
第三产业	万元	19 503	67 319	97 083
国内生产总值指数(以上年=100,按可比价计算)	%		126.0	133.4
区县级财政收入	万元	9 757	7 376	8 018
区县级财政支出	万元	7 328	14 343	20 653
#教育经费支出	万元	3 050	6 276	8 078
*固定资产投资(不含农村集体和个人投资)	万元		50 399	35 958
#区县属	万元		830	946
*房屋施工面积(不含农村集体和个人投资)	万元		68.77	38.92
#区县属	万元		0.97	0.77
*房屋竣工面积(不含农村集体和个人投资)	万元		23.94	12.55
#区县属	万元		0.97	0.47
乡以上工业企业单位数	个	238	314	305
从业人员	万人	1.00	0.84	0.79
总产值(现价)	万元	11 441	26 673	30 380
产品销售收入	万元	11 272	26 928	27 922
利税总额	万元	2 271	2 937	3 103
资产总额	万元	9 525	26 634	31 247
固定资产原值	万元	3 254	7 517	7 970
流动资产合计	万元	7 247	18 785	21 787
社会消费品零售总额	万元	30 939	39 300	48 888
批发零售贸易业网点	个			817
饮食业网点	个			108
*私营工商企业户数	户		554	818
雇工人数	人		5 045	6 779
注册资本	万元		10 366	20 632
总产值	万元		5 008	7 252
营业收入	万元		7 560	15 620
*个体工商业户数	户	6 062	12 936	14 276
从业人员	人	6 815	15 002	16 268
资金	万元	1 234	13 379	15 534
营业额	万元	17 662	58 999	61 925
直接利用外资协议额	万美元		526	417
外贸出口商品总值	万美元		430	518
*小学校数	所	64	67	70
在校学生数	人	49 208	53 073	49 574
*普通中学校数	所	32	38	46
在校学生	人	17 474	28 891	32 572

注:"*"为全区数据,其余为区县属数。1990年工业总产值为现价原口径,1995年和1996年为现价新口径。

19－7　塘沽区基本情况

指标名称	单　位	1990年	1995年	1996年
* 常住户数	户	135 178	145 950	147 284
＃农业户	户	26 918	27 678	23 200
* 户籍人口	万人	43.06	44.82	45.05
按农业、非农业分				
农业人口	万人	8.55	8.52	7.22
非农业人口	万人	34.51	36.30	37.83
* 人口出生率	‰	12.20	6.52	6.78
* 人口自然增长率	‰	7.30	1.65	1.73
职　工	万人	3.39	3.89	4.21
* 乡村劳动力	万人	3.65	3.09	2.99
＃农林牧渔业劳动者人数	万人	1.61	0.99	0.98
国内生产总值(现价)	万元	35 527	120 468	151 351
第一产业	万元	6 808	14 110	12 669
第二产业	万元	10 389	28 383	37 213
第三产业	万元	18 330	77 975	101 469
国内生产总值指数(以上年＝100,按可比价计算)	%	112.8	116.0	118.0
区县级财政收入	万元	30 519	23 376	27 055
区县级财政支出	万元	10 193	28 315	35 671
＃教育经费支出	万元	2 891	8 360	9 422
* 固定资产投资(不含农村集体和个人投资)	万元		623 904	633 134
＃区县属	万元		19 476	38 158
* 房屋施工面积(不含农村集体和个人投资)	万平方米		195.81	163.74
＃区县属	万平方米		19.20	19.37
* 房屋竣工面积(不含农村集体和个人投资)	万平方米		63.68	73.23
＃区县属	万平方米		11.07	12.49
* 年末实有耕地面积	万公顷	0.53	0.52	0.52
* 农业机械总动力	万千瓦	23.70	29.85	28.03
* 化肥施用实物量	吨	5 516	4 271	4 271
* 农村用电量	万千瓦小时	8 077	10 764	9 881
* 农林牧渔业总产值(现价)	万元	21 106	32 131	31 786
* 农林牧渔业总指数(以上年＝100,按可比价计算)	%	103.9	115.8	92.48
* 农作物产量				
粮　食	万吨	1.76	2.81	2.83
棉　花	吨			
油　料	吨			
水　果	吨	2 578	4 163	4 503
* 畜产品产量				
猪牛羊肉	万吨	0.38	0.26	0.34

注:"*"为全区数据,其余为区县属数。1990年工业总产值为现价原口径,1995年和1996年为现价新口径。

19－7续表

指标名称	单 位	1990年	1995年	1996年
禽 蛋	吨	523	5 523	5 016
*水产品产量	吨	16 432	15 427	15 608
*蔬菜总产量	吨	75 313	68 639	70 131
*农民人均年纯收入(抽样调查数)	元/人	1 560	3 026	3 633
乡镇企业单位数	个	329	354	338
#工 业	个	207	223	194
乡镇企业人数	万人	1.98	1.96	2.06
#工 业	万人	1.37	1.22	1.21
乡镇企业总收入	万元	24 944	101 920	123 006
#工 业	万元	16 483	59 850	71 704
村以上工业企业单位数	个	280	550	448
从业人员	万人	1.99	2.18	2.19
总产值(现价)	万元	24 756	110 369	142 848
产品销售收入	万元	20 321	105 669	128 925
利税总额	万元	1 196	6 093	6 471
资产总额	万元			196 971
固定资产原值	万元	14 000	64 988	83 679
流动资产合计	万元	8 943	75 883	106 596
社会消费品零售总额	万元	34 860	122 973	182 493
批发零售贸易业网点	个			459
饮食业网点	个			83
*私营工商企业户数	户	83	750	838
雇工人数	人	730	7 797	8 382
注册资本	万元	730	22 123	32 553
总产值	万元		6 955	8 535
营业收入	万元		22 081	26 511
*个体工商业户数	户	5 206	13 763	13 109
从业人员	人	7 436	17 258	17 625
资金	万元	2 502	21 642	28 044
营业额	万元	3 207	29 802	39 367
外贸出口商品总值	万美元	1 111	1 464	2 380
*小学校数	所	57	61	61
在校学生数	人	42 385	41 711	40 931
*普通中学校数	所	34	34	35
在校学生数	人	19 734	24 220	26 796
*学龄儿童入学率	%	100.0	100.0	99.88
卫生机构数	个	193	194	195
#医 院	个	20	26	21

19－8　汉沽区基本情况

指标名称	单　位	1990 年	1995 年	1996 年
* 常住户数	户	54 503	57 117	57 429
#农业户	户	15 157	14 575	13 876
* 户籍人口	万人	16.32	16.72	16.72
按农业、非农业分				
农业人口	万人	4.98	4.78	4.61
非农业人口	万人	11.35	11.94	12.11
* 人口出生率	‰	12.80	8.40	8.06
* 人口自然增长率	‰	7.90	3.70	2.00
职　工	万人	1.53	1.85	1.84
* 乡村劳动力	万人	2.61	2.59	2.54
#农林牧渔业劳动者人数	万人	1.31	1.26	1.27
国内生产总值(现价)	万元		67 236	86 520
第一产业	万元		14 260	17 063
第二产业	万元		25 152	30 677
第三产业	万元		27 824	38 780
国内生产总值指数(以上年＝100,按可比价计算)	%		120.2	120.4
区县级财政收入	万元	13 748	5 335	6 524
区县级财政支出	万元	4 809	11 546	11 079
#教育经费支出	万元		2 554	3 107
* 固定资产投资(不含农村集体和个人投资)	万元		34 789	69 655
#区县属	万元		1 982	16 506
* 房屋施工面积(不含农村集体和个人投资)	万平方米		11.96	13.34
#区县属	万平方米		2.54	3.68
* 房屋竣工面积(不含农村集体和个人投资)	万平方米		5.89	9.77
#区县属	万平方米		1.64	2.76
* 年末实有耕地面积	万公顷	0.46	0.45	0.45
* 农业机械总动力	万千瓦	8.66	12.9	15.19
* 化肥施用实物量	吨	4 994	5 487	5 806
* 农村用电量	万千瓦小时	9 431	7 929	10 794
* 农林牧渔业总产值(现价)	万元	14 506	33 580	40 455
* 农林牧渔业总指数(以上年＝100,按可比价计算)	%	111.9	112.1	112.3
* 农作物产量				
粮　食	万吨	2.23	1.92	1.93
棉　花	吨		96	77
油　料	吨			
水　果	吨	6 522	22 421	24 792
* 畜产品产量				
猪牛羊肉	万吨	0.06	0.09	0.11

注:"＊"为全区数据,其余为区县属数。1990 年工业总产值为现价原口径,1995 年和 1996 年为现价新口径。

19－8续表

指标名称	单　位	1990年	1995年	1996年
禽　蛋	吨	4 020	4 308	4 430
*水产品产量	吨	8 704	18 012	20 162
*蔬菜总产量	吨	33 228	35 740	36 276
*农民人均年纯收入(抽样调查数)	元/人	1 350	2 451	3 210
乡镇企业单位数	个			
#工　业	个	126	173	161
乡镇企业人数	万人			
#工　业	万人	1.48	1.57	1.50
乡镇企业总收入	万元			
#工　业	万元	24 841	68 099	88 667
村以上工业企业单位数	个	217	257	238
从业人员	万人	1.93	1.96	1.86
总产值(现价)	万元	37 821	92 634	122 907
产品销售收入	万元	31 940	86 537	111 396
利税总额	万元	2 090	6 839	8 481
资产总额	万元	22 250	79 077	119 526
固定资产原值	万元	16 503	32 793	42 399
流动资产合计	万元	10 062	53 239	76 440
社会消费品零售总额	万元	9 857	17 971	19 269
批发零售贸易业网点	个			176
饮食业网点	个			40
*私营工商企业户数	户		360	396
雇工人数	人		4 238	4 561
注册资本	万元		7 056	7 511
总产值	万元		4 658	7 500
营业收入	万元		2 039	982
*个体工商业户数	户	2 209	4 586	4 795
从业人员	人	2 628	5 052	5 291
资金	万元	1 142	3 152	3 565
营业额	万元	1 706	18 396	20 000
外贸出口商品总值	万美元		2 851	3 088
*小学校数	所	36	30	30
在校学生数	人	18 918	15 422	14 891
*普通中学校数	所	19	19	18
在校学生数	人	6 208	10 275	10 930
*学龄儿童入学率	%	100.0	100.0	99.85
卫生机构数	个	17	17	19
#医　院	个	7	7	8

19－9　大港区基本情况

指标名称	单　位	1990 年	1995 年	1996 年
* 常住户数	户	85 040	95 187	96 746
#农业户	户	32 691	33 741	33 693
* 户籍人口	万人	29.08	31.22	31.58
按农业、非农业分				
农业人口	万人	11.44	20.34	10.87
非农业人口	万人	17.64	10.88	20.71
* 人口出生率	‰	15.6	11.01	10.93
* 人口自然增长率	‰	11.4	7.21	7.05
职　工	万人	0.65	0.91	0.86
* 乡村劳动力	万人	5.10	4.18	4.10
#农林牧渔业劳动者人数	万人	1.61	1.33	1.30
国内生产总值(现价)	万元	26 263	136 384	180 000
第一产业	万元	4 182	8 734	10 000
第二产业	万元	13 220	76 050	70 000
第三产业	万元	8 861	51 600	100 000
国内生产总值指数(以上年＝100,按可比价计算)	%		128.1	126.5
区县级财政收入	万元	6 750	10 969	15 738
区县级财政支出	万元	5 118	15 262	22 523
#教育经费支出	万元	943	2 744	3 793
* 固定资产投资(不含农村集体和个人投资)	万元		463 711	529 324
#区县属	万元		3 981	9 570
* 房屋施工面积(不含农村集体和个人投资)	万平方米		79.97	101.32
#区县属	万平方米		5.01	11.40
* 房屋竣工面积(不含农村集体和个人投资)	万平方米		61.57	81.65
#区县属	万平方米		3.61	7.17
* 年末实有耕地面积	万公顷	1.32	1.32	1.32
* 农业机械总动力	万千瓦	30.10	29.84	31.14
* 化肥施用实物量	吨	4 507	5 317	5 305
* 农村用电量	万千瓦小时	9 972	10 262	12 012
* 农林牧渔业总产值(现价)	万元	9 502	19 583	21 868
* 农林牧渔业总指数(以上年＝100,按可比价计算)	%	109.1	104.8	110.3
* 农作物产量				
粮　食	万吨	4.80	4.93	4.77
棉　花	吨	21		
油　料	吨	807	547	784
水　果	吨	1 823	3 078	3 759
* 畜产品产量				
猪牛羊肉	万吨	0.20	0.22	0.25

注:“*”为全区数据,其余为区县属数。1990 年工业总产值为现价原口径,1995 年和 1996 年为现价新口径。

19－9续表

指标名称	单　位	1990年	1995年	1996年
禽　蛋	吨	3 388	4 292	5 877
*水产品产量	吨	2 650	4 276	5 770
*蔬菜总产量	吨	13 895	27 012	31 262
*农民人均年纯收入(抽样调查数)	元/人	1 061	2 511	3 250
乡镇企业单位数	个	379	470	453
#工　业	个	367	388	381
乡镇企业人数	万人	3.45	3.76	3.58
#工　业	万人	3.37	3.65	3.47
乡镇企业总收入	万元	53 194	235 481	297 070
#工　业	万元	50 145	198 288	260 245
村以上工业企业单位数	个	443	474	467
从业人员	万人	3.39	3.71	3.52
总产值(现价)	万元	56 883	259 347	367 961
产品销售收入	万元	50 153	198 321	260 825
利税总额	万元	3 884	18 546	22 443
资产总额	万元	33 130	182 474	175 509
固定资产原值	万元	19 012	66 340	76 938
流动资产合计	万元	14 118	116 134	134 875
社会消费品零售总额	万元	12 364	34 214	59 671
批发零售贸易业网点	个			368
饮食业网点	个			40
*私营工商企业户数	户	60	499	529
雇工人数	人	1 317	4 098	4 318
注册资本	万元	658	14 684	15 564
总产值	万元	3 600	7 335	7 759
营业收入	万元	340	4 137	7 523
*个体工商业户数	户	3 150	5 581	6 380
从业人员	人	5 650	10 713	11 971
资金	万元	1 507	8 426	10 693
营业额	万元	8 043	36 059	41 059
外贸出口商品总值	万美元		1 200	4 134
*小学校数	所	63	58	48
在校学生数	人	33 937	27 582	28 090
*普通中学校数	所	41	41	44
在校学生数	人	22 231	20 938	21 274
*学龄儿童入学率	%			99.86
卫生机构数	个	10	10	10
#医　院	个	2	2	2

19－10　东丽区基本情况

指标名称	单　位	1990 年	1995 年	1996 年
* 常住户数	户	85 202	93 703	94 919
#农业户	户	62 704	65 735	66 058
* 户籍人口	万人	28.61	29.71	29.85
按农业、非农业分				
农业人口	万人	20.54	20.51	20.52
非农业人口	万人	8.07	9.20	9.33
* 人口出生率	‰	14.53	11.10	10.40
* 人口自然增长率	‰	6.11	5.50	4.70
职　工	万人	1.42	2.24	2.35
* 乡村劳动力	万人	10.09	10.99	9.04
#农林牧渔业劳动者人数	万人	2.76	2.66	2.28
国内生产总值(现价)	万元	80 105	266 035	351 143
第一产业	万元	12 156	18 979	19 038
第二产业	万元	38 324	128 177	168 711
第三产业	万元	29 625	118 879	163 394
国内生产总值指数(以上年＝100,按可比价计算)	%	112.7	117.5	126.1
区县级财政收入	万元	12 285	17 449	20 082
区县级财政支出	万元	4 900	16 631	20 032
#教育经费支出	万元	1 595	4 667	6 063
* 固定资产投资(不含农村集体和个人投资)	万元		273 451	132 955
#区县属	万元		13 912	9 065
* 房屋施工面积(不含农村集体和个人投资)	万平方米		48.70	33.20
#区县属	万平方米		24.32	2.61
* 房屋竣工面积(不含农村集体和个人投资)	万平方米		29.11	13.21
#区县属	万平方米		16.77	2.08
* 年末实有耕地面积	万公顷	1.43	1.41	1.41
* 农业机械总动力	万千瓦	59.31	73.98	70.08
* 化肥施用实物量	吨	14 341	10 072	9 599
* 农村用电量	万千瓦小时	11 928	17 975	20 265
* 农林牧渔业总产值(现价)	万元	23 045	54 565	54 712
* 农林牧渔业总指数(以上年＝100,按可比价计算)	%	100.3	108.9	109.7
* 农作物产量				
粮　食	万吨	7.49	7.52	7.69
棉　花	吨			
油　料	吨			
水　果	吨	1 633	4 455	4 547
* 畜产品产量				
猪牛羊肉	万吨	0.25	0.53	0.50

注:“*”为全区数据,其余为区县属数。1990 年工业总产值为现价原口径,1995 年和 1996 年为现价新口径。

19－10续表

指标名称	单　位	1990年	1995年	1996年
禽　蛋	吨	4 938	6 645	6 340
*水产品产量	吨	5 687	8 397	8 708
*蔬菜总产量	吨	171 280	200 740	212 991
*农民人均年纯收入(抽样调查数)	元/人	1 333	2 722	3 342
乡镇企业单位数	个	1 070	1 223	1 102
#工　业	个	867	941	841
乡镇企业人数	万人	7.22	5.98	5.33
#工　业	万人	6.03	5.45	4.87
乡镇企业总收入	万元	111 714	593 564	825 746
#工　业	万元	79 546	311 920	381 215
村以上工业企业单位数	个	946	1 043	940
从业人员	万人	6.03	6.18	5.03
总产值(现价)	万元	123 297	367 007	490 731
产品销售收入	万元	81 782	321 289	391 178
利税总额	万元	11 788	26 152	48 019
资产总额	万元		304 910	336 310
固定资产原值	万元	38 076	127 793	144 594
流动资产合计	万元		177 117	191 202
社会消费品零售总额	万元	1 600	2 853	3 618
批发零售贸易业网点	个			431
饮食业网点	个			21
*私营工商企业户数	户	226	1 118	1 367
雇工人数	人	3 848	14 316	15 149
注册资本	万元	2 760	39 840	48 040
总产值	万元	16 081	71 236	99 125
营业收入	万元	16 081	56 989	79 300
*个体工商业户数	户	5 400	7 081	8 223
从业人员	人	12 959	12 816	14 065
资金	万元	6 182	15 537	18 265
营业额	万元	10 721	68 720	101 622
外贸出口商品总值	万美元	406	8 135	11 589
*小学校数	所	63	79	79
在校学生数	人	29 179	27 148	26 934
*普通中学校数	所	18	22	22
在校学生数	人	11 910	13 984	14 466
*学龄儿童入学率	%	100.0	100.0	100.0
卫生机构数	个	12	12	12
#医　院	个	4	4	4

19－11　西青区基本情况

指标名称	单　位	1990 年	1995 年	1996 年
* 常住户数	户	92 071	97 435	91 367
＃农业户	户	69 970	74 144	67 882
* 户籍人口	万人	29.05	30.23	30.57
按农业、非农业分				
农业人口	万人	22.29	22.89	22.97
非农业人口	万人	6.76	7.34	7.60
* 人口出生率	‰	14.26	11.99	10.82
* 人口自然增长率	‰	8.07	6.23	3.71
职　工	万人	1.07	1.07	1.02
* 乡村劳动力	万人	12.12	11.38	11.11
＃农林牧渔业劳动者人数	万人	4.71	3.75	3.60
国内生产总值(现价)	万元	78 150	298 998	406 800
第一产业	万元	17 980	35 730	36 400
第二产业	万元	49 954	201 257	260 400
第三产业	万元	10 216	62 011	110 000
国内生产总值指数(以上年＝100,按可比价计算)	%	111.4	132.3	130.6
区县级财政收入	万元	11 045	12 634	16 426
区县级财政支出	万元	5 199	14 356	18 861
＃教育经费支出	万元	1 476	4 418	4 560
* 固定资产投资(不含农村集体和个人投资)	万元		307 280	472 947
＃区县属	万元		26 629	2 370
* 房屋施工面积(不含农村集体和个人投资)	万平方米		67.61	62.58
＃区县属	万平方米		4.44	6.76
* 房屋竣工面积(不含农村集体和个人投资)	万平方米		17.26	21.16
＃区县属	万平方米		1.69	0.71
* 年末实有耕地面积	万公顷	1.65	1.63	1.63
* 农业机械总动力	万千瓦	39.53	38.39	43.88
* 化肥施用实物量	吨	13 701	14 760	16 096
* 农村用电量	万千瓦小时	14 478	31 290	43 569
* 农林牧渔业总产值(现价)	万元	38 099	68 908	75 501
* 农林牧渔业总指数(以上年＝100,按可比价计算)	%	105.6	107.0	108.9
* 农作物产量				
粮　食	万吨	5.48	7.26	6.92
棉　花	吨	7.3		
油　料	吨	1 454	376	61
水　果	吨	7 092	10 991	10 032
* 畜产品产量				
猪牛羊肉	万吨	0.49	0.81	1.03

注:“*”为全区数据,其余为区县属数。1990 年工业总产值为现价原口径,1995 年和 1996 年为现价新口径。

19－11续表

指标名称	单 位	1990年	1995年	1996年
禽 蛋	吨	14 741	12 645	14 305
*水产品产量	吨	20 366	27 475	28 865
*蔬菜总产量	吨	259 939	309 567	357 606
*农民人均年纯收入(抽样调查数)	元/人	1 666	3 018	3 636
乡镇企业单位数	个	3 386	6 426	8 480
#工 业	个	1 472	1 421	1 797
乡镇企业人数	万人	10.16	11.35	12.61
#工 业	万人	9.20	9.31	9.53
乡镇企业总收入	万元	222 505	1 168 470	1 612 001
#工 业	万元	206 818	924 404	1 269 390
村以上工业企业单位数	个	1 112	1 062	1 089
从业人员	万人	8.68	8.93	9.10
总产值(现价)	万元	296 507	1 047 922	1 537 417
产品销售收入	万元	202 915	901 135	1 236 748
利税总额	万元	19 455	115 345	148 351
资产总额	万元	134 652	598 342	724 844
固定资产原值	万元	71 775	265 757	337 451
流动资产合计	万元	62 877	361 269	420 434
社会消费品零售总额	万元	230	895	1 300
批发零售贸易业网点	个			343
饮食业网点	个			15
*私营工商企业户数	户	151	666	836
雇工人数	人	2 434	7 399	8 662
注册资本	万元	923	12 346	18 686
总产值	万元	1 367	2 762	8 287
营业收入	万元	393	1 656	4 735
*个体工商业户数	户	3 795	4 898	5 154
从业人员	人	6 663	8 603	9 197
资金	万元	2 036	8 774	10 778
营业额	万元	286	16 126	23 344
外贸出口商品总值	万美元	5 818	17 890	23 021
*小学校数	所	39	46	45
在校学生数	人	29 569	25 135	24 509
*普通中学校数	所	21	20	19
在校学生数	人	12 111	14 741	14 771
*学龄儿童入学率	%	100.0	100.0	100.0
卫生机构数	个	15	15	15
#医 院	个	11	11	11

19－12　津南区基本情况

指标名称	单　位	1990 年	1995 年	1996 年
* 常住户数	户	104 626	109 964	110 059
#农业户	户	79 693	83 350	83 347
* 户籍人口	万人	35.65	36.23	36.29
按农业、非农业分				
农业人口	万人	28.09	28.54	28.56
非农业人口	万人	7.56	7.69	7.72
* 人口出生率	‰	14.6	11.8	11.2
* 人口自然增长率	‰	7.9	7.2	5.6
职　工	万人	1.41	1.99	1.77
* 乡村劳动力	万人	13.21	14.79	14.68
#农林牧渔业劳动者人数	万人	3.26	3.79	3.85
国内生产总值(现价)	万元	71 115	272 882	379 143
第一产业	万元	8 811	20 201	21 996
第二产业	万元	45 393	185 041	263 890
第三产业	万元	16 911	67 640	93 257
国内生产总值指数(以上年＝100,按可比价计算)	%		127.2	135.6
区县级财政收入	万元	11 177	13 151	14 363
区县级财政支出	万元	5 382	13 007	14 857
#教育经费支出	万元		5 403	5 194
* 固定资产投资(不含农村集体和个人投资)	万元		12 212	37 179
#区县属	万元		1 535	1 482
* 房屋施工面积(不含农村集体和个人投资)	万平方米		19.81	23.51
#区县属	万平方米		3.72	3.76
* 房屋竣工面积(不含农村集体和个人投资)	万平方米		9.47	12.72
#区县属	万平方米		1.45	2.05
* 年末实有耕地面积	万公顷	1.52	1.50	1.50
* 农业机械总动力	万千瓦	43.10	42.72	44.94
* 化肥施用实物量	吨	15 671	14 064	13 064
* 农村用电量	万千瓦小时	14 943	32 821	24 045
* 农林牧渔业总产值(现价)	万元	21 777	37 497	39 611
* 农林牧渔业总指数(以上年＝100,按可比价计算)	%	102.4	109.2	96.4
* 农作物产量				
粮　食	万吨	7.00	7.24	6.39
棉　花	吨			
油　料	吨			
水　果	吨	1 336	1 700	1 552
* 畜产品产量				
猪牛羊肉	万吨	0.26	0.43	0.41

注:“*”为全区数据,其余为区县属数。1990 年工业总产值为现价原口径,1995 年和 1996 年为现价新口径。

19－12续表

指标名称	单 位	1990年	1995年	1996年
禽 蛋	吨	8 432	6 399	5 142
*水产品产量	吨	5 212	6 920	7 185
*蔬菜总产量	吨	177 067	164 119	169 547
*农民人均年纯收入(抽样调查数)	元/人	1 316	2 729	3 348
乡镇企业单位数	个			9 865
#工 业	个		2 865	2 890
乡镇企业人数	万人			13.36
#工 业	万人		9.53	9.46
乡镇企业总收入	万元			1 363 130
#工 业	万元		963 764	963 150
村以上工业企业单位数	个		963	865
从业人员	万人		7.77	7.69
总产值(现价)	万元		728 716	1 050 513
产品销售收入	万元		748 694	963 150
利税总额	万元		101 236	121 796
资产总额	万元		386 019	524 952
固定资产原值	万元		135 097	222 618
流动资产合计	万元		266 008	348 308
社会消费品零售总额	万元		8 133	8 308
批发零售贸易业网点	个			142
饮食业网点	个			4
*私营工商企业户数	户		1 059	1 165
雇工人数	人		16 783	18 932
注册资本	万元		23 243	23 104
总产值	万元		40 142	51 597
营业收入	万元		15 326	11 559
*个体工商业户数	户		11 706	12 308
从业人员	人		19 787	20 551
资金	万元		13 397	15 934
营业额	万元		33 397	45 757
外贸出口商品总值	万美元		7 644	8 551
*小学校数	所	47	48	49
在校学生数	人	33 951	31 377	31 090
*普通中学校数	所	21	25	25
在校学生数	人	15 500	14 422	14 929
*学龄儿童入学率	%	100.0	100.0	100.0
卫生机构数	个	18	19	19
#医 院	个	2	2	2

19－13　北辰区基本情况

指标名称	单　位	1990年	1995年	1996年
*常住户数	户	92 863	98 463	99 137
#农业户	户	64 096	66 725	66 336
*户籍人口	万人	30.63	31.47	31.55
按农业、非农业分				
农业人口	万人	20.87	21.08	21.03
非农业人口	万人	9.76	10.39	10.52
*人口出生率	‰	12.84	10.22	9.64
*人口自然增长率	‰	6.41	4.55	2.93
职　工	万人	1.17	1.44	1.36
*乡村劳动力	万人	8.87	8.28	8.20
#农林牧渔业劳动者人数	万人	3.06	2.76	2.77
国内生产总值(现价)	万元	59 699	258 092	350 026
第一产业	万元	16 750	45 174	42 834
第二产业	万元	30 038	139 957	193 138
第三产业	万元	12 911	72 961	114 054
国内生产总值指数(以上年＝100,按可比价计算)	%		131.7	130.5
区县级财政收入	万元	10 046	12 557	15 099
区县级财政支出	万元	4 631	11 362	17 047
#教育经费支出	万元	1 610	4 254	5 470
*固定资产投资(不含农村集体和个人投资)	万元		53 910	157 250
#区县属	万元		2 109	10 001
*房屋施工面积(不含农村集体和个人投资)	万平方米		39.23	44.27
#区县属	万平方米		3.52	7.08
*房屋竣工面积(不含农村集体和个人投资)	万平方米		9.68	20.29
#区县属	万平方米		1.12	5.72
*年末实有耕地面积	万公顷	1.91	1.87	1.87
*农业机械总动力	万千瓦	37.88	56.81	59.01
*化肥施用实物量	吨	9 838	13 953	15 047
*农村用电量	万千瓦小时	8 795	17 726	21 614
*农林牧渔业总产值(现价)	万元	28 737	81 038	90 779
*农林牧渔业总指数(以上年＝100,按可比价计算)	%	106.5	106.8	110.9
*农作物产量				
粮　食	万吨	5.21	6.28	6.72
棉　花	吨	96	18	4
油　料	吨	3 959	2 560	2 365
水　果	吨	12 158	25 426	27 441
*畜产品产量				
猪牛羊肉	万吨	0.38	0.65	0.72

注:"*"为全区数据,其余为区县属数。1990年工业总产值为现价原口径,1995年和1996年为现价新口径。

19－13续表

指标名称	单　位	1990年	1995年	1996年
禽　蛋	吨	15 637	21 178	24 490
*水产品产量	吨	3 851	5 485	6 549
*蔬菜总产量	吨	335 079	367 892	371 005
*农民人均年纯收入(抽样调查数)	元/人	1 036	2 869	3 446
乡镇企业单位数	个		3 867	1 990
#工　业	个	1 134	1 177	1 251
乡镇企业人数	万人		8.24	8.45
#工　业	万人	6.00	6.67	6.62
乡镇企业总收入	万元		717 004	968 675
#工　业	万元	117 386	519 399	724 711
村以上工业企业单位数	个	1 199	1 396	1 399
从业人员	万人	6.07	7.38	6.33
总产值(现价)	万元	176 997	643 585	867 536
产品销售收入	万元	97 437	555 940	772 999
利税总额	万元	13 402	70 670	98 554
资产总额	万元		460 521	697 849
固定资产原值	万元	48 094	178 415	262 379
流动资产合计	万元	59 459	300 141	401 315
社会消费品零售总额	万元	1 856	3 926	5 565
批发零售贸易业网点	个			477
饮食业网点	个			26
*私营工商企业户数	户	120	501	672
雇工人数	人	2 088	5 077	7 003
注册资本	万元	724	10 816	51 330
总产值	万元	819	13 129	21 800
营业收入	万元	365	3 342	14 028
*个体工商业户数	户	5 185	9 581	9 688
从业人员	人	8 997	13 130	12 258
资金	万元	2 359	11 034	14 256
营业额	万元	701	4 191	6 913
外贸出口商品总值	万美元	3 054	14 863	20 669
*小学校数	所	48	48	49
在校学生数	人	29 429	27 712	27 295
*普通中学校数	所	20	21	21
在校学生数	人	12 964	11 953	12 782
*学龄儿童入学率	%	99.81	99.80	100.0
卫生机构数	个	19	19	20
#医　院	个	7	16	16

19－14　宁河县基本情况

指标名称	单　位	1990 年	1995 年	1996 年
* 常住户数	户	91 737	97 756	99 039
#农业户	户	71 193	73 581	73 984
* 户籍人口	万人	32.91	34.72	34.90
按农业、非农业分				
农业人口	万人	27.86	28.59	28.60
非农业人口	万人	5.05	6.13	6.30
* 人口出生率	‰	16.40	10.41	9.74
* 人口自然增长率	‰	10.82	5.40	4.61
职　工	万人	2.32	3.11	2.99
* 乡村劳动力	万人	10.85	11.14	11.06
#农林牧渔业劳动者人数	万人	6.63	6.04	6.61
国内生产总值(现价)	万元	61 300	215 500	300 200
第一产业	万元	23 500	57 100	71 000
第二产业	万元	28 100	98 600	137 300
第三产业	万元	9 700	59 800	91 900
国内生产总值指数(以上年＝100,按可比价计算)	%	114.0	131.8	132.5
区县级财政收入	万元	6 255	8 051	9 108
区县级财政支出	万元	5 722	12 469	13 921
#教育经费支出	万元	1 490	3 852	4 147
* 固定资产投资(不含农村集体和个人投资)	万元		29 260	23 524
#区县属	万元		18 149	12 390
* 房屋施工面积(不含农村集体和个人投资)	万平方米		9.00	11.27
#区县属	万平方米		6.57	6.17
* 房屋竣工面积(不含农村集体和个人投资)	万平方米		6.10	2.52
#区县属	万平方米		4.90	2.91
* 年末实有耕地面积	万公顷	3.98	3.95	3.95
* 农业机械总动力	万千瓦	28.12	35.95	42.14
* 化肥施用实物量	吨	37 451	45 221	52 249
* 农村用电量	万千瓦小时	6 234	15 486	16 406
* 农林牧渔业总产值(现价)	万元	35 866	136 556	142 496
* 农林牧渔业总指数(以上年＝100,按可比价计算)	%	108.2	122.9	118.8
* 农作物产量				
粮　食	万吨	19.20	22.25	23.18
棉　花	吨	6 910	4 180	1 263
油　料	吨	1 320	2 070	813
水　果	吨	1 104	3 067	4 947
* 畜产品产量				
猪牛羊肉	万吨	0.56	0.98	1.05

注:"*"为全区数据,其余为区县属数。1990 年工业总产值为现价原口径,1995 年和 1996 年为现价新口径。

19－14续表

指标名称	单 位	1990年	1995年	1996年
禽 蛋	吨	9 970	17 302	18 086
*水产品产量	吨	43 800	11 910	11 298
*蔬菜总产量	吨	41 720	242 369	285 250
*农民人均年纯收入(抽样调查数)	元/人	989	2 452	3 153
乡镇企业单位数	个	456	466	522
#工 业	个	405	400	366
乡镇企业人数	万人	2.42	2.59	2.61
#工 业	万人	2.23	2.42	2.53
乡镇企业总收入	万元	43 538	295 229	407 048
#工 业	万元	39 865	275 517	392 386
村以上工业企业单位数	个	476	497	463
从业人员	万人	3.33	3.92	3.65
总产值(现价)	万元	95 731	377 375	481 345
产品销售收入	万元	66 331	342 701	396 287
利税总额	万元	7 014	7 841	5 784
资产总额	万元	23 185	249 479	253 618
固定资产原值	万元	30 606	81 180	131 506
流动资产合计	万元	20 516	60 092	141 813
社会消费品零售总额	万元	1 450	4 822	4 665
批发零售贸易业网点	个			79
饮食业网点	个			9
*私营工商企业户数	户	179	513	580
雇工人数	人	3 886	8 956	8 734
注册资本	万元	598	12 809	18 363
总产值	万元	17 900	50 984	74 913
营业收入	万元	1 647	4 670	5 528
*个体工商业户数	户	4 131	5 950	8 762
从业人员	人	6 263	8 546	11 726
资金	万元	1 660	5 888	7 380
营业额	万元	1 705	1 787	37 248
外贸出口商品总值	万美元	3 222	10 353	12 376
*小学校数	所	223	228	228
在校学生数	人	40 324	39 773	41 640
*普通中学校数	所	37	32	32
在校学生数	人	12 461	16 722	18 046
*学龄儿童入学率	%	99.48	98.80	100.0
卫生机构数	个	62	61	57
#医 院	个	7	8	8

19－15 武清县基本情况

指标名称	单位	1990年	1995年	1996年
*常住户数	户	217 325	225 447	227 036
#农业户	户	196 648	200 256	200 438
*户籍人口	万人	77.30	79.05	79.35
按农业、非农业分				
农业人口	万人	70.62	70.92	70.88
非农业人口	万人	6.68	8.13	8.47
*人口出生率	‰	14.9	10.7	10.2
*人口自然增长率	‰	8.4	3.7	2.6
职　工	万人	3.2	3.2	3.1
*乡村劳动力	万人	35.5	36.1	35.9
#农林牧渔业劳动者人数	万人	18.7	19.9	19.8
国内生产总值(现价)	万元	155 338	500 501	600 471
第一产业	万元	49 989	113 024	130 658
第二产业	万元	76 675	247 810	289 776
第三产业	万元	28 674	139 667	180 037
国内生产总值指数(以上年＝100,按可比价计算)	%		114.0	116.0
区县级财政收入	万元	10 209	13 310	15 759
区县级财政支出	万元	7 832	17 828	20 640
#教育经费支出	万元	2 825	6 998	8 758
*固定资产投资(不含农村集体和个人投资)	万元		39 165	28 506
#区县属	万元		24 375	8 552
*房屋施工面积(不含农村集体和个人投资)	万平方米		14.49	13.93
#区县属	万平方米		4.88	4.76
*房屋竣工面积(不含农村集体和个人投资)	万平方米		12.17	9.84
#区县属	万平方米		4.84	2.23
*年末实有耕地面积	万公顷	9.35	9.18	9.17
*农业机械总动力	万千瓦	53.00	76.96	81.11
*化肥施用实物量	吨	120 782	131 752	132 295
*农村用电量	万千瓦小时	27 244	48 369	52 275
*农林牧渔业总产值(现价)	万元	114 148	287 811	321 251
*农林牧渔业总指数(以上年＝100,按可比价计算)	%	105.6	112.2	102.6
*农作物产量				
粮　食	万吨	48.0	52.0	51.5
棉　花	吨	8 880	2 798	1 917
油　料	吨	23 330	15 795	13 720
水　果	吨	19 240	53 397	61 165
*畜产品产量				
猪牛羊肉	万吨	1.90	4.80	4.70

注:“*”为全区数据,其余为区县属数。1990年工业总产值为现价原口径,1995年和1996年为现价新口径。

19－15续表

指标名称	单 位	1990年	1995年	1996年
禽 蛋	吨	30 762	53 912	49 661
*水产品产量	吨	6 741	19 195	19 500
*蔬菜总产量	吨	743 260	1 500 000	1 965 892
*农民人均年纯收入(抽样调查数)	元/人	1 019	2 343	2 900
乡镇企业单位数	个	1 833	1 610	1 470
#工 业	个	1 667	1 440	1 328
乡镇企业人数	万人	11.7	15.6	14.5
#工 业	万人	10.80	14.34	13.75
乡镇企业总收入	万元	206 032	797 885	987 030
#工 业	万元	190 022	774 823	956 694
村以上工业企业单位数	个	1 731	1 494	1 416
从业人员	万人	12.20	15.24	14.27
总产值(现价)	万元	364 113	1 114 477	1 394 607
产品销售收入	万元	195 392	840 210	1 075 717
利税总额	万元	31 192	153 347	166 124
资产总额	万元	84 263	623 576	752 992
固定资产原值	万元	74 729	296 431	398 959
流动资产合计	万元	25 041	401 801	456 213
社会消费品零售总额	万元	11 196	12 768	16 988
批发零售贸易业网点	个			370
饮食业网点	个			29
*私营工商企业户数	户	3	413	522
雇工人数	人	56	4 489	5 316
注册资本	万元	106	8 347	13 999
总产值	万元	12	14 322	34 252
营业收入	万元	12	4 049	9 782
*个体工商业户数	户	11 629	20 417	25 925
从业人员	人	15 581	28 651	32 411
资金	万元	2 722	12 508	14 336
营业额	万元	6 836	139 832	160 269
外贸出口商品总值	万美元		26 740	30 843
*小学校数	所	522	496	487
在校学生数	人	85 975	78 231	78 852
*普通中学校数	所	92	72	68
在校学生数	人	34 745	41 289	42 610
*学龄儿童入学率	%	100.0	100.0	100.0
卫生机构数	个	73	74	74
#医 院	个	36	36	36

19－16　静海县基本情况

指标名称	单　位	1990 年	1995 年	1996 年
* 常住户数	户	134 300	142 840	142 291
#农业户	户	115 191	121 548	120 141
* 户籍人口	万人	46.55	49.01	49.41
按农业、非农业分				
农业人口	万人	40.82	42.46	42.62
非农业人口	万人	5.73	6.55	6.79
* 人口出生率	‰	14.78	12.86	11.50
* 人口自然增长率	‰	8.34	6.98	5.94
职　工	万人	3.32	3.39	3.09
* 乡村劳动力	万人	16.67	15.36	15.28
#农林牧渔业劳动者人数	万人	8.09	7.23	7.13
国内生产总值(现价)	万元	121 027	454 713	574 979
第一产业	万元	31 682	95 270	106 222
第二产业	万元	74 200	261 838	332 997
第三产业	万元	15 145	97 605	135 760
国内生产总值指数(以上年＝100,按可比价计算)	%		114.1	123.0
区县级财政收入	万元	9 921	13 148	15 402
区县级财政支出	万元	6 677	17 385	21 452
#教育经费支出	万元	2 343	6 593	7 392
* 固定资产投资(不含农村集体和个人投资)	万元		71 625	21 658
#区县属	万元		15 082	7 598
* 房屋施工面积(不含农村集体和个人投资)	万平方米		33.99	28.61
#区县属	万平方米		24.98	21.24
* 房屋竣工面积(不含农村集体和个人投资)	万平方米		23.89	25.00
#区县属	万平方米		17.88	18.08
* 年末实有耕地面积	万公顷	6.99	6.94	6.94
* 农业机械总动力	万千瓦	43.50	50.47	53.87
* 化肥施用实物量	吨	64 480	57 275	61 763
* 农村用电量	万千瓦小时	24 227	78 242	85 754
* 农林牧渔业总产值(现价)	万元	55 941	149 757	166 672
* 农林牧渔业总指数(以上年＝100,按可比价计算)	%	107.6	116.1	113.4
* 农作物产量				
粮　食	万吨	21.97	29.51	32.29
棉　花	吨	95	702	234
油　料	吨	6 562	6 920	5 727
水　果	吨	2 251	7 224	9 334
* 畜产品产量				
猪牛羊肉	万吨	0.85	0.83	0.91

注:“*”为全区数据,其余为区县属数。1990 年工业总产值为现价原口径,1995 年和 1996 年为现价新口径。

19－16续表

指标名称	单 位	1990年	1995年	1996年
禽 蛋	吨	14 267	19 118	16 731
*水产品产量	吨	3 627	6 056	8 692
*蔬菜总产量	吨	162 247	335 077	347 418
*农民人均年纯收入(抽样调查数)	元/人	1 039	2 313	2 865
乡镇企业单位数	个	1 706	1 523	1 465
#工 业	个	1 519	1 320	1 213
乡镇企业人数	万人	9.01	10.60	10.53
#工 业	万人	8.41	9.79	9.39
乡镇企业总收入	万元	196 119	1 492 688	1 944 520
#工 业	万元	184 575	1 418 073	1 824 324
村以上工业企业单位数	个	1 574	1 361	1 264
从业人员	万人	9.56	11.44	10.97
总产值(现价)	万元	324 706	1 580 244	2 071 392
产品销售收入	万元	211 571	1 519 127	1 922 040
利税总额	万元	27 120	154 425	193 936
资产总额	万元		836 012	1 063 526
固定资产原值	万元	83 023	422 753	459 032
流动资产合计	万元		480 672	602 760
社会消费品零售总额	万元	5 493	5 500	7 249
批发零售贸易业网点	个			152
饮食业网点	个			16
*私营工商企业户数	户	432	495	410
雇工人数	人	3 147	5 423	5 046
注册资本	万元		21 341	20 790
总产值	万元		15 325	12 654
营业收入	元		5 424	7 830
*个体工商业户数	户	4 678	11 900	13 000
从业人员	人	7 539	20 738	24 230
资金	万元	1 121	13 391	15 604
营业额	万元		7 695	6 299
外贸出口商品总值	万美元		5 000	8 204
*小学校数	所	299	276	276
在校学生数	人	50 924	44 338	45 735
*普通中学校数	所	48	44	43
在校学生数	人	23 093	25 098	25 707
*学龄儿童入学率	%	99.0	100.0	100.0
卫生机构数	个	68	68	78
#医 院	个	6	6	6

19－17 宝坻县基本情况

指标名称	单 位	1990 年	1995 年	1996 年
* 常住户数	户	158 288	165 474	171 296
#农业户	户	140 858	145 342	148 831
* 户籍人口	万人	60.74	63.37	63.86
按农业、非农业分				
农业人口	万人	54.62	56.22	55.86
非农业人口	万人	6.12	7.15	8.00
* 人口出生率	‰	15.60	13.40	11.30
* 人口自然增长率	‰	10.34	8.13	5.52
职 工	万人	3.54	4.00	4.01
* 乡村劳动力	万人	22.28	22.25	22.09
#农林牧渔业劳动者人数	万人	15.08	12.74	12.48
国内生产总值(现价)	万元	130 010	430 009	615 614
第一产业	万元	52 849	117 747	131 803
第二产业	万元	55 176	207 210	309 964
第三产业	万元	21 985	105 052	173 847
国内生产总值指数(以上年＝100,按可比价计算)	%	121.1	122.1	132.1
区县级财政收入	万元	6 716	10 224	15 628
区县级财政支出	万元	6 982	14 539	22 775
#教育经费支出	万元	2 546	6 016	8 366
* 固定资产投资(不含农村集体和个人投资)	万元		13 841	28 046
#区县属	万元		6 253	11 597
* 房屋施工面积(不含农村集体和个人投资)	万平方米		10.40	19.91
#区县属	万平方米		7.15	9.63
* 房屋竣工面积(不含农村集体和个人投资)	万平方米		5.82	9.91
#区县属	万平方米		3.83	6.81
* 年末实有耕地面积	万公顷	8.20	7.76	7.75
* 农业机械总动力	万千瓦	31.61	37.76	40.13
* 化肥施用实物量	吨	46 306	69 312	71 749
* 农村用电量	万千瓦小时	11 730	21 779	33 033
* 农林牧渔业总产值(现价)	万元	84 050	227 949	221 678
* 农林牧渔业总指数(以上年＝100,按可比价计算)	%	107.9	111.8	108.0
* 农作物产量				
粮 食	万吨	36.40	45.51	47.39
棉 花	吨	2 827	3 122	1 495
油 料	吨	8 890	6 769	5 349
水 果	吨	6 079	11 395	9 013
* 畜产品产量				
猪牛羊肉	万吨	1.50	3.15	3.72

注:"*"为全区数据,其余为区县属数。1990 年工业总产值为现价原口径,1995 年和 1996 年为现价新口径。

19－17 续表

指标名称	单　位	1990年	1995年	1996年
禽　蛋	吨	19 411	45 000	46 585
*水产品产量	吨	5 784	16 111	17 404
*蔬菜总产量	吨	315 101	450 225	435 514
*农民人均年纯收入(抽样调查数)	元/人	843	2 560	3 264
乡镇企业单位数	个	840	780	716
#工　业	个	759	720	678
乡镇企业人数	万人	5.40	7.53	8.59
#工　业	万人	4.66	6.62	7.79
乡镇企业总收入	万元	83 870	434 128	661 243
#工　业	万元	79 395	410 846	639 818
村以上工业企业单位数	个	709	915	836
从业人员	万人	5.54	7.79	8.67
总产值(现价)	万元	169 855	522 180	782 509
产品销售收入	万元	90 425	447 776	681 631
利税总额	万元	8 730	59 548	89 578
资产总额	万元	183 200	347 346	402 858
固定资产原值	万元	37 731	60 967	164 623
流动资产合计	万元	101 964	212 569	247 344
社会消费品零售总额	万元		13 100	17 100
批发零售贸易业网点	个			66
饮食业网点	个			3
*私营工商企业户数	户		211	160
雇工人数	人		3 355	2 617
注册资本	万元		5 358	5 646
总产值	万元		4 800	6 961
营业收入	万元		1 733	2 105
*个体工商业户数	户	8 836	14 529	15 925
从业人员	人	13 362	24 270	26 093
资金	万元	3 476	15 493	19 047
营业额	万元	390	27 056	51 747
外贸出口商品总值	万美元	6 294	31 325	32 891
*小学校数	所	695	677	671
在校学生数	人	66 567	74 530	81 534
*普通中学校数	所	71	56	53
在校学生数	人	25 333	28 811	30 419
*学龄儿童入学率	%	100.0	100.0	100.0
卫生机构数	个	42	42	43
#医　院	个	33	35	35

19－18　蓟县基本情况

指标名称	单　位	1990年	1995年	1996年
* 常住户数	户	198 442	207 675	208 827
＃农业户	户	183 808	188 138	188 236
* 户籍人口	万人	74.11	77.17	77.81
按农业、非农业分				
农业人口	万人	67.81	69.23	69.58
非农业人口	万人	6.30	7.94	8.23
* 人口出生率	‰	15.84	12.08	11.25
* 人口自然增长率	‰	10.68	5.80	4.71
职　工	万人	2.93	3.26	3.25
* 乡村劳动力	万人	29.41	30.59	30.99
＃农林牧渔业劳动者人数	万人	19.98	17.93	18.19
国内生产总值(现价)	万元	112 407	267 024	351 001
第一产业	万元	40 584	87 265	97 768
第二产业	万元	47 629	92 246	125 047
第三产业	万元	24 194	87 515	128 186
国内生产总值指数(以上年＝100,按可比价计算)	%		111.8	126.0
区县级财政收入	万元	7 273	9 614	11 853
区县级财政支出	万元	8 471	17 212	19 633
＃教育经费支出	万元	2 513	6 993	7 841
* 固定资产投资(不含农村集体和个人投资)	万元		143 583	124 999
＃区县属	万元		14 622	4 310
* 房屋施工面积(不含农村集体和个人投资)	万平方米		37.57	24.46
＃区县属	万平方米		4.65	5.11
* 房屋竣工面积(不含农村集体和个人投资)	万平方米		24.50	22.22
＃区县属	万平方米		4.65	5.11
* 年末实有耕地面积	万公顷	5.49	5.47	5.45
* 农业机械总动力	万千瓦	35.12	44.66	46.43
* 化肥施用实物量	吨	65 380	79 846	98 861
* 农村用电量	万千瓦小时	14 492	21 876	22 256
* 农林牧渔业总产值(现价)	万元	71 148	166 547	184 967
* 农林牧渔业总指数(以上年＝100,按可比价计算)	%	107.6	108.9	110.1
* 农作物产量				
粮　食	万吨	31.88	36.51	32.35
棉　花	吨	422	300	87
油　料	吨	2 620	4 660	2 283
水　果	吨	41 734	47 263	48 086
* 畜产品产量				
猪牛羊肉	万吨	3.28	3.77	4.03

注:“*”为全区数据,其余为区县属数。1990年工业总产值为现价原口径,1995年和1996年为现价新口径。

19－18续表

指标名称	单　位	1990年	1995年	1996年
禽　蛋	吨	22 830	30 701	37 583
*水产品产量	吨	6 202	11 743	12 685
*蔬菜总产量	吨	330 451	638 440	707 562
*农民人均年纯收入(抽样调查数)	元/人	903	1 856	2 390
乡镇企业单位数	个	976	904	833
#工　业	个	840	796	739
乡镇企业人数	万人	5.08	5.19	5.14
#工　业	万人	4.00	4.11	4.08
乡镇企业总收入	万元	51 975	201 564	249 854
#工　业	万元	45 644	168 609	224 163
村以上工业企业单位数	个	935	919	843
从业人员	万人	5.15	5.33	5.32
总产值(现价)	万元	116 786	250 140	382 645
产品销售收入	万元	69 062	231 084	284 585
利税总额	万元	7 069	19 639	22 822
资产总额	万元	58 342	253 479	288 694
固定资产原值	万元	42 396	111 867	123 150
流动资产合计	万元		131 612	143 184
社会消费品零售总额	万元	29 313	69 419	77 640
批发零售贸易业网点	个			340
饮食业网点	个			21
*私营工商企业户数	户	17	306	329
雇工人数	人	250	2 800	2 935
注册资本	万元	297	9 126	10 289
总产值	万元	136	4 728	3 903
营业收入	万元	82	1 131	795
*个体工商业户数	户	9 935	16 289	17 537
从业人员	人	15 361	24 389	26 259
资金	万元	3 682	17 928	20 420
营业额	万元	7 930	34 130	40 861
外贸出口商品总值	万美元	3 186	11 101	15 787
*小学校数	所	775	745	728
在校学生数	人	73 985	113 225	120 800
*普通中学校数	所	81	72	72
在校学生数	人	28 964	37 386	41 084
*学龄儿童入学率	%	98.0	100.0	100.0
卫生机构数	个	105	103	142
#医　院	个	43	44	44

附一

主要统计指标解释

一、综　合

国内生产总值:是指一个国家(或地区)在一定时期内,所生产和提供最终使用的产品和劳务的价值。它不仅能够反映物质生产的发展情况,而且能够反映各种劳务的增长情况,能够全面反映国民经济和社会发展的规模和水平。

国内生产总值从生产角度来说,是国民经济各部门的增加值之和;从分配角度来说,是这些部门劳动者报酬、生产税净额、营业盈余和固定资产折旧四个项目之和;从使用角度来说,是最终使用于消费、投资以及净出口的产品和劳务之和。

总产出:反映国民经济各部门在一定时期(一年)内所进行的生产活动的总成果。

中间使用:指为国民经济各部门的本期生产活动所提供的、包括国内生产和国外进口在内的各类产品和服务。

最终使用:指已退出或暂时退出本期生产活动而为最终需求所提供的产品和服务。根据使用性质分为三部分:

1.总消费:指一定时期内,我国居民和社会、集体对物质产品和服务的最终消费。

(1)居民总消费:指我国农业居民和非农业居民在国内的各种消费,它既包括由居民个人承担的各种货币性消费支出和自给性消费(投资性支出除外),还包括由国家和集体以补贴或福利形式支付的而由居民享用的各种物质产品和服务的消费。但不包括我国居民在国外的消费和外国居民在我国的消费。

(2)社会总消费:它包括政府消费和集体消费两部分。政府消费是指政府部门(包括各种行政事业和公共服务部门)的最终消费支出。它包括政府财政拨款形式的支出、自筹经费的支出和行政事业单位固定资产的虚拟折旧;集体消费是指各企事业单位用于集体事务的非生产性的物品消费。

2.资本形成总额:指本期形成的各类固定资产与新增库存。

(1)固定资本形成:指本期内通过大修理、更新改造、基本建设等所形成的各类固定资产的总和。

(2)库存增加:指一定时期内全社会库存产品的变化量(库存减少时为负数)。

3.净出口:指当年各类产品和服务的进出口差额。即:净出口 = 出口 - 进口

中间投入:指各部门在生产活动中所消耗的各种物质产品(如原材料、燃料、动力等)和服务。

总投入:指国民经济各部门进行生产活动所投入的总费用。

直接消耗系数:也称为投入系数,是指某一部门生产单位产品(或劳务)所直接消耗的各部门产品(或劳务)的数量(价值)。计算方法是:用某部门的“总产出”分别去除该部门所直接消耗的各部门产品(或劳务)的数量(价值)

完全消耗系数:是指单位最终产品的生产对其他部门总产出的全部需要量,它是直接消耗、间接消耗和最终需求的合计数。

三次产业:是根据社会生产活动历史发展的顺序对产业结构的划分。产品直接取自自然界的部门称为第一产业,对初级产品进行加工的部门称为第二产业,为生产和消费提供各种服务的部门称为第三产业。它是世界上通用的产业结构分类,但各国的划分不尽一致。我国的三次产业划分是:

第一产业:农业(包括农业、林业、牧业和渔业,不含农、林、牧、渔服务业)。

第二产业:工业(包括采掘业、制造业、电力、煤气及水的生产和供应业)和建筑业。

第三产业:除第一、第二产业以外的其他各部门。具体包括交通运输、仓储及邮电通信业、批发零售贸易餐饮业、金融保险业、房地产业、农林牧渔服务业、地质勘察业、水利管理业、社会服务业、卫生体育和社会福利业、教育文化艺术及广播电影电视业、科学研究和综合技术服务业、国家机关、政党机关和社会团体及其他行业。

现行价格:(或称当年价格)是指报告期的实际价格,如工业品的出厂价格,农副产品的收购价格,商业的零售价格等。它反映当年的实际情况,使国民经济各项指标互相衔接,便于对生产、流通、分配、消费之间进行综合平衡。

不变价格:不变价格是用某一时期同类产品的平均价格做为固定价格,来计算各个时期的产品价值,目的是为了消除各时期价格变动的影响,保证前后时期之间、地区之间、计划与实际之间指标的可比性。不变

价格在使用过一定时期后，它和现行价格的差距愈来愈大，为此国家统计局先后五次制订了全国统一的工业产品和农产品不变价格。从1949—1957年使用的1952年工(农)业产品不变价格，从1957—1970年使用1957年不变价格，从1971—1980年使用1970年不变价格，从1981—1990年使用1980年不变价格，从1991年开始使用1990年不变价格。

可比价格：可比价格在不同时期的价值量指标对比时，扣除了价格变动的因素，以确切表示物量的变化。

“三资”企业：指外商、华侨或港澳台工商业者与大陆投资者以合资经营、合作经营(或开发)、或独资的形式在我国大陆直接投资开办的企业。

合资经营企业：是指两国(地区)或两国(地区)以上的投资者在一国境内根据所在国的法律，通过签订合同，按一定的比例(股份)共同投资建立、共同管理、分享利润、分担亏损和风险的股权式企业。

合作经营企业：指两国(地区)或两国(地区)以上的合营者在一国境内根据所在国的法律，通过签订合同建立的契约式合营企业。合作双方的责任、权利、义务由双方通过协议(合同)加以规定。

合作开发：指拥有矿产等资源的国家政府或企业，与外国(地区)开发公司、企业合作对本国的矿产资源进行开发。投资分为外商风险投资和双方共同投资。在合作开发中，用开采的产品偿还外商投资。

独资企业：指外国(地区)投资者直接到某一国家(地区)单独设厂，属于纯外资股权的经济实体。独资企业的生产、采购、销售、资金筹措和运用、人事安排、利润分配等，都由外国(地区)投资者集中控制和监督。

建成区面积：指市行政区范围内经过征用的土地和实际建设发展起来的非农业生产建设地段。它包括市区集中连片的部分，以及分散在近郊区与城市有着密切连系，具有基本完善的市政公用设施的城市建设用地(如机场、铁路编组站、污水处理厂、通讯电台等)。建成区范围，一般是指建成区外轮廓线所能包括的地区，也就是这个城市实际建设用地所达到的境界范围。因此，它是一个闭合的完整区域，一城多镇分散布点的城市，其建成区范围则可能由几个相应的闭合区域组成。

二、人口和劳动工资

常住人口：指在一定时点有常住户口的人数，不包括①未落常住户口的人②被撤销户口的在押犯、劳改、劳教人员。③现役军人和人民武装警察。

人口密度：指一定时点一定地区的人口数与该地区的土地面积之比，通常以每平方公里的居民人数来表示。

人口出生率：指在一定时期内(通常为一年内)该地区平均每千人口中出生的人数，一般用千分率表示。

人口死亡率：指在一定时期内(通常为一年内)该地区平均每千人口中死亡的人数，一般用千分率表示。

人口自然增长率：指在一定时期内(通常为一年内)该地区人口自然增加数(出生人数减死亡人数)与年平均人口数之比，一般用千分率表示。

人口迁入率：指在一定时期内(通常为一年内)从外地办理户口迁入手续，落常住户口的人数与年平均人口数的比率。

人口迁出率：指在一定时期内(通常为一年内)常住人口办理户口迁出手续的人数与年平均人口数的比率。

人口机械增长率：指在一定时期内(通常为一年内)社会增加人口数(迁入人数减迁出人数)与年平均人口数的比率。

婚姻状况：人口调查登记的婚姻是指实际的婚姻，包括未在主管婚姻部门登记而实际结婚的人。

计划生育率：指在一定时期内每百名出生人口中符合计划生育政策出生的人口数与出生人口总数的比率。

受教育程度：指本人接受国家实施的最高一级教育或具有同等程度的人。

社会从业人员：指从事一定社会劳动并取得劳动报酬或经营收入的全部劳动力。包括职工、城镇私营企业从业人员、城镇个体劳动者、农村社会劳动者和聘用或留用的离休、退休人员、民办教师、宗教职业者以及在各单位中工作的外方人员和港、澳、台方人员。

职工人数：指在国有经济、城镇集体经济、联营经济、股份制经济、外商和港、澳、台投资经济、其他经济单位及其附属机构工作，并由其支付工资的各类人员。不包括乡镇企业和私营企业从业人员、城镇个体从业人员、再就业的离、退休人员、民办教师以及在各单位中工作的外方人员和港、澳、台方人员。

城镇个体劳动者：指市区和各镇在工商管理部门登记并领取营业执照的人，称个体劳动者。

职工工资总额：指各单位在一定时期内直接支付给本单位全部职工的劳动报酬总额。包括计时工资、计件工资、奖金、津贴和补贴，加班加点工资、特殊情况下支付的工资。

三、固定资产投资

固定资产投资额：是以货币表现的建造和购置固定资产的工作量以及与此有关的费用总称。它即是反映固定资产投资规模、速度、比例关系的综合指标，又是观察工程进度、检查投资计划执行情况和考核投资效果的重要依据。固定资产投资活动的内容是多种多样的,有的要兴工动料组织施工,有的要购置工业、建筑业产品作为劳动资料转为固定资产,还有的要做必要的准备工作和管理工作等等。这些不同工作内容的数量不可能用实物单位来加以汇总,必须以价值作为尺度综合地表现投资活动的工作成果。

固定资产投资就其统计范围,可分为全社会固定资产投资和固定资产投资。全社会固定资产投资的统计范围包括国有经济单位投资、城乡集体所有制单位投资和城乡个人投资。固定资产投资的统计范围包括国有经济单位投资和城镇集体所有制单位投资。按照我国现行管理体制,国有经济单位固定资产再生产,划分为基本建设、更新改造、其他固定资产和房地产开发投资四部分,在投资计划上分别安排,分别管理。因此在固定资产投资统计上也相应划分:

基本建设:是以扩大生产能力(或工程效益)为主要目的的新建、扩建、改建和恢复工程以及设备购置等有关活动。基本建设投资额是以货币表现的基本建设工作量,是反映一定时期内基本建设规模和建设进度的综合指标。

更新改造措施:是指利用企事业单位自有的基本折旧基金、国家更新改造拨款和国内外技术改造贷款等资金,对原有设施进行技术改造和更新,以及相应配套的辅助性生产、生活福利设施等工程(不包括大修理和维护工程)。其目的是要在技术进步的前提下,通过采取新技术、新工艺、新设备、新材料,努力提高产品质量、增加品种,促进产品升级换代,降低能源和原材料消耗,增强资源综合利用和污染治理等,提高社会综合经济效益和实现以内涵为主的扩大再生产。更新改造措施投资额,是以货币表现的更新改造措施完成的工作量。

其他固定资产投资:指不划分基本建设和更新改造的固定资产投资,包括国有经济单位按规定不纳入基本建设计划和更新改造措施计划管理,总投资在五万元以上的固定资产投资。即:用油田维护费和石油开发基金进行的油田维护和开发工程;矿山、森林等采掘、采伐工业用维持简单再生产费用进行的开拓延伸工程;交通部门用养路费对原有公路、桥梁进行的改建工程和商业部门用简易建筑费建造的仓库工程。还包括城镇集体所有制及其它经济类型企业、事业单位的固定资产投资。

房地产开发投资:是指房地产开发公司、商品房建设公司及其他房地产开发单位进行土地开发工程、商品房屋建设工程所完成的投资额。是以货币表现的房地产开发工作量。

商品房屋:指有资格的商品房屋开发公司为了出售而统一开发的全部商品房屋,包括商品住宅和其他商品房屋。但不包括开发区内的非商品房屋项目,也不包括开发公司自建自用的房屋和承建的统建住宅。①商品住宅的建设投资包括:a.开发区内的征地、拆迁等实际费用;b.商品住宅建筑安装工程费用;c.开发区红线内的市政配套;d.为开发区内商品住宅配套的服务网点。②其他商品房屋的建设投资包括:由开发公司统一开发建设的厂房、仓库等其他商品房屋的建筑安装工程费用,以及由此而发生征地、拆迁费用和配套设施建设。

固定资产投资按构成分组:

建筑工程:是指各种房屋建筑物的建造工程,又称建筑工程量。这部分投资额必须兴工动料,通过施工才能实现。建筑工程包括各种房屋的建造,设备基础及各种窑炉的砌筑和金属结构工程,为施工而进行的建筑场地布置、地质勘探、平整场地、施工用水、电、汽、路和清理绿化等。矿井的开凿、铁路、公路、桥梁、水利及防空、地下建筑等特殊工程。

安装工程:是指各种设备、装置的安装工程,又称安装工作量。在安装工程投资额中,不包括被安装设备本身的价值。安装工程包括生产、动力、起重、运输、传动和医疗试验等各种需安装设备的装配与设备相连的工作台、梯子栏杆以及管线敷设、保温、油漆、防腐和单机试运系统联动无负簧试运(不包括投料试运)。

设备、工具、器具购置:是指购置和自制达到固定资产标准的设备、工具、器具的价值。但新建单位、扩建单位的新建车间,按照设计和计划要求购置或自制的全部设备、工具、器具,不论是否达到固定资产标准均计入"设备、工具、器具购置"中。

其他费用:是指除建筑安装、设备工具器具购置和商品房屋购置以外的构成固定资产投资完成额的各种费用。主要包括牲畜购置费、林木营建费、办公和生活家具、器具购置费、土地青苗补偿费和安置补助费、建设单位管理费、研究试验费、勘察设计费、联合试运转费、引进技术和进口设备项目的其他费用、生产职工培训费、施工机构迁移费、报废工程损失费和供电站费、矿山巷道维修费等。

固定资产投资按建设性质分组:是反映固定资产投资使用方向,研究各类性质的比重和对比分析投资效果。具体包括:

新建:一般指从无到有"平地起家"新开始建设的企事

业和行政单位,及新建输电线路、输油管道、铁路、公路等独立工程。有的项目原有基础很小,经扩大建设后,其新增加的固定资产价值(原值)超过原有固定资产价值三倍以上的也应算为新建。

扩建:是指为扩大原有产品生产能力或新的产品能力,在厂内或其他地点增建主要生产车间(或主要工程),独立的生产线等。事业单位和行政单位在原单位增建业务用房,也作为扩建。

改建或更新改造:现有企事业单位为了技术进步对现有设施、工艺条件进行技术改造或更新(包括相应配套的辅助性生产、生活设施建设)。有的还充分发挥现有的生产能力,进行填平补齐而增建不直接增加本单位主要产品生产能力的车间等,也属于改建。

新增固定资产(又称交付使用的固定资产):是指已经完成建造和购置过程,并以交付生产或使用单位的固定资产价值。

固定资产交付使用率:是指报告期内新增固定资产价值和同期投资完成额的比率。

四、能源和原材料

能源消耗量:是指企业在报告期内直接用于产品生产过程的原材料、燃料动力消耗和工艺消耗的各种能源。

能源折标准煤:各种能源由于原始计量单位不同,热值也不一样,因此必须折算成同一标准计量单位,才能汇总、对比和分析。本资料采用的标准计量单位是"标准煤"。

五、财政和物价

城市商品零售价格指数:这是1994年国家价格统计制度实行改革后,新增编的价格指数。它是反映本市市场零售物价水平变动趋势和程度的相对数。按现行分类有食品、饮料、烟酒、服装鞋帽、纺织品、中西药品、化妆品、书报杂志、文化体育用品、日用品、家用电器、首饰、燃料、建筑装璜材料、机电产品十四个大类,300多种商品。以其各该商品的实际调查的综合平均价格,按加权算术平均公式计算。权数是社会商品零售额中各类商品零售额的构成比重。

城市居民消费价格指数:1994年取消城市职工生活费用价格指数,采用居民消费价格指数反映城市居民购买生活消费品和支付服务收费的价格变动趋势和变动程度。调查范围和内容是居民用于日常生活消费品的全部商品和服务项目价格。包括食品、衣着、家庭设备及用品、医疗保健、交通和通讯、娱乐教育和文化用品、居住、服务项目等八大类商品及服务项目价格。既包括居民从商店、工厂、集市所购买商品的价格,也包括从餐饮行业购买商品的价格。以实际调查的综合平均单价,根据住户调查有关资料确定的权数,按加权算术平均公式计算。

农产品成交价格指数:1994年将集市贸易价格总指数改为该指数。它是反映本市农副产品市场商品价格变动趋势和程度的相对数。它采用加权倒数平均公式,根据粮食、油脂类、鲜菜、干菜、肉禽蛋、水产品、鲜果、干果、这八类农产品在农贸市场成交的平均价格计算。

原材料、燃料及动力购进价格指数:是反映工业企业通过各种价格形式购进的主要原材料、燃料、动力价格水平变动趋势和程度的相对数。它是依据我市部分重点企业中主要原材料、燃料、动力购进价格的定期调查资料,按加权算术平均公式计算的。

工业产品出厂价格指数:是反映各种工业产品以各种价格形式的出厂价格水平变动趋势和程度的相对数。它是依据我市部分重点企业的部分产品出厂价格定期调查资料,按加权算术平均公式计算的。

固定资产投资价格指数:是反映固定资产投资活动中所涉及的建筑安装工程投资价格、设备及工器具投资价格和其他费用投资价格水平变动趋势和程度的相对数。它是在编制建筑安装工程投资价格指数、设备及工器具价格指数和其它费用投资价格指数的基础上,采用加权算术平均法计算出来的。

六、城市建设和环境保护

城市园林绿地面积:是指公共绿地、专用绿地、生产绿地、防护绿地和风景名胜区的全部绿地面积。

建成区绿化覆盖率:是指建成区园林绿地面积+建成区道路绿化面积之和与建成区面积之比。用百分数表示。

公共绿地:是指各类开放公园、(包括植物园、陵园、游乐园和风景名胜公园等)、动物园、广场绿地、河(湖)滨绿地和宽度在八米以上设置有行人休息设施的林荫道绿地等。

人均公共绿地面积:是指市区公共绿地面积与市区非农业人口之比。市区包括市内六个区和滨海三个区的城市部分。

城市人口平均每人居住面积:是指按城市人口(市辖

区的非农业人口)计算的平均居住面积。其中的居住面积是指全部住宅中,专供日常生活起居使用的卧室、起居室的房间面积,不包括客厅、厨房、厕所等附属面积。居住面积按居住用房的内墙线计算。

七、人民生活和社会福利

城镇居民家庭就业人口:指从事社会劳动并取得报酬或经营收入的人口,不论在全民、集体所有制单位工作或从事个体劳动,不论有固定性职业或临时性职业都是就业人口。

城镇居民家庭实际收入:指调查户的全部现金收入,包括经常或固定得到的收入和一次性收入。不包括周转性的收入和提取银行存款、借入款、收回借出款以及其他各种暂收款。

城镇居民家庭生活费收入:指调查户家庭实际收入中能用于安排日常生活的收入。即用实际收入减掉"赡养支出"、"赠送支出"、调查户记帐所得的"记帐补贴"、非家庭人口中的经常用饭人口所交的"搭伙费"及家庭副业生产支出。

城镇居民家庭消费性支出:指调查户用于日常生活的全部支出,包括食品、衣着、家庭设备用品及服务医疗保健、交通和通讯、娱乐教育文化服务、居住、杂项商品和服务等八大类支出。

城镇居民家庭非消费性支出:包括直接税、消费性贷款利息支出、经常性转移支出等支出。

农民家庭总收入:指农民年内从各种来源得到的全部实际收入。它包括从集体统一经营中得到的收入,从经济联合体得到的收入,家庭经营收入和其他非生产性收入。

农民家庭纯收入:指农民全年总收入扣除费用性支出后可以直接用于进行生产和非生产性建设投资、改善生活的那部分收入,是反映农民家庭实际收入水平和经济效益的主要指标。

农民家庭总支出:指农民家庭全年用于生产、生活等方面的全部实际支出。包括家庭经费支出、缴纳税收、上交集体的承包任务、购买生产性固定资产支出、生活消费支出和其他非生产性支出。

劳保福利费:是指企业、事业、机关根据国家有关劳保福利规定在工资以外实际支付给职工个人和用于集体的劳动保险和福利的费用。不包括用于职工的劳动保护费用,以及劳动保险福利费中的洗理卫生费,上下班交通费补贴,从企业来讲,劳保福利费不仅包括由职工福利基金支出的部分,而且还包括由企业营业外支出、企业基金或利润留成、工会文教费、企业管理费支出的部分。

人口平均期望寿命:也称人口平均预期寿命。指假设一个国家或地区同时出生的一代人,根据当时的社会、经济、文化和卫生条件,从出生开始到全部死去为止,平均每个人预期可以活多少岁。平均期望寿命是对同时出生的全体出生者平均可能生存的年数而言,至于具体每一个人的寿命,则有长有短。

八、农村经济

农林牧渔业总产值:是指以货币表现的农林牧渔业全部产品总量。它用价值量形式综合说明了一定时期(通常指一年)农林牧渔业生产的总成果和总规模,是观察农林牧渔业生产水平和发展速度;研究农林牧渔业内部比例关系和农林牧渔业在国民经济中的产业布局的一个重要指标,同时,也是计算农林牧渔业劳动生产率和农林牧渔业增加值的基础资料。

农林牧渔业总产值的计算方法,一般采用"产品法"进行计算,即凡是有产品产量的,都按产品产量乘以其产品单价求得每一种产品的产值,然后将四业产品的产值相加求得。

农业产值:包括种植业和其他农业的主产品和副产品产值。

1.**种植业产值**:是指从事农作物栽培取得的产品的产值。包括谷物、棉花、麻类、糖类、烟叶、药材、薯类、蔬菜、瓜类及其他种植业产值。

2.**其他农业产值**

(1)采集野生植物产值:按采集到的各种野生药材、纤维原料、油料、淀粉原料、柴草等原料产品(未经加工)的数量乘以产品的单价计算。

(2)农民家庭兼营的商品性工业产值:是指以经营农业为主的农民家庭所兼营的商品性工业产值。根据我国农村的实际情况。只计算农民家庭为出售而生产的工业品价值。

工业生产活动又分为农产品简单加工(如碾米、磨面、屠宰、轧花、饲料加工等)、颗粒肥料制造及肥料简单加工、缝纫、农具修理、家具修理和其它属于工业性作业活动的生产活动,一律按加工价值计算产值。除上述这些活动以外,全部其他工业活动如榨油、制糖、造酒、酿醋、采矿、炼焦、炼铁、烧砖瓦、制造工具和农具,制造土化肥、造纸、编织等等都要按这些生产活动成品产量乘单价(全部价值)计算产值。农民对企业承做的零配件加工不计算产值。

农林牧渔业增加值:是指各种经济类型的农业生产单位和农户从事农业生产经营活动所提供的社会最终产品的货币表现。增加值的计算方法有两种,一是生产法:农林牧渔业增加值=农林牧渔业总产出-农林牧渔业中间消耗;二是分配法:农林牧渔业增加值=固定资产折旧+劳动者报酬+生产税净额(生产税-生产补贴)+营业盈余。

固定资产折旧:是指固定资产在生产经营过程中逐步消耗并转移到产品成本和流通费用中的那部分价值。它包括两个部分:一是当年按一定标准提取的固定资产折旧;二是农业生产单位实际发生或预提的固定资产修理费。

劳动者报酬:是指各种经济类型的农业生产单位的劳动者和农户,在从事农业生产经营活动中取得的以各种形式支付的报酬和收入。对于农业企业,是指列入成本和销售费用的工资,不包括从利润、营业外收入、专用经费等列支的工资。对于农村集体和农户,是指农民从农业集体生产单位取得的劳动报酬和农民的农业纯收入(扣除生产性固定资产折旧)。

生产税:指农业生产单位和农户在生产、销售过程中向国家缴纳的农业税、农林特产税 、屠宰税、渔业税、牧业税、销售税等利前税。

生产补贴:指国家直接支付给农业生产单位的补贴。

营业盈余:是指生产要素在生产过程中创造的剩余价值,具体是指社会总产品扣除中间投入、固定资产折旧、劳动者报酬、生产税净额后的剩余部分。

农业商品产值:是指本生产年度内全社会(包括国营、农村集体经济组织和农户)全年生产的农产品总产量中实际出售的商品价值。按日历年度内实际出售的商品价值来计算。不论是出售给国家的,还是直接出售给城镇居民的或农民的,都应计算为商品产值。

农业机械总动力:是指主要用于农、林、牧、渔业的各种动力机械的动力总和。包括耕作机械、排灌机械、收获机械、农产品加工机械、运输机械、植保机械、牧业机械、林业机械、渔业机械和其它农业机械。内燃机按引擎马力折成瓦特计算。电动机按功率计算。

有效灌溉面积:是指具有一定的水源,地块比较平整,灌溉工程或设备已经配套,在一般年景下当年能够进行正常灌溉的耕地面积。在一般情况下,有效灌溉面积应等于灌溉工程或设备已经配套,能够进行灌溉的水田和水浇地面积之和。

造林面积:是指报告期内在荒地、荒山、沙丘等一切可造林的土地上,采用人工播种、植苗、飞机播种等方法新植的成片乔木林和灌木林,经过检查验收符合“造林技术规程”要求株数,成活率达40%以上的面积。四旁植树如一侧在四行以上,连续面积0.066公顷以上,应统计在造林面积内。

当年出栏头数:指农林牧渔企业生产单位饲养的,供屠宰并已出栏的全部牲畜头数。包括交售给国家,集市上出售的部分。

九、工 业

工业总产值:工业总产值是以货币表现的工业企业在报告期内生产的工业产品总量。它是反映一定时间内工业生产总规模和总水平的重要指标。工业总产值采用“工厂法”计算。全国第三次工业普查对工业总产值的范围和计算方法作出新规定。工业总产值包括本年生产成品价值,对外加工费收入,自制半成品、在产品期末期初差额价值。新规定与原规定的变化:一是对工业产值中凡自备原材料,不论其加工繁简程度如何,一律按全价计算产值。凡来料加工,一律按加工费计算总产值;二是自制半成品、在产品期末期初差额价值的计算改变了生产周期六个月以上的原则,而以当期会计是否将其计入成本核算作为是否计入产值的依据;三是现价产值按不含增值税的价格计算,而按1990年不变价格计算的本年生产成品价值、工业性加工、修理价值,与原规定一样,一律按不扣除增值税的价格计算。由于以上不同,因此在用1995年工业总产值数时,应注意其可比性。

工业行业类别:国家1994年制定的《国民经济行业分类与代码》(GB/T4754-94),将现行的“工业”门类调整为“采掘业”“制造业”和“电力、煤气和水的生产和供应业”三个门类。依据产业活动单位其经济活动性质的同一性进行分类,即按企业生产的产品经济用途、使用的原材料、生产工艺性质来划分,而不是按其所属行政管理系统分类。

轻工业:一般是指提供生活消费品和制作手工工具的工业,按其使用的原料不同,可分为两大类:

以农产品为原料的轻工业:是指直接和间接以农产品为基本原料的轻工业,主要包括:棉、毛、麻、丝、纺织和缝纫、皮革及其制品、纸浆和造纸、食品制造、饮料制造、烟草加工等工业。

以非农产品为原料的工业:主要是指以工业品为原料的工业,包括日用金属品、日用化工品、化学纤维及其制品、制盐、日用玻璃陶瓷以及铁制小农具、竹木农具、匠作工具等工业。

重工业:一般是指生产生产资料为国民经济部门提供

物质技术基础的工业。包括下列三类：

采掘工业：是指石油开采、煤炭开采、金属矿开采、非金属矿开采和木材采伐工业等。

原料工业：它是提供国民经济各部门使用的原材料和动力、燃料工业。包括金属冶炼及加工、炼焦及焦炭化学、化工原料、水泥等原材料工业以及电力、石油、煤炭等能源工业。

加工工业：是指对原材料进行加工制造的工业。包括装备国民经济各部门的机械设备制造工业和金属结构，以及为农业提供的生产资料和化肥、农药等工业。

大、中、小型企业：是根据国家统一标准划分的，划分标准有两种：一种是按企业产品的年生产能力划分，凡产品比较单一的行业如电力、原煤、石油、钢铁、有色金属、硫酸、烧碱、纯碱、合成氨、发电设备、汽车、拖拉机、手表、缝纫机、自行车等均属这类划分标准；另一种是按企业拥有的固定资产原值划分，凡产品种类繁多，难以按生产能力划分的，则以企业拥有的固定资产原值作为划分标准。

资本金：是指企业在工商行政管理部门登记的注册资金。资本金按照投资主体分为国家资本金、法人资本金、个人资本金及外商资本金，还有集体单位等其他形式筹集的资本金等。其中，国家资本金为有权代表国家投资的政府部门或者机构，以国有资产投入企业形成的资本金；外商资本金为外国投资者以及我国香港、澳门和台湾地区投资者投入企业形成的资本金。

产品销售收入：是指企业销售产品的销售收入和提供劳务等主要经营业务取得的收入总额。新会计制度计算产品收入是"以产品已经发出、劳务已经提供，同时收讫或者取得收取价款的凭据为原则"，由此计算范围扩大。1994 年实行税制改革后，增值税成为价外税，因此产品销售收入中不含增值税。与 1994 年前产品销售收入指标不可比。

产品销售成本：是指企业销售产品和提供劳务等主要经营业务的实际成本。它是按制造成本法计算的，不同于旧制度中的按完全成本法计算的实际成本。所谓完全成本法，就是将企业在生产经营过程中发生的所有费用，都摊到产品成本中去，形成产品的完全成本。制造成本法则是在计算产品成本时，只分配与生产经营有密切关系的部分，而将与生产经营没有直接联系的部分直接计入当期损益。现产品销售成本经济函义的变化，使其包括的范围小了。

产品销售费用：是指企业销售产品和提供劳务等主要经营业务过程中所发生的各种费用。包括运输费、装卸费、包装费、保险费、展览费、广告费，以及为销售本企业产品而专设的销售机构的职工工资、福利费、业务费等经常费用。新制度中的产品销售费用包括范围比旧制度要小，因此同 1994 年前数不尽可比。

产品销售税金及附加：1994 年实行新税制后，取消了产品税，产品销售收入中不再含增值税。因此现在的"产品销售税金及附加"指标包括消费税、城市建设维护税、资源税和教育费附加。与 1994 以前年度数不可比。

产品销售利润：是指企业销售产品和提供劳务等主要经营业务收入，扣除其成本、费用、税金后的利润。由于产品销售收入、产品销售成本、产品销售费用、产品销售税金及附加等指标都有变化，因此，今年产品销售利润与 1994 年以前同一指标不可比。

营业利润：是指企业生产经营活动所发生的利润。分为主营业务利润和其他业务利润。营业利润是企业营业收入减去营业成本、营业费用（包括销售费用、管理费用、财务费用）再减去营业收入应负担的营业税金（流转税金）后的余额。

利润总额：是指企业在一定时期内实现的利润（亏损以负数表示）。它集中反映企业生产经营活动各方面的效益，是企业的最终财务成果，是衡量企业生产经营管理水平的重要综合性指标。该项指标由于营业利润的变化，特别是新增加了一项投资收益指标，因此与 1994 年前不尽可比。

利税总额：是指利润总额、产品销售税金及附加和本期应交增值税之和。

十、建筑业

施工产值：是指建筑安装企业或单位自行完成的按工程进度计算的建筑安装生产总值，其中包括(1)建筑工程产值，(2)设备安装工程产值，(3)房屋，构筑物修理产值，(4)非标准设备制造产值。

(1)建筑工程产值：是指列入建筑工程预算内的各种工程价值，主要包括：各种用途的房屋、构筑物的建筑工程和暖气、卫生、通风、照明、煤气等设备安装价值；设备基础、支柱、操作台、梯子、烟囱、凉水塔的砌筑工程；各种锅炉炉体砌筑和金属结构安装工程；施工现场布置、场地平整、施工临时用水、电、道路的铺筑与架设；矿井的开凿、井巷掘进延伸、露天矿的剥离、石油、天然气钻井工程；铁路、公路、港口、桥梁的建筑工程；水利工程；防空、地下建筑等特殊工程，和对建筑物内部或外部进行装饰、装修的价值。

(2)设备安装工程产值:是指设备安装工程价值,主要包括生产、动力、起重、运输、传动、医疗、实验、电讯、光纤、电话、计算机和电子设备等各种需要安装设备的装配与安装,与设备相联接的工作台、梯子、栏杆等装设工程;附属于被安装设备的管线敷设工程;被安装设备的绝缘、防腐保温、油漆等工作;为测定安装工作质量,对单个设备、系统设备进行单机试车和系统联动无负荷试运转工作,但产值中不包括被安装设备的价值。

(3)房屋、构筑物修理产值:是指房屋和构筑物修理所完成的价值,但不包括被修理房屋、构筑物本身价值和生产设备的修理价值。

(4)非标准设备制造产值:是指加工制造没有定型的非标准生产设备的加工费和原材料价值。

十一、交通运输和邮电通信

货运量:是指在一定时期内,由各种运输工具实际完成运送过程的货物数量。

货物周转量:是指在一定时期内,由各种运输工具实际完成运送过程的以重量和运送距离的复合单位(吨公里)计算的货物运输量。

把各种运输工具采用各种运输形式(铁路、公路、水运、空运、管道)完成的货运量或货物周转量相加,就得到货运总量和货物总周转量。

港口货物吞吐量:是表示港口生产能力的指标之一,指由水运进出港区并经过装卸的货物数量,吞吐量分为进口、出口。

邮电业务总量:是指以货币表现的邮电通信部门,为用户传递信息和提供其他邮电服务的总量,它是由函件件数、电报份数、长途电话、市内电话和农村电话的年平均户数,订销报刊累计份数等各类业务的实物量,分别乘以相应的不变单价之和,再加上出租代维及其他业务收入。邮电业务总量综合反映一定时期邮电工作的总成果。

市内电话平均户数:指报告期内每天实有用户的平均户数。月平均用户可以用上月末到达户数和本月末到达户数相加除以2求得。年平均户数,以1至12月各月平均用户相加除以12求得。

十二、批发零售贸易和餐饮业

批发和零售贸易业:根据国家1994年新制定的行业分类标准《国民经济行业分类与代码》(GB/T4754－94)将原国内商业、对外贸易业、物资供销业,统一调整为批发和零售贸易业。包括流通环节批发贸易和零售商业。

社会消费品零售总额:指各种经济类型的批发零售贸易业、餐饮业、制造业和其他行业对城乡居民和社会集团的消费品零售额和农民对非农业居民零售额的总和。

商品购进总额:指从本企业以外的单位和个人购进(包括从国外直接进口)作为转卖或加工后转卖的商品。包括从工农业生产者购进额,从批发零售贸易业购进额,进口额和其他项目组成。这个指标反映批发零售贸易企业从国内外市场上购进商品的总量。

商品销售总额:指对本企业以外的单位和个人出售(包括对国(境)外直接出口)的商品(包括售给本单位消费用的商品)。本指标由对生产经营单位批发额、对批发零售贸易业批发额、出口额、对居民和社会集团商品零售额项目组成。这个指标反映批发零售贸易企业在国内市场上销售商品以及出口商品总量。

城乡集市贸易成交额:指农民在集市和集市外售给城镇居民和社会团体的消费品零售额。

商品销售收入(营业收入):指批发零售贸易企业商品销售收入、接受其他单位委托代销商品的收入和餐饮企业的营业收入。1994年实行增值税为价外税,因此商品销售收入不含增值税。与1994年前数字不可比。

商品销售收入净额:指批发零售贸易企业商品销售收入,减去商品销售折价与折让后的净额。

商品销售税金及附加:实行新税制后,商业批发零售改征增值税。是价外税不含在销售收入中。因此,商品销售税金及附加中也不含增值税。现在的商品销售税金及附加中,只包括城市建设维护税和教育费附加。与1994年前对比口径不同。

十三、对外经济贸易和旅游

利用外资:包括三部分,一是对外借款;二是客商直接投资;三是外商其他投资。外资包括现金、实物、工业产权或专有技术等。

对外借款:是指由我国政府、部门、企业和中国银行等单位向境外借入的外资,借款按不同渠道划分为:①外国政府贷款;②国际金融组织贷款;③外国银行现汇贷款;④外国银行提供的买方信贷:⑤其他:包括对外发行债券、股票和以地方部门、企业名义直接借入的外资。

客商直接投资：是指外国企业和经济组织或个人(包括华侨、港澳同胞)以及我国在境外注册的企业，按我国有关政策、法规，在我国境内开办独资企业、合资企业、合作经营企业或合作开发资源的投资。

客商其他投资：凡不属上述两类方式吸收的外资，均列入本类。主要有：①补偿贸易；②加工装配客商作价提供设备；③国际租赁；④其他。凡是本年内实际投资，不论是执行本年签订的或是执行过去几年签订的协议均应计算在内。

协议(合同)外资金额：是指经有关部门批准并签有正式协议(合同)的外方与客商规定可使用的贷款额。客商投资额和中方对外发行债券、股票总值，以及客商提供的设备等价款总值。

实际利用外资：是指根据投资协议(合同)实际执行的投资额。贷款按实际提取或拨交的使用数；客商直接投资项目(合同)的实际投资额；外商其他投资，按到货数计算。

海关进出口总额：海关进出口总额是指实际进出我国国境的货物总金额。包括对外贸易实际进出口货物，来料加工装配进出口货物，中外合资企业、合作企业和外商独资企业进出口货物以及国家间、联合国及国际组织无偿援助的物资和赠送品，华侨、港澳同胞、外籍华人的捐赠品的金额。

外贸出口总额：是指离开我国口岸或国境的向国外销售货物数量，以金额表示。

地方外汇进口总额：地方外汇是指由地方掌握使用的外汇，包括中央分配给地方的外汇，出口商品留成外汇，非贸易留成外汇，地方货款外汇等，使用这部分外汇组织进口称地方外汇进口总额。

十四、金融和保险业

贸易外汇："非贸易外汇"的对称。属于对外贸易款项结算范围以内的外汇。主要指对外贸易中因收付贸易货款以及交易佣金、运输费和保险费等而发生的那部分外汇。

非贸易外汇："贸易外汇"的对称。是指不需要组织商品进出口而发生收付的那部分外汇，主要是相互提供劳务的外汇。主要包括：国际收支中的侨民汇款；团体、个人的出口旅杂费和生活费；文化、外交、军事驻外代表机关经费等。按我国现行规定，某些虽然在性质上属于进出口贸易的项目，但由于不是通过外贸部门统一经营的，其外汇收入也列入非贸易外汇的范围。如进出口书刊、影片、邮票等收支的外汇。

十五、教育和科学技术

基础研究：为获得新知识而进行的独立性研究。其目的是揭示观察到的现象和事实的基本原理和规律，而不以任何特定的实际应用为目的。

应用研究：为获得新的科学技术知识而进行的独创性研究。它主要针对某一特定的实际应用目的。应用研究是为了确定基础研究成果或知识的可能的用途，或为达到某一具体的、预定的实际目的确定新的方法(原理性)或用途。

试验发展：利用从研究或实际经验获得的知识，为生产新的材料、、产品和装置，建立新的工艺和系统，以及对已生产或建立的上述各项进行实质性的改进，而进行的系统性工作。

研究与试验发展成果应用：为解决研究与试验发展活动阶段产生的新产品、新装置、新工艺、新技术、新方法、新系统和服务等能投入生产或在实际中应用所存在的技术问题而进行的系统性活动。它不具有创新成份。此类活动包括为达到生产目的而进行的定型设计和试制以及为扩大新产品的生产规模和新方法、新技术、新工艺等应用领域而进行的适应性试验。

科技服务：与科学研究与试验发展有关并有助于科学技术知识的产生、传播和应用的活动，包括为扩大科技成果的使用范围而进行的示范性推广工作；为用户提供科技信息和文献服务的系统性工作；为用户提供可行性报告、技术方案、建议及进行技术论证等技术咨询工作；自然、生物现象的日常观测、监测，资源的考察和勘探；有关社会、人文、经济现象的通用资料的收集，如统计、市场调查等，以及这些资料的常规分析与整理；为社会和公众提供的测试、标准化、计量、计算、质量控制和专利服务，不包括工商企业为进行正常生产而开展的上述活动。

十六、文化体育卫生及其他

电视人口覆盖率：指用普通的电视接收机，室外天线在离地面4米高处能在晚上正常收看电视节目的人数与全市总人口数之比。

广播人口覆盖率：指用普通的收音机在中午能正常收听广播节目的人数与全市总人口数之比。

文化事业机构：指从事专业文化工作和为专业文化工作服务的单独核算、独立建制的单位，不包括文化主管部门直属单位举办的其他行业和各部门的业余文化组织。

艺术表演团体:指从事戏曲、音乐、舞蹈、杂技等专业艺术表演有独立帐户、实行单独核算的团体。

电影放映单位:指具有放映机器设备,固定或不固定的放映场所与专职或兼职的放映技术人员,经文化部门登记批准,经常为一定的观众对象映出电影的机构。包括经批准对外开放进行营业、并与电影发行放映管理机构分帐的专用放映单位或军委系统租片在内。

体育场:指有米跑道(中心含足球场),有固定车道,跑道6条以上,并有固定看台的田径场。

体育馆:指有固定看台可供篮球、排球、羽毛球、乒乓球、体操等项目训练比赛活动用的室内场地。

等级运动员人数:指经考核正式批准授予等级运动员称号的人数。分为国际级运动健将、运动健将、一、二、三级运动员和少年级运动员。

等级裁判员人数:指经考核正式批准授予等级裁判员称号的人数。分为国际裁判、国家级裁判、一、二、三级裁判。

卫生技术人员:指卫生事业机构支付工资的全部固定职工和合同制职工中现任职务为卫生技术工作的人员。包括中医师、西医师、中西医结合高级医师、护师、中药师、西药师、检验师、其他技师、中医士、西医士、护士、助产士、中药剂士、西药剂士、检验士、其他技士、其他中医、护理员、中药剂员、西药剂员、检验员和其他初级卫生技术人员。

医生:指经卫生部门审查合格,从事医疗工作的专业人员。分为中医医生和西医医生。包括卫生技术人员中的中医师、西医师、中西医结合高级医师、中医士、西医士和其他中医。

十七、改革开放和滨海新区

消费品批发市场主要商品成交情况:是指在集贸市场上,由买卖双方直接见面,按照集市价格成交的各种主要消费品的数量和金额。

生产资料市场:是指组织供需单位集中进行商品交易活动,并提供咨询服务和管理的场所或交易中心。

商品交易总量:是指凡在市场上成交的商品,不论交易的次数多少,均按买卖双方发生交易的次数统计商品交易的总数量和总金额。其中远期现货合约交易,是指三个月以上合约交易;期货合约交易是指在交易达成的标准化的、受法律约束并规定在将来某一特定地点和时间交收某一特定商品的合约交易。

金融市场:从狭义讲,指资金市场。即证券交易所,如股票、债券发行、买卖等。从广义讲包括货币市场、资本市场、外汇市场和黄金市场。

外汇市场:是由经营外汇业务的金融机构所组成,从事外汇买卖、调剂外汇供求的交易场所。调剂外汇业务是国家外汇管理部门,根据国家有关规定和金融体制改革进程的要求开办的一项外汇市场业务。所谓外汇调剂是指部门企业之间有偿转让外汇使用权的经济活动。也就是说一部分单位企业把自己多余的留成外汇,通过调剂市场以调剂市场价格,卖给其他急需用汇但又缺少外汇的企业单位。主要指标有成交额、调剂价格等。

劳务人才市场交易情况:劳务人才市场是指劳动力供求双方实现劳务交换和劳动力流动的场所。主要反映进场单位数、进场人次、达成意向人次等情况。

技术市场:从狭义看,是指在一定时间、地点进行技术转让和技术商品交易的场所。目前统计反映的是企业购买技术开发、技术转让、技术咨询、技术服务项目的合同数和成交额。

房地产交易市场:主要反映房地产的开发、生产、交换、消费活动等情况。如国有土地使用权出让的地块数、面积、收入;房产买卖的成交面积和成交金额;房屋租赁的出租面积和出租金额,以及向个人出售住宅的面积和收回资金数等。

附二、世界主要国家(城市)统计资料

国内生产总值

单位:百万美元

国家(地区)	1980	1985	1990	1994	国家(地区)	1980	1985	1990	1994
阿尔巴尼亚	1 636	1 965	2 102	1 808	爱沙尼亚			7 490	4 578
阿尔及利亚	42 347	57 997	59 902	42 306	埃塞俄比亚		6 696	8 608	5 366
安提瓜和巴布达	112	202	395		斐济	1 204	1 141	1 381	1 867
阿根廷	76 962	88 151	141 352	281 922	芬兰	51 306	53 507	134 806	
亚美尼亚		4 978	7 650	4 346	法国	664 595	523 097	1 195 439	
澳大利亚	159 728	167 590	296 046		法属圭亚那	213			
奥地利	76 882	65 174	158 429		加蓬	4 279	3 663	5 456	3 945
阿塞拜疆			9 740	3 647	冈比亚	233	218	331	379
巴哈马	1 335	2 321	3 135		格鲁吉亚			12 167	2 143
巴林	3 073	3 705	4 032		德国	809 850	619 293	1 501 488	
孟加拉国	12 950	15 651	22 397	26 163	加纳	4 445	4 504	6 226	8 004
巴巴多斯	835	1 204	1 743		希腊	40 147	33 433	66 561	
白俄罗斯			34 188	20 287	格林纳达	75	116	202	
比利时	118 021	79 926	192 175		瓜德罗普	1 426	1 074		
伯利兹	195	209	397	550	危地马拉	7 879	9 722	7 650	12 855
贝宁	1 405	1 046	1 845	1 522	几内亚			2 818	3 502
百慕大	624	1 058			几内亚比绍	105	158	236	243
不丹	142	193	285	278	圭亚那	591	459	396	540
玻利维亚	3 074	2 973	4 487	5 512	海地	1 462	2 009	3 001	1 645
博茨瓦纳	971	1 137	3 176	4 011	洪都拉斯	2 566	3 640	2 943	3 161
巴西	234 909	222 974	479 213	639 562	匈牙利	22 163	20 625	33 055	41 175
文莱	4 906	3 483	3 591		冰岛	3 373	2 913	6 242	
保加利亚	20 040	17 562	20 726	10 115	印度	172 321	214 303	298 356	291 054
布基纳法索	1 484	1 242	2 581		印度尼西亚	78 013	87 207	106 142	174 638
布隆迪	920	1 150	1 132	909	伊朗	92 664	179 812	120 404	
柬埔寨			1 432		伊拉克	47 562	44 204	48 657	
喀麦隆	7 499	8 324	11 038	7 470	爱尔兰	20 231	19 787	44 812	
加拿大	263 192	347 379	568 072		以色列	22 690	25 835	54 911	
佛得角	107	107	269	334	意大利	452 648	424 512	1 095 122	
中非共和国	797	704	1 304	980	牙买加	2 679	2 018	4 242	4 231
乍得	727	727	1 213	910	日本	1 059 257	1 343 273	2 932 055	
智利	27 572	16 464	30 387	52 181	约旦		4 992	4 020	6 105
哥伦比亚	33 399	34 894	40 274	64 371	哈萨克斯坦			39 831	18 328
科摩罗	124	114	244	211	肯尼亚	7 265	6 131	8 533	6 956
刚果	1 706	2 161	2 799	1 578	吉里巴斯	28	23	34	
哥斯达黎加	4 831	3 923	5 710	8 284	韩国	63 661	94 322	253 671	376 505
科特迪瓦	10 175	6 982	9 899	6 716	科威特	28 639	21 446	18 428	
克罗地亚				13 460	吉尔吉斯		3 049	5 593	2 726
塞浦路斯	2 154	2 420	5 561		老挝		2 368	868	1 534
捷克共和国	29 123	27 573	31 599	36 024	拉脱维亚			12 008	5 817
丹麦	66 322	58 045	129 127		黎巴嫩			2 838	9 240
吉布提	296	344	418		莱索托	368	247	604	886
多米尼克	58	99	171		利比里亚	1 117	1 095		
多米尼加	6 631	4 489	7 609	10 416	利比亚	35 545	27 366		
厄瓜多尔	11 733	12 130	10 686	16 557	立陶宛			12 757	5 224
埃及	22 912	34 690	35 396	42 923	卢森堡	4 950	3 764	10 557	
萨尔瓦多	3 567	4 060	5 409	8 806	马其顿			2 313	1 678
赤道几内亚		80	132	178	马达加斯加	4 042	2 858	3 081	2 817
厄立特里亚					马拉维	1 238	1 131	1 858	1 302

资料来源:世界银行《世界数据表》1996 年。

续表

单位:百万美元

国家(地区)	1980	1985	1990	1994	国家(地区)	1980	1985	1990	1994
马来西亚	24 488	31 200	42 822	70 634	所罗门群岛	116	160	211	
马尔代夫		85	146	267	索马里	604	876	917	
马里	1 629	1 057	2 477	1 870	南非	78 743	55 246	106 713	124 726
马耳他	1 135	1 018	2 313		西班牙	211 543	165 845	491 938	
毛里塔尼亚	709	683	1 020	1 027	斯里兰卡	4 024	6 078	8 140	11 715
毛里求斯	1 132	1 076	2 559	3 361	苏丹	6 760	10 284	9 014	
墨西哥	194 905	184 504	244 047	375 465	苏里南	891	978	533	252
摩尔多瓦			7 681	3 727	斯威士兰	582	361	904	1 102
蒙古	2 329	2 526	2 241	741	瑞典	125 557	100 722	229 756	
摩洛哥	18 821	12 870	25 825	31 503	瑞士	101 646	92 771	226 029	
莫桑比亚	2 028	2 563	1 443	1 467	叙利亚	13 062	16 404	14 408	
缅甸	5 780	6 860	24 415	62 213	塔吉克斯坦			4 680	2 069
纳米比亚	2 190	1 357	2 304	2 884	坦桑尼亚	5 138	6 904	2 590	
尼泊尔	1 946	2 621	3 628	3 971	泰国	32 354	38 900	85 640	143 209
荷兰	172 280	128 063	283 518		多哥	1 136	762	1 636	973
新西兰	22 469	22 624	43 625		汤加	52	61	112	
尼加拉瓜	2 144	2 684	1 540	1 771	特立尼达和多巴哥	822	6 236	5 068	4 795
尼日尔	2 538	1 440	2 481	1 540	突尼斯	8 743	8 280	12 291	15 770
尼日利亚	93 082	80 956	32 424	35 200	土耳其	56 919	52 783	150 677	131 014
挪威	57 711	58 181	105 524		土库曼斯坦			5 558	
阿曼	5 982	10 006	10 535	11 628	乌干达	1 267	3 926	4 341	4 032
巴基斯坦	23 690	31 148	40 013	52 011	乌克兰			155 618	76 139
巴拿马	3 592	4 948	5 009	6 852	阿联酋	29 625	27 021	33 653	
巴布亚新几内亚	2 548	2 424	3 221	4 724	英国	537 383	457 073	975 512	
巴拉圭	4 579	3 163	5 265	7 752	美国	2 708 147	4 016 650	5 489 600	
秘鲁	20 661	16 096	30 996	50 385	乌拉圭	10 133	4 719	8 355	16 154
菲律宾	32 451	30 735	44 311	63 876	乌兹别克斯坦			22 615	21 249
波兰	56 793	70 986	58 976	95 406	瓦努阿图	113	118	154	181
葡萄牙	28 526	23 514	67 238		委内瑞拉	69 377	61 965	48 599	58 882
波多黎各	14 436	20 289	30 604		越南		17 046	6 472	15 570
卡塔尔	7 829	6 153	7 360		美属维尔京群岛	219	728	1 344	
罗马尼亚			38 244	29 206	西萨摩亚	112	88	146	
俄罗斯		363 706	608 121	274 929	也门共和国			6 868	4 654
卢旺达	1 163	1 715	2 305		扎伊尔	14 391	7 193		
圣基茨尼维斯	48	78	160		赞比亚	3 884	2 252	3 288	3 481
圣卢西亚	133	217	399		津巴布韦	5 355	4 519	6 779	5 432
圣文森特	59	113	198		撒哈拉以南非洲	295 717	250 185	288 794	289 145
圣多美和普林西比	43	35	50	29	南亚	219 309	274 861	379 568	392 285
沙特阿拉伯	156 487	86 676	104 670						
塞内加尔	3 016	2 578	5 703	3 881	中、低收入国家	3 174 537	3 293 548	4 748 757	5 429 263
塞舌尔	147	169	373	442	低收入国家	727 918	830 460	979 705	1 174 372
塞拉利昂	1 100	1 315	857	834	中等收入国家	2 446 619	2 463 088	63 769 052	4 254 891
新加坡	11 718	17 691	36 510	68 949	高收入国家	7 653 861	90 408 031	16 274 670	
斯洛伐克	12 027	12 491	14 321	12 370	经合组织成员国	7 470 624	8 832 447	15 868 840	
斯洛文尼亚			17 327	12 825	世界	10 828 400	12 334 350	21 023 420	

第一、二、三产业对国内生产总值增长的贡献率

单位:%

国家(地区)	第一产业			第二产业			第三产业		
	1985	1990	1994	1985	1990	1994	1985	1990	1994
世界	0.20	0.10		1.30	0.80		1.80	1.20	
孟加拉国	0.45	3.80	0.65	0.45	0.99	1.42	3.04	1.86	2.46
印度	0.08	1.18	0.73	1.24	1.92	2.15	4.08	2.55	2.28
印度尼西亚	1.04	0.45	0.08	-0.15	3.59	3.98	1.76	3.01	3.04
伊朗	1.58	2.10	1.10	-0.62	3.95	-2.97	1.44	4.22	-9.37
日本	-0.01	0.01		2.48	3.12		2.52	1.69	
哈萨克斯坦			-8.39			-11.55			-5.02
马来西亚	0.40	0.04	0.47	-1.26	5.40	4.48	-0.26	4.30	3.80
蒙古	2.08	-0.34	0.36	2.37	-0.11	0.12	1.30	-1.86	1.83
缅甸	1.17	1.01	3.45	0.29	0.59	0.94	1.30	1.08	1.98
韩国	0.50	-0.43		7.20	5.90		-0.48	4.20	
巴基斯坦	2.89	0.78	0.68	1.83	1.61	1.22	2.83	2.08	1.22
菲律宾	-0.43	0.11	0.53	-6.05	0.91	2.08	-0.80	1.66	1.67
新加坡	-0.08	-0.03	0.01	-3.83	3.45	4.99	2.07	5.31	5.17
斯里兰卡	2.46	2.20	0.79	0.92	2.20	2.45	1.73	1.90	1.64
泰国	0.82	-0.56	0.40	0.46	5.87	4.37	3.41	6.45	3.79
土耳其	0.44	1.25	-0.16	1.72	2.02	-1.19	2.95	5.87	-3.99
越南	1.53	0.61	1.40		0.65	3.56		3.22	3.88
埃及	0.69	0.31	0.53	2.31	-0.15	-0.07	3.60	2.24	1.54
尼日利亚	5.45	1.50	0.80	2.53	2.04	-1.67	2.71	4.25	1.14
南非	0.99	-0.48	0.52	-1.46	-10.51	0.81	-0.55	9.98	1.07
加拿大	-0.10	0.09		2.01	-0.92		2.82	0.54	
墨西哥	0.32	0.47		1.71	2.09		0.71	1.74	
美国	0.29	0.16		1.03	0.05		1.80	1.05	
阿根廷	-0.15	1.00	0.31	-3.62	0.01	2.37	-2.82	-0.84	4.72
巴西	1.04	-0.38	0.26	3.75	-3.30	2.20	3.15	-0.89	1.65
委内瑞拉	0.45	-0.11		-0.42	4.18		0.16	2.81	
白俄罗斯	-1.45	-3.24		2.28	2.35		3.39	-0.52	
保加利亚	-3.39	-0.41	0.56	3.10	-7.91	-2.19	4.48	-1.56	1.99
法国	0.03	0.07			0.56		1.88	1.89	
意大利	0.03	-0.11		0.75	0.80		1.83	1.46	
荷兰		0.39			0.85			2.90	
波兰	1.30	-1.90		3.14	-16.32		-0.09	15.84	
罗马尼亚	0.17	1.97	0.88	-1.11	-7.62	1.17	0.50	-0.87	0.33
俄罗斯	-0.19	-0.89	-1.39	1.23	-1.58	-10.15	1.21	-1.13	-3.46
西班牙		0.15			1.34			2.25	
乌克兰	-1.26	-1.54	-1.24	0.95	-0.88	-11.77	3.01	-0.89	-13.69
澳大利亚	-0.12	0.29		1.23	-0.53		2.64	-0.47	
新西兰	1.12	1.05		-0.25	-1.28		-0.33	-0.29	

资料来源:世界银行《世界数据表》1996年。

总投资对国内生产总值增长的贡献率

单位:%

国家(地区)	1980	1985	1987	1988	1989	1990	1991	1992	1993	1994
世界总计	**-0.20**	**0.70**	**1.00**	**1.70**	**1.30**	**0.40**	**-0.20**	**-0.10**	**0.20**	
孟加拉国	5.08	1.51	1.34	0.30	0.46	0.34	-1.13	0.95	1.01	0.92
印度	-0.79	4.04	1.28	5.06	-0.06	3.42	-3.27	1.85	-0.93	2.96
印度尼西亚	0.28	-0.35	1.38	0.78	3.69	5.06	0.95	1.61	1.81	3.64
伊朗	10.00	-4.98	0.01	-7.75	4.38	5.49	6.44	3.37	-8.22	-11.96
以色列	-3.14	-2.13	0.55	0.13	-0.78	4.56	8.37	1.98	0.05	
日本	-0.30	1.77	2.32	3.98	2.97	2.49	1.47	-0.84	-0.73	
哈萨克斯坦		6.94	-1.16	1.72	-3.12	0.09				-5.99
马来西亚	5.21	-7.08	-0.65	5.40	5.01	5.91	8.47	1.67	5.02	7.79
蒙古		10.55	-18.85	1.43	4.55	-4.55	-16.17	-15.15	4.21	2.40
缅甸	1.13	0.86	-0.34	-0.92	-0.09	3.35	2.29	0.17	1.15	0.73
韩国	-7.61	1.15	4.85	5.02	5.32	6.49	5.52	-0.82	0.22	3.49
巴基斯坦	1.53	1.98	0.77	-0.10	1.18	0.94	0.55	1.88	0.72	-0.16
菲律宾	-0.76	-6.25	2.29	2.03	4.18	3.24	-4.42	1.44	2.31	2.27
新加坡	6.96	-6.21	3.44	0.41	2.94	9.50	2.32	0.75	6.01	-0.14
斯里兰卡	5.36	-1.11	2.00	-0.12	-1.24	-1.25	1.54	2.60	2.61	2.54
泰国	0.48	-1.09	4.86	8.07	5.39	10.18	4.82	2.14	3.85	4.57
土耳其	2.24	3.25	1.47	-0.63	0.52	6.62	-2.86	1.46	7.92	-7.39
越南						-1.12	1.23	5.88	6.35	7.47
埃及	-0.39	1.98	-4.01	5.76	-0.01	-0.20	-0.98	-1.96	0.26	0.82
尼日利亚	4.80	-1.85	-2.54	0.32	3.29	2.52	2.62	0.30	-2.75	-1.96
南非	5.59	-5.65	0.66	2.39	-0.99	-3.54	-0.52	-0.62	0.37	2.90
加拿大	0.11	1.41	2.30	2.05	1.58	-1.79	-0.70	-0.73	0.75	
墨西哥	6.41	2.13	1.46	2.23	1.04	2.29	1.85	3.35	-0.88	2.20
美国	-1.99	-0.05	0.30	0.35	0.81	-0.44	-1.24	1.12	2.26	
阿根廷	2.32	-3.30	2.59	-0.39	-4.76	-1.56	3.56	5.03	2.69	3.99
巴西	3.54	3.18	-0.27	-1.08	0.26	-1.69	-0.83	-0.46	0.95	1.28
委内瑞拉	-5.37	0.91	3.15	3.75	-14.07	-1.09	9.79	7.35	-4.72	-9.30
白俄罗斯		-5.62	0.07	-1.56	4.79	-1.27	3.44	-4.12	-2.23	
保加利亚		-0.14	-0.99	6.54	0.13	-13.55	-0.59	-6.46	-3.52	2.44
捷克共和国		0.88	0.96	-1.45	0.58	0.98	-6.28	-2.72	-2.55	1.01
法国	0.41	0.52	1.01	1.98	1.86	0.75	-0.66	-1.06	-2.29	
德国	-0.60	-0.37	0.14	1.41	1.47	1.57	4.91	0.38	-1.18	
意大利	2.77	0.37	0.96	1.32	0.50	0.79	-0.01	-0.17	-3.68	
荷兰	-0.28	1.41	-0.69	0.99	2.14	0.59	-0.27	-0.58	-0.92	
波兰		0.66	0.69	2.50	1.60	-7.96	-4.96	-2.64	2.54	0.38
罗马尼亚	-4.71	-1.09	-9.43	-3.13	-4.43	12.37	-10.59	-2.05	0.42	-4.44
俄罗斯		1.28	-0.26	2.90	-0.25	-3.08	4.53	-13.00	-6.23	-6.92
西班牙	0.56	0.30	2.96	3.30	3.08	1.66	0.30	-0.90	-3.44	
乌克兰		-0.08	0.93	-1.48	1.80	-3.99	-3.05	-10.04	-4.67	-5.55
英国	-2.99	0.60	1.73	3.24	1.05	-1.52	-2.51	0.69	0.35	
澳大利亚	2.00	0.99	1.99	3.89	-0.06	-4.10	-1.59	0.96	0.88	
新西兰	-1.48	-0.95	0.17	-0.61	5.24	-0.12	-7.46	3.68	4.26	

资料来源:世界银行《世界数据表》1996年。

总消费对国内生产总值增长的贡献率

单位:%

国家(地区)	1980	1985	1987	1988	1989	1990	1991	1992	1993	1994
世　　界	1.50	2.70	2.50	2.70	2.10	1.60	0.60	1.30	1.50	
孟加拉国	1.22	5.93	3.28	4.29	1.77	6.06	1.85	2.51	3.51	3.31
印　　度	8.82	2.61	2.62	6.00	5.76	1.93	1.86	3.33	3.63	2.83
印度尼西亚	7.94	5.96	0.75	0.57	3.63	6.09	7.61	0.21	3.85	4.50
伊　　朗	-19.31	6.31	-2.14	0.64	-0.17	5.31	4.52	2.86	8.91	-1.32
以 色 列	5.85	2.67	10.03	1.76	-2.28	4.45	4.97	4.41	5.97	
日　　本	1.69	2.48	2.32	2.86	2.22	2.30	1.85	1.33	0.61	
马来西亚	10.38	0.03	1.18	7.89	7.09	7.18	6.55	2.80	4.10	5.31
蒙　　古		-0.48	14.83	8.15	6.92	-4.47	-14.84	3.65	-6.62	1.00
缅　　甸	6.93	1.75	-3.22	-12.04	2.54	1.04	-3.64	7.73	5.86	5.55
韩　　国	0.49	4.81	4.91	5.50	8.19	6.87	6.88	4.06	3.88	4.07
巴基斯坦	8.17	7.51	7.09	7.77	2.61	1.36	-0.59	8.11	3.58	0.64
菲 律 宾	3.20	0.17	6.42	5.96	3.43	2.26	1.24	1.46	2.36	2.67
新 加 坡	3.64	3.15	4.34	5.35	4.70	4.57	3.18	2.80	5.17	-0.23
斯里兰卡	6.39	5.92	0.46	0.69	1.45	4.87	4.80	1.79	5.45	4.37
泰　　国	2.93	-0.21	6.87	8.57	7.45	6.43	3.73	3.92	4.67	5.83
土 耳 其	-3.06	1.35	8.54	-0.68	1.22	7.43	2.06	4.72	5.65	-5.61
越　　南						1.01	-4.88	0.16	10.94	2.60
埃　　及	12.01	5.17	-0.06	-2.39	1.17	3.85	0.30	-0.11	4.77	1.97
尼日利亚	15.74	4.68	-8.60	7.13	3.42	5.28	4.04	1.91	2.93	0.84
南　　非	5.86	-1.36	2.66	3.55	1.95	0.62	-0.02	-1.05	0.60	3.34
加 拿 大	1.69	3.76	2.65	3.93	2.30	0.94	-0.57	0.96	1.10	
墨 西 哥	7.45	2.78	0.07	2.81	5.80	5.46	5.23	4.79	0.21	4.06
美　　国	0.17	3.65	2.55	2.80	1.43	1.37	0.17	1.80	2.19	
阿 根 廷	6.06	-5.44	1.14	-3.72	-3.32	-0.27	10.25	9.22	4.29	4.92
巴　　西	4.35	4.05	1.82	-0.49	3.01	-1.70	1.31	-1.82	5.14	3.08
委内瑞拉	4.98	-0.61	2.51	6.18	-4.20	2.83	6.61	5.02	0.23	-3.50
白俄罗斯		-17.25	1.58	-3.35	6.19	8.50	-2.65	-17.53	0.06	
保加利亚		4.01	6.98	4.21	-2.52	2.99	-15.29	-0.03	-0.29	-3.56
法　　国	1.15	1.82	2.15	2.64	1.94	1.91	1.23	1.21	0.56	
德　　国	1.15	1.26	2.20	1.95	1.18	3.30	14.15	2.62	0.04	
意 大 利	3.75	2.35	3.01	3.18	2.28	1.73	1.74	1.05	-1.13	
荷　　兰	0.30	1.52	2.03	0.74	2.37	2.79	2.07	1.73	0.41	
波　　兰		3.65	-0.08	-0.98	-0.18	-0.12	8.49	3.38	3.36	2.43
罗马尼亚		-10.43	4.69	5.88	2.67				0.96	2.27
俄 罗 斯		3.29	1.40	5.78	4.36	-1.10	-23.42	-8.22	-2.26	-7.37
西 班 牙	0.91	2.94	4.83	3.65	4.74	3.29	2.66	1.92	-0.84	
乌 克 兰		2.93	2.56	3.47	2.02	0.54	-6.02	-4.13	-3.17	-20.88
英　　国	0.58	2.12	3.66	4.97	2.10	0.82	-0.87	-0.22	1.77	
澳大利亚	3.47	2.33	3.48	4.58	3.17	0.35	0.84	2.56	3.01	
新 西 兰	0.18	1.43	1.79	-0.34	0.72	-1.83	3.68	0.89	2.04	

资料来源:世界银行《世界数据表》1996年。

总投资占国内生产总值的比重

单位:%

国家(地区)	1980	1985	1987	1988	1989	1990	1991	1992	1993	1994
世　　界	24.1	22.3	22.5	23.3	24.0	23.2	22.5	21.7	21.5	
孟加拉国	14.9	12.9	12.9	12.4	12.9	12.8	11.5	12.1	13.8	14.0
印　　度	20.9	23.9	23.7	25.6	25.6	25.7	22.9	23.3	21.3	23.0
印度尼西亚	24.3	26.2	27.3	28.2	29.5	30.9	31.5	30.3	27.8	29.1
伊　　朗	29.6	21.1	25.5	19.1	23.8	28.6	33.2	35.4	29.2	14.9
以色列	21.8	17.8	17.6	16.9	15.8	18.5	23.6	23.2	22.3	
日　　本	32.2	28.2	28.7	30.6	31.8	32.8	32.5	31.1	29.9	
哈萨克斯坦	37.7	47.5	42.5	39.9	40.1	42.6	31.3		24.0	24.0
马来西亚	30.4	27.6	23.2	26.0	28.6	31.5	37.0	33.8	35.0	38.5
蒙　　古	46.2	58.4	45.7	43.4	46.0	42.3	28.9	14.5	19.0	20.9
缅　　甸	21.5	15.5	11.6	12.8	9.2	13.4	15.3	13.6	12.1	12.5
韩　　国	32.0	29.6	29.8	31.1	33.6	36.9	38.9	36.6	34.3	38.4
巴基斯坦	18.5	18.3	19.1	18.0	18.9	18.9	19.0	20.2	20.7	19.5
菲律宾	29.1	15.3	17.5	18.7	21.6	24.2	20.2	21.3	24.5	25.3
新加坡	46.3	42.5	39.0	36.5	34.8	39.5	38.0	36.4	38.4	32.2
斯里兰卡	33.8	23.4	22.9	22.3	21.4	21.9	22.6	24.6	25.6	26.9
泰　　国	29.1	28.2	27.9	32.6	35.1	41.1	42.2	39.6	39.9	40.1
土耳其	21.9	21.0	25.7	26.2	22.5	25.5	23.5	23.1	26.8	21.6
越　　南			14.6	19.2	14.6	13.0	15.0	17.6	20.5	24.2
埃　　及	27.5	26.7	18.0	24.2	23.3	21.9	20.4	18.0	17.0	17.5
尼日利亚	22.2	9.0	12.5	13.6	13.5	13.6	16.6	16.6	15.1	10.1
南　　非	28.3	20.1	18.5	21.0	21.1	17.1	16.3	14.8	15.3	17.7
加拿大	23.6	20.3	21.9	22.7	23.2	20.9	19.3	18.3	18.2	
墨西哥	27.2	21.2	19.3	20.4	21.4	21.9	23.4	24.4	22.8	24.5
美　　国	19.9	20.2	19.0	18.4	18.4	17.2	15.6	15.7	16.5	
阿根廷	25.3	17.6	19.6	18.6	15.5	14.0	14.6	16.7	18.2	19.9
巴　　西	23.3	19.2	22.3	22.7	24.8	21.5	18.9	19.1	19.2	16.5
委内瑞拉	26.4	18.5	24.6	28.0	12.7	10.2	18.7	23.7	18.7	9.4
白俄罗斯	19.5	21.3	23.3	22.4	27.4	27.4	30.0	32.3	35.0	
保加利亚	34.0	32.2	32.9	34.4	33.1	25.6	27.9	22.3	18.9	20.3
捷克共和国	31.0	27.6	29.3	27.4	26.8	28.6	29.8	26.6	17.8	
法　　国	24.2	18.9	20.2	21.4	22.3	22.5	21.4	19.7	17.6	
德　　国	23.4	19.6	19.4	20.0	20.9	21.4	23.6	23.2	22.0	
意大利	27.0	22.5	21.0	21.5	21.3	21.0	20.4	19.4	16.9	
荷　　兰	21.8	20.0	20.7	21.4	22.6	22.2	21.4	20.5	19.4	
波　　兰	26.3	27.7	28.8	32.6	38.5	25.6	19.9	15.2	15.6	14.6
罗马尼亚	39.8	33.0	31.8	28.4	26.8	30.2	28.0	31.0	27.1	26.6
俄罗斯	22.4	26.6	25.3	27.3	33.8	30.1	39.1	30.2	28.0	27.0
西班牙	23.2	19.2	21.5	23.7	25.1	25.4	24.6	22.7	19.9	
乌克兰	23.8	27.3	27.3	25.5	27.3	26.3	18.6	11.6	8.4	5.0
英　　国	16.9	17.2	17.9	20.1	20.7	19.0	15.7	15.5	15.1	
澳大利亚	25.4	25.3	24.0	26.2	25.4	21.0	19.2	19.5	19.7	
新西兰	20.8	26.2	21.7	19.8	23.4	21.3	17.5	19.7	21.1	

资料来源:世界银行《世界数据表》1996年。

按购买力平价法计算的人均国民生产总值

国家(地区)	1994 年国民生产总值(百万美元)	人均国民生产总值(美元)			1994 年按购买力平价法计算的人均 GNP(国际元)
		1993 年	1994 年	增长率(1985－1994 年)%	
孟加拉国	26 636	220	230	2.1	1 350
印　度	278 739	290	310	2.9	1 290
印度尼西亚	167 632	810	880	6.0	3 690
伊　朗				－1.0	4 650
以色列	78 113	13 880	14 410	2.5	15 690
日　本	4 321 136	31 360	34 630	3.2	21 350
哈萨克斯坦	18 896	1 410	1 110	－6.5	2 830
韩　国	366 484	7 660	8 220	7.8	10 540
马来西亚	68 674	3 140	3 520	5.7	8 610
蒙　古	801	320	340	－3.3	2 020
巴基斯坦	55 565	440	440	1.6	2 210
菲律宾	63 311	850	960	1.8	2 800
新加坡	65 842	20 130	23 360	6.9	21 430
斯里兰卡	11 634	600	640	2.8	3 150
泰　国	129 864	2 110	2 210	8.2	6 870
土耳其	149 002	2 970	2 450	1.5	4 610
越　南	13 775	170	190		
埃　及	40 950	660	710	1.6	3 610
尼日利亚	29 995	280	280	1.2	1 430
南　非	125 225	2 910	3 010	－1.4	
加拿大	569 949	19 960	19 570	0.4	21 320
墨西哥	368 679	3 730	4 010	0.6	7 050
美　国	6 737 367	24 780	25 860	1.3	25 860
阿根廷	275 657	7 270	8 060	1.9	8 920
巴　西	536 309	2 930	3 370	－0.4	5 630
委内瑞拉	59 025	2 840	2 760	0.6	7 890
白俄罗斯	21 937	2 850	2 160	－1.7	5 010
保加利亚	10 255	1 170	1 160	－3.2	4 230
捷克共和国	33 051	2 710	3 210	－2.1	7 910
法　国	1 355 039	22 490	23 470	1.7	19 820
德　国	2 075 452	23 980	25 580	1.9	19 890
意大利	1 101 258	19 840	19 270	1.8	18 610
荷　兰	338 144	20 950	21 970	1.9	18 080
波　兰	94 613	2 250	2 470	0.9	5 380
罗马尼亚	27 921	1 150	1 230	－6.2	2 920
俄罗斯	392 496	3 000	2 650	－4.4	5 260
西班牙	525 334	13 580	13 280	2.7	14 040
英　国	1 069 457	18 050	18 410	1.4	18 170
乌克兰	80 921	2 210	1 570	－5.1	3 330
澳大利亚	320 705	17 490	17 980	1.2	19 000
新西兰	46 578	12 600	13 190	0.5	16 780

资料来源:世界银行《世界图表集》1996 年。

1994 年人均主要经济指标

国家(地区)	国民生产总值(美元)	主要农产品产量(公斤)						
		谷 物	棉 花	肉 类	牛 奶	油菜籽	原糖产量	水产品①
孟加拉国	230	244.0	0.13	3.0	6.6	2.03	18.3	9.1
印 度	310	231.3	2.46	4.5	32.7	6.21	2.4	4.9
印度尼西亚	880	277.2	0.04	8.7	2.2		11.3	19.4
伊 朗		293.1	1.56	20.1	32.3		36.1	5.9
以色列	14 410	29.1	6.30	51.9	204.6			3.5
日 本	34 630	126.3		26.7	66.9	0.01	17.3	65.2
哈萨克斯坦	1 110	962.7	2.94	72.6	311.2	1.29	126.8	4.4
朝 鲜		192.7	0.47	9.8	3.8			77.2
韩 国	8 220	170.7		32.4	44.7	0.07		60.1
马来西亚	3 520	105.9		45.5	1.7		109.9	35.7
蒙 古	340	187.7		87.3	106.4			0.1
缅 甸		446.4	0.32	7.1	10.0		49.2	19.4
巴基斯坦	440	176.0	10.67	13.2	32.4	1.56	17.1	5.1
菲律宾	960	232.0	0.10	18.7	0.2		32.2	34.5
新加坡	23 360			51.9				4.1
斯里兰卡	640	146.7		3.2	12.7		120.9	12.5
泰 国	2 110	380.1	0.24	25.1	4.5		36.4	57.2
土耳其	2 450	441.3	9.64	16.8	146.3		35.3	9.2
越 南	190	323.5	0.08	17.5	0.6		29.8	15.5
埃 及	710	253.1	5.38	14.7	17.1		37.0	5.4
尼日利亚	280	124.6	1.06	8.6	3.6		19.9	2.4
南 非	3 010	356.6	0.69	28.4	58.1		53.4	14.2
加拿大	19 570	1 608.7		102.7	263.2	245.71	73.9	40.5
墨西哥	4 010	294.7	1.05	38.2	81.1	0.05	23.2	13.2
美 国	25 860	1 371.0	16.48	126.5	267.3	0.78	8.3	23.0
阿根廷	8 060	721.7	7.28	104.6	230.2	1.17	63.2	27.6
巴 西	3 370	298.8	3.26	52.6	102.6	0.07	14.1	5.1
委内瑞拉	2 760	96.8	1.17	50.5	75.4		101.0	18.8
白俄罗斯	2 160	572.9		82.0	512.1	9.66	208.7	1.4
保加利亚	1 160	761.1	0.36	53.0	134.5		255.9	2.5
捷克共和国	3 210	656.1		84.7	312.8	43.76	209.1	2.4
法 国	23 470	926.4		106.0	430.7	30.59	37.3	14.4
德 国	25 580	446.5		71.1	346.4	34.42	26.4	3.9
意大利	19 270	330.8		70.5	180.1	0.21	37.8	9.7
荷 兰	21 970	88.1		183.7	699.3	0.52	140.4	31.8
波 兰	2 470	564.7		62.8	317.0	19.62	56.1	11.0
罗马尼亚	1 230	770.1		63.0	158.3	0.04	95.0	1.5
俄罗斯	2 650	531.9		2.0	297.4	0.77	14.6	30.1
西班牙	13 280	391.5	1.02	96.1	146.7	0.28	55.1	33.0
英 国	18 410	336.9		56.3	257.0	22.66	37.0	15.4
乌克兰	1 570	633.1		51.4	345.5	0.35	41.6	7.1
南斯拉夫		847.0		44.8	142.6	0.19	205.3	0.6
澳大利亚	17 980	810.7	18.44	188.1	466.7	12.78	121.1	12.4
新西兰	13 190	223.2		341.3	2 400.9	0.86		136.3

注:①1993 年.②不包括黄金.③煤、电、水泥、钢指原联邦德国地域的数据。

资料来源:联合国《统计月报》1996 年 4 月;粮农组织《生产年鉴》1994 年、《渔业年鉴》1993 年;世界银行《世界图表集》1996 年。

续表 1

国家(地区)	主要工业产品产量(公斤)						出口额	外汇储备
	煤	原　油	电(千瓦小时)	水　泥	化　肥	钢	(美元)	(美元)②
孟加拉国			86.0	2.9	9.1		22.6	26.6
印　　度	294.9	33.6	382.1	67.3	10.3	15.4①	27.2	21.4
印度尼西亚	149.7	389.4		114.9	15.5		210.1	63.6
伊　　朗		2 922.1①			8.9			
以 色 列			4 943.7①		305.5		3 126.1	1 257.8
日　　本	55.5	5.9	7 272.9①	732.4	10.0	764.7	3 177.4	1 007.2
哈萨克斯坦	6 900.2①	1 132.4	3 828.3		19.2		64.3	
朝　　鲜					34.3			
韩　　国	160.6		3 713.1	1 171.7	24.2	759.1	2 162.2	576.8
马来西亚		1 689.8	2 034.2	505.0	15.3		2 990.1	1 293.8
蒙　　古							137.3	34.3
缅　　甸			76.5①	10.7	2.3		17.4	9.6
巴基斯坦	25.4	21.8	394.1	62.7	13.5		58.2	23.2
菲 律 宾	25.6①		333.4①	142.8	5.2		198.4	89.8
新 加 坡			7 056.7				33 046.4	19 855.6
斯里兰卡			244.6	34.1①	0.5		179.7	114.6
泰　　国	287.9		1 196.2	503.8			761.5	493.8
土 耳 其	934.4	60.2	1 296.9	481.7	22.5	199.1	295.9	117.2
越　　南					2.0		49.6	
埃　　及		819.1①		239.8①	16.4		59.6	231.1
尼日利亚		893.2①	112.1①	30.9①	3.0		94.3①	12.8
南　　非	4 593.2①		4 511.6	164.7	20.9	205.3		41.7
加 拿 大	2 489.8	2 935.4	18 257.2	359.0	381.1	862.1①	5 654.0	420.0
墨 西 哥		1 496.7	1 479.3①	326.8	16.0	94.2	371.3	67.5
美　　国	3 595.6		12 186.8①	295.8	98.7	340.7	1 966.2	242.8
阿 根 廷	5.0①	949.3	1 751.1①	184.7	1.4	88.8	458.1	419.2
巴　　西	33.8	215.4	1 659.4①	164.2	14.1	167.5	283.3	241.1
委内瑞拉	207.7	6 169.8①		332.0①	18.9	124.0①	783.2	377.3
白俄罗斯					239.3		69.0①	
保加利亚	3 394.6①	4.3①	4 546.9	226.1	81.9	295.7	492.5	
捷克共和国	8 132.8①		5 682.9		20.7	655.2①	1 382.4	
法　　国	193.4①	47.7①	8 177.7①	348.8	54.0	311.3	4 077.2	453.5
德　　国③	3 252.1	36.0	5 569.7	494.5	52.9	501.6	5 239.8	950.3
意 大 利	17.5①	81.0①	3 903.8	591.7①	15.9	456.8	3 322.6	564.2
荷　　兰		223.1	5 168.3	205.6①	119.7	401.0	9 525.0	2 245.3
波　　兰	5 163.2①		3 498.5	360.2	37.0	288.3	442.2	151.6
罗马尼亚	1 748.3	294.5	2 422.7	293.4	55.1	254.9	270.5	91.7
俄 罗 斯	2 091.0①	2 388.8①	6 456.9①	251.4	68.2		427.4	26.9
西 班 牙	359.3①		4 005.3①	641.5	51.0	342.9	1 870.2	1 060.1
英　　国	817.1	1 614.5①	5 679.8	192.4①	42.9	295.3	3 493.9	702.4
乌 克 兰	2 267.3①	81.6①	4 406.1①		27.6		187.0	
南斯拉夫	3 557.8	108.8①	3 375.3	152.9	20.1	3.4		276.4
澳大利亚	12 694.5①	1 309.6	9 161.0	369.3	31.8	427.8	2 664.0	632.6
新 西 兰	928.4	484.8	9 060.2	198.3①	112.2		3 490.3	1 062.8

各年龄平均预期寿命

国家(地区)	年 份	0 岁		10 岁		20 岁		40 岁		60 岁		80 岁	
		男性	女性	男性	女性	男性	女性	男性	女性	男性	女性	男性	女性
孟加拉国	1988	56.91	55.97	58.73	57.26	49.53	48.30	31.58	31.44	15.50	15.76		
印 度	1981-85	55.40	55.67	56.08	57.98	46.99	49.18	29.39	32.12	14.61	16.42		
印度尼西亚	1985-90	58.50	62.00										
伊 朗	1976	55.75	55.04	53.87	54.38	45.19	44.97	29.19	30.47	14.58	15.39	5.02	5.24
以色列	1990	74.93	78.53	65.94	69.49	56.15	59.61	36.99	40.08	19.28	21.86	6.79	8.20
日 本	1993	76.25	82.51	66.81	73.02	57.02	63.13	37.80	43.55	20.17	24.94	7.09	9.18
韩 国	1989	66.92	74.96	58.18	66.23	48.58	56.54	30.34	37.51	14.92	19.89	5.01	6.60
缅 甸	1978	58.93	63.66	54.87	59.42	45.86	50.30	28.88	33.07	14.63	17.40	5.05	5.95
菲律宾	1991	63.10	66.70	58.20	61.10	48.90	51.70	31.20	33.80	15.50	17.30	5.10	5.60
斯里兰卡	1981	67.78	71.66	60.99	64.75	51.64	55.36	33.19	39.96	17.74	19.57	5.81	6.43
泰 国	1985-86	63.82	68.85	58.28	62.68	48.86	53.43	31.34	35.05	15.52	18.56	5.20	6.17
土耳其	1985-90	62.80	68.00										
埃 及	1991	62.86	66.39	57.90	61.69	48.49	52.17	30.16	33.43	14.85	16.48	6.09	6.03
南 非	1985-90	57.50	63.50										
加拿大	1985-87	73.02	79.79	63.87	70.52	54.26	60.71	35.51	41.27	18.40	23.24	6.91	9.04
墨西哥	1979	62.10	66.00										
美 国	1989	71.80	78.60	62.80	69.50	53.30	59.70	35.10	40.50	18.60	22.70	7.10	9.00
阿根廷	1980-81	65.48	72.70	58.83	65.70	49.29	56.03	30.95	37.22	15.58	17.95	5.23	6.55
巴 西	1985-90	62.30	67.60										
法 国	1990	72.75	80.94	63.56	71.61	53.87	61.77	35.51	42.45	19.02	24.19	6.85	8.68
原联邦德国	1985-87	71.81	78.37	62.73	69.15	53.01	59.30	34.07	39.87	17.26	21.72	5.99	7.46
意大利	1989	73.49	80.02	64.33	70.78	54.63	60.90	35.69	41.37	18.31	22.90	6.41	7.96
荷 兰	1990-91	73.95	80.18	64.73	70.83	54.94	60.97	35.74	41.48	18.13	23.18	6.43	8.37
波 兰	1991	66.11	75.27	57.48	66.47	47.83	56.65	29.76	37.33	15.09	19.74	5.51	6.62
罗马尼亚	1989-91	66.59	73.05	59.27	65.38	49.71	55.63	31.54	36.54	16.26	19.01	5.55	5.95
原苏联	1991	63.46	74.27	55.29	65.80	45.87	56.10	28.85	37.06	14.73	19.67	5.74	6.90
西班牙	1985-86	73.27	79.69	64.26	70.53	54.57	60.70	35.76	41.22	18.69	22.71	6.66	7.73
英 国	1988-90	72.73	78.27	63.61	68.99	53.88	59.13	34.78	39.63	17.40	21.57	6.36	8.09
澳大利亚	1991	74.35	80.29	65.12	70.94	55.44	61.10	36.68	41.68	19.07	23.30	6.84	8.68
新西兰	1989-91	72.44	78.34	63.47	69.11	53.98	59.34	35.49	40.03	18.21	22.24	6.81	8.44

注:法国、意大利、荷兰、西班牙、澳大利亚为完全生命表,其余国家为简易生命表。

资料来源:《日本统计年鉴》1996年。

按死亡原因分类的死亡率

单位:1/100000

国家(地区)	年份	合 计	恶性肿瘤		脑血管疾病	心脏病	高血压	肺炎	结 核	肠道传染病①	未确诊	交通事故	自 杀
			乳腺和宫颈	其他									
以色列	1989	632.6	37.8	107.9	56.6	130.1	6.6	13.7	0.4	0.3	30.2	9.7	7.8
日 本	1991	669.6	15.6	173.8	95.6	42.6	7.3	56.5	2.7	0.6	24.3	11.6	16.0
韩 国	1990	445.6	5.7	87.4	61.4	8.7	28.9	5.0	9.5	1.2	59.0	30.4	7.4
菲律宾	1981	598.6	31.5②		20.2	66.6	19.1	87.1	55.2	32.7	54.5	4.1	0.5
新加坡	1990	513.4	25.6	111.1	61.6	99.8	7.8	44.0	4.2	1.6	7.3	9.1	13.1
埃 及	1987	950.4		20.1	18.9	24.3	16.4	53.3	2.6	82.1	196.3	6.6	
加拿大	1990	722.1	47.9	177.8	52.7	166.9	4.6	24.1	0.4	0.2	18.5	13.7	12.7
墨西哥	1990	489.5		40.3	22.9	36.3	7.9	25.3	7.2	25.0	11.2	16.2	2.2
美 国	1989	869.4	46.8	181.5	58.8	203.7	13.0	30.3	0.8	0.2	10.9	18.8	12.2
阿根廷	1989	785.6		128.4	79.7	75.5	11.6	19.9	4.0	3.5	20.9	9.7	7.1
巴 西	1987	564.7	17.0	47.5	51.8	46.6	10.4	22.5	3.6	15.4	112.0	19.5	3.3
委内瑞拉	1989	449.8		45.3	28.9	47.9	12.0	15.6	3.3	13.0	56.4	20.7	4.8
法 国	1990	927.5	47.0	223.9	85.5	88.8	10.9	22.3	1.7	1.1	55.5	17.6	20.1
原联邦德国	1990	1 161.0	57.7	233.1	133.1	220.6	26.5	25.5	1.3	0.4	34.8	13.3	17.5
意大利	1989	924.3		228.2	125.6	126.0	25.5	11.8	1.1	0.2	21.5	15.1	7.5
荷 兰	1990	861.6	57.5	211.3	82.9	150.1	5.2	23.4	0.1	0.2	36.4	8.6	9.7
波 兰	1991	1 056.2	14.0	177.0	70.0	121.5	21.4	14.3	3.6	0.2	75.0	22.6	13.9
罗马尼亚	1991	1 085.9	43.2	126.0	172.6	197.9	88.8	30.7	7.3	1.0	0.6	16.4	9.3
原苏联	1988	1 012.1	32.7	160.6	192.9	306.0	5.8	20.3	7.6		6.3	18.0	19.5
西班牙	1989	835.2	36.3	178.0	112.9	88.6	6.5	17.6	2.1	0.6	19.2	21.1	7.7
英 国③	1991	1 118.7		251.4	134.8	298.9	6.6	56.0	0.8	0.3	10.4	8.6	7.6
澳大利亚	1988	725.7	41.6	162.6	75.3	193.7	6.8	9.4	0.3	0.3	4.7	18.6	13.3
新西兰	1989	816.5	52.8	179.5	80.6	216.0	6.5	35.2	0.6	0.2	7.8	23.1	14.0

注:①不包括霍乱和伤寒。②为恶性肿瘤合计数。③仅包括英格兰和威尔士。
资料来源:《日本统计年鉴》1996年。

居民文化程度构成

单位:%

国家(地区)	年 份	25岁和25岁以上人口总计(万人)	大 学	中学		小学		文盲及文化程度不明确者
				初 中	高 中	肄 业	毕 业	
孟加拉国	1981	3 159	1.3	7.4	4.2	16.7	③	70.4
印　　度	1981	28 060	2.5	13.7	④	11.3	③	72.5
印度尼西亚	1980	5 844	0.8	4.7	4.9	31.6	16.8	41.1
以 色 列	1982	200	23.1	36.6	④	30.6	③	9.7
日　　本	1990	8 049	21.2	⑤	44.5	②	34.3	
哈萨克斯坦	1989	841	12.4	50.7	④	29.2	③	7.7
科 威 特	1985	57	12.7	10.7	19.0	7.2	③	50.3
韩　　国	1990	2 341	13.4	18.9	35.0	0.8	20.9	11.0
缅　　甸	1983	1 395	2.0	14.5	④	27.7	③	55.8
尼 伯 尔	1981	615	1.1	3.7	④	4.8	③	90.3
巴基斯坦	1990		2.5	5.8	8.2	9.7	③	73.8
菲 律 宾	1980	1 787	15.2	18.9	④	31.3	22.8	11.7
新 加 坡	1990	160	4.7	23.2	8.1	①	①	64.0
斯里兰卡	1981	649	1.1	34.1	④	48.9	③	15.9
泰　　国	1980	1 749	2.9	4.5	2.3	67.3	2.4	20.5
土 耳 其	1980	1 828	3.6	8.7	④	35.3	③	52.4
埃　　及	1986	1 944	4.6	14.8	④	16.5	③	64.1
南　　非	1985	1 039	2.3	20.6	5.9	41.6	4.8	24.8
加 拿 大	1991	1 747	21.4	34.3	27.7	4.0	11.7	1.0
墨 西 哥	1990	3 119	9.2	12.7	10.7	28.6	19.9	18.8
美　　国	1990	15 868	45.2	44.4	④	9.1	③	1.2
阿 根 廷	1991	1 734	12.0	25.3	④	22.3	34.6	5.7
巴　　西⑥	1989	11 016	⑤	11.9	5.5	57.0	6.9	18.7
委内瑞拉	1990	768	11.8	12.0	④	55.0	③	21.2
保加利亚	1992	565	15.0	35.7	④	12.5	31.9	4.7
捷克共和国	1991	658	8.5	58.6	④	31.4	③	0.3
芬　　兰	1990	339	15.4	②	35.3		49.4	
匈 牙 利	1990	680	10.1	②	30.7	24.3	33.6	1.3
意 大 利	1981	3 560	4.1	18.0	11.2	47.4	③	19.3
挪　　威	1990	280	17.9	32.9	46.4	0.1	③	0.1
波　　兰	1988	2 299	7.9	47.8	④	5.6	37.2	1.5
罗马尼亚	1992	1 360	6.9	63.2	④	24.4	③	5.4
西 班 牙	1986	2 316	7.0	8.9	8.7	40.3	29.9	5.2
南斯拉夫	1981	1 308	6.8	23.4	④	53.9	③	15.8
新 西 兰	1991	199	39.1	16.3	7.8	①	39.5	
俄 罗 斯	1989	8 602	14.1	49.0	④	36.9	③	

注:①本栏数据包括在文盲及文化程度不明确栏内。②本栏数字包括在小学毕业栏中。③本栏数字包括在小学肄业栏中。④本栏数字包括在初中栏中。⑤本栏数字包括在高中栏中。⑥为10岁及10岁以上人口。

资料来源:联合国教科文组织《统计年鉴》1995年。

电话、报纸、电视机及收音机普及率

国家(地区)	每百人电话用户 1994	每十万户蜂窝电话用户 1992	每千居民日报发量 1980	1990	1992	每千居民拥有收音机 1980	1990	1993	每千居民拥有电视机 1980	1990	1993
孟加拉国			3	6	6	17	45	47	1	5	6
印　　度	1		21	31	31	38	79	80	4	32	40
印度尼西亚	1	19	15	28	24	99	145	148	20	57	62
伊　　朗	7		25	25	20	163	228	230	51	61	63
以 色 列	37	696	258	258	246	245	468	478	232	267	272
日　　本	48	1 260	567	587	577	678	899	911	539	611	618
朝　　鲜			219	230	221	82	119	124	7	15	19
韩　　国	40	623	210	280	412	525	1 011	1 013	165	210	215
马来西亚	15	442	59	140	117	411	429	430	87	148	151
蒙　　古			106	74	92	96	133	136	3	39	41
缅　　甸			10	7	7	23	81	82		2	3
巴基斯坦	1	12	12	15	6	64	87	88	11	16	18
菲 律 宾	2	17	41	56	50	43	141	143	22	44	47
新 加 坡	47	4 270	286	282	336	373	636	644	311	377	381
斯里兰卡			30	32	27	98	197	201	2	35	49
泰　　国	4	431	57	81	85	140	185	189	21	106	113
土 耳 其	20	104	56	71		113	160	162	79	174	176
越　　南			10	8	8	93	103	104		39	42
埃　　及	4	13	39	42	41	137	302	307	32	101	113
尼日利亚			15	18	18	97	194	196	8	36	38
南　　非	9	31	48	36	32	274	309	314	69	100	101
加 拿 大	58	3 727	221	212	204	721	983	992	432	612	618
墨 西 哥	9	298	124	133	116	134	254	255	57	146	150
美　　国	59	4 326	273	249	236	1 996	2 118	2 120	684	812	816
阿 根 廷	14	136	142	123	143	427	670	672	183	218	220
巴　　西	7	20	45	55	55	313	384	390	124	207	209
委内瑞拉	11	101	195	144	205	391	441	443	113	159	163
保加利亚	34		253	452	164	395	439	450	243	250	260
捷克共和国	21		313	507	583	509	793	631	280	297	476
法　　国	55	568	192	208	205	741	888	890	353	402	412
德　　国	48	958	335	331	323	893	878	890	439	554	559
意 大 利	43	1 355	85	105	106	602	798	802	390	424	429
荷　　兰	51	1 097	326	301	303	650	906	907	399	482	491
波　　兰	13	7	236	128	159	298	433	439	246	295	298
罗马尼亚	12		181	272	324	177	198	202	184	195	200
俄 罗 斯	16	4	423	503	387	504	336	338	296	365	372
西 班 牙	37	461	93	88	104	258	306	311	253	395	400
英　　国	47	2 595	417	389	383	950	1 143	1 146	401	434	435
南斯拉夫			119	36	52	224	246	207	190	198	179
澳大利亚	50	2 150	323	249	265	1 098	1 279	1 290	384	486	489
新 西 兰	47	2 938	340	327	305	885	931	935	332	446	451

资料来源:《美国统计摘要》1995 年,联合国教科文组织《统计年鉴》1995 年。

世界主要城市面积、人口及人口密度

地　区	年份	面　积（平方公里）	人　口（人）	人口密度（人/平方公里）	地　区	年份	面　积（平方公里）	人　口（人）	人口密度（人/平方公里）
印度					美国				
德里	1992	1 483	9 756 500	6 579	休斯顿	1992	1 520	1 635 827	1 076
海德拉巴	1992	175	2 981 348	17 036	纽约	1992	824	7 322 564	8 886
马德拉斯	1992	174	3 851 181	22 133	阿根廷				
印度尼西亚					布宜诺斯艾利斯	1991	200	2 965 403	14 827
雅加达	1990	661	8 222 515	12 435	巴西				
三宝垄	1992	290	2 595 451	8 937	圣保罗	1991	1 500	11 380 300	7 620
伊朗					保加利亚				
马什哈德	1991		1 759 155		索非亚	1992	1 310	1 190 126	908
德黑兰	1991		6 475 527		捷克共和国				
日本					布拉格	1992	496	1 217 315	2 452
大阪	1992	220	2 603 272	11 809	法国				
东京	1992	618	8 129 377	13 158	巴黎	1990	105	2 154 678	20 445
横滨	1992	433	3 272 180	7 554	德国				
名古屋	1992	326	2 162 007	6 624	柏林	1992	889	3 465 748	3 898
韩国					汉堡	1992	755	1 688 785	2 237
仁川	1992	339	2 070 616	6 111	慕尼黑	1992	311	1 320 634	4 253
斧山	1992	529	3 887 278	7 350	意大利				
汉城	1993	605	10 925 464	18 047	罗马	1993	1 508	2 829 003	1 876
哈萨克斯坦					米兰	1992	182	1 358 627	7 474
阿拉木图	1992	183	1 193 200	6 524	波兰				
马来西亚					华沙	1992	495	1 644 515	3 322
吉隆坡	1992	243	1 285 000	5 288	罗马尼亚				
菲律宾					布加勒斯特	1992	228	2 065 651	9 060
马尼拉	1992	38	1 584 490	41 392	俄罗斯				
新加坡					莫斯科	1993	994	8 881 600	8 935
新加坡	1992	641	2 818 200	4 397	圣彼德堡	1992	143(1)	4 971 038	3 455
泰国					西班牙				
曼谷	1992	1 565	5 562 141	3 554	马德里	1992	607	3 017 439	4 970
土耳其					巴塞罗那	1992	99	1 630 635	16 459
伊斯坦布尔	1990	1 630	7 600 000	4 663	乌克兰				
伊兹密尔	1990	11 973	2 694 770	225	基辅	1993	828	2 617 512	3 161
埃及					英国				
开罗	1992	214	6 800 000	31 522	伯明翰	1992	265	1 009 100	3 801
加拿大					伦敦	1991	1 579	6 889 900	4 363
蒙特利尔	1991	500	1 775 870	3 552	澳大利亚				
墨西哥					珀斯	1992	5 400	1 205 342	223
墨西哥城	1990	1 499	8 235 744	5 494					

注：(1)包括郊区。

资料来源：《世界大都市比较统计年表》1994年。

世界主要城市道路和公园情况

地区	年份	道路		公园	
		长度(公里)	面积(万平方米)	数量(座)	面积(万平方米)
印度					
德里	1992	24 402		14 551	7 473
海德拉巴	1992	3 000		3	
马德拉斯	1994	2 204		88	2 300
印度尼西亚					
雅加达		5 010		394	177
泗水	1992	731			38
日本					
大阪	1992	3 899	3 881	835	797
东京	1992	11 546	9 226	4 870	3 364
横滨	1992	8 809	5 339	2 283	1 347
哈萨克斯坦					
阿拉木图	1993	1 336	1 397	5	84
韩国					
仁川	1992	1 027	1 728	253	2 961
斧山	1992	1 879	2 058	231	3 896
汉城	1992	7 516	7 104	1 348	15 042
马来西亚					
吉隆坡	1991	1 054	908	244	225
新加坡					
新加坡	1992	2 967	6 910	392	1 771
泰国					
曼谷	1992			131	83
土耳其					
伊斯坦布尔	1 985	44 000			
埃及					
开罗		7 200		548	
加拿大					
蒙特利尔	1992	2 019	3 000	300	4 149
墨西哥					
墨西哥城	1992	7 607			
瓜达拉哈拉	1992	2 650	2 600	266	458
美国					
休斯顿	1993	14 449		449	82 525
纽约	1990	10 200			10 670
阿根廷					
布宜诺斯艾利斯		3 589			2 864
巴西					
圣保罗	1991	18 000		34	2 963
萨尔瓦多	1993	419	377	6	2 712
捷克共和国					
布拉格	1992	2 838			
法国					
巴黎	1990	1 576			2 736
德国					
柏林	1993	5 132	7 526		8 340
汉堡	1992	3 893			3 232
慕尼黑	1993	2 273			3 800
意大利					
罗马	1991	4 621			
米兰	1992	1 396	1 741	14	856
波兰					
华沙	1992	2 168	1 646	84	750
罗马尼亚					
布加勒斯特	1992	2 121	1 950	30	4 670
俄罗斯					
莫斯科		4 541	8 075		4 520
圣彼德堡					
西班牙					
马德里	1992			1 264	3 879
巴塞罗那	1992	1 291	1 576	42	504
乌克兰					
基辅	1993	1 560	3 890		
英国					
伯明翰	1992	2 191		301	3 923
伦敦		14 693			45 370
澳大利亚					
珀斯	1992	10 666		500	

资料来源:《世界大都市比较统计年表》1994 年。